The Evolution of Development Policy

A Reinterpretation

The Evolution of Development Policy

A Reinterpretation

SYED NAWAB HAIDER NAQVI

OXFORD
UNIVERSITY PRESS

OXFORD
UNIVERSITY PRESS

Great Clarendon Street, Oxford OX2 6DP

Oxford University Press is a department of the University of Oxford.
It furthers the University's objective of excellence in research, scholarship,
and education by publishing worldwide in

Oxford New York

Auckland Cape Town Dar es Salaam Hong Kong Karachi
Kuala Lumpur Madrid Melbourne Mexico City Nairobi
New Delhi Shanghai Taipei Toronto

With offices in

Argentina Austria Brazil Chile Czech Republic France Greece
Guatemala Hungary Italy Japan Poland Portugal Singapore
South Korea Switzerland Turkey Ukraine Vietnam

Oxford is a registered trademark of Oxford University Press
in the UK and in certain other countries

ISBN 978-0-19-547773-3

Second Impression 2010

Typeset in Minion Pro
Printed in Pakistan by
Kagzi Printers, Karachi.
Published by
Ameena Saiyid, Oxford University Press
No. 38, Sector 15, Korangi Industrial Area, P.O. Box 8214,
Karachi-74900, Pakistan.

To the hallowed memory of my parents;
To my wife Saeeda;
To our daughters Andalib, Tehmina, Qurrat-ul-Ain, Neelofar and;
To our grandchildren Akbar, Roheena, Zara, Aiyza, Masum, Abbas

Contents

List of Tables

List of Figures

Preface

The developmental progress that the developing countries have been experiencing for more than half a century, preceded by approximately two centuries of a steady march from rags to riches presents us with a fascinating story of humankind's struggle to cross the Rubicon in the quest for economic prosperity. It is also a story of the developing countries moving along a high growth path with a resolute stride; of many an intrepid 'newcomer' eventually catching up with the 'pioneers' in an unprecedented short period of time. This is indeed an accomplishment which deserves the envy of pessimists and the amazement of optimists. But on the other hand, this exhilarating period was also marred by many a dismal development failure, that was a cause for much despair. However, observing successes elsewhere must have encouraged those stuck in the quagmire of negative growth, poverty and deprivation to struggle a little longer and take philosophically their failures as a timely warning that development success cannot be taken for granted. Like everything worthwhile, it must be earned the hard way, requiring national governments and the global community to 'exhaust the limits of the possible'. On balance, one can see signs of sanguine expectations writ large on the horizon. This book, therefore, paints a rather optimistic picture of the developing countries' future growth possibilities—that unswerving devotion to duty and determined human effort, enlivened by independence of mind and imaginative vision, can make miracles. It, however, insists that such effort can be crowned with success only by the timely intercession of 'correct' development policies—namely, those which forsake anti-progress prejudices, urge the desirability of the freedom to experiment, bring about an essentially egalitarian systemic change, and raise the welfare of the least-privileged people in society so that they too have reason to live. That is how 'well-ordered societies' have fared forward in the West; that is how they will progress in the East.

MANY ROADS TO DEVELOPMENT

A lot has been documented about the successes and failures that have occurred during the developmental process that different countries have experienced. One finds a deep difference of opinion about the road that one needs to follow which would lead a country towards developmental success and preventing the evils that exist.

For some, this path to success is through sacrifice and pain that maximizing rates of growth of per capita income and unusually high rates of saving and investment impose on the present generation for the greater good of posterity (not caring much for intergenerational equity). This is the road that many communist countries took. This strand of thought can be identified as one of universal government success, in which the mere passage of resources from private hands to public hands would guarantee developmental success.

The outcome of this strategy, as long as it held sway, was to extinguish human volition and private initiative. And yet those countries who followed this path achieved fast growth rates, lesser inequalities of income and wealth, and universal access to health and education. However, success came after much privations and suffering.

Some others identified the road to success as that which goes through free markets and minimum government interference, which presumably presents humankind of individual freedom and right to own property. This way of thinking could be referred to as 'universal market success'. Structural Adjustment Programs have taken this path in the developing countries which would lead them towards progress. They have been advised, rather condescendingly, to aim at 'sustainable growth' rather than 'maximal growth' of per capita income so that they move towards a steady rate of progress. It is interesting to note that, like the communist countries, the free-marketers too have freely employed 'shock therapies', which have proved disastrous to vigorous life. Like them, the Structural Adjustment Programs also have enforced fast-paced privatization and liberalization of control on trade and capital flows and the sovereignty of the corporate interests as worthwhile objectives in their own right, regardless of what they do to human welfare. The result of this is listlessness and lack of private initiative just as it was experienced in countries where Communism was practiced.

However, unlike the Communists who contributed a lot towards the enhancing social justice and reduction of poverty, the Structural Adjustment Programs have taken social justice off their reformist agenda. And yet these programs are regarded as the acme of wisdom, which excludes nothing that is significant and includes nothing that is redundant.

To questions about the downside of these programs, which have caused immense pain and suffering to the common man, the ready answer has been that the greater the pain that adjustment to change causes, the more assured a country would eventually be to grasp the Holy Grail of economic prosperity. But going by available evidence, the net outcome of this policy-imposed catharsis has been rather unpleasant for the developing countries: it has brought in its trail slow growth; higher unemployment; lower wages; and greater inequalities of income. But perhaps 'the most unkindly cut of all' is the fact that liberalist reformism has unleashed a kind of an unvarnished capitalism on the developing countries, that social philosophers, including economists (with the exception of those from the Chicago School) have unreservedly decried for centuries. Individual freedom has degenerated into a license for the privileged few, and free enterprise (minus free competition) has turned out to be no more than a subterfuge for the unabashed pursuit of profits by a handful of Multi-National Corporations (MNCs). Worse still, the liberalist moral-rights philosophy has given a *carte blanche* to capitalist greed on the pretext of protecting individual private property rights, even though it has invariably caused the economic enslavement of the poor.

Both these approaches have seemed, to some development economists, as economically impoverishing and morally unacceptable, and rightly so. They have offered a hectoring vision of the economic processes rather than a humbler one that respects the institutional and organizational constraints in the developing countries. They have, therefore, opted to tread a 'friendly' road to human happiness. Its major benefit, so the argument goes, is that one could maximize human development for much less input of sacrifice. The road to success would presumably lead 'directly' to an ample provision of health and education to people in much shorter time than the one that requires maximizing the growth of per capita income. Sri Lanka, the Indian state of Kerala, pre-reform China and some Eastern European countries (before they decided to ride the bandwagon of free markets) took this shorter road to human development. They were duly rewarded by an unprecedented, indeed, miraculous reduction in illiteracy, mortality and poverty, which are highly valued achievements in themselves. But these countries/regions have also been burdened with slow growth, high unemployment rates and morbidity. It appears that, in these cases, the elusive search for happiness through the most direct route has kindled a vacuous happiness, which withers away for its lack of vitality, vibrancy and durability. On balance, much as we applaud the rush to human development and happiness, it has entailed a significant opportunity cost in terms of lost economic development, which might nullify human development with the passage of time.

One would think that economists, learning from the many mishaps that these rather exclusive roads to prosperity have caused, would take the Smithian road to maximizing the wealth of nations within a mixed-economy framework that was recommended by some committed development economists in the 1950s. This should have been the obvious choice because the models of universal government success and universal market success, being highly simplified perceptions of the reality, have failed to deliver development. The task of development policy should, therefore, have been to strike a balance between the extremes of giving freedom and opportunities to few, as unvarnished capitalism does, and ensuring a kind servile security to all, which Communism offers.

This philosophy was adopted consciously by Latin America, Asia and Africa from 1950 to 1980 which indeed resulted in an upsurge of economic prosperity in these countries. They succeeded in harnessing the power of individual initiative to the cause of harmonious development. Land reforms were instituted to limit the right to private property so as to bring it in harmony with the requirements of high agricultural productivity and rapid overall growth, as well as with the dictates of social justice. These countries have attained the highest rate of growth of per capita income ever recorded in history. Indeed, East Asia achieved miraculous growth, poverty reduction and human development but, relatively, to other strategies, imposed the least sacrifice on the part of the poor people. Yet, for reasons that will be elaborated at length in this book, the middle road that most developing countries tread successfully for thirty or more years had to be abandoned under unremitting 'hostile fire' of the liberalist ideas around 1980. This book argues for a return to the abandoned middle road to economic prosperity that ushered the dawn of human understanding of the mystery of development, with a clear focus on maximizing the growth of per capita income, achieving the deepest possible cuts in poverty and ensuring social justice. But to attain such results yet again, all controversies befogging the policy maker's vision must first be settled.

CAULDRON OF CONTROVERSY

Underlying the divergences between the roads taken towards development, is the economists' failure to reach a common understanding about the structure of values that should guide development effort; the principal factors that have contributed to widely shared growth (which I shall refer to in this book as 'inclusive growth'); and those which precipitate economic regress. Each of these differences in outlook and about the best strategy to translate them in concrete policies will be discussed in this book. Let me note them down briefly in the Preface.

This divergence of opinion on developmental issues seems to have revolved round the rather familiar divide on some old and new 'talking points' on development: Firstly, as noted above, there has been this debate as to the most appropriate institutional framework which should be adopted for achieving economic progress. Is it the one in which the dominating role is assigned to socially committed development states, or that which the invisible hand airily performs all by itself? The present study maintains that this dialogue has been unrewarding and pointless as a kind of a surreal war between order and chaos. The fact is that historically, the government and the market have together 'caused' an outward shift of the production-possibility frontiers in the developed as well as the developing countries. It is, therefore, misleading to press claims for either universal market success or inevitable government failure.

Secondly, more off beam than enlightening have been the controversies about trade *versus* protection, and import substitution versus export expansion. Ever since development economics established itself firmly as a separate discipline around the 1950s, the analysis has been generally conducted (until 1980) in an open-economy framework for estimating the net gains from trade. Quite expectedly, the focus of development policy has been on mitigating the undesirable consequences of unequal exchange for the developing countries. These rather pessimistic estimates of the gains from trade and foreign investment reflected the inbuilt de-equalizing tendency of the historical patterns of trade and investment to compromise the growth possibilities of the developing countries, a tendency that has become only more persistent with the passage of time. Hence, the development economist's insistence that the gains from trade and investment be equitably divided between the developed and the developing countries could not be construed as an argument for protection, much less autarky. Similarly, one would be hard put to interpret the recognition of the inescapability of knowledge-enhancing, import-substitution activities that the traditional development policy once highlighted as an argument against export expansion. Indeed, recent research has shown that without making a determined, yet selective import-substitution effort that aims to expand the domestic market on a priority basis, developing countries cannot face the challenges of integrating into the world economy with confidence. In other words, one can imagine import-substitution and export-expansion activities as joined together at both ends with a view to maximizing the growth rate of per capita income, ensuring distributive equity and minimizing poverty as an irreducible policy package. Any attempt to separate these strategies as working independently of each other, or, one at the expense of the other would be counterproductive. Fortunately, developing countries have followed both the activities together.

Thirdly, yet another acrimonious debate has centred on the relative contributions of physical capital formation and human capital formation to economic growth. In fact, in all developing countries (including East Asia), physical capital formation has been a lot more important than human capital formation as a contributor to growth. Yet again, the debate has been unfairly cast in either-or-terms, even though common sense would suggest that both types of capital are needed to fire the engine of growth—a suggestion that has been duly supported by empirical research. In addition to the instances of the fruitless debate just given, many more examples will be presented in this book of controversies that have subjected development policy to frequent and unhealthy twists and turns rather than letting it move steadily along a learning curve. It is mostly because of lack of clarity on these and other questions that developing countries are 'slipping and floundering about like ducks [that] have alighted on a pond and found it frozen over'. It is, therefore, high time that these sterile controversies, which have fractured development policy cease.

The proverbial visitor from Mars, whose opinion economists have routinely solicited, would most probably be wonder-struck by this on-going clatter of debate on the most proper focus of development policy as well as on the causative factors that have contributed to development. She/he might recognize it as a proof of the economists' propensity to endlessly indulge in nitpicking about almost everything and their tendency to excel at shooting down Aunt Sally. There have been many other reasons why economists have uncompromisingly insisted on the veracity of their own points of view notwithstanding contrary empirical evidence. We will analyze these matters in detail in this book, and briefly in the next section. But our distinguished Martian visitor would be justified in still demanding that we convince her/him about the relevance to the real world of these perceptual differences of which the potential to changing the destiny of humankind for the better might on first sight appear as vanishing small? After all, what else would be the ultimate criterion to judge the rightness of specific perceptions and of actions if not the consequences that different perceptions of reality are most likely to have for the welfare of humankind? Would that she/he would be favourably impressed if we showed that the glorious history of 'right' ideas leading to high rates of growth of per capita income and greater social justice and a miraculous reduction in income and non-income poverty and human deprivation in the West can be repeated in the developing countries? Separating what we have recognized as the 'right ideas' (those which helped development) from the ones identified as 'wrong ideas' (those which hinder development), this book shows that entertaining such optimism is by no means a Midsummer Night's Dream; indeed, it is the stuff of which all adventures in the realm of ideas are made. It, therefore, recounts the evolution of development policy from this rather triumphal, though by no means Utopian, point of view. But let us first look closely at the wide differences in the extant points of view on development strategies and policies to achieve socially agreed ends.

PERCEPTION AND REALITY

During my frequent and prolonged tryst with problems of development and especially in the two-and-a-half years spent on thinking about this book and actually writing it, I have often wondered as to how could it be that perceptions of reality in the developing countries have tended to differ, sometimes radically, from each other; and why it is that perfectly level-headed economists should take pride in their 'trained incapacity', to use Hirschman's suggestive phrase, to learn from contrary theoretical and empirical evidence? It may be instructive to answer this question in some detail. One possible reason why there has not been a meeting of minds on the elemental issues of human existence may be the researchers' loyalty to their long-held opinions. They find themselves confronted with an honest dilemma like the one a soldier faces who is 'fighting for a cause in which he has lost faith [and thinks] that it is a treachery to stop, and it is treachery to go on'. Yet another reason, which has been elaborated at length later in this book, may be that the economists' respective points of view flow logically from their worldviews and value systems, which colour their perceptions of reality, their choice of the kind of transformations they wish to promote and the ones they would rather resist. These are probably good enough reasons for saying things differently as well as saying different things about reality. But, in this section, I pursue a related train of thought, which to some extent unifies the reasons given above and in the rest of the book. It is that, in the nature of things, perceptions can and do differ from reality.

True, there are some philosophers who have held the position that reality has taken a permanent abode in our perceptions so that in effect the two are one and same. It has been argued, that reality is no more than illusions, which like a kaleidoscope, take different shapes and colours as our perceptions of it, for whatever reasons, change. There is some truth in this point of view, but in the present context we take the position that reality, though related to perceptions of it, has an independent existence of its own as well. Indeed, it is only through contact with reality that perceptions acquire a recognizable face and tell a tale of human failures and triumphs. If this position is accepted then, given that they subscribe to the 'right' kind of moral values (i.e., pay close attention to the consequences of specific policies and actions for human welfare), the predilections of the economists who must translate perceptions into clear visions and specific policies are vital for judging the worth of their recommendations for changing the reality for the betterment of humankind. As a general rule, the chances are that neither the economists who are not sufficiently familiar with real-life developing economies, nor do they commiserate with their structure of values, but generalize about them on the basis of what they see in developed societies would be prone to committing serious mistakes of judgment. This class of analysts has been referred to below as 'outsiders' regardless of their place of residence. The presumption is that their perceptions or rather, preconceived notions about reality would more likely be a positive hindrance rather than help in understanding reality in the developing countries. The reason is that they would 'naturally' train only on those elements of reality that they understand and are most interested in, and not necessarily on those that are widely regarded as most important in the developing countries. It is the inevitable consequence of viewing reality as an 'outsider' that 'we become instantly vulnerable to distortions in perceptions, the more so when we remain—voluntarily or otherwise—the prisoners of our system of values'. In that case too, we can and do 'impoverish the object' of our observation and consciously or unconsciously 'manipulate it and dominate it' [Yaqub-Khan (2005), p. 96]. These rather abstract notions can be best illustrated with reference to the wide range of contrasting explanations given of the luminous East Asian Miracle, those which have veered between uncontrolled adulation and condescending exhortations. The 'outsiders' have deliberately 'manipulated' and 'dominated' empirical evidence to prove the veracity of their interpretations (preconceived notions) of the East Asian Miracle. More often than not, the outcome of such pedantic attitudes and efforts has been to 'impoverish' the object of enquiry.

An alternative, and in my view a superior way to approach reality, is to do as an 'insider'—namely, a person familiar with the developing countries and subscribing to their structure of values—would do on viewing it. It is safe to assert that only the insiders' perceptions of reality should become the basis of their generalizations.

Economic processes are not independent of the social, cultural and geographical milieu in which they take place, so that vivid perceptions of it can only be made if the observer has been able to imbibe its cultural and moral values, its traditions, its outlook on life and its prejudices, its geographical and socio-economic compulsions and coordinates.

Once the essential duality of perceptions and reality is accepted, it should become immediately clear that the opinions of the insiders and those of the outsiders are more likely to diverge than converge. Thus, for instance, an 'insider', whose perceptions of reality are formed by daily exposure to the problems of slow growth, poverty and human deprivation, would be impelled to analyze and redress the causes of pain and poverty that afflict the majority of humankind? In sharp contrast, an 'outsider' would most probably veer between exhortation and contempt to make up their mind on the most proper course of action. I think it is a fair bet that they would be repelled by the surfeit of human suffering, thinking it to be more hopeless and final than ever. To take a concrete example, the 'insiders' view of the East Asian Miracle turned out to be totally at variance with the 'outsiders' view, because the formers perceptions were based on a deep understanding of the factors that promoted economic growth and bred social justice. Unlike the liberalist 'outsider', the knowledgeable 'insiders' consistently held government-sponsored import substitution policy aimed to expand the domestic market first, and then export. Yet another example of the superiority of the 'insiders' vision is their knowledge that miracles do not happen if individuals indulge in self-interest maximization; they happen only when human societies in general, and the developing ones in particular, are driven by a sense of commitment to a higher cause, which is, to create at least as much as to possess. True, as liberalist 'outsiders' would contend, individual liberty and freedom have an intrinsic worth, apart from the use to which they are put; but 'insiders' would know that the need for social justice and rights is no less to make liberty and freedom accessible to the least privileged who must endure what they cannot change. As Russell (1973) once pointed out, 'It is clear that some liberty ought to be sacrificed for the sake of justice, and justice for the sake of liberty' (p. 7). The problem for the development policy to resolve is achieving the right balance between the two which each society must find for itself. This book argues that a society that resolves this problem satisfactorily could not for long be deprived of the results of a job well done.

About this Book

This book leans heavily on my (insider's) perceptions of reality that were formed during my extensive visits to Thailand, the Philippines, Malaysia, South Korea, Singapore and China. This period of learning lasted through the 1980s, early 1990s and the first three years of the present century. No silent watcher of the unfolding reality in the developing countries from an ivory tower, I have been very much 'in the thick of things' in Pakistan and elsewhere in the Asian region and positively inclined to change reality in the developing countries rather than be content with explaining it by cold and insensitive reasoning. During these highly educational trips, I got the rare opportunity of sharing my perceptions of reality, both with other 'insiders' in the region and with sympathetic and non-sympathetic 'outsiders', which helped me form a holistic and balanced vision of the development process.

These visits also gave me an invaluable opportunity to talk to some of the most important development economists about what was responsible for the miraculous growth of East Asia and less than miraculous growth in the non-East Asian countries. I got strong impressions about their lack of sympathy for what I identify in this book as the liberalist thinking on development. Above all, I was convinced that the story of the creation of miracle and outstanding growth in the developing countries must be retold in terms of precise chronological marker, and in a manner that would help reinterpret the changes in thinking on development policy over time. Some of the impressions I garnered from my visits are as follows:

Firstly, the regional 'insiders' treated with a barely disguised disapproval the liberalist viewpoint that free (or freer) markets, minimalist governments, and export fetishism (rather than import substitution) were primarily responsible for causing the Miracle. They thought that the liberalist 'outsiders' explanations of the factors responsible for miracle or non-miracle growth were examples of 'dominating' and 'manipulating' available evidence to reach pre-arranged conclusions, which inevitably hark back to their neo-classical roots. In particular, the economists I talked to did not agree with the World Bank's (1993) version of the East Asian Miracle. Indeed, they could not. It was a time of intellectual ferment throughout the developing world, including East Asia, when the economists' main preoccupation was a quest for a middle way between the harsh realities of economic competition and the stultifying embrace of egalitarian socialism. The exact location of the mid-point between state control and free markets would depend on the stage of development reached and the needs of the society, but in the 'initial period', state regulation has typically been heavy. The focus of development policy during these fateful times remained practically fixed—namely, to maximize the growth of per capita income and minimize poverty within an egalitarian framework.

Secondly, I came away from these meetings convinced that though the East Asian Miracle was indeed a miracle, it was by no means non-replicable (as the World Bank asserted), nor was it the largesse of unanticipated exogenous factors. Rather, the roots of the miracle lay in their strongest possible 'fundamentals' (saving rate at the unheard of rates of 40 per cent of GDP and investing over 35 per cent of GDP), far in excess of what Arthur Lewis had prescribed (increasing the saving and investment rates from 5 per cent to 12 per cent) as the primary task of development policy.

Thirdly, contrary to the opinion held rather widely at the time, the 'insiders' in Asia, Pacific region, Latin America and Africa (the latter two I could not visit) did not subscribe to the opinion that a rapid increase in per capita income did not matter for increasing the level of well-being of the people. On the other hand, on repeated visits to the fastest growing countries in the region, especially to South Korea, Singapore, and China, I, like every sympathetic observer, could clearly see the difference that a rapid increase in per capita income within an egalitarian framework in which a strong middle class also rises, could make to the life of the common man. Indeed, the 'skyline' in these countries underwent a transformation—more than once, each time pushing back the retrograde forces that perpetuate poverty and helplessness. On seeing the reality unfold, thus, in the most growth-prone areas in the world, I was left with no doubt that the usual flamboyant agnosticism about the relevance of a rapidly multiplying per capita income for human well-being was, in fact, nothing but economic dilettantism.

Fourthly, yet another impression was the remarkable degree of interaction between the region's economists, which led to a convergence of opinion about the essence of development policy, and its focus. For instance, there was no difference of opinion among the regional economists about the right policies needed to initiate and sustain high rates of growth, ensure social justice and occasion deep reduction in poverty. Thus, nobody quarrelled about the necessity of industrialization as the engine of economic and social transformation.

Fifthly, the non-East Asians were visibly worried about the wide difference between their growth rates and those of East Asia which they would like to diminish as soon as possible. In other words, convergence was a real issue that policy makers tackled with varying degrees of success. But many thought the job to be too difficult, still others philosophized that wealth was not everything, and that the happiness that sprang out of leisurely growth—and not 'helter-skelter' growth—bred a sense of contentment that must be valued independently of what it meant for economic growth. However, viewing the East Asian's heart-warming development achievements and those of many others, many felt that the job could be done, if proper policies were implemented efficiently, and provided that the system of values one held (especially commitment to a cause, rather than unabashed pursuit of self-interest, cupidity and greed) was consistent with the challenge of development.

Lastly, a rather disconcerting conclusion of my visits was that, while most economists I met believed in an egalitarian economic and social system, gender equity was no part of it. It is worth recalling that a rather nice person and a competent Korean economist, in response to my query as to how many women specialized in economics, stated with an air of insouciance that they perhaps specialized in home economics. This led me to conclude that fast economic growth could move mountains but not the deeply ingrained prejudice against women—the more so in the developing countries where it was most needed for all round development.

My chance to translate these perceptions of the reality in developing countries into a specific set of growth-promoting policies came in 1991 on my appointment as a Chairman of the Strategy Committee for the Eighth Five Year Plan (1993–94/1997–98). The Committee was entrusted with the task of suggesting to the Government of Pakistan alternative policy scenarios in order to achieve the highest feasible growth rates and social change. The Committee took a little more than one year to finalize its recommendations. I decided to write my own Chairman's Report, based partly on the 16 sub-committees' reports, and partly on my own impressions about the multifarious aspects of the development process. The following brief quotes from the above-mentioned Report (1992) summarize some of the relevant aspects of my thinking on the proposed strategy at the time are still by-and-large valid:

(a) 'The overarching vision of the proposed strategy for the Eighth Five Year Plan is that public policy should be committed to doubling per capita income in as short a time as possible—say in 12 years or so' (p. 5).

(b) 'This Committee rejects this line of reasoning [that development policy should concentrate on ends rather than the means] because recognizing the ends of development is not necessarily to discredit the [only available] means of development...' (pp. 6–7).

(c) 'It must be emphasized that the proposed strategy of economic development [does not suggest] that the trickle-down effects of growth will be sufficient to solve the problems of distributive justice and poverty. Public policy must deal with these problems partly, by strengthening market forces, and partly, by strong legislative action' (p. 9).

(d) 'There is no 'direct' route to development that may bypass this basic income-generating mechanism [which maximizes the growth rate of per capita income]' (p. 226).

(e) 'This report makes it absolutely clear that trying to accelerate growth without improving the distribution of its fruits among the largest number of people, or trying to gain points on some egalitarian scale without bothering about economic growth, is a pointless exercise, because trying to accomplish one without the other would not result in improving the level of economic well-being of the people' (p. 149).

(f) 'This Committee strongly feels that all forms of discrimination against women should be eliminated, so that women are accorded a status equal to men in every walk of life' (p. 272).

I have further refined these early impressions, based on my personal experiences and a close reading of the extensive literature on development issues, in my two books (1993 and 2002), and four articles on the subject (1995; 1996; 2004; 2006). In the present work, I have elaborated on these ideas. In particular, I have greatly expanded on my earlier notions about the paradigmatic taxonomy used rather effectively in this book to explain the rival views on the development process in unusual detail and to highlight the differences between them. This taxonomy has also served me well, in organizing the large literature on the subject (reported in the References section) around foundational old/new development themes.

I must state frankly at the beginning of this book an important aspect of my cumulative thinking on development economics and development policy. It is that the fastest possible growth rate of per capita income within an essentially egalitarian institutional framework has historically been central to the process of development, and to uplifting the spirit of the people mired for centuries in the hopelessness of static growth, poverty and deprivation. To the least-privileged, it has shown the light at the end of the tunnel—that their living conditions can be transformed by institutionalizing the forces that cause and sustain high rates of growth of per capita income. That being the case, we should keep this candle of hope burning brightly to be able to attain other socially desirable ends (social justice, poverty reduction) as well.

It is hoped that my 'insiders' perceptions of the reality in developing countries would help scatter the pervading clouds of confusion that have enshrouded the current thinking on development, at least for the last thirty years or so. With a burning passion to find out the truth, I have carefully sifted through a large literature that, either directly or indirectly, is relevant to the central hypotheses advanced in this book. To this end, I have highlighted the original contributions made to our knowledge of the mystique of the development process in the last half a century or so; but I did not shrink from stating what I consider to be the right position to take on specific development issues, and from exposing the hollowness of 'conventional' wisdom forcefully, though without rancour. In particular, I have been careful not to let a reasonable criticism of the received ideas, especially those which have for long dominated intellectual dialogue in one guise or another, degenerate into an unreasonable slander. For instance, I have rejected the nearly universal belief among liberalist economists that the traditional development paradigm that ruled the waves in the developing countries for the first thirty years of the post-colonial period (from 1950 to 1980) was just a bundle of mistaken policies that damaged the development prospects of the developing countries, and which, for that reason had to be cast out unceremoniously from the realm of development thought and policies. By the same token, I have shown that substituting the so-called liberalist development policy for the traditional development policy in 1980 in most developing countries, was based on a total misunderstanding of the ground reality in the developing countries. And yet I have explicitly acknowledged the positive contribution of liberalist thinking to our understanding of the development process.

This book has argued that the zigzag, meandering pattern of the evolution of development thinking in the last fifty-seven years or so—from maximizing growth to sustainable growth to human development to pro-poor growth—has not always been conducive to clarity of thought about the future direction of development policy. And yet it will be something of an exaggeration to assert that that the history of development policy has been no more than 'a quixotic quest to find the 'right answer', disappointment in the failure of one strategy leading to the hope that the next will work'. Nothing can be farther from the truth. True, the history of the evolution of ideas on development policy has been marked by ups and downs, which this study describes in detail; yet there is nothing quixotic about it. Instead, this book shows that finding efficient and morally acceptable answers to development problems has been a highly successful adventure into the unknown and has yielded a rich harvest of universally valid economic and moral principles, which are scientifically rigorous, empirically verifiable and strictly relevant to the reality in the developing countries.

When stakes are as high as they are in the developing countries—three-fourth of the humankind being deprived of an honoured place on the table of successful nations—the economists' only concern should be to tell the bitter truth that the situation in the developing countries is deteriorating and that they should do whatever is possible to undo blatant social injustices etc. However bleak the landscape, the search must go on for the light of hope. Be it ours to give succour to the failing courage of the 'voiceless millions' whose plight is so moving and yet so unmoved. It is to the discharge of this duty that this book is dedicated.

Acknowledgements

Firstly, I would like to acknowledge my deepest gratitude to Professors Paul Streeten, John Mellor, Ismail Sirageldin and Solomon Cohen who went through the entire typescript and made invaluable comments, which also helped to sharpen and hone the insights I gleaned from my frequent visits to several countries of Asia and the Pacific region. More generally, I thank those who, in addition to the internationally acclaimed scholars just mentioned, have helped me in forming my own views, through their writings and sometimes by personal communications on the development policy. They are: Arthur Lewis, Jan Tinbergen, Amartya Sen, Lawrence Klein, Hans Singer, Lloyd Reynolds, Jagdish Bhagwati, and Edmond Malinvaud, I.M.D. Little, and many others with whom I have had the privilege of forming personal relationships over the years. However, as is usual, the entire responsibility is mine for the views expressed in this book, which in effect is a personal manifesto. Secondly, I wish to record my thanks to Rehana Khandwalla, editor at the Oxford University Press (OUP) for efficiently tackling complex issues relating to the preparation of the book for publication and for making excellent suggestions for improving the text. Many thanks are also due to Ameena Saiyid, Managing Director, OUP, for making excellent arrangements for the publication of the book in the best possible manner. Thirdly, I most gratefully acknowledge the labour of love of my colleagues at the Federal Urdu University of Arts, Science and Technology, Islamabad: Dr Rehana Siddiqui for her invaluable help in doing the difficult computations reported in this book; Mr Saeed Ahmed Sheikh, for making a significant contribution to improving the original draft with dedication and patience; Professor Abdul Salam for diligently going through the entire typescript twice and making helpful suggestions for improving it; Ms Adiqa Kausar Kiani for making many useful and innovative suggestions to improve the argument in the book and straighten out several technical aspects of the typescript with great patience and utmost competence; and Professor Ather Akbari for reading through some parts of the book. Fourthly, I am most grateful to the Higher Education Commission Pakistan, and especially to its resourceful former Chairman, Professor Atta-ur-Rahman, and energetic Executive Director, Professor Sohail H. Naqvi for arranging the necessary research grant, and to Director Academics, Mr Abdul Ghaffar Khan for administering the grant efficiently and with a sense of urgency which is rare among administrators of funds. Lastly, my unbounded gratitude is reserved for my deceased parents Syed

Mohammed, Hasan Fatima, and Hameed Fatima, my uncle and aunt Syed Mustafa Hasan and Haideri Begum who taught me to care for the poor and least-privileged in the society. The beneficence of their love has continued beyond their graves. I also owe a lot to my sisters Naseem Zehra and Aley Zehra whose selfless love has been a source of strength for me, and to my brothers Syed Aley Mustafa Naqvi and Syed Aftab Haider Naqvi. No less is my gratitude for the constant support I have received from my wife and four daughters to whom this book is dedicated, and my sons-in-law Imran, Ali Raza and Saklain.

Part I

Preliminaries

1

An Overview

This chapter gives a bird's eye view of the basic themes of this book. It is the study of the evolution of thinking on development policy from the beginning—when the developing countries threw off the yoke of colonial rule around 1940s—to the present times. To this end, it identifies the outstanding milestones along this evolutionary path with the help of a paradigmatic taxonomy that provides at once an effective organizational principle, a basis for evaluating different points of view about the 'best' development policy in terms of their consequences for the welfare of the developing countries; and a set of fruitful recommendations for reorganizing the entire intellectual basis of development thinking. This analytical framework also highlights the fault lines in the structure of development policy as it has evolved over time. Needless to point out, a pattern of evolution that at every stop wiped the slate clean and made every intellectual initiative a new beginning and an adventure into the unknown cannot be conducive to creative thinking on development policy, if only because it necessitates the rejection of the existing stock of knowledge and its replacement with new ideas. This practice must be given up. A wiser course of action would be one that does not fail to acknowledge the belief that there is nothing altogether new under the sun and that it would be foolhardy to reject all that has been accomplished by the best minds in our profession. When the need arises adjustments, the new paradigm should indicate what must be done to re-order development priorities rather than make a clean break from the past. These points are elaborated below.

1.1. THE GENESIS STORY

A full narrative of the evolutionary perspective on development policy has required a detailed analysis of the major 'turning points' in development thinking—namely, the Traditional Development Paradigm, the Liberalist Paradigm, and the Human Development Paradigm.[1] This analytical framework, which is original to this book, has the distinct advantage of integrating a diverse and large body of contributions to development policy around a reasonable organizing principle, which is that specific development policies should be traced to their paradigmatic roots.[2] The existing differences in development policies would then be seen to flow logically from the differences (divergences) in the basic assumptions of rival paradigms. This perhaps is a more reasonable way to look at specific development policies rather than follow the many conspiracy theories that trace them to some sinister western design to exploit the rest of the world. They may very well be true; but they do not leave much room for rigorous economic analysis. An additional bonus of this approach is that, depending on its paradigmatic affiliation, each staple development issue—e.g., growth, poverty, distributive inequity (including gender inequity), export expansion and import substitution, to cite only a few of them—gets analyzed from more than one angle.

Yet another merit of the proposed analytical framework is that it requires an *explicit* consideration of the moral aspects of the development problems and policies. This is absolutely foundational; because many life-and-death problems do not get the analytical and policy attention they deserve if one insists on strict positivism, which mandates explaining specific situations as they are, rather than prescribing what they should be. For instance, a high rate of unemployment may be neglected if viewed on efficiency grounds alone, leaving out of account the moral aspects of it. The classical and neo-classical analyses have termed it as voluntary, attributed it to labour-market inflexibility and regarded it as the necessary price paid to ensure the efficient working of the labour market.[3] But this elemental issue can no longer be ignored once a state of economy in which a large number of people have to bear the indignities of being without a job is declared to be morally unacceptable. That this should be the proper thing to do can be appreciated by the fact that even the high rate of European unemployment, which is fully covered by social-security payments, has contributed to social unrest and led a large number of people to commit suicide.[4] Things will be much worse in the developing countries where the unemployed are not as fortunate as their European brethren.

Another example of moral considerations causing an issue that is generally ignored on efficiency grounds to become a burning issue is that of 'distributive justice'.[5] If, on moral grounds it is decided, 'Undeserved inequalities call for redress; and since inequalities of birth and natural endowment are undeserved, these inequalities are somehow to be compensated for', then this should be a decisive argument for development policy to address them.[6] The problem of gender inequity can be recognized and adequately analyzed only on moral grounds. An important implication of these examples is that there is no such thing as a strictly positivistic development policy.

An important aspect of the suggested analytical scheme is that it provides a valid basis for making inter-paradigmatic comparisons in terms of their respective value premises and moral perspectives; and furnishes an objective basis for making a choice between different paradigms in order to arrive at a cherished and desired pattern of development policy. Thus, for example, if the objective of development policy is to ensure maximal growth of per capita income along with 'distributive justice' and poverty reduction, one would look to the Traditional Development Paradigm (see Part II of this book). On the other hand, once high growth rates have been achieved, if it is decided that the policy focus should shift to translating increments in income into valuable functioning and capabilities, and human happiness, then one would have to turn to the Human Development Paradigm to gain an understanding of the issues (see Part V of this book). Similarly, with a view to thinking systematically about issues of macroeconomic stability (in the narrow sense) and analyzing the dangers of unbalanced budgets, overvalued exchange rates and high rates of inflation, the Liberalist Paradigm would be the obvious source of ideas to seek guidance from (see Part III of this book). The place to look for a systematic, even devastating criticism of the liberalist point of view is the Anti-Liberalist Consensus, which shares neither the liberalist worldview nor its value premises (Part IV of the book). If, however, it is understood that all these problems should be considered together with a clear focus on growth, 'distributive justice' (including gender equity) and poverty reduction, then we need to refer to what I have christened as the New Development Paradigm (see Part VI of the book).

But, perhaps, one of the most important justifications of the proposed analytical scheme is that a chronologically arranged story of the evolution of ideas on development policy related in this book could not have been told in a better way. By the same token, it is expected to give a clearer view of an adequate development policy. An important moral of this story is that, with the outstanding exception of the Traditional Development Paradigm, major changes in the structure and focus of development policy in the last half a century or so have been dictated more by a sudden surge of ideological unease with the existing economic order, than by a deep understanding of the ground realities in the developing countries.[7] Yet another moral is that the evolution of development ideas has, despite occasional diversions, been guided by an irrepressible urge to understand the mysterious historical forces that, when fully harnessed, have transformed static, 'ill-ordered' societies into dynamic 'well-ordered' ones—the ones organized along the universal egalitarian principles of justice and fairness and a compelling compassion for the downtrodden.

1.2. Economic Development and Development Policy

At this point, it will be instructive to illustrate the 'marginal utility' of the analytical scheme proposed in this book by reference to the rival interpretations of the *observed* persistent tendency for the growth rates of per capita income to wildly accelerate and for the incidence of poverty and glaring 'distributive injustice' (mainly that traceable to the dominance of rental income in total national income) to dramatically decline in the first thirty three years of the post-colonial era.[8] These tendencies were clearly evident to be at work throughout the developing world, but most convincingly, in East Asia and China.[9] So, one would expect that there would be little disagreement about their quintessential beneficence.

Yet, unbelievable as it may sound, a mere shaking of the paradigmatic kaleidoscope would cause a radical perceptional change about such a visible phenomenon, its implications for development policy and the basic recommendations for changing the 'reality' in the developing countries for the better. Alone among the paradigms, the Traditional Development Paradigm, whose prescriptions helped to bring about a sea-change in economic outlook as long as it formed the basis of development policy (from 1950 to 1980 in most developing countries), regarded maximization of the growth of per capita income at an increasing rate within an egalitarian institutional framework as the vehicle for reducing poverty and giving people greater freedom to make the choices they would voluntarily make for their happiness and well-being.[10] The mechanisms for achieving these beneficial results were identified as quickening the pace of Structural Transformation (i.e., the share of manufacturing activity steadily rising as a percentage of GDP) and implementing sweeping land reforms.[11] As the former reduced the size of the rural sector and rendered it more productive by reducing the land/labour ratio, the latter made it more egalitarian by transferring the ownership of land from the unproductive, rent-seeking and exploitative landlords to the more productive owner-cultivators for whom efficient cultivation strategies are a way of life. Furthermore, such reforms were confidently expected to eliminate or minimize unproductive rental income and increase the productive profit income.[12] At the same time, the demand for industrialization (and for mass produced goods that urban dwellers prefer rather than the luxury goods that rural landlords and the urban elite crave for) would intensify with the gradual rise of an urban middle class, which would also raise agricultural productivity as an integral part of the dynamics of systemic change.

Contrary to popular opinion, the Traditional Development Paradigm's was a highly focused rather than a scattershot approach to economic progress. It regarded agriculture as the leading sector in initiating the growth process. The argument was that the demand for industrialization, at least in the beginning, would flow from the developing country's success in raising agricultural productivity.[13] Also, while export expansion was regarded as generally beneficial, it was not considered as the engine of growth. Hence, the

Traditional Development Paradigm gave priority to expanding the domestic market through knowledge-creating import substitution for achieving accelerated growth of national income. The development strategy it recommended was viewed as the safest road to modernity that would also nullify the developed countries' historical advantage by adding non-traditional high value added goods to their traditional exports and allowing the former to engage in mutually beneficial exchange with the latter. Furthermore, it was expected to help the developing countries achieve independence from an unsustainable dependence on concessionary foreign aid, and in time to converge with the developed countries. Even a cursory comparison of the growth rates (of both agricultural and manufacturing activities), distributional inequities, and the incidence of poverty, as well as the rates of growth of both imports and exports in the post-colonial period with those prevalent in the colonial period would verify the quintessential wisdom of the Traditional Development Paradigm.[14]

The Liberalist Paradigm, however, pedantically decided on ideological grounds that the unprecedented growth and industrialization accomplished during the first three decades must have been either an illusion, or if a reality, then it could not be sustained in the long run. It, therefore, viewed with extraordinary suspicion the accomplishments of the Traditional Development Paradigm—especially the unusually high growth rate of per capita income and a reduction of poverty that it helped to achieve. The main source of the liberalist worry about the observed high growth rates in the post-colonial period was that they were 'artificially' stimulated by government intervention—artificially, because these were seen as having been caused by the acceleration of input accumulation rather than supported by steady increases in total factor productivity that propelled European and American ascension to their modern greatness [Pack (1988)]. The developing countries' heavy reliance on input accumulation and forced industrialization *rather than* on steady improvements in productivity, referred to in the literature as 'extensive growth', has been (mistakenly, in my opinion) regarded as inevitably unsustainable, precisely because it could not be kept going except by an increase in the capital/output ratio. Assuming the elasticity of substitution to be less than one, this tendency would be rewarded in due course of time by the declining marginal productivity of capital. Thus, growth rates would eventually decline, even though, capital accumulation continued unabated.[15] It has, therefore, been argued that the traditional development policy should have aimed at a *sustainable* (read, slower), rather than *maximal*, growth rate of per capita income—one that would cause the growth process to flow 'naturally' and serenely from secular improvements in total factor productivity.[16]

An essential characteristic of the Liberalist Paradigm has been its insouciance towards the inevitable consequences of its policies for growth, unemployment, incidence of poverty, and distributive inequity. It is remarkable that these unfavourable consequences of liberalist reforms were the most pronounced in countries that implemented them most punctiliously (e.g., Latin America, Eastern Europe and sub-Saharan Africa). And yet these policies have been prescribed in the belief that what is (theoretically) 'first-best' must also yield 'first-best' outcomes in the long run—and that what is efficient must also be equitable (at least, in the Pareto-sense). In the short run, it was argued that sacrifices must be made and pain endured, mainly by the poor, for the sake of a better future.[17]

One of the most notable features about the Liberalist Paradigm is essentially the absolutist character of its basic propositions. Indeed, though touting its unalloyed commitment to scientific probity and hard-boiled positivism, it has often taken on a fundamentalist colouring that leaves little room for a reasoned dialogue. An outstanding example of this tendency has been its uncompromising condemnation of anything that smacked of government intervention. The main point of the liberalist criticism has been that any development policy that relied on extensive government intervention must be wrong, for the simple reason that it would be economically unsound (it would violate the sacrosanct Pareto-optimality criterion). It would also be ideologically unsettling because any government intervention to redistribute income and/or reduce poverty constituted, by definition, a serious violation of individual's moral rights to hold on to whatever they earn by the dint of their alleged superior merit. Thus, in the liberalist calculus, extreme inequalities of income and wealth get condoned on moral grounds [Hayek (1960)]. Likewise, the liberalists contend that the prevalence of extreme poverty is 'unfortunate' but not unjust.[18] In the same spirit, high rates of unemployment are regarded as essentially voluntary and assumed to flow from labour market rigidities (i.e., the observed downward inflexibility of the wage rate).

Furthermore, the Liberalist Paradigm would not be the least concerned about breaking down the institutional barriers to growth and development, partly because doing so would disturb the existing pattern of the distribution of power and privileges in the society. For example, land reforms, which the Traditional Development Paradigm emphasized so much, have all been forgotten in the liberalist scheme of things. The fundamental reason for this neglect is that the Liberalist Paradigm regards status quo as essentially the best possible arrangement in the sense of reflecting the 'unanimity' principle. For all these reasons, it has 'solved' the distributional problem by taking it off the reformist agenda. Instead, it has focused first and last on restoring, even extending, the writ of the 'Invisible Hand' to all sectors of the economy so that the Natural Economic Order that Adam Smith had allegedly discovered could re-emerge in its resplendent splendour from the apparent chaos of the market place [Buchanan (1985)]. An absolute and unquestioning 'submission to the markets' has been recommended because it is 'something that is greater than any of us can fully comprehend' [Hayek (1944/1994), p. 224].[19] However, a more important argument for insisting on the untrammelled sway of the markets is that, for want of a better alternative, they are seen as the best guarantees against the state's encroachment on individual liberty on the pretext of improving distribution of income or reducing poverty.

The Human Development Paradigm would accept the reality of positive rate of growth and the necessity for reducing (income) poverty; but it would link its beneficence to what it does to enhancing individual 'functioning's' and 'capabilities'. [20] In this framework of thought, wealth and income are only the means for achieving some basic functioning's and capabilities in order to live a life one has reason to value most. It was argued that the success achieved on the income scale during the first thirty years though invaluable, was wanting when weighed on the human development scale. It, therefore, has shifted the focus of development policy from maximizing the growth rate of per capita income to building up elementary, yet foundational, individual 'functioning's' and 'capabilities', i.e. to be more literate, healthy and be able to move about in the society 'without shame'.[21] It has emphasized the need for positive growth rates of per capita income (expressed in PPP dollars) but only as much as required to support a 'decent standard of living'. An increasing share of social expenditure is also regarded as the surest means to reduce income and non-income poverty and human deprivation—and eventually to increase the growth rate of per capita income.[22]

The present study maintains that, notwithstanding its great merits in analyzing the distributional problems with complete confidence in its scientific rigor, the Human Development Paradigm fails to offer a viable strategy of systemic change and does not offer a meaningful alternative strategy of economic growth and development. Its preferred 'direct' (or the 'support-led') approach to development, as opposed to the 'indirect' (or the 'growth-mediated') approach does not seem to be a promising growth strategy. Indeed, it constitutes the paradigm's Achilles' heel. Development experience shows that the few countries (for example, Sri Lanka, Eastern Europe) and regions (Kerala) that took the shorter road to happiness have not been able to convert the gains in human development into faster and more equitable rate of economic development [Dreze and Sen (1995)]. This crucial failure of the support-led strategy is an eloquent testimony to its weakness as a reliable engine of long-term growth. The empirical evidence presented in Part VI of this book shows that this weakness of the paradigm can be traced mainly to its making too sharp a distinction between the growth of income and the corresponding increments in human happiness, and its failure to understand that human development expenditures contain a significant consumption element, so that increasing such expenditure might, beyond a certain limit, affect investment and growth adversely.[23] Furthermore, contrary to the Human Development Paradigm's assertions, it would not be realistic to run the engine of growth on human capital alone; physical capital must be brought in to pull it towards economic prosperity and human happiness.[24] Furthermore, like the endogenous growth theory on which it seems to have drawn rather heavily in the formulation of its views, on the link between human capital and economic growth, it too ignores the critical role of Structural Transformation in powering the growth process.[25]

This rather critical comment about what the Human Development Paradigm has not handled well does not, however, diminish in any way what it has accomplished superbly. It makes the important point that it would be extremely limiting to think about the advantages flowing from human development expenditure *only* in terms of what it does to the growth of per capita income. Rather, insofar as greater social expenditure directly contributes to some vital elements of human happiness, an increase in them will be demanded beyond what is required for promoting growth and/or reducing poverty.[26] The present book asserts that the Human Development Paradigm's non-Utilitarian consequential moral philosophy, which judges specific policies by reference to their consequences for human well-being, and holds humankind responsible for the choices they voluntarily make, has been its most original and enduring contribution to a clearer understanding of the nature of such elemental problems as distributive injustice, poverty and human deprivation.[27] No less has been its contribution to making human-development concerns an integral part of everyday economic thinking. It is a tribute to the power of its advocacy of the socially and morally relevant issues of our social existence that 'human development' has become a household word. There is no doubt that it has *caused* social expenditures to increase substantially in all countries and, thereby, helped alleviate income and non-income poverty.[28] Yet another of its outstanding contributions has been its overarching emphasis on the justness of the 'background' social institutions, because without them 'the outcome of the distributive process will not be just' [Rawls (1999), p. 243].

1.3. A Legacy Not Worth Preserving

Before getting on with the main themes of this book, it will be useful to identify the set of ideas that have generally misguided economic development in many a developing country since 1980. These ideas, which the liberalists seem to have advanced with intense sincerity, share a simple property: they are dead wrong for development. To put it rather sharply, development experience has amply shown that in one country after one another the so-called liberalist first-best policies have produced the least-best outcomes. On the other hand, nearly all the successful development episodes owe their success to policies that liberalists routinely condemn as injurious to development [Hausman and Rodrik (2003)].[29] These arguments have been analyzed at length in Parts III and IV of this book.

1.3. (i). The Unwise Rejection of Traditional Development Paradigm

An important aspect of the liberalist academic opinion has been to reject outright the entire body of the development policies associated with the Traditional Development Paradigm with a view to making real-life economies approximate the mythical first-best economic universe. I do not wish to sound overly judgmental, but this indeed was a colossal mistake. It would be, perhaps, a major project that adequately estimated the total damage that the liberalist development policies since 1980 have caused to the developing countries' growth prospects in terms of lost output, employment creation and poverty reduction and the possibilities of creating a fair and just society. It has not been wise for the Human Development Paradigm to repeat the same mistake by rejecting the Traditional Development Paradigm for sins it did *not* commit—that it allegedly suffered from 'commodity fetishism', focused entirely on growth of per capita income as *the* means for achieving human happiness and neglected the contribution of knowledge formation to economic growth and development. It is the contention of this book that such accusations are mostly based on an incomplete understanding, if not a total misunderstanding of the rationale, salience and reach of the Traditional Development Paradigm.[30] This book features the policies associated with it as a huge success in responding vigorously to the monumental economic challenges that developing countries faced in the post-colonial period. Taking a leaf from the Marxian and Keynesian Revolutions and based on a close reading of the European economic history, the traditional policies emphasized the fundamental point that a modern capitalistic economy must be *managed* to accelerate the engine of growth to 'full-throttle'. To this end, it recommended *systemic* change of an essentially egalitarian nature, without which the fruits of economic progress would not reach the common man. In particular, it emphasized the need for making revolutionary changes (through peaceful means gradually implemented) in the basic institutions, with a view to sustaining a steady structural transformation of rural societies with static values into urban entities possessing dynamic values. And it understood early on that that doing this job would be beyond the ken of the so-called free market; and that it must be handled by a full-blooded development state endowed with a forward-looking vision of economic progress. There is solid empirical evidence to prove that its chosen strategy was crowned with success—most emphatically in the East Asian countries, but quite convincingly in the other developing countries of Asia, Latin America, Africa and the Middle East.[31] The fact is that the Traditional Development Paradigm deliberately chose the best development strategy—in the sense that it was superior to any other alternative strategy available at the time.[32] Thus, for instance, it would have been economically incorrect, politically suicidal, and morally unacceptable to have chosen the so-called first-best prescriptions— namely, unfettered markets, minimal government and *laissez-faire* as the guiding principles of development policy in the aftermath of the developing countries' emancipation from colonial rule. How could any sane person recommend to the policy-makers the very 'first-best' policies that had yielded the worst possible economic scenario in the developing countries? The colonial governments had forged an essentially exploitative relationship with the colonies: they aimed to transfer from them maximum resources to the colonists, leaving the former stuck in the quagmire of economic stagnation, high unemployment, widespread poverty and an unhealthy dependence on the western countries for meeting their demand for high-value added goods, technological knowledge and technical know-how. No different would have been the fate of the human development aficionado, if people were advised by someone at the dawn of Independence: 'forget about growing at the fastest possible rate because the growth of per capita income is only a means to happiness'. It would not be unrealistic to think that such a person would have been promptly condemned (if not actually lynched) as an enemy agent. It can, therefore, be stated without fear of contradiction that no development policy, other than the one actually implemented, would have been politically acceptable at the time, and none would have produced better economic results.

1.3. (ii). Irrelevance of Market-only 'Solution'

One of the main contentions of this book is that an undiluted faith in the first-best nature of market-only solutions would be, as it has been, misplaced. Many studies, cited in this book, show that when information is incomplete (which is always the case) competitive equilibrium is not pareto-optimal; and that in such a milieu persistent widespread unemployment is best treated as a case of market failure [Stiglitz (1991)]. Then there is the persuasive thesis that in the context of the unrivalled growth-generating prowess, the capitalist system innovation has replaced price as the name of the game in a number of important industries' [Baumol (2002), p. 4]. These arguments are even more compelling in the development context. It is, therefore, hazardous at best, to base real-life development strategies on assertions about the un-improvability of the market solutions. At any rate, their unsuitability has been amply demonstrated by the manifest failure of the so-called first-best market reforms throughout the developing world. The Transition Economies provide the most tragic illustration of the damage that standard (elementary) textbook market-only or market-friendly remedies can cause, if not accompanied by the creation of the basic institutions and universally accepted ethical norms (e.g., trust, honouring of contracts etc.) that have sustained the Western market economies [Stiglitz (2003); Campos and Coricelli (2002)].[33] But their failure has been universal. The market-only idea is also wrong because it hypothesizes that there actually exists somewhere between heaven and earth an economy where markets are free and unfettered, and the government is ideally non-existent, or at best Lilliputian in size. This is obviously an incomplete picture of capitalism, which has, in the West and the East, lived peacefully and productively with large and intrusive governments. Indeed, the European Welfare States have been no less intrusive than any of the East Asian economies.

Luckily, the initial enthusiasm about the un-improvability of the market solutions and their relevance for economic and human development seems to have subsided somewhat, though, not significantly—at least in the academic circles, if not at the policy-making level. The present author believes that the mixed-economy model, which John Maynard Keynes first proposed to save capitalism from itself, is the *only* model that has succeeded to combine economic growth and social justice within an essentially democratic framework. In practice, the problem is to find a *juste milieu* that makes judicious use of both the market and the government. It has succeeded everywhere in the West; it will do so no less in the East.

1.3. (iii). The Inadequacy of Self-help Liberalist Prescription

It is quite common to hear the advice that, what with their many misfortunes (most of them inherited from their colonial past and the historical inequities of the international economic system) the developing countries should be encouraged to develop through their own efforts. In particular, they must carry the cross of painful structural adjustments before qualifying for any aid or loans. They are also advised not to disturb the working of the domestic and global markets in order to achieve growth and egalitarian objectives (because efficiency has priority over growth/distribution). It is also argued that domestic or international aid cannot be claimed as a fundamental right of the poor people or countries, except what the rich people cough up voluntarily. On the other hand, the rich should be given maximum freedom to own what they earn by dint of their superior merit [Hayek (1960)].[34] The most debatable aspect of this line of thinking is that it has lent intellectual support to the notion that the existing distribution of income based supposedly on 'merit' should not be disturbed by a redistributive policy [Nozick (1974)]. On the same ground, it would be morally wrong to 'coerce' the rich countries into helping the poorer countries. Regardless of its many theoretical blemishes that economists and social philosophers have pointed beginning with Adam Smith and John Stuart Mills, the uncritical acceptance of meritocracy (even as an ideal) has had undesirable consequences for the size of the aid given to the developing countries. The reluctance of the developed countries to write off the debt of the African countries (and to implement that promise after making it with great fanfare) flows from the same faulty reasoning; so does their even greater reluctance to make unilateral concessions to increase market access for the developing countries at the WTO multilateral negotiations.[35]

1.3. (iv). The Self-Interest Maximization Principle

The idea that has for long held economists in thrall, but is not very relevant in the development context, is to regard the principle of self-interest maximization as the sole, or even the primary, source of human motivation. But this is a completely wrong idea. It has given rise to many a faulty economic proposition. But a little reflection should show that accepting it as a lynchpin of any serious programme of systemic change would be counterproductive, to say the least. Firstly, collective goals, even the universally accepted ones, have never been achieved only with individuals acting for their self-interest, which has a tendency to drift into incapacitating isolation. Secondly, development entails a systemic transformation, and replacing old institutions with new ones—a process that is beyond the reach of the Invisible Hand even at its vanishing best. Thirdly, knowing that information about the future possibilities of a typical developing country is costly, public policy is needed to canalize individual initiative into socially desirable activities. Indeed, it has always been a creative symbiosis of enlightened self-interest and moral considerations like commitment to a cause that has moved people to action throughout human history. Theoretical considerations also do not support the self-interest-only (or even predominantly self-interest) hypothesis. (a) The pursuit of self-interest alone may lead to non-optimal solutions. (b) Pareto-optimality in real-life situations can (and does) coexist with inefficiency [Stiglitz (1988)]. (c) Even if optimal solutions do flow from the exercise of self-interest, these may not be socially the most desirable ones [Solow (1980)]. (d) Ostensibly moral motives (gift exchanges, being honest, keeping one's trust and observing contracts that under-gird a capitalist system), rather than cupidity and greed, are more likely to lead to superior outcomes both in terms of equity and efficiency [Hirsch (1977)]. All this may sound heretical to liberalist ears; but it came naturally to the Adam and the Smith of modern economics.[36]

1.3. (v). The Sterility of Lilliputian Governments

Another idea that has misguided development policy since 1980, and is now overdue for an unceremonious burial, is that state is an inherently evil institution: it works only for lobbies if it at all works; curtails people's liberties; and once allowed to get hold of people's minds paves 'the road to serfdom'. Highly influential has been the thesis (which forms the basis of the so-called New School of Political Economy) that the state maximizes its own welfare and is, therefore, unable to act in the larger national interest. Yet for all their influence, these notions are anti-history and contrary to everyday experience. No less absurd is the liberalist prescription that the state should, therefore, be minimized.[37] The empirical evidence presented in this book shows that there is not a single instance of a developing country in the post-1950 period, including the miracle economies, where high rates of economic development have been achieved without state intervention. Indeed, this is true of the developed countries as well. It is known that the period before the emergence of the state as a dominant player in the development game, when presumably unfettered markets and *laissez-faire* dominated economic life, was marked by static growth rates of per capita incomes and the exploitation of the poor by the rich [Reynolds (1983); Rondinelli and Lacono (1996); Stiglitz (2003); (2006)].[38] Socially committed governments have changed all that directly as well as by helping the evolution of progressive institutions and development-oriented coalitions. Together, they have made possible rapid, even miraculous, growth rates of per capita incomes and a significant reduction in human suffering in developing countries. The process of 'getting the institutions right', something that North (1990; 1994) has emphasized of late, is a historical struggle in which the old static institutions (e.g., the feudal system) have got uprooted with the active help of governments to make room for new ones.[39] But there are strong theoretical reasons for such a proposition as well.[40] Thus, for instance, coordinated investment decisions might become necessary to initiate and sustain economic activity. But such decisions would fail to materialize if private profit were the sole indicator of the social profitability of making additional investment. Indeed, without government assistance, private investors will have no incentive to make the necessary transition from the low-income equilibrium associated with the traditional way of production to the high-level equilibrium associated with industrialization.[41] But the role of the government would be no less at a higher stage of economic development. As amply illustrated by the East Asian miracle and the Chinese super-miracle growth performances, socially committed states have typically acted as Stackelberg leaders, taking the private actors along the largely uncertain and (from the point of view of the private investor) risky path of economic and human development.[42] At any rate, the 'government versus the private sector' debate has only generated heat but no light. The fact is that there has never been a time when, notwithstanding ambitious planning exercises, government or the private sector could crowd each other out of development. [43]

1.3. (vi). Lack of Development with 'Undistorted' World Prices

There is enough empirical and theoretical evidence against the liberalist principle, also enshrined in the Structural Adjustment Programmes, that domestic investment decisions should be dictated, exclusively or mainly, by undistorted world prices rather than the 'distorted' domestic prices, i.e. those which foster 'forced-draft' industrialization [Little, Scitovsky and Scott (1970); Lipton and Ravallion (1995)]. But this is false reasoning because world prices (for example, the world prices of the agricultural products) have seldom, if ever, been undistorted. They are heavily subsidized by the OECD countries, and can hardly be regarded as helpful guide for a socially beneficial, or even an efficient, allocation of national or global resources. Indeed, these prices have been accused of 'killing' the developing countries' agriculture. The same is the case with the world prices of primary exports of the developing countries, which have been falling down since long, even as the prices of the developed countries' exports have steadily risen. But even assuming that world prices are truly and honestly undistorted, the current world prices and opportunity costs (determined by and for the developed countries) could not possibly reflect the future development possibilities of a developing country. The reason is that what a country is good at producing (or where the country has a dynamic comparative advantage) could seldom, if ever, be foreseen with certainty. On the other hand, in many cases, the goods and processes in which a country eventually comes to enjoy comparative advantage have been discovered as an unanticipated by-product of the learning process.[44]

1.3. (vii). *Laissez-Faire* as an Invalid Development Principle

Yet another idea that has been most actively, even aggressively, advertised for the good of the developing countries is that development policy should unquestioningly follow the dictates of the (static) Ricardian Law of Comparative Advantage, or the Heckscher-Ohlin version of it. This idea has been revived recently to lend intellectual support to globalization; but is most definitely due for burial in the development context in its static form. The time has come to accept without reservation 'the end of the *laissez-faire*' that

John Maynard Keynes once recommended. Insofar as conditions approximating *laissez-faire* prevailed ever, they did the developing countries more harm than good. Lewis (1978) observed that the *laissez-faire* in the nineteenth century mainly benefited the Western countries, but it offered the developing countries 'the opportunity to stay poor' (p. 19).[45] The terms of trade losses of the developing countries have tended to increase over time, with no end in sight. The 'income losses [of the developing countries] were greater in the 1990s than in 1980s not only because of the larger terms-of-trade losses but also because of the increase in share of trade in the GDP' [UNCTAD (1999), p. 85]. Not only that; there is strong evidence that the terms of trade of the manufactured goods of the developing countries have declined relative to those exported by the developed countries [Grilli and Yang (1988)]. But the development prospects of the developing countries are much grimmer than is indicated by the terms-of-trade statistics, which have been interpreted both differently and indifferently. Indeed, they have been misinterpreted to reach prearranged conclusions. The bigger problem is that the tapestry of the world economic order represented by the WTO has tended to solidify, rather than weaken the dynamics of 'unequal exchange'.[46] A widespread recognition now exists of the inherent inequities of the WTO that derive from an unequal bargaining between the rich and the poor in which the brute power of the rich always comes out triumphant.[47] Perhaps the most objectionable aspect of it is that it has tended to penalize the creation of knowledge by the mushroom growth of monopolies all over (which are 'un-contestable' as far as the developing countries are concerned); indeed, it has condoned an open piracy (including bio-piracy) of the traditional knowledge in the developing countries. There is not much empirical support for the argument usually adduced in favour of *laissez-faire*, that foreign trade is the primary determinant of growth, and for that reason of poverty reduction.[48] Indeed, the Asian growth experience (which has been a parent to many a generalization about the strong linkage between growth and export expansion) shows that a rise in the export/GDP ratio has seldom been a sure indicator of an increase in the GDP and employment. Instead, growth has mostly been determined by domestic factors, with international trade playing second fiddle, though a 'significant' one in a strict statistical sense. Whatever the situation was in the nineteenth century, when most developing countries were helpless colonies unable to decide their economic and political destiny, this has not been the case since these countries obtained their independence from colonial rule around 1947. Once the focus of attention shifted to raising the incomes of the developing countries in the shortest possible period of time, it was inevitable that the primary emphasis would be initially on the expansion of the domestic market, rather than on the continued acceptance of the colonial pattern of development (indeed, non-development) in which foreign trade dominated.

A careful examination of the cross-country data shows unmistakably that growth of the Asian countries during 1965 to 2000 period can mainly be explained in terms of the growth of the domestic variables (i.e., physical and human capital formation, and government investment) and only secondarily, though significantly, by their degree of openness. (The regression results of this elaborate exercise are reported in Part VI of this book).[49] The same conclusion holds with respect to the secondary, though significant, effect of trade on poverty reduction. Furthermore, an over-reliance on export promotion as an engine of growth could reduce a developing country's ability to adjust to external shocks. Indeed, there have been cases in which a deeper integration with the world economy has resulted 'in immersing growth, where increased export production is not absorbed in world markets, causing severe damage to terms of trade and a loss of real income' [UNDP (2003b), p. 27]. Why then revive in the twenty-first century, the dying ambers of faith in the eventual beneficence of *laissez-faire* that has never been beneficial to the developing countries?

1.3. (viii). Perils of Free Capital Market

Yet another aspect of *laissez-faire* that has done great damage to the developing countries is the freeing of capital markets from all controls, even in times of financial crisis. The argument in favour of such policy is basically that capital-market controls simply prevent foreign capital from flowing in; they do not prevent it from flowing out. But experience has shown that each time a developing country, even with strong fundamentals, liberalized trade and capital flows rapidly without advance preparation, it has faced severe balance-of-payment problems owing to a net movement of (short-term) capital out of the country in times of crisis. Even worse, labour has been forced out of low-productivity activities to the zero-productivity activity of becoming unemployed. Furthermore, the essentially pro-cyclical movement of short-term capital ('hot money') in and out of a developing country doing liberalization has caused financial instability, which discouraged even the flow of long-term capital. Contrary to the best of liberalist intentions, the net result of trade and capital-market liberalization done in a hurry has led to infernal situations. This is one of the reasons why capital-market liberalization has nearly always been followed by increased macroeconomic instability, higher unemployment and slower growth—all of which have tended to reduce growth and enhance poverty. This is one of the abiding lessons of the 1997/98 financial meltdown of the East Asian miracle economies, which nearly washed away decades of hard work and development.[50] There is, therefore, a grudging acceptance of temporary controls on the movement of hot-money transfers, which have contributed to financial instability—something that John Maynard Keynes pointed out long ago.

1.3. (ix). Export Fetishism can be Harmful

Yet another misguided notion has been the liberalist advocacy of an open-ended Export-Expansion (EE) strategy as opposed to the Import-Substitution (IS) strategy that the Traditional Development Paradigm was accused of advocating.[51] What is wrong with this notion is not so much its emphasis on export expansion but to contra-pose it to import substitution. Indeed, one would be hard put to find examples in the economic history of the last 200 years or so of cases where one activity had been carried out consistently to the exclusion of the other, either of the developing Europe or the United States, in their formative stages and, especially, since 1950, when economic change began to emerge in developing countries. True, import substitution might have been emphasized for some time at an early stage of economic development; but this does not bespeak a systematic bias against export expansion. The point of such exercise might have been the developing countries' quest for dynamic comparative advantage in the knowledge-expanding, skill-creating and innovation-promoting activities, so that they too could participate in world trade on a mutually beneficial footing with the developed countries.[52] Historically, export orientation has been the outcome of a comprehensive and 'balanced' development effort.[53] Indeed, contrary to the frequent claims made in the liberalist literature, outward orientation has nowhere been the engine of growth in any of the modern miracle growth countries (East Asia since the 1960s, and China since the 1980s); nor in any of the reasonably high-growth economies of Latin America and South Asia.[54] This is because learning and knowledge accumulation, which are powerful engines of economic growth, have more often been associated with carefully chosen import-substitution activities rather than with all-out export fetishism [Bruton (1998)]. Indeed, generous export incentives have been at least as 'distorted' as import restrictions. The real task of development policy is to seek a balanced expansion of the domestic market and the foreign market so that the contribution to growth is maximized without exposing the economy to unnecessary risks.

1.3. (x). Immorality of Inconsequential Moral Rights

Yet another liberalist idea that has positively hindered the formulation of an effective development policy is that it should be strictly positivist to be scientifically acceptable. The Pareto-optimality principle, Libertarianism and Benthamite Utilitarianism all belong to this category of unhelpful ideas, which have the added disadvantage that they harbour some (essentially perverse) moral principle 'deep down' but do not explicitly state it for fear of being branded as irrational. Thus the Pareto-optimality principle claims to be value-free and in terms of distribution, neutral; but, in fact, it makes a strong case for the preservation of the status quo as opposed to social change on the grounds that the latter might lack unanimity. If a consistent application of this principle does not result in economic development or social justice, then so much the worse for both. The liberalist recommendation would still be to stick to the efficiency criterion in the quest for economic bliss. Furthermore, by its very definition, a Pareto-optimal state is deemed to be perfectly consistent even with a famine-like situation so long as the agony of the poor cannot be relieved without cutting into the ecstasy of the rich. Libertarianism is no less flint-hearted; its withering contempt for human welfare would be unbelievable if not true. It regards individual liberty as an intrinsically valuable objective, which must be defended even if that means a total neglect of all other socially worthwhile objectives. It too prefers status quo to social change, because the latter would inevitably involve hurting some while benefiting others. A policy of studied inaction towards distributional matters has, therefore, been supported on the grounds that 'redistribution is a serious matter indeed involving the violation of people's rights' [Nozick (1974), p. 168]. Libertarianism is, in effect, a philosophy of exquisite moral ambiguity. It offers a kind of savage justice whereby 'the right to life is the right not to be killed, it is not the right to be given sustenance' [Hausmann and McPherson (1993), p. 703]. Benthamite Utilitarianism, though paraded for more than a century as a moral principle, does no better as a principle of redistribution. It also does not offer any coherent poverty reduction policy. The reason is that it measures an individual's happiness *exclusively* in terms of the metric of mentally experienced increments in total utility but does not worry about the distribution of utility among people. Sticking to the Utilitarian formula— seek the greatest good of the greatest number—would simply perpetuate poverty rather than reduce it. This is because if the aim of public policy were to choose a distribution of resources that maximized social welfare, and choose a population size that maximized this number, then such a policy would give no more than is necessary to keep the largest number at the starvation level [Roemer (1996)]. Indeed, it is possible to conceive of situations in which Utilitarian policies may worsen distributive injustice and enhance poverty.[55] Thus, for instance, political 'freedom' may peacefully coexist with blatant economic 'un-freedom'. This is obviously not a satisfactory state because economic 'un-freedom' in the form of extreme poverty can make a person helpless prey in the violations of other kind of freedom' [Sen (1999b), p. 8].

1.4. A BRIEF 'HISTORY OF THE FUTURE'

A basic stance of this book is that, each of the paradigms analyzed above, notwithstanding its blemishes, has helped us understand some important aspects of the development problem, while neglecting matters that require equal, even greater, focus. The Traditional Development Paradigm, identified as the only genuine paradigm so far, provided a fairly satisfactory theory of economic growth and development within an egalitarian framework. It also explicitly dealt with the inter-relatedness of growth, distributive justice (including gender equity) and poverty reduction—though it lacked clarity on some of the important interactions between these vital variables. It had the rare distinction of seeing its policy prescriptions produce excellent results during the genesis of modern growth and development. For all its weaknesses, the Liberalist Paradigm has sensitized us to the need for maintaining macroeconomic stability, with a view to making the long-run growth 'sustainable'. In this context, its emphasis on keeping the budgetary and trade deficits within manageable limits and holding the rate of inflation down to a tolerable level must find an important place in any successful development policy. The Human Development Paradigm has given us a full treatment of the moral foundations of the elemental issues like distributive injustice, and poverty and human deprivation. Most valuable is its emphasis on the creation of just institutions so that people voluntarily defend them in times of crisis. And yet, as noted in the preceding section, each of these paradigms is lacking in some important respects. The Traditional Development Paradigm did not possess, or spell out, a theory of moral philosophy, that could analyze satisfactorily the egalitarian aspects of its reformist agenda. The Liberalist Paradigm has dealt with the most existential development issues only insofar as achieving them is consistent with macroeconomic stability. Most problems with the Liberalist Paradigm arise from its tendency to regard fiscal and monetary stability, trade liberalization and privatization as valuable ends in themselves; and also because it does not adequately take into account their relationship with growth, distributive justice and poverty reduction. The Human Development Paradigm, for all its theoretical virtuosity, people-friendliness and social concern, does not possess an economically valid theory of growth within an essentially egalitarian framework.[56] It has overdone the distinction between income and non-income variables and (incorrectly) regarded the 'direct' route to human development as somehow superior to the traditional 'indirect' route that goes through the maximization of income per capita. Real world events seem to have disproved this claim.

Thus, notwithstanding the efforts made so far to understand the chemistry of a fruitful development policy, there remains on this count a residue of 'emptiness' that, if not addressed explicitly, will only grow with the passage of time. To some extent, the malady in question has arisen from the tendency of each of the paradigms reviewed so far to reject all previous knowledge as irrelevant or wrong. The need for doing so was, however, pressing only in the case of the Traditional Development Paradigm because the reality on the ground as well as the rules governing it had undergone a total transformation in the post-colonial period.[57] The same, however, cannot be said of the paradigms that followed, which, in most cases have spent too much time on 'differentiating their products', or worse still, on reinventing the wheel without acknowledging the ones who invented it first. But needed or not, they caused drastic, though avoidable changes in the direction of development policy that must have imposed heavy opportunity cost on the developing countries in the form of lost output and employment. It is argued, therefore, that policy makers should be mercifully spared the loss of equilibrium that ideologically motivated paradigm shifts have produced in the past. The next phase in the evolution of development policy should be to design a New Development Paradigm that respects the demands for preserving continuity in the evolution of ideas on development policy, while making its own original contribution to knowledge.[58] It should be informed by the accumulated stock of knowledge about the functioning of the past development policies, and must include those hypotheses and recommendations of the preceding paradigms, the validity of which has been confirmed by sound theoretical reasoning and empirical research. The brief description of the New Development Paradigm given below would suggest that it would be a creative symbiosis of the Traditional Development Paradigm, the Human Development Paradigm and will contain some valid insights of the Liberalist Paradigm. But, hopefully, the whole will be greater than its constituent elements. More important, it will refocus development policy on the elemental problems of growth, equity and poverty reduction with a view to facilitating systematic change. While its full elaboration would appear only in Part VI of this book, it may be interesting to drop some broad hints at this stage about the likely position it would take on some of the issues that the preceding paradigms have also tackled, though not always with success.

1.4. (i). The Case for 'Inclusive' Growth

The New Development Paradigm would gain superiority in its goal for achieving the highest feasible rate of economic growth of per capita income; for it is the flame that burns brightly in the lantern of systemic change, which is what economic and human development, should be all about. However, this end would be most effectively achieved if a high rate of growth of per capita income, distributive justice, and poverty reduction and a rising social expenditure on education and health were pursued as an irreducible set of policy objectives. Such an 'inclusive' development strategy would play a central role in the emergence of progressive, essentially egalitarian and democratic societies in developing countries that are both 'good' and 'just'.[59] The basic contention here is that it is only when the economy is strongly growing, that egalitarian policies can best be implemented. There should, therefore, be no paltering with the spirit of a broad-based and widely shared development. The extra policy sensitivity to high growth rates of per capita income also links up with the need to achieve independence from foreign aid and attain convergence with the developed countries in the shortest period of time. We know now that a growth rate of per capita income of 3 per cent plus per annum is the 'minimum critical effort' needed to achieve the basic development objectives. The real success, however, comes when growth rates of 6 per cent or more are sustained for several decades that double per capita income in a decade or so. The heart-warming stories of East Asian miracle economies and the Chinese super-miracle economy demonstrate convincingly the great changes, both in economic and human development terms, that can be wrought when developing societies brace themselves for making the required effort to grow at the fastest possible rate and effecting the required institutional and other changes required to sustain it in the long run. It is only then that poverty can be definitely reduced in both percentage terms (the percentage of total population living below the one or two-dollar-a-day poverty line) as well as in absolute terms (the total number of people living below the poverty line). The evidence that the fastest rate of poverty reduction in particular, and human development in general, has occurred in countries that registered the fastest (e.g., China, East Asia) has been too compelling to be ignored in any sensible poverty and human development analyses, be it in terms of income poverty or capability deprivation.[60] True, Table 20.1 of this book shows that human development expenditures reduce poverty by a larger percentage than high growth rate of per capita income; but this does not obviate the need for a strong growth regime. Indeed, without it, human development would wither on the vine for lack of availability of the required financial and physical resources. It may be noted that the focus on high rates of the 'inclusive' growth as the only durable means to achieving human happiness is not necessarily inconsistent with the Human Development Paradigm's view of development process as enlarging the people's substantive freedoms. The reason is that judging individual advantages and making inter-personal comparisons in terms of people's capabilities does not rule out the possibility of using the real income metric for achieving some of the freedom-giving capabilities. By the same token, poverty reduction efforts need not (indeed, should not) ignore the income space in order to grapple with capability deprivation; all that the latter requires is that a concentration of focus on income alone (which incidentally no sensible development economist has ever suggested) must be avoided. The link between the growth of income and the expansion of people's capabilities and freedoms can be made tighter by appropriately adjusting the income space, using the information on the determinants of capabilities other than income. It is, therefore, mystifying as to why the UNDP's *Human Development Report* should each year assert that increasing per capita income at the fastest possible rate is not the primary policy objective and that one needs income only insofar as it leads to achieving basic functioning and capabilities.

1.4. (ii). Strategy of 'Inclusive' Growth: Balanced Growth

To sustain high rates of economic growth, the development process should follow consistently a 'balanced-growth' trajectory—that is, one that ensures a harmonious inter-sector and inter-temporal development of the economy.[61] Indeed, the idea of balanced growth, which was first proposed by the Traditional Development Paradigm, is quite general in its applicability. Thus, for instance, inter-sector balance would require agriculture and industry achieving maximum rates of growth so that the economy holds firmly to the high growth path.[62] This is because the manufacturing activity would not be profitable if the agricultural sector did not also grow at the maximal rate; though by the inexorable working of the Engel's Law, the share of agriculture in the GDP must decline no matter how fast it grows. The tendency of the growth of the industrial sector to exceed significantly that of agriculture has historically (in the last 200 years or so) been a universal tendency in all the growing economies. This obvious point needs emphasis because in recent discussions of the so-called 'pro-poor growth' strategies the centrality of industrialization for economic development has sometimes been questioned on the ground that agricultural development is essential for poverty reduction. However, such arguments are really off-beam because effective poverty reduction policies also require the relative growth rate of industry to be higher than that of agriculture; and since without it, labour productivity will not rise (through a reduction of labour force in agriculture as a proportion of total labour force).

1.4. (iii). Strategy of 'Inclusive Growth': Primacy of Expanding Domestic Market

The New Development Paradigm should eschew the 'which-comes-first' debate about the expansion of the domestic markets and/or encouraging foreign trade.[63] Development experience has confirmed that economic growth (and development) has primarily flowed from the expansion of the domestic market, which the knowledge-enhancing import-substitution activities caused. In certain cases, however, the growth process has been ignited by an export boom and in some others by a sharp rise in agricultural productivity. But, regardless of how it began, growth process has historically been most 'stable' when it relied, at least initially, relatively more on expanding the domestic market than on export expansion. As is shown at some length in this book, the miracle economies as well as the super-miracle grower (China) have been primarily driven by import substitution, which has played a more decisive role in 'internalizing' high rates of growth of per capita income—and eventually in making China as one of the most, if not the most, formidable exporting countries in the world. The recent upsurge of the Indian economy, which was earlier attributed entirely to liberalist reforms (e.g., privatization, trade and capital market liberalization, and emphasizing export promotion rather than import substitution), has on deeper analysis been seen as flowing from the growth of the intra-marginal import-substitution (manufacturing) activities [Rodrik and Subramanian (2004)].

1.4. (iv). Macroeconomic Stability

The New Development Paradigm must keep in view the requirement of macroeconomic stability as one of the preconditions, though not necessarily an over-riding one, for strong long-run growth. In this context, there is a broad agreement that the 'twin deficits' (i.e., budgetary and trade deficits) should stay within safe limits (say about 3–5 per cent of GDP); and that, to this end, the inflation rate be kept on average at about 5 per cent and the level of external indebtedness stays at say 30–40 per cent of GDP. It may be noted that most of the high-growth Asian economies have had low inflation rates; but it is an open question as to what has been the 'threshold inflation rate'— that is, above which it hurts growth. The general rule seems to be that, while it is advisable to keep inflation rate low, it would also be unwise to fall prey to fiscal and monetary radicalism, which invariably hurts growth and investment. Thus, the chosen regime of macroeconomic stability should neither be too lax nor too tight—the optimal level should be found through a process of trial and error, keeping in view its likely effects on the growth rate of per capita income, the unemployment rate, distributive inequity and the incidence of poverty. Unfortunately, in practice, the pursuit of macroeconomic stability has ended up slowing down the growth rate of per capita income, which is then explained ex-post as the only sustainable rate feasible. Insofar as this practice forecloses the possibility of inclusive growth it is counterproductive. A fatal flaw of the macroeconomic-stability-first approach is, as the Latin American case clearly shows, that it allows the economy to grow only at the *sustainable* rate, a synonym for a significantly slower growth rate, which then raises poverty and lowers employment creation.

1.4. (v). Globalization and Development

One of the most outstanding features of the New Development Paradigm would inevitably be to restate the innately unjust 'unequal exchange' doctrine in order to make it more convincing in the modern context and serve as a starting point of a global effort to make it equal and just. There is an urgent need for doing so, because if there ever was any doubt about the inherent inequity of the world trading system, there should be none now. The terms of trade of the goods exported by the developing countries have had a free fall; the domestic manufacturing has suffered mainly because of the many institutional constraints on all kinds of import substitution that the WTO has enacted and imposed on them while letting the developed countries flout them with impunity. In addition to its severe adverse effects on economic growth in the developing countries and on the withered lives of the common man, there is also the question of the gross unfairness of the WTO, which denies to the developing countries what the developed countries themselves practiced in their days of underdevelopment [UNDP (2005)]. Also, innovation and knowledge-creation have been arrested by a feckless enforcement of the so-called intellectual property rights by a handful of multi-nationals (MNCs) [Stiglitz (2006)]. The net result of these and other related constraints is that globalization has for all practical purposes decimated multilateralism. It should be recognized that the WTO has not been able to create a level playing field for all the participants in international trade. Indeed, it was not meant to achieve any such a noble objective. The WTO has kept legitimatizing departures from multilateralism, i.e. free-trade areas and bilateral negotiations, both of which have given the developed countries ample room to exploit the developing countries.[64] True, it has provided a rule-based world trading system in which the poorer countries also have equal votes and can (theoretically) change the bargaining process in their favour. Yet the 'chemistry' of the uneven distribution of economic and political power has worked against them; and there are no encouraging signs on the horizon that the world economic order is going to become more equitable any time soon.[65] To make it worse, excessive export orientation and capital-market liberalization, which the WTO and other international donor institutions have enthusiastically enforced as a matter of their ideological commitment to *laissez-faire*, have exposed the fragile developing economies to the vagaries of the world commodity and capital markets. They have also made the maintenance of a stable exchange-rate regime well-nigh impossible. The WTO, therefore, faces the challenge that it has so far failed to meet—namely, of graduating from an apparently rule-based organization that caters primarily to the interests of the developed countries to the one that cares for development and poverty reduction and strives for international amity and peace. In this context, the long suspension of the Doha round of negotiations, which was meant to enhance the development content of the WTO but has accomplished nothing on that count so far, does not betoken a healthy evolution of the world trading and financial system. The perverse part of the story is that, while differential and preferential treatment of the developing countries' exports has been phased out because it allegedly did not serve developing countries' interests, the differential and preferential treatment of the developed countries' exports has been justified on grounds that it serves their interests. Furthermore, the developed countries do not want to give up the massive subsidies to their agriculture, even though the net effect of their policies has literally been to 'kill agriculture' in some developing countries, like Mexico.[66] At the same time, they demand unrestricted access to the developing countries' markets for their manufactured goods (including textiles) exports, which threaten to destroy the nascent manufacturing activities in Africa and many other developing countries. The dynamics of unequal exchange fed primarily by Northern greed, which the failure of the Doha Round of Negotiations has made amply clear, has come back to haunt international relationship with a vengeance, if ever it retreated. The New Development Paradigm must, therefore, focus on enhancing the development orientation of the WTO.

1.4. (vi). Gender Equity

A sharp focus on promoting gender equity should be one of the defining characteristics of the New Development Paradigm—in the sense that a development policy with more gender equity would be unequivocally preferred to one that has less of it. Gender equity involves both the welfare aspect (development should give a better deal to women than is the case now) and the agency aspect (women should be viewed as active agents of social transformation). Both aspects require increasing woman's participation in economic activities, so that she acquires an independent say in family decisions. This aspect of the equity issues needs a separate and emphatic mention because, as the example of the miracle growers shows, gender inequity can coexist both with high growth and an equitable distribution of income and wealth. The importance of gender equity lies in the fact that giving a better deal to women is a desirable end in itself (regardless of any other reason for doing so). No society can be called a truly civilized one if it maltreats its women in a systematic way. However, the issue gets added support from the fact that gender equity also makes a direct contribution to general human happiness and well-being by lowering fertility and infant mortality rates. Furthermore, since poverty is basically concentrated in women, no sensible anti-poverty policy can leave out of reckoning an explicit mention of the gender dimension of development.

1.4. (vii). Morality and Development

Yet another defining characteristic of the New Development Paradigm would be the explicitness of its moral foundations.[67] Correspondingly, there would be little room for unalloyed self-interest maximization in promoting systemic change. By the same token, there would not be much justification for regarding it as the acme of rationality. The fact is that in real-life situations, especially when the focus is on systemic change, it is neither irrational to act morally nor immoral to act rationally. Indeed, to restrict rational behaviour to self-interest maximization alone would be to greatly underrate the human capacity to be compassionate, selfless and committed to a cause.[68] Sen (1999b) has argued that it would be a gross misreading of development history to equate capitalism with the pursuit of narrow self-interest. The fact is that ethical values like trust and adherence to mutually agreed contracts have been no less important in making capitalism successful. Thus, rather than glorify self-interest and greed as worthy traits of human character (which is what the Liberalist Paradigm routinely does without any compunction), the New Development Paradigm should reflect the modern thinking on behavioural choice, which goes much beyond self-interest to highlight 'reflective selection, concordant behaviour, public discussion, and evolutionary selection' in the making of individual and social decisions.[69] The point to remember is that self-interested behaviour cannot be accepted as the dominant, much less exclusive, motivation in a strongly growing society. It is one of the central contentions of this book that successful development episodes cannot be implemented, much less be sustained over long periods of time, without a systematic pattern of self-sacrifice and a recognizable repudiation of the dominance of self-interested behaviour. In other words, it can be stated as a general rule that individuals' free riding on a large scale to serve their narrow self-interest is inconsistent with development.[70] This proposition has been all the more true in miracle economies, where extra-ordinarily high rates of saving and investment (that is, acts of abstaining from present consumption and comforts) have prevailed for about four generations. Such abstemious acts have reflected a widely held belief among people that what is good for the society is also good for their individual well-being. The same spirit of self-abnegation comes to be universally accepted when people decide, as they have done on many occasions in history, that new and egalitarian institutions must be created—through sweeping land reforms and/or by agreeing to progressive taxation of income and wealth—to solidify the great development accomplishments. Going beyond that, it is not possible to create a 'stable society'—one that people would voluntarily defend—without a moral commitment on their part that they would accept greater advantages for themselves only 'under a scheme in which this works out for the benefit of the less fortunate' [Rawls (1971/1999), p. 90]. In this context, the New Development Paradigm should recognize explicitly the binary relationship between 'claimable rights' of the poor and the 'counterpart obligations' of the rich to help them. It should reflect the global consensus about observing this relationship in letter and spirit. Fortunately, this valuable global consensus is now enshrined in the basic values identified in the Millennium Declaration (2000)—especially, Equality, Solidarity, and Shared Responsibility—and the Millennium Development Goals. What remains is the real task of implementing these global agreements in letter and spirit and reflecting them in national development policies.

1.5. CONCLUDING REMARKS

The evolution of ideas is mercifully an on-going, never-ending process and it seldom leads to clear-cut all-bad or all-good outcomes 'in the affairs of men'. It flows meandering through the thickets of inspiration and delusion, visionary insights and flights of idealism, dogmatic blindness and hypnotic enslavement to some absolutist pre-conceived notions about what is good and what is bad. As we trace the unfolding of this process in development policy in search of an identity and a mobilizing theme, we find examples of all kinds of ideas—the right ones, the wrong ones, and the shadows of which fall in between these extremes. We take note of the ideas that have tried to impose low-brow uniformity on what is an essentially diverse phenomenon. These ideas have done the society no good. But our main focus is on those ideas which have opened up new opportunities for human advancement, without claiming to have actually 'exhausted the limits of the possible'. They exemplify what humankind can achieve with deep thought, reasoned dialogue and selfless commitment to the 'higher' cause of widely shared development. The account presented in these pages of the evolution of ideas about development policy is essentially optimistic, without being Utopian. It is in the spirit of knowing better what was only inadequately known before, that an effort has been made in this book to tell the story of the evolution of development policy in a manner that is both 'constructive' and 'revealing'—constructive in the sense that it gives a step-by-step account of its evolution through time; and revealing, in that it makes audible the silent symphony that echoes the deepest secrets of the development process. Inescapably the story also offers a judgment on the adequacy or otherwise of each of the paradigms to guide developing countries along the road to economic prosperity and well-being. The point is that, with the exception of watershed events that render existing thinking and doing science obsolete (something that happened at the time of the independence of the developing countries from centuries of colonial rule), constructive changes in development policy need not come in fits and starts, propelled by pseudo-paradigmatic shifts in thinking. Indeed, the premise in this book is that such changes should rather flow smoothly and incrementally from a deep understanding of the shifting reality in the developing countries—in a manner that ideally preserves good parts of the preceding developments strategies and discards the bad ones. An implication of this approach is that in formulating ideas about the future path of intellectual evolution, one need not indulge in some grand paradigm-building exercise; rather its texture must be woven by picking and choosing from the available menu of ideas—namely, the ones whose validity has been proven by sustained theoretical and empirical verification. And new ideas should be added to this menu through the process of reasoned scrutiny. The New Development Paradigm should seek to accomplish exactly this act of 'choosing and picking' as dexterously as possible. It would combine efficiency and growth criteria for evaluating the net worth of a strongly growing economy. It would, at the same time, satisfy some well-known overarching moral principle, which this book identifies as the creation of a 'well-ordered society'—one that is democratic so that its members are 'free and equal', effectively 'regulated by a public conception of justice', and where human freedom is incomplete without a compelling sense of sharing the fruits of economic progress with the least-privileged members of society. In such a society, selfish free riding on a large scale would be inconsistent with a general code of conduct that glorifies selfless behaviour.[71] These assertions become self-evident once it is remembered that 'major advances in civilizations are processes that all but wreck the societies in which they occur' [Whitehead (1972)]. Needless to say, such a gigantic undertaking is beyond the reach of the Invisible Hand, which is assumed to be guided solely by self-interest maximization behaviour. There is room for the exercise of one's narrow selfish interests as the society fares forward to meet its destiny, but the history of the future can only be envisioned optimistically when man can bury the hatchet of personal greed and commits himself towards the pursuit of unexplored horizons of development.

NOTES

1. Yet another important broad category of contributions has been labelled in this study as the Anti-Liberalist Consensus. It has shown that the development process, resting as it does on incomplete information, is essentially an externality that invites state intervention on an almost regular basis for effecting Pareto improvements—something that is beyond the

grasp of the Invisible Hand. There are also some other contributions that have clarified the relative roles of the government and the market in guiding the course of economic development. This literature has been reviewed in Part IV of this book.

2. Thus, for instance, the paradigmatic perspective used to great advantage in this book helps to rope in a much larger and diverse literature on development than the one that equates the development process with the 'factors that impede the efficient and equitable working of the market' [Ray (1998)]. For one thing, the latter view leaves out of account the moral aspect of the development process, which this book emphasizes. In particular, unlike the suggested analytical scheme suggested in this book, such a market-focused view would not include gender equity as one of the central aspects of the development process.

3. The efficiency argument justifying unemployment has been shown as vacuous [Greenwald and Stiglitz (1988)].

4. For an insightful analysis of European unemployment see Malinvaud (1984); and Sen (1999b).

5. The moral argument in favour of greater equality is that 'it puts in the hands of citizens generally, and not only of a few, the productive means to be fully cooperating members of a society' [Rawls (1999), p. xv]. This argument should be decisive enough to actively pursue greater equality as a desirable policy goal.

6. The quotation in the text is from Rawls (1999), p. 86.

7. Thus, for instance, the meteoric rise of the Liberalist Paradigm has been unrelated to anything that happened to the developing countries; it directly flowed from the universal acceptance of neo-classical economics by the economic profession in most American universities and to the fact that the international donors embraced it. The Human Development Paradigm had a more substantial basis in facts: it, like the Anti-Liberalist Consensus (see Part IV of this book), rejected the liberalist case for imposing market solutions on the developing countries; and, disputing the liberalist arguments for *laissez-faire*, has pleaded for a just international order. But in rejecting the traditional case for focusing on maximizing per capita income in the inclusive sense, it has been guided by moral considerations that devalue income as an end of development. However, as argued in this book, this rejection of the Traditional Development Paradigm has been based on a gross misunderstanding of its basic message; no one among the founding fathers of development economics argued for unalloyed capitalism.

8. The post-Colonial era in most developing countries commenced around the late 1940s.

9. See Table 2.1 (in Chapter 2) of this book for the empirical basis of the statement made in the text.

10. Lewis explicitly states, 'the advantage of growth is not that wealth increases happiness, but that it increases the range of human choice,' and that it gives 'man greater control over his environment and, thereby, increase his freedom' [Lewis (1955), pp. 420–1].

11. It may be noted that Structural Transformation soon comes to encompass agricultural transformation, migration, and urbanization [Chenery and Srinivasan (1988)].

12. However, it is important to note that, unlike the common perception, the Traditional Development Paradigm did not regard greater inequalities of income as a pre-condition for high rate of growth. This point is discussed at length in Part II of this book.

13. The point in the text needs emphasis because, contrary to folk wisdom, the Traditional Development Paradigm regarded agriculture as the leading sector. See, Parts II and IV of this book for an elaboration of this point of view.

14. Reliable empirical evidence, presented in this study, shows that the developing countries following the Traditional Development Paradigm scored significant development success in the first thirty years of economic development, especially when their performance is seen against the background of a nearly static growth of per capita income in the Colonial period [Maddison (1970)]. For instance, the best estimates of long-run growth rate of per capita income in India (and Pakistan) were no better than 0.5 per cent per annum before 1947;

and that most economists at the time did not expect it to be any higher than this figure in the future. Belying these pessimistic evaluations of the growth possibilities, the growth rate of per capita income 'subsequently attained has been about three times the rate expected' [Colin Clark (1984), p. 63]. Indeed, it has been a lot higher than Clark's figures show. See also Reynolds (1983) for a detailed comparison of the post-colonial era with the colonial times.

15. The tendency for the marginal productivity of capital to decline has been cited as one of the reasons for the eventual decline in growth rate of output in the Soviet Union towards the end of the thirty-six years of solid growth, from 1950 to 1986. It, however, remains to be explained as to why a faster rate of input accumulation did not lead to a decline in growth of output in Japan, Korea and China. Furthermore, it also remains to be investigated what happens if the elasticity of substitution turns out to be greater than one.

16. By definition, unsustainable growth is that which is consistent with a strict regime of macroeconomic stability, which the Liberalist Paradigm has limited to fiscal and monetary variables (inflation, budgetary deficits), pointedly excluding from consideration such real variables as GNP, the rate of unemployment etc. which every textbook since the time of John Maynard Keynes has treated as part of the macroeconomic picture of an economy.

17. It may be noted that, borrowing from the neo-classical economics, the Liberalist Paradigm defines first-best policies as those, which mimic competitive equilibrium in the real world.

18. Thus, Hayek (1960) insisted, it is wrong 'to suggest that those who are poor, merely in the sense that there are those in the same society who are richer, are entitled to a share in the wealth of the latter—' (p. 101). See Part III of this book for a detailed analysis of this point of view.

19. An extremist formulation of the neo-classical point of view (known as the Rational Expectants or the RATS, for short) is that private market agents have access to all the information that the government can possibly have, so that the former can anticipate and defeat the latter's every move (say to control inflation). The RATS were once very influential both in the academic and the policy-making circles, especially in the 1980s. See, Naqvi (2003) for a detailed analysis of the RATS in the development context.

20. The present study interprets Human Development Paradigm more broadly than is done in practice. In addition to the UNDP's Research Programme, it also includes the entire body of non-Utilitarian consequentialist moral philosophy, and the United Nation's Covenant on Economic, Social and Cultural Rights, the Millennium Development Declaration and the Millennium Development Goals. This redefinition of the paradigm has the merit of also bringing into its scope some of the essential elements of a just society. Indeed, without this broadening, the UNDP's Research Programme alone would not satisfy the requirements of a complete paradigm.

21. It is somewhat odd that the Human Development Paradigm does not include unhindered access to food needed for human survival as an integral element of the capability build-up—all the more so because the UN's Covenant on Economic, Social and Cultural Rights (1976) declared it as one of the fundamental rights of the individual.

22. The basic assumption here, borrowed from the endogenous growth theory, is that human capital formation, rather than physical capital formation, is the dominant driver of growth of per capita income. Indeed, the Human Development Paradigm postulates a virtuous circle that links growth and human development *via* greater human capital formation. This hypothesis has been analyzed at length in Chapter 14 of this book.

23. Empirical evidence to support the assertion in the text is given in Part VI of this book.

24. Empirical studies of the East Asian miracle growth show that human capital accounts for only one-third of the growth, the remaining two-thirds being the contribution of physical capital. These findings are significant because folk wisdom has attributed East Asian miracle almost entirely to their superior human capital formation record.

25. The link between endogenous growth theory and human development paradigm is explicitly mentioned in [UNDP (1996)]. For an evaluation of the endogenous growth theory and the limited nature of its contribution to the development policy see Part II of this book.

26. The distinction between the direct and indirect contribution that human capital formation makes to social and economic change is given in Sen (1999b). An earlier account of contribution of knowledge formation to economic growth is given in Lewis (1955).

27. Sen (1999a) summarizes the social choice theory's contribution, which this book regards as an integral part of the Human Development Paradigm, to resolving the problems of poverty and distributive injustice as follows: 'it would not be possible to talk about injustice and unfairness without having to face the accusation [delete] that such diagnoses must be inescapably arbitrary or intellectually despotic' (p. 365).

28. The empirical evidence presented towards the end of this book shows that increasing human development expenditures has been the most effective means of reducing poverty in Asia and the Pacific Region during 1965 to 2000. Next in importance, as reducers of poverty have been the decline in inequality and the growth rate of per capita income respectively.

29. Wade (2006) makes the point in the text: 'Which countries have had the fastest sustained growth rates since World War II? Japan (8 per cent from 1950 to 1980), Taiwan (8.6 per cent from 1960 to 1995), Hong Kong (7.7 per cent from 1960 to 1995), Malaysia (6.9 per cent from 1960 to 1995), Singapore (8.4 per cent from 1960 to 1995), South Korea (8.1 per cent from 1960 to 1995), Thailand (7.5 per cent from 1960 to 1995), China (8.9 per cent from 1980 to 2006), and India (6 per cent from 1980 to 2006). Botswana, Ireland, and Vietnam are also in the same league. What is striking is that all but two of the twelve are in East or South Asia, and virtually all have maintained policy regimes that would mark them as serious failures by neo-liberal criteria. Some of the worst pupils of neo-liberalism have gotten high grades, while many of the best pupils have gotten low ones'. Thus, Latin America comes out right on top of the countries that have implemented first-best policies with religious fervour only to be condemned to persistent economic stagnation, rising inequality and poverty.

30. These misunderstandings about the Traditional Development Paradigm seem to have arisen from an exclusive reading of Lewis's 1954 article, neglecting his 1955 book that contains the most definitive articulation of his ideas. The relatively more informed commentators seem to have read only the last chapter of his book.

31. Contrary to popular practice, the present study regards East Asian economies as having been the best practitioners of the Traditional Development Paradigm. Nothing they did to achieve spectacular economic success contradicted any of the prescriptions of the Traditional Development Paradigm. It, therefore, does not matter from an analytical point of view whether they practiced it consciously or unconsciously. This point has been elaborated in Part II of this book.

32. To put it more formally, the chosen alternative might not have been an optimal one, but it was manifestly maximal because there was available at the time no better alternative than the one actually chosen. For the distinction between optimization and maximization, see Sen (1997b). Even as an empirical statement, it was the best option available, in the sense that no counter-factual exercise has ever been done to show that an alternative policy would have proved to be more successful.

33. It is interesting that competent observers of the pre-reform Russian economy did not comprehend the reasons for its post-reform debacle. To give only two examples: Blanchard (1997) wrote: 'The fact that transition to come with an often large initial decrease in output should be seen as a puzzle' (p. v.); and Kornai (2000) 'My prognosis was wrong. I did not predict the deep depression that followed' (p. 21).

34. Hayek (1960) frankly states that it is wrong 'to suggest that those who are poor, merely in the sense that there are others in the same society who are richer are entitled to a share in the wealth of the latter—' (p. 101).

35. Indeed, the liberalist logic of self-help was responsible for substituting the WTO for the GATT. While the GATT emphasized that developing countries be allowed preferential entry into the developed countries' markets, they should not be required to return the favour to the latter in each case. The WTO looks at these clauses with disfavour. This point is examined at length in the ensuing chapters.

36. Adam Smith (1790) was explicit in denying that self-interest was in any way the only or the dominant principle of human motivation. 'How selfish so ever man may be supposed, there are some principles in his nature, which interest him in the fortune of others, and render their happiness necessary to him, though he derives nothing from it, except the pleasure of seeing it'.

37. A pertinent question is: if the state is in fact a selfish maximizer like any other individual, then would not the chances that it would minimize itself be close to zero [Bruton (1998)]?

38. To the argument that the government expenditure may go to waste, Lewis (1955) replied: 'The pessimists remark that there have been many cases where these vast expenditures [on public utility project normally undertaken by the government] have led to nothing, because they have been misplaced, but to conclude from this that economic growth is possible without such expenditure is an absurd non-sequitur; for his observations will not reveal to him any community where economic growth has taken place without tremendous expenditures of this kind' (p. 265).

39. Lewis (1955) emphasized the necessity of institutional change for economic growth much earlier.

40. The theoretical contributions, made in the early 1980s, showed that, 'there are, in principle, government interventions, consistent with the limitations on markets and information, which can make some individuals better off without making anyone else worse off' [Stiglitz (1991), p. 138]. These contributions have been referred to in the present study as the anti-Liberalist Consensus.

41. The argument in the text is based on Murphy, Shleifer and Vishny (1989b). It will be elaborated later in this book.

42. The reference in the text is to the Stackelberg Duopoly Model in which one firm plays the aggressive role in the market (assumes the mantle of a leader) and the other plays a passive role (that of a follower). The Stackelberg equilibrium is reached when the leader finds a point on the follower's reaction function where its profit will be maximized.

43. Development plans specifically featured the market along with the specified role of the public sector investment, mainly in areas where the private sector was not forthcoming or where the market did not exist or were liable to failure [Waterston (1965)].

44. These arguments are discussed later in this study; and in Hausman and Rodrik (2003). Feenstra (1990) Grossman and Helpman (1991).

45. A truly diabolical event in the history of nineteenth century *laissez-faire* was the forced opening of the Chinese market for the Western opium exports so that the Chinese would become addicted to opium [Stiglitz (2003)].

46. The greatest impediment in the way of a truly multilateral world system that works in the interests of the poor countries as it does for the rich is the one billion dollar-a-day subsidies paid out to the farmers in the OECD countries that have nearly destroyed African agriculture and compromised the growth possibilities of the agriculture in other developing countries. Ironically, this is happening at the time when the poverty-reducing potential of agriculture is being emphasized. Yet another impediment has been the extensive and growing use of anti-dumping duties to protect the developed countries' sunset industries from cheaper imports from developing countries. Ironically, the use of anti-dumping duties

as a protectionist instrument, mainly by the OECD countries, has witnessed an exponential increase since the creation of the rule-based WTO in 1995: during 1995 to 2003 the total number of anti-dumping initiations by reporting countries was 2,284. It is also interesting to note that rise in the use of anti-dumping measures by the West coincided with the tariff reductions agreed to during the Uruguay Round Agreement.

47. The inequities of the existing trading, payments and financial system has been most thoroughly analyzed in Stiglitz (2006).

48. Thus, for example, WTO (2004a) asserts: 'the proponents of the favourable [trade-poverty nexus] have a two-step argument: that trade promotes growth, and that growth reduces poverty—the evidence for both these propositions as dominant tendencies is very strong in our post-Second World War experience' (p. 12).

49. The Asian region has been chosen for the verification of the most important development hypotheses is that this has been the highest growing region in the world for about 40 years.

50. The adverse impact of enforced capital-market liberalization on employment and growth was indeed immense on the East Asian miracle economies: the unemployment rate increased fourfold in Korea and tenfold in Indonesia. The GDP fell by 13.1 per cent in Indonesia, by 6.7 per cent in Korea and 10.8 per cent in Thailand [Stiglitz (2003), p. 97].

51. It will be shown in Part II of this book that this is false statement. The fact is that the Traditional Development Paradigm never claimed that import substitution is superior to export expansion at all stages of economic development. It rather viewed import substitution in a historical sequence. It preceded export expansion when the primary task was to expand the domestic market and the export base; but both activities have gone together when at an advanced stage of economic development the domestic market alone could not provide enough outlets for domestic production. This tendency has been faithfully mirrored in the secular unfolding of the development process: in the pursuit of high and sustained growth all countries have had to combine both the activities in some kind of optimal proportion [Reynolds (1983)]. The fact is that even this evolutionary view is an oversimplification of what is a complex process of simultaneous determination: import substitution scoring new 'points' on the learning curve, and export expansion then helping to solidify these gains.

52. The most frequent charge; that import substitution has entailed immense resource allocation costs on the economy remains to be established. Indeed, most empirical studies show that such costs have been rather small and a necessary price paid for achieving the much more urgent developmental objectives of economic and human development.

53. Development economists have long emphasized the point made in the text. See, for instance, Chenery (1965) for a review of the relevant literature. More recently, it has been demonstrated that India's recent growth performance is more properly attributable to the expansion of the traditional import-substitution industries [(Rodrik and Subramanian [2004]].

54. Lewis (1978) observed that international trade was not the engine of growth. 'The engine of growth should rather be technological change with international trade serving as lubricating oil and not as a fuel' (p. 74).

55. The perverse scenario in the text can happen because Utilitarianism permits only mental state comparisons of inter-personal utility. Thus, more income may well be given to the hard-to-please type of rich people who many feel deprived in a given scheme of distribution and less to those poor who may feel content with the same scheme of distribution [Sen (1999a)].

56. The present book also recounts at length the significant contribution of the Anti-Liberalist Consensus to clarifying important aspects of the development problem e.g., the identification of the cases of market failure that are relevant to development context and which underline the need for state intervention to achieve Pareto-optimal results. But, going beyond the recognition of market failure, a full statement of the development problem also

requires a clear statement of a workable strategy for achieving high rates of growth of per capita income together with greater distributive justice and lower poverty. The consensus tells us that in such cases state intervention will produce Pareto-optimal results, but does not tell us how. Some theoretical contributions in the neo-classical tradition show that Big-Push strategy will be required to initiate and sustain industrialization, but it is simply an elegant re-statement of the Traditional Development Paradigm's known hypotheses. They lie outside the scope of the Anti-Liberalist Paradigm's main component, i.e. the Imperfect Information Paradigm.

57. It is one of the basic contentions of this book that only the Traditional Development Paradigm represented a correct paradigm change, in the sense that it addressed real-life development issues, which the previous economic order did not tackle. On the other hand, the rise of the Liberalist Paradigm was totally unrelated to anything adverse happening to the developing countries. The Human Development Paradigm can, however, be seen as falling between these two extreme cases. At a theoretical level, it filled a serious gap in our knowledge by bringing moral issues into economics, which also served the purpose of undermining the moral basis of the Liberalist Paradigm and its worldview. At the same time, its rejection of the Traditional Development Paradigm has been ill advised. These matters are discussed at length in this book.

58. It can be validly objected that by its very chemistry the New Development Paradigm is not a paradigm in the true sense of the term—because it does not reject the extant way of doing science. The justification for the practice followed in this book is that, notwithstanding its accommodating attitude towards rival paradigm, it has something significant to offer that others do not possess. Thus, for instance, its emphasis on inclusive growth in the sense of dealing with growth, distributive equity and poverty reduction as an irreducible policy package and its implication for development policy, are new. These matters are clarified in Part VI of this book.

59. The words 'good' and 'just' in the text are the attributes of a 'well-ordered society', as defined in Rawls (1999).These matters have been analyzed in Part VI of this book.

60. Thus, for instance, it is estimated that the 'deaths of about half a million children in 1990 would have been averted if Africa's growth rate in the 1980s had been 1.5 percentage point higher' [Easterly (2001)].

61. An elaborate statement of the balanced-growth principle is given in Chenery (1965).

62. Inter-sector balance also requires that the production for the home market be at least as much encouraged as production for exports.

63. The Traditional Development Paradigm has been routinely condemned for consciously advocating an Import Substitution (IS) strategy as opposed to an export-led strategy. Even a sympathetic reviewer of development economics, Bruton (1998) identifies the Traditional Development Paradigm as 'import-oriented as well as import-substituting' (p. 909). He, however, does not consider this to be one of its defects.

64. However, the WTO's commitment to multilateralism is not very strong. It has condoned an outbreak of bilateral and preferential trade and payments arrangements that the developed countries have concluded among themselves and with some selected developing countries. Through this strategy the developed countries have succeeded in maintaining a winning position both in bilateral arrangements and in multilateral negotiations.

65. For instance, reflecting the increasing influence of liberalist thinking, the principle of giving special and preferential treatment to the developing countries to offset their weaker bargaining position in international economic relations is now no longer looked at favourably by WTO. As a result, it has now become difficult for developing countries to practice knowledge-creating and growth-promoting import substitution policies.

66. 'WTO kills the farmers' was the refrain of the protestors at the WTO's Cancun Meeting (September 2003). The issue was dramatized by the protest suicide of a prominent farmer, Lee Kyung Hae, whose family farm had been destroyed by the WTO and IMF forced

liberalization of Mexican agriculture [Juhasz (2006)]. For a detailed analysis of the economic, social and moral aspects of globalization, see Naqvi (2006/2004); Sirageldin (2001, 2007).

67. Part of the reason for thinking about economic issues in moral terms is that, 'ethical behaviour is essentially an expression of individual volition' based on an implicit social contract of such nature that each performs duties for the other in a way calculated to enhance the satisfaction of all' [Arrow (1974), p. 348].

68. Sen (2002c) refers to persons who profess to be guided only by self-interest maximization rule as 'rational fools', a person who gives the same answer to such distinct ideas as 'what serves my interest best'; 'what are my goals'; 'what shall I do' and have no use even 'for different reasons for choice' (p. 7).

69. Sen (1999b and 2002c) and Lewin (1996) contain an illuminating discussion of the variety of behavioural traits noted in the text.

70. The point in the text is worth noting. It is that the acceptance of self-interest as one of the major traits of human character does not mean that it is its dominant characteristic. Considerations like 'commitment' (which involves self-sacrifice in actual situations) provide a much better explanation of the human behaviour, especially in times of grave crises. To put it rather differently, the fact that people have within themselves to act selfishly does not mean that they always will so act—especially, when the cause is to commit oneself to improving the well-being of one's and other's children and grandchildren through participation in development-related activities.

71. The definition of a 'well-ordered society' noted in the text is from Rawls (1999). The members of such a society are actually motivated by a sense of justice and sharing. The dimension of this concept in the context of economic and human development will be given at different places in this book.

2

Introduction

John Maynard Keynes (1936) had famously remarked, 'Soon or late, it is ideas, not vested interests, which are dangerous for good or evil' (p. 384). But no set of ideas has been as 'dangerous for good or evil' as that relating to the economic and human development of poorer countries where the majority of humankind resides. There have been attempts to alleviate the sufferings of the poor people, but the unfinished development agenda remains large and daunting. However, a consistent application of the 'right' ideas in many developing countries (located mostly in Asia) has been crowned with remarkable success: measured against their pre-colonial economic heritage of economic stagnation, unacceptable inequity and entrenched poverty, per capita incomes and the quality of life have risen dramatically. In some of these countries (East Asia and China), development success has been miraculous—their per capita incomes have doubled within a decade, for the first time in human history. Millions of people have been pulled out of the quagmire of poverty, most convincingly in the high-growth countries. But, contrary to widespread misconception, high growth rates have not been unique to the East Asian tiger economies.[1] As shown in subsequent chapters, 'development leaders' (those with the highest rates of growth) in the last fifty years or so have come from all the developing regions, including Africa and Latin America, at different time periods during the last fifty years or so. These feats in growing leadership are a befitting tribute to the creative application of 'right ideas' in the domain of public policy. It also proves that infirmities of human condition can be (and have been) overcome by determined and sustained development effort. They have also shed new light on the intricacies of the development process and what it takes to accelerate it. There has arisen a reality of development, the brilliance of which cannot be denied. There is a universal upsurge of reverence for high growth achievers; and the urge to move forward economically has caught on in most developing countries, no less because of a conviction that high growth and reduction of poverty is possible, though not inevitable, whenever the link between the two is held tightly by deft management. Indeed, a longing for economic prosperity has informed politics as well. The 'fluent' political rhetoric, in which the developing countries have enjoyed an absolute as well as a comparative advantage, is gradually being replaced by a national commitment to becoming economically 'affluent' as well. Political power is now seen as emanating from fast rates of economic and human development that promise to transform, through essentially peaceful means, man's life within a generation and attain convergence with the developed countries.[2] In many developing countries, the target for achieving 6-8 per cent growth of the GDP or more—not long ago regarded as untrue—has been repeatedly mentioned as a practical economic objective to aim at. Human development has, on average, risen in tandem with the growth rate of per capita income.[3] Development experience shows that once high growth rates are sustained for long enough periods in essentially democratic and egalitarian economies then human capabilities also expand. The Chinese example shows that extraordinary development performance, rather than aggressive sabre-rattling, can project developing countries towards international publicity.

2.1. A SOBERING THOUGHT

Developing countries and development economists can be justly proud of these solid development achievements.[4] But a lot remains to be done (and be undone). Notwithstanding the impressive episodes of economic success in some developing countries, there are others where extreme poverty and famines still persist. There are, more worryingly, cases of development reversals caused mainly by exogenous causes—the most devastating of which has been the AIDS pandemic, which, in Africa alone has killed countless millions and has cancelled development gains.[5] These are also the countries where the burden of external debt is the highest. The cases of growth success and failure have, however, one element in common: they suggest that, going beyond achieving high growth rates of per capita income, one must take several additional steps to alleviate (income and non-income) poverty on a lasting basis, and achieve distributive equity within nations and between nations. To this end, developing countries must clear the decks of the 'wrong ideas', whose faithful observance has practically upended economic and human development in economies that once had grown reasonably fast for a decade or so (those located in Latin America and Africa and Eastern Europe).[6] Their advancement has been arrested: relative to their development achievements in 1990, fifty-four countries became poorer, twenty-one experienced the incidence of acute hunger, and fourteen saw primary school enrolment decline in 2003.[7] More specifically, six million children under the age of five still die of diseases that could have been easily and cheaply controlled; forty million people are unable to go to school, three hundred million Africans lack access to clean water, and so on. A recent World Bank assessment points out that extreme poverty in Africa (spending less than a dollar-a-day on the basic necessities of life) rose from 36 per cent of the population in 1970 to around 50 per cent of the population (300 million people) in 2000. It has 10 per cent of the global population but accounts for 30 per cent of the world's poor.

The scourge of economic regress resulted in a rise in global unemployment to 185.7 million people between 1990 and 2000; and 59 per cent of the world population lived in countries where inequality of income and wealth has increased, and only 5 per cent where it has declined.[8] Furthermore, the distances between the developing and developed countries and the rich and poor peoples have generally widened with the passage of time, and have bred mutual distrust, ill-will and discord between them.[9] But these rather extreme cases of development failure are not the only ones that have poisoned international economic relations: no less important is the fact that, with the exception of the miracle growers and some others, the developing countries have not been able to achieve absolute convergence with the developed countries—which was once accepted widely as an achievable major developmental objective [Pritchett (1995); IMF (2000)]. The need to accelerate economic and human development at the fastest feasible rates, therefore, remains as pressing as ever. In particular, the long-lost growth momentum in Africa and Latin America must be revived and the high growth rates already achieved in South Asia and East Asia sustained, to bring hope to the millions of dispossessed people throughout the developing world.

2.2. GLOBAL RESPONSIBILITY FOR DEVELOPMENT

Fortunately, more widely understood than in the past is that the challenge facing most developing countries is enormous, and that it cannot be met by their own efforts alone, for the simple reason, that they cannot be held entirely responsible for their state of underdevelopment, past or present. The fact is that world trade and financial systems have not let the developing countries grow 'to the full complements of their riches'. Notwithstanding the creation of rule-based international organizations (the WTO, in particular), and freer international flows of goods, services, knowledge and technologies, a disproportionate share of the benefits of globalization has accrued to the rich countries while the poor countries have generally come out as net losers in the development game. Through unguarded and relentless implementation of market-friendly national and global policies, 'the benefits of the world trading system are very unevenly shared, while its costs are [also] unevenly shared' [UN (2000)]. Unfortunately, there is nothing unintended about it; the developing countries have reaped what the developed countries sowed. So the developing countries have a long struggle ahead of them. For them to succeed, the responsibility for their current misfortunes has to be globally shared. The

Millennium Development Goals reflect such a global understanding of the causes of the 'poverty of nations'. However, to translate this noble global commitment into solid achievements, the current intellectual and moral ambiguity about what constitutes 'right' development policies must be dispelled. A wise and informed development policy with a clear divide of 'right' and 'wrong' ideas is the need of the day for moving towards economic progress.

A lot is at stake. Africa and the Transition Economies have collapsed in on them, with no end in sight. True, South Asia and East Asia have moved resolutely towards economic prosperity, but the authorship of their prosperity has been a subject of endless debate—has it been the handiwork of the Invisible Hand, or that of the socially committed governments, or of both? It is important that we, avoiding such sterile debates apply time-tested ideas to get the right answers to the elemental developmental questions. But to get such answers we need to critically examine the pattern of the evolution of development policy and prescribe ways and means of doing the needed course-correction.

2.3. THE EVOLUTION OF DEVELOPMENT POLICY

The present study offers an apparently self-evident suggestion: In the quest for economic prosperity, eschew the 'wrong' ideas (i.e., the ideas which have ostensibly led to development failures, even disasters) and hold firmly onto the 'right' ones (those whose contribution to notable, even miraculous, development success has been empirically established). But the reasons behind this suggestion are by no means self-evident. Understanding them requires a detailed theoretical and empirical analysis of development history in the last half a century or so. In order to comprehend the development process in its essential multi-dimensionality, and to guide developing economies on the fastest road to modernity, this book has sought to highlight the elemental inter-relationships among growth, distributive equity and poverty reduction as linked together in an indissoluble chain so that achieving them together, rather than one at a time, is the only way to attain success. Its general approach can be variously described as: 'revisionist' (it makes a case for the revival of the valid core of the Traditional Development Paradigm), 'radical' (it finds the Liberalist Paradigm wanting in the development context) and 'reformist' (it modifies somewhat the Human Development Paradigm to bring out its essential contribution to knowledge). But insofar as the New Development Paradigm proposed in this book consciously seeks to incorporate the empirically valid features of all past and present development paradigms, it is inescapably 'eclectic'. In the Marxian vein, it tries to understand not only the nature and significance of reality, and the perceptions of it in the developing countries, but change it for the betterment of poor peoples. This analytical framework has permitted us to look at nearly all the foundational development problems and issues—namely, growth, equity and poverty reduction; market and government, export expansion and import substitution, domestic market expansion and foreign trade as drivers of economic progress, and the morality's role in development—from different, and in some cases original, analytical angles. We then present empirical evidence, which is spread throughout the book, to decide some of these basic issues.

2.3. (i). The Paradigmatic Taxonomy[10]

In order to see the formation of development policies together with the basic value systems on which these are based, the present study has sought to trace their evolution in paradigmatic terms—from the Traditional Development Paradigm to the Liberalist Paradigm, and to the Human Development Paradigm. Then there are sets of ideas, which have emanated from a fundamental revision of the Arrow-Debreu neo-classical research programme. These ideas have been brought together in this book under a suggestive title: Anti-Liberalist Consensus, to highlight the basic thrust of its large and varied academic output. This paradigmatic narrative is then used to highlight the need for an informed New Development Paradigm, which is expected to yield a 'rightly guided' development policy. The aim of this exercise is to clear the intellectual confusion that has engulfed the academia and policy-makers alike for at least the last three decades.

The Traditional Development Paradigm: One of the recognizable features of this book is the unusually large space (Chapters 3 to 6) given to the analysis of the Traditional Development Paradigm—for a very important reason. This book regards the Traditional Development Paradigm as the undisputed 'keeper of the flame': it is the repository of most of the 'right' ideas about the mechanics of growth and development that have transformed the lives of the people in an unbelievably short period of time. It, therefore, argues that the near-universal decision of the academic community and the international donors to scuttle the Traditional Development Paradigm in the 1980s was both wrong and harmful. A somewhat scandalous aspect of that fateful rejection of what was essentially right is that it was done for the wrong reasons. Thus, contrary to folk wisdom, this book denies that it advocated a one-point growth-only agenda through state-directed industrialization. Much nearer the truth is that it offered a broad-based development agenda that focused on societal transformation and the creation of the growth-oriented institutions as the fastest road to modernity. Similarly, there is not much substance in the charge that it advocated flint-hearted 'growth fundamentalism' that did not care about equity or poverty reduction. In fact, it emphasized the quintessentially egalitarian nature of economic growth. Land reforms were actively advocated as beneficial to equity and growth; and the gradual urbanization of the economy was expected to help the emergence of a financially and socially strong middle class—both of which would stimulate the demand for industrialization and economic development. It also advocated the view that economic development, in a deeper sense, contributed to human freedom from want, hunger, drudgery and outdated feudal structures; and that economic, social and moral objectives of economic development could best be achieved within the framework of the elementary political freedom that democratic societies routinely provide.

The empirical evidence that is usually cited against the accomplishments of the Traditional Development Paradigm is also questionable. Most reliable studies show that it helped to bring about an overall improvement in the major economic and human development indicators that was ubiquitous and persistent throughout the developing world, but most convincing in East Asia, on a scale which could not be anticipated by the most prescient of the observers at the time. The source of much intellectual confusion has been the near-universal misunderstanding that the geographical writ of the Traditional Development Paradigm was limited to the relatively slower growing economies of Latin America and South Asia. The fact is that the same policies (the ones that Traditional Development Paradigm advocated) were used in both the slow growing and the miracle growing countries. The observed differential between the growth performances of developing countries was mainly due to the efficiency with which the same ideas and policies were implemented.[11] The empirical work reported in this study establishes this point convincingly.

This book, therefore, relates the story of the evolution of development policy in constructive fashion: it first evaluates the success or otherwise of the development strategies that most developing countries pursued between 1950 and 1980. These strategies emphasized the urgency of achieving high rates of economic and human development in the post-colonial period, with a view to reducing poverty and achieving convergence with the developed countries, even if that meant incurring some static efficiency cost. To this end, it focused, among others, on an essentially growth-oriented strategy, which shared three common characteristics: (a) it aimed at bringing about a systemic transformation of the society from a rural based society to an urban-based social entity; (b) it required a dominant role of the government to implement such a 'revolutionary' vision of economic progress, for the simple reason, that the market could not handle such a Herculean assignment; (c) its near-universal validity has been established both theoretically and empirically.

The Liberalist Paradigm: The next step in the evolution of development policy is the emergence of the Liberalist Paradigm from nowhere in 1980, with a view to extending the writ of unfettered markets from esoteric neo-classical models to the real world. It has actively been implemented since then in the developing countries through the Structural Adjustment Programmes of the IMF and the World Bank. It has radically altered the policy framework of the Traditional Development Paradigm in the name of scientific probity, which invariably has meant an uncompromising insistence on: efficiency to the exclusion of all other worthwhile objectives of public policy; minimization of government intervention in economic affairs, so that domestic and global markets can work freely; and falling back on the principle of (static) comparative advantage as the best possible guide to achieving economic development at least cost. Assuming no significant trade-offs between the winners and losers from growth and development, the Liberalist Paradigm has blithely ignored equity-related reformist issue. That important omission allowed it to accord overarching primacy to maintaining macroeconomic stability, which has been defined narrowly to focus only on low inflation rate, low budgetary and trade deficits as a percentage of the GDP, and a 'realistic' exchange rate.[12] A fairly detailed analysis of the Liberalist Paradigm is given in Chapters 7, 8 and 9. Much of this material should be familiar to most readers. The only thing different about it may be that the manifest inadequacy of the Liberalist Paradigm is traced to its non-consequentialist moral philosophy, and not to any ulterior motives that its practitioners might harbour towards the developing countries. Even a perfectly honest man with the best of intentions for the developing countries would probably think in roughly the same manner as long as he subscribed to its underlying economic priorities and moral philosophy.[13]

Anti-Liberalist Consensus: Next in order is a fairly detailed discussion of what this book christens as the anti-Liberalist Consensus, which has essentially challenged (since 1980 or so) the market-can-do-no-wrong libertarian contention. It shows that with imperfect information and incomplete markets, competitive equilibrium is not generally un-improvable. That demonstration has created immense policy space for Pareto-improving government intervention. It also shows that, contrary to the neo-classical (and classical) argument, unemployment is by no means a sign of market imperfection—the inevitable result of wages being too high. Whence, it follows that reducing the going (efficiency) wage rate would not necessarily improve market efficiency and create additional effective demand.[14] Indeed, doing so might lower industrial productivity. Another set of studies in the Consensus's fold shows that, in a dynamic context, when account is taken of dynamic external economies, static comparative advantage would no longer be suitable as a criterion for optimal resource allocation, nor would it optimize growth or social welfare. An implication of this line of research is to turn one of the basic recommendations of the Liberalist Paradigm on its head and show that import substitution, rather than export fetishism would most likely lead to maximal growth. Under this heading are included contributions, made in a self-consciously neo-classical tradition, that provide a modern and analytical rendering of the some of the basic ideas of the Traditional Development Paradigm—namely, the Structural Transformation and the Big-Push hypotheses, and their distributive implications. Chapters 10, 11 and 12 recapitulate the highlights of this large literature in some detail. The book, however, makes the point that, for all its originality and perspicacity, this literature does not qualify as a new development paradigm, if only because a deeper understanding of the factors that lead to market failure does not exhaust the growth-promoting and inequity and poverty-reducing possibilities of development policy.[15] However, this 'defect' does not detract from the critical importance of these contributions to a clearer understanding of several aspects development process, which the Liberalist Paradigm had obscured from view. No less important is the fact that these seminal analyses have brought neo-classical economics 'closer' to reality.

Human Development Paradigm: Partly as a reaction to the Liberalist Paradigm's excesses, but also as the outcome of an essentially endogenous evolution of economic science to deal effectively with the equity-related issues, the Human Development Paradigm has shifted rather radically (and not always fruitfully) the analytical and policy focus to a broader vision of human freedoms—one that allows individuals to make the choices they value most within the framework of an egalitarian, democratic and caring society. Towards these ends, it emphasizes the centrality of creating just social institutions with a view to helping the passage of the ill-ordered societies to a 'well-ordered society. An important implication of this principle is that, 'we cannot preserve our sense of justice and all it implies, while at the same time holding ourselves ready to act unjustly should, in doing so, promise some personal advantage' [Rawls (1999), pp. 497–498]. While admitting the 'natural' human urge to maximize one's self-interest, the Human Development Paradigm clarifies that it is no less natural to be committed to the cause of human development, or to recognize fulfilling contracts or acting honestly even if that means some personal loss. To this end, it focuses on the complex relationship between rationality, freedom and justice to get a complete view of human motivation.[16] A fairly detailed analysis of the Human Development Paradigm is given in Chapters 13 to 18. The reader will note that the analysis presented in these chapters differs from the conventional expositions in several ways. Firstly, it defines the paradigm much more broadly than is usually the case. The highly original UNDP Research Programme appears as one, though perhaps the most visible, element of the Human Development

Paradigm; its other elements being the entire modern non-Utilitarian consequentialist moral philosophy, due mainly to the path-breaking works of John Rawls and Amartya Sen, and the United Nations many resolutions—especially the Convention on Economic, Social and Cultural Rights (1976); the Universal Declaration of Human Rights (2000) and; the Millennium Development Goals. It is contended that such broadening of scope of the Human Development Paradigm is essential for establishing its paradigmatic character. Secondly, the present study points out that the Human Development Paradigm draws much too sharply, the distinction between growth of income and non-income aspects of development, and generally between economic development and human development. Even though they are not the same, the fact remains that the one cannot live without the other. Thirdly, it is argued that the Human Development Paradigm has been in error in downgrading the importance of the growth of per capita income for achieving human development. Indeed, for that omission, it does not possess any satisfactory mechanism for explaining and sustaining high rates of growth of per capita income, which are so vital for poverty reduction. It will be shown later on in this book that greater expenditures on education and health help to distribute the fruits of economic progress but they do not directly contribute to growth in a statistically significant way.[17] Furthermore, empirical evidence presented in this book strongly suggests, contrary to what the Human Development Paradigm does, that physical capital formation has been one of the most 'stable' and significant factors contributing to growth in the developing countries, including the miracle growers (in the sense that addition of new variables on the right-hand side of the regression equation does not much alter its statistical significance). The implication is not that human capital formation is unimportant; rather it is that both are required to fire the engine of growth.

The New Development Paradigm: The preceding analysis points to the need for an essentially eclectic and 'well-informed' paradigm—one that affirms some of the conventional wisdom about what an adequate development policy should focus on. These issues are analyzed in Chapters 19 to 22. Their main point is that the New Development Paradigm though sympathetic to the Traditional Development Paradigm, it does not just recall its silent memory; rather it essentially consists of its creative symbiosis with the wisdom of the Human Development Paradigm. It aims at forming a comprehensive, well-informed overarching vision of economic processes in general and seeing the inter-connections between growth, distributive justice (including gender equity) and poverty reduction as an irreducible policy package in particular. Yet another of its defining characteristics is that, rather than seeing the key development issues in a futile confrontational posture of this-*versus*-that—namely, government *versus* the market, agriculture *versus* industry, physical *versus* human capital formation, factor (input) accumulation *versus* productivity growth, export expansion *versus* import substitution, economic development versus human development etc.—the New Development Paradigm looks at these important matters in a 'balanced' way. It pays attention to some of the key insights of the Liberalist Paradigm—that is, the inflation rate; the budget and trade deficits, and exchange rates should be kept within safe limits. But, it does not accept liberalist absolutism with respect to macroeconomic stability; instead, it argues for broadening its area of concern to the adverse consequences of this exercise on growth, unemployment and poverty. These issues are discussed at length in Chapters 19 to 22. The last two chapters conclude the argument and offer a constructive vision of a fruitful development policy.

2.4. DEVELOPMENT EXPERIENCE

It may be noted at the outset that one of the important reasons for reinterpreting the evolution development policy which this book presents, is to strengthen the skimpy empirical foundations on which much of the extant thinking on development policy rests. To this end, pooled data for 18 developing countries for the years 1965 to 2000, from the Asia-Pacific region, have been used to re-examine nearly all the basic propositions of rival paradigms concerning the relationship between: growth and structural transformation; growth and human development,; growth and macroeconomic stability; growth and inequity and; growth and poverty. The equation for poverty, in particular, is one of the most important aspects of this exercise. It unifies many points of view and corrects some common misconceptions about how best to go about reducing poverty. An additional attraction of this exercise is to disaggregate the regional data into East Asian and non-East Asian countries to see the differences between them with respect to their choice of development policies. The outcome of this empirical exercise is to confirm the point of view that the same set of policies caused the miracle in East Asia, and in the relatively slower-growth non-East Asian economies— namely, above all, higher-than-trend rate of physical and human capital formation and saving rate required to finance the highest ever rate of Structural Transformation. But it does not confirm the general view that a higher rate of human capital formation in East Asia made the difference between it and the non-East Asia. This result, however, does not contradict the fact that human capital formation was a significant contributor to growth.

As a preface to the detailed presentation of the results of the empirical exercise done for this book, it will be instructive at this point to note some of the key characteristics of developing countries and their experiences with economic and human development since the 1960s. Table 2.1 computed from the different sources, on as comparable basis as possible, summarizes the relevant information. The pooled data presented in the table should help us read, at a glance, their absolute and relative inter-temporal economic perform-ance in relation to some of the key variables routinely cited in the develop-ment literature.[18] The information given in the table gives a fairly suggestive picture of the developing economies, spread over a large non-oil producing geographic area—including Africa, Latin America, East Asia (including China) and South Asia (including India). Some tentative observations can legitimately be made even at this preliminary stage about the reasonableness of the many hypotheses that the rival paradigm have made—even though a definitive confirmation or rejection of these must await a more sophisticated regression analysis presented towards the end of the book.

2.4. (i). Growth Rate of GDP and Per Capita GDP (first and second rows)

The growth rates of the GDP in developing countries have generally improved over time, with East Asia on top of the growth performers list. Thus, through the 1960s and 1970s, East Asia growth rate at above 8 per cent was well above the rest of the developed countries. However, other regions' growth record has also been impressive, though it has varied over time. Yet another notable event is Africa's faster growth rate than that of Latin America and South Asia. However, the tide began to turn for it from the 1980s onwards and it slipped well below the rest of the pack. Latin America's growth also began to founder from 1980s onwards. These events have some important implications for the changes in development policy over time; and will be analyzed later in this book. South Asia surpassed both Latin America and Africa during 1980s and 1990s.

The second row paints a similar, though clearer picture of growth performance of the developing countries in per capita terms. It can be seen that the growth differential between the regions is significant; but with the exception of South Asia, there is a definite slackening of growth rates after the 1970s. The polar case is that of Africa where growth rate sunk to a very low level. Nothing definite can be said just by looking at these figures about the causative factors that might have caused the growth rates, outside of South Asia, to generally decelerate after the 1970s. However, these figures do confirm the overall superiority of East Asia in its development performance, both, absolutely and in relation to others. It may be noted that the 'African problem' arose only after the 1970s. Latin America is the other hard-hit area, whose performance generally decelerated after 1970s. It is well known that the main factors causing the growth rates to decline in Latin America and Africa were the exogenous shock; a steep rise in the global interest rates and;

the two oil shocks—which practically pulverized these economies. These shocks also affected East Asia adversely but to a much smaller extent. However, the relatively 'closed' economies of South Asia remained virtually unaffected by these shocks. A couple of points may be made at this very preliminary stage of our empirical investigation. (a) With the exception of Africa in the 'post-shock' period, none of the developing countries experienced 'development failure'. (b) Many exogenous shocks in the 1970s seem to have been correlated with the slackening of development effort throughout the developing world, with the exception of South Asia, which was the least 'open' of the developing world. This watershed event suggests that openness has not always been an unmixed blessing.

2.4. (ii). Saving and Investment Rates (third and fourth rows)

The table shows that saving and investment rates have steadily risen all over the developing world, far beyond anybody's expectations in the 1950s. (a) The (high) saving rates exceeded the investment rates in East Asia and Latin America in the 1980s and 1990s suggesting that they might have become capital exporters. Elsewhere, the saving and investment rates increased but the former consistently fell short of investment rates, so that their dependence on capital imports has continued. This seems to have been a pervasive phenomenon in the developing countries. (b) Read along with the first two lines, it is obvious that high growth rates have always been associated with high saving and investment rates. As a general tendency, the reverse of this statement has also been true over the 1965 to 2000 period.

2.4. (iii). Structural Transformation (fifth and sixth rows)

Table 2.1 highlights yet another fact—indeed, it can be called a 'stylized fact' for its regularity and universality. It is that the Structural Transformation of the developing countries increased at a fairly rapid pace throughout the developing world, but especially so in East Asia and Latin America. An implication of this tendency is that import substitution has not been limited to the slow-growing countries or regions; it has taken place throughout the developing world. Also, while Africa's per capita income has grown at a much slower rate than that of South Asia, the rate of Structural Transformation in the former is much higher than in latter. What do these trends suggest about the relationship between growth of per capita income and the degree of Structural Transformation? It does show that the causes of Africa's failure lie more in its stars (i.e., in the exogenous factors) than in its weak economic fundamentals or to its lesser degree of industrialization. The relationship between investment, Structural Transformation and growth of per capita

Table 2.1: Selected Development Indicators (1960–2000). (In percentage terms)

Indicators	South Asia				East Asia				Latin America				Africa			
	1960s	1970s	1980s	1990s	1960s	1970s	1980s	1990s	1960s	1970s	1980s	1990s	1960s	1970s	1980s	1990s
Growth Rate of GDP	3.59	3.38	4.79	4.98	8.12	8.08	7.78	6.79	5.38	5.56	4.48	4.48	5.73	5.19	3.19	3.29
Growth Rate of GDP per capita	1.15	0.96	2.48	3.04	5.87	5.99	5.93	5.24	2.72	3.20	2.82	2.82	3.02	2.16	0.09	0.94
Saving GDP Ratio	9.30	9.90	11.4	14.1	18.36	27.50	35.29	36.93	18.86	21.14	23.29	21.57	17.00	15.10	15.10	13.0
Investment GDP Ratio	12.80	17.0	21.2	19.8	21.79	29.07	33.86	31.07	19.64	22.14	22.14	20.07	18.80	21.90	20.90	20.0
Industry GDP Ratio	15.40	19.8	22.6	24.4	27.86	33.57	37.79	38.14	32.14	35.93	36.57	33.00	26.00	28.70	30.60	28.0
Agriculture GDP Ratio	43.20	44.0	37.3	30.2	24.21	19.93	14.43	11.07	19.07	13.00	10.21	9.57	31.50	31.70	26.60	23.0
Export GDP Ratio	11.80	11.9	13.8	17.7	31.21	44.71	69.86	84.43	11.64	13.71	19.57	27.14	23.40	25.50	26.50	25.0
Public investment GDP Ratio	9.40	9.9	9.1	10.9	11.14	11.07	11.00	9.57	9.64	10.64	10.36	10.57	13.20	16.90	17.60	17.0
Inflation	4.72	11.6	9.26	8.48	7.79	11.24	5.39	6.06	18.66	61.54	152.83	46.13	3.34	13.82	17.40	19.6
Poverty	-	-	39.5	36.8	-	-	12.70	12.67	-	-	25.71	26.20	-	-	55.00	54.5
Gini Coefficient	-	-	-	34.4	-	-	-	39.66	-	-	-	52.87	-	-	-	40.0
Share of Lowest 20 per cent income group	7.10	-	-	8.38	7.22	-	-	6.46	3.53	-	-	3.73	-	-	-	6.53
Share of Highest 20 per cent income group	39.30	-	-	43.2	42.10	-	-	46.64	49.75	-	-	57.47	-	-	-	45.5

Sources: Computed from Penn World Tables-Version 6.1, *The Human Development Reports* (various issues) and *World Development Reports* (various issues)

Note: Following countries are included in the regional classification. South Asia: Bangladesh, India, Nepal, Pakistan and Sri Lanka. East Asia: Hong Kong, Korea (leader in 1980s at a growth rate of 7.46 per cent), Indonesia, Malaysia, Singapore (leader in 1960s at a growth rate of 11 per cent), Thailand and China (leader in 1990s at growth rate of 8.02 per cent). Latin America: Argentina, Brazil, Chile, Colombia, Ecuador, México, Peru. Africa: Botswana (leader in 1970s at growth rate of 9.82 per cent), Egypt, Ethiopia, Kenya, and Zambia.

income, however, raises some fundamental questions about the mechanics of development. A satisfactory answer to them cannot be given just by looking at the relevant figures in Table 2.1; it requires a deeper empirical analysis, which will be presented later in this book.

An implication of the Structural Transformation, or more accurately its essential characteristic, is the declining trend in the share of agriculture in GDP through the developing world. A couple of aspects of this trend should be noted: (a) The secular decline in the percentage share of agriculture in the GDP should by no means be confused with the decline in its growth rate. This is an elementary point but has often been a source of confusion; the share of agriculture in GDP must decline by the inexorable working of the Engel's Law, no matter how fast it grows. (b) The share of agriculture has declined the fastest in Latin America followed by East Asia, Africa and South Asia in that order. However, it can be seen that this historical tendency does not seem to be strongly correlated with the growth rate of per capita income. It has declined more in Latin America than in East Asia, even though the growth rates in the latter have been consistently higher than those of the former. Similarly, Africa's per capita income has practically stagnated in the post-Shock period while that of South Asia has grown steadily; and predictably the share of agriculture has been consistently lower in Africa than in South Asia. This suggests that growth of per capita income is probably more directly influenced by the rising share of manufacturing than a decline in the share of agriculture. But this is only a guess that needs investigation.

2.4. (iv). Openness (seventh row)

The export/GDP ratio has increased in all the developing countries, but more so in East Asia. Does this suggest that the growth rate of per capita income there has been export-led? This claim has been made, but it remains to be established. The high export ratio in Africa has been associated with a stagnant growth of the economy, and with a slackening of the growth momentum in Latin America. Also, the significantly lower export-GDP ratio in South Asia sustained a much faster growth rate of income than has been the case in Africa and Latin America. In other words, a steep rise in the export/GDP ratio might as well have been associated with higher rate of growth of per capita income as with a lower growth rate. There is every reason to believe, on the other hand, that one of the reasons for the economic decline of Africa might have been its unduly high export/GDP ratio; excessive openness made it a 'sitting duck' when recessionary forces (increase in the price of oil and the steep increase in the interest rates) struck the region. (b) Depending as it does rather heavily on international trade, the secular decline in the prices of the commodities that Africa exports, and the corresponding reduction in the purchasing power to import goods needed for its development must have affected its growth potential more than that of other countries that are not so open. (c) The sharp rise in the export/GDP ratio has been cited as a proof of the oft-repeated statement that growth was higher there because it was export-led. But this statement is only partly true. The fact is that the gradual rise in the export/GDP ratio from 1960s to 1970s and a sharp increase, thereafter, in East Asia is more a sign of export expansion coming on the heels of a successful import-substitution programme that diversified its exports. At any rate, not much can be inferred from reading Table 2.1 about the phenomenon of export-led growth. This matter is investigated in more detail at appropriate places in the book.

2.4. (v). The Size of Government (eighth row)

However, the table clearly shows that the size of the government (as measured by the ratio of public expenditure to the GDP) has by no means been excessive in the developing world. The demand for a minimalist government is, therefore, misplaced. Furthermore, the size of the government has remained practically stagnant in most of the developing world, around 10 per cent of GDP, but in Africa, it increased significantly at a time when its growth stagnated. Does it mean that larger government was in any way responsible for the much slower growth in Africa? Such a correlation has been asserted but it must be far-fetched at best. A better explanation could be that a slower growth of their economies might have spurred on the African governments to act in time to save the situation from getting worse. The fact is that the secular decline in world prices of African exports has been a very important factor in the decline of the economic fortunes of Africa. This would warrant government intervention, not leaving it to the free markets, which caused this decline in the first place. A reasonable suggestion would, therefore, be that without such intervention, its downward slide might have been sharper and more disastrous.

2.4. (vi). Inflation Rate (ninth row)

A striking fact about the developing countries is that, with the exception of Latin America, inflation rates have been confined to low-to-moderate range. Yet another important consideration is that low-to-moderate inflation rates seem to have been more frequently correlated with high, rather than low, rate of growth of per capita income. The point is that firm generalizations about inflation growth cannot be made just on the basis of reading the two time-series together. This statement does not lend support to monetary or fiscal policy radicalism, nor does it suggest that we can be careless about high inflation rates.

2.4. (vii). Growth and Poverty (tenth row)

On the poverty-growth relationship, the rather skimpy evidence in the table does suggest that poverty has declined most rapidly in the highest growing East Asia; but it increased in Latin America when growth slackened. Also, the level of poverty has been the lowest in East Asia and the highest in Africa. One would, therefore, be probably justified in associating high growth rate of per capita income with a reduction in poverty. But here too one must be cautious: the level of poverty has been higher in South Asia (where growth has been somewhat higher) than in Latin America, even though the growth rate of income has been higher in the former than in the latter. Furthermore, somewhat paradoxically, poverty slightly declined in Africa in 1990s while the growth rate of per capita income remained stagnant.[19] However, the paucity of comparable data should be taken into account when making generalizations about it.

2.4. (viii). Growth and Inequity (eleventh, twelfth and thirteenth rows)

The connection between growth and inequity, measured by the Gini coefficient, and the differential between the shares of the lowest and the highest 20 per cent of the total population, seems to be more ambiguous than that between growth and poverty. Thus, inequality seems to increase with high rate of economic growth: inequality is higher in East Asia than in South Asia; but it is less than in the slower-growing Latin America. And the slowest-growing Africa is the least egalitarian. In other words, greater inequality goes with faster growth as well as slower growth. No firm generalization, therefore, can be made by just looking at Table 2.1. More rigorous regression analysis is required to establish the relationships between growth and poverty on the one hand; and growth and inequity on the other.

2.5. Concluding Remarks

A series of paradigmatic shifts in the realm of ideas have been responsible for making abrupt changes in the focus of development policy in the developing countries. Thus, even such a manifestly beneficial phenomenon as the high rate of economic growth of per capita income in the post-colonial era has fallen prey to the vagaries of interpretation: development policy has been refocused, by turn, on maximal growth (Traditional Development Paradigm);

on sustainable growth (the Liberalist Paradigm); on pro-poor growth and yet again; on building up capabilities (the Human Development Paradigm). This rather discontinuous evolution of development policy has not proved to be fruitful, partly because at each turn of paradigmatic growth path, all previous knowledge about how best to deal with the mysteries of the development process has been rejected outright. This has led to intellectual confusion and a confrontational position-taking on the vital issues—such as how to go about achieving the highest possible growth rates, distributive justice and the lowest levels of poverty and human deprivation as an irreducible policy package. The development potential of the developing countries, as a result, has remained grossly under-utilized. A more promising approach to the future evolution of development policy would, therefore, be to learn from the past, if only because no set of ideas are completely wrong or right. What is needed is achieving a creative synthesis of the theoretically and empirically valid hypotheses and recommendations of each of the paradigms discussed in this book. This should lead to a better-informed New Development Paradigm that eschews the unhelpful controversies about what caused development. It should, instead, focus on the gradual construction of a new intellectual architecture that could avoid the mistakes of the past, and lead development policy in the future for the good of mankind.

NOTES

1. The statement made in the text is an implicit rejection of the liberalist position that the miraculous growth episodes have been unique to the miracle growers of East Asia; and that these are not replicable in other developing countries. [World Bank (1993)].
2. The break-up of the Soviet Union has, to a large extent, been attributed to a gross disparity between its economic power and political ambitions to be counted as a first-world military power. Its tragic example is one more reason for the countries to be as strong on economic performance. Indeed, as compared with the situation in the early 1950s and 1960s, the demand for populist leaders who are strong on pretentious rhetoric but fail to deliver development seems to have sharply declined.
3. The statement in the text is not inconsistent with the finding that in some cases economic growth and human development indicators have not risen in tandem.
4. Lewis (1984b) wrote: 'My overwhelming impression is that the LDC's have done much by their efforts than we had considered likely. This is an achievement on which a country should be congratulated, as should the economists who pushed in this direction' (p. 137).
5. *The Economist* (London) in 1991 noted that pandemic's reach knew no bounds, given that some 250 million people contracted sexually transmitted infections annually [cited in Mallaby (2004), p. 318].
6. The observation made in the text refers to the liberalists' persistent tendency to offer 'simple' solutions—e.g., leave it all to the market—to the highly complex problems of the developing countries. Of late, neo-classical paradigm has again been attacked for the unrealism of its basic assumptions and its total inability to explain the growth of the developing countries [Stiglitz (1991), p. 140].
7. The information in the text is taken from [UNDP (2003b), p. 34].

8. The figures cited in the text, cited in Stiglitz (2006) are based on the findings of the ILO's World Commission on the Social Dimensions of Development (2001).

9. The inequalities of income and wealth between the poor and the rich are large and have risen over time: The richest 5 per cent of world's peoples receive 114 times the incomes of the poorest 5 per cent, and the richest 1 per cent receive as much as the poorest 57 per cent [Milanovic (2002), pp. 51–92].

10. The term Scientific Research Programme (SRP) was coined by Lakatos (1970) while the term paradigm was suggested by Kuhn (1962) and more fully developed by Popper (1980). A detailed discussion of the relevance of these ideas is given in Blaug (1983). The common suggestion of both these terms is to distinguish doing normal science—elaborating, refining and applying the existing principles of a ruling paradigm—from a sharp break in the scientific world-view. Every paradigm is also defined as a distinctive research programme that has 'additional empirical content' and is 'progressive' [Naqvi (1993, 2002)]. See also Schmalensee (1991).

11. The point that the policy instruments used for the agreed objectives were similar in all the developing countries, the slow-growing as well as the miracle growers, is brought out forcefully in Findlay (1979); Rodrik (1995); and Bruton (1998) and many others.

12. The liberalist definition of macroeconomic stability is narrow, because a fuller definition of the term would also monitor, as any modern text on macroeconomics would show, the effect of the monetary, fiscal and foreign exchange rate policies on growth rates of GDP and the unemployment rate. The essence of public policy would then be to strike a balance between the monetary and real indices of macroeconomic stability.

13. However, the considerations noted in the text do not absolve the 'honest practitioner' of the responsibility for choosing a paradigm that does not allow an explicit consideration of the elemental development issues.

14. The argument is that efficiency wage (which is typically higher than the going market wage) may have to be paid to increase labour productivity to ensure a fuller employment of skilled labour.

15. The suggestion that economic development is basically a matter of the greater frequency of market failure in developing countries is made in Stiglitz (1989b). This argument overlooks that the ubiquity of market failures in a developing country simply proves a developmental role for the government. It says nothing about the shape and forms of state intervention to bring about development in the shortest period of time—that, for instance, it should encourage Structural Transformation with the help of an acceleration of the rate of physical and human capital formation; and that in certain cases it should take the form of Big-Push.

16. Sen (2000c) has clarified the link between rationality, freedom and justice. See, Sen (2000c).

17. Many studies show that greater aid has not always increased the total expenditure on education and health in many developing countries due mainly to its essential fungibility and whatever is spent does not always translate into greater access to education and health because of corruption among public officials [Dollar and Pritchett (1998)].

18. Unfortunately, there is not much information about the first decade of development, 1950s, when the foundations of the post-colonial pattern of growth and development were laid under the direct guidance of the Traditional Development Paradigm.

19. However, in Africa, the decline in poverty was so slight that it might have been due to measurement error.

Part II

The Traditional Development Paradigm

3

The Traditional Development Paradigm I: Rationale and Salience

One of the principal aims of this book is to reclaim the Traditional Development Paradigm from the vaults of a forgotten development history. Contrary to the universal academic practice of consigning it to the heap of intellectual rubbish, it will be shown that the paradigm spelled out a 'non-improvable' development policy for the first thirty years of development in the post-colonial period—in the sense that nothing else would have worked better at that time. This effort has been motivated by a desire to put right a grave historical wrong in the realm of ideas, do some fresh thinking on its nature and significance, and determine its relevance in today's developing world. Yet another reason for reinstating it to a place of honour in the annals of post-colonial development history is, that the Traditional Development Paradigm spelt out satisfactorily, the laws of motion that govern the developing societies with a combination of pith and exactitude at a time when their understanding was next to nil in the developed countries. Indeed, it has held an uncontested monopoly with respect to its understanding of the factors that contribute to fast, even miraculous, growth of per capita income in an essentially egalitarian institutional framework; and for highlighting the dynamic relationship between growth, distributive inequity (including gender inequity), and poverty reduction. An important reason for the success of the Traditional Development Paradigm was that it exhibited an exquisite sense of economic history and of contemporary thought. At a time when political and economic considerations demanded an immediate reversal of the colonial policies that deliberately perpetuated *laissez-faire*, it struck the right cord by emphasizing the necessity to expand the domestic market through government-supported import-substitution industrialization. Also, it held a correct view of the economic development of Europe after the Industrial Revolution, the Keynesian Revolution, as well as the Marxian critique of a capitalist society.[1] It is, therefore, an urgent matter that its central ideas should be allowed to re-ascend to their prominent place in the overall strategy of economic development. Such exercise has been long overdue because most recent theoretical and empirical works tend to support its fundamental propositions (e.g., Structural Transformation, Big-Push, and Dynamic Comparative Advantage, Dynamic External Economies, 'Unequal Exchange' etc). The unfolding of the international politics also points in the same direction. Seldom in the realm of ideas has the vision of the development process been so prescient, accurate and enduring.

3.1. THE RATIONALE OF THE TRADITIONAL DEVELOPMENT PARADIGM

It is important to remember that the Traditional Development Paradigm faithfully reflected the widespread consensus of the academic and informed public opinion in the late 1940s that the predominance of private sector (and minimal government), and *laissez-faire* were mainly responsible for the long night of economic stagnation, persistent poverty in the developing countries, and for widening the gap between the rich and poor people within and between nations.[2] Industrialization at the fastest pace was regarded as the necessary pre-condition for achieving the central objectives of development policy. However, doing all these demanded nothing less than a complete departure—a paradigmatic change in the purest sense of doing science in a new way—from past development perceptions and policies.[3] It would be useful to recapture the highlights of the development thinking at the time.

3.1. (i). The Nature of Development Challenge

The newly independent developing countries had inherited a long and undistinguished history of static growth rates of per capita income and widespread unemployment and poverty—and the total absence of the sparks of innovation and bursts of technological change [Reynolds (1983)]. The development policies in the pre-independence period clearly promoted a culture of total dependence on the colonial powers. Against that historical background, it was strongly believed that only a proactive development policy could convert the vicious circle of static growth, underdevelopment and dependence into a 'home-grown' virtuous circle of high growth and widely shared development. The most important item on the new agenda for the post-colonial period was, in the Marxian vein, to change (and not just explain) the historical patterns of growth and development. This central insight had several implications for development policy.

Firstly, the developing countries had no option but to focus on achieving the fastest rate of economic growth of per capita income as the quickest means to achieve economic independence and cement their political independence from the developed countries. This was regarded as the surest way to scatter the shadows of widespread poverty and inequity and social injustice in the colonial period. Like most founders of the Traditional Development Paradigm, Rostow saw the growth process in this light: 'Successful movement into reasonably well-balanced self-sustained growth, rooted in national aspirations, was judged to represent a way of minimizing the likelihood of successful external intrusion, communist or otherwise' [Rostow (1984), p. 239].

Secondly, the only feasible prescription to break free from the colonial legacy was to industrialize, which alone could make increasing returns to scale technologies economical. It was known at the time that not a single country (including the developed countries in their days of underdevelopment) in the last 200 years had achieved high rates of economic growth on a sustained basis without industrialization. This was regarded as the key to create an exportable surplus in the manufacturing goods in the developing countries. Indeed, the success in achieving this objective was regarded as the very acme of development wisdom. The developing countries, therefore, had to undergo rapid Structural Transformation of their economies, i.e. the share of industrial production in total output should secularly rise—to rekindle economic growth. It was designed to achieve the widely advertised objectives of development policy—namely, encourage technological change, raise agricultural productivity, expand and diversify the production structure and the export base, increase the volume of saving and investment, help the creation of an urban-based middle class and achieve convergence with the developed countries in the shortest period of time. All this was expected to raise the share of profits (and that of saving) and reduce that of rents in total national income; draw on the surplus agriculture labour; ensure that the factors of production moved from low-productivity into high-productivity uses with a view to expanding the size of the domestic market; make industrialization privately profitable, and above all; to promote systemic change. The requirements of static economic efficiency (i.e., that the structure of output and trade should be Pareto-optimal) were naturally regarded to be of secondary importance at best. It was not considered then as economically absurd for the policy makers to sacrifice a certain percentage of GDP for the sake of achieving a faster (and in the long run efficient) economic growth.[4] Indeed, doing anything else in the name of scientific rectitude would have been condemned at the time as economically and politically irresponsible.

Thirdly, having opted for achieving maximal rate of growth of per capita income through industrialization, it was only logical to demand that the government should play its historic catalytic role of a development leader. This is because much of industrialization, at least at the initial stage of development, could only come about by the government acting to coordinate investment decisions across sectors to expand the size of the domestic market, and realize economies of large-scale production.[5] Such coordination of investment decisions could not, however, be achieved through the private profit motive alone.[6] Lewis (1955) stated: 'In practice, it is also clear that the role of governments in economic development is, and ought to be much greater now than it has been in the past, if only because of the greater rate of economic growth which has now come to be generally expected' (p. 84). Quite predictably, then, the share of government investment in total investment, and the size of total investment itself, increased markedly.[7]

3.2. Some Common Misconceptions about the Traditional Development Paradigm

To set the stage for promoting an informed and unprejudiced development dialogue, it will be shown that the standard liberalist characterization of the Traditional Development Paradigm is no more than a caricatured representation, if not a wilful misinterpretation, of its world-view, salience and reach. To this end, we rebut three principal charges routinely brought against the Traditional Development Paradigm—namely, that it was anti-agriculture, anti-trade (i.e., that it discriminated against export expansion), and anti-human development.

3.2. (i). Did the Traditional Development Paradigm Discriminate Against Agriculture?

Several studies have highlighted the anti-agriculture colours of the Traditional Development Paradigm. However, nothing could be farther from the truth. The fact is that agriculture grew rapidly from 1950 onwards (Table 2.1). It was helped in large part by technological change (like the Green Revolution), and through large investments made in agricultural research and extension services. In a sample of 22 countries, the average agricultural growth rate was 3.7 per cent during 1949/51 to 1964/66, which exceeded by a large margin the pre-war to 1949/51 average growth rate of only 1.7 per cent. Indeed, 'most developing countries [pursued] a reasonably balanced policy towards agriculture, and in two countries where it was neglected, India and Pakistan, there has been a substantial revision of policy that augurs well for the future' [Maddison (1970), p. 160]. It follows that even if, for the sake of argument, it is accepted that the structure of price incentives at the time discriminated against agriculture, the severity of discrimination was not serious enough to impede agricultural growth. The ready adoption of the Green Revolution technologies by the farmers in the developing countries proves the absence or ineffectiveness of agricultural discrimination, if any, at the time. At any rate, the terms of trade had decisively moved, by the beginning of the 1970s, in favour of agriculture in the expectation of a robust supply response, which did materialize.[8] In addition, steps had already been taken to improve the productivity and output growth of agriculture e.g., controlling water logging and salinity, installation of tube wells, and the construction of dams to ensure ample irrigation water throughout the year. In particular, many countries (Pakistan, India, and Egypt among others) had taken concrete measures to achieve self-sufficiency in food.[9] As a general trend, in nearly two-thirds of the developing countries, the output of food increased rapidly and broadly in line with the growth rates of the GDP in this period. There is also no evidence to support the charge that the Traditional Development Paradigm systematically favoured industry at the expense of agriculture.[10] Lewis (1978) specifically singled out an increase in agricultural productivity as a pre-condition for industrialization.[11] It is thus fair to assert that the cases of a lack of agricultural development (e.g., in Africa) were the exception rather than the rule; and, to the extent that they existed, were due to political reasons and occurred 'in systems where the small cultivator carries little political weight' [Lewis (1984b), p. 128]. Although, an elementary point, it needs to be noted that a secular decline in the share of agriculture in GDP and a corresponding rise in that of industry could by no means be regarded as a sign of discrimination against agriculture. It is rather a historical tendency, which has asserted itself in every growing economy.

3.2. (ii). Did the Traditional Development Paradigm Discriminate Against Export Expansion?

Yet another widely advertised, but no less unfounded, charge against the Traditional Development Paradigm is that it deliberately biased the structure of incentives in favour of import substitution and against export expansion— in fact, against international trade generally. In evaluating the force of this charge, it may be remembered that the Traditional Development Paradigm did not invent the import-substitution policies; indeed, in some cases, the post-colonial governments simply continued the import-substitution activities of the colonial period. Historically, the collapse of world trade after 1929 had pushed many a developing country to protectionist policies mainly with a view to protecting balance of payments. It is, therefore, from 'this time that inward-looking development policies can be dated' [Maddison (1970), p. 63]. However, it is a fact that the Traditional Development Paradigm continued using the import-substitution policy as a way to gain economic independence; expand the domestic market and; broaden the export base. The reason was that, notwithstanding their contribution to the establishment of physical and administrative infrastructure, the colonial governments 'were typically hostile to domestic industrialization, preferring continued imports of manufactures from the metropolis. Education, particularly secondary and higher education, was typically under-supported' [Reynolds (1983), p. 957]. In particular, it was seen that the coordination failures would be large and frequent in economic activities and 'characterized by high forward linkage, large size, output-market orientation, and production of tradable or import substitutes rather than exports' [Jones and Sakong (1980)]. It was, therefore, quite natural to think at the time that there was an inbuilt externality and public goodness in the industrialization process and that it required determined state intervention to correct the anti-industrialization bias of the market.[12] Indeed, industrialization was seen as an important 'regularity' of economic development in the post-colonial era, for sound economic reasons. Given the decision to industrialize because, among other things, world trade was neither costless nor free, no alternative development policy could have yielded better results in terms of achieving the fastest possible rate of growth of output.[13] The expansion of the domestic market through import substitution was accorded priority to facilitate the adoption of the increasing returns technologies, without which industrialization could not have become socially and privately profitable. However, once developing countries' dynamic comparative advantage had taken some concrete shape, export-expansion efforts invariably followed in all the developing countries. Indeed, a deliberate sequencing of import-substituting industrialization prefacing export expansion in all the developing countries must be counted as yet another 'regularity' of economic development.[14]

The preceding analysis suggests that there is no evidence of an avoidable anti-trade or anti-export bias in development policy in the developing countries in the post-colonial period.[15] It would, therefore, be disingenuous to discredit the Traditional Development Paradigm on the grounds that it was irrevocably 'state-directed, inward-oriented, import-substituting industrialization' [Behrman and Srinivasan (1995), p. 2467]. In fact, it generally maintained a delicate balance between the government and the market; agriculture and industry and; import substitution and export expansion—a balance that was subsequently lost with the advent of the Liberalist Paradigm.

3.2. (iii). Was the Traditional Development Paradigm Anti-Human Development?

The human development aficionados have persistently accused the Traditional Development Paradigm of neglecting human development. But there does not seem to be much evidence to support this charge. On the other hand, it was as much concerned with the acceleration of economic growth as with adequate human development. It clearly envisaged an increase in social spending on education and health. It was pointed out that there was no excuse for 'not developing a proper range of social services—medical services, unemployment pay, pensions and the like [for urban labour]. The effect would be a healthier labour force, more settled, and more anxious for improvement on the job. These things cost more, but they also pay off in extra productivity, as well as in human happiness' [Lewis (1955), pp. 193–94]. The important point, however, is that it did not deem the primary emphasis on high growth of per capita income as inconsistent with the pursuit of human development. Indeed, a high growth rate of per capita income was regarded as essential for achieving any lasting human development. And in this respect, as will be shown later in Part VI of the present study, empirical evidence strongly supports the veracity of the Traditional Development Paradigm's point of view.

3.3. The Evolution of the Traditional Development Paradigm

In evaluating the worth of the Traditional Development Paradigm, it is important to remember that it was not meant to be a fixed doctrine, irrevocably bound to what it was at the time of its birth around the 1950s. Like a living doctrine, it remained single-mindedly beholden to the needs of the developing countries as long as it lasted. Its shape changed over time in predictable ways and for the better. It learned from the implementation of its basic ideas in different developing countries through an on-going dialogue and review. There is evidence that policy-makers in different countries interacted with each other throughout the 1950 to 1980.[16] Learning by doing, the paradigm designed a variety of prescriptions it offered to deal with specific developmental issues. Simultaneously, a consensus was evolved about the validity of some of the paradigm's fundamental contentions. That explains why the developing countries in Asia (including East Asia), and Latin America in particular, followed more or less similar development policies, as has been widely noted by many an acute observer of the development experience [Bruton (1998); Amsden (1989); Wade (1990); Rodrik (1996)].[17] However, while there was flexibility about the exact policy mix, the Traditional Development Paradigm remained focused, as long as it ruled the waves of policy making, on bringing about systemic change—from a predominantly rural society to an urban-based society. Four examples should illustrate these remarks.

Firstly, there occurred a gradual shift of development policy from heavy import substitution in the 1950s towards a balanced growth of import substitution and export expansion activities during the 1960s and 1970s. The shift came about in a somewhat 'natural' way: as the domestic market for import substitutes became too small, many developing countries moved 'towards a more outward-looking policy stance, involving trade and exchange-rate policies which were more nearly neutral as between exports and import substituting activities—' [Reynolds (1983), p. 973]. It is important to note that the pattern of development in this respect was no different in East Asia from the rest of the developing countries.

Secondly, from an initial over-emphasis on growth considerations alone, development policy sought a better balance between satisfying the requirements of efficiency and the dictates of achieving high growth. However, an uncompromising focus on efficiency never became the overarching principle of the Traditional Development Paradigm. This was because one simply could not remain inexorably wedded to (static) economic efficiency while aiming at high rates of economic growth of per capita income, distributive justice, poverty reduction and convergence with the developed countries. In other words, an over-riding preoccupation with static efficiency was widely regarded as inconsistent with the dynamics of social and economic change.

Thirdly, its initial somewhat unfavourable perception of the role of international trade in national development (e.g., that international trade was an instrument of economic imperialism and exploitation of the developing countries) was suitably modified with the passage of time. The share of international trade in GDP generally grew faster in the 1960s and 1970s than in 1950s. Correspondingly, the initial protectionist sentiment was moderated as the size of the domestic market and the export base expanded significantly, both of which enabled the developing countries to export non-traditional higher value-added goods. Indeed, the developing countries took great pride in exporting manufactured goods to the developed countries. As evidence of the policy shift towards export expansion, the earlier preference for having multiple exchange rates, mainly to offset the over-valued exchange rates, gave way to more realistic and unified exchange rates, sometime around the early 1970s.[18] And, yet, it was clearly understood that there was simply no way to achieve a steady Structural Transformation of a developing country while remaining religiously loyal to the neo-classical (and classical) *laissez-faire* ideal.

Fourthly, as some of the key markets were created and private sector overcame its earlier diffidence to take risks, development policy sought to achieve a better balance between the market and government. There came about a gradual shift from direct controls of economic activity to more indirect controls (from quota restrictions to tariffs constraints on trade; from physical control of investment activity to fiscal and monetary control of the economy, and so on). The main point to grasp is that remaining true to its basic value system and worldview; it did not prevent the Traditional Development Paradigm from changing the relative emphasis it accorded to the different components of development policy. The reason for the paradigm's 'open-mindedness' to development experience and its readiness to change accordingly reflected the non-doctrinaire nature of the Traditional Development Paradigm and its readiness to learn from experience. At no point did it try consciously to confine the process of change within the procrustean bed of a preconceived ideological mould. In that context, it explicitly repudiated both the Communist pattern of development and that which untrammelled capitalism prescribed. Overall, it evolved a system of thought that sought to achieve a fine balance between individual freedom and social responsibility within a mixed economy framework.

3.4. THE GEOGRAPHICAL LIMITS OF THE TRADITIONAL DEVELOPMENT PARADIGM

A fundamental misunderstanding about the Traditional Development Paradigm is that it was responsible for the slower growth of the non-East Asian countries as opposed to the greater export orientation and lack of government intervention in East Asia. This line of thinking has artificially limited the writ of the Traditional Development Paradigm to the slower-growing non-East Asian countries. This book rejects this practice as totally unwarranted. Some of the reasons for rejecting this practice have already been given; but let us restate them here:

(i) There is no evidence that the fast-developing countries of East Asia followed development policies different from those practiced by the relatively slower-growing countries of South Asia and Latin America. If anything, the so-called inefficient (interventionist) policies were followed with greater intensity in East Asia than elsewhere [Amsden (1989); Wade (1990); Bruton (1998)]. Thus, government intervention was perhaps more severe, though highly efficient, in the East Asia and took the form of a 'strong government discipline over the private sector' [Rodrik (1995), p. 2948]. If, as has been vigorously argued in the liberalist literature e.g., [Little, Scitovsky and Scott (1970)]—state intervention in non-East Asia was the principal cause of slower growth there, then East Asia, which practiced the so-called second-best policies much more vigorously, should have grown at a much slower rate than the rest of Asia. The fact that it kept galloping along the high growth path notwithstanding a heavy-handed government can be taken as a sufficient confirmation of the unambiguous superiority of the second-best over the so called first-best policies.

(ii) On the other hand, all available evidence shows that roughly similar policies have been followed by both groups of countries, and that they, everywhere, produced excellent results in relation to their respective historical growth rates.

(iii) The assertion that East Asia grew faster than the rest of the developing countries, because the former relied on human capital formation and the latter on physical capital is also factually incorrect. All evidence shows that 60 to 70 per cent of the growth of per capita income in East Asia can be explained by physical capital formation, with the remaining 20 to 30 per cent being contributed by the residual by improvements in total factor productivity [Bosworth and Collins (1996); IMF (2000)].[19] This is not to suggest that human capital formation has not been one of the principal causative factors of growth, but only that it did not make a significant difference between the growth performances of the East Asia and non-East Asia. The regressions presented in the later part of this book show that physical capital formation has been statistically the most 'stable' factor contributing to the growth of both East Asia and the non-East Asia.

True, there have been significant differences in the relative growth performances of the East Asian and non-East Asian countries; but the explanation for these observed differences lay elsewhere. There is a consensus now that the East Asian growth was more a miracle of 'input accumulation' (the highest ever rates of saving and physical and human capital formation) rather than of a miraculous improvement in total factor productivity [Young (1993)]. Furthermore, the reason for the superlatively fast rate of growth of the East Asian economies lay not so much in the policy mix they followed, as in the efficacy of its implementation. A look at Table 2.1 should make clear that all the developing countries, the slow growers as well as the fast growers, scored extra-ordinarily high rates of human and physical capital formation and domestic saving—the centrality of which was first highlighted by the Traditional Development Paradigm. Even the stagnant African economies enjoyed strong fundamentals.

There is also no evidence to suggest that the East Asian countries did not know about the Traditional Development Paradigm's basic precepts. There are two points to be noted in this context. (a) It will be a case of unbelievable information blockage if the East Asians did not know what the non-East Asians were doing. After all, Arthur Lewis and Raul Prebisch (both non-Asians) were known everywhere in the developing world; and most of the most colourful of the Western contributors e.g., Gunnar Myrdal, Jan Tinbergen, Albert Hirschman, Paul Streeten, John Mellor, to name only a few of them to the Traditional Development Paradigm travelled far and wide, and also worked as advisors in both East Asia and non-East Asian countries. Even more important, the World Bank till 1970s broadly agreed with the paradigm's broad priorities and strategies; and it was responsible for disseminating the paradigm's message across the globe through its highly influential *World Development Reports* and international meetings [Bruton (1998)]. (b) Even if it were accepted that the East Asians did not know what they were doing, this is not relevant to the point we are making in this section. Like Moliers' M. Jourdain, who was not conscious that he was writing great prose but still was its indisputable author, the East Asians practiced Traditional Development Paradigm to perfection even if it is accepted that they were not aware of it.

To put positively, the basic point of this section: the Traditional Development Paradigm was practiced throughout the developing world till the 1980s in Latin America and Africa, till late 1980s in Pakistan, and till 1996 in East Asia, China and India are still practicing it, as will be argued a little later in this chapter. True, there have been observable differences in the degree of success achieved by them but what unites them is the commonality of their worldview; their commitment to high rates of economic growth within an essentially egalitarian institutional set-up; the similarities of development objectives they set themselves to achieve and; the near-identity of the development policies they pursued to attain them.

3.5. CAN SLOW GROWTH BE EQUATED WITH DEVELOPMENT FAILURE?

There has been a tendency in the development literature to regard the slower-growth of South Asia and Latin America relative to the much faster growth of East Asia as 'development failure', which is then attributed to the Traditional Development Paradigm. On the other hand, when the very same policies worked superbly (in East Asia, China) then the credit for their success has been routinely attributed to market orientation. These contradictory statements betray a multi-layered misunderstanding and misinterpretation of available empirical evidence. Table 2.1 tells a story of development success, miraculous in East Asia and nearly so in Latin America, but not less impressive in Africa during the foundation years of the Traditional Development Paradigm. The exception to the rule was South Asia where the growth momentum built up slowly but steadily, partly a reflection of the relatively poorer state of their economies in the pre-colonial times. One cannot escape the obvious conclusion that the Traditional Developmental Paradigm led to unprecedented all-round growth in the developing countries during its thirty-year reign (from 1950 to 1980). It coincided with the 'Golden Period of Growth' in Latin America, during which per capita income increased by nearly 3 per cent per year—a performance that has not been equalled since then. The Brazilian miracle also happened in this period, with its per capita income increasing at the rate of 4.2 per cent [Cardoso and Fishlow (1992)]. Pakistan achieved in this period a growth performance similar to that of Brazil. This is also the period when 41 developing countries in Reynolds (1983) sample (drawn from Latin America, North Africa and Middle East, Africa, Asia) crossed over from their early 'extensive growth' stage (i.e., in which growth rate of GDP and the population growth rate are equal, so that the per capita income does not display an uptrend) to the 'intensive growth' stage (i.e., when the formers growth outpaces the latter, so that the per capita income rises). There is, therefore, no need to investigate the oft-repeated 'puzzle' as to why the policies that produced economic miracles in the East Asia brought other developing countries to their ruin?[20] The reason is that no such puzzle has ever existed.

3.6. What Explains China's Super-Miracle and India's Growth Revival?

It may be interesting to comment briefly on the claim that China's super-miracle has been the handiwork of market-oriented policies as opposed to the interventionist policies that it practiced before its 'take-off' into self-sustained growth. To some extent, it is true that there has been a gradual shift in the Chinese development policy from total government control of economic activity to a relatively greater reliance on markets. But, contrary to the usual academic practice, China's transition from a centrally controlled economy has been not so much towards a full market economy as towards a mixed economy—something that the Traditional Development Paradigm actively advocated. The role of the state in the Chinese economy continues to be heavy and the emphasis is on forging some kind of public-private partnership, with the government in a commanding position. It would, therefore, be more accurate to state that in the case of China, the highest ever rate of growth was achieved by the application of ideas similar to those of the Traditional Development Paradigm rather than the market-oriented policies. The policies that helped China to attain a super-miracle have been no different from those followed by other developing countries. It is interesting to note that, very much like the East Asian case that was at first declared to be the paradise for free traders, similar claims have been made with respect to the Chinese super-miracle—to find a black cat in a dark room that is not there.[21] Empirical evidence, however, offers little support to such generalizations. The fact is that the pace of reform in China remains gradual and the reason for undertaking it was not that it faced any crisis that required immediate change, 'only dissatisfaction with the pace of economic growth' [Perkins (1994), p. 23)]. Yet another point is that an important aspect in China has been, to achieve economic efficiency by promoting competition and not by post-haste privatization, which is what the Structural Adjustment Programmes have routinely prescribed.[22] The most radical reform was in the rural areas where the collectivized farms were transformed into cooperative units; but even these reforms have been gradual under the vigilant eyes of the state. The necessary steps to define property rights in agriculture have been taken very gradually; and the fundamental step to extend the right to property to the entire Chinese society was taken in the year 2003, when these rights were enshrined in the Chinese constitution. Similarly, the same spirit of gradualism permeated in 'freeing up' the foreign trade sector, where the task performed by state corporations at the centre was first delegated to regional corporations, which did not diminish the involvement of the state but only shifted its focus [Perkins (1988)]. Once again the aim has been to promote competition without privatization. The same has been the approach to opening up the industrial sector to the private investor. There still remain important constraints on the ownership of equity by the private citizens: while individuals can hold one-third of the stock, the remaining two-thirds must be held by the state. Yet another constraint is that the state-owned enterprises, rather than the state itself, have traditionally provided the social safety nets to the Chinese poor—a role that it is not expected to cede any time soon to the private sector. It is, therefore, most unlikely that the privatized units will come to enjoy significant powers to hire or fire the staff or make other important operational decisions [Megginson and Netter (2001)].[23] Fundamentally, the problem is to balance out the requirements of efficiency with those of providing a minimum of social security to the Chinese citizens—one of the basic concerns of the Traditional Development Paradigm.

Yet another case of misattribution of economic success to liberal economic policies is India's recent strong growth revival beginning in 1992. The present study takes the view that it will be inaccurate to give all, or, even most of the credit for the recent resurgence of the Indian economy to the market reforms initiated in 1992, and apportion all the blame to the Traditional Development Paradigm for its presumably lacklustre economic performance before that.[24] It would be more realistic to state that economic policies during 1950 to 1990 laid down the basic structure of the Indian economy and the reforms removed the unnecessary restrictions on trade and the domestic sectors. Indeed, it has been asserted that India's surge to high growth began in the late 1980s, well before the 1991 reforms, and even that the growth surge has mostly come from the old-fashioned import-substitution activities [Rodrik and Subramanian (2004); De Long (2003)]. Indeed, it can be legitimately claimed that the determined efforts to expand the domestic markets on a priority basis that the Indian policy-makers made from 1950 onwards has helped India achieve a more balanced pattern of development (that gave export orientation a much greater role than in the past) in the 1990s than other high-growth countries, including East Asia and China, which, because of their unusually high saving rates might have experienced a relatively more stunted expansion of the domestic market.[25]

3.7. THE ORIGINALITY OF THE TRADITIONAL DEVELOPMENT PARADIGM

Before proceeding any further, it is proper to make some general comments about the originality of the Traditional Development Paradigm, its wide scope and extensive reach. Firstly, it focused on an essentially egalitarian systemic transformation of the developing countries, and was opposed to a single-cause explanation of the process of development (such as remedying the insufficiency of effective demand, promoting the right institutional framework, facilitating accumulation of knowledge and capital, and making up the lack of technical skill) taken one at a time. It understood that the many factors contributing to growth were quintessentially inter-related and that they were singled out only for analytical purposes.[26] Also, it visualized the development process as an outcome of a series of fundamental changes in attitudes of the people to such foundational matters as risk-taking, scientific thought and innovation, as well as the ones that contributed to these changes.[27] It is, therefore, highly misleading to assert, as is the almost universal practice in the academia, that the Traditional Development Paradigm advocated a one-point agenda of 'growth fundamentalism' [Gillis, Perkins, Roemer and Snodgrass (1983)].

Secondly, simultaneously with maximizing the growth of per capita income, the Traditional Development Paradigm insisted on the creation of growth-friendly and essentially egalitarian institutions to internalize the beneficial growth-promoting upsurge and establish a tight link between growth, distributive equity and poverty reduction. In this context, it is totally incorrect to suggest, as has often been done, that the Traditional Development Paradigm postulated a positive relationship between growth and inequality. Quite the contrary; it explicitly stated that significant economic growth could be achieved 'even if there were no differentials [of income and wealth] at all' [Lewis (1955), p. 429]. Indeed, it saw great advantages flowing from the emergence of a strong middle class as the process of Structural Transformation spread its wings wider (This aspect of the traditional paradigm is explored in Chapter 6). The fact is that its was a broad enough message that treated the key human development variables (like education and health) at par with income per capita in terms of their potential contribution to economic progress and human happiness.[28] It is, therefore, unfair to accuse the Traditional Development Paradigm of imprisoning the development process in a 'little box'—focusing narrowly and irrevocably on GNP per capita, or industrialization or just capital accumulation. Most definitely, this is a crime that it did not commit.

Thirdly, it explicitly recognized that 'it is hard to correlate wealth and happiness' [Lewis (1955), p. 420]. In other words, it understood that the acquisition of wealth would not necessarily translate into human happiness.

Yet, it confidently laid down that there was no other way to bring happiness to the people other than the ones it prescribed—by implementing a set of policies (especially, industrialization) that would initiate and sustain high rates of growth of per capita income for decades. And to this end, maximum effort should be made to raise physical and human capital formation, create knowledge and spark innovation and technological change. By implication, it denied that there existed a direct route to human happiness that could bypass the basic income-generating mechanism.

Fourthly, the Traditional Development Paradigm changed the ways in which economists viewed the world at the time.[29] Not content with doing 'normal science', elaborating, refining, and applying existing principles, it generated a 'new research programme' that possessed 'extra empirical content' and a value system of its own and made predictions radically different from the academic practice at the time [Naqvi (2002)].[30] This aspect of the paradigm (that it made an original contribution to development thinking) is explored at length in the next chapter. Suffice it to note here that, as if to prove its paradigmatic credentials, it departed sharply from the then in-fashion models of economic development and social change. For instance, while sympathizing with its egalitarian message, it rejected the Marxian vision of class war and social revolution as the only means to achieving systemic change [Baran (1957)]. Similarly, it rejected the eighteenth century *laissez-faire* capitalistic prescription of development as a flint-hearted process, regularly fed by the sweat, blood and tears of the working class. Instead, it opted for a mixed economy that would seek a creative symbiosis of individual initiative and state direction, and pave the way for a gradual and non-violent transformation of a decadent rural society into a vibrant urban society. It was no less sceptical of the relevance of the Harrod-Domar type of models of growth for conceptualizing correctly, the problems of developing countries. These models regarded capital formation to be the only constraint on growth. On the other hand, the Traditional Development Paradigm emphasized that accumulation of knowledge and a thoroughgoing change in the institutional set-up and the structure of values were as important, if not more, than the capital accumulation, as engines of growth.

Fifthly, with respect to implementation strategy, it provided both: a set of readily understood evaluative criteria to measure economic progress and; a carefully chosen catalogue of the contributory factors to economic and social development. To this end, it replaced the contemporary models of growth by a model of economic development driven mainly by Structural Transformation that focused on the growth-promoting inter-sector movement of capital and labour from low-productivity to high-productivity activities. This concept, solidly based in development history, can justifiably be called as the 'Fundamental Law of Development' and one of the defining characteristics of the Traditional Development Paradigm. This point is elaborated at length in the next chapter.

3.8. CONCLUDING REMARKS

A central theme of this chapter is that developing countries managed their development-related affairs with varying degrees of success in the first thirty years of development. Some of them have done so with a remarkable degree of success; but all seem to have done very well, absolutely as well as relatively to their performance under colonial rule. Contrary to what has been asserted, much of the credit for this resplendent record goes to the development policies that the Traditional Development Paradigm prescribed. It is, therefore, important that the nature and motivation of the criticism against it are clearly understood. To this end, the present chapter highlights many aspects of the Traditional Development Paradigm that have been generally glossed over, even misrepresented, in academic discussions. This chapter demonstrates fairly conclusively that nearly all the criticism directed against it betrays a gross misinterpretation of its central message. For instance, It would be wrong to insist that: (a) it was innately inward-looking and generally hostile to export expansion; (b) it discriminated against agriculture to finance industrialization; (c) it did not care for efficiency or equity; (d) it neglected human development, and that; (e) for all these very reasons, it contributed to development failures in countries where it ruled the roost (i.e., in non-East Asian economies) by comparison with the allegedly market-oriented, outward-looking policies that were crowned with great success wherever these were practiced (i.e., in East Asian miracle economies).

This characterization of the paradigm is misleading because it ignores that: (a) both the fast-growing and the relatively slow-growing economies practiced similar development policies and focused on the same set of variables that the Traditional Development Paradigm advocated; (b) in both sets of countries these policies, judged by reasonable criteria of success, proved to be eminently successful; (c) the Traditional Development Paradigm was not an unchangeable doctrine, it rather evolved in response to the stage of development attained by different countries. Indubitably, the Traditional Development Paradigm has been a huge success;[31] yet the unstoppable onslaught of liberalist ideas throughout the world forced it to retire hurt from the game of growth in utter humiliation on grounds that were totally unrelated to reality. The fact is that the severe exogenous shocks that derailed development in the developing countries (most decisively in Latin America and Africa) originated in the West, but were used as an excuse for introducing sweeping changes in domestic policies. This suggests that the real reasons for making a sudden paradigmatic change were essentially ideological—that is, 'to begin to move the developing countries from a highly distorted price incentives and investment frameworks to something that was more stable, more oriented to the market system of prices, and more open and less protectionist' [Stern (1991), pp. 1–2]. This theme is explored at length in Part III of this book.

NOTES

1. Even a cursory reading of Lewis's magnum opus (1955) should convince the reader of the veracity of the claims made in the text. It is interesting to note that the first (1948) edition of Paul Samuelson's classic economics textbook contained no more than three sentences on development problems. Also, the discussion of the first draft of the World Bank that Harry Dexter White wrote and which John Maynard Keynes endorsed in the immediate post-Second World War period was primarily motivated by the problems of the reconstruction of Europe and only marginally with those of the development of the developing countries [Mallaby (2004), pp. 15–16].

2. The dominant political opinion at the time of independence was to view *laissez-faire* as a tool of capitalist exploitation. Mohammad Ali Jinnah, the founder of Pakistan, explicitly stated that Pakistan would be a welfare state and free from capitalist exploitation. Jawaharlal Nehru, the first prime minister of India, held similar views, and singled out international trade (in the sense of *laissez-faire*), as an instrument of imperialism rather than being an engine of growth. He explicitly stated, 'International trade was certainly not excluded, but we were anxious to avoid being drawn into the whirlpool of economic imperialism' [Nehru (1946), p. 403)].

3. Incidentally, the birth of the Traditional Development Paradigm coincided with the ending of the Longest Depression of 1914–45 and the beginning of the Greatest Boom of 1945–73. This must have created an air of optimism about the potential achievements of a development policy.

4. The last line in the text above is based on Maddison's (1970) argument: 'We must remember that it is rational to subsidize and protect home production temporarily in the initial stage of industrialization—efficiency will also increase over time because of the learning process—it may be worthwhile for an economy like Pakistan to sacrifice 3 per cent of the GNP to cover these 'learning' costs' (p. 196).

5. Rosenstein-Rodan (1943) was the first to see the point made in the text. It is known as the Big-Push hypothesis.

6. The argument in the text is set out in full later in this book.

7. Maddison (1970) notes: 'In the pre-war years the government revenues were usually only about 10 per cent of GNP. Investment was also low. In the post-war period this has changed. There has been great emphasis on the role of investment, particularly public investment. Governments have also increased spending on education and other services which increase their supply potential' (p. 64).

8. Reynolds (1983) observes: 'It is probably fair to say also that, in most countries, government policies were more favourable to agriculture in the seventies than in the fifties—the importance of agricultural output is more widely appreciated and requirements for agricultural progress are better understood' (p. 970).

9. It is interesting that the policy of achieving food self-sufficiency was hotly resisted by the international donors on the grounds that it was more economical to import wheat from the US under the PL-480 programme. The present author himself saw the foreign adviser's

adverse reaction to President Ayub Khan's proposal immediately after he took over in the late 1950s to attain self-sufficiency in wheat production in Pakistan. The policy was, nevertheless, pursued and has paid handsome dividends. Furthermore, as a part of a generally pro-agriculture policy, the terms of trade had already moved in favour of agriculture in the early 1960s.

10. In fact, as noted later in this book, it was during the currency of the Liberalist Paradigm that agriculture suffered because government allocations for infra-structural development were sharply cut to achieve macroeconomic stability [Lipton and Ravallion (1995)].

11. The proposition in the text was supported by practically the entire spectrum of development economists like Rosenstein-Rodan (1943), Nurkse (1953), Lewis (1954, 1978), Ranis and Fei (1961), Johnston and Mellor (1961), to name only a few.

12. See, Murphy, Shleifer, and Vishny (1989a) for a formal statement of the argument in the text.

13. Historically, it is a rarity for a developing country to proceed directly from an export boom to industrialization, even though it (along with the rise in agricultural productivity) does tend to stimulate the demand for industrialization by raising the income of the exporting country [Lewis (1978)].

14. A major World Bank sponsored empirical study of the patterns of structural transformation in the developing countries concluded: 'there may be a necessary sequence from growth dominated by import substitution to a shift to manufacturing exports as major engine of economic growth. It appears that an economy must develop a certain industrial base and a set of technical skills before it can pursue manufactured exports' [Chenery, Robinson and Syrquin (1986), p. 358].

15. 'In most of the growing economies of Asia and Latin America, though not in Africa, import substitution in consumer goods is now substantially complete—indeed, a half-dozen countries have substantial exports of consumer goods. Except in China and Brazil, import substitution in intermediates and capital goods is less—many countries still importing one-third to two-thirds of the requirements' [Reynolds (1983), p. 972].

16. An interesting instance of this learning from each other is the widely known fact of the South Korean policy makers visiting Pakistan to learn about the latter's development policies. As it turned out, the South Koreans proved to be much better practitioners of the policies they learned from Pakistan.

17. The liberalist view is, of course, radically different from that cited in the text. Krueger (1995a) states: 'Whatever else was evident about the rapid growth of the East Asian NICs, it was clear that all of them had altered their foreign trade regimes and abandoned policies of import substitution in favour of an outer-oriented trade strategy' (p. 2517).

18. For instance, the *Pakistan Development Review* in the 1960s featured several articles that aimed to create greater sensitivity to efficiency concerns in policy-making. They consistently argued against multiple exchange rates and overvalued exchange rates and also warned against keeping the cost of capital too low because that would lead to the creation of excess capacity in the industrial sector [e.g., Naqvi (1963; 1964; 1966; 1971)]. See also Islam (1967); and the many articles collected in (1970).

19. Ray (1998) reaches similar conclusion: 'It appears that the East Asian countries have grown rapidly, but they have grown the old-fashioned way, through an extraordinary process of improvement in labour force, as well as sustained capital accumulation' (p. 122).

20. This puzzle has been stated as follows: 'How could the East Asian countries avoid the disasters that accompanied interventionist policies elsewhere' [Rodrik (1996)]. It is indeed a greater puzzle to ponder as to how economists of stature have declared slower-than-miracle rate of economic growth in most developing countries a 'development disaster'.

21. Perkins (1994), an avid advocate of full market reforms in China as necessary for realizing its full potential, has this to say about the nature of the market reforms implemented in China so far: 'What will be left once the reforms of the large scale enterprises is well along,

is a market economy with all kinds of government interventions at both the local and central level, perhaps on the pattern of South Korea or Taiwan in the 1970s'. He then asks, 'whether these continuing state interventions in an essentially market economy will slow growth markedly, or whether growth will continue at the torrid pace for the first 15 years of reform' (p. 44). There is little dispute that China has continued its growth 'at the torrid pace', since Perkins wrote. There is also no indication that it is going to adopt a full-market capitalist economy any time soon.

22. Stiglitz (2003) describes the shape of reforms in China. He recalls that Arrow and he himself gave the Chinese the advice to worry about infusing competition in the economy but not to worry about privatization immediately. The latter must await the creation of the supporting institutions. The Chinese came up with the two-tier price system that nevertheless equalized the incentives at the margin. This system 'avoided the huge redistributions that would have occurred if the new prices were instantaneously to prevail over the entire range of output' (p. 183). The system, however, was abolished once its purpose was achieved.

23. The same point has been made in Perkins (1994); and in Ahmad and Hussein (1989).

24. Behrman and Srinivasan (1995) take the position that market reforms should be given the entire credit for India's growth revival: 'The government of Prime Minister Rao that took power on 21 June 1991 recognized the systemic and long-term failures of India's development strategy and embarked on major reforms by dismantling regulatory apparatus governing investment, foreign trade and the financial sector' (p. 2471).

25. John Mellor in a private correspondence with the author suggested the point made in the text.

26. Lewis (1955) reviewing the history of the identification of the causes of economic growth from Adam Smith (lack of the right institutional framework) to Malthus (insufficiency of effective demand) to the present day fads about capital accumulation, or technical assistance or natural resource availability, observes: 'though the reformer may begin by working upon one factor only, he has to bear in mind that if he is to have full success, much other change is involved beyond the factor with which he is immediately concerned'. He made clear that, 'we separate the various [essentially inter-related] causes for analytical purposes only' (p. 20).

27. Rostow (1953) saw capital formation as, 'not merely a matter of profit maximization; it is a matter of a society's effective attitude towards and response to basic science, applied science, and risk-taking of innovation and innovational lending' (p. vii). He affirmed later, 'the analysis of growth, as I envisaged it, became an exercise in the dynamic analysis of the whole societies' [Rostow (1984), p. 239].

28. Thus, in evaluating the role of the government in economic development, Lewis (1984b) emphasized the traditional development policy's accomplishments in satisfying human development concerns: 'Taken as a group, LDC governments have, in fact, passed reasonable tests. There are four times as many children in schools as there were in 1950. The infant mortality rate has fallen by three-quarters. The multiplication of hospital beds, village water pipes, all-season village roads, and other mass services is faster than at any time in the history of the countries now developed' (p. 132).

29. Lewis, writing his own magnum opus on economic growth, could claim, 'A book of this kind seemed to be necessary because the theory of growth once more engages world-wide interest, and because no comprehensive treatise on the subject has been published for about a century' [Lewis (1955), p. 5].

30. A look at the table of contents of Lewis (1955) should convince even its most trenchant critics of the wide reach of the Traditional Development Paradigm. Fairly exhaustive chapters deal with the will to economize on institutions, knowledge, capital, population and resources, and government. The book gives no hint that he was proposing one-point agenda of growth-man-ship.

31. Temple (1999) records ten cases of growth miracles, in which annual growth rates of per capita income during the 1960–90 period ranged from 6.1 per cent for South Korea to 4.4 per cent for Lesotho; and ten cases of growth disaster ranging from -2.1 per cent for Guyana to -0.3 per cent for Ghana (p. 116).

4

The Traditional Development
Paradigm II: The Foundational Issues

The Traditional Development Paradigm focused explicitly on 'the high theme of economic progress' [Alfred Marshall (1920), p. 461]—a theme that neither Marshall nor his neo-classical progeny had the time or the inclination to analyze adequately. But, fortunately, while mainstream (read, neo-classical) economics engaged full-time in finessing the fine points of steady-state growth in a hypothetical industrialized economy, the Traditional Development Paradigm set its sights on discovering the laws of motion that increase the wealth of real-life developing nations with social justice and harnessing these laws for the good of humankind. Chapter 3 shows that in this momentous task it succeeded superbly. It moved mountains of backward looking tradition-bound institutions that abhorred change and rolled back the forces of static growth of per capita income, high unemployment rates and widespread (income and non-income) poverty. This intellectual iconoclasm helped the developing countries grow at the fastest growth rates of per capita income ever recorded in human history. Some of these countries managed to double per capita income in about a decade as compared with what Europe could do in more than 100 years, and that which Japan accomplished in 50 years in modern times. It achieved this remarkable feat by breaking the hold of what are identified in this book as 'wrong ideas' on the minds of the academic community and policy-makers and replacing them by a forward-looking, 'constructive' research programme in the quest for economic prosperity for the least-privileged countries and peoples. It kindled the candle of hope in the hearts of countless women and men that their withered lives could be transformed in an orderly and peaceful manner by commitment and devotion to a cause and through means that are scientifically and morally correct.

4.1. STRUCTURAL TRANSFORMATION

One of the regnant ideas of the Traditional Development Paradigm that guided development policy in the developing countries in the foundational post-colonial period was to mobilize the labour surplus in agriculture and related activities in the pre-modern era without neglecting the need for raising agricultural productivity. It unequivocally emphasized that a vibrant agriculture (indeed, an agrarian revolution) would create the demand for industrialization. The surplus food production and the labour transferred to the industrial sector were expected to fire up the process of Structural Transformation—the complex development process through which the share of industrial production in total output would increase secularly; but the process once begun vigorously would not stop at that. It would, in time, touch off 'an overall structural transformation of the structure of demand, trade, production, and employment as the central feature of development, in contrast to the steady-state conclusions of earlier growth theory for developed economies' [Chenery and Srinivasan (1988), p. 198]. The Traditional Development Paradigm explicitly envisaged the process to presage a systemic transformation of the rural, stagnant society into a modern strongly growing urbanized society with a progressive set of values. It was also seen as the surest way to break out of the vicious circle of static growth and poverty that had trapped the development effort at low levels of per capita income during the colonial rule. The paradigm focused on those forces that keep the development effort moored at the pre-industrialization equilibrium, rather than letting it proceed full throttle to the post-industrialization equilibrium.[1] The originality of the Traditional Development Paradigm lay in its forceful questioning of the neo-classical (and classical) explanation of the development process: that the flexibility, especially of the labour markets, the profit motive, and *laissez-faire* will ensure a market-friendly transition of a developing country to a higher stage of economic development.[2] In sharp contrast, it underscored that there was no hope to break away from 'multiple equilibria' with the help of the market forces alone.[3] This is because the profit motive would not by itself create a sustained demand for industrialization. There would be no incentive for the private investor, driven by profit motive alone, to move on to a higher-income level of the equilibrium. It, therefore, highlighted the need for forceful government intervention to expand the domestic market through import-substitution industrialization with a view to smoothing the path of sustained economic progress. To this end, it subordinated efficiency concerns (about the rightness of the structure of relative prices prevailing in unfettered markets in the pre-development stage) of neo-classical economics, though not ignoring them altogether, to the over-riding objective of Structural Transformation leading to systemic change. The main argument in support of this idea was that static efficiency losses arising from relative price distortions would be small, relative to the substantial dynamic efficiency gains flowing from a restructuring of a low-productivity rural economy into a high productivity urban economy, which would eventually raise the productivity of the agriculture sector as well. Furthermore, economic development would, in due course, create its own structure of relative prices that would better reflect the realities and requirements of economic development.

4.1. (i). Lewis's Two-Sector Model

Lewis's two-sector model (1954b; 1955) succeeded, to a superlative degree, in capturing the basics of the development process. It envisaged economy-wide inter-sector shift of labour from low-productivity agriculture to the high-productivity manufacturing sector by drawing upon a perfectly elastic (or 'unlimited') supply of labour in the rural sector. This process would help meet the excess demand for labour in the urban sector where, combined with the necessary capital, it would be more productive. As a result, the new inter-sector input/output configurations would stimulate overall economic growth.[4] The purpose of Lewis's two-sector model was 'to provide a mechanism explaining the rapid growth of the proportion of domestic savings in the national income in the early stages of an economy whose growth is due to expansion of capitalist forms of production' [Lewis (1972)]. It postulated, as a simplification of reality, that capital was used only in the industrial sector and, for that reason, output per-worker would be significantly higher in the industrial than in the agriculture sector.[5] The model predicted that, as long as the agricultural wage lagged behind its marginal product and there was a gap between the agricultural wage and the urban wage, the growth-promoting reallocation of labour to urban manufacturing activity would continue.[6] The saving and the investment rates and total output and employment would rise together as the speed of structural transformation picked up, i.e. as the capitalistic (urban) sector expanded relative to the agriculture sector with an elastic supply of labour. Structural Transformation would raise the share of industrial output in total output while requiring that agriculture sector also grew at the maximal rate. The process would be completed if and when the dualistic characteristic of the economy, i.e. the labour surplus condition was eliminated [Fei and Ranis (1963)]. However, contrary to a widely held view, the process would not come to an end any time soon because the surplus labour was by no means a fixed reserve army; its numbers would be swelled by an increasing population, a greater labour force participation rate, especially of women, as economic growth picked up, and by what Marx identified as 'technological unemployment' [Lewis (1954]. Thus, the development process financed by labour surplus would continue for quite some time, long enough to carry the economy to a high-income equilibrium. The central policy issue in this two-sector model was to resolve the initial inter-sector production asymmetry between a large agricultural sector and a smaller manufacturing sector in order to satisfy the preconditions for sustained growth. Furthermore, the growth of national output would increase by moving 'the composition of output in the direction of an efficient outcome' [Kanbur and MacIntosh (1990), p. 116]. The process would also be equitable because the share of wages in total income would typically rise with an increase in employment. At the centre of this transformation were the (productive) capitalist entrepreneurs who would replace the (unproductive) rent-seeking landowners. The common reason for the convergence of the growth, efficiency and equity considerations in the two-sector model is that the overall productivity of the economy would rise, as labour was used up increasingly to finance industrial growth and as both agriculture and industry grew in a self-supporting manner. The productivity of the former would increase both because of greater industrial demand for agriculture products and because of land reforms, which the Traditional Development Paradigm had fervently advocated.[7] The net result of Structural Transformation would be to lower the overall capital/output ratio in the economy and increase the share of wages in the total national income [Johnston and Mellor (1961)]. Here we have the process of creative destruction at work; as the new urban values supplant the old agrarian ones, the traditional sector would give way to the fluorescence of the modern industrialization sector. It was also expected to change radically the ways in which people in the rural backwater viewed the world. The process would definitely lay the basic framework for ushering widespread social change for the good of mankind.

4.1. (ii). Agricultural Development as the Basis of Industrialization

The Lewis's two-sector model explicitly envisaged a vibrant agriculture to sustain the process of Structural Transformation. Firmly rooted in development history, it identified the main feature of Industrial Revolution as Britain's highest agricultural productivity, which created a large demand for industrialization. Subsequently, the Industrial Revolution spread to those European countries, which had attained high levels of agricultural productivity.[8] The important point to note here is that, contrary to the popular notion, agriculture was expected to play a leading role in initiating and sustaining the Structural Transformation process. Lewis (1978) put this very forcefully: 'The most important item on the agenda of development is to transform the food sector, create agricultural surpluses to feed the urban population, and thereby create the domestic basis for industry and modern services' (p. 75). It is important to remember that an increase in agricultural productivity was clearly seen as a necessary condition for the progressive adoption of increasing returns to scale technologies in the industrial sector. It was not, however, seen as a sufficient condition for it.

4.1. (III). THE BIG-PUSH HYPOTHESIS

The process of Structural Transformation would lower the overall man/land ratio and increase agricultural productivity. This would, in turn, create a demand for industrialization and start off a series of connected events within the industrial sector (a simultaneous expansion of industries) to make the adoption of increasing-scale technologies profitable. This is Rosenstein-Rodan's (1957) Big-Push hypothesis, which essentially complements Lewis's Structural Transformation hypothesis. It describes the process through which industrialization would internalize the higher demand for industrial goods. Furthermore, enabling changes must occur in the distribution of income that would eventually raise the share of the middle class in total income.[9] It stipulated that since the domestic markets were typically small in the developing countries, uncoordinated private investment decisions would generally fail to exploit the increasing returns to scale inherent in the manufacturing activity. But a state-sponsored coordinated investment programme of a critical minimum size would most probably succeed where individual acts of investment undertaken by the private sector were doomed to fail. This is because through mutual demand support, the enlargement of the market would make subsequent investment and growth privately profitable as well.[10] More specifically, disguised unemployment, pecuniary external economies, social overhead capital, and technological external economies required that a critical minimum effort be made to get the growth process started and keep it moving along the long run growth path. 'A minimum level of resources...must be devoted to... a development programme if it is to have any chance of success.' (p. 70).[11] However, undertaking such an investment programme was a necessary, though not a sufficient, condition for successful development. It would fructify only in the urban-based manufacturing activities. 'Industrialization has to be promoted not because of terms of trade, but because external economies are greater in industry than in agriculture alone' [Rosenstein-Rodan (1984)].[12] A higher level of industrial activity was expected to yield technological spillover that would become a new source of wealth creation. The wage earners spend part of their higher wages (as wages are assumed to be higher in the industrial employment than in agricultural employment) on the goods produced in the industrial sector, as well as on agricultural products. This increase in demand would then expand the domestic market and raise overall output growth. Here is a potential virtuous circle that was expected to take the economy to a higher-equilibrium growth path with the help of strategically focused state intervention.[13] The price implication of the Big-Push hypothesis is developed in the next chapter.

4.1. (iv). A Proactive Role for Government

The Structural Transformation hypothesis adequately captured the essence of the history of economic progress that featured industrialization as its linchpin. It could be described as stylized history on a grand scale, covering a time span of nearly two centuries. It is especially applicable to the story of industrialization and economic progress of the developing countries after 1945. Two main forces have principally characterized the modern era of growth in the developing countries: (i) A marked change in the responsibilities of the government—from one confined to the maintenance of law and order to a development-oriented state. In particular, it has involved raising substantially public investment as a percentage of the GDP and 'a marked increase in public ownership of economic activities, extending beyond infrastructure to mining, manufacturing, finance and trade'. (ii) Furthermore, there was an irrepressible 'urge to launch new enterprises in a situation where government seemed best able to mobilize the necessary investment funds'. Thus, 'rapid, government-propelled industrialization was preferred to the slower pace which would have resulted from relying on private initiative and finance' [Reynolds (1983), p. 971].

4.2. THE EMPIRICAL BASIS OF THE STRUCTURAL TRANSFORMATION HYPOTHESIS

Empirical studies confirm Structural Transformation—that manufacturing production has tended to increase at a faster pace than total output—to be a widely observed 'stylized fact' of economic development since 1950 [Kuznets (1955)]. In a wide-ranging study of the structural evolution of the developing countries Chenery, Robinson and Syrquin (1986) find Structural Transformation to be the unifying theme of economic progress, which has manifested itself in the increasing share of the industry in total output, the growing intermediate use of industrial products, and the transformation of comparative advantage as factor proportions changed. They identified 'a period in which the share of manufacturing rises substantially as a universal feature of the structural transformation' (p. 350). They also confirm the expansion of the domestic market brought about mainly by exploiting inter-industry linkages to be the dominant force driving Structural Transformation, which has been shown as the single-most important factor responsible for the higher rates of total and per capita output in the post-colonial period; and the one that has directly contributed to a significant geographical redistribution of world manufacturing production from the developed to the developing countries, even though the former still dominated world trade in manufactured goods.[14] Chenery, Robinson, and Syrquin (1986) further reported that in a sample of 100 countries during 1950 to 1983, about 8 per cent of the change in the GDP was accounted for by the rise in the investment share, and 11 per cent of the change by the rise in savings share. A part of the reason for this extraordinary increase in the saving and investment rates might have been a steady decline in the inflow of foreign capital in this period. The greater observed role of savings in the growth of GDP is broadly consistent with Lewis's emphasis on increasing the savings rate as the most crucial element in the development process. The regressions done on a sample of 40 developing countries for the 1979–90 period tell a similar story. They highlight the rate of investment and the share of manufacturing in GDP, financed by a corresponding increase in the domestic and/or foreign saving, to be among the most significant variables explaining the higher-than-trend growth rate of per capita income in the developing countries. Yet another set of cross-country regression for the developed and the developing countries during the 1960–73 and 1973–85 periods showed that inter-sector factor reallocations made a significant contribution to the GDP growth, and that 'industrial development is at the heart of the development process' in both the developed and the developing countries; indeed, more in the former than in the latter [Dorwick and Gemmel (1991), p. 273]. Many more research studies confirm the close association between the growth of manufacturing and the growth rate of the GDP: 'GDP growth is the faster the greater the excess of industrial growth relative to GDP growth, that is, when the share of industry in total GDP is rising the fastest' [Thirlwall (1999)].

4.2. (i). Stages of Structural Transformation

Yet another aspect of Structural Transformation, which Mahalanobis (1953) first emphasized, was the critical role of 'heavy' (machine-making) industry in raising the growth rate of per capita income.[15] It assumed that the domestic production of capital goods would limit the rate of investment in the economy. 'As the capacity to manufacture both heavy and light machinery and other capital goods increases, the capacity to invest (by using home-produced capital goods) would also increase steadily, and India would become more and more independent of the import of foreign machinery and capital goods' (p. 18).[16] Here we have another regularity of Structural Transformation— namely, its steady progression from the consumer goods industries to heavy industries throughout the developing countries. The median share of manufacturing in the developing countries rose from below 10 to 16 per cent, and to 30 per cent in the case of 12 developing countries. The latter group included Latin America, Egypt, Turkey, Sri Lanka, the Philippines, Taiwan, South Korea, and China [Reynolds (1983), p. 972]. Another study showed that, during 1965–95 period, a 3 per cent growth rate of GDP was correlated with an even higher growth rate of manufacturing, especially in the heavy industry. A less than 3 per cent growth would reflect an even lower manufacturing growth; and a zero growth of GDP was always a combined result of a negative growth in manufacturing and a positive growth in other sectors [UNIDO (1996)]. However, it could be argued that, while the broad message here is essentially correct, at least some of the industrial requirements for machines could be satisfied by imports that could be paid for by converting domestic savings into foreign exchange earnings through additional exports. But the fact is that, since the capacity of the developing countries to convert domestic saving into foreign exchange is severely limited by the inadequacy of external demand at the time, the development of heavy industries was perhaps the only feasible option to promote self-sustaining economic growth. These industries, generally more intensive in physical and human capital and R&D expenditure, were expected to yield the largest 'spillover' effects on the long-run growth of the economy. This strategy would be especially effective in strengthening the economy's 'fundamentals'. This is because the growth of such industries would simultaneously help generate greater (forced) savings to finance higher rate of investment and encourage innovation activity required for sustaining rates of economic growth significantly higher than the trend rates, and achieving convergence with the developed countries. In addition, it would enable developing countries to move up the ladder of comparative advantage so that they, in due course, become producers and exporters of higher value-added goods.[17]

4.2. (ii). Structural Transformation in Asia and Pacific Region (1965–2000)

Using pooled data for 18 high, medium and low-growth developing countries in Asia and Pacific region, we have tried to test quite a few of the basic hypotheses that have had wide currency in the development literature. The results of this extensive empirical exercise will be presented at different places in this book. The Asia-Pacific region has been chosen because, for quite some time, it is here that the game of growth has been played with great success. It, therefore, provides the ideal laboratory to test many of the standard prescriptions about development success.[18] Figure 4.1 provides a striking confirmation of the Structural Transformation thesis. It shows that during the 35 years of development experience (1965 to 2000), none of the countries that achieved growth rate of per capita income of above 4.02 per cent could do so with a lower-than-average share of industry (29.7 per cent in total GDP). The left-hand upper corner of the box is empty. On the other hand, all countries that attained higher-than-average growth rate of per capita income—in excess of 4.02 per cent per annum (Thailand, Singapore, South Korea, Vietnam,

China and Malaysia) had attained industry-GDP ratio in excess of the average figure, which is 31.99 per cent. Moreover, most of the slow growers, located in the lower left-hand side of box (Pakistan, India, Bangladesh, Nepal, and Sri Lanka) could attain only lower-than-average industry GDP ratio. For reasons that will become clearer as we move on, Sri Lanka's case needs to be noted. It has been correctly cited as a special case which succeeded in achieving high rates of human development directly, not waiting for the growth rate of per capita income to occur first. However, for all its heart-warming achievement which must be valued for significantly reducing the burden of poverty, low literacy and inadequate access to health facilities, Sri Lanka has been trapped in low-growth and high-unemployment equilibrium. There may be many reasons for its lacklustre growth performance, but one stands out clearly: it is that it has failed to achieve a more-than-average rate of Structural Transformation. There is also the outlier case of countries, located in the lower right-hand corner (Papua New Guinea, Indonesia and Japan), where high industrial-output to GDP ratio has coexisted with low growth rates. This simply shows that attaining the requirement of a high manufacturing output can sometimes be offset by other growth-reducing factors. For instance, in the case of Japan, the failure to invest its large domestic saving and generate adequate domestic demand seem to have outweighed all other growth-promoting factors, including Structural Transformation. The importance of Structural Transformation as a key factor of growth and development will be examined more rigorously in Part VI of this book.

Figure 4.1: Growth Rate of Per Capita Income and Share of Manufacturing in Gross Domestic Product in Asia and Pacific Region (1965–2000)

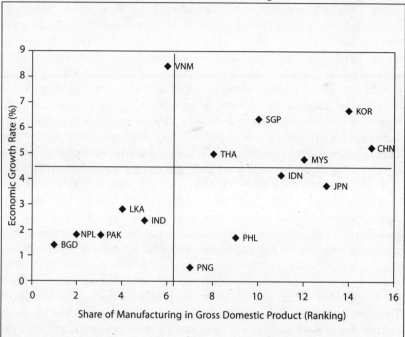

Note: Economic growth is measured as growth rate of GDP per capita. Share of manufacturing in GDP is ranked in ascending order. Higher rank means higher share of manufacturing in GDP. Average growth rate of GDP per capita for sample countries is 4.02 per cent for the period 1965–2000. Average share of manufacturing in GDP is 31.99.

◆ Following countries are included in the sample: Bangladesh (BGD), China (CHN), Fiji (FIJ), Hong Kong (HKG), India (IND), Nepal (NPL), Indonesia (IDN), Japan (JPN), Papua New Guinea (PNG), Korea (KOR), Malaysia (MYN), Pakistan (PAK), Philippines (PHL), Sri Lanka (SLK), Singapore (SGP), Taiwan (TWN), Thailand (THA), and Vietnam (VNM).

4.3. STRUCTURAL TRANSFORMATION AND THE CLASSICAL AND NEO-CLASSICAL THEORIES OF GROWTH

It may be of some interest to compare the Structural Transformation hypothesis with other growth theories. Let us first give a sample of the views of some of the outstanding classical economists of the time, who were the early expositors of the liberalist point of view that has consistently opposed Structural Transformation. We will then briefly discuss the classical and neo-classical views on the mechanics of growth.[19] This discussion, notwithstanding its brevity, should bring out the originality of the Traditional Development Paradigm and its paradigmatic character in sharper relief.

4.3. (i). Liberalist Critique

At about the same time that the Traditional Development Paradigm had gained currency, Nobel Laureate Schultz (1956) wrote, 'I know of no evidence for any poor country anywhere that would even suggest that a transfer of some small fraction, say 5 per cent, of the existing labour force out of agriculture, with other things equal, could be made without reducing its production'. Viner (1958) argued, 'the degree of industrialization may be and often is a consequence rather than the cause of prosperity' and because it tends to lower per capita income than it would be, 'if the urban industry were not artificially stimulated'. He instead preferred that development policy concentrated on agricultural prosperity and let the tertiary and service industries grow 'spontaneously' (p. 97). Haberler (1959) argued for a development policy that would work through, and with the help of, the powerful forces of the price mechanism instead of opposing and counteracting the market forces. The price mechanism would work equally effectively in the case of 'measures [taken] in the area of international trade as well as in the domestic field' (p. 6). These views show that the leading classical economists of the time had little understanding of development history, or of what an adequate development policy must focus on to spur on the process of growth and development.

4.3. (ii). Harrod-Domar Model

The Harrod-Domar (1939; 1946) model was intended to provide an explanation of the growth of Western economies; but somehow it has been cited quite widely as encapsulating the basics of growth in the developing countries as well—a practice that is open to question. Both by its structure and what it aimed to achieve, this model at best represents, 'a mythical state of affairs not likely to obtain in any actual economy', [Robinson (1956), p. 99].[20] However, it has the merit of identifying some of the key variables that determine rate of the growth of the economy. The model highlighted the role of the saving (s) and investment rates, and the capital/output ratio (v), in order to sustain the long-run growth of output ($g = \frac{s}{v}$) of an industrialized economy. An important implication of the Harrod-Domar model is that a high rate of saving means that the equilibrium growth rate (s/v) is high because a high rate of investment is required to absorb the available savings. Conversely, a low rate of saving would mean a low rate of growth [Hahn and Mathews (1965)].[21] But its highly restrictive assumptions (e.g. a single-sector economy, and one commodity that served both as consumption and an investment) precluded any detailed description of such a mechanism. Essentially, an extension of the Keynesian static model, its primary motivation was to explore the properties of the steady-state growth path of a developed economy, i.e. when the growth rate of all the relevant variables would remain constant over time. Obviously, that would not be a matter of great concern for a typical developing economy.[22] One of the chief drawbacks of the model is that it does not specify the exact mechanism through which a high rate of saving would be generated, nor does it tell us about a meaningful scenario in which it would contribute to a high rate of growth in a developing country. With a given capital/output ratio (v), a higher rate of growth (g) would obviously require a higher rate of saving(s). But in the absence of a saving generation mechanism like the one specified in the Lewis model (by transferring resources from a low saving rural sector to a high saving manufacturing sector), a higher rate of saving could only be generated in the Harrod-Domar framework by further cutting down on prevailing low levels of consumption. By making effective demand even more deficient than it was to begin with, it would act as a drag on the growth process rather than be a spur to it.

4.3. (iii). The Solow-Swan Type Model

Like the Harrod-Domar model, the Solow-Swan classical model of growth (1957) has also been cited in many standard texts on development economics as having relevance to analyzing the development-related issues—a claim, however, which the authors of the model would most certainly deny.[23] The model sought to demonstrate the possibilities of growth of a developed economy by letting the capital/output ratio vary. Once again, this analytical framework basically sought to remedy the knife-edge problem of the Harrod-Domar model; it was not suitable to analyze the development problem. Thus, in it, raising the saving rate is not at all crucial to the growth process: it would raise the growth of output only in the short run because a high saving rate would soon be offset by an increase in the capital/output ratio. Furthermore, the assumption of diminishing returns to capital implied that, 'the long-run rate of growth is completely independent of the saving-investment quota' [Solow (1994), p. 48]. Thus, comparing two states of economy with the same population rate of growth, an economy with the higher saving rate would have a higher capital/output ratio and a higher level of income but the growth rates in the two states would be the same. This left capital/output ratio as the only control variable to bring the economy back to the steady-state growth path.[24] In fact, in the Solow-Swan model, the growth rate of population would sustain the long-run growth of the economy. Furthermore, thanks to diminishing returns to capital, an economy could not generate long-run growth of output per capita, in the absence of technological change. By sharp contrast, in the Lewis's model, raising the saving rate by stimulating the productivity-enhancing inter-sector transfer of resources would raise per capita income on a long-run basis. Also, in it, an increase in population is a double-edged sword: it would swell the reserve army of surplus labour that would support growth; but it would also subtract from a given growth achievement (measured by growth of the GDP) by lowering per capita income, and prolong the time it took to eliminate the dual character of the economy. It would also worsen the wage/rental ratio, a result that Lewis openly rejected as contrary to the egalitarian intent of his model.

4.3. (iv). Uzawa Two-Sector Model

One would think that perhaps the two-sector classical growth models would offer some inkling into the working out of the process of development. But once again, here the appearances are deceptive—and misleading. In the standard Uzawa's 1961 two-sector model, the inter-sector movement of capital and labour would not take place, for the simple reason, that the profit rate would be the same in both the sectors; which implied that the wage-rental ratio would also be the same in the two sectors and so would be the rate of increase of the output in them. This shows that there is no mechanism in this model to wean a rural economy and no need to industrialize a developing economy to maximize the growth rate of per capita income. Once again, this result is exactly the opposite to that of the Lewis model.

4.3. (v). Endogenous Growth Model

The modern endogenous growth theory due to Romer (1986) and Lucas (1988) has contributed to the feeling of self-sufficiency among the liberalists: that after all, they have enough understanding of process of growth and development. Indeed, it was confidently claimed that the endogenous growth theory made the Lewis model and the Traditional Development Paradigm redundant for analyzing the development-related issues. Let us examine this important claim. True, the endogenous growth models overcome the diffidence (or indifference) of the neo-classical growth models to problems of long run-growth of per capita income.[25] In the Solow-type models long-term growth is pinned down by the ubiquitous diminishing returns to capital. In sharp contrast, the endogenous growth theory allows non-decreasing returns to reproducible assets, like knowledge and capital which leads to greater R&D activities that increases growth from within by the creation of 'new products' and improving the old ones. Technological progress is driven in the new models by the profit-seeking actions of individuals in an essentially imperfect market setting. The spillover effects that flow from the productivity-enhancing acts of individuals and those which materialize through positive effects of the investment made by a specific firm on the production possibilities of other firms in the economy, constitute yet another mechanism to raise the long run growth of per capita income. However, it has been shown that the new theory does not quite succeed in capturing the essence of the development process because increasing scale economies are neither necessary, nor sufficient to generate long run growth of output [Srinivasan (1993)]. Furthermore, like the neo-classical theory, the endogenous growth theory too is hampered by its neo-classical (and unrealistic) assumptions of a single-sector economy and that all sectors are symmetric. Yet another inadequacy of the endogenous growth theory is that its research agenda does not reflect the concerns of a development oriented policy.[26] Indeed, by virtue of its simplifying (or, perhaps, simplistic) assumptions, it fails to provide, 'a powerful organizing framework for thinking about actual growth phenomenon' [Pack (1994); Naqvi (1995), (2002)]. Its insight regarding the role of human capital in the growth process is an important one.[27] But this fact has been known all along to development economists. And what has not been known to them—namely, the new theory's assertion that helping human capital formation is all that matters—is really an oversimplification of the complexity of the development process. For one thing, while accepting the great importance of human capital, it would not be proper to underestimate the importance of physical capital for economic and human development. As noted in the previous chapter, even in East Asia physical capital formation explained most of the miracle growth. Probably, human capital is a luxury good, the importance of which increases at higher stages of economic development.[28] Furthermore, contrary to what it claims, the new theory's concern has not been so much with the growth of real-life economies along a high-growth path; nor has it enlarged much on the theme of multiple equilibria, which the Traditional Development Paradigm highlighted—that the essence of development is to move the underdeveloped economies out of the low-productivity equilibrium to high-productivity equilibrium. For all these reasons, endogenous growth theory could not contribute significantly, if at all, to an understanding of the vital development issues—namely, slow growth, higher unemployment rate, increased inequity and poverty.[29]

A more basic contribution of the new theory to an understanding of the development issues has probably been to show that international trade and investment open possibilities of growth by making available new goods (through imports), and by avoiding unnecessary (and costly) duplication of research and development. But these possibilities are more apparent than real for the developing countries, because trade would reduce the profitability of new investment in R&D in the developing countries by opening up the local investors to the superior knowledge and techniques of the foreign investor. Thus, the local investor would end up imitating the foreign investor rather than creating new ideas if trade and investment were open, than if the domestic investor was protected. The problem here is that the pool of knowledge that international trade creates is highly localized in developed countries that already have an edge over the developing countries with respect to the creation of new knowledge, so that with free trade, the richer countries are likely to capture a large part of the market in goods created by their superior learning (and learning to learn). In sharp contrast, the poorer countries, not enjoying such advantages in the opportunities to learn, would be left to specialize in inferior type of goods not intensive in learning. They would, therefore, specialize in less sophisticated varieties of goods. It is therefore fair to conclude, that endogenous growth theory offers little that is new to development economists. The pervasiveness of externalities in the innovation process, emphasized by the new growth theory, has been the standard fare in development theory and policy. And what is new in it— formalizing these ideas in the framework of perfect competition models, and later on in imperfect competition models—is not of much direct, or even indirect, relevance to development policy. On the other hand, 'the new literature [on endogenous growth theory] in some ways diverts our attention from the abiding concern of development economists with the problems of structural transformation and with those of reallocation of resources from the traditional sectors to other sectors with different organizational and technological dynamics' [Bardhan (1995), p. 2992].

4.4. BALANCE BETWEEN AGRICULTURE AND INDUSTRY

Yet another foundational concern of the Traditional Development Paradigm was to ensure inter-sector balance—especially that between the agriculture and industrial sectors. As noted above, the Structural Transformation conjecture did not imply a bias against agriculture. Indeed, keeping a dynamic balance between the two sectors was an integral part of the Structural Transformation process and a precondition for its success in bringing about systemic change. It is, therefore, important to have a clear understanding of the mechanism through which the impulses generated by high agricultural productivity get transformed into the demand for industrialization and vice versa. The chain of events would be as follows: A rise in the agricultural productivity, spurred on by technological change has the effect of raising agricultural (food) surplus. At the same time, it expands the domestic market for industrialization, which is defined as the progressive substitution of the increasing returns technologies for constant returns to scale technologies. A key element here is that an expanding domestic market creates the demand for industrialization, increases employment in industry, and helps agricultural transformation from a low-productivity to a high-productivity activity. A technological change in the agriculture sector increases the production (and supply) of food, while the demand for it in the agriculture sector does not rise by as much—a food surplus is created. At the same time, employment in agriculture falls, farm output rises, and labour flows out of agriculture into industry as the output of existing industries increases and industrialization gathers momentum. As industry expands to absorb the labour released by agriculture, the frequency of the adoption of the increasing scale technologies increases and with it industrial output.[30] As the creator of new wealth and technological spillover for the rest of the economy, the manufacturing sector would take the economy to a higher growth path—'from cottage-production equilibrium to industrial production equilibrium.'[31] What this analysis shows is that industrialization would be initially financed by the surplus labour in the rural sector, as Nurkse (1953) pointed out; but that it would help agriculture productivity to increase as well. In other words, both agriculture and industry would need to grow in tandem. This is the reason why 'industrial and agrarian revolutions always go together, and [that is] why economies in which agriculture is stagnant do not show industrial development' [Lewis (1954), p. 433]. Indeed, the manufacturing activity would not be profitable, unless agriculture was growing simultaneously as well.[32] This is because, 'economic development is characterized by a substantial increase in the demand for agricultural products, and the failure to expand food supplies in pace with the growth of demand can seriously impede economic growth' [Johnston and Mellor (1961), p. 590]. Kuznets (1961) emphasized the same point: 'One of the crucial problems of modern economic growth is how to extract from agriculture a surplus for financing of capital formation necessary for industrial growth, without, at the same time, blighting the growth of agriculture, under conditions where no easy quid pro quo for surplus is available in the country' (p. 115).

Empirical studies confirm the predictions of the Traditional Development Paradigm: successful developing countries have had their agricultural sector growing at the maximal rates and their industrial sector growing even faster. A high rate of agricultural growth has been generally significantly correlated with industrial growth and factor productivity [Chenery, Robinson and Syrquin (1986), pp. 241–42]. This strategy of the balanced growth of agriculture (with a low capital/output ratio), and industry (with a much higher capital/output ratio) would make the long-run growth of the economy sustainable by lowering the overall capital intensity of the development process. Thus, government policy would help transform an economy with low saving and investment into an economy with high rates of saving and investment.[33] The important point about this conceptualization of the development process is that once begun, it leads to a chain of events that eventually culminates in a progressive decline, by the Engel's Law, in the weight of agricultural output in total output and a rise in that of the industrial output. Going beyond that, it would lead to the discovery of new frontiers of growth that would facilitate an economy-wide transformation of the entire structure of demand, trade, production, and employment, together with the accumulation of physical and human capital [Chenery and Srinivasan (1988)]. These are the essential first steps to a societal transformation that would eventually guide the transition from agrarian values to urban values and from feudalism to capitalism. For instance, Rostow (1984) placed, 'the process of growth explicitly in the setting of the whole societies' (p. 232).

4.5. BALANCED-GROWTH STRATEGY

The requirement of inter-sector balance between agriculture and industry is a special case of the general phenomenon of balanced growth, which, along with the Structural Transformation and the Big-push processes, constitutes yet another original contribution that Traditional Development Paradigm made. It also lent itself to the construction of sophisticated planning models. A balanced-growth strategy was recommended basically to break out of the vicious circle of poverty and underdevelopment, if the supply of key industrial inputs was assumed to be elastic [Nurkse (1953); Scitovsky (1954); Fleming (1955)]. However, the growth path could be 'unbalanced' to begin with, if investment resources were assumed to be fixed, but only to achieve eventually, a dynamic inter-sector balance economy-wide. It may be noted that, contrary to a common misunderstanding, both these concepts—balanced growth and unbalanced growth—are complementary in nature. They take into account the input-type of linkages between different sectors of the economy and within the industrial sector. Together, they convey the essence of the development process. The balanced (or unbalanced) strategy requires that the worth of specific acts of investment be judged with reference to their feasibility and productivity or efficiency. Hirschman (1958) advocated unbalanced growth because it would economize on scarce entrepreneurial skills and internalize the inter-sector investment spillover in the form of backward and forward linkages. Streeten (1959) favoured the same strategy on the grounds, that the greater gains in output would accrue in the form of technological progress, if some key industries were to grow faster than others. In either case, faster growth would occur in those sectors and industries where the output and income elasticity was relatively high, while industries and sectors where the relevant elasticity was lower would grow more slowly [Scitovsky (1990)]. Another way of looking at these complementary growth strategies, is to view the balanced-growth strategy coming into play as the limits of unbalanced growth are reached—that is, when the constraints imposed by inter-sector dependence get violated so that investment and growth in one sector goes too far out of line with the rest of the economy. The basic motivation here is to exploit the technological complementarities and the demand spillover that lead to an increase in the demand faced by neighbouring firms and/or a reduction in their costs of production.

Yet another misunderstood point is that the balanced-growth models are not closed in the sense of excluding the possibilities of international trade altogether. Indeed, the two-gap models, initiated by Chenery and Bruno (1962), explicitly featured the external sector in the development process. In these models, export growth is exogenous and domestic saving seen as a function of income. Domestic investment, however, needs both domestic and foreign saving. Insofar, as export growth is insufficiently strong, foreign capital would act as a powerful stimulus to growth by alleviating foreign-exchange bottlenecks. Furthermore, the operational counterpart of the balanced-growth model, i.e. the programming approach to resource allocation—explicitly allowed for international trade. Thus, in a typical linear-programming model, 'the activities of importing and exporting are also included in the system, and the price solution contains the equilibrium prices of foreign exchange' [Chenery (1965), p. 138]. In these models, the requirements of efficiency and consistency are met by regarding domestic production and imports as alternative activities to satisfy the domestic demand for commodities and factors. The feasible solution (in the programming sense) is represented by a production or import activity for each of the commodities included in the programme, plus an export activity for foreign exchange.

4.6. DYNAMIC COMPARATIVE ADVANTAGE DOCTRINE

One of the central elements of the Traditional Development Paradigm—and one of its greatest sins in the liberalist eyes—was to question the relevance of the classical (neo-classical) Law of Comparative Advantage for determining the allocation of domestic resources, and that between exports and imports in a typical developing country.[34] It considered as inimical to achieving fast growth of per capita income, the basic recommendations of the Law, i.e. whatever goods can be imported at cheaper price than if produced at home need never be domestically produced; and the production for exports should be expanded to the point of equality between marginal revenue and marginal cost.[35] Indeed, it argued that, static comparative advantage might as well obstruct the emergence of a sector-pattern of production that would maximize growth, and a more advantageous pattern of outward orientation in the developing countries. The Traditional Development Paradigm was quick to see that, in a dynamic setting, it would not be correct to derive an optimal pattern of resource allocation from a mere comparison of the present domestic and foreign prices of traded goods. It, therefore, concluded that a religious attachment to the Law would preclude a concerted search for discovering the country's long-term Dynamic Comparative Advantage, which would emerge from the growth process itself. In other words, far from being the determinant of the process of Structural Transformation and economic growth, the developing country's long-term comparative advantage would be determined only after an explicit analysis of the growth process itself [Chenery (1965)].[36] This should be clear once it is recognized that international trade should not merely be seen, as the static Heckscher-Ohlin model does, as forcing a change in the inter-sector allocation of resources in the efficient direction—or more formally, as moving along the trading country's production-possibility frontier. In a more fundamental sense, international trade is one of the key factors (though not the only one) that cause an outward shift in each trading country's production-possibility frontier associated with the inter-sector shift in allocation of resources in the efficient and growth-generating direction. Such shifts would themselves be triggered by the accumulation of skills and physical capital, the availability of intermediate inputs and a fuller exploitation of the increasing-scale technologies that industrialization requires and promotes.

4.6. (i). The Primacy of Expanding the Domestic Market

The Traditional Development Paradigm put forward the seminal idea that economic growth, driven by Structural Transformation and the Big-push, would create its own pattern of comparative advantage by causing a change in the composition of imports and exports. In sharp contrast to neo-classical (or classical) economics, which held that trade primarily determined growth and the allocation of domestic resources between alternative uses, it accorded primacy to the factors that expanded the domestic market as the basic determinant of the pattern of resource allocation. A clear understanding of this fundamental point marked a paradigmatic shift in development thinking in that it led to a major reorientation of the development effort in the form of a vigorous import-substitution activity; it also reshaped the patterns of production and trade in the developing countries. This policy shift proved to be especially fruitful in East Asia, where the dominant government policy was to promote exports as a subset of overall industrialization of a developing society that steadily progressed from the import-substitution stage to the export-expansion stage. In this progression, the governments 'have not so much as picked winners as made them' [Wade (1990), p. 334].

4.7. 'UNEQUAL EXCHANGE': THE LEWIS-SINGER-PREBISCH THESIS

The Traditional Development Paradigm highlighted the asymmetry in international economic relations between the developed and developing countries to be the general rule rather than the exception. This was cited as the basic reason why developing countries could not leave their development to the vagaries of the international trade that historically favoured the developed countries. Lewis (1978) explicitly stated that the distribution of world trade on the principle that the tropical (the developing) countries had a comparative advantage in agricultural products, and the temperate (the developed) countries in manufacturing was no more than an 'optical illusion' (p. 11). It was, he argued, a product of the special conditions prevailing in the nineteenth century, when the factorial terms of trade available to the developed countries ensured them higher income, savings and greater opportunities for import substitution and industrialization. On the other hand, the factorial terms of trade available to the developing countries offered them 'the opportunity to stay poor' (p. 19). This pattern of comparative advantage was harmful, because it limited the (required) growth rates in the developing countries to the (lower-than-required) realized growth rates of the developed countries. Such a policy would, therefore, not generate growth rates needed for the developing countries to develop fast and converge with the developed countries (p. 68). He, therefore, concluded, 'international trade which became an engine of growth in the nineteenth century is not its proper role'. The engine of growth should, therefore, 'be technological change, with international trade serving as lubricating oil and not as fuel' (p. 74). Earlier, Prebisch (1950) and Singer (1950) had pointed out that the historical asymmetries in trade relationship essentially reflected the highly uneven distribution of wealth and economic power between the developed and the developing countries. The developed countries would, therefore, be the principal gainers from international trade and investment in a *laissez-faire* regime.[37] Indeed, thanks to the inequities in the distribution of economic and political power, the rich and the powerful nations would reap the 'best of both the worlds' [Singer (1950)].[38] The main point of the Lewis-Singer-Prebisch thesis was, that structural differences between the developed countries (which typically were exporters of high value-added, non-resource-based manufacturing), and the developing countries (which exported lower value-added primary goods and resource-based manufacturing) introduced an inherent bias in the international trading system. For this bias, a regime of free trade and investment would tend to hinder, rather than help, the growth-promoting process of Structural Transformation in the developing countries.[39] That being the case, free trade would not work necessarily to the developing countries' advantage. Indeed, it might as well hurt them for the following reasons: (a) Specializing in the production of traditional exports would not, as a rule, allocate resources to the high-productivity manufacturing production. (b) Foreign investment in the low-productivity sectors would benefit the investing countries and not the countries where such investment was made. The newly developing countries would, therefore, not be the principal beneficiaries of the potential gains from international trade and investment.[40] By the same token, the development efforts in the developing countries would be constrained by the systemic asymmetries in international economic relations in which the superior bargaining and financial powers of the developed countries and their virtual control of marketing, processing and distribution mattered a great deal to decide the principal gainer from the international trading system. The point was (it still is), that free trade would prevent the graduation of a low-income economy into a high-income economy.[41]

Recent research seems to support Lewis-Singer-Prebisch thesis. It has been shown that the terms of trade of the primary commodities have experienced a secular decline during the twentieth century [Grilli and Yang (1988); and Diakosavvas and Scandizzo (1991)]. Since the pioneers wrote, the gravity of the situation for the developing countries has only increased. The 'income losses [of the developing countries] were greater in the 1990s than in the 1980s, not only because of larger terms of trade losses, *but also because of the increase in the share of trade in the GDP*' [UNCTAD (1999), p. 85; italics added]. The italicized phrase says that, contrary to what the advocates of free trade have claimed, an increase in the share of exports in their national income—that is, notwithstanding their greater export orientation—has added to, rather than subtracted from, the developing countries' economic difficulties. The terms of trade of the non-oil producing developing countries have declined at about 1.5 per cent per annum since the early 1980s. This adverse movement of the terms of trade, which Lewis-Singer-Prebisch hypothesis predicted, has cut the purchasing power of the developing countries exports. Not only that; there is strong evidence that the terms of trade of the manufactured exports of the developing countries have declined relative to those exported by the developed countries. And there is a presumption that the income terms of trade have also been generally unfavourable to the developed countries [Thirlwall (1999), pp. 441–4]. Both the Pearson Commission Report, 1969, and the Brandt Commission Report, 1980, endorsed the need for a new international pattern of trade and investment that would free the developing countries from the straitjacket of the nineteenth century *laissez-faire*, and provide full opportunities for their economic and human development. These sentiments have also been echoed in the successive UNCTAD reports, which emphasized that: 'economic relations between un-equals have never delivered fast growth and shared prosperity even in to-day's developed countries, and it has at times been destructive' [UNCTAD (1999), p. 1].

The Traditional Paradigm's strong scepticism of the eventual beneficence of the static Comparative Advantage principle also seems to have been confirmed by the modern international trade theory, which admits of the possibility of the poor countries being better off under autarky than with free trade. Thus, for instance, free capital flows among the developed countries are generally seen as beneficial, because they economize on the expenditure made on R&D by different countries. However, it can be objected, that this result may not necessarily hold in respect of the flows of capital between the developed and the developing countries. There is a distinct possibility that the former, because of their greater stock of scientific knowledge, might capture a disproportionate share of the world market in R&D to the detriment of the developing countries. On the other hand, the latter might get hurt, because the developed countries' unbeatable (at least in the short run) superiority in technological knowledge would lead entrepreneurs in developing countries to under-invest in R&D, in the expectation of making losses on their investment, would then lower their long-run economic growth [Feenstra (1990); Grossman and Helpman (1991)]. Furthermore, in such situations, 'trade may drive the [poorer] country to specialize in production rather than research, and within production from high-tech products to traditional, possibly stagnant industries which use its relatively plentiful supply of unskilled workers—thus slowing down innovation and growth' [Bardhan (1995), p. 2987].

4.7. (i). Open Economy or a Closed One?

Contrary to the liberalist insinuations, the Traditional Development Paradigm did not use the preceding argument to deny the importance of international trade and investment for the growth of the developing countries. Its point was not to choose between free trade and autarky. What it meant was that international trade be conducted on a fairer basis than that provided by the traditional *laissez-faire*, and that the division of the gains from trade should be equitable. There is, therefore, no substance in the liberalist charge that the Traditional Development Paradigm modelled a closed economy.[42] On the other hand, it explicitly factored international trade into the model and sought to explore the consequences of such opening to the development prospects of the developing countries. Lewis (1955) explicitly recognized that, 'the extension of trade and specialization are a vital part of economic growth' (p. 69). However, he warned against the likelihood that the international economic system might not facilitate Structural Transformation, unless proper safeguards were taken to regulate trade and capital flows. Prebisch

(1950) also derived his major theses in the context of an international economic framework. Within the centre-periphery system, his interest in the working of the international trade was excited by, 'the question of the dissemination of technology and the distribution of its fruits, since the empirical evidence revealed considerable inequality between the producers and the exporters of manufactured goods on the one hand, and exporters of primary commodities on the other hand' [Prebisch (1984), p. 176]. Singer (1984) clarified that his 1950 paper, 'did not deny the existence of [gains from trade], nor did it claim that the deteriorating barter terms of trade are direct evidence of a welfare loss by developing countries.' All that it asserted was that, 'deteriorating terms of trade mean a welfare loss for developing countries as compared with a situation in which their terms of trade do not deteriorate...' (p. 284).[43] Rosenstein-Rodan (1984) rejected, 'a strategy of self-sufficiency or an inward-looking strategy of industrialization.' Instead, he argued, 'for industrialization with the help of international investment and for a pattern of industrialization that would preserve the advantages of an international division of labour and would in the end produce more for everybody.' (p. 211). Myrdal (1957) explicitly conceptualized the problems of the developing countries in an open economy context. He focused on, 'the biases of the inherited theory of international trade, particularly by the unrealistic idea then becoming prevalent among economists, that trade in commodities worked for the equalization of factor prices, more especially of wages.' [Myrdal (1984), p. 152]. The point is that the Traditional Development Paradigm's doubts about the fairness of the distribution gains from international trade and investment between the rich and the poor nations, which recent world events have only confirmed, could not, by any stretch of imagination be construed as a denial of the obvious advantages that can, and do, flow from a greater integration with the world economy if adequate preparations were made to repair at least some of the obvious disabilities of unequal exchange. In other words, a denial of the proposition that a regime of *laissez-faire* was the surest means to promoting growth and development is not the same thing as denying the importance of international trade and investment as vital for achieving fast rate of economic growth.

4.8. Concluding Remarks

It may be interesting to conclude this chapter by making a few observations on the central thrust of Traditional Paradigm's foundational hypotheses—namely, the Structural Transformation, Big-push, Inter-Sector Balance, the Balanced-Growth Doctrine, the Dynamic Comparative Advantage Principle, and the principle of Unequal Exchange—that have spilled new light on the pages of development history. These seemingly unrelated concepts weave a single tapestry of the Traditional Development Paradigm, which transformed our thinking about the meaning and focus of development policy. A striking thing about them is that latter-day research has confirmed their essential truth and statistical robustness—that they correctly described the basic regularities of the development process in the developing as well as the developed countries. Yet another is that, a set of apparently heretical doctrines metamorphosed into a development orthodoxy that readily captured the minds and hearts of the policy-makers throughout the developing countries for a full three decades—and for some time of the international donors as well. It may be noted that these hypotheses were inspired in part by the development history of the Western countries (the so-called 'pioneers' in development). Rostow (1956) and Gerschenkron (1952) concluded that the developed countries' experience had shown that the balanced-growth scenario set the pattern of development there. However, the similarities in developed countries' experience and that of today's developing countries do not cover the entire range of the Traditional Development Paradigm's contributions to development thinking.[44] It can be stated with confidence that the Traditional Development Paradigm was not wrong in focusing on increasing the supply of the constraining factors, especially the human and physical capital, so as to achieve a balanced growth of the economy as a prelude to 'self-sustaining' growth, as Rostow (1956) put it. The planning models, which were duly reflected in the development plans, gave empirical and theoretical support to the Traditional Development Paradigm. An important feature of the balanced-growth hypothesis, which recent theoretical contributions have confirmed as valid, is that new employment would increasingly be created in the more productive manufacturing sector to more than offset the employment destroyed in the less productive agriculture sector. It emphasized the complementary nature of the balanced-growth doctrine, in the sense, of different sectors growing in approximate (not exact) balance, in proportion to their demand and supply elasticity. However, in actual practice, it is not difficult to find instances of disproportionate sector or regional growth than could be explained by their differential demand and supply elasticity. Such imbalances have created problems, like urban unemployment, which some developing countries experienced in the 1950 to 1980 period.[45] But the point to grasp is that a defect in the implementation of certain policies need never be construed as a fundamental defect of the development strategy.

NOTES

1. Nurkse (1953) identified the forces that trap an underdeveloped economy in the pre-industrialized equilibrium, as well as the proper policies that would transform a low-income equilibrium economy into one with higher-level income equilibrium.

2. These neo-classical explanations of the growth process are referred to as the staple theories of growth, which rely on the exploitation of natural resources and their exports. See, Baldwin (1956), Watkins (1963), and Caves (1965) for a detailed exposition of such theories.

3. In the neo-classical literature, multiple equilibria signify a state when market forces do not lead to a single price, as is the case with 'adverse selection' phenomenon.

4. Lewis (1984b) explains that it was essential to postulate an elastic supply of labour to show that the profit share would rise with a rising productivity of the capitalistic sector.

5. Later on, Kaldor (1967) also restated the Structural Transformation hypothesis as an empirically testable statement: 'the fast rate of growth of income is almost invariably associated with the fast rate of growth of the secondary sector, mainly the manufacturing, and this is an attribute of an intermediate stage of development' (p. 7).

6. It may be noted that, contrary to the common perception, the constancy of the agriculture wage and its being equal to zero marginal product are not essential elements of the Lewis's model. Furthermore, labour is not surplus in the Lewis's model in the sense that agricultural output will not be affected if any amount of it was removed from agriculture.

7. Lewis (1984b) states: 'Nothing was more popular with us in the 1950s than land reforms, on ground of both equity and of expected effect on output' (p. 128). The output-raising effect of land reforms would flow from the greater productivity of owner-cultivated smaller sized farms. Binswanger and Rosenzweig (1986) and; Binswanger, Deininger and Feder (1995) have shown that small farms are generally more productive than small farms.

8. Lewis (1978) states: 'The [Industrial] revolution spread rapidly in other countries that were also revolutionizing their agriculture, especially in Western Europe and North America. But countries with low agricultural productivity, such as central and Southern Europe, or Latin America or China, had rather small industrial sectors, and there it made slow progress' (p. 10). See also Timmer (1988) on the greater productivity of European agriculture mainly because of a quicker reduction of labour/land ratio there than has been the case with the developing countries.

9. Baldwin (1956) showed that if the extra income generated by the agricultural revolution got concentrated in the hands of the very rich then a strong and self-sustaining industrial base might not be established. This point is elaborated later in this book.

10. Myrdal (1957) referred to the process as one of 'cumulative causation' that helped a developing economy to develop on a self-sustaining basis.

11. Murphy, Shleifer and Vishny (1989a,b) in a companion set of seminal papers formalize the argument and draw out its distributional implications as well. These papers also made the central message of the Big-Push and the Structural Transformation hypotheses audible to neo-classical ears. See, Krugman (1999). But it may be noted that, contrary to what Krugman states, Rosenstein-Rodan had a clear idea of the 'centrality of interaction between scale economies and the market size.'

12. Scitovsky (1954) termed the positive effect of investment in one sector on the profitability of other sectors through reduced costs or higher demand as 'dynamic external economies'.

13. Stern (1989) points out that the originality of the Structural Transformation and the Big-Push hypotheses was to combine 'the Keynesian notions of effective demand and the Smithian ideas of the size of the market'.

14. See Chenery (1955) and Syrquin (1988) for a complete exposition of the ideas noted in the text.

15. It would not be inaccurate to state that Mahalanobis formalized the political demand for the creation of a heavy industry base. This demand had been put forward by no less a person than Jawaharlal Nehru, the first Prime Minister of India. His ideas are worth quoting: 'No modern nation can exist without certain essential articles which can be produced only by big industry. Not to produce these is to rely on imports from abroad and,

thus, to be subservient to the economy of foreign country. It means economic bondage and probably also political subjugation' [Nehru (1941)].

16. Komiya (1959) showed Mahalanobis approach completely ignored the price and demand considerations. Furthermore, not much regard was paid to the considerations of comparative advantage and the dictates of efficiency. Mahalanobis's conjecture has recurred in some important recent research. Bradford, de Long, and Summers (1991), and Grossman and Helpman (1994) show that greater investment in heavy industries pays off because of its large spillover effect.

17. To the same end, Kaldor (1955), and Galenson and Leibenstein (1955) supported a policy of generating investible surplus in the manufacturing sector. In Kaldor's model, which assumed the marginal propensity to save of the wage earners to be zero and that of the capitalists to be one, the savings of the capitalist class exclusively determined the long-run growth equilibrium. Given the extreme assumption of classical saving function, the inter-sector transfer of resources was expected to accelerate capital accumulation and increase the saving rate to finance high rate of investment, in direct proportion to the greater weight of the capitalist class in an increasingly urbanized society.

18. The empirical results reported in the text in this and the subsequent chapters are a revised version of those given in Naqvi (2004).

19. See Cass (1965) and Koopmans (1965) for a good discussion of the neo-classical growth models.

20. It is interesting to recall that Abramovitz (1952) in the survey of growth theory excluded Harrod-Domar model on the ground that these models did not make any assertion about the development of real-life economies over time.

21. The formula further stipulated that population (n) grow at a constant growth rate, and that $n = g$ in long-run equilibrium.

22. Indeed, the concern for the problems of the developing countries is totally absent from the entire corpus of the classical theory of growth. Thus, Hahn and Mathews (1965) in their classic survey of the theory of economic growth explicitly excluded a discussion of 'the optimal saving and the development of backward areas' (p. 1).

23. Indeed, the planning models of several developing countries have made use of the Harrod-Domar model to compute capital requirements of the five-year and perspective plans (usually of 25 years length).

24. Empirical evidence now contradicts the view that economic growth is independent of investment. On the other hand, there is a robust relationship between investment rate and growth [Temple (1999)]. However, if the endogeneity of the investment rate were allowed for then the contribution of investment to growth would probably fall to zero.

25. About the neo-classical theory's inadequacy to deal with the growth-related issues, Stern says that it was 'concerned not with policy but with understanding what determines growth' [Stern (1991), p. 123]. From the mid-1970 to 1980s, when the going was not generally good for the developing countries, 'mainstream economics practically lost all interest in growth issues' (p. 126).

26. Baumol (1991), recognizing their predilection for the surreal advised (mainstream) economists to 'return to the wealth of nations as a leading focus for the economists' research.' But, he lamented that, 'the pertinent theory has a long way to go' to having one (p. 7).

27. Romer (1986) correctly pointed out that since 'the creation of new knowledge by one firm is assumed to have a positive external effect on the production possibilities of other firms...knowledge may have an increasing marginal product' (p. 1003).

28. However, it can also be argued that the cost of human capital formation is lower at lower rather than at higher stage of economic development.

29. Indeed, the endogenous growth theory does not help much in analyzing the standard neo-classical issues. Solow (1994) showed that the essence of the endogenous growth theory is

not that it modelled imperfect competition and increasing returns to scale. On the contrary, everything in the endogenous model turned on the unrealistic assumption of the *constancy* of the returns to capital. Make this assumption and increasing returns to scale follow as a logical necessity, 'because otherwise the assumption of constant returns to capital would imply negative marginal productivity for non-capital factors' (p. 49). Furthermore, the efforts to translate the theory into empirical models have been confounded by using steady states of different countries as the benchmark against which to measure growth performance of a country [Evenson and Westphal (1995)].

30. The last few lines in the text have been adapted from Murphy, Shleifer and Vishny (1989a).

31. The quotation in the text is from Murphy, Shleifer and Vishny (1989b, p. 1004).

32. Lewis (1954) emphatically stated that the industrial and agrarian revolutions always went together and that, 'economies in which agriculture is stagnant do not show industrial development'. Later on, Johnston and Mellor (1961) stated: 'It is our contention that balanced growth is needed in the sense of simultaneous efforts to promote agriculture and industrial development.' Yet another reason for a balanced growth of agricultural production and industrial output was that such a policy would not let a marked shift to occur in the internal terms of trade against agriculture [Fei and Ranis (1963); (1964)]. Mellor (1986) emphasized the interactions between agriculture and industry through the product and factor markets.

33. There is evidence that the saving and investment got endogenized at least in East Asia [Stiglitz and Uy (1996)]. In particular, 'government policies that enhance productive investments and raise income may have a compound effect on growth by increasing saving rates' (p. 255).

34. Robinson (1962) called the Law of Comparative Advantage as the pseudo-internationalist doctrine of *laissez-faire*.

35. More generally, the classical principles held that the market prices of factors and commodities would under perfect competition be indicative of their best alternative use or opportunity cost [Haberler (1950)]. According to this doctrine, the opening up of trade would have an instantaneous resource pull effect in the direction of the low-wage, labour-intensive goods produced in the export sector and away from the high-wage, capital-intensive goods produced in the import-substitution sector. The net effect of the resource-allocation effect would, therefore, be to help growth and the functional distribution of income [Rodrik (1995)].

36. The observations in the text are based on the Nurkse's (1958) remarks to Viner's reformulation of the classical comparative cost doctrine (1958). Viner conceded that in developing countries the classical comparative cost doctrine should allow for external economies, the divergence of market prices from their opportunity costs, and that the efficiency of production may change over time. But once these concessions were made, Nurkse observed, the comparative-cost doctrine could no longer be used to determine the optimal pattern of production and trade.

37. It may be noted that the point of the Traditional Development Paradigm was not to support protectionism. On the other hand, it warned the developing countries against misplaced optimism about the mutually beneficial nature of international trade and investment. Furthermore, it argued that it was only by an explicit understanding of the reality of 'unequal exchange' that free trade and investment could be made to work to the developing countries' advantage without necessarily putting the developed countries at a disadvantage.

38. The same position was taken by Myrdal (1956), who saw international trade as contributing to inequality between nations through the backwash effect. Later on, the Kemp-Ohyama model (1978) highlighted the fundamental asymmetry in international economic relations that is inherently biased against the South. The term unequal exchange appears in the title

of Emmanuel's book (1972). In his model, the inequality of wages between the developed and the developing countries, that they are lower in the latter than in the former, explains the unequal exchange between the two. In this and the related, though distinct models, unequal exchange leads to the unequal development of the developed and developing countries. This unequal development is considered to be the integral part of world capitalism.

39. Singer (1984) tracing the evolution of his ideas on the gains from trade and investment, remarks, 'the assumption of equal exchange in impartial 'fair' markets seemed in conflict with the facts of unequal market and technological power—my interest was in structural differences between the industrial countries exporting manufactures and exporters of primary commodities—these structural differences between the countries and markets would set up a tendency for primary commodity prices to decline relative to those of manufactured goods, and for asymmetrical changes in demand and volume' (p. 281).

40. Streeten (1981) observes: '...in the world economy there are forces at work that make for an uneven distribution of the gains from trade and economic progress generally, so that the lion's share goes to the lions, while the poor lambs are themselves swallowed up in the process' (p. 217).

41. Singer's main thesis about the deterioration of the terms of trade against the developing countries was that, as he himself later clarified, 'it is a fallacy of composition to assume that what is possible for one or some of the LDC's or newly industrializing countries can work, if at all, for the great majority of developing countries seek to pursue export substitution (export-led growth) at the same time' [1984, p. 294)].

42. Thus, it has been maintained that the central doctrines of the Traditional Development Paradigm—especially the Structural Transformation and the Balanced Growth doctrines, presumed a closed economy and that they would not hold in an open economy [Bell (1990)]. The argument in the text showed that this reasoning is not correct.

43. Singer (1984) elaborates on the same point: 'The title of Distribution of Gains article also indicates that it did not question the basic doctrine of comparative advantage and that trade is a positive-sum game resulting in gains to the trading partners. But it did seem to be legitimate to ask further questions as to *who* gains' (p. 287, italics in the original). At another place he asserts, 'my formulation of the 'Distribution of the Gains' paper did not question the likelihood of gains all-round from international trade, only the likely distribution of such gains; a compromise between *laissez-faire* and exploitation' (p. 280, footnote 13).

44. It has been noted that, contrary to earlier expectations of the Traditional Development Paradigm, the accumulation of physical capital did not impose a constraint on growth given rapidly rising saving rates, the possibilities of international borrowing, and the availability of direct foreign investment' [Pack (1988), p. 339]. The same was true of the skill constraint. The Traditional Development Paradigm also may not have adequately anticipated that the supply of all the constraining factors can increase in tandem—as it, in fact, did in the successful developing countries, most decisively in the East Asian countries. For if this were not the case, the relative factor prices would have increased fast, thus creating growing inequalities of income of the scarce factor, something that did not, in fact, happen [Fei, Ranis, and Kuo (1980)]. However, notwithstanding these caveats the validity of the main elements of the Traditional Development Paradigm remains unaffected.

45. The problem noted in the text was formalized in the Harris-Todaro model (1970), which explained urban unemployment as an in-built tendency of the Structural Transformation that results from the labour-market distortion caused by an institutionally set urban wage. The process of inter-sector migration, however, would continue in the hope (measured by the relevant probability) of finding a job that was not always fulfilled. Khan (1980) has generalized the Harris-Todaro conjecture. Khan and Naqvi (1983) look at the Harris-Todaro equilibrium as one, in which capital earns differential rates of return in the rural and urban sectors and show that a reduction in this differential is always welfare increasing.

5

The Traditional Development Paradigm III: Key Development Policy Issues

The Traditional Development Paradigm's position on the foundational aspects of the development process discussed in the previous two chapters has strong implications for such policy-relevant issues as the function of prices in the design of development programmes, the developmental role of government, as opposed to that of the market in furthering the 'cause' of development, the notorious import-substitution *versus* export expansion debate etc. Several questions arise in this context. What should be done when the market prices fail to perform their appointed signalling function (e.g., because of information blockage) about the future development possibilities of a developing country? Should we still leave a satisfactory resolution of these vital development-related problems to the inscrutable forces of free markets in the hope that order will be born from the womb of apparent disorder? These questions do not have obvious answers. Thus, for instance, the suggestion that, if not market prices, let 'shadow prices' (especially of capital and foreign exchange) be the guide, does not decide the case in favour of the market or against it. This is because shadow prices are generally computed by a planning agency as a substitute for market prices. These questions have been answered to some extent in the traditional development literature with considerable scientific sophistication. This chapter will endeavour to re-examine these answers in a non-doctrinaire fashion. The unifying theme of these answers is that their worth must not be judged on procedural (doctrinaire) grounds alone. Rather, it should be evaluated by their effects, likely or actual, on growth, distributive justice and poverty reduction. Some interesting empirical evidence will also be presented to buttress the theoretical arguments.

5.1. 'RIGHT' (MARKET) PRICES BECOME WRONG PRICES

It has been pointed out that one of the principal features of the Traditional Development Paradigm has been its 'distrust of the proposition that [development] matters can be left to the market' [Bell (1990), p. 15]. Folk wisdom would assert that this distrust flows directly from its anti-market ideological predilection. As always, folk wisdom is folksier than wisdom. The fact is that the paradigm's position on this and related matters had nothing to do with idealism.[1] It flowed logically from the Structural Transformation and the Big-Push hypotheses, both of which furnish ironclad arguments for market failure and an intrusive government.[2]

5.1. (i). Big-Push and Market Prices

The Big-Push case, when investment in any one sector depends on a close coordination of acts of investment between different sectors, occasions a market failure because of an important externality—namely, that mutual demand support and technological spillover from one sector to another must be factored in the investment decisions made in all the other sectors. The hypothesis has been discussed in the preceding chapter; here we look at it again in relation to the role of market prices in effecting an efficient allocation of resources. The externality in question can be internalized by undertaking investments in several connected sectors. Nurkse (1953) explicitly stated: 'Economic progress is not an automatic affair. On the contrary, there are forces within the system tending to keep it moored to a given level—a frontal attack—a wave of capital investments in a number of different industries—can economically succeed while any substantial application of capital by an individual entrepreneur may be blocked or discouraged by the limitation of the pre-existing markets...' (pp. 10 and 13). The central point of departure of the Traditional Development Paradigm was that, in this and similar cases, market prices would not typically lead to an optimal allocation of resources, nor would they suffice to generate maximal growth rate of output. In general, it was argued, present market prices do not reflect future demand and cost configurations in a typical developing country, nor do they convey the necessary information regarding the opportunity cost attached to different investment activities. Rosenstein-Rodan (1943), the original author of the Big-Push hypothesis, gave four reasons why market prices could not be trusted to guide investment in the socially desirable direction—namely, disguised unemployment, pecuniary external economies, technological external economies, and the need to create an elaborate social and physical infrastructure to make industrialization socially and privately profitable. He focused on the indivisibility in production and the feature of complements of demand as responsible for the interdependence of investment decisions. In other words, there would be a high degree of risk involved in isolated acts of investment so that the private entrepreneurs would face considerable uncertainty in finding a market for their produce. Hence, if investments could occur on a large enough scale, the complements of demand would overcome the investor's uncertainty about finding a ready market. He pointed out that risk reduction is, in this sense, a special case of external economies. 'Reducing such interdependent risks increases naturally the incentive to invest' [Rosenstein-Rodan (1984), p. 213]. The same position has, of late, been restated more rigorously. It has been shown that the profit motive alone would not be a sufficient basis for industrialization for the simple reason that, 'when the profits are the only channel of [demand] spillover, the industrialized equilibrium cannot coexist with the unindustrialized one' [Murphy, Shleifer and Vishny (1989b), p. 1005].[3] Based on the same argument, market prices would not facilitate the Structural Transformation process—indeed, they would most likely block it.

5.1. (ii). 'Governed Market Economy' With 'Wrong Prices'

As the old adage goes, nothing succeeds like success. And the success of the East Asian Miracle has buried the liberalist case of unfettered market-led development in a deep grave. What it has shown is that the appropriate frame of thinking about the drivers of development is that of a 'governed market economy'. It is shown that in such milieu, the level (and also the rate) of investment in some key industries would also be typically lower in the absence of government investment (there is a market failure here), than its optimal level. In all such cases, the governments in East Asia acted in anticipation of the emergence of the dynamic comparative advantage [Wade (1990]. It has been asserted that the key to success in East Asia has been 'getting the prices wrong' and distorting the incentives to accelerate industrial development. Thus, in the case of Korea, 'wrong prices have been right because the government discipline over business has enabled subsidies and protection to be less than elsewhere and more effective' [Amsden (1989), p. vi].[4] The point is that in cases of market failure, the government cannot rely on the market prices; rather, ignoring the price signals, it has to go ahead making investment in lines of production where private investment would not be profitable. It is for this reason that the Traditional Development Paradigm advocated state intervention to accelerate the output in industries that have in them a large element of 'public goodness', i.e. ones that can be jointly consumed by different individuals without diminishing each other's share. And, in such cases, which are quite common in developing countries, output will not be optimally supplied if left to the market [Laffont (1989)]. Indeed, in developing countries where many crucial markets are absent and/or work imperfectly, and information about the functioning of the economy is as a rule deficient, the creation of well-functioning markets are themselves public goods that require state intervention.

5.1. (iii). More Cases of Market Failure

For reasons just stated, the Traditional Development Paradigm asserted that market prices were part of the development problem rather than its solution. Lewis (1955) voicing the universally accepted position at the time stated, 'The price mechanism, which mainly determines the use of resources, gives results which are not always socially acceptable' (p. 378).[5] Government intervention is required precisely because market prices do not, as a rule, contain all the relevant information required to affect a far-reaching Structural Transformation of developing societies. Nor would market prices issue the right signals to help reduce (income and capability) poverty, and/or ensure convergence with developed countries. Streeten (1993) noted that, 'the right prices by themselves, without the complementary state action, can be ineffective or counterproductive' (p. 1285). Yet another case where market prices do not lead to correct allocation of resources is when there are imperfections in the labour market. In cases where the efficiency wage must be paid to raise productivity, it could not perform the textbook job of labour-market clearing. The wage would, therefore, have to be set at above the market clearing level [Leibenstein (1957)]. Here is an example where market equilibrium, even when it existed, would not be socially demanded. In general, market prices could not be relied upon to ensure sector balance in a dynamic setting because the structure of supply and demand would change in a regime of accelerated growth and inconsistencies would emerge over time between commodity demand and factor supplies. Hence, as an operational counterpart of the requirements of balanced growth, it emphasized that there should be some kind of a planning framework that ensured consistency between supply and demand and dynamic social profitability [Klein (1978; 1983].[6] The need to have such a framework led to the use of high-powered computational techniques of input/output analyses, linear programming and optimal control in the planning literature.[7] An important consideration here is to find the price implications of a given allocation of scarce resources. The resulting set of prices of goods, factors and foreign exchange would reflect their true scarcities. Such prices, referred to as shadow or accounting prices, were used extensively—in particular, by [Tinbergen (1956, 1958)]; Chenery (1965)]—to evaluate investment projects and determine the social worth of investment projects. Even more important, these have been used to establish the necessary linkage between the feasibility and efficiency of large investment programmes undertaken to maximize national output subject to the constraint that the demand for commodities and factors does not exceed their supplies. These and a whole lot of factors explained why market prices would not necessarily be socially right—namely, that they would diverge from their opportunity costs.

5.2. Markets and State Intervention

The Traditional Development Paradigm faced the ubiquitous question in macroeconomics—namely, the relative roles of the market and the state in the context of a developing economy. However, rather than taking an extremist position on this vital issue, it deliberately stuck to the middle ground between overactive states that stifle individual initiative and under-active states that neglect their heavy duty developmental role—in particular, to provide education and health care and a minimal of social protection to the poor.[8] Its been an attitude of relaxed eclecticism rather than one of uptight dogmatism on this sensitive issue. Thus, on the one hand, it emphasized that developing countries should operate as market economies with private property rights in the means of production (as opposed to being centrally planned ones with no private property rights); but, on the other hand, it cautioned that much social loss could occur in a world driven exclusively, or even dominantly, by the profit motive of the private investors/entrepreneurs. The most important point about the paradigm's position is that it saw both these institutions as working together in a complementary rather than in a competitive relationship. It argued that no single formula existed to decide once and for all, the relative roles of the state and the market.[9] Nor do we need one because, 'sensible people do not get involved in arguments about whether economic progress is due to government activity or to individual initiative, they know that it is due to both, and they concern themselves only with asking what is the proper contribution of each' [Lewis (1955), p. 336)]. Thus, the Traditional Development Paradigm rejected the liberalist position that a total or overwhelming reliance on the market would open the doors to heaven, or that an intrusive state inevitably pave the 'road to serfdom'. Also, notwithstanding the manifest weaknesses of the governments in performing their social and developmental functions in the developing countries, it did not fall for a somewhat circular (liberalist) argument that government failures, as a rule, more than offset government successes in delivering development.[10] Rather, based on historical precedence and actual development experience of the developing countries, it viewed governments as having been, by and large, a force for the good in promoting growth, investment and equity, in creating the infra-structure of the markets where none existed before, and in providing public goods of various kind that every efficient and compassionate modern economy must provide.[11] Yet, the Traditional Development Paradigm did not regard state intervention to be good *per se*; but because the transfer of real resources from the private sector to the public sector would help overcome the deficiencies of the market in financing the requirements of economic and human development. For instance, in the absence of well-developed financial institutions, the government would be expected to step in to finance economic and human development. However, it did reject quite firmly the proposition that state minimalism and economic and human development could go together in the developing (or even the developed) countries.

5.2. (i). Planning for Development

As noted above, the Traditional Development Paradigm never advocated centralized development planning as a tool of development policy. Rather, it opted consciously for 'indicative' planning exercises that would give broad directions to development policy, accepting the private sector as an active agency for development. The dominant view was that selective government intervention in the form of planning would be required to meet situations of information-imperfection about marketable commodities. Such planning exercises were limited in most countries (e.g., India, Pakistan) to deriving a set of macro-goals and principal action directives from a logically consistent and empirically feasible plan. Indeed, detailed planning exercises were not generally favoured. Lewis (1955) rejected 'detailed central planning' on the grounds that, 'it is undemocratic, bureaucratic, inflexible, and subject to great error and confusion. It is also unnecessary' (p. 384). Prebisch (1984) regarded planning to be compatible with the market and private initiative. It was needed to establish certain basic conditions for the adequate functioning of the market in the context of a dynamic economy. But it did not necessarily require detailed state investment, except in infrastructure and development promotion.' (p. 180). Rosenstein-Rodan (1984) argued that investment programming in the form of a plan was necessary to correct for 'indivisibilities, externalities, and information failures'. Programming was regarded as just another name for rational, deliberate, consistent, and coordinated economic policy. Yet these programming activities would in no way make markets redundant. Indeed, programming was regarded as, 'a supplement to the price mechanism and, also, an instrument for supplying additional information which the market mechanism cannot supply. The development programme is to make use of the market mechanism, but is not dominated by it' (p. 216).[12] Tinbergen (1956) viewed planning as a relationship between economic objectives (or targets) and policy instruments available. He stressed that, 'this use of the word 'planning' has nothing to do with the type of policy involved' (p. 10). It was the universal belief among development economists that some sort of planning exercise would have to be undertaken, at least in order to prepare an economy in the early stage of development to the 'take-off' stage.[13] Yet another was to estimate the time it would take for a developing country to achieve independence from foreign aid.[14] These, perhaps, were the most important functions of the planning exercises, the rationale for which seems to be quite convincing.

The general consensus among economists and policy makers was that the initial stage of development could last for about 25 to 50 years; and that the detailed guidelines for national development must be framed in the form of the Perspective Plans of that duration. In this period, the basic idea of the planning process was to initiate and sustain multi-sector industrialization that could internalize the economies of scale at the plant level to achieve a balanced growth of the economy—something that could not be accomplished without an active government involvement. One of the basic objectives of the Perspective Plans was to transform, via an integrated programme of industrialization, the entire range of economic relationships at unprecedented rates—and, in due time, to achieve economic independence, which was deemed necessary to cement political independence. And yet the developing countries preferred what has sometimes been referred to as instrumental inference to planning as an alternative to market system, based on command and fulfilment. The former type of planning, which Lewis (1955) referred to as 'piecemeal planning', was recommended for 'those sectors of the economy where demand and supply are out of equilibrium at the ruling market prices' (p. 384). Five-Year Plans and the Annual Development Programmes were the standard analytical and policy tools to implement the development guidelines of the perspective plans.

5.2. (ii). Jobs that Only a Socially Committed Government could Do

The Traditional Development Paradigm emphasized the complementary role of the government, and yet it noted that there were some jobs that only a government would do. A little-noticed reason for this assertion was that, in the absence of government intervention, the ratio of private profit to GDP would be the sole determinant of the saving rate, and yet, 'there is no obvious reason why the rate so determined should be regarded as socially acceptable' [Lewis (1955), p. 381]. The foundational issue was, then, basically that of finding equilibrium between what is privately justified and that which was socially desirable and just. It was argued that only a socially committed government could perform such a delicate balancing act. The role of the state was regarded as the most compelling, when a domestic and/or global public good must be consumed and produced; and when large self-supporting investments must be undertaken within a policy determined time period. Thus, it was reasonably believed that the goal of high rates of saving and investment required for financing significantly higher-than-trend growth rates and achieving convergence with the developed countries could not be attained without active government intervention. The reason is that a decision must be made about how much consumption today must be sacrificed for securing higher consumption in the future, depending upon the society's accepted norms about inter-generational equity. Furthermore, only the government could bring about structural change required to redistribute private property rights (through coercive land reforms) in the initial period of the development process—because an equitable distribution of the losses and gains among the population is a job that only a government can do. It might botch up the job, but no market can even begin to comprehend the enormity of the challenge. A case in point is that of effecting land reforms. There is no alternative to government action here because land markets would normally not facilitate efficiency-enhancing and growth-promoting transfer of land from the large (and unproductive) farms to small (and productive) family-operated farms. The reason is that large landed estates that characterize feudalism, which the Traditional Development Paradigm passionately opposed, had come into being as part of a historical evolution of power relationships [Binswanger, Deininger and Feder (1995)]. In general, market prices alone could not be relied upon because they would need to be modified in a number of ways to arrive at the optimal social value of specific investment projects. These corrections were needed both to balance supply and demand under conditions of initial disequilibrium, and promote accelerated growth, something that the market prices could not do.[15]

5.2. (iii). Evidence on Large Government Developmental Role

The East Asian experience—as also of other developing countries in general—shows that efficiently implemented government intervention has been one of the most important 'causes' of systemic change in these countries. A comprehensive study of the East Asian miracle [World Bank (1993)] highlighted the useful, though, still market-friendly role of the government in making a decisive contribution to extraordinary growth by stimulating physical and human capital accumulation, allocation, and productivity, and to wider sharing of the fruits of economic progress. Amsden (1989) found that, 'all economic expansion depends on state intervention to create price distortions that direct economic activity towards greater investment' (p. 14); and Wade (1990) underscored the need for 'governing the markets' to achieve accelerated development. What happened in East Asia was, however, a special (and superlative) case of a general tendency throughout the developing countries in the post-1950 period, when the role of public sector increased. This increase was most marked in the manufacturing production: 'The public-sector share of manufacturing is often 20 to 25 per cent, and sometimes reaches 75 to 80 per cent' [Reynolds (1983), p. 973]. In view of compelling empirical evidence, a consensus has emerged (which even the liberalists now agree with) about the fact and nature of government intervention in East Asia. This consensus concerns, among other things, about the following propositions: 'there has been a lot of government intervention and an active trade and industrial policy'; and that intervention has taken place, 'in an institutional setting characterized by a hard state and a strong government discipline over the private sector' [Rodrik (1995), p. 2948)].[16]

5.2. (iv). Empirical Evidence on the Role of Government in Asia and Pacific Region (1965–2000)

It will be interesting to see how important the role of the government (measured by the ratio of government expenditure to the GDP) has actually been in Asia and the Pacific region, including East Asia, where the rate of growth has been the fastest in the world. Figure 5.1 portrays the dominant role of the government with remarkable clarity. It shows that, with the exception of Hong Kong, and to some extent Indonesia, the government expenditure/GDP ratio has been higher-than the average (11 per cent) for all the countries that have grown at a higher-than-average growth rate of per capita income (4.02 per cent) during 1960 to 2000 (Singapore, South Korea, Thailand, China and Malaysia). Among the slow-growers are countries where the role of the government has also been low (Bangladesh and Nepal), but also some cases where it has been high (India, Pakistan, Sri Lanka, and Vietnam). These contrasting results strongly suggest that, with few exceptions, high government expenditure has been associated with a higher-than average growth rate of per capita income. Yet another point is that the government role has been high in all the fast growing countries, regardless of location— South Asia or East Asia. Furthermore, the figure shows that all fast growing countries have followed the same growth strategy. This issue will be revisited later in this book, where it is shown that there has been a significant causal relationship, going from government expenditure to economic growth.

5.3. THE VALIDITY OF THE IMPORT-SUBSTITUTING INDUSTRIALIZATION STRATEGY

Because an open-door policy would not necessarily help growth, employment generation and poverty reduction, the Traditional Development Paradigm recommended a policy of carefully chosen import substitution as an essential tool of development policy. The reliance on it was expected to be heavy, by design, in the initial stages of economic development—to get the process of growth and development started, provide the necessary cover to import-substitution activities and facilitate learning-by-doing, internalize extant knowledge and generate new knowledge, spark innovation and technological change, broaden the industrial base, and lay down the foundations of a durable export-expansion activity. It also helped the developing countries to move to higher stages of industrialization.[17] There evolved a broad consensus among the principal contributors to the Traditional Development Paradigm about the merits of the import-substitution strategy. Prebisch (1984) believed that 'import substitution stimulated by a moderate and selective protection policy was an economically sound way to achieve certain desirable effects' (p. 179).[18] Singer (1984) held that the shift from primary production to the production of manufactured products through import substitution was the engine of growth (p. 287). Hirschman argued that import substitution would internalize the external economies inherent in the industrialization process. 'Once the indirect employment effects (via the backward and forward linkages) are taken into account, investment in large-scale (capital intensive) industry turns out to be just as employment-creating as investment in small-scale (labour-intensive) industry...' [Hirschman (1984), p. 97].

Figure 5.1: Economic Growth and the Role of Government in Asia and Pacific Region (1965–2000)

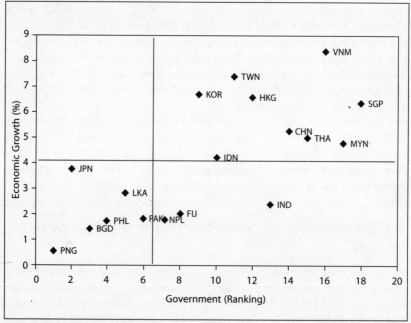

Data Source: *Penn World Table* 6.1 (PWT 6.1). The number of countries and the abbreviations are as given under Figure 5.1.

Notes: The horizontal line in the Figure 5.1 represents average growth rate of GDP per capita in the sample countries and the vertical line represents average of percentage of Government-GDP ratio. Average growth rate of GDP per capita is 4.02 per cent per annum during 1960–2000 and average of Government-GDP ratio is 11.0 per cent during the same period.

◆ Following countries are included in the sample: Bangladesh (BGD), China (CHN), Fiji (FIJ), Hong Kong (HKG), India (IND), Nepal (NPL), Indonesia (IDN), Japan (JPN), Papua New Guinea (PNG), Korea (KOR), Malaysia (MYN), Pakistan (PAK), Philippines (PHL), Sri Lanka (LKA), Singapore (SGP), Taiwan (TWN), Thailand (THA) and Vietnam (VNM).

Empirical studies on the linkages between growth and learning have shown that knowledge creation, so crucial to economic development has required processes like social values and incentives and a commitment to growth that are internal to a society [Bruton (1998)]. But these internal factors could not possibly be captured in their entirety by an overwhelming reliance on export orientation, to the exclusion of import substitution [Hobday (1995)]. They also show that successful developing countries initiated, without any exception, the development process and sustained it for quite a while (for at least 25 years or so) by producing for the more secure home market; and that this policy did not, in any way, obstruct technological progress. Indeed, many firm-level studies of technological change and learning-by-doing have found that there is a considerable amount of technological tinkering that goes on even when firms are cut off from foreign markets [Rodrik (1995), p. 2935]; and the firms scoring the highest level of technological growth have mostly been those which could rely on a safe captive market [Pearson (1987), p. 421]. As it is, the 'Brazilian miracle' of the 1960s and 1970s was clearly attributable to the policy of enlarging the domestic market through creative import substitution [Cardoso and Fishlow (1992)]. Figure 5.1 can also be used for showing the universality of the import-substituting industrialization strategy in the Asia and Pacific Region during the 1965 to 2000 period—in East Asia as well as non-East Asia. It is interesting to see that there is not a single fast-growing country (in which growth rate of per capita income exceeded 4.02 per cent) where the contribution of manufacturing to GDP fell short of the regional average: the left-hand top box is empty. Also, in all the fast-growing countries including the miracle growers, the share of manufacturing in GDP was much above average.

5.4. Has Export Expansion Been a Clear Winner?

The dominant classical (or neo-classical) position has been to advise the developing countries against import substitution and push for an all-out export-promotion strategy on efficiency grounds. The Traditional Development Paradigm contested this type of anti-historical argument vigorously.

5.4. (i). Does 'Export Fetishism' Help?

The Traditional Development Paradigm's position on export-versus-import substitution debate followed logically from its foundational hypotheses—namely, Structural Transformation, Big-Push, Dynamic External Economies, and Unequal Exchange. Though underlining the importance of foreign trade for growth and development, it asserted that 'export fetishism' was not beneficial for the developing countries; and, that it was not wise to begin the development process by prematurely opening up the domestic economy to external competition, without first creating a favourable investment climate at home through selective (but temporary) import restrictions. This is because free trade would only strengthen the dynamics of Unequal Exchange and make it all the more unequal with the passage of time. By the same token, a *laissez-faire* solution to the development issues would not help because world prices do not typically reflect opportunity costs.[19] The reason is that to decide on the structure of exports simply by a comparison of the current market prices of the traded goods with their international prices would not help the steady Structural Transformation of the economy. Thus, the classical prescription that exports should be expanded till marginal revenue equalled marginal cost would not necessarily maximize growth when account was taken of 'dynamic external economies' (i.e., those associated with a simultaneous expansion of related activities by a reduction of cost or an increase of demand) [Scitovsky (1954)]. Also, a heavy reliance on expanding exports without first broadening the export base through knowledge-creating import substitution would not generate high growth rates; instead, it would prevent developing countries from a constructive search for their long-term Dynamic Comparative Advantage. As a rule, economic growth would remain modest at best if export expansion were to be the engine of growth and if it were an integral part of a balanced-growth strategy.

5.4. (ii). Empirical Evidence from Asia and Pacific Region (1965–2000)

It is instructive to look once again at the extent to which openness helped the East Asian countries particularly and the Asia and Pacific region generally. The question then is: did they rely overwhelmingly on openness to generate the growth rates that they did achieve? This is a relevant issue because it has been claimed that the East Asian miracle could be attributed, among other things, to their greater openness. Figure 5.2 helps to form some fairly vivid impressions about the openness-growth relationship.

Firstly, the upper-left hand box shows that, with the big exception of China (which scored the highest growth rates ever achieved); no high growth rate country has had lower-than average degree of openness (45.12 per cent).

Secondly, as the other side of same coin, the lower left-hand box clarifies that some low-growth countries also have had lower-than-average openness (India, Bangladesh and Japan). Thirdly, there are a large number of countries, shown in lower right-hand side of the diagram, where a high degree of openness is associated with low growth (Nepal, Pakistan, Sri Lanka, the Philippines, Fiji Islands, Indonesia and Papua New Guinea). Fourthly, the upper right-hand box shows that most high-growth countries, especially the East Asian miracle growers (Korea, Taiwan, Singapore, Hong Kong, Malaysia). Thailand) and a rather late-comer, Vietnam have had a high degree of openness. It this kind of suggestive evidence that might have led some observers to conclude that higher-than-average degree of openness has caused high growth, especially in East Asia. However, one should evaluate these results with care. It is clear that both the high growth (China) and relatively low growth (India) big countries were characterized by a low degree of openness. On the other hand, the smaller sized countries have been more open. Thus, it can be concluded that openness has been a geographical imperative, not a general principle.

Furthermore, one cannot deduce a causative explanation from the correlations observed in the figure. This issue is explored in Part VI where it is shown that while openness is a significant factor in growth, it has not been the dominant factor in either the East Asian or the non-East Asian countries. This conclusion supports the predictions of the Traditional Development Paradigm.

Figure 5.2: Economic Growth—Openness Linkage in Asia and Pacific Region (1965–2000)

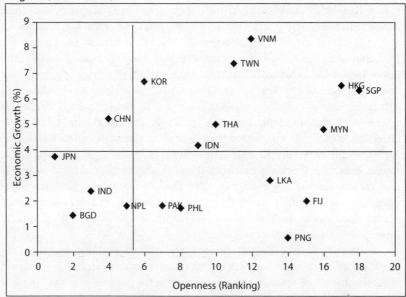

Note: Economic growth is defined as growth rate of GDP per capita. Openness, defined as share of total trade (imports + exports) in total GDP, is ranked in ascending order. Higher rank means higher openness. Average growth rate of GDP per capita for the sample countries is 4.02 per cent for the period 1965–2000. Average for openness is 45.12.

◆ Following countries are included in the sample: Bangladesh (BGD), China (CHN), Fiji (FIJ), Hong Kong (HKG), India (IND), Nepal (NPL), Indonesia (IDN), Japan (JPN), Papua New Guinea (PNG), Korea (KOR), Malaysia (MYN), Pakistan (PAK), Philippines (PHL), Sri Lanka (LKA), Singapore (SGP), Taiwan (TWN), Thailand (THA) and Vietnam (VNM).

5.5. CONCLUDING REMARKS

The Traditional Development Paradigm's fundamental hypotheses, especially Structural Transformation, Big-Push, Balanced Growth, the Dynamic Comparative Advantage and Unequal Exchange practically fixed its attitude towards such momentous issues as right prices *versus* wrong prices, market versus the government and export expansion *versus* import substitution. Given that increasing the pace of industrialization (which was seen as dependent on the maximal growth of agriculture) was the surest route to achieving high rates of economic growth, and that in the growth context the static Law of Comparative Advantage would be observed more in the breach than in the observance, it followed logically that import-substituting industrialization should be adopted as the dominant strategy to help developing countries achieve high rates of growth of per capita income and expand their export base by adding higher value-added goods. Similarly, since industrialization essentially involves an externality, market prices could not be trusted for sending the right signals to private investors for achieving maximal rate of industrialization. It is of fundamental importance to remember that both the fast growers (the East Asian countries) and the relatively slow growers (the non-East Asian countries) have followed broadly similar development strategies. And these policies paid off handsomely in all the developing countries, though much more in the former because they followed the Traditional Development Paradigm more efficiently and faithfully than did the latter. Thus, for instance, government intervention was much heavier in the fast-growing countries than in the slow-growing countries. However, one can legitimately claim that heavy government intervention paid off in East Asia not just because it was heavy, but because it was efficient as well, in the sense that it was focused sharply on strategic points and its intensity changed over time. Empirical evidence on country experiences presented so far generally confirms the validity and wisdom of the Traditional Development Paradigm. With the bitter memories of the long night of the Colonial rule still green in people's minds (which might have been exaggerated to serve a political purpose but were relevant nevertheless) no other strategy of development would have been politically acceptable. To reinstate *laissez-faire* as the dominant strategy would have looked like an ingenious plot to substitute economic colonialism for political colonialism. By accident or by design, the Traditional Development Paradigm succeeded in conceptualizing in the same flight of thought a set of doctrines that was theoretically sound and empirically robust. Did it also have a 'warm heart' for the poor and under-privileged? This question is addressed in the next chapter.

NOTES

1. It is important to remember that the acceptance of the market institutions even in early years of Independence, when socialist idealism was the in-fashion thing, was based not only on economic but on political grounds as well. Thus, the liberalist assertions about the innate anti-market tendencies of the Traditional Development Paradigm are no more than economic humbug.

2. There were voices of dissent among development economists, who warned against a price-less development policy and argued that the government should not intervene in the working of the price system [Bauer and Yamey (1957)]. But, as noted in the text, this concern was unnecessary because not a single development economist ever argued for a price-less economic system.

3. The reason for the result noted in the text is that a move from a low income pre-industrialized equilibrium with constant returns production technologies to a higher level of income associated with increasing returns to scale technology will not take place if each firm takes into account only the profits made by the other firm. Thus, if one firm loses

money on its investment (as it most likely would because it did take into account the social profitability of increasing-returns technologies) then other firms would not make the required investment effort to move to the higher income equilibrium. The economy would, therefore, remain trapped in the low-level equilibrium.

4. Amsden's terminology of getting the prices wrong may sound somewhat confusing, although the meaning is clear by the context in which it is used. It is confusing because, for instance, if the government encourages potential export industries where it does not have a comparative advantage then in a perfect-competition framework such a policy would lead to a reduction of potential output by an inefficient use of resources. It is only when increasing returns to scale, and imperfect competition are admitted that there would be a possibility of permanently altering the economy's comparative advantage by trade policy [Rodrik (1995), pp. 2948–2949]. But this argument takes for granted the very question to be asked: how do we determine in advance the industries in which a developing country has a long-term comparative disadvantage so that investing in them will reduce output? It is known that finding long-term comparative advantage is a matter of trial and error; and like great inventions it is discovered as an unexpected outcome of unintended acts of investment.

5. Adam Smith, the universally acknowledged guru of free markets, did not favour leaving it all to the profit motive to achieve social goals. He castigated, in his *Theory of Moral Sentiments* (1790), private profit seekers, who 'in their natural selfishness and rapacity' pursue 'their vain and insatiable desires' (p. 184). Sen (1999b) develops this theme at length.

6. Klein (1978; 1983) has reformulated the problem as one of liking up the Keynesian income-and-product accounts (the demand side);,the Leontief input-output framework (the supply side) and; the flow of funds accounts (the financial side) to get a complete picture of the economic universe.

7. Chenery (1965) emphasized the use of linear programming in solving development problems. The application of optimal control techniques to planning has been recommended, among others, by Chakravarty (1969).

8. Lewis (1955) stated: 'The governments may fail either because they do little or because they do too much' (p. 376).

9. The 'rebels' among the development economists did not share the view that a middle road existed between the government and the market. Thus, Bauer (1984) recalls that he had always opposed central planning: 'I noted then that comprehensive central planning was certainly not necessary for economic advance; it was much likely to retard it' (p. 42). On the other hand, he thought that unplanned and spontaneous responses of individual economic agents to emerging opportunities 'brought to their notice through the operation of the market' would be surer route to economic development of the developing countries (p. 32). See for details, Naqvi (2002).

10. The argument that government failure is worse than market failure is incorrect because while there is an elaborate theory, there is none for government failure [Stiglitz (1998)].

11. Historically, the government fostered industrialization, and helped raise agricultural productivity in the nineteenth and twentieth centuries [Adelman and Morris (1973); Adelman, (1989)]. For instance, in the United States of the nineteenth century, 'the markets were not left to develop willy-nilly on their own; the government played a vital role in shaping the evolution of the economy. The central government not only played a central role in promoting economic growth…[It also] provided a minimum opportunity to all Americans' [Stiglitz (2003), p. 21].

12. In fact, the essentially complementary role of the government was emphasized from the very beginning of the discipline without ever rejecting the information economies that free markets achieve at minimal cost [Waterston (1965)].

13. It is interesting to note that planned development in this period enjoyed the full blessings of international donors e.g., World Bank (1978). Indeed, an operational plan would be regarded as one of the preconditions for receiving foreign aid [Bruton (1998)]. However, it turned neo-classical from 1980 onwards e.g., World Bank (1987); (1990).

14. The planning exercises inevitably involved an estimate of the time it would take for a country to achieve independence from foreign aid. They highlighted two important aspects of foreign aid. (a) Foreign aid is necessary to supplement domestic savings in order to finance a level of investment far higher than domestic saving would support. (b) It also imposes a net cost on the economy in the form of an outflow of resources to finance amortization and interest payments on past loans. So outflows would outlast inflows if the borrowed money was not used productively so as to be able to raise domestic savings to a level that covers the additional financial requirements to finance domestic investment as well as the obligation to repay past debt, which continues to grow at a compound rate. For a discussion of these problems in Pakistan's context see Naqvi (1970).

15. In addition to the traditional arguments for government intervention, there are now some new ones (which in many cases are mere elaborations of the traditional position), i.e. the imperfect and missing markets, moral hazard, asymmetric information, multiple equilibrium, principal-agency syndrome, dynamic external economies, etc. These are instances where the market solutions can normally be improved upon by state intervention of some sort because the two-way link between Pareto-optimality and competitive efficiency does not necessarily hold. These are also the cases where, because of agency costs and coordination problems, government intervention might improve productive efficiency as well as equity [Bardhan (1993; 1996)]. These matters are discussed in more detail in Part IV this book.

16. Thus, even the World Bank (1991) while emphasizing that state intervention must, as a rule, be 'market friendly', conceded, 'The government needs to do more where the markets cannot be relied upon' (p. 9).

17. It may be interesting to quote Lewis in full in support of the development strategy advocated in the text. He stated that a backlog of underdevelopment on the eve of the post-colonial period 'permitted manufacturing for the home market to grow by as much as 7 to 10 per cent a year for a couple of decades, after which it was exhausted, and fast industrialization could then be sustained only by exporting manufactures. This was like breaking a spell. For over a century tropical people had been told that manufacturing industry was unsuitable for them, and that their comparative advantage lay in exporting agricultural commodities. Then suddenly they were selling manufacturers in the markets of the developed countries, and the leaders of these developed countries were running around in a panic and adopting special discriminatory measures to keep out LDC manufactures. It involved a spiritual revolution as great as that experienced by economists over the age of thirty who were converted to Keynesianism in 1936' [Lewis (1984), p. 129].

18. The emphasis on the selectivity and the moderation of protection by one of the most sceptical of the development economists of the virtues of the market solutions should be sufficient to refute the charge that the traditional development policy favoured indiscriminate protectionism. That, in fact, in some cases what was intended to be a temporary strategy turned into a semi-permanent position in some cases is not, therefore, a valid criticism of the traditional development policy.

19. Adelman (1997) supports the argument in the text on the grounds that, 'the Heckscher-Ohlin Theorem will not prevent the emergence of low-level equilibrium trap' (p. 832).

6

The Traditional Development Paradigm IV: Distributional and Related Matters

This chapter seeks to determine in detail the Traditional Development Paradigm's views on such matters as the place of moral judgments in development policy, distributive equity and social justice, poverty reduction, and the participation of women in economic activities. This analysis should also clarify some of the common misunderstandings about the Traditional Development Paradigm's position on each of these matters—that it was thoroughly positivistic and narrowly focused on growth of income; that it did not care much for distribution of income and wealth (and in fact favoured increasing inequalities as good for growth) and glorified an overly materialistic vision of human happiness; and that it was silent, or not explicit enough, on such modern concerns like gender inequity. Some of these misconceptions might have flowed from a selective reading of the statements of development economists of the time. For instance, Lewis (1955) puts his readers on notice at the very outset of his *magnum opus*: 'We shall have to consider the relationship between growth and the distribution of income of output, but our primary concern is in analyzing not distribution but growth' (p. 9).[1] This quote may be cited as a proof of the paradigm's sang-froid towards distributive equity. It will be shown that this impression is not correct. The fact is that the Traditional Development Paradigm had deep social penetration. Which social philosopher's heart would be so dispossessed as not to feel the urge to relieve the poverty and pain around him? Insensitive positivism is a luxury for those who do not have first-hand experience of the intensity of hard times and whom a wrong moral philosophy made immune to human suffering. Fortunately, the economists and social philosophers that contributed to the formation of the Traditional Development Paradigm did not belong in this category. They were men of compassion and learning and the most distinguished among them (Lewis, Tinbergen, Myrdal, Streeten, Singer, Mellor, Hirschman) had direct knowledge of the developing countries where two-third of the world's poor reside and felt the intensity of their misery.

6.1. THE NORMATIVE NATURE OF TRADITIONAL DEVELOPMENT PARADIGM

It has been alleged that the Traditional Development Paradigm was essentially positivist in orientation, focused rather narrowly on the mechanics of growth; that it held on to the view that income generation was good as long as it got created fast enough, secure in the belief that whatever was created would 'trickle down' to the poor. These impressions are, however, incorrect. While it is true that it focused most of all on maximization of growth of per capita income, but it made explicit that this objective could be fully achieved only within the framework of an egalitarian institutional change. Part of the reason for the persistence of these false impressions might have been that it did not spell out its moral point of view explicitly; but it is also a fact that the paradigm did not subscribe to a moral philosophy that would have prevented it from being egalitarian. Thus, it can be confidently stated that it did not subscribe to Benthamite Utilitarianism or Pareto-optimality as distributive principles. Or else, it could not have offered a substantive agenda for enhancing the quality of social justice and made meaningful recommendations on the ways and means of enhancing human welfare. Let us consider these matters at some length.

6.1. (i). Was the Traditional Development Paradigm Insensitive to Moral Issues?

Contrary to popular perceptions, the Traditional Development Paradigm was very much concerned with the distributive implications of its basic recommendations and with the broader issues of human happiness, which was not regarded as synonymous with the material prosperity.[2] Lewis (1984b) dismissed the charge that early development economists did not care for distribution. He pointed out, 'We were all in favour of land reforms, for reasons of equity and output' (p. 130). The fact is that he and other founders of the discipline of development economics regarded feudalism as incompatible with economic and human development on both moral and economic grounds.[3] Indeed, they were careful not to give the impression of being overly positivistic in their approach to development problems. Thus, for instance, one of Lewis's basic recommendations for promoting self-sustaining growth—namely, 'the central problem of the theory of economic growth is to understand the process by which a community is converted from being a 5 per cent saver to a 12 per cent saver' was made conditional on 'all the changes in attitudes, in institutions, and in techniques which accompany this conversion' [Lewis (1955), p. 226]. In other words, the growth of per capita income, which the higher-than-trend saving would finance, was seen to be the outcome of a complex process involving changes in economic, social and institutional variables, which also involved changes in cultural mores and moral values. Indeed, without such institutional, cultural and moral changes, the development process was not expected to yield the desired social results. Consequently, he and others argued that high rates of economic growth would not be sustained if not accompanied by thorough-going systemic change. Even more significant in the context of today's concern for human development, Lewis stressed the need for providing a whole range of social services for alleviating economic distress on a priority basis at all stages of economic development. As briefly noted in Chapter 3, he did not subscribe to the view prevalent in colonial times that an adequate provisioning of these services could be postponed for an advanced stage of economic development: 'These things cost more, but they also pay off in extra productivity, as well as in human happiness.' [Lewis (1955), pp. 193–194]. Other leading development economists were no less concerned about distributive matters. Singer (1984), reflecting on his 1950 paper, noted that he had 'concentrated on the issue of distributive justice or fairness or desirability in sharing out the gains from trade' (p. 284). Tinbergen (1985), the most egalitarian development economist of all, advocated an optimum regime that would require making large transfers of resources from the rich to the poor as basic to the establishment of a just society. He rejected the liberalist definition of equity as equality of each person's income to the contribution she/he makes to total output; and also that extra income (or rather rent) that a person gets can be attributed to her/his merits. Rather he saw these differences as flowing from such factors as inherited endowments, socio-economic status of one's parents etc. for which a person is not 'responsible'. He, therefore, advocated that all existing scarcities should be eliminated by a 'sufficient expansion of education and training', (p. 102). Hirschman (1985; 1998) dwelt at length on the moral aspects of economic development. In response to Arrow's warning (1972) against an excessive use of the scarce resources of altruism, he pointed out that altruism was a scarce resource that would increase, rather than decrease, with more frequent use, partly because doing well to others would be its own reward. Streeten (1989) has been explicit on the quintessential morality of the development process. He emphasized the central importance of adhering to a set of moral principles in order to devise a fairer basis of international cooperation. The fact is that the makers of the Traditional Development Paradigm knew their development history and social philosophy very well; and they definitely did not wish to repeat the excesses of the Industrial Revolution that were adversely commented upon at length by the leading philosophers of the time.

6.1. (ii). Was the Traditional Development Paradigm Utilitarian?

The next question to answer is, whether the Traditional Development Paradigm was explicitly or implicitly utilitarian? The answer is, of course, in the negative; because Utilitarianism does not offer any meaningful agenda for egalitarian reform. In sharp contrast, the Traditional Development Paradigm has left a rich egalitarian heritage.[4] To determine the Traditional Development Paradigm's position with respect to Utilitarianism we need to ask whether: (a) it was consequential in temperament (it insisted on evaluating a change in terms of the consequences that it has on the welfare of the people); (b) it sought to measure human well-being exclusively in terms of the utility that it purportedly generated, neglecting any other indicator of social welfare like income; (c) it required sum-ranking of individual utilities to arrive at total utility, so that the distribution of total utility among members of the society would not matter?[5] Now, there is no doubt that the Traditional Development Paradigm was quintessentially consequential in nature, in that it would evaluate the worth of a development policy by the consequences it is likely to have for the economic well-being of the people. But, in direct violation of the Utilitarian yardstick to measure happiness, it did so in non-Utilitarian terms—that is, in terms of the effect of development policy on growth of per capita income, employment, income (and wealth) equity, gender equity, and poverty alleviation. Also, violating sum ranking, it would not care about the increase in (non-measurable) total utility, but about the growth of (quantifiable) output and its equitable distribution and poverty reduction.

It may be noted that there is no reference to Utilitarianism or pleasure/pain calculus or any other such concept that can be termed as Utilitarian in Lewis's 1955 book.[6] Nor is there any such reference to it in the works of other development economists of the time. The only exception is Tinbergen, but his definition of utility is radically different from the one just noted above and it generally does not suffer from the informational deficiency of the Benthamite rendition of utilitarianism or its present-day variants. Unlike many mainstream economists, he believed in the measurability and the comparability of different person's welfare.[7] But, even more significantly, he expressed social welfare in terms of national expenditure, which could be measured sufficiently accurately, rather than in terms of the mental-state comparisons of utilities.[8] Such a procedure enabled him to define an equitable distribution as one that would equalize welfare among all individuals, with the important proviso that with sufficient expansion of education and training, all existing unearned rents (i.e., those attributable to personality traits) were eliminated. Furthermore, departing from the utilitarian practice, he reformulated the concept of welfare or utility as 'capability', and proceeded to measure its 'intensity or the degree of that capability required doing the job properly' [Tinbergen (1985), p. 102].[9]

6.2. Growth and Income Inequality

In this section we take a closer look at the routine charge against the Traditional Development Paradigm that it was generally flint-hearted, insensitive to the distributional consequences of economic growth. But, as has been argued above, this impression is not correct. The Kuznets hypothesis about the distribution of income being inverted U-shaped, which indicated a historical tendency in both, the developed and the developing countries, cannot by any stretch of imagination be cited as a positive recommendation for increasing inequalities of income in the service of growth; nor can it be seen as a proof of the paradigm's sang-froid in dealing with the distributional issues as opposed to its enthusiastic espousal of the growth-related 'causes'. Similarly, the centrality that the Traditional Development Paradigm accorded to increasing the share of profits in GDP as a precondition for accelerating the growth of per capita income has also been cited as evidence of its positivism; but this assertion is also off-the-mark. The reason is that this recommendation was conditional on the assumption that only private savings were available for financing investment. The question to ponder, therefore, remains: Did the Traditional Development Paradigm's acceptance of the Kuznets hypothesis and its broad support to a rising share of profit in national income imply its anti-egalitarian bias and a positive policy recommendation that an inequality-increasing policy should be adopted to promote growth in the developing countries? However, before answering these important questions, it may be of some interest to understand the true message of both these hypotheses.

6.2. (i). The Kuznets Inverted-U Hypothesis

Kuznets (1955) spelled out in considerable detail (without proving it) the famous inverted U-hypothesis relationship.[10] He regarded it 'as central to much of economic analysis and thinking.' The hypothesis envisaged that the economies that are developed now, and some of the present-day developing countries like India, Sri Lanka, Prussia and Puerto Rico, had been marked by greater equality and a low average income at the beginning of the development process; but that inequalities first rose, then reached a plateau (inequality remaining stay-put in the middle range of the development spectrum) before starting to decline. This is the Kuznets Process, which conceptualized inter-sector movement of labour and capital from a low-inequality, low-income rural sector to a relatively higher income urban sector, where the inequality of income is assumed to be greater [Anand, Sen and Kanbur (1985); Anand and Sen (1993)]. Then, almost by definition, the average inequality of income would rise. This tendency was expected to continue for some time as a developing country reached a higher stage of economic development. It also implied that higher growth will 'spread' (a la Myrdal's 'spread' effects) out of the 'growth poles'.[11] In this scenario, the long-run relationship between growth and poverty would, indeed, turn out to be negative: that the higher the growth rate the lower the incidence of poverty would become through some kind of a trickle-down effect. Furthermore, it expected poverty to decline if it was higher initially in the rural sector. Needless to point out, given a lower inequality of income and wealth, high growth would tend to reduce poverty faster than slow growth would. Indeed, as some modern studies on poverty (which are discussed in Part VI of this book) show, the initial increase in inequality that the Kuznets Process envisaged may not come about; and that poverty would, therefore, decline even if inequality of income does increase initially [Fields (1989); Squire (1993)].[12] The latter outcome would materialize if the agricultural sector got enriched as growth takes place, which was the most likely sequence of events that the Traditional Development Paradigm envisaged.[13]

There are two important points about the Kuznets Process that are generally overlooked. Firstly, as Robinson (1976) pointed out, the increase in average inequality flowed from shifting the locus of economic activity from the rural to the urban sector.[14] There is nothing non-egalitarian about it. Secondly, it would not be legitimate to interpret Kuznets' conjecture as necessarily ruling out the necessity for putting in place a redistributive mechanism; nor would it be correct to suggest that income inequality might even be seen as the necessary price to be paid for the sake of growth, which would, in time, make the distribution of income more egalitarian. The specification of a historical mechanism is not the same thing as a positive recommendation to increase inequality of income and wealth.

6.2. (ii). The Lewis Hypothesis

Lewis (1954; 1955) made increasing share of profits in total factor income as the centrepiece in his growth model. He seemed to be not bothered by the possibility of the distribution of income getting skewed with the passage of time: 'We are not interested in the people in general, but only say in the 10 per cent of them with the largest income....' [(Lewis (1954), p. 416]. The reason for the apparent lack of concern for distributive matters was, however, of a technical nature. Firstly, it is obvious that with the migration of the last man/woman from the rural area to the urban area, the inequality of income would increase; but then it would be eventually eliminated as wages rose (presumably at a rate higher than the rental on capital) at a higher average level of income [Fei and Ranis (1961); (1963) (1964)]. There can be a reasonable presumption that the inequalities that emerged from this source would either be self-correcting or not harmful for the society. Secondly, it is true that some contributors to Traditional Development Paradigm accepted the classical saving function as a reasonable description of the process of saving generation. It hypothesized that all saving was done by the capitalists, while the wage earners save nothing of their incremental income or save very negligible amounts [Kaldor (1955); Robinson (1956)]. This function yields the proposition that a rising inequality in the functional distribution of income (a rising profit income) has a positive role in the development process.[15] Thus a change in the distribution of functional income in favour of labour may hurt saving and accumulation and growth. It may, therefore, be unhelpful to enforce egalitarianism at too early a stage of economic development.[16] However, this assumption, though influential for some time, was not the dominant trend of the traditional thought on distributional problems. Thirdly, Lewis's concern about the share of profits rising did not imply a transfer of resources from the rich to the poor but from the rent-seekers to the productive investors.[17]

6.3. Was Inequality Considered Good for Growth?

There is a widespread impression that Kuznets and Lewis supported a more unequal distribution of income and wealth as good for growth and did not believe in a proactive egalitarian policy (because it would be corrected in good time and/or because it will hurt growth by reducing potential saving).[18] But this is not the position that the Traditional Development Paradigm took on the question. In fact, there are strong grounds for suggesting that it supported a more equal distribution of income and wealth as desirable in itself as well as good for growth. Firstly, as noted above, the Kuznets thesis simply stated a historical tendency; there is nothing to suggest that he would have supported a deliberate policy of skewing the distribution of income in favour of the rich because they save more. Secondly, Lewis (1955) did not regard inequality of income and wealth *per se* as helpful to economic growth and development: 'It is only the inequality that goes with profits that favours capital accumulation and not the inequality that goes with rents' (pp. 419–420). In other words, what he proposed was raising the profit income relative to an increase in rents, which he correctly considered to be totally unproductive. Thirdly, Lewis's favourable disposition towards profit income as opposed to labour income as a source of saving and investment was limited to private saving only. It did not say anything about *total* saving. What he said was that 'in the absence of government intervention, the rate of domestic saving is determined principally by the ratio of profits to income' [italics added]. But he did not suggest that an over-reliance on private saving was the best way to generate the resources needed for high growth rate of per capita income: 'But there is no very obvious reason why the rate [of profit] so determined should be regarded as the most desirable rate.' (p. 381). Indeed, he did not consider creating inequality as essential to economic growth: '...significant economic growth could be achieved even if there were no [income or wealth] differentials at all' (p. 429). Fourthly, Lewis's support to inequality in factor incomes did not amount to an advocacy of increasing the share of the rich in total GDP: 'A relative increase in profits is not necessarily the same thing as an increase in inequality of income distribution, since this increase may be associated with a corresponding decline in the relative importance of income from rent' [Lewis (1955), p. 226]. In general, he associated growth with greater humanitarianism (p. 227).There is no evidence that any of the founders of the Traditional Development Paradigm differed from Lewis on these matters. If anything, such distinguished exponents of the discipline as Tinbergen, Myrdal, Streeten and Hirschman only deepened the egalitarian colour of traditional thought.

6.3. (i). The Trickle-Down Effect and the Traditional Development Paradigm

It has sometimes been suggested that the Traditional Development Paradigm believed in the sufficiency of growth, as opposed to just its necessity in which everyone believed, for reducing inequities of human condition and lowering poverty. It is true that it envisaged a more egalitarian distribution of income to flow from the dynamics of industrialization from three principal channels. Firstly, industrialization would lower agricultural employment and labour/ land ratio, raise agricultural productivity and the real wages of agriculture labour, and reduce rural poverty.[19] Secondly, an increase in agricultural productivity would, other things being equal, increase the size of the domestic market for industrial goods and accelerate industrialization. Thirdly, the Lewis model (and the Traditional Development Paradigm) clearly understood that industrialization could not proceed very far with too much or too little inequity, because the former would inhibit the emergence of a strong middle class and the latter might have undefined effect on incentive to save and invest, assuming that the government saving was not a significant part of total saving.[20] However, an analysis of the channels through which trickle-down effect works does not necessarily amount to an assertion that they would be large enough to render redistribution policy redundant. Rather, such an analysis should be helpful in focusing redistributive policy on broadening them to release the growth-promoting forces.

6.4. Did the Traditional Development Paradigm Oppose an Egalitarian Redistribution of Income and Wealth?

As the preceding analysis suggests, the routine claim trotted out about the paradigm's lack of concern for egalitarianism is totally unwarranted. The source of error has been to think that the Traditional Development Paradigm envisaged only profit income to finance growth. But, as noted above, it also envisaged a strong developmental role of the government. To that end, the government was supposed to reduce unproductive inequalities of income and wealth, which would then improve growth and equity.[21] Lewis favoured the redistribution of wealth (from landed gentry) through land reforms and also of rental income, both of which were seen as inimical to growth.[22] He and other development economists at the time argued strongly for land reforms because that would help increase agricultural productivity, which would in turn widen the domestic market for industrialization. Land reforms were also expected to promote an egalitarian distribution of income that would increase the demand for manufacturing. In addition, it would lead to growth and social-justice-friendly institutional change. This is the fundamental point: The Traditional Development Paradigm considered an egalitarian distribution of income and wealth as an integral part of the process in which a vibrant middle class would emerge as the basic factor in the expansion of the domestic market, which would then accelerate the process of Structural Transformation. It explicitly stated that the emergence of a strong middle class would tend to create a demand for mass-produced necessities of life rather than for luxuries and favour broad-based industrialization that would produce goods of mass consumption rather than cater to the wasteful requirements of the rich: 'countries which have a well developed middle class may offer a better market for mass produced goods than countries of equal wealth which have only rich and poor' [Lewis (1955), p. 73]. Myrdal (1957; 1968) and Tinbergen (1958) were perhaps the most outspoken development economists at the time who emphasized the necessity of making redistribution of income and wealth for a socially stable and vibrant economy. Tinbergen recognized that, 'one of the basic ingredients for a more efficient and less equitable development was a better understanding of the main inter-relations and the orders of magnitude of the phenomenon at stake—and hence of the limits to what a nation with modest endowments could achieve' [Tinbergen (1985), p. 318]. His was a pioneering effort to combine the concerns of growth, equity, efficiency, and feasibility of the development effort required to promote and consolidate economic and political emancipation of the developing societies. Myrdal (1984) regarded greater equality as a condition for more growth' (p. 153). He emphasized that, 'radical institutional reforms' (including land reforms) would be needed to raise the consumption levels of the poor. Indeed, he regarded that equalization of income would have even greater effect on the quality of life and the productivity of the people in the developing countries than in the developed countries, by raising the consumption levels of the people, which he considered to be 'a necessary condition for a more rapid and stable growth' (p. 154).

6.5. SOME CROSS-COUNTRY EVIDENCE ABOUT THE RELATIONSHIP BETWEEN GROWTH, DISTRIBUTIVE EQUITY AND POVERTY REDUCTION

It will be interesting at this stage to explore briefly the actual country experiences about the vital relationship between growth, distributive justice and poverty reduction, both in the East Asian miracle growers as well as in the non-miracle (but still fast enough) growers. Can we say something definite in support of or against the Traditional Paradigm's position on the issue? Figure 6.1 based on the pooled data for the Asia and Pacific Region for 1965 to 2000 tells an interesting, though an ambiguous story.

6.5. (i). Growth and Inequality

Firstly, high-growth has been associated with low inequity in China, Korea and Vietnam. Secondly, low inequity has also gone with low growth in India, Pakistan, Nepal and Indonesia. Thirdly, low growth and high inequity relationship has held in Bangladesh, Philippines, Sri Lanka, and Papua New Guinea. Fourthly, high growth has been associated with high inequity in Malaysia, Thailand, and Singapore. Three points need to be noted about these relationships: (a) High growth has been associated with high as well as low inequity, so that one cannot infer an unambiguous relationship between these variables. (b) Contrary to the general impression, East Asian countries (excluding China) do not present a seamless relationship between high growth and high equity. It holds only in Korea; but in Singapore and Malaysia the opposite relationship holds. (c) Sri Lanka has been unequal notwithstanding its excellent human development record. This aspect will be elaborated upon in Part V of this book. The only conclusion that follows from Figure 6.1 is that one must be careful about drawing definitive conclusions from the cross-country data on these variables. This requires a deeper analysis to decide the issue one way or the other. In particular, one must look at the behaviour of the other variables that also have an effect on growth and distribution. Detailed regression analysis, based on pooled time-series and cross-country data, will be presented in Part VI of this book.

Figure 6.1: Economic Growth—Distribution Linkage in Asia and Pacific Region (1965–2000)

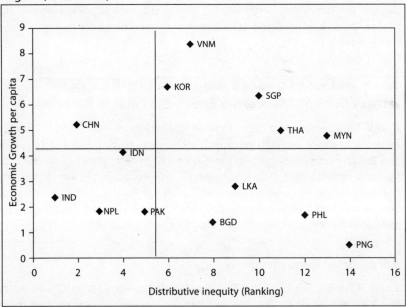

Note: Economic growth is measured as growth rate of GDP per capita. For distribution, Gini coefficient is ranked in ascending order. Higher rank means higher inequality. Average growth rate of GDP per capita for the sample countries is 4.02 per cent for the period 1965–2000. Average for distribution is 37.

◆ Following countries are included in the sample: Bangladesh (BGD), China (CHN), Fiji (FIJ), Hong Kong (HKG), India (IND), Nepal (NPL), Indonesia (IDN), Japan (JPN), Papua New Guinea (PNG), Korea (KOR), Malaysia (MYN), Pakistan (PAK), Philippines (PHL), Sri Lanka (LKA), Singapore (SGP), Taiwan (TWN), Thailand (THA), and Vietnam (VNM).

6.5. (ii). Growth and Poverty

The issue of the growth-poverty linkage is more complicated than is sometimes suggested in the literature. Whether growth is good for poverty reduction or not cannot be decided by looking at simple correlation of these variables. Figure 6.2, based on the same data set as other figures presented in this book, clarifies the following important features of growth in the region: (a) In China, Korea and Malaysia high growth has been associated with low poverty. This confirms the point of view that lower inequality implies a tighter negative relationship between growth and poverty. (b) A very striking result is that there is no country where poverty reduction has been associated with low growth: the lower-left hand box is empty. (c) There are 6 countries (India, Pakistan, Sri Lanka, Bangladesh, the Philippines, Nepal and Indonesia) where low growth has gone with high poverty, as one would expect. (d) There are only two countries where high growth and high poverty have gone together (Thailand and Vietnam), which seems to be an unexpected result.

Thus, one can fairly confidently make only two claims: (a) poverty reduction does not, if ever, go with low growth; (b) which supports the same point, low growth is mostly associated with higher-than-average poverty. Beyond these claims, the high growth and low poverty linkage is tenuous and requires more explanation. Once again, a more detailed analysis is required to come to a more definitive conclusion on the matter. This is done in Part VI of this book

Figure 6.2: Economic Growth—Poverty Linkage in Asia and Pacific Region (1965–2000)

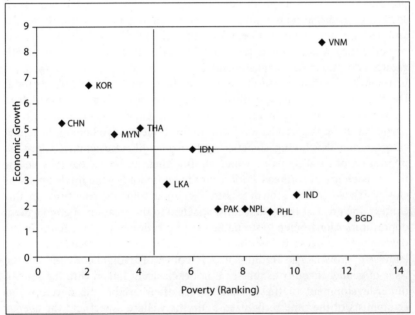

Note: Economic growth is defined as growth rate of GDP per capita. Poverty is ranked in ascending order. Higher rank means higher poverty. Average growth rate of GDP per capita for the sample countries is 4.02 per cent for the period 1965–2000. Average for poverty is 32.4.

◆ Following countries are included in the sample: Bangladesh (BGD), China (CHN), Fiji (FIJ), India (IND), Nepal (NPL), Indonesia (IDN), Korea (KOR), Malaysia (MYN), Pakistan (PAK), Philippines (PHL), Sri Lanka (LKA), Thailand (THA), and Vietnam (VNM).

6.6. GENDER INEQUALITY

What was the Traditional Development Paradigm's position on gender inequity? The question is important because even some of the great philosophers and humanists have been deafeningly silent on this foundational issue—some of them have regarded it as only 'natural'. The problem is complex because women, as a rule, do not get their fair share in the fruits of economic progress (the well-being aspect), which is bad enough; even worse, the society does not allow them the voice, the authority and the discretion to do something about their deprivation (the agency aspect), which denotes an even worse social condition. In both forms, gender inequity has survived unprecedented intellectual and technological advancement, economic prosperity and social progress in the developed countries as well. But the problem is more severe in the developing countries where the process of societal transformation has not progressed far enough to overcome the feudal and patriarchal systems that deny women their rightful place in the society; nor have they attained the required intellectual sophistication that goes with greater educational accomplishments and economic prosperity. However, it is remarkable that contrary to widely held opinion, the Traditional Development Paradigm explicitly focused on the harmful effects of feudalism on the growth process in general and on the issue of gender inequity in particular. It emphasized land reforms to break the stranglehold of the feudal class on the developing societies and also to liberate women from the oppression of rural societies, which confine them to household jobs. It saw the transference of women's work from the household to the market place as closely related to the growth possibilities of developing countries. In this context, the greatest importance was attached to the creation of employment opportunities for women to strengthen their position as positive actors in the development process rather than being just the passive recipients of the largesse of growth. The Traditional Development Paradigm correctly saw the issue of gender inequity as mostly, if not exclusively, linked with the state of underdevelopment of these societies. To their credit, the development economists of the time recognized both, the welfare aspect and the agency aspect of gender inequity and that these are closely related to each other.[23] Lewis (1955) explicitly noted while, 'It is open for men to debate whether economic progress is good for men or not, but for women to debate the desirability of economic growth is to debate whether women should have the chance to cease to be beasts of burden, and to join the human race'. It is important to note here that Lewis linked economic growth to the generation of employment for women in particular so that they could be emancipated from the drudgery of unpaid household work that reduced them to the unenviable status of the 'beasts of burden'. Going beyond the economic aspects, gaining the freedom to enter the labour market at their own discretion is also crucial to women gaining 'at last the chance to become a full human being, exercising her mind and talents in the same way as men' (p. 422). Indeed, Lewis (1955) also highlighted the important reverse link going from giving women the freedom to work to economic growth: 'To create more jobs for women is the surest way to raise their status, to reduce their drudgery, and to raise national output' (p. 117). The other contributors to the Traditional Development Paradigm (especially Jan Tinbergen and Streeten) held similar opinion on the issue of gender inequity. However, not unexpectedly, Lewis and others could not fully anticipate in that foundational period of development history the essential separateness of gender inequity from economic growth: that economic growth is probably a necessary condition, but it is definitely not a sufficient condition for achieving gender equity. To some extent this failure may be understandable. Thanks to the paradigm's optimism that the rising tide of per capita income could wash ashore anything socially untoward (including gender inequity), the problem did not receive as much attention as it deserved. But, as the latter events would show, their optimism in this respect was not all that well placed; many an untoward social evil, gender inequity most of all, was not washed ashore even as the waves of prosperity rose higher and higher with greater frequency and intensity. The unpalatable fact is that economic growth—indeed, even the very high rates of growth in East Asia—has not solved the problem of gender inequity, especially the agency aspect of it. The same has been the case with China where an incorrigible son preference has led to an unsustainable 111 males to 100 female's ratio, notwithstanding its stellar economic growth record.[24] A comprehensive study of gender inequity in Taiwan provides a disturbing example of how even essentially equitable growth does not translate into greater equity for women. A 1978–80 survey showed that 25 per cent of sons, but only 4 per cent of daughters had been apprenticed. Even worse, in the poorest 80 per cent of families, as the number of sisters rose from 0 to 4, the mean schooling per-brother rose from 6.8 to 11.4 per cent. The latter piece of evidence demonstrates that daughters have been sacrificing their prospects of an independent escape from poverty to finance their brothers' bid to escape from poverty through greater and higher education [Greenhalgh (1985); UN (2005)]. Perhaps, Lewis and other founders of the paradigm would probably have replied to such criticism that the plight of women would have been worse if these and other developing countries had not developed as fast as they in fact did; and conversely that they could have grown even faster had they succeeded in putting away their historical prejudices against women. The fact is that if developing countries have not succeeded in resolving the problem, the blame lies more on a much slower change in the institutions and ideas of men than on the inability of high growth of per capita income to solve the problem.

6.7. Concluding Remarks

Ploughing a lonely furrow in the hard under-developed territory, the Traditional Development Paradigm made development history—a feat that has not been repeated since then. The Traditional Development Paradigm's efforts were crowned with splendid success. As Table 2.1 (in Chapter 2) shows the growth rates of per capita income and employment creation were significantly higher than the historical rates of growth, and the incidence of poverty declined significantly throughout the developing world. In cases of miraculous growth, the quality of life of the people underwent a radical transformation within a single generation—an unprecedented event in the annals of development history. The standards of health and literacy improved, life expectancy at birth increased, and death rates generally declined faster than at any time in the past in developing countries. Above all, the wave of expectations of a better future never surged so high.

It is important to note that the paradigm's success did not come about accidentally or by the courtesy of exogenous factors, but for reasons that the Traditional Development Paradigm had explicitly stated. The pace of Structural Transformation increased dramatically, and so did the saving and investment rates. The urban-based cultural values came to gradually replace the preceding rural values in countries that faithfully tread the trail that Traditional Development Paradigm lighted so brightly. The greatest merit of the development policies that the Traditional Development Paradigm recommended was their gradualist approach to economic development, which gave ample time to the traditional institutions and cultural mores to adjust to the realities of societal transformation. Though not given to the revolutionary rhetoric of class conflict (which the in-fashion Marxian philosophy propagated and which some leading intellectuals in the early days of independence from colonial rule subscribed to show off their progressive credentials), Traditional Development Paradigm, following John Maynard Keynes, achieved a resplendent development outcome by the less colourful, yet more practical means of adapting capitalism to the needs of economic and human development. Seldom, if ever, the unintended outcomes of development policies have coincided so perfectly with the intentions of the policy makers.

Notes

1. The quote in the text when read with the rest of the book makes clear that Lewis is concerned with growth and distribution.
2. Lewis (1955) explicitly stated: 'it is very hard to correlate wealth and happiness—or that individuals grow happier as they grow richer' (p. 421).
3. This aversion to feudalism was in line with the classical economist's position on the subject (including, Adam Smith, David Ricardo and Karl Marx), who all saw its end as one of the momentous contributions of capitalism to human progress.
4. The famous utilitarian formula—'seek the greatest good of the greatest number'—offers no more than a very hazy idea about its impact on the well being of the people. For, if this instruction is taken to mean that for any given population maximize social welfare (measured by the sum-total of total utilities) and then choose a population size that maximizes this number, then such a policy would, at best, give no more than necessary to keep the largest number of population so chosen at the starvation level [Roemer (1996)].
5. The analysis in the text uses Sen's (1987; 1999b) factoring of Utilitarianism into three basic elements—namely, consequentialism, welfarism and sum-ranking
6. Nor did the Traditional Development Paradigm refer to the Pareto-optimality principle. It is interesting that Lewis referred to Pareto only twice in his 1955 book and that too with regard to the rather obscure Pareto Law, which is about the number of towns of each size following a certain statistical distribution.
7. Like Harsanyi (1982), he thought that man/woman had 'the capability to put oneself in others shoes, which implies a projection of different persons' welfare on a common yardstick' [Tinbergen (1985), p. 113].
8. Tinbergen (1985) states: 'This author believes in the measurability of welfare or utility and starts such measurements from national expenditure—' (p. 120).
9. He identified such parameters as leadership, intelligence, persistence, creativity, health and family size as the most important components of 'productive capability'. Incidentally, his definition of capability is somewhat different from that of Sen (1999b). Interesting, both the Noble Laureates were simply unaware of each other's contribution.
10. Initially, the hypothesis sparked off a flurry of cross-country studies. Some found it to be the accident of history. Thus, Adelman and Morris (1973) and Adelman and Robinson (1989) confirmed the Kuznets conjecture for the developing countries, though the average Gini Coefficient for the developing countries was higher than the one Kuznets estimated. Others thought it to be the outcome of economic policies, and found it as J-shaped [Papanek and Kyn (1986)]. However, of late, the earlier enthusiasm about the hypothesis seemed to have worn off, and much of the air of immutability around it has disappeared. The historical antecedents of the Kuznets Curve have been questioned, which, it is asserted, does not seem to correctly characterize the British industrialization experience in that, 'any changes in the overall income inequality were probably small' [Craft (2001), p. 313].
11. The spread effects worked in Europe and the United States (regarded as 'pioneers' of development) as follows: an increase in the demand for labour in the fast-expanding sectors of the economy eventually raised employment and real wages first around the growth poles and then throughout the economy, and thereby altered the functional distribution in favour of labour [Leontief (1983)].
12. On the other hand, poverty might increase with the rural-to-urban migration if it took place in response to the expected income differentials—which is the Harris-Todaro hypothesis (1970)—because in that case many workers would remain unemployed and their income may decline below their pre-migration income [Anand and Kanbur (1985)].
13. Fields (1980) generalized the Lewis model to n-sectors and showed that the increase in aggregate income in the structural transformation process could be decomposed into sector-enlargement and sector-enrichment effects plus an interactive term. In this model,

inequality remains tolerable and poverty stays the same in case of the industrial sector enrichment (as average income rises). But the enlargement of the manufacturing sector leads to the U-type phenomenon. However, if it is the traditional sector that gets enriched, then inequality and poverty can both decline. However, as pointed out above, this reasoning does not take into account the inter-sector linkages between an increase in agricultural productivity and the industrialization process. Once this is done, a reduction in poverty would not depend exclusively on the enrichment of the rural sector.

14. However, S. Robinson (1976) demonstrated that the existence of the Kuznets Process did not depend either on whether the high-productivity sector had higher income or higher inequality; it rather depended on only on the inter-sector differences in inequality.

15. Other useful references are Ranis (1988); (1989). It may be noted that the classical saving function was used in proofs of the steady-state properties of the neo-classical models of growth. A special case of the classical saving function is the extreme classical saving function, whereby the propensity to save out of profit income is equal to unity, in which case overall saving ratio is simply a function of the proportion of profit to income [Hahn and Mathews (1965), pp. 15–16]. However, there is nothing to suggest that the Traditional Development Paradigm accepted this type of saving function as a basis for making policy recommendation.

16. A special case of the Robinson (1956) and Kaldor (1955) conjecture is that the propensity to save of the wage earners is zero while that of profit earners is positive and constant. In this special case, therefore, the overall propensity to save becomes both equal to the profit-earners times the ratio of profit to income. This is the classical saving function, also known as Kaldorian or the Robinsonian or the Cambridge saving function.

17. Lewis (1955) stated explicitly that the reason why a country cannot save 12 per cent of its national income was not because they were poor but 'because 40 per cent or so of the national income is squandered by the top 10 per cent of the income receivers, living luxuriously on rents. In such countries productive investment is so small because the surplus is used to maintain hordes of retainers, and to build pyramids, temples and other durable consumer goods, instead of to create productive capital' (p. 236).

18. Thus, for instance, Stiglitz (2003) states: 'One Nobel Prize winner, Arthur Lewis, argued that inequality was good for growth, since the rich save more than the poor, and key to growth was capital accumulation. Another Nobel prize winner, Simon Kuznets, argued that while in the initial stages of development inequality increased, later on the trend reversed' (p. 79). He thinks that the East Asian experience disproved both Kuznets and Lewis.

19. It is important to remember that the Traditional Development Paradigm regarded agriculture and rural sectors as linked together both through the product market and the factor markets. Indeed, the growth in one sector was expected to be transmitted to other sectors mainly through these markets. See also Johnston and Mellor (1961); Mellor and Johnston (2003) for a further elaboration of this theme.

20. These aspects of Lewis's and Rosenstein-Rodan's models have been worked out in detail in Murphy, Shleifer and Vishny (1989b).

21. Lewis (1955) states this point at another place even more explicitly: 'Given that growth is not incompatible with a high level of savings, the next question is how far large profits are necessary in order to have large savings. It is true that the non-capitalist classes tend to save very little, but it is not necessary for saving to depend entirely on individual effort. It is feasible for the government also to act as saver, imposing taxes upon the public, which are used either for capital formation in public utilities, or else for lending to private producers. However, if government cannot or will not be a productive saver, it is certainly true that a developing country needs large profits if it has to have an adequate level of savings' (pp. 100–101). It is clear here that large profits are not necessary for generating large saving if the government does its job as a saver properly. He put the same point clearly in Lewis (1966) where he saw profits income as not exclusively being generated by the private sector;

it could be 'private and public, corporate or unincorporated' (p. 93). Profits would be generated only by the capitalistic sector if the government had no development role.

22. Thus, 'as far as the land is concerned, its productive capacity would not be reduced if the rent were kept by the farmers (i.e., if the landlords were liquidated and the rent passed into the freehold ownership of the farmers)...' [(Lewis), p. 123)].

23. The distinction between the agency aspect and the welfare aspect of gender equity is due to Sen (1999b).

24. A strict enforcement of the one-child rule has been responsible for the practice of selling baby girls in the Chinese Guangsi Province [Rosenthal (2003)]. She reports that a typical answer to the question as to what happens to a new-born baby girl goes like this: end the pregnancy, or if you still have her then find another family for her, or simply put her up on sale. The same problem has been observed in India where the proportion of female to male has declined over time.

Part III

The Liberalist Paradigm

7

The Liberalist Paradigm I:
Its Immaculate Birth and
Ready Acceptance

The analysis presented in the preceding chapters should lead one to expect that, with more information about the development process, there would come about a broad agreement about the essential soundness of Traditional Development Paradigm; and the analytical and policy focus would be on amending and finessing it, so that it could meet more effectively the new economic challenges that developing countries faced. For instance, amendments could be made to strengthen the links from growth to distributive equity to poverty reduction, and accommodate more adequately the concerns of macroeconomic stability. But there did not seem to be any need for outright rejecting a successful paradigm. Yet, beginning in 1980, the most outré event did happen. With an unsettling suddenness liberalist thinking overtook traditional thought and an established set of doctrine metamorphosed into a disreputable anachronism. The 'reasons', or rather, the charges against the traditional development policy, though wrong, were long. These were read out to the developing world with a sardonic sense of intellectual superiority. The Liberalist Paradigm was, therefore, divined to save the developing world from its sins and follies.[1] The new paradigm distilled its wisdom—or 'frenzy', as Keynes would have put it—from the neo-classical idealization of real-world economies. It preached the new economic gospel with proselytizing zeal and confidently predicted that a first-best regime of freer trade, open economy, minimal government and overwhelming export orientation must deliver first-best development results. The developing countries were, therefore, strongly advised to undertake major 'reforms', mainly in the trade and public sectors, with a view to correcting a (relative) price structure that was badly 'distorted' by the traditional interventionist development policy.

7.1. The Fall of Traditional Development Paradigm

Five events have been principally responsible for the fall from grace of the Traditional Development Paradigm.

7.1. (i). The Unravelling of Keynesian Revolution

Firstly, there began a strong intellectual movement, in 1970s, to diminish significantly the influence of the Keynesian Revolution in the academic and policy-making circles, especially in the United States. To some extent this could be regarded as an essentially endogenous evolution of economic science, which led to a renewed focus on micro issues, i.e. the primary role of relative prices and markets in the efficient allocation of resources—as opposed to the macro issues (like growth, inflation, employment) that the Keynesian Revolution had made fashionable. It, thus, became a matter of policy concern that (relative) prices should be kept undistorted to let them do their socially beneficial signalling duties. The Keynesian Revolution, which had made state intervention in economic life intellectually acceptable (that it was consistent with individual freedom), fell out of favour on the grounds that it saddled the Western democracies with unsustainable fiscal deficits and inflation—and if not stopped in its tracks would pave the 'road to serfdom'.

It should have been clear to a discerning observer that if an essentially conservative Victorian, John Maynard Keynes, could be pilloried posthumously (partly because no one could take him on while he was alive.) for recommending temporary government intervention to reclaim a capitalistic economy felled by deep depression, much worse fate would await the Traditional Development Paradigm for having violated the classical and neo-classical orthodoxy of mainstream economics in more than one ways. The expected did happen: the Traditional Development Paradigm was committed to the hell-fire of studied neglect and ridicule and formally charged for sinning against the universality of economic science.

7.1. (ii). Ascendancy of the Individualistic Moral Rights Philosophy

Secondly, the resurgence of the pro-market (and anti-state interventionist) sentiment was bolstered by a moral-rights philosophy, which emphasized the absolute priority of individual moral rights (to own what individuals earn by virtue of their alleged 'superior merit') over all other social objectives, like growth, unemployment, poverty reduction etc. It confined the state, on moral grounds, to safeguarding individual liberty in general and her/his right to own private property in particular. It asserted that a system of unfettered markets offered the best guarantees for the preservation of individual liberty and must, therefore, be reinstated, regardless of the consequences of such market-friendly 'reforms' on human welfare. The demonstration of its moral inferiority must have tightened the hangman's noose around the Traditional Development Paradigm neck.

7.1. (iii). The Exogenous Shocks

Thirdly, a serious debt crisis, major macroeconomic imbalances and hyperinflation must have come as godsend to the liberalists who had been looking for the right opportunity to send the Traditional Development Paradigm into oblivion. The financial crisis of the 1970s, caused by such exogenous shocks as the sharp increase in the price of oil, a steep rise in international interest rates, and the decline in the terms of trade had a tsunami-like impact on the developing countries. It ended two decades of economic prosperity in Latin America and Africa. The enormity of the crisis can be seen by the fact that the steep rise in interest rate and the decline in the developing countries' terms of trade together accounted for as much as a reduction of 5 per cent of the GDP of the affected countries in 1981–85 over 1971–80; and of 4.9 per cent of the GDP over 1986–90 [Corbo and Fischer (1995), Table 44.1, p. 2654]. These shocks were large enough to upset any economy's applecart; and yet, by the strange twist of liberalist logic, it became commonplace to view the debt crisis as the consequence of import-substitution (inward-oriented) policies. The decks were, therefore, cleared for the wholesale 'reform' of prevailing development policies in Latin America, Africa, Asia [Rodrik (1996), p. 17].

7.1. (iv). The Disintegration of the Soviet Union and Eastern Europe

Fourthly, the economic disintegration of the centrally planned economies of Soviet Union and much of Eastern Europe, which was essentially a political development, was widely attributed to the failure of the central planning model and the non-existence of open-market institutions. Generally, the failure of the communist system was seen as a victory for capitalism and capitalistic values.[2] More broadly, the cataclysmic event was (incorrectly) interpreted as a proof of the essentially counter-productive nature of state intervention in economic affairs; and of the innate inefficiency of the 'extensive' growth strategies of the developing countries as well—those which supported economic growth mostly by input accumulation rather than by an increase in productivity [Ofer (1987)]. That argument was used to silence those who pointed out that the communist system, which, for full forty years (from 1950 to 1990) had helped growth, employment creation, poverty eradication and human development (a 100 per cent adult literacy was achieved), could not possibly be dismissed as inefficient. It was asserted that the government-induced distortions had already become significant enough to slow down and eventually disintegrate the entire communistic system. Did not the Solow-type neo-classical models of growth predict that such growth was fated to run into sharply diminishing returns to capital and a steeply rising capital/output ratio, both of which would cause the growth rate to slacken and eventually cease? In other words, while the growth rates under the communist rule were very high by comparison with those attained by the 'free world', these could not have been sustained much longer because of their innate inefficiency and reliance on input accumulation. This pattern of growth and the incidence of high degree of government intervention in the Soviet system have also been seen as a warning to the developing countries (including East Asian countries) that have suffered at the hands of hyperactive states [Easterly and Fischer (1995)].[3] Even though not strictly relevant for the developing countries, these events were taken to be a repudiation of even the much milder form of state of intervention that the developing countries practiced.

7.1. (v). The East Asian Miracle

Fifthly, somewhat oddly, the remarkable success of East Asia to achieve unprecedented rate of economic growth of per capita income and a sharp reduction of poverty was also seen as a refutation of the Traditional Development Paradigm. The argument was that, unlike the slow-growing non-East Asia, the East Asian countries followed first-best policies—namely, open markets, minimal governments, and all-out export-orientation. What else could it be, the question was asked?[4] Going a step further, the wide differential between the miracle East Asian growth rates and the relatively modest ones achieved by the non-East Asian countries was taken to be a decisive argument against the allegedly 'distorted' policies of the non-East Asian economies. One would more logically attribute their success to the greater supply of human capital and much higher degree of equity in the initial conditions, both of which allowed the East Asian governments to concentrate almost single-mindedly on physical capital formation and economic growth. Their previous experience with industrialization also mattered a great deal in jumping the historical barrier of growth and development after their liberation from colonial rule.[5] And yet, once the liberalist interpretation of the actual circumstances surrounding the miracle growth came to be accepted, it closed off all avenues to explore the real reasons for the observed differential between the stellar growth performance of East Asia and the non-stellar (but reasonably high) performance of non-East Asia. So it was that, the liberalist argued, the experience of the East Asian countries finally convinced the 'policy makers that there was a feasible and desirable alternative set of policies—to the import substitution, government-control model of development' [Krueger (1995a), p. 2514)].

7.2. THE NEO-CLASSICAL RESURGENCE

Yet another factor that helped the intellectual ascendancy of the Liberalist Paradigm has been the universal resurgence of the neo-classical consensus, which was widely accepted as 'mainstream economics' and its practitioners regarded as the illuminati of the economic profession. Making such somewhat exaggerated claims would not be a cardinal sin, if the Liberalist Paradigm had not illegitimately extended the writ of neo-classical economics to the development arena—illegitimately, because the neo-classical doctrine is not suitable for studying the elemental problems of growth, distribution and poverty.[6] Legitimate or not, the Liberalist Paradigm has, by and large, uncritically accepted neo-classical economics as its pith and core and advertised the latter as universally valid and perfectly suitable for practical applications in developing countries. The 'reason' given for this somewhat uncharacteristic behaviour of the economics profession has been that a universally valid body of doctrine would be no less applicable to the understanding and resolution of the development problems [Schultz (1981)]. This statement implies that neo-classical economics is applicable in the developed countries. A brief description of the reasons for the neo-classical resurgence worldwide—which sounded like the spread of a 'universal contagion' [(Sen (1983), p. 746)]—should, therefore, help understand better the new paradigm's resolute confidence in the beneficence of its reformist agenda. These reasons are diverse but share a common love for unfettered markets and an implacable aversion to state intervention in economic affairs.

7.2. (i). The Mainstream Academic Profession Turns Liberalist

It can be plausibly suggested that a dramatic increase in the representation of the economists of liberalist persuasion in the academic community (especially in the United States) greatly strengthened its longing to revert to free markets, run by rational utility and profit-maximizing economic agents, as a first-best solution to development problems.[7] The availability of research grants to work on liberalist 'causes' must have oiled the research efforts on aspects of the Liberalist Paradigm that would demonstrate the quintessential munificence of free domestic and international markets for developing countries. The result has been the expected one: a near-total capitulation of the economics profession to the World Bank's and IMF's lucrative research agenda—which, with the benefit of hindsight, looks like a Faustian bargain. True to its profit-maximizing instincts, the academic community's attention got shifted from the development issues regarded most important in the 1950s and 1960s, i.e. 'planning and development, balanced and unbalanced growth two-gap model, import substitution industrialization, growth theories and dualism'—to such neo-classical fads in 1980s as 'structural adjustment, debt, neo-classical growth theory, household behaviour, imperfect competition, trade and industrialization theories' [Stern and Ferreira (1993), Table 1, p. 104]. It, became academically correct to look at developing (and the developed) world through the prism of neo-classical economics of Arrow-Debreu vintage. The real leap of faith (though not of economic reasoning), however, was the further claim that the Arrow-Debreu Theorem was not just a theoretical construct subject to many caveats, but that it also could serve as a fairly faithful model of a real-life developing economy—indeed, as the closest approximation to it. It could, therefore, be used readily to cut the Gordian knot of economic and human development.[8] In this frame of thought any other way of looking at the development problem would be regarded a second-best option—indeed, dead wrong. In particular, government intervention that altered the structure of relative prices must, by definition, distort the micro and macro performances of the economy, impose an avoidable excess cost on the economy and lower potential social welfare. To put the same point formally, a Pareto-optimal situation, which the unfettered markets would approximate, depicted an un-improvable state of the economy that government intervention could only worsen. An important implication of this kind of reasoning was that an interventionist Traditional Development Paradigm could not have been right for the developing countries. Furthermore, whatever good it apparently did to the developing countries must have been illusory; and could, at any rate, be improved upon by a consistent application of the first-best remedies.[9] So for the academic profession and the international donors, the demise of the Traditional Development Paradigm, far from being an occasion for recalling its great services to the developing world, was in fact celebrated as a triumph of commonsense and scientific probity over economic dilettantism.

7.2. (ii). Monetarists and Rational Expectants

As part of the revival of the neo-classical vision of the economic processes, many an attempt was made quite early to show the total irrelevance of government intervention in economic affairs. The cult of monetarism, led by Friedman (1968), and the Rational Expectants under the leadership of Lucas (1972), and Lucas and Sargent (1978) conquered the hearts and minds of the academia completely and kept them in thrall for quite some time. (It is no accident that all the members of this tribe belong to the University of Chicago, that citadel of economic and political conservatism). The monetarists emphasized the importance of regulating the real money supply to control inflation—which was seen as a purely monetary phenomenon—and ensure full employment. Furthermore, since involuntary unemployment could not exist in such an economy, it could only be caused and undone by the voluntary actions of the wage earners. The Rational Expectants (also code-named as RATEX) introduced the idea of omniscient private economic agents who could anticipate each and every significant regulatory government action and adjust their expectations and behaviour accordingly. In such a scenario the government could not change, even in the short run, the course of the economy—for the simple reason that the smart private market agents would alter their behaviour instantaneously.[10] So government intervention, whose effectiveness depended on its unexpectedness, would be doomed for its sheer ineffectiveness.

7.2. (iii). The Neo-Classical Political Economy

With a view to proving the unsuitability of government intervention in economic affairs, especially in the foreign-trade sector, a new (and financially affluent) school of neo-Classical Political Economy has arisen. It has shown—to the satisfaction of the members of the so-called School—that government intervention would inexorably lead to rent-seeking activities [Krueger (1974)] and to directly unproductive profit-seeking activities [Bhagwati (1982)], both of which depicted a sub-optimal state of the economy, and entailed a significant waste of scarce economic resources. This economic waste, which was assumed to be quite substantial as a per cent of GDP, could only be rectified by minimizing government intervention. A leading member of this School, Krueger (1993), who has done more than anyone else to highlight the critical importance of market institutions for developing countries, succinctly put what was wrong with the Traditional Development Paradigm: 'There was strong emphasis on the primacy of market imperfections. Market imperfections were thought to be strong while it was assumed that governments could correctly identify and perform economic functions. Virtually no attention was given to the possibility that there might be government failures' (p. 49). Even in the absence of any well-established theory of government failure, she and others of this School have contradicted the traditional market-failure arguments by the counter-contention that the incidence of government failure would, as a rule, be greater and more costly. It was confidently asserted that the government typically did not have the information that the market had. Whence, it followed that government failure would always be much more costly and disruptive than market failure. It was also argued that while the private sector worked for profits and eventually for the benefit of the society (didn't Adam Smith say so?), the government normally pandered to the vested interests of the lobbies rather than working for public weal. Buchanan (1985), therefore, nostalgically pleaded for a return to the Smithian principle, 'of spontaneous order, or spontaneous coordination' (p. 20). In this Natural Order, 'there are narrow limits on the exploitation of man by man, markets tend to maximize freedom from government control' and individual liberty 'is best preserved in a regime that allows markets a major role' (p. 5). At best, a necessary though costly evil, the government could (perhaps, should) be tolerated to perform some very specific market-friendly chores like creating a conducive working environment for the utility and profit-maximizing individuals [World Bank (1991)].[11] The question as to whether there ever existed a place anywhere in the West or the East or in between where the governments had not been deeply involved with economic and human development (especially for the adequate provisioning of public goods) has been quietly sidestepped. Nor much thought seems to have been given to the obvious possibility that, in the absence of a functioning government, the institutional infrastructure required for a market economy might, indeed would, break down completely.

7.2. (iv). The 'Distortion(ist)' School

A whole research industry (promising large private profits) sprung up to focus whole time on proving the inefficient nature of industrialization in the developing countries—most of the blame for this undesirable outcome was heaped on the sub-optimality of their foreign-trade regimes. These studies showed that industrialization done at the distorted domestic prices greatly overstated its true contribution at the world prices to national income [Little, Scitovsky and Scott (1970)].[12] There has occurred an outpouring of the liberalist literature which has focused on industrialization as having been, 'inefficient, in-egalitarian, and source of deleterious impacts on other productive sectors' [Pack (1988), p. 334].The main reason given for the alleged inherent inefficiency of the government-sponsored, import-substituting industrialization in the developing countries was that in the (essentially, irrational) bid to converge with the developed countries the industrialization process was greatly 'compressed': industrial progress during the first twenty years (1950–70) averaged at 7 per cent plus, which far outstripped the growth record of the industrialized countries in their formative growth period (an average rate of 3.5 per cent).[13] In particular, the East Asian miracle economies experienced extra-ordinary economic and human development, faster and better than anything achieved by the Western 'pioneers'. But, it was argued, that such rapid-fire industrial progress allegedly exacted a stiff price in the form of making it highly capital-intensive—and for that reason unsustainable. It also relied a lot more on factor accumulation than on increasing productivity.[14] It has been argued that, an equally undesirable aspect of this 'industrial compression' was its excessive reliance on government intervention, which entailed more inefficiency.

The empirical studies, mostly contracted out by the international donors, have gone out of their way to demonstrate the sub-optimality of the foreign-trade regimes which the Traditional Development Paradigm had installed. They have invariably reached the (prearranged) conclusion that such trade practices did the most damage to the growth possibilities of the non-East Asian countries by stimulating the demand for domestically produced goods and imposing an implicit tax on the agricultural sector.[15] In other words, industrial growth was achieved at the allegedly large (static) resource cost because the high rate of growth attained in the manufacturing sector did not so much reflect improvement in total factor productivity as it did the uneconomical (and rising) capital/labour ratios and excessive rates of protection accorded to the manufacturing sector. Thus, the non-manufacturing sector had to pay higher prices of industrial products than they would have otherwise done. In fact, it was claimed that the Structural Transformation of the developing economies under the protectionist regimes might have been perverse in that they caused a 'reallocation of primary factors from the higher (agricultural) to lower (manufacturing) marginal productivity pursuits'. What made it worse was that rapid industrialization of developing countries created a large excess demand for low cost sources of energy, making them vulnerable to fluctuations in the prices of oil [World Bank (1982)]. More fundamentally, the complaint was that a (static) resource misallocation of domestic resources to import-substitution activities rather than to export-expansion industries imposed a net cost on the economy that greatly reduced its long–run growth potential [Bhagwati (1978)]; prevented the developing countries from learning the best practice in industrial development and technological change [Balassa (1988)]; and exposed them to exogenous shocks (on the grounds that export-oriented economies were better able to absorb these shocks)[Balassa (1978; 1981)]. All this could be remedied, it was argued, by doing away with such regimes, abolishing import restrictions of all kinds and adopting instead uniform and 'realistic' exchange rates. The combined effect of these reforms was expected to significantly increase export-expansion activities, reduce the costly import-substitution activities and enhance social welfare.[16] And, also, if such reforms have not produced the expected results so far, the fault must have been of the allegedly nth-best implementation of the first-best policies.

7.3. Law of Comparative Advantage and Economic Development

An important consequence of the revival of the neo-classical economics and the apparent triumph of the Liberalist Paradigm has been the re-ascension of the static Law of Comparative Advantage as the correct principle of resource allocation in the developing countries. Indeed, this 'event' has been celebrated as the triumph of common sense over economic insanity.[17] The liberalist (compulsory) advice has, therefore, been to go back to the neo-classical guiding principle of equating the marginal rate of substitution with the marginal rates of domestic and international transformation *via* the equalization of domestic price with international price [Krueger (1997), p. 18)].[18] It is argued that, to achieve this end, the government intervention must be eliminated, or at least minimized, from the foreign-trade sector on a priority basis. The underlying assumption here is that international trade could be a perfect substitute for domestic development effort for achieving efficient allocation of resources, with the added advantage, that the former would avoid the waste (measured by the Domestic Resource Cost) of scarce resources that protectionist policies impose on the economy. Once these statements are accepted, the only logical position would be to 'open up' developing countries to foreign competition. The beneficial outcome of these 'first-best' policies, it is confidently argued, would be to cut down wasteful rent seeking and offer opportunities for profit making to domestic firms [Kruger (1978]. In the pursuit of economic efficiency, economic development could then safely be entrusted to the theoretically robust Heckscher-Ohlin-Samuelson (HOS) Theorem, which proves that (free) trade is superior to no-trade and that it is also the surest way to maximize the gains from trade.[19] The HOS Theorem also assures that if international economic relations are so organized that each country specialized (though not completely) in activities that most intensively used its most abundant factor, then world economic resources would be most efficiently deployed in the rich and the poor countries. The outcome of this optimal deployment of each trading country's resources would also be equitable, because the relative and absolute rewards of its most abundant factor (labour) would increase, while that of the scarce factor (capital) decline [Metzler (1949)]. The real wage of the unskilled worker would rise, while the rental on capital decline if each labour-surplus country exported its labour-intensive goods. Such a move would also reduce poverty. An important implication of following the Law, the liberalist argued, would be to go all out for export expansion in order to maximize growth and employment creation. Indeed, it has been argued that to *err* on the side of export expansion would be unambiguously superior to doing so on the side of import-substitution.[20] In sum, once a bagful of first-best assumptions are accepted as a faithful approximation to reality, then logic would lead to a world of universal bliss in which all policies produce first-best results with perfect certainty. The reasonableness of these assumptions and the statements flowing from them will be discussed in Part IV.

7.4. WASHINGTON CONSENSUS

One of the most important events that sealed the fate of the Traditional Development Paradigm was the forging of the so-called Washington Consensus which, in fact, represented an official endorsement of the Liberalist Paradigm. It spelled out, initially, a series of reforms specifically to deal with Latin America's severe financial crisis.[21] However, soon these principles were generalized into a set of policy prescriptions that developing countries had to implement in order to receive a certificate of good economic health, which would then qualify them to receive financial aid from official and non-official sources. What made these prescriptions authentic and hallow is that they have been regarded as universally valid, in the North as well as in the South; and that any argument about their lack of generality is promptly condemned as perpetuating 'apartheid' in the realm of economics.[22] The Consensus proposed a 10-point agenda aimed at promoting economic growth without (consciously) hurting distribution of income and wealth within the general framework of a globalizing market economy. It required developing countries to deregulate, liberalize trade and capital flows with a view to installing a regime of competitive exchange rates, and doing privatization and financial liberalization to 'un-distort' market prices. The aim of all this was to push developing countries back to the path of 'sustainable' growth.[23] This system of 'beliefs' put a heavy premium on outward orientation, prized making greater use of the market mechanism and the price incentives, and desisting from import substitution and government intervention. It accorded primacy to restoring macroeconomic stability in all the developing countries on the assumption that only the growth rates achieved within the framework of macroeconomic stability could be sustained in the long run without inviting a debt crisis. The international donors subscribed whole-heartedly to the Washington Consensus and undertook to spread its message throughout the world with reformist zeal in the belief that, 'the sort of economic policies that worked in OECD countries were also applicable in Latin America', and by implication in the rest of the developing countries [Kuczynski and Williamson (2003)].[24] There is a solid body of empirical evidence to prove that such policies produced low growth, high unemployment, distributive injustice and increased poverty everywhere—in OECD countries as well as Latin America. If these outcomes can be described as a sign of economic success, one wonders what sobriquet would denote economic failure.

7.4. (iv). The Ready 'Acceptance' of the Washington Consensus

One might wonder as to why the reformist creed could gain ground throughout the developing world in such a short time. An obvious explanation, noted above, is that the developing countries coming to the Washington-based institutions for financial help had no option but to unquestioningly submit to their absolutist, non-consequential worldview. The only alternative was to leave the badly needed money. Obviously, most, if not all, took the money, even if that meant implementing reforms that, they knew, would not serve their national interests. Yet another explanation of the ready acceptance of the liberalist programme by the donor institutions and the recipients of funds from them alike laid in its apparent simplicity. One can predict with reasonable confidence, that in a contest of acceptability, a mindless simple dogma will be strictly preferred to good hard thinking. This is what the liberalist programme has done. It has offered a ready-made formula that would radically curtail in one swoop the writ of the state in economic matters, redefine private property rights as clearly as possible, and make rules to prevent the violations of individual freedom, no matter what the economic and social consequence would be of implementing such a policy. The actual running of the economic universe should be left to prices and private profits, which could be relied upon to produce, all by themselves (i.e., without state intervention), efficient, un-improvable and universally valid solutions. An added attraction of the proposed prescription for the hard-pressed policy-maker would be the assurance of development success with the minimum input of his rather scarce intellectual resources.

When a faith-based message is enforced on unwilling takers, reason becomes its first casualty: proselytizers do not appeal to their victim's reason but astound it. This is exactly what Washington Consensus has done to developing countries. To keep the message simple, and beyond the grasp of reason, its basic underlying assumptions have never been explained to the recipients of its assistance. Thus, for instance, the developing countries have seldom, if ever, been invited to engage in a reasoned dialogue on the conditions under which markets work; nor have they been informed that they work if the legal, administrative and institutional infrastructures are also put in place first to ensure competition, and if the economic actors voluntarily observe certain principles like trust, a minimum of honesty, the sanctity of contracts. Considering the very high cost that the implantation of its worldview has normally imposed on developing countries such dialogues would have enhanced their ownership. Instead, driven by a strong desire to replicate European experience in the developing countries, the authors of the Washington consensus have, 'tried to take a shortcut to capitalism, creating a market economy without the underlying institutions, and institutions without the underlying institutional infrastructure' [Stiglitz (2003), p. 139].[25]

7.5. THE 'CONVERSION' OF INTERNATIONAL DONORS

The World Bank and the IMF have dutifully suffused the Washington Consensus's message into the very texture of the Structural Adjustment Programmes. These programmes openly assumed the mantle of the defenders of the faith in neo-classical economics.[26] They helped complete the changeover from the old to the new paradigm throughout the developing world rather quickly, without giving recipients the time to think through the implications of the new ideological 'realities' for their welfare. The entire process of change was consummated in the first half of the 1980s in most of the developing countries. 'By the beginning of the 1990s, the structural adjustment model had, to an extraordinary extent, become the accepted model for reform, with the erstwhile critics increasingly accepting the general approach while attempting to soften the rigors of its application' [Corbo and Fischer (1995), p. 2853]. During the 1980 to 1991 time period, seventy-five countries had already accepted to undergo one or the other 258 programmes launched by these agencies. The range of policies that the 'conditions' of the Structural Adjustment Programmes have prescribed for the crisis-bitten countries is normally quite vast and in most cases covers nearly every sector of the economy. Regardless of the nature of the crisis (defined as a situation when current account deficits can no longer be financed by commercial borrowing), the developing countries are routinely required to implement restrictive fiscal and monetary policies that are religiously enforced to reduce the domestic absorption of the internationally traded goods, while the expenditure-switching policies have sought to make exchange rates more 'realistic' (i.e., market-determined). But their main area of concentration has been a thorough restructuring of the trade and payments regimes to liberalize imports and encourage exports and permit unhindered international flow of private capital. Yet another area of their concentration has been the restructuring of the operations of the public sector and reducing its size [Corbo and Fischer (1995)]. The so-called price distortions allegedly caused by tariff and non-tariff import restrictions should be dealt with, it was recommended, by opting, to begin with, for 'optimal' government intervention (domestic subsidies in place of tariffs, which should replace quantitative restrictions). Furthermore, in the belief that markets are infallible in all circumstances and locations, these programmes invariably demanded of all the developing countries to abandon the government-supported, inward-looking, import-substitution policies forthwith to minimize the cost of distortions. In its place, privatization of the public-sector enterprises has been diagnosed to be the ultimate remedy for infusing efficiency in the production and financial sectors on the assumption, that defining private property rights tightly would, by itself, create strong forces to generate the rule of law that would provide the mechanism to settle disputes about the ownership rights. Above all, it requires ensuring a regime of macroeconomic stability at all times within the framework of undistorted markets and free (or at least freer) international trade and capital flows. Furthermore, these policies have aimed at reducing 'price distortions', lowering the inflation rate, increasing the flow of private domestic and foreign investments and paring down government intervention in economic affairs.[27] Also, they are meant to increase the supply response of the economy to the price signals and help restore macro-economic balance so that 'the present social value of the future sequence of consumptions is higher with adjustment than without it' [Lipton and Ravallion (1995), p. 261].[28] Together, these reforms have sought to put the crisis-bitten countries on the long-run growth path by providing stable macroeconomic conditions; an appropriate structure of market incentives; an adequate physical and human capital base and saving rate and; by establishing efficient institutions that help to plough savings into productive investments.

It is an interesting commentary on the advent of the new paradigm that the Structural Adjustment programmes begun rather sensibly as a cure for the acute macroeconomic instability (mainly astronomical inflation rates and unsustainable external debt) that Latin American countries were suffering from, soon became, not so sensibly, the cure-all for all sorts of real or imagined crises, regardless of their origin, nature and intensity.[29] For instance, if reducing excess demand was prescribed to reduce the very high inflation rates in Latin America (in the 1980s), the same remedy was diagnosed for East Asia in its hour of crisis (in 1996), even though inflation rates there were moderate, even by textbook standards. The air of certainty and exactitude that normally surrounds the Structural Adjustment Programmes is somewhat surprising, considering that while they have been specific about the preconditions to long-run growth; there is not much clarity about what happens to growth once these preconditions are satisfied. Worse still, they are totally at a loss about what happens to the conditions if growth does not revive, which has happened quite often. All that is done is to state that the period required to position the economy for long-term growth path would be a long one in which painful adjustments will have to be made, especially by the poor.[30] However, the quintessential questions about the time it takes for the Structural Adjustment Programmes to actually initiate long-term growth, and about the duration and intensity of the promised pain, have seldom been answered with clarity and confidence.[31]

7.6. Concluding Remarks

The cataclysmic events that shook developing countries, and Latin America and Africa in particular, in the 1970s, i.e. a steep rise in the interest rates, the oil price shocks—presented the liberalists with the perfect opportunity to impose the liberalist views on all the developing countries. Inspired by the vision of the first-best universe, the liberalist set about minimizing the size of the government, mostly achieved through post-haste privatization, and abolishing most restrictions on the international flow of goods (even short-term) capital. But, above all, the new economic dispensation aimed to restore individual freedom to own property, which must be prized as an absolute good, regardless of what it does to development. The Structural Adjustment Programmes sought to produce these first-best results by requiring a faithful implementation of their conditions, which, among other things, tilted the incentive structure in favour of exports and agriculture with a view to raising the threshold of sustainable growth and poverty reduction. Yet another important aspect of the debut of the Liberalist Paradigm has been its insistence that what is good for the developed countries must be good for the developing countries as well.[32]

It is, however, not the Liberalist Paradigm's lack of understanding of the realities of the developing world that is surprising (after all most of them have had no more than a nodding acquaintance with the developing countries); it is rather the astonishing information blockage that its practitioners have apparently suffered from. It is difficult to believe that the highly erudite mainstream economists would, disregarding the latest advancements in neo-classical economics and international trade theory, let the pendulum of academic opinion swing all the way from traditional paradigm's point of view to the opposite extreme of using unfettered markets and the static Law of Comparative Advantage as the best principle to guide the allocation of domestic resources between alternative economic activities. Surely, they must have been aware of the historical irrelevance of *laissez-faire* and the well-known unrealism of the assumptions of the static Law of Comparative Advantage and the Heckscher-Ohlin-Samuelson Theorem.[33] They must also have known that all advanced countries including Japan, climbed the development ladder by practicing protectionism—nursing their infant industries till the attained adult hood.[34] Why then must they 'kick the ladder' away from the grasp of the developing countries in this day and age?

Notes

1. The liberal ideology, formulated in the Mont Pellerin Society, was fully formulated by Milton Friedman and Friedrich von Hayek. Margaret Thatcher implemented it in England and Ronald Reagan in the United States.

2. Heilbroner's (1990) evaluation of the fall of Soviet Union and the march to the market of the entire Soviet Bloc was typical of the euphoria at the time: 'with few exceptions, socialism has experienced a public deligitimization—whereas capitalism, despite its failures had enjoyed—a rising degree of political support' (p. 1097).

3. There seems to be major disconnect between the cause and the effect in the type of thinking cited in the text. This is because there is a world of difference between centrally planned economic systems and the mixed economies of the developing countries. The latter, it will be recalled, had explicitly rejected the communist model of development back in the 1950s. However, as things have turned out, the East European and Soviet system's experiment with the market system has proved to be a big embarrassment for the free-market aficionados: it can now more properly be cited as an example of the utter failure of the market-based system. These matters are discussed later in the book.

4. The logic behind the argument in the text seems to be the following: since the sub-optimal policies of the Traditional Development Paradigm were the proximate cause of the developing countries' misfortunes (outside East Asia), the only possible explanation of the East Asian success could be that these countries must have followed the liberalist first-best policies—a kind of implicit theorizing that economists do not normally accept.

5. That initial conditions matter a great deal in determining the future growth path has also been substantiated by the inter-country differences in their respective industrialization success. Pack (1988) observes: '...it is difficult to identify a country with a record of industrial manufacturing growth which had not substantial industrial experience before the Second World War. Korea and Taiwan certainly had such experience—policy is important but so is inheritance' (p. 338).

6. Thus, for instance, the rush to privatization was an illegitimate extension of the neo-classical paradigm (the Arrow-Debreu model). Arrow reportedly advised the Chinese against rushing to privatization without first creating the institutional infrastructure for a market economy. He also emphasized that the important thing for the success of a market economy was competition not privatization *per se* [Stiglitz (2003), p. 182]. Similarly, there was no theoretical or historical antecedent for a post-haste liberalization of the international flow of short-term capital, which too the Liberalist Paradigm imposed on the financially beleaguered developing countries.

7. In this context, the World Bank was seen, in 1980, as 'leading the charge of neo-classical resurgence'. And to this end, it provided finances to the academic profession to work on market-related research. Indeed, it set the latter's research agenda by a powerful advocacy of the neo-causes through its *Annual Development Reports*. The reports for years 1983, 1985 and 1987 especially focused academic attention on such neo-classical issues 'as price, trade, tax, and institutional reforms to increase the efficiency of resource allocation—crucially, domestic investment—' [Stern and Ferreira (1993), p. 19].

8. It may be noted that the rather dismissive comments in the text should not be construed as a criticism of the theoretical validity of the neo-classical paradigm, which continues to be one of the finest achievements of the economics profession. The comments relate rather to the liberalist belief that it can be used as a ready-made formula for the design of an optimal development policy.

9. The point noted in the text explains the liberalist perception that development success, especially that achieved in East Asia could not have been caused by the Traditional Development Paradigm. Not finding any other logical explanation, Krueger (1995a) has attempted to explain away development success of the developing countries, including that of East Asia, by reference to the favourable exogenous factors prevailing in the post-War era: 'it may be that in the late 1940s and early 1950s any economic policy that did not entirely thwart these investments would have generated rates of economic growth significantly above long-term growth' (p. 2508) The exogenous factors she cites as the main causes of the development success of the developing countries are: the buoyancy of the

international economy, the availability of the sterling balances or other foreign exchange reserves as the outcome of the Second World War, increased expenditure on health and education, and significant backlog of worthwhile investments that could not be undertaken during the War, etc. In other words, the success of the developing countries was not the result of any policy, but owed itself to fortuitous circumstances. However, these assertions, if true, would falsify the other liberalist claim that their success was due to liberalist policies.

10. For a detailed analysis of the monetarist and rational expectationists schools see, Naqvi (1993) and (2002).

11. But, strictly speaking, such concessions to reality cannot logically be given in the neo-classical scheme of thought because these are not consistent with the claims that markets are both perfect and rational. Any departure from the markets, big or small, would, in the neo-classical scheme, mean irrational behaviour on the part of the economic agents and signify imperfections (distortions) in the economy.

12. These studies used estimates of the world prices as a proxy for undistorted prices, ignoring the well-known fact that these prices have been routinely distorted by large government subsidies given by the OECD governments to their producers.

13. Kuznets (1956, 1957) reports growth rates of 6.2 per cent for lower middle income, 7.0 per cent for the middle-income oil importers, and 9.1 per cent for the upper middle-income developing countries during 1950–70. By contrast, the United States grew at the rate of 5 per cent during 1874–1914; Sweden's growth rate was 4.8 per cent during 1865–1914; Germany's growth rate was 4.2 per cent during 1860–1914; Italy's growth performance was 1.6 per cent during 1863–1913.

14. 'The attempt to compress centuries of skill formation into four decades while achieving rates of industrial growth exceeding those of the current developed countries in their early period of industrial development has resulted in slow rates of productivity growth and in current production that is highly inefficient' [Pack (1988), p. 336]. Cipolla (1976) has tried to show the inherent inefficiency of compressing industrialization in a short period, not waiting for the slow build-up of technological skills necessary for efficient industrialization.

15. Krueger, Schiff and Valdes (1991) have estimated that the implicit taxation in the Asian and Mediterranean countries was 25 per cent and that it was 50 per cent in the case of sub-Saharan Africa.

16. However, subsequent studies of the static allocative effects of the import-substitution losses have shown that the efficiency losses on this count were generally small: no more than a couple of percentage points of the GDP (ranging from 1 to 5 per cent) [Srinivasan and Whalley (1986)]. Furthermore, the claim that the removal of protection-induced price distortions would make a significant impact on growth has not been proven. For one thing it is not always clear whether a high rate of growth of output leads to lesser protection or vice versa (if the case is that the government loosens trade restrictions in times of prosperity). If that is the case, the statistical relationship between lesser distortion and higher growth (the former causing the latter) would be a spurious one.

17. Krueger (1997) upbraided development economists for their open disregard of the time-honoured Law in the making of development policies: 'How could it happen that a profession, for which the principle of comparative advantage was one of its key tenets, embraced such protectionist policies?' (p. 2) The probable reason given for their professional misbehaviour was that they chose the wrong 'stylized facts' to represent reality in the developing countries (e.g., that economic development meant industrialization, and that supply response was lacking), and used bad economics (e.g., that infant-industry argument was misused) to support inefficient industrialization; and typically misapplied a correct theory (e.g., free trade was misinterpreted as implying that developing countries would forever specialize in the production of primary goods).

18. Lal (1983) recommended that developing countries had better be guided by the Pareto-optimality principle to conduct their policies (indeed, non-policies) according to a principle that regarded government intervention as redundant and counter-productive.

19. While we speak of the Law of Comparative Advantage and the H-O-S theorems in the text as essentially complementary propositions, the two are, in effect, alternative models of reality. While the former assumes a one-factor world and attributes to differences in the production functions the main predictions of international trade; the latter postulates a world of two factors of production world so that the composition of international trade flowed from differences in the factor endowments. The latter also rules out differences in production functions as explaining international trade. Furthermore, the former seeks to prove the welfare propositions of trade theory; but the latter is meant to be a positive contribution to theory of international trade [Bhagwati (1965), p. 173].

20. Krueger (1983) has tried to provide an empirical confirmation of this proposition in a static context.

21. The term Washington Consensus was born at a conference held at the Institute of International Economics in November 1989 under the title 'Latin American Adjustment: How Much Has Happened'. Later on, Williamson (1990) reported on the conference. To him, by common consent, goes the credit for coining the term in 1989.

22. Williamson expresses appreciation for the liberalists who 'freed themselves of the intellectual apartheid that earlier in the post-War period had divided the world into industrial countries (those belonging to the Organization for Economic Cooperation and Development) where price stability, the market economy, and open trade were good things; and developing countries where inflation was due to structural causes, the state had to play a leading role, and import substituting industrialization provided a royal road to growth' [Kuczynski and Williamson] (p. 325).

23. In addition to the elements of the Consensus noted in the text, there were others: fiscal discipline, redirection of public expenditure towards health and education, tax reforms that would call for broadening the tax base and cutting down the tax rates, and ensuring secure private property rights. There could be little doubt that it is always good to exercise fiscal probity (though not to the extent that it crowds out development expenditures) or to ensure that the domestic currency be not overvalued. But the same could not always be said about such liberalist cure-alls as privatization and the deregulation of international flow of capital. The Washington Consensus has been restated in Kuczynski and Williamson (2003).

24. Williamson has disputed the usage of the Washington Consensus as synonymous with market fundamentalism; but now it is quite common in the development literature. Thus, Thirlwall (1999) states: 'The Washington Consensus, which is essentially neo-liberal, is based on the alleged superiority of the free market and free trade for the achievement of rapid economic progress.' (p. 472). Stiglitz (2003) has used market fundamentalism and Washington Consensus synonymously. However, out of deference to the sensitivities of the 'father' of Washington Consensus, we have avoided using either of these terms in favour of the more dignified and neutral term Liberalist Paradigm throughout this book.

25. No country perhaps suffered more than Russia from this rather simplistic view of market capitalism: It suffered a greater loss of income and output than it did in the Second World War. In 1990–98 the Russian industrial production fell by 42.9 per cent as compared with a 24 per cent fall during the fateful years of 1940 to 1946. The GDP in 2000 was only a third of what it was in 1989. Poverty in 1998 was 23.8 per cent as compared to only 2 per cent in 1989. And life expectancy in the same period fell by three years mainly because of the massive unemployment caused by market-friendly policies [Stiglitz (2003), pp. 152–53]. On this, see also Campos and Coricelli (2002).

26. The World Bank's structural adjustment programmes are handed down to the crisis-bitten developing countries in the form of the Structural Adjustment Loans (SALs) and the Sectoral Adjustment Loans (SECALs); while the IMF's programmes are known as the

Structural Adjustment Facility (SAF) and Extended Structural Adjustment Facility (ESAF).

27. A more complete treatment of the Structural Adjustment Programmes is given in the next chapter. It may be noted here, that if the purpose of the programme was to improve the developing economies' capacity to sustain long-term growth, then this expectation has not been fulfilled, or at least not convincingly. The studies carried out by the World Bank and others generally report that between 1970–80 and 1980–88, the investment to GDP ratio at constant prices decreased by 5.6 percentage points [Corbo and Fischer (1995)]. Furthermore, a common complaint has been that the Structural Adjustment Programmes paid scant attention to income distribution [Edwards (1989)].

28. The broad thrust of '*structural adjustment is a process of market-oriented reforms in policies and institutions, with the goals of restoring a sustainable balance of payments, reducing inflation, and creating conditions for sustainable growth in per capita income*' [Corbo and Fischer (1995), p. 2847; emphasis appear in the original]. Structural adjustment has also been defined as the 'combination of supply and demand side policies [just described] directed towards the transformation of the structure of the economy—aiming both to restore macroeconomic equilibrium and to improve microeconomic efficiency' [Stern and Ferreira (1993), p. 20].

29. There is an extensive literature on the political economy of reforms debating whether it was the crisis that prompted them. See, Rodrik (1996) for an analysis of this debate, which remains inconclusive. For instance, Krueger (1993) prescribed that, 'economic conditions deteriorated sufficiently so that there emerged a political imperative for better economic performance' (p. 109). That might well have been the case, but as a refutable hypothesis the contention that crisis caused the reform is as enlightening as the assertion that fire caused the smoke. What would then explain those cases where the governments did not institute reforms in the face of a crisis? Or what could be the explanation of the cases where the reforms were instituted even though not faced with a crisis (for instance in South Asia, which did not face the serious debt crisis of the 1980s or the very high inflation rates that only Latin America experienced)? The answers given to these questions have been unsatisfactory, if not totally absurd. In particular, the liberalist literature is silent on the most important issue of the nature of reforms to sort out different types of crises.

30. The emphasis of these programmes is generally on the intensity of the pain they cause to the (poorer) people, in the masochistic belief that the greater the pain tolerated by them the more receptive would they become to structural adjustments.

31. An authentic and sympathetic evaluation of the structural adjustment programmes states: 'This is obviously a question that has no unique answer, for it depends on the extent of the disarray at the start of the reform programmes, on the speed and comprehensiveness of the adjustment programme, on the stability of government policies. Nonetheless, observation of even such successful programmes as those of Chile and Mexico in the 1980s suggests that it takes a long time, perhaps five or more years, until growth begins to revive. The delays are due to the complexity of the necessary policy changes, and on lags in the investment response of the private sector. Such a long transition period increases the political difficulty of sustaining the adjustment programme' [Corbo and Fischer (1995), p. 2893].

32. Thus, Nobel Laureate Schultz (1981) held: 'Standard economic theory is as applicable to the scarcity problems that confront the low-income countries as to the corresponding problems of the high-developed economies' (p. 4). The problem, however, is that they are not applicable anywhere.

33. It is well-known that, for instance, differences in production functions between developing and the developed countries would introduce contradictions in the predictions of the HOS model. No less unrealistic is the assumption, which the Law of Comparative Advantage makes, that factor supplies are irrelevant in the determination of the trade pattern especially

in the case of the developing countries. Furthermore, as discussed below, not much success has been achieved in testing the empirical validity of the intuitively obvious Heckscher-Ohlin-Samuelson Theorem.

34. All reliable historical studies support the point of view that restrictions on the imports and on foreign direct investment have stimulated R&D efforts. Something like this had happened in Japan in the 1970s [Odagiri and Goto (1993)].

8

The Liberalist Paradigm II:
Transformation of Policy Focus

The Liberalist Paradigm, like any other paradigm, is an internally consistent system of values, basic economic statements and policy implications. Thus for instance, the belief in the efficiency of privatization follows from the priority it attaches to individual freedom to hold on to what she/he has acquired through his/her alleged superior merit, and from the theoretical demonstration of the un-improvability of market solutions. Similarly, the Law of Comparative Advantage, which has been universally accepted (quite legitimately) as one of the crowning achievements of the economic profession, has lent support to the revival of the *laissez-faire* ideal as an oriflamme of international economic relations. The rejection of an extensive role of the government in economic affairs flows from the same values and the principal statements of the Liberalist Paradigm. The preceding chapter spelled out the main factors that led to its swift (though, Pyrrhic) victory over the Traditional Development Paradigm. It will be of some interest to highlight in the present chapter the radical change in the policy focus that the victory of the liberalist ideals has caused.

8.1. 'Wrong' (Market) Prices Become 'Right' Prices

As noted above, a focal recommendation of the Liberalist Paradigm has been to rely on 'unfettered' market prices as the most reliable and economical means to guide domestic resources into the most efficient activities and sectors—unaided by government intervention. An interesting aspect of this recommendation is that the economic profession has shifted ground, both with respect to the specification of the 'right prices' and where to find them [Streeten (1993); Naqvi (2002)]. In the beginning (in the 1960s-70s), economists fervently advocated using shadow prices, rather than the market prices, to evaluate the worth of investment programmes. But with the ascendancy of the Liberalist Paradigm in economic affairs (from 1980 onwards) it has reverted to the use of the market prices.

8.1. (i). Use Shadow Prices not Market Prices

The liberalist literature (though the Liberalist Paradigm in its present form was not yet officially born) initially asserted that market prices, robbed of their quintessential signalling function by government-induced distortions, would not ensure an efficient allocation of resource, nor would they serve the cause of equity [Little, Scitovsky and Scott (1970)]. Thus, it recommended that 'shadow (accounting) prices', rather than the market prices (especially of capital and foreign exchange), should be used to evaluate the efficiency of inter-sector resource allocation between agriculture and manufacturing, on one hand, and that between domestic and foreign trade sector, on the other. Great reputations were made at the time on just doing such calculations with a view to deflating the growth rates (especially industrial growth rates) achieved by the developing countries. The outcome of these exercises was almost pre-determined: restructure the relative prices so that agriculture received more policy attention relative to industry and, within the latter category, light industry more than heavy industry. The necessity of undertaking such a corrective exercise was emphasized on the grounds that the bias against agriculture arising from a distortion of the price structure was assumed to be very substantial.[1] It was 'considerably greater than comparison of the border price with the domestic price to farmers indicated. Moreover, the reduction in the agricultural producers' incomes was considerably greater than had been thought' [Krueger (1995), p. 2527]. It was, therefore, recommended that the developing countries must 'grow in an off-set, unbalanced fashion, by specializing on its comparative advantage in agricultural production, and also by growing at a much slower rate, given the much lower elasticity of demand [as compared to that of the developed countries] for food than for the industrial products' [Scitovsky (1990), p. 56].[2] The intended effect of the change in policy focus was to pull the developing countries away from the allegedly distorted industrialization patterns towards a more efficient and sustainable growth path—namely, one that flowed from TFP growth rather than capital accumulation, from agriculture rather than industry and; from export expansion rather than import substitution.

It may be noted that the very purpose of the exercises done to compute shadow prices was to reject the need for, or the desirability of, comprehensive investment programmes as guides to economic policy, and to revert to the Law of Comparative Advantage to decide on the social profitability of specific investment projects. The importance of this principle for the liberalist recommendations can be gauged by the fact that it made the international prices of imported goods (especially of capital goods) the pivot around which the estimates of all the factor scarcities would turn. However, it is interesting to note that the standard procedure for computing shadow prices—namely, estimating them from the dual of an economy-wide investment programme—has not been followed for this purpose.[3] Instead, as a short-cut, the international prices of traded goods have been used to evaluate domestic output of the import substitutes. This procedure was justified by reference to the important theoretical result that these prices reflected the relative scarcities of the traded goods [Diamond and Mirrlees (1971)]. The uncomfortable fact that non-traded inputs used in the production of the import substitutes would not be represented by international prices of the traded goods was taken care of by yet another mathematical result. It was that, the 'non-tradable goods are produced by means of tradable, non-tradable and labour; and labour, in turn, produces both tradable and non-tradable goods in alternative employments and spends extra income on tradable and non-tradable goods. Thus, non-tradable goods and labour can be decomposed into tradable goods valued at world prices' [Bell (1990), p. 14]. It would, therefore, be justified to evaluate non-tradable goods as well by international prices [Little and Mirrlees (1969)]. The end result of this exercise would be the same as the one produced by the method used in the previous paragraph. The 'systems of shadow prices [would] seem to impose the discipline of free trade by stealth' [Bell (1990), p. 15]. The proposed reform would end the 'forced draft industrialization', reduce rural poverty and encourage 'pro-poor growth'.[4] It was further recommended that interest rates must be increased and domestic currencies devalued to reflect their domestic scarcities. Doing this would have the effect of dampening down the 'overheated' developing economies and increasing social welfare by depriving the domestic producers of the implicit subsidy on the domestic production of the import substitutes, and saving the domestic consumers from an implicit tax it imposed on them. Furthermore, by abolishing the implicit tax on agriculture such reforms were expected to promote agricultural productivity.

8.1. (ii). Use Market Prices not Shadow Prices

However, much of the enthusiasm for computing shadow prices evaporated as the Liberalist Paradigm spread its wings, even though the markets were far from fully unfettered. In a reversal of the neo-classically correct policies of relying on shadow prices, it was recommended that domestic market prices, not their shadows, should be reassigned their traditionally allocated duties as guides to domestic development policies. The argument probably was that once the markets were unfettered, domestic prices would no longer be distorted and rent seeking would disappear. Similarly, it was argued that the computation of the shadow price of foreign exchange would become unnecessary to conduct international trade and investment efficiently as and when: the price of foreign exchange (through repeated devaluation) drifted downwards, the currency overvaluations of the early years of development were more or less worked off, imports liberalized, and capital market reforms introduced to attract private capital flows from the developed to the developing countries. These reforms were seen as creating free trade regimes in which trade and investment would move in the most efficient direction. To prove the empirical validity of this line of thinking, it was claimed in one study after another that the revival of the markets and the minimization of government intervention had been the key to successful development in all developing countries, especially in East Asian Miracle economies [e.g., Krueger (1993); World Bank (1993)]. The promised empirical proofs of these assertions have not yet arrived.

8.2. Controlling Inflation

An important element of the new-fangled liberalist development policy has been its uncompromising insistence on reducing the inflation rate—the lower the better. To this end, one of the basic conditions of the Structural Adjustment Programmes has been to reduce the budgetary deficits to as low a level as possible, even if that means cutting into the much needed development (including human development) expenditures, and withdrawing the subsidies on food, which have invariably been the first casualty of every such programme. National governments have to literally beg the international donors into giving them some 'fiscal space', so that development expenditures are kept and some subsidies, especially those given to the poor retained. That being the importance given to the conditions, it should be of interest to look at the evidence about the beneficial effects of reducing the inflation rate. Most studies show that the adverse effects of the inflation rate on growth begin to appear only when it gets too high—that is, it exceeds 20–40 per cent per year; and that when inflation rates are brought down from those levels through structural adjustments, the pay-off in output growth tends to be significant. However, at a lower-to-moderate rate of inflation, the positive effects are not so obvious [Little, Cooper, Corden, Rajapatirana (1993)]. Bruno (1996) has reported similar findings. What is then the basis of anti-inflation radicalism? The answer that the liberalists give is somewhat tentative: it is that inflation is a persistent phenomenon, which quickly acquires a life of its own. It is, therefore, better controlled at an early stage before inflationary expectations start getting out of hand. That may be so but this consideration does not mean that one should go to the other extreme and aim at the lowest possible inflation rate. There is, of course, the Phillips Curve negative relationship between inflation rate and the unemployment rate. For some obscure reasons, this rather robust relationship seldom gets reflected in the conditions, even though unemployment has risen in nearly all countries where IMF conditions have been faithfully implemented for a long enough time.

8.2. (i). Empirical Evidence from Asia and Pacific (1965–2000)

It will be instructive in this context to examine the inflation-growth nexus in the Asia and Pacific Region. The average annual growth rate of per capita income in the region has been high (4.02 per cent), while the average inflation rates in the region a modest 7 per cent. What does this say about the correlation between growth and inflation relationship? In particular, is there much warrant in applying the lessons learnt in Latin America in this region? Figure 8.1 highlights some important facts. Firstly, five high-growth countries (Hong Kong, China, Thailand, South Korea and Vietnam) fall in the higher-than-average inflation region (upper right-hand side box).[5] On the other hand, three high-growth countries (Singapore, Taiwan and Malaysia) are located in the lower-than-average inflation box as well (upper left-hand box). Secondly, a fairly large number of slower-growing countries are in the high-inflation rate (lower right-hand box). Thirdly, a striking feature of the figure is that, with the exception of Japan, the low-growth and low-inflation (lower-left) box is empty.

One can extract the following conclusions even at this preliminary stage of economic analysis: (a) Low-inflation and low-growth combination seems to be the unlikeliest of all the possible scenarios. Japan's case, where a prolonged recession has been the cause of this unlikely combination, can be treated as an exception to this rule. (b) Next in the order of probabilities is the high-growth and low-inflation case. Here the three countries (Singapore, Malaysia and Taiwan) are those where growth has been accompanied by some degree of fiscal prudence, thus, ruling out both, fiscal laxity as well as fiscal radicalism. One can look at this possibility as the ideal scenario which will keep both the Traditional Development Paradigm as well as the Liberalist Paradigm happy. (c) A more likely scenario is that of fast-growth going with higher-than-average inflation. These countries will be well advised to watch for lowering the inflation rate, so that it does not get out of hand. However, the required degree of fiscal discipline should not squelch growth under its feet. What does the inflation-growth relationship suggest? Obviously, nothing very specific follows from these comparisons. More important, however, is the point that the inflation-growth link cannot be read by just looking at the correlation of these two variables. We need to go beyond these correlations to discover the causative relationships and arrive at a more satisfactory policy implication. Detailed multivariate regression analysis is required to establish the growth-inflation linkage in a proper perspective. Such exercise is presented in Part VI of this book.

Figure 8.1: Economic Growth—Inflation Linkage in Asia and Pacific Region (1965–2000)

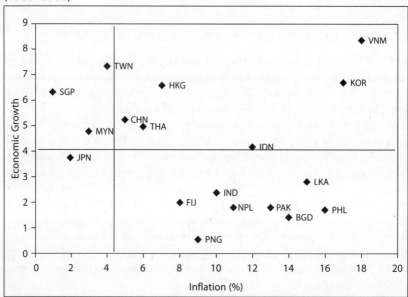

Note: Growth rate is defined as growth rate of GDP per capita. The inflation rate is ranked in ascending order. Higher rank means higher inequality. Average growth rate of GDP per capita for the sample countries is 4.02 per cent for the period 1965–2000. Average rate of inflation is 7.02.

◆ Following countries are included in the sample: Bangladesh (BGD), China (CHN), Fiji (FIJ), Hong Kong (HKG), India (IND), Nepal (NPL), Indonesia (IDN), Japan (JPN), Papua New Guinea (PNG), Korea (KOR), Malaysia (MYN), Pakistan (PAK), Philippines (PHL), Sri Lanka (LKA), Singapore (SGP), Taiwan (TWN), Thailand (THA), and Vietnam (VNM).

8.3. EXPORT FETISHISM

An important consequence of the liberalists emotional return to the fold of the static Law of Comparative Advantage has been its rather one-sided emphasis on export orientation. It may be interesting to examine more closely the arguments in favour of export fetishism.[6] Three important generalizations have been advanced in support of this contention: (1) the outer-oriented strategy is unambiguously superior to the import-substitution strategy; the East Asian experience, it is argued, demonstrated the superiority of export-led growth strategy; (2) export growth, or rather outward orientation, is uniquely related to the growth rate of GDP, with the chain of causation running from the former to the latter; (3) an import-substitution regime is alleged to be intervention-intensive and for that reason more distorted and would entail rent-seeking. By the same token, export orientation would be 'undistorted' and encourage profit-seeking. Each of these propositions requires careful scrutiny.

Available evidence seems to suggest that the following conclusions are not true: (a) The East Asian countries were the only ones that shifted from an import substitution to export orientation around the 1960s. (b) Only they had the foresight to see the merits of a neutral trade policy. (c) In these countries exceptionally high growth with equity could be attributed mostly, if not exclusively, to outward orientation.

The fact is that once the limits of the domestic market were reached, nearly all developing countries had started to shift towards export expansion with the help of a nearly neutral trade policy. Reynolds (1983) recounts that as the limitations of an overly import-substitution bias in industrialization became clear 'some countries moved from the early sixties onwards toward a more outward-looking policy stance, involving trade and exchange rate policies that were more nearly neutral as between export-expansion and import-substituting activities, plus higher interest rates and flexible exchange rates. Notable examples are Brazil, Colombia, Taiwan, Korea, Pakistan, and recently Sri Lanka. The growing efficiency of manufacturing industries in these countries, and their success in export markets, can be traced partly to this policy shift (p. 973). The poor man's second question that still begs an answer is: what was the growth differential attributable to? There is not much unanimity on the answer; but it is clear that their growth performance owed itself to a variety of factors. Thus, even those who insist that export orientation has been the most important factor that contributed to growth concede that outward orientation alone could not have succeeded in achieving these superlative results without the 'development of infrastructure (ports, roads, railroads, electric power, communications), increasing educational attainments, and a number of other policies' [Krueger (1995a), p. 23]. Furthermore, land reforms had created in these countries the preconditions for agricultural growth and for a favourable development of the society free from the stranglehold of the landed aristocracy. Furthermore, their high achievement with respect to literacy and health must have a created, propitious climate for widely shared growth and development [Abramovitz (1992); Adelman (1978); Adelman and Robinson (1989)].

The available cross-country evidence would support the following generalizations: (a) The shift from a less to more balanced import-substituting and export-promoting regimes has been a gradual historical process that inevitably necessitated neutral trade and exchange rate policies. These policies were duly introduced by all the developing countries when the proper time for such policies came. In other words, there is no unique causation here going from these policies to export-promotion regimes. Any statistical relationship here might as well be a spurious one. (b) The shift has not been from import substitution-only regimes to export promotion-only regimes, but from one set of mixed regimes (in which import substitution had a relatively greater weight), to another set of mixed regimes (that gave greater weight to export expansion activities). Each such regime reflected the stage of development reached by the countries that implemented it. (c) The shift from the former to the latter has not been decisive in explaining the growth differential between the East Asian countries and the rest of the developing countries that have been disparagingly labelled as inward-looking countries in the liberalist trade-policy literature.

The chain of causation running from outward orientation to economic growth need not be unique. The reasons are many. The choice of the indicator of openness has not been an unambiguous one. Thus, as Esfahani (1991), and Jung and Marshall (1985) point out, the most frequently cited candidates for measuring the degree of openness (the share of exports in income or its growth rate)—the ones used by Balassa and Associates (1971); Balassa (1978); Feder (1983); Michaely (1977), Easterly (1992) suffer from reverse causality. We then have the bizarre situation that the many empirical studies, having expended immense amount of time, money and energy did not succeed in establishing a firm link between trade policy, trade orientation and growth.[7] The reason is that, as noted above, the chain of causation going unambiguously from export expansion to GDP growth has not been satisfactorily dealt with in these studies. Even more damaging is that the method used to prove the causality relation going from export expansion to growth of output has been plainly wrong. Surprisingly, Krueger, Balassa and others used Spearman's correlation coefficient to prove the chain of causation going from export expansion to output growth. Equally questionable is the practice of using a country's trade policy in a regression. The fact is that the question still begs for a conclusive answer. Frankel and Romer (1999) do seem to address the issue in a more explicit way; but they have had to appeal to rather far-fetched geographical factors to measure the effects of trade on growth.[8] Yet even this somewhat roundabout method does not provide unambiguous guidance on what type of trade policy developing countries should follow because trade policy does not affect trade in the same way as geography does. At any rate, their findings cannot possibly explain relationship between the export performance and the miracle growth of the geographically small countries of East Asia.[9] In other words, their study is not relevant to deciding the liberalist contention that the East Asia proved that export expansion rather than import substitution was the best policy for the developing countries.

In general, the quality of the empirical work done on the openness growth problem has suffered from severe statistical problems: (i) the trade-regime indicator used is typically measured very badly, and is often an endogenous variable itself; (ii) the direction of causality is not always clear, even when a policy variable is used as the trade indicator: government may choose to relax trade restrictions when economic performance is good; (iii) openness in the sense of lack of trade restrictions is often confused with macroeconomic aspects of the policy regime, notably the exchange-rate stance; (iv) the causal mechanisms that link openness to beneficial dynamic effects are rarely laid out carefully and subjected to test themselves; this makes it very difficult for policy conclusions to be drawn [Rodrik (1995), p. 2941].[10]

The real issue here is that there is no simple way to test causality because the amount that countries trade is not exogenously determined. Perhaps, an even more important reason for the failure of the causality tests is that growth is driven by many factors of which export growth would be one.

8.3. (i). Empirical Evidence from Asia and Pacific (1965–2000)

Figure 8.2 suggests that the relationship between the growth of per capita income and the export/GDP ratio is a complex one even in the high-growth Asia and Pacific region, which has been export-oriented as well. It does not lend itself to unambiguous generalizations, such as those examined above. The following points may be noted in this connection.

Firstly, the upper left-hand box shows that the fastest growing China achieved super-miracle growth with a lower-than average export/GDP ratio (20.96 per cent). The same has been the case with South Korea, one of the original miracle growers; and with Thailand, which joined the high-growth club later on. Secondly, some of the fast-growing countries (Vietnam, Hong Kong, Singapore, and Malaysia) have enjoyed high growth rates of exports. Thirdly, it is also true that most of the slower-growing countries (Japan, India, Pakistan, Bangladesh, the Philippines and Nepal) also had lower-than-average export/GDP ratio. Fourthly, there are only two countries (Sri Lanka and Papua New Guinea) where higher-than-average export/GDP ratio and low growth have gone together. This preliminary evidence suggests that there are only six countries in our sample (those located in the upper-left hand and the lower-right hand boxes) where the relationship between export/GDP ratio is tenuous. (b) In the remaining ten countries (those located in the lower left-hand and upper right-hand boxes) the relationship is tight. Thus, counting the number of countries in each group, one can say that the relationship seems to be strong when one talks in (un-weighted) average term, not taking into account the size of the countries. However, this finding does not entitle us to stake out the (liberalist) claim that higher exports cause higher growth of GDP, for the simple reason that the relationship can work both ways. It requires doing some rigorous regression exercises to establish the relationship on a firm empirical basis. This is done in Part VI of this book.

Figure 8.2: Economic Growth and Export–GDP Ratio in Asia and Pacific Region (1965–2000)

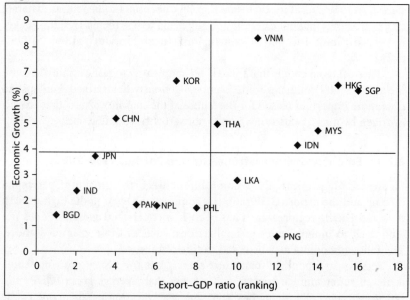

Note: Economic growth is defined as growth rate of GDP per capita. Export–GDP ratio is ranked in ascending order. Average growth rate of GDP per capita for the sample countries is 4.02 per cent for the period 1965–2000. Average for Export–GDP ratio is 20.96 per cent.

◆ Following countries are included in the sample: Bangladesh (BGD), China (CHN), Hong Kong (HKG), India (IND), Nepal (NPL), Indonesia (IDN), Japan (JPN), Papua New Guinea (PNG), Korea (KOR), Malaysia (MYS), Pakistan (PAK), Philippines (PHL), Sri Lanka (LKA), Singapore (SGP), Thailand (THA), and Vietnam (VNM). The data for Taiwan and Fiji was not available.

8.4. RENT-SEEKING, DOMESTIC RESOURCE COSTS AND ECONOMIC GROWTH

Perhaps, one of the most influential liberalist arguments against the traditional development policy has been that the latter led to a severe 'distortion' of relative prices, which, in turn, prevented the market mechanism from issuing the correct signals for an efficient allocation of domestic resources between rival activities and sectors. A large number of the so-called 'path-breaking' studies about the protection regimes prevalent throughout the developing world during 1950 to 1980 have sought to prove that government intervention invariably has led to wasteful 'rent-seeking' and widespread inefficiencies in the external trade sector [Little, Scitovsky and Scott (1970); Krueger (1974); Balassa and Associates (1971)]. Novel computational measures, like the effective protection rates (EPRs) and domestic resource costs (DRCs) were extensively used to estimate the opportunity cost of import substitution in terms of lost output or the loss of foreign exchange, respectively. These formulae have also sought to prove that industries are typically much more protected than the nominal protection rates suggest; and that the protection given to import-substitution activities tends to exceed that accorded to the export-expansion activities; and that protection accorded to the domestic industries has been generally variable. These results have been taken to establish that government-supported industrialization (almost) always discriminates against exports and agriculture and would, *a fortiori*, lower the potential long-run growth of output. Once again, we see the argument that a more efficient dispensation for the developing countries would be one in which agriculture is emphasized more than industries. The use of these measures of protection had at one time become universal—especially before the initiation of the Liberalist Paradigm. But these days one does not hear much about them. What has happened? To some extent, one can argue that once the economies have been restored to the market discipline (courtesy the extensive privatization already done throughout the developing world); there is not much need for EPRs and DRCs. But that begs the question whether privatization has, in fact, restored developing economies to a competitive dispensation. The answer is, of course, in the negative, as the analysis in the next section shows. The reason for virtually abandoning what was once regarded as one of the most fundamental contributions to international trade theory and practice, in fact, lies elsewhere. Many empirical studies show that, contrary to the expectations, the relationship between these measures of protection and the sector-resource allocation pattern has not always been tight. Many attempts have been made to explain away the dissonance between the measures of allocated efficiency and their impact on the growth of output that could be attributed unambiguously to the removal of distortions. For example, it has been shown that a given EPR regime could be consistent with different allocation patterns that corresponded to different nominal tariff structures; the EPRs are essentially static measures of costs while industrialization involves a change of sector-allocations over time; and that the protected sectors might not offer many opportunities for further investment if they already experienced much expansion [Bhagwati and Srinivasan (1979)]. Then there is the additional problem of translating tariff reform measures into the desired structure of EPRs. Thus, suppose that a given tariff reform requires equalizing the effective protection across industries or sectors. Now this result cannot be achieved by simply equalizing nominal protective measures (i.e., nominal tariffs, domestic subsidies) across industries. Or, take the case of reducing the EPRs to promote industrial efficiency. The only way to do it is to reduce nominal tariff. But tariffs will be redundant if quotas are binding; the former, therefore, would not exercise a decisive effect on domestic prices. Thus, with quotas high and binding, reducing tariffs would simply enhance the importer's rent [Naqvi (1966)]. In other words, there is no one-to-one relationship between nominal protection measures and the computed effective protective measures even though the two measures are related to each other. There are complicated ways to translate reductions in nominal tariffs in the effective protective rates but to be of any use, there must be simple ways of introducing such policy changes. There is yet another problem. It is that, notwithstanding the assertions to the contrary, rent seeking does not cease once an import-substitution activity is converted into an export activity. The reason is that such reversal of the policy bias does not come about by market forces, but, as noted above, it takes substantial government intervention to achieve it. The overall incidence of government intervention would most likely not decrease after the policy shift than it was before it. Thus, Onis (1991) shows that in Turkey the shift to export orientation has simply meant that the rent-seekers started running after export subsidies just as they were running after import licenses. The same thing has happened in Pakistan, where the subsidies replaced tariffs and quotas in the 1970s and exercised the same distorting effects on output [Naqvi and Kemal (1991a)].

Yet another factor contributing to the same state of affairs is that most studies trying to prove the superiority of export-expansion to import substitution activities did not correct for the country size or for the changing conditions of world demand in estimating the contribution of export orientation to output [Edwards (1993)]. This practice is obviously inappropriate because the trade share of large countries tends to be lower than that of smaller countries. Furthermore, these studies ignore the historical fact that a country must have reached a minimum level of industrialization and general development before it could take full advantage of export activity [Helleiner (1986)].

8.5. MACROECONOMIC BALANCE AND MICRO-LEVEL ADJUSTMENTS

In evaluating the liberalist development policy a distinction must be made between the need to achieve macroeconomic balance (fiscal rectitude, monetary and exchange rate policies), and the requirements of micro-level structural adjustment (removal of price distortions, minimizing government intervention) programmes. The two, though related, are not the same. It is, therefore, useful to keep these de-equilibrating factors separate for analytical and policy-making purposes. Yet the tendency in the economic profession has been to mix up the two and attribute to the latter the economic difficulties caused by the former. But such ambiguity can be harmful because it amounts to misattributing the economic difficulties brought on by overvalued exchange rates and budgetary deficits to price distortion caused by trade policy. According to this view, 'what eventually drove many import-substituting countries to ruin were not so much micro-economic inefficiencies, but macroeconomic imbalances and the inability to correct them with sufficient speed' [Rodrik (1996), p. 16]. While trade restrictions create microeconomic distortions, large budgetary deficits and overvalued exchange rates could produce truly large macroeconomic imbalances.[11] Conversely, if macroeconomic balance is maintained, then the economy can get along well with some price distortions. This explains, it is argued, why the East Asian regimes that did not let their currencies to be overvalued got away with major price distortions caused by protective trade regimes. The lesson is that, while microeconomic imbalances presumably impose modest losses in terms of lost GDP, but they would not lead to economic instability or to a reduction of the long-run growth of the economy. However, the same is not the case with macroeconomic imbalances, which could be very costly in both these respects.[12] Thus, while large budgetary deficits and grossly overvalued exchange rates must be avoided, the same is not necessarily the case for trade restrictions.[13] This view has merits in so far as it recommends keeping the policy focus on the foreign exchange rates (that they remain realistic) and on observing fiscal rectitude. But there is another view, which maintains that macroeconomic instability is endogenous to a typical import-substitution regime. Bhagwati and Srinivasan (2002) point out, 'there are several cases of macroeconomic stability and absence of outward orientation (India and China), but there are none of successful outward orientation and absence of macroeconomic stability' (p. 180).[14]

There is something to be said on both sides. On the one hand, it is a fact that macroeconomic instability has, to some extent, been endogenous to a policy regime that favours tariff and non-tariff barriers to trade for promoting industrialization. Thus, for instance, overvalued exchange rates and import restrictions have gone together, even though it would be rash to make one the cause of the other. Indeed, the alternative to devaluation has almost always been the use of import restrictions; and a country that sought to maintain overvalued exchange rates in the face of a serious balance-of-payments problem would normally tighten import restrictions (when it does not have sufficient foreign-exchange reserves of its own or it does not receive help under a bailout programme from the IMF). 'Econometric evidence confirms the hypothesis that trade policy tightening and devaluations were substitutes up to 1983'; and that, in general, 'it cannot be concluded that a country that has a flexible exchange-rate regime, or that is willing to devalue when there is a balance-of-payments problem, will necessarily avoid imposing or tightening trade restrictions' [Little, Cooper, Corden, Rajapatirana (1993), p. 273]. Also there have been cases of keeping intact high (protective) import tariffs even those with considerable 'water' in it, i.e. even when redundant, in the sense of not making a net impact on domestic prices—and well past the corrections of the exchange rate overvaluation. Such oddities have been justified mainly for revenue reasons. More paradoxically, high import tariffs have been sustained even when, because of smuggling, they did not produce much revenue as well and when devaluation had taken place [Naqvi and Kemal (1991a)]. Thus, a sensible compromise between these rival points of view is neither to make an over-sharp distinction between macro-and-micro-economic difficulties, nor to regard the one as the cause of the other. What is needed is restoring a sense of balance to policy-making—that is, keeping the exchange rates from getting too overvalued and observing rules of fiscal probity, but at the same time minimizing quantitative import restrictions, except when they are required to protect knowledge-creating import substitution activities or those which are needed to encourage innovation and technological change. Furthermore, many studies referred to in this book as well, warn against exaggerating the real cost of import restrictions. At any rate, much of this debate has lost relevancy because import restrictions (quotas) have either been abolished or scaled down drastically (import tariffs). Furthermore, in most cases exchange rates are now, to a large extent, determined by the market and budgetary deficits now kept within low limits as part of the requirements of the Structural Adjustment Programmes.

8.6. Concluding Remarks

The Liberalist Paradigm has sought to establish its writ in developing countries through a strict implementation of the Structural Adjustment Programmes. They could be regarded as the Siamese Twins, sharing the same vital organs and characteristics. Both wear the same air of Olympian certitude refusing to be separated. They claim to have laid down conditions that are 'just right' for the economic health of the developing countries. To make known their omniscience and put the policy-makers in the developing countries on notice that 'they mean business', the Liberalist Paradigm and the Washington Consensus have claimed to have discovered some infallible universal laws of the economic universe, with its centre in Washington. Such claims must have offended the sensibilities of the developing countries; but, for one reason or another, the undivided unity of their message, which sometimes makes the ridiculous seem sublime by citing high theory to support their outlandish claims, have managed to suffuse throughout the developing world, which has been brought down to its knees by real and imaginary financial crises and the international donors' over-reaction to them. In many cases, the solutions of the crises have tended to make them worse.[15] There is a fair degree of academic and policy consensus that this was indeed the case in the East Asian crisis of 1996–97. But it seems that lessons to be learnt from such instances have not been learnt. For the international donors, it is business as usual, in the darkest hour. Without any doubt, their labours have been crowned with success, in the liberalist sense of the word. They together have brought back the essence, if not the form, of *laissez-faire*; managed a drastic reduction in the role of the government in economic affairs and; caused a substantial increase in the share of private investment in total investment, even when it has meant a net reduction in total investment, slowed down economic growth and increased unemployment. Imbued with missionary zeal, they have implemented their research programme with exemplary thoroughness. Within a decade of its launching in 1980, they have reversed the priorities of a well-entrenched and universally understood traditional development policy. They have substituted efficiency and macroeconomic stability for growth and industrialization, and social progress as the overarching principles of development policy; and have shifted the emphasis of domestic policy in developing countries from achieving fastest possible growth rate, employment creation, distributive equity and poverty reduction to an insistence on 'sustainable' growth, a reduction of budgetary and trade deficits and the inflation rates to the lowest rate (the lower the better), import liberalization, privatization and unification of exchange rates. Through these and other policies (like the liberalization of capital flows across national boundaries), they have sought to impose fiscal and monetary discipline and facilitate integration of national economies into the world economy with despotic zeal that could only be justified if the developing countries were actually under a vicious enemy attack. Yet, the net result of these reformist measures has been inconclusive, at best, if not downright counterproductive.

The fact is that even where the liberalist approach to development policy can claim a modicum of originality—namely, the empirical studies designed to link the reforms of the price-distorting trade policies (the distortion measured in terms of the associated EPRs and DRCs) to the growth of the individual sectors—have suffered from a tendency to make exaggerated claims about their beneficial effects [Pack (1988), p. 344].[16] An even more basic objection to these 'structural' exercises—about which there is nothing structural in the proper sense of the term—, is that they have never shown with the help of a counterfactual that an alternative trade regime with a minimal or no government would have fared any better. Also, it is not generally understood that the private sector might have done at least as badly in this respect as the government presumably did [Edlin and Stiglitz (1992)].

Furthermore, as noted above, a shift from import substitution to export expansion did not signal the end of rent seeking; it simply shifted its focus from the domestic sector to the foreign-trade sector. As a result, 'the benefits of policy reforms remain small in relation to the development objectives, and tend to be linked to economic growth through uncertain and unreliable channels' [Rodrik (1995), p. 2972]. It is, therefore, no wonder, that the Washington Consensus-backed remedies have been greeted with distrust, even disgust, everywhere in the developing world.[17]

NOTES

1. The recommended shift from the promotion of heavy industry to the lighter ones became a major bone of contention between the policy makers in the developing countries and the World Bank. The policy change was recommended because total factor productivity (TFP) was seen to be higher in the latter than in the former. The example of the extraordinary rise of the Korean manufacturing industry over the 1963 to 1979 period has been usually cited in this regard [Dollar and Sokoloff (1990)].

2. The quote in the text relates to the situation existing at the time of British Industrial Revolution; but the same argument has occurred each time the Law of Comparative Advantage mentioned as the regulator of domestic and global resource allocation.

3. The Traditional Development Paradigm recommended such computations to reflect the balanced-growth principle [Chenery (1965)]. Such elaborate computations were used widely in the Communist Soviet Union as well as in the developing countries. These exercises had an entirely beneficial spin off in the form of the collection of the data about almost all sectors of the economy.

4. The liberalist argument is that the 'artificial' subsidization of industry at the cost of agriculture increased poverty and hurt agricultural growth because 'agriculturally extractive and/or trade-restrictive paths to industrialization not only slow growth; they reduce its benefits to the poor' [Lipton and Ravallion (1995), p. 2561]. However, this argument ignores the fact that industrialization draws labour from agriculture and raises agricultural productivity and agricultural wage. Also, a significant part of the increase in wealth in the industrial sector gets spent on agriculture. Both these processes increase agriculture growth and reduce rural poverty.

5. It should, however, be noted that what is classified as higher-than-average inflation rate in the Asia and Pacific Region would be classed as moderate inflation rate in most of the developing countries. Also, of the five countries noted in the text as belonging to the higher-than-average category are located so close to the average line that it could be classed as really belonging to high-growth and low-inflation category (the left-hand top box)

6. Interestingly enough, Little, Scitovsky and Scott (1970), who pioneered many of the liberalists arguments long before these became a standard fare in the literature, had warned that their recommendation for achieving greater export orientation did not amount to the suggestion that, 'a country should export for export's sake' (p. 346). But the arguments in the 1980s and 1990s have strongly supported the thesis that alleged export fetishism of the East Asian economies was responsible for their miraculous growth: 'There was little question but that the shift to the outer-oriented trade strategy was a significant factor in bringing about the spectacular growth of exports, and that in turn had contributed in a major way to the accelerated growth rate of the GNP' [Krueger (1995a), p. 2518]. For an early contrary view of the East Asian miracle, see Findlay (1979).

7. The many (Granger) causality tests done to establish the causality between exports and growth of output have come up with many more cases of the latter having caused the former rather than the other way round [Jung and Marshall (1985), and Esfahani (1991)].

8. Frankel and Romer (1999), cited in the text, provide a rather complicated method of using 'geographic factors as a proxy for identifying the effects of trade on income.' They prove, 'the relation between the geographic component of trade and income suggests that a rise of one percentage point in the ratio of trade to GDP raises income per person by at least one half per cent.' (p. 394) However, even this ingenious method, whose sole claim to fame is its methodological ingenuity, does not settle the issue noted in the text because there are many other influences affecting growth other than exports. The authors, therefore, wisely conclude that although the results of their study 'bolster the case for benefits of trade they do not provide decisive evidence for it.' (p. 395) At any rate, a demonstration of the benefits of trade does not necessarily provide an argument for export orientation, and certainly not for export fetishism.

9. Thus, they find that countries that are geographically bigger (in the sense of having bigger population, size, not being landlocked, having greater access to export outlets) have higher incomes. They conclude that increasing the country size and area by 1 per cent raises income by one-tenth of 1 per cent or more.

10. An additional problem with export fetishism has been its ideological roots: 'in the late 1980s the policy debate on the merits of alternative trade regimes had become confusing and increasingly ideological' [Bradford and Branson (1987); Cooper (1987)].

11. Rodrik (1996) estimates that a 20 per cent increase in import duties will cause a loss of no more than 0.5 per cent of the GDP. Earlier, Diaz-Alejandro and Carlos (1975) faulted Little et al. (1970) for mixing up macroeconomic stabilization with structural adjustment, calling it 'guilt by association'. He pointed out that selective protection and judicious government intervention could produce excellent results within the framework of macroeconomic stability. The same would not be the case if, for instance, macroeconomic stability was restored within the context of budgetary imbalances.

12. A World Bank study concluded: '[Budgetary] deficits are bad for growth' [Easterly, Alfredo, and Schimdt-Hebbel (1994), p. 1].

13. Stiglitz (2003) recounts that the bailout operation in Russia insisted on maintaining an overvalued currency on the grounds that devaluation would cause inflation. As it is, this insistence 'ultimately crushed the [Russian] economy' (p. 135).

14. The same point has been made in Srinivasan, Ramaswami and Bhagwati (2001).

15. Stiglitz (2003) gives many examples of such cases.

16. Many reasons have been given for this lack of correspondence between the reformist policies and their effect on the allocative inefficiency e.g., a given EPR regime may be consistent with many nominal tariff structures and hence may exercise different effects on consumption and production and EPRs are measured in a static context in which no growth of resources occurs [Bhagwati and Srinivasan (1979)]. But these explanations don't inspire much confidence in the desirability of these reforms.

17. It is a testimony to the strong faith in the essential correctness of the Liberalist Paradigm that the implementers of the rather unpopular agenda of the Washington Consensus have been called the 'heroes of the economic profession'—those who faithfully and fearlessly implemented the Washington Consensus in the face of stiff opposition by the populists, who asserted that doing so would be bad politics [Harberger (1993)].

9

The Liberalist Paradigm III:
Its Moral Foundations

This chapter analyses the influence of (libertine) moral values on the formation of the new-fangled liberalist development policy. Ever since Robbins (1935) pronounced economics and ethics as irrevocably divorced, taking a stance of ethical neutrality has become an intellectual fashion.[1] In this frame of thought, rationality is defined as the full and free exercise of the self-interest maximization principle, which is regarded as perfectly consistent with social good. Far from being stigmatized as morally wrong, the exercise of the self-interest is considered as the very acme of rationality. Indeed, it does not permit bending the laws of economics, except rhetorically, to worry about 'emotionally charged' social questions for doing so would be 'irrational'. An effect of this divorce has been to sideline, if not altogether ignore, the foundational questions about the ways and means of accelerating growth of per capita income, promoting equitable distribution of income and arranging poverty reduction. To most people all this would sound confusing and morally unsettling. Yet it looks perfectly natural to those whom deep thought and reflection has convinced of the shining merit of so-called liberalist values.[2] The reason why we must analyze the moral aspects of the Liberalist Paradigm is that just below the surface of moral neutrality, one can clearly discern an inflexible commitment to retaining the status quo, one that must satisfy the 'unanimity principle'. True, such a stance would be extraordinarily conservative; but, liberalists assert, that does not disqualify it as a moral argument.

9.1. INDIVIDUAL LIBERTY, NEGATIVE FREEDOMS AND MINIMUM GOVERNMENT

A strictly procedural moral-rights philosophy informs the Liberalist Paradigm. It is non-consequential in the sense of being independent of the consequences that the exercise of moral rights by a privileged few might entail for the vast majority of the poor and the deprived. This philosophy seeks to provide a moral case for the free markets, to 'go with' the usual positivist efficiency arguments. It adopts the Pareto-optimal principle, which, notwithstanding its quintessentially distributional-neutrality, is regarded as a valid criterion for judging the moral worth of any changes in economic and social arrangements. The moral-rights philosophy emphasizes the absolute priority of individual liberty to own private property, to the exclusion of all other social objectives of development policy—for instance, the individual's right to a minimum of sustenance. As a logical corollary of the individual's unlimited right to own private property, the state's right to interfere with the individual's decision to own what has been acquired through 'legitimate' means, i.e. those sanctioned by laws, however unjust, that govern the processes of acquisition and exchange is seen as minimal, if any. In particular, the state is not permitted to perform any redistributive role, even in times of a devastating, heart-rending famine, because that would amount to trampling over individual's freedom. There is also no room in this philosophy for such redistributive measures like land reforms because the quest for egalitarianism will make a free society slip down an inclined plane at the bottom of which lies only one thing: totalitarianism. The freedom-giving free markets, which let people act in their best interests, must, therefore, be jealously safeguarded against all state encroachments.

9.1. (i). The Moral Arguments for Markets

The efficiency argument for unfettered markets (that market solutions are un-improvable) has a well-defined and elegantly self-serving moral counterpart as well. It holds that free markets alone prevent the violation of individual's moral rights. They depict a mutually advantageous arrangement, not threatened by significant inter-class conflicts and trade-offs. On the other hand, individual rights are less than secure in every other regime in which the government is involved. Since only unfettered markets provide a hospitable environment for the exercise of individual moral rights, it is argued, these must be the most preferred social and economic arrangements, regardless of what they do to the distribution of income and wealth and/or to the incidence of poverty. It may be noted that capitalism has been primarily justified on these very grounds: that it offers the best guarantees against arbitrary government intrusion in the individual's 'private domain' [Friedman (1962); Hayek (1960)]. Any proof that it also increases the wealth of nations has been a helpful, but not decisive, argument in its favour. Buchanan (1985) would prefer unfettered markets because these alone represent voluntary arrangements between individuals. By the same token, involuntary arrangements (defined as those which involve state intervention) are held inferior, partly because notwithstanding the rhetoric to maximize social welfare, governments, in fact, end up maximizing the welfare of the lobbies of vested interests. The job of the government is, therefore, simply to create a legal infrastructure within which the liberty-preserving markets could function freely, guided by little else than individual cupidity and greed and the lure of private profits. It is, therefore, not surprising that the Liberalist Paradigm has aimed primarily to minimize the incidence of government intervention in domestic and international markets, with the explicit or implicit understanding that such efforts are their own reward. In other words, it judges the worth of development policies by the contribution they make to the enhancement of individual liberty, not by their manifest consequences for growth, employment, distributive justice and poverty reduction, however distasteful they might be to most people whose moral sensibilities have not been benumbed by an overdose of liberalist philosophy. The only requirement is that the contemplated reforms satisfy the 'unanimity' and 'impartiality' of the procedures for the free exercise of individual freedom and for ensuring that individuals fulfil their contractual obligations.

9.1. (ii). The Minimalist Government

An obvious corollary of the moral-rights philosophy is that government intervention is bad, especially when it distorts the relative price structure; and that it can be justified only if it makes effective laws to protect private property and preserve law and order, so as to leave utility maximizing individuals effectively in charge of the decisions and choices they make voluntarily. Beyond this rather carefully defined limited sphere, government intervention, by its very chemistry, must be inherently inefficient and morally indefensible [Hayek (1960)]. In this watertight individualistic model, there is no room, by definition, for the government to do anything better than to remove itself from the individual's private domain and make room for unfettered markets. On the other hand, unfettered markets, in their mysterious and inscrutable ways that the human mind cannot easily comprehend, achieve insensibly but surely the ends that are economically efficient and morally acceptable to those who believe in the libertine philosophy. Similarly motivated, Nozick (1974) reached even more uncompromising conclusions. He asserted the inviolability of moral rights on the grounds that individuals enjoy virtually unlimited rights to own private property, including those in the means of production, which they come to possess by the morally just procedures of 'initial acquisition' and 'transfer'. Once these essentially legal procedures are satisfied, any interference with the results of voluntary exchange must end up violating individual moral rights and be unjust for that reason.[3] In particular, any government intervention to redistribute ('pattern') income and wealth directly (say, by land reforms), or indirectly (through progressive taxation) would constitute an unacceptable violation of the individual's moral rights because, 'from the point of view of entitlement theory, redistribution is a serious matter indeed; involving as it does the violation of individual rights' (p. 35). In other words, any state intervention to change the structure of legally acquired property rights is unjust and morally indefensible. Indeed, the argument against government intervention is a general one: it declares all actions to achieve certain specified end-states and patterns of holdings as unjust on the ground that they would necessitate, 'an unacceptable degree of disruptions of individual holdings to preserve those end-states or patterns of distribution' [Nozick (1974), pp. 160–164]. Thus, at least at a theoretical level, if not in practice, making even one hairbreadth of deviation from the straight path of free-markets, causing one shadow of (government-induced) impurity in the light of individual freedom would be condemned as a morally indefensible economic heresy.

9.1. (iii). 'Negative Freedoms'

The only morally correct role for the state is, therefore, no more than a residual one—that is, to safeguard the 'negative freedoms' of the individuals from the violation of moral rights; but, strange as it might sound to a 'normal' person, it is not allowed to protect them against their violation by 'other' individuals. In general, 'individuals have rights and there are things no person or group can do to them (without violating their rights)' [(Nozick (1974), p. ix]. These moral rights constitute side-constraints on actions, i.e. those which must be satisfied in any scheme for social change. Thus, a sufficient argument for unfettered markets is that they adequately, but inexpensively, safeguard negative individual freedoms from the (arbitrary) intrusion of the state in individual's private domain. It follows that, once the government has taken appropriate measures to prevent the violation of individual's moral rights it should leave the efficient working of the economy to the rational that is, self-interested individuals who know what is best for them.

Needless to state, this characterization of a real-life government—namely, that it could do nothing that is socially right—must be an immense exaggeration. It can be shown that there are important areas where centralization of decision-making on economic matters would dominate decentralization. This is especially the case, 'when decisions are so interdependent that they cannot be delegated; and it can also help efficiency by making recalcitrant people participate in schemes that benefit society in general' [Farrell (1987), p. 121]. Furthermore, it is much too restrictive to claim that the economic and political freedoms of individuals can best be safeguarded only in societies with unfettered markets and where the government has been cut down to a Lilliputian size. The fact is that there are welfare states where both the economic and political rights of the individuals have been well-safeguarded. Conversely, most capitalist democracies do not always treat individual economic rights at par with political rights.[4] Undeterred by such considerations that only faint-hearted individuals harbour, libertarianism would pillory state intervention on seemingly 'moral' grounds.

9.1. (iv). The 'Morality' of the Pareto-Optimality Rule

Unlike its unalloyed advocacy for political individual rights on moral grounds, the liberalist support to the individual economic rights wears thin rather quickly. For instance, the rights of the poor to a minimum of economic sustenance are not generally recognized in the same way as the rights to private property of the rich are. The fact is that when it comes to making egalitarian social change, democracies sometimes degenerate into the rich person's despotism. The degeneration process is sustained not just through the power of the purse but also by intellectual trickery done in the name of scientific rectitude. Thus, the libertarians require that steps taken to meet individual's economic rights must be efficient and morally uncontroversial, i.e. they satisfy the Pareto-optimality rule of efficient resource allocation.[5] This stance is made logically tight by the further claim that whatever is efficient is also morally just. Put together, these stipulations render social change meaningless. Let us follow this line of argument in some detail.

A libertarian would argue that if the advantages for some can be secured without disadvantaging others, or if there are no alternative states of the economy in which all could gain, or at least one person can be made better off and no one worse off, how could anyone object to its moral superiority? After all, no one would complain about a presumably morally uncontroversial move from a state in which no one could be made better off without making someone worse off to a state in which someone could be made better off without making anyone worse off [Allen Buchanan (1985)].[6] Furthermore, it is argued, that since the very best state of the economy must at least be Pareto-optimal and in competitive equilibrium, such a move should be mutually advantageous (in the sense of not failing to let go any opportunity for mutual advantage). Thus, in the domain of definitions though not substantively, the quintessentially efficient Pareto rule also becomes a moral rule—though an empty one at that.

The rather skimpy reformative credentials of the Pareto rule derive from the Second Fundamental Theorem of Welfare Economics, which stipulates that given a redistribution of initial individual property holding, every Pareto-optimal state is also in competitive equilibrium. But, the Pareto largesse is more apparent than real because given self-interested individual behaviour, no substantial egalitarian results can possibly be extracted out of it. The reason is that, as Sen (1987) points out, there is no 'mechanism by which people have the incentive to reveal the information on the basis of which the choice among Pareto-optimal states could be made and the appropriate distribution could be fixed'. Furthermore, the distributive mechanism that Second Welfare Theorem suggests—namely, making lump-sum transfer of resources from the potential gainers to compensate the potential losers in acts of exchange—is no better than a neo-classical sleight of hand. Graff (1990) pointed out the utter 'emptiness' of the rule: 'the possibility of compensation means very little unless the compensation is actually carried out'.[7] In the pusillanimous neo-classical tradition, which regards shadows of reality as more substantial than the reality itself, the Theorem is not programmed to solve any significant problems of distributive justice or equity.

9.2. The Sanctity of Private Property and Egalitarianism

A string of brilliant contributions have aimed at showing that market processes can reproduce a situation that, besides being efficient, satisfies the dictates of equity as well. Buchanan and Stubblebine (1962) demonstrated that if property rights are clearly defined and freely exchanged, then within a game-theoretic framework (though not in reality), a bargaining process could produce an equitable initial distribution of private property rights. But, it should not take too much wisdom to understand that the property rights can never be perfectly and clearly defined, if only because significant transaction costs will be inevitably involved in settling rival claims to property rights even in developed economies. The situation is made much more difficult in the developing countries where, in the absence of effective contract laws, rules, and an established tradition of business morality, transaction costs are likely to be strictly non-zero. Some of these transaction costs will have to be incurred to keep the free riders out. But in such cases, the familiar externality scenario that renders the competitive market solution inoperative would resurface [Furubotn and Pejovich (1972)]. Also, Arrow (1979) showed that such favourable outcomes (i.e., producing efficient and equitable solutions) depended on the (un-stated) assumption that the players in a cooperative game knew each other's pay-off (utility, profit etc.) as a function of the strategies played. But the existence of such knowledge is inconsistent with the basic rules of competitive markets.

9.3. Concluding Remarks

The preceding analysis suggests that one should not be surprised at the adverse economic and social consequences of the implementation of the Liberalist Paradigm—at first in the West and then in the developing countries. At least here intentions and actions point in the same direction, leaving little room for 'unintended consequences' that reportedly issue forth from every intended action. Armed with the liberalist logic, well established welfare states were pulled down in the 1970s in most OECD countries; and, for the same reasons, the emphasis of public policy has shifted there from achieving full employment and high growth to the maintenance of a low rate of inflation (the lower the better). This was to be achieved by contract-based monetary and fiscal policies, and through privatization of state-owned enterprises (SOEs). The inevitable consequences of the paradigmatic shift in public policy were to slacken the growth rates, catapult the unemployment rate to 10 per cent or more, as compared with the 3 per cent or so in the early post-war period, to worsen the distribution of income and wealth and increase poverty. It would have been more reasonable to expect that liberalists, having learned their lessons in the West, would not implement them in the developing countries where the social structures are much too fragile to withstand the stress of low growth and high unemployment rates and because they could not afford to finance the elaborate safety nets (unemployment benefits etc.) that mollified somewhat the adversities of high unemployment rates in the OECD countries. And yet these programmes have been implemented with frightening speed in the developing countries with an ever-greater confidence in their innate beneficence, unmindful that they might extinguish poor people's longing for a better tomorrow.

Many perfectly plausible explanations can be given. For instance, it could be maintained that the liberalist policies were expected to help growth, distributive justice and poverty reduction; but that such savoury consequences could not materialize. If this were indeed the case, it would be extraordinarily naïve to entertain such a forlorn hope because from the womb of liberalist reformism nothing progressive could ever be born. An alternative explanation could be that an essentially coercive implementation of the Liberalist Paradigm in the developing countries was deliberately designed as a political and social cover for the exercise of corporate influence and authority [Galbraith (1991); Stiglitz (2003)]. There are grounds for subscribing to either of these points of view.[8] This book rather takes a more charitable view of the ill-concealed liberalist disinterestedness in the resolution of vital development issues in the developing countries. It is that the liberalist ideas about development success might have coloured to a large extent their vision of the reality in the developing countries. Thus, subscribing to the logic of the Liberalist Paradigm, a well-intentioned libertarian would not be as much intellectually inclined to think about human suffering or unhappiness as she/he would about the problems of enforcing rules for guaranteeing individual liberty. By the same logic, she/he would still cast a vote for market arrangements that signify individual freedom when pressed to do something tangible about egalitarian issues. It would also not be illogical in this frame of thought to argue that government intervention is not good, however efficiently implemented. The fact that certain attitudes and policies flow logically from the premises of the Liberalist Paradigm, need not justify subscribing to it, knowing full well its adverse consequences in the developing countries. Similarly, it does not exonerate one of holding views, which are manifestly wrong.

Notes

1. Robbins (1935) laid down: 'it does not seem possible to associate the two studies [ethics and economics] in any form but mere juxtaposition' (p. 148).
2. In the preface to his important work, Nozick (1974) himself admits to a certain sense of unease about a kind of moral repulsion that this kind of thinking evokes in human hearts; but that he became convinced of the validity of this way of thinking as he thought more 'systematically' about these issues.
3. Nozick (1974) explicitly lays down the outlines of the libertarian theory of justice in property [holdings]: 'The holdings of a person are just if he is entitled to them by the principles of justice in acquisition and transfer, or by the principle of rectification of justice (as specified by the first two principles). If each person's holdings are just, then the total set is just' (p. 153).
4. Allen Buchanan (1985) cites the example of the United States as a capitalistic country where the political rights of minorities (e.g., blacks) are not adequately safeguarded; and of the Scandinavian countries where welfare (and a fairly intrusive) state has coexisted with an excellent record of political rights.
5. As is well known, a situation is Pareto optimal if once it is reached no further Pareto-improvement in it is possible (which is equivalent to saying that not everyone's utility could be raised by a change in a Pareto-optimal state; or, that there is no state of the economy that is Pareto superior to it). It is now widely understood that the rule is not helpful at all in resolving distributive issues (because it would not recognize any conflicts of interest, say between the rich and the poor). And yet the liberalists regard it as morally correct.
6. See also Feldman (1991) for a concise statement of the Two Fundamental Theorems of Welfare Economics. .
7. Graff (1990) puts the same point more emphatically at another place in the same article: 'What does it help to say that, although several men will starve, the cost to the society is low, because they could be given sufficient food to prevent their starving (p. 254)?
8. Stiglitz (2003) gives many examples of public policy in the US pandering to corporate greed. Thus, in 1993, on the question of introducing capital market reforms in South Korea, which, for decades had achieved economic prosperity without the help of foreign capital, the decision to push Korea to open up was eventually taken, overruling the evidence presented by the Council of Economic Advisers to the effect that the US national interest would not be hurt if Korea did not follow open-up policy. The decision to push Korea against their national interests was still taken to please the corporate interests in the US (pp. 102–104). Juhasz (2006) gives many examples to show that the American emphasis on free trade has essentially served the interests of a handful of corporations—especially Betchel, Chevron, Halliburton, Lockheed Martin.

Part IV

The Anti-Liberalist Consensus

10

The Anti-Liberalist Consensus I:
Its Genesis

When the Liberalist Paradigm started making the waves in policy-making circles in the 1980s, the strongest criticism of its basic postulates came from a respectable body of contrary ideas. These ideas have been cobbled together in this book under the amorphous, but somewhat nihilistic title, Anti-Liberalist Consensus, because they are united in their opposition to the Liberalist Paradigm, whatever else they say.[1] The Consensus has effectively challenged the liberalist claims about universal market success, minimal government and *laissez-faire*; and emphasized the necessity for Pareto-improving state intervention in a variety of situations, some of which the classical literature on market failure did not envisage. It also discredited the liberalists anti-egalitarian agenda on both economic and moral grounds. On the other hand, it confirmed the quintessential validity of some of the 'heretical' hypotheses of the Traditional Development Paradigm (e.g., the Structural Transformation, the Big-Push, and the Dynamic Comparative Advantage). What is most extraordinary about the coexistence of the equally powerful liberalist and anti-liberalist currents of thought is their seeming lack of convergence with each other. Here too one finds an example of interacting contradictions within the heart of neo-classical economics. A significant merit of the Anti-Liberalist ideas is that they are theoretically sound and have received support from real-world experience with privatization, trade liberalization and the revisionist view of the East Asian miracle. This and the next two chapters attempt to capture the highlights of a large and diverse debate, which has given a new sense of direction to neo-classical economics and brought it nearer to the reality in the developing countries.[2] At the same time, it has taken the shine off the evangelical market-only rhetoric—the unabashed deification of the free domestic and international markets and the uncontrolled demonizing of the government—in the academic circles, even though they continue to hold the international donors in thrall. We also bring out some obvious implications of the Anti-Liberalist Consensus for development policy.

10.1. THE 'IMPERFECT INFORMATION PARADIGM'

The first element of the Anti-Liberalist Consensus is a forceful refutation of the Arrow-Debreu (A-D) neo-classical model, which sought to prove the existence of an idealized model of universal market success. Within the limits of its assumptions, A-D model has been a great achievement. The objectionable part, however, is that the Liberalist Paradigm has extended the idealized outcomes of the model to real-life situations in the ill-ordered developing economies, on the assumption that what can be shown as valid within the framework of a model will also hold in the real world—something which seldom, if ever, is true. What has greatly reduced the legitimacy of the liberalist application of the model (indeed, has made a mockery of it) is that the model itself has been successfully challenged by the so-called Imperfect Information Paradigm, which aims to modify the Arrow-Debreu (A-D) neo-classical paradigm by showing the extreme unrealism of its central assumptions—namely, market prices contain all the information required for the efficient functioning of a competitive market economy, and that such information is costless and perfect.[3] It has shown that the principal results of the A-D model do not hold once these assumptions are relaxed. To repair the relevance deficit of the A-D model, it has highlighted such real-world phenomena as incomplete markets, asymmetric information, moral hazard, strategic behaviour, principal-agency syndrome, dynamic external economies, and multiple equilibria etc. In particular, it proves that the celebrated 'un-improvability' results (i.e., market solutions are Pareto optimal so that their efficiency cannot be improved upon by government intervention) will not hold once it is explicitly recognized that markets are generally incomplete and information costly. Instead, the free-market solutions would then almost always be Pareto-inefficient [Stiglitz (1986); Rothschild and Stiglitz (1976)]. On the rather reasonable assumption that it has at least as much information as the private sector does, and that it has the incentive and the inclination to implement socially desirable policies, the government can almost always affect Pareto improvements. Yet another important contribution here is to show that, contrary to the implications of the A-D model (which regards all unemployment as voluntary that can be eliminated by sufficiently lowering the wage rate), the persistence of unemployment and low wage testify to the Pareto-inefficiency of (free) market economies.[4] These formulations show that, 'market economies with search and efficiency wages are, in general, not constrained Pareto-efficient' The implication is that there *is* scope for welfare-raising interventions—those which can increase employment and wages [Greenwald and Stiglitz (1988), p. 352].[5] These findings provide a powerful argument for government intervention that can make everyone better off (or, which is the same thing, to make at least one person better off without making anyone worse off) and induce egalitarian change in the distribution of income between labour and capital. The latter implication follows from the finding that, contrary to what the A-D model predicts, market-clearing wages and the unemployment rate apparently associated with it are not Pareto-efficient. A fundamental policy implication of this result is that unemployment is not a sign of the efficiency of the markets nor is high wage the cause of it. The government cannot sit back and watch the efficient working of the labour market to create the requisite amount of employment, by pushing the wage down to the market-clearing level. Quite the contrary; the government intervention aimed at enhancing wages to the efficiency level and increasing employment can indeed be welfare-raising. A non-trivial solution in all such cases is to design state interventions that will succeed in making the socially desired Pareto-improvements in terms of employment creation and raising the wage rate.

Imperfections of the Market for Knowledge and Information: Perhaps, the strongest case for government intervention occurs in cases where the markets are most imperfect—namely, with respect to knowledge and information, both of which are essentially public goods. These areas are most crucial for enhancing the growth possibilities of the developing countries. In these cases, private investors will have hard time appropriating all the benefits flowing from knowledge creation, acquisition and transfer. That being the case, the private supply of these 'goods' will be less than optimal. It has been pointed out that such imperfections (and the associated market failures) are universal. But their incidence would be greater in the developing countries, partly because the non-market institutions designed to cure these imperfections are also much weaker there [Stiglitz (1989b)].[6] Once the costly nature of information is taken into account, it would no longer be legitimate to compare the information economy that markets reportedly make possible with the information-intensive nature of government intervention. This is because gathering the required information will be at least as costly for the private sector as it is for the government.[7] The assertion that markets typically use up less information than the government normally does not appear to be an empirically verifiable proposition, especially because the state typically handles projects that involve considerations of public benefits, which require a lot more information than the private sector can buy or use up. Likewise, once it is conceded that with costly information, incomplete markets, and inadequate price signals Pareto-optimal situations would normally be inefficient, it would be illegitimate to dismiss state intervention in real-life situations on the grounds that it would make the situation worse with respect to efficiency. In particular, there is no logical basis for the oft-repeated argument that one should go for the market-based solutions because the inefficiencies of the markets are relatively small and those of the government big.[8] Indeed, a stronger statement is possible: it is that market solutions can almost always be improved upon by informed and socially motivated state intervention.[9] This is so because the government's role has historically not been limited just to correcting market failures, but it has been decisive in dealing with cases where the requirements of growth must be combined with the imperatives of social justice. Of course, it does not mean that any amount of state intervention is justified; what it does imply is that the state must not be regarded as innately counterproductive, much less a social abomination that the liberalists make it.

10.2. The Limits of the Coase Theorem

In this context, it is of interest to note that recent research has discredited not just the A-D model but also a weaker statement of it due to Coase. What the Coase Theorem says is that even if the markets are not normally complete and competitive, an efficient outcome is still possible if nothing obstructs bargaining between individuals.[10] Or to put it positively, efficient outcomes can be achieved so long as people are allowed to bargain their way to an optimal outcome and if no mutually beneficial bargain is missed. What with the standard obstacles to market efficiency—the existence of monopoly or of a public good—the Coase Theorem proves that they can be overcome as long as the bargaining option is open to individuals and the private property rights are well-defined [Calabresi (1968)]. This result underlies much of the liberalist thinking on development policy. But these assertions are subject to some important qualifications, which should be noted in evaluating the policy relevance of the Coase Theorem.

The Decentralization Results: It may be noted that the liberalist case for unfettered markets essentially rests on Hayek's assertion that they alone can ensure the decentralization result.[11] It has been asserted that the superiority of the market over the government primarily rests on the most efficient use it enables the society to make of the private information—which, typically, only an individual possesses while others do not know about it.[12] Such information, it has been argued, is not available in a concentrated form such that a central authority can make use of it; but solely as dispersed bits of incomplete knowledge that different individuals possess. However, the demonstration that individuals possess private information is not necessarily an argument against government intervention. The reason is that a situation in which people come to enter mutually beneficial contracts (voluntarily) knowing their 'private information' a first-best outcome may not be attainable. In such situations the individuals may have no incentive to enter into such contracts. Rather they would walk away from them [Myerson and Satterthwaite (1983); Farrell (1987)]. An implication of this result is that, contrary to what

Hayek asserts, the state may do a better job of making individuals reveal their private information. It is also better placed in such situations to use its coercive powers to make people participate in an efficiency-enhancing contract.[13] The only condition in which the markets can do the job better than the government is when everyone knows about everyone else's private information—or when there is no private information. But when this is the case the Coase Theorem ceases to be interesting. Also, in that case the government can do the job equally well.[14]

Coase Theorem and Privatization: A rather outlandish, indeed illegitimate application of the Coase Theorem is that it also proves the innate efficiency of privatization. To understand why such extension is illegitimate, let us look at the development problem as one of undertaking a project or a collection of projects that are beneficial to the society as a whole so that it pays to provide inducements to the individuals to participate in such schemes. The result is that 'central authority helps when decisions are so interdependent that they cannot be delegated; and [when the problem is to make] recalcitrant people participate in schemes that benefit society in general' [Farrell (1987), p. 121]. In such cases, which occur quite commonly in developing countries, the Coase Theorem cannot be used as a blanket endorsement of privatization. Indeed, its basic assumptions are so utterly unrealistic (e.g., zero transaction costs and perfect information) that no one should be invoking it in support of the privatization, even in specific cases. Even more unwarranted is the generalization of the Coase Theorem that privatization done in a sustained fashion generates its own support by the beneficiaries of privatization [Shleifer and Vishny (1999)]. The fact is that privatization is more likely to create oligarchies that obstruct a democratic set up in which they are likely to lose public support. Indeed, many empirical studies show that this has been the standard outcome. At any rate, the point is that privatization does not necessarily mean a net enhancement in industrial efficiency. Sappington and Stiglitz (1987) and Stiglitz (1989a) have conclusively shown that there is no a priori case for privatization. Furthermore, the incidence of rent-seeking behaviour and 'fraud' is no less, if not more, in the private sector [Bebchuck, Fried and Walker (2002); Darby and Karni (1973)].

Specification of Private Property Rights: A more fundamental problem with the Coase Theorem is that when bargaining is done with incomplete information negotiations will not assuredly lead to efficiency result [Samuelson (1985)]. That being the case, there is not much justification for citing Coase Theorem in support of the specification of private property rights, which the liberalists generally make a linchpin of their so-called reformative agenda. Furthermore, even when it is possible to do so, it may not be the most desirable thing to do. To illustrate, if, in a feudal system, the existing property rights of landlords are more precisely defined, it would simply institutionalize the inequalities of income and wealth in the rural areas. And in so far as smaller farms are more productive than small farms, this step would also slow down agricultural development by dispossessing the peasant-cultivators of the land they cultivated for several generations [Binswanger et al. (1995)].

The 'Private Information' and Non-Minimal Government: It may be noted that the validity of the Coase Theorem depends crucially on the possibility of striking all the mutually beneficial bargains to arrive at the optimal outcome. However, this result is not as robust as it appears on first sight. The reason is that such bargains cannot be struck if people come to the bargaining table with private information. In this case no arrangement exists that will lead them to trade voluntarily to arrive at an efficient outcome. In such circumstances, the problem is to provide the necessary incentive to parties to the bargain to reveal their private information. However, this is also a problem that the government would be better placed to resolve. On the other hand, if people do not have 'private information, then too it is most likely that voluntary bargaining would be dominated by a centralized decision-making body'. As if to make life more difficult for the Coase Theorem, in this case, the specification of private property rights and bargaining cannot by themselves produce efficient solutions [Laffont and Maskin (1982)].

Mechanism Design and Coase Theorem: Yet another problem with the Coase Theorem is that in case people have private information they may not reveal it for fear that it might be used against them. For instance, people strongly prefer a project when they expect that they will be taxed less than the benefits that will accrue to them. Indeed, in this case, they are likely to exaggerate their preference for the project in question; but those who expect the opposite are likely to pretend that they do not like the project to be undertaken at all. In such situations voluntary bargaining will not work because it takes some mechanism design to make people reveal private information when they know how it will be used.[15] This process becomes easier (more efficient) when the holders of private information about some project that is beneficial to them but not necessarily to others can be induced to make side-payments for the expected externality that they create to demonstrate their willingness that a specific project is undertaken. In such a case, decentralized bargaining is inefficient; but centralized decision-making can design an expected-externality scheme that causes such projects to be undertaken [Farrell (1987)].[16]

10.3. BALANCED GROWTH ONCE AGAIN

The second foundational contribution of the Anti-Liberalist Consensus is to have revived interest in the validity of the government-sponsored import-substituting industrialization. The Traditional Development Paradigm regarded it as an integral part of the development process, but the Liberalist Paradigm consigned it to the heap of the unhelpful ideas on the grounds that it was innately inefficient and one of the principal sources of the economic misfortunes of the developing countries.

10.3. (i). The Validation of the Big-Push Hypothesis

In a seminal contribution, made in the neo-classical tradition, Murphy, Shleifer, and Vishny (1989a,b) clarify the basic mechanisms that generate a demand for industrialization and sustain it as part of the balanced-growth scenario.[17] Their point is that, since international trade is neither costless nor free of constraints, the primary source of economic growth in a developing country is an increase in the domestic demand for industrialization and a progressive substitution of increasing-scale technologies for the pre-industrialization constant-returns-to-scale technologies that it inevitably entails. True, the demand for industrialization can also flow, as it sometimes does, from an export boom or an autonomous increase in agricultural productivity, but it gets internalized only by an expansion of the size of the domestic market that comes about by the acts of coordinated investment across industries. Furthermore, this scenario of strategically placed acts of investment can be initiated and sustained only by active government intervention. The basic reasoning involved here is as follows. A common characteristic of a typical developing country is that it can basically sustain 'multiple equilibria', one without industrialization and the other with industrialization. Since the former is inefficient, the latter will be Pareto-superior to it, making an opening for government intervention. However, multiple equilibria cannot exist if a firm's profits are the only link between it and other firms that contemplate making similar investment. When this is the case, there are only two possibilities worth the worry of a Prince of Denmark: to industrialize or not to industrialize. It may seem that the option to industrialize will be exercised when firms make profits and other firms factor this fact in making their investment decision. But firms will definitely not industrialize when one firm makes a loss, because in that case the profitability of other firms also gets reduced. In either case, there is no argument for a Big-Push involving the government. The case for a Big-Push industrialization strategy rests on the possibility that the link between the profits made by a firm and its contribution to the demand for the products of the other sectors can be broken by government intervention. There are many possibilities here, two of which are basic to the development process.

(1) The productivity gain from the adoption of the increasing-returns technology is greater than the compensating differential that must be paid to

labour in order to make her/him indifferent between being employed in firms using the constant-returns technology and those using the increasing-returns technology. The extra wage that is paid to entice labour to move to the latter rather than sticking with the former is the source for the additional demand for industrialization and for it being a net producer of wealth. Since private firms would not normally factor in their investment decisions the contribution they make by this means to the demand for the other firm's products they will tend to stick with the inefficient no-industrialization option. The incentive to move out of this inefficient equilibrium to a more efficient and higher-income equilibrium must be created by a government subsidy to industrialization. But the need for government intervention does not end once industrialization gets going. This is because the process must also be made self-sustaining by overcoming the problem of inadequate market size that prevents a profit-maximizing firm from adopting increasing-returns technologies. This is the problem of the existence of strategic complementarities between industries in relation to the relatively small size of the domestic market at the initial stages of economic development that can be resolved by taking advantage of the demand spillover between them. Obviously, an assurance problem is involved here: a profit-maximizing firm would undertake modernization if it were assured that others would do the same. This assurance comes handy in the form of a government-sponsored coordinated programme of industrialization of large enough size, which internalizes the economies of scale of industrialization.

(2) The Big-Push hypothesis scores high as the most economical alternative in all situations where the demand spillover between sectors are important and the 'industrialized firms capture only a fraction of the total contribution of their investment to the profits of other industrializing firms'. It follows that 'Simultaneous industrialization of many sectors can be self-sustaining even if no sector could break even industrializing alone' [Murphy, Shleifer and Vishny, (1989b), pp. 1004 and 1024 respectively]. This option is most compelling when a fixed-cost infrastructure must be built, the cost of which can be covered only if there is actual demand for it by its potential users. It is also the case when the existence of multiple equilibria (and of the pre-industrialization equilibrium being Pareto inefficient) is the obvious possibility because industrialization would most emphatically bring down the total cost of production of other sectors. In this case the coordination problems are most severe because infrastructure serves many sectors simultaneously. In this case also it will not be enough to pay subsidy on such investment to the private investor. It, therefore, follows that, depending on the market size, 'a coordinated investment programme can achieve industrialization of each sector at a lower explicit cost in terms of temporary tariffs and subsidies than a country that industrializes piecemeal' (p. 1025).

The point here is that Pareto improvements can be most confidently made if such socially profitable investments are made an integral part of a comprehensive state-sponsored programme of industrialization.

It has been objected that in situations like the ones envisaged above, it would pay the producers to take advantage of the wider international market. That being the case, it is argued, the balanced-growth nature of industrialization would be an argument for free trade rather than for government intervention, because the latter is generally regarded as an impediment to trade [Rodrik (1995), p. 2953]. However, as Bardhan (1995) points out, such objections usually underestimate the importance of the domestic market even in an open economy. These markets are supported by a chain of non-traded support services and infrastructure and financial, communication and distributions channels, which are crucially important in exploiting the potential economies of scale. Indeed, a lot of this infrastructure will not be built if the entrepreneur's expectations are not coordinated around high future investment—that is, if there are not enough users of these services. It is this coordination failure of the free markets that the government must rectify by encouraging simultaneous industrialization, in the manner suggested by the Big-Push hypothesis.

10.4. *Laissez-Faire* and New International Trade Theory

Yet another element of the Anti-Liberalist Consensus is the set of studies that question the inevitability of the beneficial effects of trade and capital flows, *via* a diffusion of technological knowledge, on the long-run growth of the trading countries. These beneficial effects are assumed to work by enhancing expenditure and the productivity of the R&D sector that are subject to increasing returns to scale and by saving on the duplication of expenditure on similar types of R&D activities that the trading countries normally incur and by freeing up resources of each country for undertaking the production of *new* products, which then increase the beneficial effects of international trade and investment on a country's development [Rivera-Batiz and Romer (1991); Grossman and Helpman (1991)]. However, there are important circumstances when international trade and investment can be detrimental for the developing countries. An important consideration in this context is the technological superiority of the developed countries that is basically traceable to their greater capability of learning by doing and 'learning to learn'. But since both these processes are highly localized, the productivity-enhancing spillover from them to the developing countries would be severely limited [Stiglitz (1987)]. That being the case, the productivity differential, insofar as it depended on learning-by-doing and a greater investment in R&D expenditure, between the developed countries would grow in a regime of *laissez-faire.* The developed countries with their bigger initial stock of capital and technological know-how are likely to end up by capturing the lion's share of the world market. Correspondingly, the developing countries will be unable to take full advantage of technological development precisely because they are usually imitators rather than the innovators of new products. The cumulative effect of these asymmetrical developments on the developing countries may 'drive [them] to specialize in production rather than research, and within the production from high-tech products to traditional, possibly stagnant, industries which use its relatively plentiful supply of unskilled workers—thus slowing innovation and growth. For the lagging country isolation would have been more advantageous for the pace of innovation' [Bardhan (1995), p. 2987]. Insofar as these trends cause a reverse flow of capital from the developing to the developed country, it would solidify, rather than weaken, the latter's superiority with respect to its higher initial average stock of knowledge capital [Lucas (1990)]. In the event of free trade, therefore, the developing countries might under-invest in R&D (a kind of market failure imposed on them by the developed countries' superiority of knowledge) because the investors there would normally expect making a loss on their knowledge-creating activities.

10.5. PRIVATIZATION OF THE STATE-OWNED ENTERPRISES

Yet another event that has dented faith in the Liberalist Paradigm is the somewhat spotty, if not altogether dismal, record of the privatization experiment throughout the world. It has proceeded at top-speed throughout the world since 1980, though the outcome of this 'radical' faith-based therapy has been mixed, at best.[18] It has been undertaken even in areas like education and health—which have historically been the exclusive preserve of the public sector even in the developed countries. Within a space of just a decade (from 1979 to 1989) more than eighty countries had already launched efforts to privatize in excess of 2,600 state-owned enterprises (SOEs). Their share, in the high-income countries, fell from 8.5 per cent in 1984 to 6 per cent of GDP in 1991; and it probably stood at 5 per cent by the end of the 1990s. Even more striking is the fact that the share of SOEs fell from 16 per cent of the GDP in 1980 to only 7 per cent of GDP in 1995, and to barely 5 per cent since then. The middle-income countries and the transition economies have also experienced large privatization sales [Megginson and Netter (2001)]. The usually listed objectives of privatization have been to raise revenues for the state, promote efficiency, reduce government interference in economic activity and provide opportunities for competition within the private sector [Price Waterhouse (1989)]. However, in fact, privatization has been done for the least convincing reasons: that is to raise revenue for the cash-strapped governments. Even more fundamentally, the primary impetus to privatize throughout the world has come from an ideological commitment to phasing out the government from the economic sector rather than by a strong enough commitment to securing net efficiency gains.[19] It is, therefore, not surprising that the international donors continue emphasizing privatization exercises, even though their average outcome worldwide has been by and large adverse for efficiency, growth and equity. The following analysis should substantiate these remarks.

10.5. (i). Cross-Country Evidence on Privatization

There does not appear to be much empirical support for the Liberalist Paradigm's central contention that privatization of public-sector must, of necessity, lead to an efficient operations of the privatized public units. Cross-country studies done so far do not lend unambiguous support to the efficacy of privatization, except in a very narrow sense of an increase in private profits. Apart from the fact that an increase in private profit is not necessarily a sign of competitive efficiency, a complete analysis of privatized firms' efficiency must also reckon such variables as new investment made by the private sector in infrastructure development, development and research leading to higher quality and lower prices of its output etc. On that wider reckoning there is not much to establish the prima facie supremacy of privatization. Megginson and Netter's (2001) comprehensive study presents a rather mixed picture of the success of privatization done so far in both the developed and the developing countries. On the one hand, it finds 'at least limited support for the proposition that privatization is associated with operating and financial improvements of divested firms' (p. 356); and that 'privatization 'works', in the sense that 'the divested firms almost always become more profitable, and financially healthier, and increase their capital investment spending' (p. 381)]. It has also reportedly encouraged some private investment in the privatized state-owned enterprises (SOEs) in the developed and the developing countries, including the Transition Economies, even though the evidence here does not seem to be compelling. On the other hand, these apparently encouraging results are subject to several important caveats, which should dampen the runaway enthusiasm of those who wish to present privatization the flagship of development policy.

Firstly, the Megginson and Netter's (2001) study gives disproportionately greater weight to the privatization of the most efficient firms located in the developed countries, where in most cases privatized units have been the beneficiaries of the 'shakeout effect'—namely, the privatized SOEs attained a modicum of market efficiency at state expense before privatization. Therefore, the reported efficiency gains in these 'privileged' cases do not establish a general case for privatization in the developed countries, much less in the developing countries. Even more important, the studies on the subject have not corrected for the greater exercise of monopoly power by the privatized units. They, therefore, do not prove that privatization must promote allocate-efficiency in the privatized units. Indeed, in such cases, it is not possible to make an a *priori* claim that privatization would add to industrial efficiency and social welfare. While monopolistic practices can widen the market and raise the profits of the privatized units, they do not necessarily imply that public interest would be best served by monopoly gains.[20] These cases are symptomatic of the monopolist's skill at maximizing their profits by exploiting the consumer; it does not signify greater efficiency as measured by a reduction in cost of production through innovation. Quite predictably, therefore, the consumers and workers, paying higher prices and receiving lower wages, have had to take the entire burden of the so-called structural adjustment in the overwhelming majority of the privatization exercises done so far.

Secondly, some other important studies have cast doubt on the efficacy of privatization. Newberry and Pollitt (1997) show that producers and shareholders have typically captured all the benefits while the consumers and the government have lost out in one of the best instances of privatization—of electricity in Britain—even though a permanent cost reduction of 5 per cent per annum took place there. This is a typical case of which there are many instances elsewhere in the world. On the other hand, there are cases of achieving an increase in productivity and avoiding asset stripping while retaining state ownership [Vickers and Yarrow (1988); (1991)]. But, unfortunately, in many cases, outright privatization has led to asset stripping in most developing countries. There is, therefore, a strong case for going slow on privatization where deregulation and internal restructuring can take care of a large number of deficiencies of the SOEs. The Chinese experience illustrates that, 'enterprise restructuring, concentrating on improving the allocation of property rights can yield large benefits even without privatization' [Megginson and Netter (2001), p. 338].

Thirdly, it has been shown that almost as important as privatization is the method used to privatize the SOEs. For instance, privatization has helped the growth of capital-market capitalization and trading volume only when it is done by the SIP (share-issue privatization) method. On the other hand, voucher privatization done in Russia has only led to asset stripping on a massive scale, bordering on loot and plunder of public assets by the oligarchs. Indeed, a variation on the voucher privatization—namely, the loan-for-share programme—amounted to open theft in the name of privatization.[21] It has been observed that this method was adopted only in the transitional economies because of the non-availability of a better alternative. But the point is that in such cases it would have been better to do first everything to improve the structural weaknesses of the state-owned enterprises and then go for limited privatization. The worth of this method has been demonstrated in the case of the telecommunication industry where a combination of deregulation and liberalization has produced dramatic improvements [Noll (2000); D' Souza and Megginson (2000)]. The case of China, briefly described below is another example of the success of such method.

Fourthly, most of the privatization-induced efficiency gains have been secured by a sharp reduction in the wage bill (secured through greater unemployment and lower wages), rather than as a result of innovative activity undertaken to lower production costs. Thus, for example, an increase in output by 54 per cent was associated with a cut in employment by 50 per cent in Mexico [La Porta and Lopez-de Silanes (1999)]. Rather than being an exception, this result illustrates a general tendency in the wake of privatization. Large-scale unemployment of even highly skilled workers, not to speak of the unskilled workers who get unceremoniously thrown out of jobs in droves in a rather mechanical fashion, has happened in nearly all the privatization exercises done so far throughout the world. Needless to state this is an aspect of privatization that cannot be easily overlooked. Indeed, these opportunity costs, which, in many cases are large and irreversible, must be factored in computing the profitability of privatization.[22] Yet another factor, not sufficiently emphasized, is that while privatized firms have almost always lowered wages, they seldom, if ever, created new employment. Now, as the efficiency wage theory shows, lowering wages does not enhance the efficiency level in the privatized firms. It is, therefore, not very reassuring to know that, 'whenever employment is cut, there is almost invariably a large compensating performance improvements' [Megginson and Netter (2001), p. 381]. The question begged here is: how do we know that performance improvements in question are large enough to offset the employment losses in specific enterprises, not to speak of the misery they cause. The fact is that the labour economics of privatization still remains an unexplored territory; especially whether privatization causes employment creation large enough to compensate for the job destruction it very surely causes. The proper conclusion to draw from our state of ignorance about the employment aspects of privatization is that, because the social suffering it causes is so vast, one should not go all-out for it even when some significant performance gains are expected to be garnered. Here is yet another example of the need to achieve equity and efficiency (in the narrow sense of high private profits) together as a package deal.

Fifthly, and this is a basic point, Megginson and Netter (2001) warn against taking the evidence they provide for privatization as establishing an a priori superiority of the unfettered markets over government intervention in the production sector. This is because no counterfactual exercise has yet been carried out to determine that privatization in each (successful) case was the only or the best alternative course of action under the circumstances in which it was undertaken. They sensibly argue, 'Unless [all the alternative policies] have been identified and the interactions between various policy options are established launching large-scale privatization will be a leap of faith.' (p. 382).

Sixthly, it is often forgotten in evaluating the costs and benefits of privatization that the emergence of the SOEs in the developing countries was meant to serve as an instrument for growth and for remedying the informational and knowledge imperfections of the private investor. Both these objectives typically entail an externality in the sense that the private sector would not be able to appropriate the returns to knowledge creation and growth acceleration through the price mechanism. And to the extent that they do succeed in appropriating these returns under-utilization would be the inevitable outcome. That in some cases, the SOEs have not been able to perform the functions they were supposed to perform is an argument for making them more efficient in the wider sense—of achieving the declared social objectives at least cost to the society.

To summarize: these general remarks are not meant to discredit privatization altogether or to assert the unambiguous superiority of government regulation and control of economic activity over private-sector activity. Each has a place in the repertoire of development policy. The point here is that it is not safe to conclude that privatization must, of necessity, lead to efficient market solutions. Indeed, an important lesson of privatization done so far is that, with the exception of raising revenue for the government, it has not registered any noteworthy success with respect to its proclaimed objectives. In particular, in most cases it has not led to greater efficiency by encouraging competition; instead it has tended to create profit-maximizing private monopolies. It is clear now that privatization, if not accompanied by a clear-headed regulatory framework to suppress the emergence of monopolies, would not succeed in achieving competitive efficiency, reducing production costs and creating jobs, and in lowering prices. Instead, the newly created private monopolies would more likely impose the textbook excess burden on the economy on top of the large social costs of greater unemployment noted above.

10.5. (i). a. Case Studies: Privatization in Soviet Russia

The privatization exercise undertaken in post-reform Soviet Russia is an example of the great damage that an unregulated privatization can do to the economy and the nation's psyche. It has led to higher unemployment, made the oligarchs richer and the consumers poorer. All in all, privatization has not contributed to industrial efficiency; instead, it has undermined confidence in the fairness, efficiency and competence of the post-reform (and geographically and economically much reduced) Soviet Russia. The fact that people still do not want to go back to the collectivization of the pre-reform Soviet Union does not show that they are happy with the present economic malaise. A more convincing argument seems to be that once an industry has been privatized, it would not be transferred back without imposing a substantial cost on the economy even when the disadvantages of privatization become transparent. Indeed, the Russian case illustrates two basic points about privatization. Firstly, privatization is essentially a gradual affair and it takes institutional 'preparation' so that a competitive market economy can function to the benefit of the common man and not just for the chosen few. In particular, a set of rules for corporate governance must be put in place to ensure that private corporations do not steal assets from the minority shareholders and the managers are not given the opportunity to defraud the shareholders. Secondly, in the absence of such preparations, or while these are not yet complete, it would be counterproductive to rush with such reforms in the hope that a shift to unfettered markets would by itself create wealth—indeed, it is more likely to subtract from wealth. The reason is that in the absence of a system of checks and balances, privatization has a tendency to degenerate into open theft. And this scandalous saga of public corruption has not been unique to Soviet Russia; it illustrates a general tendency, of which there are many instances with varying degrees of institutionalized dishonesty. After all, 'why expend energy in creating wealth when it is so much easier to steal it' [Stiglitz (2003), pp. 157–158].

10.5. (ii).b. Case Studies: Privatization in Pakistan

Pakistan's experience with the privatization of SOEs is interesting in that, contrary to the East European and Russian experience, a fairly elaborate regulatory mechanism has been created to ensure the transparency of the privatization process; and yet the results of the exercise done so far have not been altogether satisfactory.[23] There have been complaints of pandering to the exigencies, caprices and prejudices of influential people who, behind the charade of privatization, have indulged in asset stripping and massive public corruption.[24] The fact is that the performance of the State Owned Enterprises (SOEs) before and after privatization has not inspired confidence in the hearts and minds of the people so that whatever is done to enhance the transparency of the procedures, a significant residue of doubt still remains. The empirical studies have not established an a priori case for the efficiency of the privatized industrial units. What they have shown is that the mere passage of public ownership to the private sector is neither a necessary nor a sufficient condition for improving productive efficiency [Naqvi and Kemal (1991b)]. Indeed, the evidence is strong that in most cases when the public sector units have been made corporate, they have produced better results. The reason is that, even though a regulatory structure exists, yet in most cases private monopolies have simply replaced public monopolies so that the gains in efficiency have been indeterminate at best. Indeed, the privatized monopolies have done worse in an overwhelming number of cases. In most privatized industrial units, commodity prices have risen and the quantities produced reduced. Furthermore, it has been shown that the incidence of inefficiency, measured by the effective protective rates (EPRs) and the domestic resource costs (DRCs) has tended to be higher in the private-sector production units than in the public-sector units; and the percentage of the inefficient units is roughly the same in both the private and public sectors. Even more ominous, privatization has directly contributed to the highest ever rates of unemployment in the country. The reason is that the privatized units have tended to substitute capital-intensive for labour-intensive production technologies and contract labour for regular employees. In addition, job security and the service conditions of those remaining employed have, in general, deteriorated significantly [e.g., Naqvi and Kemal (1999)].

10.5. (iii). c. Case Studies: The Chinese Privatization

The Chinese privatization of the SOEs, begun in 1984, much later than the initiation of its market reforms in December 1978, illustrates how an over-regulated economy should work to produce efficiency results without hurting the interests of the common man. It has generally taken the form of co-production between the domestic production units and the foreign private sector, with the former retaining heavy government presence. However, domestically the selling of large state enterprises to private investors was ruled out in 1980s and 1990s on both political and ideological grounds. Instead, the state and private sectors have operated side by side with the result that the productivity of both has increased in both over time. The key to success has been a strategy that has sought to achieve the principal objective of privatization (that is, fostering competition to lower production costs and product prices) without actually transferring ownership to the private sector. The fact is that large-scale enterprises are still a long way off from the stage where most private individuals would come to hold most of the shares [Perkins (1994)]. Of late, the government has taken the most important step of giving constitutional protection to private property. The exact details of the Chinese experience are largely unique to that country, which has made a shift from totally controlled economy to an economy that could be more accurately called 'mixed', but a couple of points are of general interest too:

Firstly, the privatization in the best of cases needs to be done on a case-by-case basis and mainly to achieve efficiency gains. But this should be done by bringing about efficiency improvement through cost reduction and not by reducing the employment of skilled and unskilled workers.

Secondly, it should be remembered that the SOEs in many cases produce wage goods, demanded by the less well-to-do people. The supply of these goods should be maintained, even subsidized. In these cases, they perform essentially the job of providing safety nets to the poor whom the government cannot possibly leave at the mercy of the private sector [Megginson and Netter (2001); Ahmad and Hussein (1989)]. In such cases, an abrupt transfer of SOE's to the private control would most likely lead to social turmoil, which would then make the country doing the privatization unattractive for both the domestic and the foreign private sector. Perhaps, the Chinese, either consciously or unconsciously, have tried to avoid the economic, social and political fall-out of the post-haste privatization in Russia. And so far they seem to have succeeded remarkably in their economic tight-rope walking.

10.6. THE REVISIONIST VIEW OF THE EAST ASIAN MIRACLE

No amount of theoretical contributions could have tilted the scale of academic and policy opinion against the Liberalist Paradigm as decisively as the East Asian miraculous growth experience accomplished. The reversal of the academic opinion has surprised even the most inveterate liberalist. But the transition to the present consensus has come about rather slowly. In the beginning, some self-serving liberalist explanations were offered. The weak-to-moderate growth elsewhere in the developing world was attributed to excessive government intervention and the dominance of import-substitution policies and a refusal to revise these policies well past their social utility [Ranis and Mahmood (1992)].[25] So by elimination, that left first-best free market remedies that could pull off the miraculous growth and poverty reduction.[26] Little (1982) was explicit: 'apart from the creation of [these neo-classical conditions] it is hard to find any good explanation for the sustained industrial boom in Taiwan'. But this oft-repeated suggestion begs the fundamental question: how come such miraculous growth did not occur in free-market economies, at any other time in development history? Now, there are only two logical possibilities here. Either, the free-market economies were in the past run on first-best principles, or they were not run on these principles. The first case should more properly be interpreted as a failure of the first-best remedies; while the second case would beg yet another question: if these principles did not produce high growth rates in the advanced countries when they were still underdeveloped, why would they produce better results in the developing countries? The fact is that the so-called first-best policies have never produced miraculous rates in advanced countries; they would not promise to do so in the developing countries. One of the concerns of the traditional development policy was, therefore, to ensure that the growth rates in the developing countries were not too tightly linked to the industrialized countries where they have been consistently much lower than those required to enable the developing countries to achieve any of the stated objectives of development policy.

10.6. (i). Are Development States Unique to East Asia?

When the reality of government intervention and its beneficial effects on growth in East Asia became too obvious and emphatic to be ignored, the liberalists shifted grounds to claim that the reason why the government could do it there (and only there) was that the state intervention was highly selective, market-friendly and was promptly ended once its objective was achieved.[27] Once again, however, such essentially impressionistic explanations of the role of the state in bringing about a highly unusual phenomenon are thoroughly unconvincing. How do we know when the just-right time has arrived for ending government intervention; and why only the East Asians have possessed this alchemic sense of anticipation? The fact is that all attempts to explain away the crucial importance of the development state lead the analyst and the policy-maker to a dead-end street. The starting point of all such explanations should, therefore, be the clear acceptance of the endogenous character of government in all episodes of development success. Figure 5.1 (Chapter 5) shows quite convincingly that all cases of higher-than-average growth of per capita income (in excess of 4 per cent) have been associated with higher-than-average government expenditure. Even more striking is the fact that there has not been a single case in the Asia and Pacific regions, including East Asia, where the higher-than-average growth has been accompanied by lower-than average government expenditure.

The World Bank's comprehensive study of the East Asian Miracle (1993) presented an apparently more nuanced view of the matter. It conceded: 'In a few economies, mainly in Northeast Asia, in some instances, government interventions resulted in higher and more equal growth than otherwise would have occurred' (p. 6). But, it has offered yet another—though least convincing—twist in its finest hour of lucidity. It argued that the East Asian experiment was unique to East Asia and could not be 'replicated' elsewhere in the developing world.[28] However, the 'non-replicable' argument does not hold much ground. Indeed, Figure 5.1 rules out this possibility also. The fact is that same (or at least similar) policies have been fruitful in both the East Asian and non-East Asian countries, but the more so in the former because they were more effectively (though not necessarily more efficiently in the neo-classical sense) carried out there. In addition, the superior initial conditions in East Asia—in particular, a more educated labour force, greater equity, and a substantial experience with industrialization in the post-Second World War period—must have also contributed significantly to the observed growth differential between them and the rest of Asia [Adelman and Morris (1973); Adelman (1978)] The 'replicating' argument is indecisive also because such 'distortions' explain only the relative profitability of different industries affected by protection; they cannot account for their overall performance. This is because the adverse (static or dynamic) effects of protection on import-substitution industries would be offset by the greater gains of the export industries [Rodrik (1995)].[29] Similarly motivated, and incorrect, is the argument that higher factor productivity of the East Asians, bred by market-friendly policies, was to a great extent responsible for their higher growth rates. [30] But the factual evidence is that it was not productivity but an extraordinary saving and investment effort that accounted for the miracle [Young (1993); Ray (1998)]. The saving and investment rates in the former rose together and were much higher (in the 25 to 35 per cent range) than in the latter (in the 15 to 20 per cent range). Also, like in Europe and America in the days of their underdevelopment, the import-substitution industrialization played a crucial role in increasing the rate of growth of the manufacturing activity: its share in the GDP rose to 25–30 per cent, as compared with about 19–20 per cent in the latter. These 'facts' do not detract from the miraculous nature of the East Asian achievements; but, what is more significant, they make the miracles replicable. By their acts of superlative growth-man ship, East Asia has lighted a trail that many more will tread, hopefully with even greater success. China has done it even better; so has Vietnam. India is going to achieve it; and there may be many more miracle workers in the making. Indeed, the 'replicating' of East Asia's miraculous growth in every country that tries hard enough to achieve it is one of the brightest aspects of recent development history. It offers the optimistic lesson that there are no limits to human ingenuity when it comes to improving upon past success.

A common factor which runs like a silver thread through all the modern miracle stories of growth and poverty reduction is that the road to success lies in a phased implementation of the reformist agenda. It begins by expanding the domestic market by a government-sponsored programme of coordinated industrialization, using the very same instruments of protection employed by the relatively slow-growing developing countries [(Bruton (1998)].[31] The World Bank study cited above concedes, 'All [East Asian countries] (except possibly Hong Kong) began with a period of import substitution, and a strong bias against exports. But each moved to establish pro-export regime more quickly than other developing economies' (p. 12). Table 2.1 (Chapter 2) shows that the much superior speed of Structural

Transformation in East Asia as compared with that experienced by other regions should explain, to some extent, their superior performance in overall growth. Their better export performance was very much endogenous to the state-sponsored industrialization there. On the other hand, all the developing countries, in particular those located in sub-Saharan Africa, that did not follow this roundabout historical route to economic progress and went straight to export expansion, ended up courting development disaster.[32] And the African countries that did relatively better did not owe their success to a free-trade strategy or the one routinely prescribed by the structural adjustment programmes. It can, therefore, be stated as one of the stylized facts of economic development that the countries that did knowledge-creating import substituted first and then exported, or the ones which did both in quick succession, have generally done better than those which started off with export expansion and then persisted with it [Linder (1961)]. The reason is that accumulation and learning, along with the traditional emphasis on physical and human capital formation have determined the speed and quality of economic development of all the successful developing countries; and that these factors have worked most effectively in the context of knowledge-promoting import substitution that relies primarily, though not exclusively, on the domestic market [Bruton (1998)]. This was done with superlative success in East Asia but reasonably satisfactorily elsewhere in the developing world as well. To maintain that accumulation and innovation flowed wholly or mainly from export orientation (interpreted by the liberalists to signify the absence or a lesser incidence of government regulation and control) is really to oversimplify a more complex story. There is, therefore, not much substance in the claim that the East Asian experience demonstrated most of all that, 'a developing country could achieve industrialization without relying on domestic market to absorb almost all additional output' [Krueger (1997), p. 17].[33] Indeed, they demonstrated exactly the opposite.

Notwithstanding the contrary liberalist opinion, there is a broad enough academic consensus now that one of the most important features of the East Asian economies has not been minimal government but 'hard 'governments that 'governed the markets'. These governments, which were more interventionist in East Asia than in non-East Asian countries, actively nurtured infant-industries and set stringent performance standards for them. Such policies of selective protectionism helped promote very high overall rates of investments all over as well as in key industries where the spillover of knowledge formation to the rest of the economy is supposed to have been the maximum [Westphal (1990); Amsden (1989); Wade (1990)]. In particular, the heavy industries (steel mills) that were bitterly opposed by the World Bank and the IMF on efficiency grounds were, nevertheless, promoted with great success in South Korea and contributed significantly to its raising the long-run growth of their economies. In retrospect, one can state without fear of contradiction that if South Korea had taken to the first-best advice of the multi-lateral donors it would still have been specializing in the production of rice.

10.7. Concluding Remarks

The Anti-Liberalist Consensus has refuted the basic tenets of the Liberalist Paradigm—namely, the latter's steely support to the superiority of unfettered market solutions and the *laissez-faire* regimes; its unqualified opposition to state supported import-substitution industrialization and to all forms of state interference with economic activities; its advocacy of the idea of a minimal state on economic and moral grounds; and its insistence that the role of the state should be confined to creating an infrastructure of rules that would let (rich) individuals pursue their projects as they see fit. These important theoretical and empirical results have struck the Liberalist Paradigm at its weakest points, i.e. their advocacy of privatization without regard to their adverse consequences for individual and national welfare, their insatiable tolerance for rising unemployment and their unqualified support to *laissez-faire* regime. The liberalist plea for the unrestricted reach of the market has been challenged on the grounds that with imperfect markets and costly information, free-market solutions are, as a rule, Pareto-inefficient. In other words, it would be possible, in practically all the real-life situations, to increase someone's welfare without lowering the welfare of anyone else by suitable government intervention. The same result holds in the factor (labour) market, where unemployment in the presence of non-market-clearing efficiency wage does not necessarily signify efficiency. In addition, the limited reach of the Coase Theorem, which has been cited in support of privatization even when markets are imperfect and to settle important distributional issues by a 'correct' definition of private property rights and by absenting all constraints on free bargaining, has been noted. And the empirical studies that question the beneficence of privatization have been noted. Perhaps, no less important for development policy have been the new theoretical contributions that lend support to the Big-Push and Structural Transformation hypotheses and those which question the limited use of *laissez-faire* solutions for developing countries. Then there is the revisionist view of the East Asian miracle, which, more than any theoretical contributions has finally weaned away academics and policy makers from addiction to the magic of the market. It has also made the idea of a legitimate and substantial development role of the state once more intellectually acceptable—indeed, fashionable. It is no exaggeration to say that the Anti-Liberalist Paradigm has effectively pushed the Liberalist Paradigm into an irreversible hibernation by demonstrating the extreme fragility of its theoretical foundations and inapplicability of its policy prescriptions.

NOTES

1. In this book this important development in neo-classical economics has, however, not been recognized as a distinct paradigm in development policy. But that does not make it any the less foundational for understanding some of the essentials of a successful development policy.

2. The Anti-Liberalist Consensus has redefined the research programme of neo-classical economics, even though it would be a little premature to state that mainstream economics has abandoned the Arrow-Debreu model. For this reason, in this book we have preserved the current practice of most modern textbooks, which identify neo-classical economics with the Arrow-Debreu model and show the new developments under the heading 'The Incomplete Information Paradigm'.

3. Bardhan (1993) remarks: 'The international donors proffered market fundamentalism at a time when new neo-classical economists had effectively undermined faith in it. Contrary to the perfect information Arrow-Debreu model, the Anti-Liberalist Paradigm emphasized 'information asymmetry, imperfect and incomplete markets, dynamic externalities and increasing returns to scale, multiple equilibria and self-reinforcing mechanisms of path dependence' (p. 131). All these innovations of the Anti-Liberalist Consensus, and their implications for development policy, have been analyzed at different places in this and the ensuing two chapters.

4. It will be recalled that the Keynesian Revolution (1937) made a similar demonstration: That a substantial part of unemployment is of the involuntary variety and can be cured only by state intervention; and that lowering the wage rate towards zero would not cure the unemployment.

5. The hypothesis about efficiency wage is that productivity depends on the wages paid. This has the implication that the wages may exceed the market-clearing wage level in equilibrium. In other words, the market-clearing wage is not Pareto efficient and government intervention will obviously be welfare-raising. The search costs relate to the fact that searching for a job entails some unemployment, particularly if off-the-job search is more likely to succeed than in-job search. While search unemployment may justifiably be regarded as market equilibrium, it need not be Pareto-efficient.

6. Stiglitz (1989b) emphasizes the costly and imperfect nature of information, the more so in the developing countries. But surprisingly he shies away from recommending a substantial role for the government in this respect: 'While market failures with which I have been concerned do provide a rationale for a variety of types of government interventions, governments face information and incentive problems no less than does private markets' (p. 202). In particular, he rules out any role for the government with respect to the provision of credit and to cure capital market imperfections. Where does it lead us then? It would have been more logical for him to show that there is a role for the government even when faced with the same imperfect information. Fortunately, he no longer holds that position. In a more recent work he clearly states: 'wherever there is market imperfection (that is, always) there are, in principle, interventions by the government—*even a government that suffers from the same imperfections of information*—which can increase the market efficiency' [Stiglitz (2003), p. 213. Italics added].

7. An explicit recognition of costly information leads to the following important results: market equilibrium may not exist even when all the underlying preferences and production sets are well behaved; when equilibrium exists it is in general not Pareto-efficient; and when

the separation between equity and efficiency considerations may not hold etc. [Stiglitz (1988)].

8. It is interesting to note in this connection that the theoretical arguments against the state-owned enterprises (SOEs) and for their privatization are in effect against *state ownership* and not against *state regulation*. Thus, it would not be legitimate to conclude: 'the harmful effects of public ownership can be eliminated through privatization' [Megginson and Netter (2001), p. 331].

9. A related argument that has dented faith in the efficacy of the free markets is the recognition of the centrality of the acquisition of knowledge for sustaining high rates of economic growth. It too warrants state intervention because knowledge has an element of externality that cannot be internalized by a profit-maximization [World Bank (1999)].

10. Cooter (1990) gives three versions of the Coase Theorem: (i) the initial allocation of legal entitlements is a matter of unconcern from the view point of efficiency so long as they can be freely exchanged; (ii) the initial allocations of legal entitlements do not matter for efficiency so long as they can be exchanged in a competitive market and; (iii) these provisions of the Theorem would hold if the transaction costs are zero.

11. The argument in this section draws heavily on Farrell (1987).

12. The significance of private information (which others don't know about) is that individuals may not reveal it in case they anticipate that it will be used against them. This requires the specification of 'mechanism design' to induce (sometimes, bribe) individual to reveal it.

13. The proposition in the text is due to the non-cooperative models of bargaining—that bargaining would be typically inefficient when each bargainer knew some things that would benefit only him/her if a successful agreement were reached as a result of Coase type bargaining [Sutton (1986)]. Varian (1974) proved that Pareto-optimal outcomes arrived at through a bargaining process could be envy-free and equitable only if the consumer's tastes were identical, which is obviously an unrealistic assumption to make.

14. The really extraordinary aspect of the liberalist line of thought is that it has rested confidently on the belief that no-government situations do actually exist in both the developed and the developing countries; so that both must seize the opportunities that unfettered markets offer, even when these are not complete or competitive. To give only one example of such extraordinary belief, the central recommendations for the developing countries to achieve greater (indeed, maximum) trade orientation and maximize growth has been defined as one that led 'a country to neutrality in the sense of bringing its economy closer to the situation that would prevail if there were no governmental interferences' [(Michaely, Papageorgiou, and Choski (1989), p. 20].

15. The theory of mechanism design offers the basic insight that where it is difficult to monitor people's private information and actions, then there is need to give people incentive to share information; and that the efforts made in that direction impose constraints on the economic system that are as binding as the availability of raw materials. Thus, the theory requires that incentive constraints should be considered at par with the resource constraints to deal with real economic problems [Myerson (1990)].

16. Decentralized bargaining when people have private information is costly and inefficient. This is because in such cases, the negotiations may be protracted and costly—including situations when such negotiations simply break down [Roth and Murnighan (1982]. This latter possibility arises when a potential buyer of a good likes to buy it but not as much as the seller may think; in that case the seller may not lower the price to the market-clearing level. The only case when voluntary bargaining can work is the uninteresting case when people know each other only too well. But in these cases decentralization is least useful.

17. Since Murphy, Shleifer and Vishny, (1989b) put industrialization at the centre of the development process, their research also lends support to the Structural Transformation hypothesis, which too can be interpreted as helping a developing country 'out of the non-industrialization trap' (p. 1004) by a balanced growth of the agriculture and the industrial

sectors of the economy. An important point of difference between the Big-Push and the Structural Transformation hypotheses is that, while the former focuses on the demand for industrialization, the latter highlights the mechanism—the transfer of labour and capital from low-productivity agriculture to high-productivity industrial sector—that increases the average productivity of the economy.

18. The term privatization in the sense it is used now was first coined by Peter Drucker [Yergin and Stanislaw (1998), p. 114]. However, its first influential adoption, in place of deregulation, was by the Thatcher government in 1979. But it was not till 1984 that privatization became an established tool of economic policy in the UK and elsewhere. However, there are other claimants to the privatization ancestry—namely, the German ideologically motivated denationalization in 1961; and even earlier, the British denationalization of the steel industry in 1950. Yet the fact remains that these early episodes of privatization remained isolated instances that were not copied elsewhere, certainly not in the developing countries.

19. The amounts raised through privatization have been massive: The cumulative value of the proceeds rose through privatization exceeded $ I trillion in 1997; peaked at $160 billion in 1999; and have levelled off at $140 billion since then [Gibbon (2000)].

20. It may be interesting to cite a passage from Adam Smith (1776) on this point: 'To widen the market and to narrow competition is always the interest of the dealers. To widen the market may frequently be agreeable enough to the interest of the public; but to narrow the competition must always be against it, and can serve only to enable the dealers, by raising their profits above what they naturally would be, to levy for their own benefit, an absurd tax upon the rest of their fellow-citizens' (pp. 266–7). Incidentally, here is also an early statement of the proposition cited in the text that there is no a priori guarantee that privatization *per se* will be socially beneficial.

21. Under this infamous programme the government asked for loans from the private banks (not the Central Bank) in return for the shares of the SOEs. Later on, the government defaulted on these loans letting the private banks (owned by the oligarchs) take over these SOEs at a fraction of its value. Much of this wealth was quickly sent abroad for fear that a future government would annul these sales [Stiglitz (2003), p. 159].

22. These social costs include job anxiety even among workers who have managed to keep their jobs, a total sense of alienation and shame among those laid off (the incidence of suicide invariably rises in prolonged periods of unemployment, even among western countries with strong social security systems) and the unbearable burden of supporting their children's education, which, in many cases has had to be terminated.

23. It may be noted that the remarks on Pakistan do not cover the privatization of banks and the telecommunication sector. But, with the exception of the telecommunication sector where the beneficial effects of privatization have been obvious enough, the same cannot be said of the privatization of banks. The persistence of a wide 'spread' between the lending and the deposit rates is an example of uncontrolled use of oligopolistic power by the private banks at the expense of the public. Furthermore, the cases where influential people get their loans written off have not diminished with privatization. Since one of the main reasons for privatization was to stop this practice, this fact must be counted as a failure of the entire experiment.

24. It is interesting to note that many high officials of the Privatization Commission in Pakistan have been accused of wrong doing in the disposal of the pubic enterprises at throw away prices and without observing proper procedures, and many have had to go to jail on the charges of corruption; and many more potential jail birds might be in the making.

25. Ranis and Mahmood (1992) attribute the success of Taiwan and South Korea to the willingness of their governments 'to allow growth to proceed along a 'natural' path, and an aversion to use covert measures of resource transfers in order to promote growth artificially' (p. 138). It is interesting to note here that the miracle growth of East Asian economies has

been characterized here as 'natural' because it supposedly came about in the absence of government intervention. These observations leave open the questions: (a) On what definition of the term can a miracle growth be called natural? (b) What differentiates an artificial growth from the real one? The answers given are that growth achieved through government intervention is unnatural and artificial, while market-promoted growth is natural and real. Needless to point out, these arguments are simply a restatement of the definitions used by the authors to characterize what is natural and real.

26. Bhagwati (1988) expressed a similar sentiment: 'The intellectual orthodoxy, therefore, shifted rather sharply away from the emphasis on the virtues of protectionism and the attendant import-substitution strategy toward the merits of trade liberalization and the outward-looking strategy of export promotion' (p. 94).

27. An authentic representation of this point of view is the following statement: 'To be sure the Korean economy has not been characterized by *laissez-faire*. But, in contrast to the over controlled, over regulated, highly distorted economies described above, the Korean economy has been characterized by a diminishing intervention in most spheres of economic activity and the degree of distortion is considerably smaller.' [Krueger (1993), p. 30)]. What this argument, in effect, means is that when economies grow, then government intervention must have fallen in them. On the other hand, if the economies fall behind, then it must have been the case that they were over-regulated, etc. Needless to point out these arguments are examples of implicit theorizing.

28. The World Bank study, argued: 'The prerequisites for success [achieved by the East Asian countries] were so rigorous that policy makers seeking to follow similar paths in other developing countries have often met with failure' (p. 6). No convincing example has, however, been given of the countries that tried such a policy and failed. These other countries might not have scored similar miraculous success but, as noted in Chapter 3, lesser (though still impressive) development success can by no stretch of imagination be called a development failure.

29. It is not reasonable to explain the large observed differentials between the East Asian and non-East Asian growth rates in terms of the distortion-related static cost of protection being less in the former than in the latter. This is because these costs have never exceeded couple of percentage points of the GDP [Srinivasan and Whalley (1986)].

30. Furthermore, such claims—that Krueger and Tuncer (1982) among others made—have not succeeded in establishing the proposition that total factor productivity (TFP) has been higher in less protected industries than in the more protected industries. Indeed, there are industry studies that show that the most protected countries have been more successful in TFP growth. Thus Argentina, one of the much-closed economies, experienced the greatest TFP growth in the automobile industry [Waverman and Murphy (1992); (2001)]. Furthermore, 'the virtual impossibility of accurate cross-country measurement of distortions, as well as the prevalence of distortions in Taiwan and Korea in the 1960s and the 1970s, should make us cautious with regard to the presumption of improved technological performance in any specific country contemplating liberalization' [Rodrik (1995), p. 2941].

31. Rodrik (1996) compares the East Asian experience with the prescriptions of the Washington Consensus. He observes that these countries did not follow deregulation, trade liberalization, privatization, elimination of barriers to the DFI and financial liberalization. Thus, for instance, South Korea far from encouraging the private sector, imprisoned prominent businessmen and threatened to confiscate their assets. However, they maintained macroeconomic stability, without hurting economic growth and distributive equity. Yet all this was done in a manner that was not consistent with the policies that the Structural Adjustment Programmes would approve. See, Table 3 and the accompanying text on p. 17 of Rodrik's paper. This argument has been examined at some length in Chapter 8.

32. A large body of literature, however, tries to explain the African growth disaster in liberalist terms. Sachs and Warner (1997) find that restrictive trade policy, poor access to sea, and Dutch disease between them explained 1.2 per cent of the shortfall between the African growth rates and those of the other developing countries. But they are the only ones to have made such a claim. Most authors attribute a much more modest proportion of the African poor growth to these factors. For instance, Easterly and Levine (1997) attribute only 0.4 per cent of the growth shortfall in Africa to these factors. An interesting point about these cross-country studies is that in them the African dummy remains by-and-large inexplicable. In a comprehensive survey of the literature, Collier and Gunning (1999) report that lack of openness and social capital, high risk and poor public services are the four most cited factors in the empirical studies on the African development disaster. Yet they conclude: 'The relative importance of macroeconomic and microeconomic policies cannot be quantified because the latter are so poorly proxied in the regression literature' (p. 101). It follows that it would be no more than a leap of faith to attribute an overwhelming proportion of the differential growth in Africa to its failure to liberalize domestic and international markets. In fact, they overdid it and were heavily penalized for their indiscretion.

33. Fairly decisive empirical evidence on the causative factors responsible for the growth differential between the East Asian and non-Eastern economies are given in Part VI.

11

The Anti-Liberalist Consensus: Some Practical Policy Aspects

In addition to the points made in the preceding chapter, the Anti-Liberalist Consensus has trained on some of the pet liberalist positions—namely, the likely favourable effects of trade liberalization on growth, the alleged superior merit of export expansion strategy as opposed to the one that favours import substitution, and the essentially beneficial character of the international trading system. Ironically, in these matters, as well the ones analyzed in the preceding chapter, the drift of the anti-liberalist criticism seems to be similar to that of the Traditional Development Paradigm—namely, a sturdy scepticism of the beneficence of trade liberalization, a rejection of the liberalist obsession with *laissez-faire* (that it be used as the fulcrum with which to move the economic universe), a reaffirmation of the grim reality of unequal exchange and a general distrust of the existing world trading system's capability to work for the benefit of the developing countries. It has also supported import-substitution industrialization on both theoretical and empirical grounds, without compromising the possibilities of export promotion.

It will be useful to begin the analysis of the anti-liberalist position on the above-mentioned issues with an evaluation of the Structural Adjustment Programmes, which faithfully reflect the spirit of the Liberalist Paradigm.

11.1. WHAT TO MAKE OF STRUCTURAL ADJUSTMENT PROGRAMMES?

The announced purpose of the Structural Adjustment Programmes has been to create the pre-conditions of long-run growth of the crisis-hit economies and to reduce their excessive exposure to external shocks. As noted in Chapter 7, these programmes have been truly comprehensive in the sense of encompassing every sector of the economy. An interesting aspect of these programmes is that while the efforts to determine the net impact of the Structural Adjustment Programmes on the real variables have not borne fruit so far, yet the international donors' belief in the eventual beneficence of these reform programmes remains intact. One important reason for the multilateral donors romantic attitude is that market reforms have been pursued as desirable ends in themselves. This aspect of the paradigm will be dealt with in greater detail in Chapter 12. Yet another reason, analyzed below, is the liberalist belief that, although, many of their important aspects remain to be fully understood but they are theoretically sound so that one can predict their beneficial long-run consequences with a fair degree of confidence.

11.1. (i). Difficulties in Estimating the Net Impact of the Structural Adjustment Programme

The usual demonstrations of the good that the Structural Adjustment Programmes must do to the developing countries are, in fact, a rather inconclusive exercise in proof by contradiction: to the criticism that these programmes have generally worsened the performance of the economy and have hurt the poor people, it has been asserted that a non-adjustment to crises in line with their advice would have yielded even worse consequences for the poor; and that the poor would ultimately gain if the structure of incentives were such as promoted an efficient allocation of resources, labour-intensive industrialization and non-interventionist government. This line of reasoning, however, lacks credibility because the veracity of these claims cannot be verified. To so-called 'before-and-after approach' to evaluate the economic consequences of specific policies usually runs into serious statistical problems [Behrman and Srinivasan (1995)].[1] The only way to make valid comparisons between the situation with the Structural Adjustment Programmes and that without them is to do a detailed counterfactual, for which the hard-pressed domestic or international civil servants officials have little time, assuming that they know how to do it. The same observation applies to claims that the countries that implemented the Structural Adjustment Programmes have outperformed those that didn't. Yet the evidence here does not seem to be unambiguous. Much less is there an agreed upon position about the distributive consequences of these programmes. Corbo and Fischer (1995) conclude their sympathetic review of the Structural Adjustment Programmes as follows: 'The absence of agreed-upon analytic or econometric models to analyze some of the basic problems of adjustment is striking. For instance, the analysis of sequencing problems is still under-developed. The important issue of the distributional impact of adjustment has received attention in computable models—but it is fair to say that this work has not yet had a wide impact. It is also striking how few empirical generalizations are yet widely accepted' (p. 2917). The debate on these issues has gone on and its outcome has been far from decisive. The fact, however, is that the general approach to establish the superiority of the Structural Adjustment Programmes has been to appeal to the elusive common sense criterion and assert that market-oriented reforms cannot go far wrong. It is sincerely believed that growth and foreign investment would start flowing once the conditions of the programme were satisfied. But unfortunately sincerity of purpose is a poor substitute for hard economic thinking and rigorous statistical testing of hypotheses.

11.1. (ii). Structural Adjustment Programmes and Growth

The problems with the implementation of the Structural Adjustment Programmes have generally arisen from the donor agencies' failure to estimate the costs and the benefits of the implementation of the conditions attached to the programmes. In particular, an air of studied ambiguity hangs on their probable impact on growth and poverty. There are some obvious reasons, in addition to those stated above, why doing so is not always easy. In both cases, a great deal would depend on the speed of the supply response, which itself depends crucially on the initial conditions, the state of physical and educational infrastructures, among others. No wonder, therefore, the chances of the Structural Adjustment Programmes making a decisive and favourable impact on growth and poverty have been evenly balanced at best; in fact, the record has generally been unfavourable in this respect. Thus, a large number of studies of the impact of these programmes on the economy, mostly done by the staff of the Fund and the Bank and by those who are in broad sympathy with their logic, have come up with ambiguous results, at best. Khan (1990) has shown that the effects of the programmes on the current balance of payments have been positive; but that these effects have been negative on growth. Edwards (1989) demonstrates that these programmes have paid scant attention to income distribution. Also, the output effects of devaluations that usually accompany these programmes have been negative in the twelve countries he examined. The World Bank's own study (1990) reaches an ambiguous conclusion: while the performance of the economies hit by external shocks has generally improved when the situation in 1985–88 is compared with that in 1981–84; it generally deteriorated when the post-reform performance in the 1980s is compared with that of the 1970s. Mosley, Harrington and Toye (1991) and Corbo and Rojas (1992) find that the Structural Adjustment Programmes have generally adversely affected the investment rate, even though they have had a weak positive effect on growth. Another evaluation of the Structural Adjustment Programmes concludes that many of the arguments on which rest, 'high expectations of supply-side response to adjustment, and hence to a rapid transition to a more favourable growth path' have proved to be, by and large, implausible [Lipton and Ravallion (1995)]. Indeed, most empirical studies suggest that it normally takes a fairly long period of at least five years, for the growth rate of the GDP to revive in the aftermath of a successful Structural Adjustment Programme. The blame for this tardy performance of the liberalist reforms has been conveniently heaped on 'the extent of disarray at the start of the reform programme, on the speed and comprehensiveness of the adjustment programmes, on the financing available to cushion the reforms, and on the credibility and stability of the government policies' [Corbo and Fischer (1995), p. 2893]. Calvo (1989) has shown that the lack of credibility of these programmes makes them harmful rather than beneficial. Thus, considering that our understanding of the way in which the Structural Adjustment Programmes work through the economy to make the desired impact on the choice variable is at best hazy, the resolute confidence with which they are imposed on the developing countries is somewhat puzzling, to put it mildly.

11.1. (iii). Structural Adjustment Programmes and Poverty Reduction

The record of the programmes is spottier still with respect to poverty reduction. This is because while strong growth is one of the preconditions for poverty reduction, it alone is not sufficient to achieve it. Thus, even when it can be demonstrated that they have impacted growth positively, though weakly, it would not necessarily follow that they would reduce poverty to the desired extent. As shown in Chapter 17 (Table 17.1), a significant increase in human development related expenditures is required, most of all, to reduce poverty. But, unfortunately, under the Structural Adjustment Programmes the axe falls most decisively on these very expenditures. In addition, they tend to raise food prices, reduce public expenditure and employment and curtail anti-poverty programmes, all of which add up to a net reduction in human development. Next in order of importance is a reduction in inequality; but there is a widespread agreement that the programmes have been de-equalizing. So a decisive verdict against the Structural Adjustment Programmes is that they have usually been relatively more successful in fulfilling the pre-conditions to long-run growth, than in achieving growth itself and poverty reduction.

11.1. (iv). Latin America's Case

A direct confirmation of the adverse impacts of the Structural Adjustment Programmes comes from Latin America, which has gone farther than most in abandoning the much maligned state-controlled import-substitution policy and in implementing the conditions of the Structural Adjustments Programmes. Thus, the Lora's index (2001) of structural reforms rose steadily from 0.34 in 1985 to 0.58 in 1999. Yet the effect of these reforms on the real variables has been most disappointing. 'Per capita income declined in these countries from an average of 22.9 per cent of the US level in 1985 to 17.7 per cent in 1999, a relative decline of 22.7 per cent' [Hausmann and Rodrik

(2003), p. 604]. Indeed, Mexico, Bolivia, and Argentina, to cite some of the more distinguished examples, 'have undertaken more trade and financial liberalization and privatization within five years than East Asian countries have managed in three decades' [Rodrik (1996), p. 18]. Yet, for all we know, Latin America has waited in vain for the dawn of economic prosperity for years now, longer than the Keynesian long run. A rather undistinguished result of these programmes is that they have made Latin America distinctly un-egalitarian.

This section can be concluded by noting that a faithful implementation of the Structural Adjustment Programmes is neither a necessary nor a sufficient condition for achieving high growth and poverty reduction. For reasons given above, the most probable effect of the policy docility shown by the developing countries has been to reduce growth, increase poverty and worsen distributive inequity. This is what has actually happened in the post-reform Latin America, which is not even a pale shadow of what the East Asians achieved with lesser degree of reforms and what Latin America itself achieved in the distortion-filled Golden Growth Age of 1950–80. And whatever little growth it posted has made little difference to poverty reduction. Indeed, more than after a decade of reforms, 'Latin America suffers from a vicious circle in which low growth contributes to the persistence of poverty, particularly given high inequality, and high poverty and inequality contribute to low growth' [Birdsall and Szekely (2003), p. 51].

What has gone wrong? Obviously, one cannot blame the developing countries, as IMF does often, for being half-hearted about the implementation of the Structural Adjustment Programmes—that they have not shown firmness in the fulfilment of the conditions attached to the programmes. How can they be expected to be enthusiastic in implementing programmes, the consequences of which they do not know; and whatever little they do know about them is essentially adverse?

11.2. TRADE LIBERALIZATION AND ECONOMIC GROWTH

The pro-liberalization studies analyzed in Chapter 8 have one thing in common: it is their failure to prove that trade liberalization has played a decisive role in promoting strong export growth [Sachs (1987)]. Indeed, as if to prove that the economist's propensity to assume the most implausible is close to one, the general tendency has been to regard the export-led growth sequence as a self-evident truth. However, like all self-evident truths, this too is far from evident. The general presumption in support of the liberalist assertion is probably that since exports have tended to grow faster than output one could not be too wrong in concluding that the former must have led output expansion [Bhagwati (1988)]. But this line of argument smacks more of casual empiricism than of a rigorous attempt to settle a vital issue. Partly due to the weak empirical foundations of this proposition, the liberalist position on it has changed over time. Once it became clear that price distortions, if there were any in fact, did not prevent development successes—most certainly not in East Asia—the goal-post of research got insensibly shifted to disproving the benefits of its opposite, i.e. import-substitution [Balassa and Associates (1982); Westphal (1978); Pack and Westphal (1986)]. Needless to state, disproving one is not necessarily to prove its polar opposite because there is a third possibility of combining the two in proper proportion, one that would change with the stage of development. As it is, the liberalist line of research also failed to demonstrate that import substitution did not compromise the growth potential of the developing countries; nor has it been proved—at least not yet—that export expansion would of itself be growth-promoting and welfare-raising. Thus, for instance, Pack (1988) concluded, 'Export orientation, whatever its other merits, does not appear to yield higher total factor productivity growth than does import substitution' (p. 372). Furthermore, these studies have not established the claim—by [Krueger (1978)] for instance—that government intervention to promote exports is less distorted than that favouring import substitution, and that the net result of the policy bias in favour of export expansion would be to push scarce resources into more productive activities. The main reason for the unsoundness of the claim is that an efficient trade regime would be one that equalized the effective exchange rates—defined as one unit of the domestic currency actually paid out for one unit of foreign exchange—for exports and imports [Naqvi (1971); Bhagwati (1978)]; it is not necessarily the one that favoured export expansion at the expense of import substitution or vice versa. Furthermore, the tendency has been to compare the actual situation with the cooked up counterfactual in which rational behaviour sufficed to produce optimal solutions and where the government had no economic role whatsoever. But this stance amounts to the nihilistic conclusion that best trade policy is one that recreated a *laissez-faire* regime—a regime that never really existed except in the classical (and neo-classical) economist's febrile imagination.[2] Furthermore, it is not fully understood, or is at least not reflected in liberalist policies, that becoming internationally competitive with the help of best-practice technology is not uniquely related to the degree of a country's outward orientation. It rather requires an understanding of the, 'more fundamental aspects of the society—entrepreneurship, institutions, values, social incentives, commitment to growth, and a variety of other factors that define a society'. The impossibility of 'leapfrogging' to a higher state of international competitiveness with the help of outward orientation alone is established by the historical fact that, 'some form of the protection for learning is necessary. Korea and Taiwan (and Japan) have always had numerous forms of protection that (along with government influence) induced learning' [Bruton (1998), p. 930].

11.2. (i). The Futility of the Import-Substitution *versus* the Export-Expansion Debate

The preceding analysis of the debate about the relative merits of import substitution and export expansion suggests that, perhaps, the only defensible generalization about it is that the research effort, time and money spent on proving or disproving it has been an exercise in utter futility. The fact is that no sensible development economist has ever denied that export expansion helps growth. Thus, Lewis (1955) explicitly stated that an export boom might stimulate the demand for industrialization, but that it would not sustain it. Furthermore, it could do it by making the production process more efficient, permitting the installation of larger sized plants, and shifting to the best-practice production technology. It is factually wrong to suggest, as the liberalists do, that the transition from import substitution to export expansion does not normally happen because infant-industries have refused to grow. In nearly all the developing countries (including the highly protectionist ones like Pakistan and India), import-substitution industries have gradually converted into export-expansion industries; and both government policy and the normal profit-maximizing behaviour have facilitated such conversion.[3] Chenery (1980) showed that, 'after a period of strong import substitution, export expansion became the major source of industrial growth in Korea and Taiwan in each sector, and also led to an acceleration of growth in each' (p. 286). The emphasis here is, 'primarily on the role of manufactured exports in the structural transformation of the economy' (p. 284). In this context, the main policy advice has been to eliminate the trade policy bias against export expansion for sustaining the growth momentum achieved by import-substituting industrialization.

The fact is that, in the post-1980 period, in terms of its beneficial effects on the economy, export orientation alone does not seem to have emerged as a clear winner; nor did import substitution come out to be the villain of the piece. It is now widely accepted that the most fruitful strategy for all developing countries has been to use import substitution for exploring new areas of comparative advantage (adding higher-value added products to the export list) and export expansion to achieve efficient scale of production of the exportable goods [UNDP (2005)]. An additional argument in favour of this strategy is that the aggregate supply response with respect to agricultural products is typically less than unity: it has ranged from 0.3–0.9, with the poorer developing countries lying at the lower end of the range [Chhibber (1989)]. In other words, the right policy has always been to move away from the exports of primary goods (and the lower-value added light manufacturing) to those of the higher value-added manufacturing products where the relevant price elasticity is typically higher. That is how the development process in all developing countries, and not just in the East Asian countries, has progressed. This is how it is going to be in the future.

11.3. Unequal Exchange Once Again

Perhaps, one of the most important reasons for a reconsideration of the Liberalist Paradigm is the realization that its assertions about the relevance of the Ricardian Law of Comparative Advantage, the Heckscher-Ohlin Theorem, the Stolper-Samuelson Theorem, and the Samuelson's Factor-Price Equalization Theorem for development policy have been utterly wrong-headed. Both the modern theory of international trade (briefly discussed in the preceding chapter) and practical considerations have shown that an international economic system based on the *laissez-faire* ideal, which the above-mentioned theorems reflect, might well be unfair in the sense of being unhelpful in arranging a fair distribution of the gains from trade, even if it were shown to be theoretically efficient. Not much weight in this context can be given to the liberalist assurances that free trade-induced growth would typically enhance the potential for compensating the losers, for the simple reason that just pointing out the possibility of such compensation is no guarantee that it would in fact be paid out in a distribution-neutral *laissez-faire* world trading system.

11.3.1. Learning and Dynamic External Economies

Of late, new international trade models have questioned the validity of the above-mentioned theorems in cases of dynamic external economies arising from the learning-by-doing process. They have demonstrated that the balance of advantage that developed countries have traditionally enjoyed over the developing countries normally shows up in the differential between their respective rates of human capital accumulation; and that this differential is more likely to increase, rather than decrease, with human-resource intensive technological change. In other words, the opening up of trade and investment might, on balance, impede the growth-promoting structural transformation in the developing countries. These models also highlight that yet another source of discrimination arises from the fact that the opening up of a developing country to international competition adversely affects R&D activities in the developing countries. For instance, it has been pointed out that a development policy based on the Law of Comparative Advantage would discriminate against activities that are intensive in human capital and R&D,

and where the spillover effects are the most growth-promoting [Grossman and Helpman (1994)].[4] There is yet another route through which the adverse effects of trade on the developing countries can (and do) materialize. It is that when the trading countries are asymmetric in terms of their respective economic size (as is the case between the developed and the developing countries), the superior comparative advantage of the former is decisive, and the size of the market matters for economic growth, then free trade is likely to hurt the latter since it might crowd out their relatively weaker R&D activities [Rodrik (1995)]. For all these reasons, a regime of autarky may be superior to the one with free trade and investment. These findings are supported by the historical studies of the innovation-intensive activities, which show that restrictions on imports and foreign investment might have played a significant role in the fluorescence of innovation and R&D in Japan in the early 1970s [Odagiri and Goto (1993)]. The most influential modelling of this relationship is of an innovating north and an imitating south [Grossman and Helpman (1991)]. In this type of unequal relationship, there is no room for a meaningful, not to speak of a fair, sharing of the common pool of knowledge that the international spillovers of technological knowledge create. When the South can do a good job of imitation it must incur a significant cost by way of the obligation to pay large royalties to the innovators in North who are now protected by the Intellectual Property Rights. But even if the developing countries do succeed in imitating the North without incurring such costs the North will be freed up to concentrate on new high-tech innovations and then protect them through the Intellectual Property Rights, in the creation of which it has enjoyed an overwhelming advantage over the developing countries. Needless, to point out these are not blanket arguments in favour of protectionism; but they do highlight the fragility of the liberalist claims about the unambiguous superiority of free-trade regime over trade regimes that selectively protect the learning process, at least in the initial period of development. They also show that it would not be wise to exaggerate the gains from free international trade and investment.

However, it may be noted that much of the focus of the anti-liberalist writings just reviewed has been on proving that in some cases autarky may be superior to free trade. But this is seldom the question that engages the attention of development economist and the policy-maker. Rather the problem they normally face is: how to minimize the likely adverse impact of freer trade on the speed of Structural Transformation and the distribution of gains from trade? Two observations are in order about the relevance of the anti-liberalist writings reviewed above to development policy. One is what it directly proves—namely, that free trade is not the option in a development context. The second is that if the extreme option of autarky is a legitimate one in the development context then a milder restriction of free trade that the Traditional Development Paradigm advocated should be even more so.

11.4. THE WTO AND THE UNEQUAL EXCHANGE

More than any theoretical arguments, the recent trends in world trade and development have tended to confirm the long-held scepticism about the inevitable munificence of *laissez-faire* regimes. Indeed, the inequitable distribution of the gains from trade and investment that followed in the wake of WTO has helped in building up an international consensus *against* the Liberalist Paradigm. It is now widely appreciated that the new rules of the game, enshrined in the WTO charter, reflect the dominant Liberalist Paradigm; and they, by and large, have not been helpful to the developing countries. One of its most objectionable aspects has been its uncritical acceptance of the liberalist position that the developing countries are primarily responsible for keeping themselves in good economic health. International assistance would help too, it is argued, but to benefit from it the developing countries themselves must undertake deep and painful structural reforms, which means that they open up their economies for the developed countries' exports, even if there is no reciprocal action by the developed countries. Thus, the WTO insists, 'it is their own trade policy reforms that would produce a large share of benefit to themselves and to other developing countries from liberalization of trade in agricultural and manufactured goods—This lesson, that a large part of the economic gains from liberalization of trade accrue domestically, should not be overlooked in the context of reciprocal bargaining for market access' [WTO (2004a), p. 2]. The basic problem with the WTO is that it has bound its body and soul in total servitude to the tenets of the Liberalist Paradigm. As if to prove that the spirit of progress and reform has fled from its new-fangled charter, it has effectively tilted the balance of advantage against the developing countries. To that end, it has replaced those clauses of the GATT that favoured the Special and Differential Treatment of developing countries. This, in effect, represents a reversal of the line of thinking of the world community since 1955, which had gradually made GATT more receptive to the developing countries' concerns.[5] But the WTO has put all that global effort to naught. It has, in effect, run the engine of global change in the reverse: by going for 'big-bang' liberalization of trade and capital flows, and doing precious little to improve the bargaining position of the developing countries in multilateral bargaining. The recent collapse of the Doha round of negotiations illustrates the ineffectiveness of the WTO in doing any good to the developing countries. It practically has stood with folded hands while the developed countries insisted on the opening up of the developing countries markets for their exports, though doing practically nothing to stop the increasing misuse of the Intellectual Property Rights and reduce subsidies on their exports.

The net effect of the recent trends in international economic relations as they have evolved under the aegis of the WTO, has been to greatly concentrate trade and investment in few hands: the top fifth of the world's people in the richest countries control 82 per cent of the export trade and 68 per cent of direct foreign investment, while the bottom fifth (located in the developing countries) receive only 1 per cent [UNDP (1999)]. Also, the massive flow of foreign direct investment (FDI) in the 1990s that was praised to sky as only the first drop of rain of the globalization largesse on the investment famished developing countries has in fact added little to the productive capacity of those emerging countries that unfortunately received them. This is because these countries, with their high rates of saving, had little use for foreign capital; and because the FDI got used up in activities that are generally considered as inefficient (e.g., in real estate).

As it is, the world distribution of inome and wealth has unequivocally worsened. The East Asian melt-down in 1998–9, notwithstanding these countries' strong fundamentals, has shown that the discipline that free (capital) markets claim to impose on the policy-makers in developing countries simply 'reinforces the advantages of existing wealth holders[in the rich countries' [UNCTAD (1998)]. Indeed, the rapid capital-market liberalization, which the IMF, the World Bank and WTO have forced on the developing countries, was one of the most important causes of the East Asian meltdown: it facilitated speculative attacks on the region's currencies, thereby de-stabilizing their domestic capital markets. A recent analysis shows that too hasty a liberalization of foreign capital inflows might have been an important factor in precipitating the severe banking crises in Thailand, Korea and Indonesia [Kaminsky and Rheinhart (1999)]. The only remedy that helped negotiate the crisis with least damage to growth and employment (which the IMF severely criticized) was the Malaysian decision to impose temporary capital controls. There is now a broad unanimity of academic opinion that this was the right thing to do under the circumstances. Highlighting the growing anti-liberalist consensus, the UNCTAD (1999) warned: 'the twentieth century is closing on a note of crisis and a growing sense of unease about the [free market] policy that was proffered in the past decade.'

11.5. Concluding Remarks

This chapter completes a brief review of the Anti-Liberalist Consensus, which has dealt sensibly with some of basic hypotheses of the Liberalist Paradigm. Opinions may differ but the present author regards that the Anti-Liberalist

Consensus has decisively uprooted the following liberalist hypotheses: the claims about the unambiguous superiority of export-led growth to that propelled by import-substitution activities; the innate beneficence of trade liberalization; the inherent superiority of a *laissez-faire* regime (including a free movement of capital across international borders) to all other trading systems; and the capability of the WTO to ensure a fair deal to the developing countries. In addition to its remarkable theoretical contributions, the real world events have supported its basic contention—namely, that the basic liberalist suppositions are based on weak empirical and historical foundations. The adverse effects of the *laissez-faire* regime on the developing countries have long been established, the dynamics of unequal exchange seems to be in full swing in many developing countries and the failure of the WTO to establish a level playing field has become much too manifest to prevaricate about. What are the sources of the failure of the Liberalist Paradigm? One does not have to go very far to find an answer to this question. The source of the decline of its influence in the academic circles, though not reflected fully in policy-making quarters, has been its tendency to slavishly follow grand theoretical systems that cannot come to grips with the ground realities of life in the developing countries. An ideological belief in the universality of some of the least relevant generalizations of neo-classical economics at a time when they have been discredited on theoretical grounds has only added to the sense of disillusionment with it.

But there seems to be something more substantive about the Liberalist Paradigm's 'trained incapacity' to do any good to the developing countries. It has been argued with considerable truth that the liberalist idealism seems to be Janus-faced: on the one hand, it has openly advocated and enforced protectionist policies in the developed countries; but on the other hand, it has heaped praised on the likely benefits that free-trade policies must bring to the developing countries.[6] For instance, on what reasonable grounds would liberalists explain the widespread discrepancy between the developed countries' practice with respect to the subsidization of their agriculture and protecting their light industries on the one hand, and their insistence that the developing countries should not subsidize their agriculture or industries on the other? Furthermore, what honest logic would justify upbraiding the developing countries for implementing distorted policies (import-substitution industrialization) which the developed countries themselves indulged in with missionary zeal in their own state of underdevelopment?[7] Has it not been known all along that international trade cannot be carried on efficiently, equitably and durably without adding to their skimpy traditional list new non-traditional export goods that can only be produced through knowledge-based import-substitution industrialization? What then remains of the Liberalist Paradigm's advice on restructuring international trading system?

Precious little, the present book would argue. Indeed, going by the recent trend of theoretical and empirical research, the legacy of the Liberalist Paradigm promises to be more acute than lasting.

Notes

1. The problem of determining the effects of the Structural Adjustment Programmes ex-ante or ex-post has been the subject of some debate, but its outcome has been indeterminate, at best. The reason is that there are insuperable problems in performing such an exercise. 'An ex-ante evaluation of any proposed programme is difficult, if not impossible, given the multiplicity of its objectives, some of the which are often vaguely defined at best, and the difficulty of controlling for myriad other factors besides the adjustment programme that would influence the course of the economy. An ex-post evaluation that limits itself to the question whether the economy was performing better in some well defined sense after adjustment is difficult, if not unfeasible, primarily because the relevant comparison, namely, with a counterfactual scenario of a continuation pre-adjustment disequilibria, distortion and weakness without adjustment is not easy to construct' [Behrman and Srinivasan (1995), p. 2483]. That being the case, it is hard to see any wisdom in pushing Structural Adjustment Programmes on the developing countries with total confidence in their efficacy. Here is a case where something is worse than nothing.
2. Indeed, far from being a deciding factor in dealing with the central economic issues of the time, *laissez-faire* has, more often than not, 'played a notable role in contemporary lobbying and propaganda' [Coats (1971), p. 126].
3. It may be noted that—for instance, in Pakistan, India and Turkey—the conversion of import substitution industries into export industries in most cases led to a lot of rent seeking rather than profit-seeking. Being declared an export industry would qualify it for all sorts of incentives—including tax holidays. See the relevant references cited at different places in the book.
4. For instance Aw and Batra (1994), using firm-level Taiwanese data, show that there is no necessary connection between openness and growth.
5. Thus Article 18, sections A and C, Part IV, and the Enabling Clause of the GATT, 1994 have been watered down by making the compensation requirements so onerous as to defeat the very intent of the Article.
6. Galbraith (1991) opposed the implementation of the market economy, as Hayek recommended, in the Soviet Union on the ground that, 'this was not the design which in its rejection of the regulatory, welfare and ameliorating action by the state, we in the United States or elsewhere in the non-socialist world would find intolerable.' (p. 45). Stiglitz supports the same point of view: 'The Western countries pushed trade liberalization for the products that they exported, but at the same time continued to protect those sectors in which competition from developing countries might have threatened their economies' [Stiglitz (2003), p. 60]. Similar views have been aired in UNDP (2003a; 2005).
7. 'All of the late industrialists of the nineteenth century practiced import substitution before shifting to export promotion' [Adelman (2001), p. 120].

12

The Anti-Liberalist Consensus II: The Moral Dimension

The central point of this chapter is to show that the liberalist moral case for free markets is logically invalid and empirically unsound. In this context, it groups together all the arguments that have uprooted the Liberalist Paradigm's moral foundations by demonstrating the limited reach of the self-interest maximization principle and the utter irrelevance of the liberalist moral rights philosophy to development policy. Most of these arguments are reviewed in detail in Part V.

12.1. THE LIMITED REACH OF SELF-INTEREST MAXIMIZATION PRINCIPLE

The Liberalist Paradigm regularly refers to the self-interest maximization principle as the sole manifestation of the rational behaviour. The principle is focused on the maximization of one's self-interest to the exclusion of all other social and economic objectives. If, indeed, rational behaviour were synonymous with self-interest maximization alone, as the liberalists are convinced it is, then the 'raging insatiability' of the human spirit, which forsakes self-love for the greater good of others, would be promptly put down as irrational behaviour. Yet another implication of this drastic simplification (indeed distortion) of reality is that it leaves out of account altruistic aspects of human behaviour that make life worth living for. In this radically exclusivist outlook of rational behaviour one does not find even the fleeting shadows of warm-hearted egalitarianism; it also leaves little space for a socially committed development policy—without which, as we shall argue towards the end of this book, systemic change of ill-ordered societies into well-ordered cannot come about.[1] Fortunately, there have been some foundational contributions made to rescue human rationality from the narrow box in which the liberalists seem to have imprisoned it for life. It may be of interest to briefly review the highlights of some of these contributions.

Firstly, the liberalists claim about the universal reach of the self-interest principle, and it being an 'empirically testable hypothesis', cannot be established just by casual observation.[2] The fact is that the universal appeal of such an 'unsocial' view lies in its remaining untested. It should not be too difficult to visualize situations in which a socially desired end is not in the individual's self-interest. Indeed, it would be odd if it were otherwise—that is, if that which is in one's self-interest is morally correct as well. On the contrary, one should normally expect a conflict between morality and self-interested behaviour. For instance, even though it may be in somebody's interest to break one's promises, most reasonable people will still regard keeping one's promises as moral and rational [Allen Buchanan (1985)]. Also, it has been shown that this 'narrow view of rationality is not only arbitrary; it can also lead to serious descriptive and predictive problems in economics (given the assumption of rational behaviour)' [Sen (2002c), p. 23].

Secondly, it is arbitrary to limit rationality to self-interest maximization alone. Indeed, a person who insists on remaining irrevocably wedded to self-interestedness but does not know whether she/he should be self-interested at all, or if so, then to what extent, is more of a 'rational fool' who gives the same answer to related but distinct questions [Sen (1976–77)].[3] This is an example of the 'authoritarianism of artificial definitions'. Fortunately, rational behaviour is not that limited in its reach and salience; it is essentially about making a reasoned choice out of the available alternatives or, as Sen (2002c) puts it, subjecting one's choices to 'reasoned scrutiny'. It follows that there has to be a great diversity in the reasons for choice. Hence, to pin down human motivation to just one object namely, self-interest, would greatly compromise the possibilities of human reason. It would also artificially limit the exercise of human volition and her/his capacity to make a reasoned choice when confronted with a thistle of difficult problems.

Thirdly, the modern advances in game theory show that rationality as self-interest principle cannot adequately explain rational behaviour [Lewin (1996); Mansfield (1990); Binmore (1987; 1988)]. Even the simple Prisoner's Dilemma game illustrates the divergence between private rationality and collective rationality—that is, between the (inferior) outcomes if each prisoner played by the rules of a dominant self-interest strategy and a (superior) cooperative strategy that will give each one of the prisoners a better individual and collective outcome. The moral of playing these alternative game strategies is that things in real-world situations will greatly improve if rules of cooperative strategies (denoting non-self-interested behaviour) are actually observed, even though individuals may prefer to play by the rules of a non-cooperative strategy. Fehr and Fishbacher (2003) have fairly conclusively proved that the self-interest principle is not the exclusive basis for human motivation.[4] On the contrary, one must admit 'small irrationalities' to explain human behaviour adequately. What makes these entities important is that the exact nature of equilibrium happens to depend on these small irrationalities [Fudenberg and Maskin (1990)].

Fourthly, it has been shown that self-interested behaviour cannot form the sole, or even a significant, basis for achieving collective good. Olson (1971) showed that in large groups (i.e., big corporations, the nation state etc.), 'unless there is some coercion or some other device to make individuals act in their common interest, rational, self-interested individuals will not achieve their common or group interests' (p. 2). Not only that; with no binding moral norms to self-regulate, voluntary selfish behaviour of the members of a large community or society would be inconsistent with achieving the common good, even if the members of such a group know that they would gain by acting in such a manner. This is because individual members of a large group can easily free ride on the assumption that others will not notice her/his act of not giving. On the other hand, with some kind 'of explicit or internalized social cooperation' people will act in the interest of the society [Hirsch (1977), p. 138].

Finally, perhaps the most important limitation of the self-interest principle is that it runs counter to internationally agreed treaties and covenants, which seek to prevent the outbreak of universal selfishness—or at least minimize its virulence. Thus, for instance, the International Covenant on Economic, Social and Cultural Rights (1966) and the Universal Declaration of Human Rights (2000) illustrate the tendency of global policies to move away from the liberalists advocacy of the principles of meritocracy and self-help. These matters are discussed in Chapter 13. The moral of the story is that in a world that retains an ethical core, the onslaught of the love of the self cannot go unchecked. There would then be hope for collective social advancement, and not just the rush to self-aggrandizement.

12.2. 'AN IDEOLOGY TO END IDEOLOGIES'[5]

It may be appropriate at this point to evaluate the Liberalist Paradigm's point of view on egalitarian reforms in general and on helping the poor in particular. A general comment in this regard is that it has popularized a somewhat nihilistic economic and moral philosophy that rejects an individual or a social commitment to doing anything positive (especially one that involves government intervention) to alleviate the sufferings and the degradation of the poor peoples and nations. The Liberalist Paradigm has made intellectually acceptable an uncompromising insistence on non-coercive, un-improvable Pareto-optimal market solutions, according absolute priority to individual liberty, and a consequence-independent moral-rights philosophy that would reject all trade-offs between individual (political) liberty and other socially desirable policy objectives like poverty alleviation and distributive justice. The consequences of such an uncompromisingly individualistic philosophy, intended or unintended, should have been easily anticipated: 'In the mid-

1980s it was widely alleged that poverty reduction had lost salience for LDC governments and donors' [Lipton and Ravallion (1995)]. This aspect of the Liberalist Paradigm needs some elaboration, if only because normally one would not subscribe to these views.

12.2. (i). The Consequence-Insensitivity of Liberalist Paradigm

One of the defining characteristics of the Liberalist Paradigm is its manifest hostility towards any programme to redistribute income and wealth that has been acquired through legally sanctioned procedures. On strictly moral grounds as well, it does not treat the individual's economic rights against starvation at par with her/his political rights. Instead, it argues, that all government interventions constitute arbitrary infringement on individual moral rights. Nozick (1974) is explicit on this point: 'The state may not use its coercive apparatus for the purpose of getting some [rich] citizens to aid the [poor]' (p. ix). Thus, to take an extreme example, an honest libertarian will come out morally clean in a famine situation so long as the government does not 'coerce' the rich to help the famine-stricken people. The reason is that extreme poverty may be 'morally unfortunate' but it is not 'morally unjust', because starvation and famine do not constitute a violation of (the well-fed) individual's moral rights. It is, therefore, no exaggeration to state that the Liberalist Paradigm has aimed to lay down the rules of a 'savage justice', whereby 'the right to life is the right not to be killed, it is not the right to be given sustenance' [Hausmann and McPherson (1993), p. 703].

12.2. (ii). The Doctrine of Self-help

Perhaps, one of the most important opinion-forming liberalist ideas has been that the poor people and countries are themselves responsible for their well-being. On the other hand, the responsibility of the rich people and countries towards the poor people and countries is considered as voluntary, or at best made conditional on the former having exhausted all possibilities of improving their well-being by their own efforts. Indeed, the word 'responsibility' is anathema to the liberalists. This is the direct corollary of the principle noted above—namely, that the rich cannot be coerced into helping the poor on moral grounds, even in such extreme situations as starvation and famines. This idea has found acceptance also in the international circles, which have framed rules that put the burden of adjustment on the developing countries. Indeed, this was the regnant idea behind the metamorphosis of the GATT into the WTO. Hayek (1960) was perhaps the most authentic proponent of this point of view. He explicitly states: it is wrong to suggest, 'that those who are poor, merely in the sense that there are others in the society who are richer, are entitled to the wealth of the latter...' (p. 101). This is because, 'even the poorest today owe their well being to the results of past inequality' (pp. 40–46). Nozick (1974), going a step further, is dead opposed to any redistribution on the grounds that any pre-existing inequities must have arisen from the differential abilities of the people so that the meritorious got (and should have got) more. That being the case, all reformative action that undermined merit would be morally wrong because that would constitute a 'violation of people's rights' (p. 168). In this forceful, though misguided, advertisement of meritocracy no thought has been given to the simple fact that such policies would in effect mean perpetuating the unearned advantages of birth and early nurture to a disproportionate extent. The only reward of this policy inaction, in an overarching regime of voluntarism, would be some kind of political egalitarianism—that is, no one has a greater right to liberty than anyone else. But for the poor to have the political freedom merely to protest against economic un-freedom for which no liberalist remedy exist, though valuable in its own right, is really pointless. It would really amount to dying for the freedom to starve.

12.2. (iii). The Absolutism of Moral Rights

It is somewhat surprising that the liberalists have not addressed the practical issues that its antiseptic moral philosophy would give rise to. What it really says is that there is precious little that one could do in this world of unequal political and economic power, if by accident or by design, the powerful decided to cheat, even oppress, the weaker members of the society. Nozick's argument simply is that, if and when everyone observed rules of moral rights then no breach of moral rights would occur. Thus, while paying due regard to rights and duties of individuals by placing side-constraints on what others (including the state) are allowed to do, Nozick would not be concerned with the 'badness' of a situation in which the rights of individuals were actually violated by the non-observance of the prescribed constraints by others in the society. Instead, he would be content with pointing out that it was wrong to have done it in the first place.[6] In this altogether extraordinarily narrow view of moral rights, the existence of individual moral rights would be sufficient to satiate the liberalist moral sensibilities, notwithstanding the obvious fact that such arrangements would not enable the weaker members of society to use their rights effectively to lessen their deprivation. To make it look tolerably humane, the liberalist response has been to point out that, while a theory of libertarian justice is concerned exclusively with the prevention of the violations of individual's rights, one also needs a 'theory of virtues', which, would take care of poor peoples' privations by inducing (rich) individual's to help them. However, the libertarians have not bothered to lay down such a theory. The important point is that they regard giving to the poor as a matter of charity, not a matter of the poor people's right in the wealth of the rich. In other words, the poor cannot claim help on moral, much less legal, grounds, nor can the rich be coerced to part with their wealth. Needless to point out, such social inactivity (indeed, insensitivity) has amounted to doing nothing substantial, if at all, to reduce the poverty and the deprivation of the poor people and countries. Fortunately, the globally agreed treaties, discussed at length in Chapter 13, have forcefully rejected this line of argument.

12.3. THE LIBERALIST INDIFFERENCE TO INEQUITY

As noted above, a strict adherence to the Pareto-optimality rule makes the Liberalist Paradigm blissfully indifferent to issues of equity. Indeed, it does not regard the equity issues as worth the attention of hard-headed social scientists.[7] Instead, it maintains that a society that keeps its market unfettered is mutually advantageous so that what is efficient must at least be reasonably equitable. True, some feeble attempts have been made to make the Pareto-optimal rule pay at least lip service to distributional issues. An influential line of enquiry has been to focus on social welfare. Bergson (1938) and Samuelson (1947) provided an elegant proof of the proposition that a solution to problems of distributive equity is equivalent to maximizing a Bergson-Samuelson social welfare function. An intellectual feat that mesmerized a whole generation of well-meaning (neo-classical) economists, the rule amounted to doing nothing tangible to improve the distribution of the gains from exchange. Its manifest egalitarianism is more apparent than real for the following reasons: (a) The distributively neutral Pareto-optimality criterion could not possibly be used as a reference point for measuring a real improvement in the distribution of income and wealth. (b) The intention of the rule is that the gainers in social acts of exchange compensate the losers through the Hicksian non-distorted, lump-sum transfers, only notionally, but not actually. However, as noted earlier on in this book, this compensation device is no better than scientific trickery—in that it in effect amounts to transferring nothing from the rich to the poor. (c) The inflexible condition that the gains or losses be exclusively measured in terms of additions to, or subtractions from, total utility has meant leaving practically every distributive concern out of its rather restrictive welfare accounting.

To make further 'progress' on the vital problem of social justice, Buchanan and Tullock (1962) would have the distributive equity issue decided at the constitutional-making stage. Rather than 'solving' it by the lump-sum tax-subsidy, they let the potential losers be compensated through constitutional procedures that ensure the impartiality and unanimity of the decisions taken at some unspecified date in the past. However, in their scheme, the impartiality and unanimity of the legislator's decisions does not survive the constitution-making stage, beyond which the self-interested individuals would still decide the day-to-day affairs. The problem with this apparently fair procedure is that, while devising impartial constitutional procedures is a fundamental principle of a credible public policy, the further requirement that these procedures be unanimously approved would, in all probability, not lead to any substantive egalitarian outcome for the following reasons: (i) Some self-interested individuals, or even one of them, might (indeed, would) decide to block a change that hurts their interests, even if a majority regarded it as socially desirable. True, unanimity about a change in the *status quo* could be negotiated through public debate and discussion, or by a trading of compromises among themselves (which is equivalent to a logrolling process), but, contrary to the Buchanan and Tullock's intentions, the intervention of the government would be necessary to get people to agree voluntarily to a change that would hurt some while making some people better off. (ii) In the absence of an effective compliance mechanism, the decisions taken at the constitution-making stage might not be voluntarily implemented at all subsequently. Once again, as at the decision-making stage, a coercive solution (one that would involve government intervention in some form) will be required to implement them. (iii) It is highly unrealistic to think that impartial constitution-makers could foresee all the distributive issues that might arise as a result of the activities of the self-interested individuals who make and break the day-to-day decision rules.

12.4. INADEQUACY OF VOLUNTARY ACTION

An important aspect of the Liberalist Paradigm that the anti-Liberalist Consensus has called in question is its assertion that the only morally correct way to address egalitarian issues is by the voluntary actions of individuals. The fundamental problem with this point of view is that it also accepts a full-blooded pursuit of self-interest, which has been variously cloaked in constitutionalism, paraded in defence of individual liberty, or played earnestly in a draughty game-theoretic framework. But all this is incompatible with substantive egalitarianism. The heart of the problem is that the liberalist argument ignores that the free-rider phenomenon and the assurance problem would normally block an adequate supply of private beneficence.[8] This would especially be the case if individuals in the society were informed by a desire that the needy be provided for (by others) regardless of their contributions, rather than they themselves participating in philanthropic acts. The fact is that the voluntary acts of individuals would not be enough to generate sufficient funds to finance a viable charitable venture, even if they want to be charitable (and are not free riders). The reason is that, unless assured that other individuals would also be making their contributions to some common fund to help the poor, even morally motivated individuals would not contribute. For this reason, 'even if all members in a large group are rational and self-interested, and would gain if, as a group, they acted to achieve their common interest or objective, they will still not voluntarily act to achieve that common or group interest' [Olson (1971), p. 2]. It follows from this argument that, 'the laudable desire to be effectively beneficent may be self-defeating, where coercion is absent' [Allen Buchanan (1986), p. 73]. Arrow (1972) recognized the non-universality and incompleteness of the price system, which for that reason needs to be, 'supplemented by an implicit or explicit social contract. Thus one might loosely say that the categorical imperative and the price system are essential complements' (p. 357). Here the role of the government would be to assure the contributing individuals that other individuals would also contribute. More generally, the government would help in the evolution of such a social contract between itself and the individuals and between the individuals.

12.5. Markets, Diversity, and Heterogeneity of Talents

It may be of some interest to examine a recent positivist statement of the centrality of the efficiency aspects of free markets and the unimportance of the concerns about the inequalities of income and wealth. The argument is that inequalities arise because 'markets value diversity, markets sort out buyers and sellers appropriately to take advantage of the heterogeneous talents and tastes'. They arise out of the natural differences in their abilities and the investment decisions that different individuals take in acquiring better education and earn more experience and that, 'such inequalities are beneficial to the individual and the society as a whole because they improve the overall standard of living' [Rosen (2002), p. 11]. Whatever might be said of such arguments about the efficiency of the markets in sorting out diversities, the same is not an economic, much less a moral, argument in favour of the inequalities that markets generate. Firstly, inequalities of income and wealth cannot be entirely explained, much less justified, by the working of the markets and its 'sorting out' machine. And it is certainly an oversimplification to attribute inequalities of income and wealth to the differentials of skill and ability between individuals alone. But this is indeed an artificially narrow calculus because there is a lot more to determine one's chances in life than her/his own efforts. Secondly, it is not morally correct to reward individuals for their inborn faculties and those arising from early nurture for which they are not 'responsible', as Dworkin (1981a,b) has shown at length. Indeed, the task of public policy is to put into operation some principle of redress to nullify the advantages that individuals come to enjoy due to the circumstances beyond their control. To this end, it will be essential to devise a mechanism to compensate the losers in development. Obviously, the momentous task of a socially beneficial and just restructuring of the extant structure of rewards and incentives cannot possibly be left to those who are going to be adversely affected by it. It can only be achieved by an informed and committed state that has the power to coerce the recalcitrant souls to fall in line with the dictates of public policy.[9] Thirdly, a demonstration that the overall standard of living rises in the process of the market 'sorting out' inequities between consumers and producers does not necessarily imply that this overall (potential) increment in the living standards will actually materialize, much less that it will be fairly distributed and morally uncontroversial.

12.6. Concluding Remarks

It should be obvious from the analysis presented in this chapter that that the liberalist brand of inconsequential moral right, to which the Liberalist Paradigm has subscribed unreservedly, has lost out in the battle of ideas. Of late, there has been a rising crescendo of opinion that morally motivated conceptions of fairness and justice should be reflected in the design of national and global development policies. The reason is that all humans have a strong moral sense of fairness, equity, and social justice and to be part of a society where the basic institutions have been restructured justly. In other words, equity is an intrinsically important goal, which needs to be cherished regardless of its instrumental worth, which too is very substantial. It is of some importance in this context that the WDR (2005) has been dedicated to issues of 'equity and development'. The Report declares, 'A focus on equity should be a central concern in the design and implementation of development and growth' (p. xi). The main reason for a focus on equity issue is that people prefer fairness regardless of the outcome, and that there is 'something deep and fundamental about our taste for fairness and equity' (p. 82). The Report also questions the universality of the self-interest principle as the sole basis of human moral motivation. It is ironical that real-world events should have forced the Bank to relinquish its cherished position of the leader of 'neo-classical resurgence' and the implementer-in-chief of the Liberalist Paradigm, and to join, or at least pose that it has joined, the Anti-Liberalist camp. If the Bank, going beyond the equity rhetoric, finally decides both in words and deeds, to assume a leadership role in highlighting the foundational developmental issues in the right earnest, it will help restore development thinking to one of its original purposes—away from the Liberalist Paradigm's exclusive focus on efficiency towards a strongly growing economy that cares. It will also be to the benefit of humankind if it did all that.

NOTES

1. It may be noted that economists have challenged self-interest principle since its birth. Thus, Adam Smith (1776/1976), who has been incorrectly interpreted as the originator of this principle, clearly stated: 'the interest of the dealers, however, in any branch of trade or manufactures, is always in some respects different from, and even opposite to that of the public' (pp. 266–267). Much latter, Keynes (1932) wrote: 'it is not a correct deduction from the principles of economics that enlightened self-interest always operates in the public interest' (pp. 312–313). But these illustrious names are exceptions to the nearly-universal support it has enjoyed among economists, as the next note shows.

2. Stigler (1981) claimed that the self-interest principle is not only logically unassailable but also an empirically testable hypothesis that would in all probability be proved right if actually tested. He asserted 'Let me predict the outcome of the systematic and comprehensive testing of behaviour in situations where self-interest and ethical values with verbal allegiance are in conflict. Much of the time, most of the time in fact, the self-interest theory (as I interpreted on Smithian lines) will win' (p. 176). Needless to point out, this statement is more an expression of faith in the likely outcome of a yet-to-be-carried out empirical testing of the self-interest hypothesis about human behaviour than a report on a statistically acceptable experiment in alternative situations. For a criticism of Stigler's assertions see Sen (1987).

3. 'Rational Fools' are defined as persons who fail to see the difference between such distinct concepts as '(1) personal well-being, (2) private self-interest, (3) one's goals and objectives, (4) individual values (including as Arrow puts it, 'values about values'), (5) or diverse reasons for what one may sensibly choose' [Sen (2002c), p. 6].

4. Fehr and Fishbacher (2003) show on the basis of extensive evidence that some people act in ways that are clearly inconsistent with selfish behaviour: '*altruistic rewarding*, a propensity to reward others for cooperative, norm abiding behaviour, and *altruistic punishment*, a propensity to impose sanctions on others for norm violations' (p. 785). Both these behaviour patterns rule out any consideration of reciprocity from others. This contribution is discussed in World Bank (2005).

5. Robinson (1979) referred to unrestrained capitalism as 'an ideology to end ideologies'. The ideology referred to in the text is the non-consequentialist moral-rights philosophy.

6. Sen (2000) points out that in case an individual assaults another person in an open violation of the side-constraint, 'the badness of the assault is not the issue in [the libertarian] approach, only its wrongness is' (p. 493).

7. Stern and Ferreira (1993) report on the state of insensitivity to distributional concerns among the World Bank's economists: 'The 1980s were dominated in the Bank by the problems of structural adjustment and debt. Direct concern with poverty and income distribution declined and, indeed, it was not uncommon to hear Reaganite denigrations of those concerned with the poor in terms of 'bleeding hearts', 'social planners' and 'flaunting of compassion' (p. 16).

8. The free-rider problem arises when I reason that in a collective charitable act my non-contribution would in all probability go unnoticed assuming that others would duly contribute their shares. The assurance problem emerges when I desire to be charitable but need assurance that others would contribute if I did. In both cases, the resolution of the problem requires some coercion by a public authority that every individual gives what he commits to give, not waiting for others to make similar contributions.

9. Thus Rawls (1999) calls for a restructuring of the basic institutions to redress the inequalities of birth and natural endowments in an essentially meritocratic society by giving most of the primary goods to those who have the least of them. Dworkin (1981a,b) recommends that equality be achieved with respect to the (internal) *resources* for which one is 'responsible', and *not* those which have been put at her/his disposal by the circumstances

of birth or early nurture. Sen (1992) would redistribute resources (primary social goods) to offset the individual capability deficits. For a detailed account of the competing perspectives on individual morality, public policy and human well-being, see Naqvi (2002). A relatively detailed account of these alternative social choices rules is given in Part VI of this book.

Part V

The Human Development Paradigm

13

The Human Development Paradigm I: The Basic Elements

The present study, departing from the conventional practice, defines the Human Development Paradigm more broadly to include the entire body of normative non-utilitarian social-choice theories, the UNDP's Research Programme, and the United Nations Covenant on Economic, Social and Cultural Rights, the Millennium Declaration, the Universal Declaration of Human Rights, and the Millennium Development Goals.[1] The reasons for 'flocking together' these apparently diverse and distinct strands of thought under a common paradigmatic denominator are that they share a similar worldview and a set of metaphysical beliefs about how the economic universe hangs together. They subscribe to a number of distinctive hypotheses about the behaviour of the economic agents and a logically consistent framework to deal with the problems of distributive justice, income and non-income poverty and human deprivation, and enhancing the women's agency as active contributors to economic development. They also use a pluralistic set of evaluation criteria, and do not commit the logical error of trying to reduce what is essentially an irreducible plurality to just one index—for instance, maximizing self-interest or per capita income. The focal point of their endeavour has been chivalrous indeed: to put 'the human beings at the centre of the development process' in order to analyze the problems of economic and human development in their multi-dimensional complexity. Rather than treating human beings as caged animals that do nothing but maximize their self-interest or remain fully focused on maximizing their income, they are seen as valuing their freedom of discretion and choice and naturally inclined to commit themselves to certain social causes, including those that might transcend one's immediate goals in life. Not terminally consumed by cupidity and greed, humankind normally possesses, as Rawls puts it, 'a sense of justice' and a 'conception of good'. Going beyond safeguarding the individual's negative freedoms (which is what the Liberalist Paradigm does), all components of the expanded Human Development Paradigm demand equitable outcomes with a view to saving human beings from injustice and letting them enjoy the freedom to lead a life they have reason to value. It is, therefore, no exaggeration to state that the Human Development Paradigm, as defined here, presents a refreshingly original and comprehensive agenda of social reform, which is scientifically sound and socially beneficial. That has meant changing the priorities of development policy as well.

It will be instructive to describe in this chapter each component of our inclusive concept of Human Development Paradigm before analyzing their collective focus on the central human development problems in the next three chapters.

13.1. Non-Utilitarian Social Choice Theories: Rawlsian Egalitarianism

Perhaps one of the most influential and profound contributions to non-Utilitarian moral philosophy in modern times has been John Rawls's theory of social justice [Rawls (1999)].[2] It comprises the twin principles of Justice as Fairness and the Difference Principle plus a theory of the 'Good of the Sense of Justice.'[3] Here we discuss only the first two and will come to the third one in Chapter 22. The Fairness criterion used to arrive at the Principles of Justice is held central to the universal acceptability and the stability of the rearrangement of the power and privilege that would emerge from the implementation of these principles. The Difference Principle is designed to ensure that 'those better circumstanced are willing to have their advantages only under a scheme in which it works out for the benefit of the less fortunate—' (p. 90). A faithful implementation of these foundational principles should create just institutions 'so that no one gains or loses from his arbitrary place in the distribution of natural assets or his initial position in society without giving or receiving compensating advantages in return' (p. 87).

13.1. (i). Procedural Fairness

In the contract-tradition of Locke (1952), Rousseau (1964) and Kant (1948), Rawls (1999) insists on the fairness of the procedures adopted to arrive at the basic principles of justice, no less than the principles themselves. The reason is that once these procedures get 'embodied in the basic structure of the society men tend to acquire the corresponding sense of justice and develop a desire to act in accordance with its principles' (p. 119). An important implication is that a strict observance of these principles would ensure 'the stability of social cooperation'. The technique used to ensure the fairness of the principles of justice is to imagine a group of individuals who are assigned the task of setting up 'a fair procedure so that any principles agreed to will be just'. To this end, this chosen group is assumed to work behind the 'veil of ignorance' so that it remains unaware of its respective position in the future social set-up that might flow from its decisions. An obvious attraction of following this rule to make the existing social and economic institutions socially just, is that the decisions so arrived at would be seen as impartial. Having passed through the veil of ignorance the members of this group arrive at their 'original position' of total equality with respect to the kind of information each possesses about her/his status in any future social order that comes into being in the light of its deliberations.

13.1. (ii). The Priority of Liberty

The Rawlsian basic principles of justice in serial order are: 'First: each person is to have an equal right to the most extensive scheme of basic equal liberties compatible with a similar scheme of liberties for others. Second: social and economic inequalities are to be arranged so that they are both: (a) reasonably expected to be to everyone's advantage and; (b) attached to positions and offices open to all' (p. 53). A more general principle, of which these two principles are special cases, is: 'All social values—liberty and opportunity, income and wealth, and the social bases of self-respect—are to be distributed equally unless an unequal distribution of any, or all, of these values is to everyone's advantage' (p. 54).[4] It may be noted here that the first principle assigns absolute priority to individual liberty, even though the exclusions of other social values (those relating to social justice, for instance) on this count are not as severe as the ones that liberalists stipulate.

13.1. (iii). The Difference Principle

The Difference Principle essentially lays down the social reach of the Rawlsian principle of justice.[5] It measures individual advantage, especially of the worst off, in terms of her/his possession of 'primary social goods', which are defined as 'rights, liberties and opportunities, income and wealth, and the social bases of self-respect', which every rational individual wants, irrespective of whatever else she/he may want (p. 79). It demands that those who possess the least of these goods must be their principal recipients, before all others in the society.

13.1. (iv). Relevance of Rawlsian Principles

It may be instructive to note some of the objections that have been levelled against the Rawlsian vision of social change: (i) Arrow (1973) pointed out that these principles do not come to the help of those who are not part of a system of cooperation—in the sense that they do not possess enough financial or real resources to enter the system of cooperation on the basis of give and take—because of their physical infirmity or of extreme poverty. Needless to state, this is a limitation of the principle because it excludes the most underprivileged group of persons from its purview.[6] (ii) The redistribution of resources from the rich to the poor contemplated under the Rawlsian system is expected to be rather moderate. It will not obviously be large enough to meet the needs of the least privileged in the developing countries. (iii) It has been pointed out that the Rawlsian principle is *not* a principle of equality. This is because in recommending the priority of the welfare of the least-privileged members of the society, Rawls does not put any limits to the process of the rich getting richer. The net result may, therefore, be to make the society more, rather than less equal.[7] However, this objection is more apparent than real. True, the Difference Principle does not require that income and wealth be equally distributed; but it does require that any inequality in their distribution must be to everyone's advantage. Institutional arrangements that guarantee the prior access of the worst-off individuals to these primary goods must, therefore, be reordered so that the access of the least privileged to these goods is ensured. In other words, income equality is directly covered in the Rawlsian scheme of equality. In fact, the choice between any two states of the economy is decided by reference to the effectiveness with which one or other satisfies the needs of the least-privileged people.[8]

At any rate, it would be unreasonable to try to evaluate the worth of the Rawlsian principles as formulae ready for application to development policy in different political and institutional set-ups. The relevant thing is their broad message, which is that any system of egalitarian reforms must ensure that the existing inequities in any society, rich or poor, should be redressed unless they are shown to benefit all; that the needs of the least-privileged in the society are accorded first priority in any scheme of societal change; and that a conscious attempt should be made to create a well-ordered society which its members would voluntarily defend against exogenous shocks and endogenous strains.

13.2. Non-Utilitarian Choice Theories: Sen's 'Functionings' and 'Capabilities'

Sen's Functionings-and-Capabilities analysis in some respects goes beyond the Rawlsian scheme because 'the appropriate space is neither that of utilities (as claimed by the upholders of the welfare system) or of primary goods (as demanded by Rawls), but that of the substantive freedoms—the capabilities—to choose a life one has reason to value' [Sen (1999b), p. 74]. His basic idea is that the evaluation of development success (failure) should be done in terms of the achieved functionings—beings and doings which are integral elements of a person's well-being or ill-being—and by taking into account the freedoms each individual has to choose between alternative functionings. The capabilities are defined as specific choices made (voluntarily) from alternative combinations of functionings [Sen (1992)]. There is a close relationship between functionings and capabilities but they are not the same. While the functionings reflect a person's actual achievements, capabilities denote her/his freedom to achieve specific functionings [Sen (1999b), pp. 74-76]. The most widely used functionings are being healthy, being educated, having a reasonable income, and one's ability to move about in the society without a sense of shame. He regards the Rawlsian social primary goods or Dworkin's 'resources' as the means to achieve certain valuable 'functionings,' which are constitutive of human well being and which give the individual the freedom—the capability—to lead a life one voluntarily wants to follow.[9] But, an equal possession of primary goods will not, as a rule, convert into equal entitlement to functionings and capabilities. The reason is that some inescapable personal heterogeneities and diversities must be taken into account to be able to convert the possession of primary social goods or resources into the 'capability' to live really well.[10] For these reasons personal circumstances need to be taken into consideration to ensure the equality of the conversion rates. The essential problem of egalitarian reforms is, therefore, to ensure an equitable 'conversion' of primary goods into valuable functionings.[11]

It should be clear that Sen's approach has greater explanatory power than the alternative utilitarian or the resource-based or the primary goods approaches because it can define in a more comprehensive way the meaning of human happiness or the lack of it (i.e., deprivation). Thus, a disabled person might have to be allowed to enjoy more utility, resources or primary goods than the amounts given to an able-bodied or a younger person if the objective is to put the two at the same level of capability. Furthermore, it is argued, focusing on income or resources alone one may not be able to discern the extent of substantive 'deprivation' of persons who, through long exposure to the adversities of life, might have come to terms with them. And yet ignoring those who stoically carry the cross of their deprivations and yet would not talk about them in public, will serve neither the ends of justice nor the imperatives of fairness. But, above all, Sen's approach jealously guards the independence of the human spirit to make the choices one has reason to value most. This is because the institutional arrangements for the foundational opportunities individuals have (i.e., 'economic opportunities, political freedom, social powers, and the enabling conditions of good health, basic education, and the encouragement and cultivation of initiatives') are basically influenced 'by the exercise of people's freedoms, through the liberty to participate in social choice and in the making of public decisions that impel the progress of these opportunities' [Sen (1999b), p. 5]. Sen's analysis makes a significant advance on: (a) the *utilitarian's* unifocal concentration on mental experiences of satisfaction expressed exclusively in terms of total utilities; (b) the *neo-classical's* non-recognition of the real trade-off between parties to exchange and their ruling out of the possibility of the interpersonal comparison of individual utilities; (c) the *libertarian's* (e.g., Nozick's or Hayek's) focus on only the procedures of achieving individual liberty and on preventing the negative freedoms in a totally non-consequential setting; and (d) the *contractarian's* (e.g., Dworkin's, Rawl's) emphasis on the processes of arriving at the principles of justice and on the means (i.e., social primary goods, resources) to achieve human happiness.

13.3. THE UNDP's RESEARCH PROGRAMME

The second, and the most 'visible', element of the Human Development Paradigm is what we have renamed as the UNDP's Research Programme. Begun in 1990, its dimension and reach have been extended and reported over the years in its justly celebrated *Human Development Reports* (HDRs), which give each member country's relative achievement with respect to its human-development achievements and provide invaluable detailed statistical information about key human development variables. But no less significant for development policy is that these reports hold up a mirror, so to speak, to each country so that it can see its real human development accomplishments and do something positive about them. It definitely exercises an 'announcement effect' on the policies of the national governments. An improvement in a country's ranking *vis-à-vis* others in terms of their human development record has been an occasion for national self-congratulation while a drop in it a cause for global embarrassment. Regardless of what it is, it brings to bear immense pressure on governments to reclaim at least their 'old' HDI rank. In addition, each year global and national attention gets focused on a 'burning' development theme. Of late, it has given special attention to the international dimension of development—especially to the inequities of the present international economic system. For both reasons, UNDP's Research Programme is regarded by its creators, 'as an entirely new perspective, a revolutionary way to recast our conventional approach to development' [Haq (1995), p. 11].

13.3. (i). The Essential Roles of the UNDP Research Programme

The UNDP Research Programme can be seen as having performed four quintessential roles—namely, the evaluative; the information broadening; the advocacy and; the agenda-setting roles—each of which it has performed with great sophistication and dedication. Firstly, rather than focusing exclusively on national income per capita, it has, consistent with its underlying philosophy noted above, sought to use pluralistic criteria for evaluating national and global development efforts. This could be referred to as the evaluative aspect of the new research programme. To this end, it has mounted monumental and unprecedented efforts for over sixteen years to supplement, though not replace, GNP per capita, with a more comprehensive Human Development Indicator (HDI). The latter reports national progress in regard to the acquisition of some valuable 'functionings'—to be literate, to live a long and healthy life (as proxies for knowledge acquisition and longevity respectively), and adjusted income per capita, expressed in Purchasing Power Parity dollars (as proxy for a reasonable command over a multiplicity of economic objects apart from literacy and life expectancy)—which everyone is expected to want whatever else he/she may want. In addition, three more basic human development indicators—the HPI (the Human Poverty Index), the GDI (the Gender-related Development Index) and GEM (the Gender Empowerment Measure)—have been designed to focus on specific aspects of human deprivations (or negative achievements). The HPI reinforces the HDI measure by looking at the same information that goes into the construction of HDI's in the mirror of individual social deprivations: the probability at birth of not surviving to age forty, the adult literacy rate, and the percentage of people without access to clean potable water, and the percentage of children under age five who are significantly underweight for their age. The GDI disaggregates the data used in the construction of HDI by sex to highlight the inequalities between men and women in terms of their differential achievements in the acquisition of knowledge and access to health and income. GEM has a similar motivation—to focus on inequalities with respect to the male-female share in legislative, senior official positions and in professional and technical openings. The statistical bases of each of these indices have been refined each year to sort out specific index number problems.[12] The manner of treating income in these indices has received particular attention. This is because, one of the defining characteristics of the UNDP's Research Programme has been its uncompromising emphasis, which is repeated each year lest the reader should forget, that income maximization is not by itself the goal of human development effort; rather it is merely an instrument for achieving specific functionings and capabilities. A logical (and intended) implication of this observation has been a significantly reduced, though still significant, role for growth of per capita income *per se* in evaluating success (failure) on the human-development scale. Income maximization is no longer the proverbial Prince of Denmark in the new scheme of things. The net effect of this head-shrinking exercise is to create a new, much emaciated, income variable: it is only one of the three *dramatis personae*, with the main policy focus being on education and health.[13] This implication of the HDI for development policy is discussed in some detail in Chapters 14 and 15 and at other places in the book.

Secondly, these indices highlight, for 172 member countries, their relative success or failures to form and exercise the individual freedoms (capabilities) to be able to make the choices individuals make, or must make, to attain a modicum of happiness. The immense data collection effort that goes into the construction of these basic indicators is reported each year in the Human Development Report.[14] This is the information broadening aspect of the UNDP Research Programme, which is perhaps one of its most uncontroversial and enduring, though not the only, contributions to the state of knowledge about human progress.

Thirdly, an equally important aspect of the UNDP Research Programme is its advocacy aspect—that is, it makes a conscious effort to change development policy in the developing as well as the developed countries. The information on the elemental issues of human development that it regularly provides has become one of the most cited sources for meaningful discussions and debates, for which the UNDP also provides funds and forums. This torrent of information regularly fertilizes thinking on, and talking about, development policy perspectives in developing countries. Indeed, it would not be an exaggeration to claim that a marked increase in the emphasis on social expenditures (especially those on education and health) since 1990 has come about through the UNDP's efforts, for which it has rightfully earned the highest commendation. Its advocacy effort has had a global dimension as well: it has pleaded the developing countries causes in the relevant international forums. An important example is its pointed and constructive—and to some extent effective—criticisms of the WTO and the globalization process—both of which routinely get thumbs up reports each year from such vital global development players as the World Bank and the IMF. However, the downside of this entirely laudable effort is that it also attracts a lot of paid research. Such research does not add much to an understanding of the paradigm's actual and potential contributions to the human-development process. Yet another is that maximization of income objective has been somewhat degraded in the national scheme of priorities—though in this respect the paradigm's success has been, fortunately, only partial.

Fourthly, no less important has been its agenda-setting role. The UNDP Research Programme has consciously sought to influence development research priorities in the academia both in the developing and the developed countries. This mission has been accomplished by funding academic research on a series of human development causes. An important input in this process has been its own evaluation of major human development themes, which is reported in the Human Development Reports e.g., globalization, WTO initiatives, structural adjustments, aid, trade and security issues, the issue of cultural liberty and human freedom, etc. It has, of late, revived many of the central development themes, like the increasing role of government in accelerating the rate of economic and human development, especially by encouraging import-substitution of goods and knowledge through selective but temporary protection—those which the Traditional Development Paradigm first discovered and implemented. An important aspect of this effort is that the traditional emphasis on reducing income and wealth inequalities has been reintroduced (in the 2005 *Human Development Report*). It has been shown that differential inequalities between countries can make a significant difference to their respective human development achievements. Most commendable, however, has been its focus on gender inequity that has, unhappily, coexisted with economic and human development. In this context, it has emphasized both the 'welfare' aspect and the 'agency' aspect of women empowerment. Perhaps, this can be labelled as one of the brightest aspects of the Human Development Paradigm in general, and of the UNDP Research Programme in particular. And truly foundational has been its emphasis on the moral dimensions of economic and human development. In this respect it has been more successful than any other paradigm so far, partly because it has brought 'high theory' and practical economics together to focus on such vital issues as social justice, poverty and human deprivation with full confidence in the scientific correctness of its approach. All these aspects of the Human Development Paradigm will be commented upon in the following chapters.

It may be noted at this point that, even though the basic motivation of the UNDP's Research Programme was to replace the allegedly 'monocentric' focus of the Traditional Development Paradigm by a more pluralistic set of criteria to measure development success, its real contribution to development policy has been to break the stranglehold of the Liberalist Paradigm on the global approach to economic and human development. These matters are discussed at some length in Chapters 14 and 15.

13.4. THE COVENANT ON ECONOMIC, SOCIAL AND CULTURAL RIGHTS AND UNIVERSAL DECLARATION OF HUMAN RIGHTS

The Covenant on Economic, Social and Cultural Rights (1966)—which entered into force in January, 1976—the Universal Declaration of Human Rights (2000), and the Millennium Development Goals (2000) supplement and reinforce the UNDP Research Programme's emphasis on social justice, education, health, freedom from hunger, poverty and human deprivation.[15] In particular, the Covenant predates all the basic ideas with respect to education and health—and some more that the UNDP Research Programme has given concrete shape to. Indeed, these global agreements in terms of their salience and reach seem to have successfully captured the essence of the poignant history of the human spirit to create a world based on justice and fairness.

13.4. (i). The Covenant

The Covenant, and the enclosed Comments on each of its articles, was in fact a revolutionary document when it came out; and in many respects it still remains un-superseded in the breadth of its vision and the clarity of its focus. It explicitly recognizes every individual's right to food (Article 11), education (Articles, 13 and 14), and health (Article 12); and imposes the corresponding obligations on the national governments and the global community to monitor progress in these respects.[16] In particular, it regards the individual's right to be free from hunger—which surprisingly the UNDP Research Programme does not include in the HDI—as fundamental to the realization of all other human rights. It does not accept the non-availability of financial resources as a valid excuse for the non-fulfilment of this right. If a poor nation cannot fulfil its obligations in this regard, it should show that it has exhausted all the domestic and internationally available means to fulfil these obligations. The same is true for education. The Covenant emphasized the obligations of the national governments and global community to provide free primary education to all people; and it mandates that all possible steps be taken to fulfil the right to free higher education. These Articles together set 'a human-rights agenda—rights to food, education, health care, and decent living standards', which if and when acted upon would revolutionalize development policy in the developing and the developed countries.

13.4. (ii). The UN's Declaration of Human Rights and the Millennium Development Goals

More recently, the United Nations has reinforced the Covenant. It emphasizes that achieving the goals set out in all these documents is not an act of charity doled out by the rich countries to the poor countries; these are, in fact, the latter's claimable rights on the wealth of the former.[17] This vital conjunction of the national and global targets has set the framework for a globally agreed upon system of rights and obligations—a set of benchmarks against which the progress that the national governments make in achieving them can be adequately measured. Under this system of 'shared responsibilities' the national governments and global development actors would be held accountable in case they fail to fulfil their obligations to satisfy the specified rights. The Covenant and the Declaration make it a national and global obligation to keep track of the gross violations of economic (and not just political) human rights, which routinely take place in both the developed and the developing countries. They widen the scope for making individual choices among alternative policies and increase the range of financial feasibility as the budget constraints at the national level are expected to be relaxed with a greater flow of development aid. An effective implementation of these revolutionary egalitarian ideas would take understanding the complex, but positive, interaction between the individual's human agency and social obligations. So too would it entail an explicit recognition of the nature of the relationship between personal and collective responsibilities for the consequences of specific acts and events. There is an essential reciprocity here, though by no means exact, between the specific acts and happenings and the consequent state of affairs and the responsibility to do what a developing country can do to remedy (or contribute significantly to remedying) that state of affairs if it gets worse for some individuals or groups of individuals.[18] These international treaties and covenants formalize a global system of values which, if implemented, would bury in a deep grave the self-help principle, which underlies much of the thinking of international donors; set the stage for a fair sharing of the fruits of economic progress nationally and globally; and put the global dialogue on national rights and obligations on a new and higher plane of understanding.

13.5. Moral Moorings of the Human Development Paradigm

The expanded Human Development Paradigm, briefly described above, makes two solid contributions to knowledge that set it apart from the competing paradigms.

13.5. (i). The 'Pluralism' of Evaluative Criteria

As noted at the outset of this chapter, a foundational characteristic of the Human Development Paradigm is the essential plurality of the criteria it would use to evaluate national and international economic progress. The point of the exercise is to highlight the importance of making progress on a wider front to measure increments in human well-being than has been the usual practice. Thus, one of the basic reasons for rejecting Utilitarianism is that it reckons just one index (utility) of human happiness for evaluating the consequences of specific policies. As opposed to this traditional logical practice, both the Rawlsian and Sen's analyses explicitly take into account a multiplicity of ethically valuable entities that must all be taken into consideration in any satisfactory evaluative exercise, because leaving out any one of them will significantly undervalue a person's actual or contemplated achievements. A person may make progress in terms of wealth, but she/he will be less happy (indeed, be miserable) if denied the freedom to choose between alternative combinations of the possible lifestyles. Needless to state, she/he would like to have the best of both the worlds. In the Rawlsian scheme, the social primary goods—'rights, liberties, and opportunities, and income and wealth [and social bases of self-respect]'—are goods that 'a rational man wants whatever else he may want' [Rawls (1999), p. 79]. An important aspect of social primary goods is that they relate to the basic structure of the society and for that reason form an irreducible minimum.[19] They together form an index of human happiness. The index-number problem in this context is not one of reducing the six (or more) elements of the set of primary goods to a single homogenous primary good that represent all others.[20] The problem is solved by first ordering serially the primary goods. Individual liberties and basic equality of opportunity come first with the requirement that access to them is the same for all groups of people. The basic index of the remaining primary goods—namely, the distribution of power and privileges of authority and income and wealth—is their differential availability to the least-privileged members of the society. There is no single index of Sen's capabilities, which too are irreducibly pluralistic. These are more than one, some more important than others. Thus, well-being achievements may cover 'a diverse range of achievements, varying from being free from under-nourishment and avoidable morbidity to achieving self-respect and self-fulfilment' [Sen (1987), p. 64]. The point is that there is no way to reduce the inherent 'internal diversity' of valuable functionings to some artificially created homogenous entity because 'heterogeneity of factors that influence is a pervasive feature of evaluation' (pp. 76–77).[21] Indeed, it is the attempt to reduce to only one number (say, utility or income) the diverse factors that make or mar our lives that is arbitrarily exclusive.

13.5. (ii). Inter-personal Comparisons of Well-being

Yet another intellectual achievement of the Human Development Paradigm is to have finally overcome the economic profession's trained diffidence, invariably clothed in the garb of scientific rectitude, to do inter-personal comparisons of welfare.[22] The momentous nature of this achievement can be appreciated by recalling that one of the foundational characteristics of mainstream economics (which the Liberalist Paradigm has imbibed) has been the academic consensus since the 1940s about the impossibility of making inter-personal comparisons of utility (well-being).[23] What implication does this Olympian detachment of high-theory (from reality) have for development issues? The answer is that it practically precludes the design of development policy. Indeed, with the possibility of making interpersonal comparisons of welfare ruled out of court, 'we cannot even understand the force of public concerns about poverty, hunger, inequality, or tyranny'; and 'it would not be possible to talk about injustice and unfairness without having to face the accusation that such diagnoses must be inescapably arbitrary or intellectually despotic' [Sen (1999a), p. 365]. It has also created an unbridgeable gulf between the tractability and relevance of the mathematical representation of the real world. An outstanding example of this gulf is the justly celebrated Arrow's Impossibility Theorem (that, given conditions U, P, I and D, it is impossible to derive a social welfare index from the welfare indices of the individual members of a society that satisfies these conditions).[24] The Theorem has practically foreclosed all possibilities of deriving a consistent social choice rule if account is taken only of the individual ordering of the relevant alternatives. One nihilistic result of the Theorem has been to limit greatly, the possibility of even discussing distributive issues or poverty reduction without violating the basic rules of neo-classical rational behaviour based only on the preference rankings of the individuals [Sen (1999b), p. 252]. The demonstration of the possibility of the interpersonal comparisons of utility has, therefore, made it possible to do what it was not possible to do before: that is, to face the vital problems of social existence with confidence. No less important from the development policy point of view is that the problem of interpersonal comparisons has been sorted out by doing such exercises in terms of the observable indices of living conditions, which is what the UNDP's Research Programme does.

It may be noted that, in the Rawlsian scheme, the problem of making interpersonal comparisons is not that complicated because they need to be made only for the 'representative' least-privileged person. This establishes the benchmark against which the comparisons for the well-off persons are made ordinally [Rawls (1999), p. 79]. However, Sen's capability analysis does require making an interpersonal comparison of the relative importance for different individuals of the factors that impede the conversion of the income, resources, and primary goods into basic capabilities of different individuals to achieve the desired functioning.[25]

13.6. Implications for Development Policy

What do these rather abstract and esoteric-looking principles of justice, capability and functioning imply for development policy? Fortunately, they do quite a lot. Firstly, as noted above, they mean that one must go for a comprehensive list of accomplishments (or a policy package) in order to be satisfied with a given development policy regime. This is fundamental. As we have noted in Part VI at length, we need to aim at economic growth, reducing poverty within the framework of an egalitarian institutional change, as an irreducible policy package, but that requires a pluralistic set of criteria to evaluate success or failure on this inescapably complex endeavour.

Secondly, a public statement of these principles would add moral clout to a reformative development policy. And it would lower the cost of sustaining a developing society by harnessing the voluntary acceptance by its members of the basic aims and objectives of such a society. The Human Development Paradigm strongly suggests that development policy should be actually motivated by certain moral principles, which naturally appeal to human ideas of justice, fairness and goodness. And it does it with a renewed confidence in the scientific validity and real-life relevance of its policy prescriptions.

Thirdly, insofar as development policy aims to bring about systemic change, the Human Development Paradigm would provide some details of this expected outcome. The expectation would be that development policy would spur on forces that metamorphose the old and unjust institutions into new and just ones that last by virtue of their essential goodness. In the process, it promises to change the entire structure of values and the supporting architecture of institutions that make growth good for all the people and not just for a selected few and one that gives priority to the needs of least-privileged in the society. Once development policy is refocused in this way, its public ownership will be guaranteed by virtue of its justness and goodness. This aspect of the new paradigm is discussed at greater length in Chapter 17.

13.7. Concluding Remarks

This chapter highlights the contribution of the Human Development Paradigm to our knowledge and understanding of the development process. We have adopted a broader definition of the new paradigm with a view to bringing out its paradigmatic character. On the one hand, it pinpoints that the true import and significance of the UNDP's Research Programme can be understood only if it is seen in the context of the innovative non-Utilitarian consequentialist moral philosophy. On the other hand, its full reach must take explicit note of the several UN Declarations that share the same values. It is, therefore, helpful, at least for expository purposes, to place the UNDP Research Programme 'in the middle' of the Human Development Paradigm, with its philosophical underpinnings to the 'left' and the UN declarations to the 'right'. Once seen in this light, the expanded Human Development Paradigm looks more like a complete, self-contained system of thought, with its own value system, its basic logical statements and the consequences of these statements for development policy. It has been shown that the new paradigm has some original features that must be kept in mind in evaluating its true import and rationale.

Firstly, the new paradigm assures us that caring for the poor and the least-privileged in the society and an uncompromising insistence on social justice is a scientific principle in the most rigorous sense of the term and the very acme of rationality. Indeed, not doing so would not only be scientifically and morally incorrect, it would also be a gross violation of internationally agreed treaties and agreements. As noted above, the Covenant and the Declaration reaffirm the principle of global commitment to poor peoples and nations. Thus, for instance, with respect to the right to food and freedom from hunger, these global documents put the signatory states under an obligation to fulfil these rights. Resource constraint on the part of an individual country, rich or poor, is not accepted as an excuse for the non-fulfilment of these rights. If a country cannot fulfil these obligations on its own then it is a global commitment to help that country.[26] These global commitments, in effect, emphasize that the individuals' economic and political freedoms are essentially interconnected and mutually reinforcing for achieving the daunting task of societal transformation in both the developed and the developing countries.[27]

Secondly, the Human Development Paradigm rejects the liberalist 'self-help' principle. While recognizing the importance of the developing countries doing their utmost to help themselves, it does not assign to them full and exclusive responsibility for their predicament. Instead, it emphasizes a global system of 'shared responsibilities' in meeting the basic human rights to food, health and education as the true principle of international economic cooperation and vital for global peace.[28] These global commitments, in effect, affirm unequivocally that individual's political freedoms are nothing if separated from economic freedoms, and vice versa. They are essentially interconnected and mutually reinforcing for achieving the daunting task of societal transformation in developing countries. A non-fulfilment of one would abridge the effective use of the other.

Notes

1. Though formally inaugurated in 1990 under the UNDP's auspices, the present study defines the Human Development Paradigm in a broader sense for reasons given in the text. To 'differentiate our product', the UNDP's seminal work is referred to as a Research Programme (which, incidentally, is a synonym for paradigm in the literature on the philosophy of science). The following analysis should, however, show that this broadening of the scope of the Human Development Paradigm is perhaps the only way in which its paradigmatic claims can be established.
2. All references to the Rawls's work are to the 1999 edition, unless otherwise indicated. To emphasize its non-Utilitarian character, Rawls specifically rejects Utilitarianism on the grounds that it does not provide' a satisfactory account of the basic rights and liberties of citizens as free and equal persons' [Rawls (1999), p. xii].

3. It will be noted that the theory of goodness is generally omitted in the standard expositions of the Rawlsian theory. But this is not correct. Its importance in the context of development policy will be explained in Chapter 22.

4. There has been some discussion about the adverse impact of the absolute priority of liberty on the force of the Rawlsian principles as universal principles of justice [Sen (1992)]. That may also reduce considerably the relevance of the Difference Principle to development policy. However, in fact, the priority of liberty is perfectly consistent with the Difference Principle because the importance of the former increases only after a society has achieved a high stage of development—which he calls 'a society of moderate scarcity'. As Mueller (1989) points out, Rawls sees liberty as 'essentially a luxury good in each individual's preference function' (p. 232). In other words, he sees liberty as a reward for a restructuring of the basic institutions of the society that facilitate the emergence of a progressive and just society.

5. It may be noted that the Difference Principle is also a principle of efficiency insofar as any change that improves the condition of all including that of the worst-off is efficient [Sen (1992), p. 26]. See also Naqvi (2003); (2004) for a fairly detailed discussion of normative social-choice theories.

6. Rawls himself admits that this indeed was a limitation of his model [Rawls (1985), p. 234]. He sought to correct some of these aspects in the 1999 edition of his magnum opus.

7. Tullock (1986) points out: 'the maximin principle of justice [as fairness] is not a plausible principle of equality, for whether or not such an alteration [in the basic social structure] would make that more just, it would certainly not make it better with respect to equality.'

8. Several limitations of the Rawlsian principles, which are more of a technical nature, have been noted in the literature. An important limitation concerns Rawls's criterion of impartiality that is basic to his scheme of social cooperation is limited in its reach because of its 'closed' nature, i.e. that it is confined to what Sen (2002a) describes as the 'focal' group that is closed to the non-members. Even more limiting is that 'closed impartiality' of the Rawlsian criterion can exclude the voice of the people who do not belong to the focal group. This issue can be problematic for the 'justice as fairness' principle, especially in dealing with justice across national borders (p. 448).

9. Dworkin (1981a) argues for 'equalizing resources' that are mostly of a subjective nature, like natural endowments, handicaps. He recommends that equality should be achieved with respect to resources for which a person is 'responsible'. The essence of his thesis is that, while no one is responsible for one's inborn talents or early nurture, she/he is responsible for the preferences one holds and the risks he takes in life.

10. The heterogeneities and diversities noted in the text are: (i) Personal heterogeneities caused by disparate personal characteristics like old age, disabilities or illness; (ii) environmental diversities that account for differences in climate and the region's greater (or lesser) susceptibility to certain diseases; (iii) variations in social climate, like having to live in a crime-infested environment; (iv) differences in relational perspectives that take into account established patterns of behaviour in certain societies. For instance, the need to have greater amenities of life in a rich country than in a poor country will make the reasonably well-off in the rich country feel like a poor person, as much as they would do in poorer countries and; (v) the intra-family distribution of income [Sen (1999a,b).

11. Sen (1999b) states: 'If the object is to concentrate on the individual's real opportunity to pursue her objectives (as Rawls explicitly recommends), then account would have to be taken not only of primary goods the persons respectively hold, but also of the relevant personal characteristics that govern the conversion of primary goods into the person's ability to promote his/her ends' (p. 74).

12. A full explanation of the procedures used in the calculation of the above-mentioned indices is given in [UNDP (2004), pp. 258–64].

13. The HDI is calculated as a simple average of three 'dimension indices'—namely, the life expectancy index, the education index and the GDP index—in which each of the dimension indices is assigned a one-third weight. The importance of income in HDI is reduced twice. Firstly, on the assumption that, 'achieving respectable human development does not require unlimited income', the GDP per capita is adjusted by taking its logarithm. The income level for this purpose is assumed to lie between PPP $100 to PPP $4000. Secondly, the income index is assigned only one-third weight in calculating the HDI [UNDP (2004), p. 259; Haq (1995), pp. 47–50].

14. The *Human Development Reports* (HDRs) contain the relevant information on nearly 200 indicators in thirty-three tables.

15. The global commitment to Millennium Declaration was reaffirmed at Monterrey, Mexico in March 2002; and again at the World Summit for Sustainable Development in Johannesburg in September 2002. These conferences added some more emphasis on the respective responsibilities of the rich and poor countries to implement the goals of the rich countries to work actively for a supportive environment in which the goals can be implemented, and of the poorer countries to improve governance and mobilize domestic resources for the realization of the goals.

16. Article 11 of the Covenant recognizes the basic individual right 'to adequate standard of living for himself and the family, including the right to food, clothing, and housing and to the continuous improvement of living standards'; and it forcefully states the fundamental right of everyone to be free from hunger'. Article 12 recognizes 'the right of everyone to the enjoyment of the highest attainable standard of physical and mental health'. Articles 13 and 14 recognize 'the right of everyone to education'. These rights and their rationale have been explained at length in general comments on each of these rights. In particular, Comment 11, 12, 13 and 14 spell out the rationale of the rights to primary education, food, education, and health; and they also mandate corrective action in cases of violations of these rights.

17. Article 28 of the Universal Declaration of Human Rights and Article 2 of the Covenant recognize that, 'human rights carry counterpart obligations on the part of others—not just refrain from violating them, but also protect and promote their realization' [UNDP (2003b), p. 28].

18. Sen (2000) perceptively remarks: 'Even if it is not specified who will have to do what to help the victimized person, there is the general need for responsible consequence-evaluating agent to consider her general duty to help others (when reasonably feasible)' (p. 494).

19. They relate to the basic structure of the society in the sense that, 'liberties and opportunities are defined by the rules of major institutions and the distribution of income and wealth is regulated by them' [Rawls (1999), p. 79].

20. Rawls reckons the index-number problem—of weighing individual elements—as relevant only in the case of the welfare of the least-advantage group of people. He suggests that the way to go about this problem is to ask each individual what combination of such goods 'it will be rational for him to prefer' (p. 80).

21. There is, therefore, not much weight in the criticism that an operational metric may not exist for capability analysis corresponding to the one for the real-income framework or like the one 'for the Marshallian consumer theory combined with the Kaldor-Hicks compensation test.' [Sugden (1993), p. 1954]. Sen correctly argues that the existence of such an operational metric for real-income framework is one of its weaknesses, not strengths.

22. An early exception to the remarks in the text is Harsanyi (1977) utilitarian scheme of maximizing social welfare function, which explicitly accepted the possibility of making interpersonal comparisons of individual welfare. It proves the remarkable result that social welfare is the sum of the individual utilities. It stipulates that individuals, though generally guided by self-interest, are also capable of being 'in someone else's shoes' and act as impartial spectators of societies' needs beyond one's own selfish interests. But the problem

with this approach is the improbability that the impartial spectator would have complete knowledge of the manner of thinking of all other members of the society so as to become another person and yet retain all his individual identities. It has been pointed out that Harsanyi confused *impartiality* with *impersonality*. While the former makes sense the latter does not [Naqvi (2002; 2003)].

23. Arrow echoes this consensus: 'Interpersonal comparison of utility has no meaning' (1951), p. 9). Even the standard microeconomics texts still echo this consensus. The impossibility of making interpersonal comparisons of utility was first enunciated as follows: 'Every mind is inscrutable to every other mind and no common denominator of feelings is possible' [Robbins (193), p. 636]. However, it has been shown that such mental state comparisons are also not that infeasible. Indeed, such interpersonal comparisons of each other's feelings are done routinely in everyday life [Davidson (1986)].

24. The U, P, I, and D conditions stand, respectively for (i) unrestricted domain; (ii) Pareto-optimality requirement; (iii) independence of irrelevant alternatives and; (iv) the absence of a dictator. Given these conditions, the theorem states that it is impossible to derive, in a non-dictatorial way, one Social Welfare Function (SWF) from individual social orderings (one per person). It has been shown that the impossibility result can be resolved if, and only if, interpersonal comparisons can be made [Sen (1999a)].

25. Yet another fundamental contribution here is to have shown the unreasonableness of the neo-classical insistence that to make a decision on such momentous issues as social justice, human deprivation and extreme poverty requires making a complete ordering of all individual preferences over *every* possible alternative. Instead, it has been shown that what is required is only a partial ordering of the relevant alternatives to evaluate real-life possibilities of social action in specific situations [Sen (1999b)].

26. The right to food and its implications for the duties of national governments and the global community are set out at length in the 'Comment' 12, which explains the true import of The Covenant and the Declaration recognize, for the first time at the global level, that the individual's economic rights to food, health, education and employment are as fundamental to human well-being as her/his civil and political rights. The former mandates the Amnesty International, to the chagrin of many a libertarian, the countries to keep track of the violations of individual economic rights, no less than of the political rights.

27. Sen (1999b) points out the close connection between individual responsibility and effective public support: 'The argument for public support in expanding peoples' freedom can, therefore, be seen as an argument *for* individual responsibility, not against it' (p. 284; Italics are in the original).

28. The right to food and its implications for the duties of national governments and the global community are set out at length in the 'Comment' 12, which explains the true import of Article 11 of the Covenant.

14

The Human Development Paradigm:
The Question of 'Identity'

This chapter seeks to settle the foundational issue regarding the identification of the paradigmatic characteristics of the Human Development Paradigm. Like every new paradigm or research programme, it has also explicitly or implicitly laid down what it includes and that which it excludes. For additional clarity, we begin by discussing the second aspect of the paradigm; this will be followed by an analysis of the first one. It will be shown that the Human Development Paradigm has gone out of its way to make its presence felt by highlighting its differences with the Traditional Development Paradigm. Unfortunately, most of this exercise has been of the 'differentiating-the-product' variety in which many an Aunt Sally has been shot down with great fanfare and to the utter puzzlement of the hapless reader.[1] On the other hand, its distancing from the core of the Liberalist Paradigm is of considerable importance—something that it has not explicitly recognized. And of late, it has embraced many of the basic themes of the Traditional Development Paradigm. These apparently contrary trends might be interpreted as a sign of the disintegrating identity of the new paradigm as it was defined in the beginning; but they might also be construed as a learning-by-doing process. This book takes the latter point of view.

14.1. RELATIONSHIP WITH TRADITIONAL DEVELOPMENT PARADIGM

The Human Development Paradigm has generally distinguished itself by rejecting the Traditional Development Paradigm. It has alleged that the Traditional Development Paradigm concentrated only on the income metric for evaluating individual advantage as well as for measuring improvements in the state of the economy, not paying attention to the wider concerns of human development. In particular, it has been accused of focusing on the means (income) rather than the ends of development (the improvement in the basic capabilities). In sharp contrast, the Human Development Paradigm, it is argued, trains on ends rather than the means of human development.[2] This change in analytical focus has been regarded as distinctive enough to earn for itself the title of a new paradigm. To some extent these claims are justified. While per capita income and the human development variables are inevitably inter-related they are not the same; and the link between increasing income and expanding human choice (capabilities) is by no means automatic. Hence, a more pluralistic measure (HDI), including (adjusted) income, has been created to supplement GNP in order to measure individual advantage and national achievements more adequately. The Human Development Reports contrast each year the HDI and the GNP estimates to show that some countries are more efficient than others in converting wealth and income into human capabilities. Thus, some have done relatively better than others with respect to the GNP levels achieved, while others have done better with respect to HDI improvements.[3] Obviously, the most successful cases are those in which the countries (or regions within the countries) have cared at least as much, if no more, for providing 'social opportunities' (measured by HDI) as they have done for accelerating the rate of 'economic development' (measured by GNP).[4] How one should evaluate the two types of cases? Evidently, the most preferred option would be to make progress with respect to both so that increments in income get adequately translated into an expansion of the corresponding functioning and capabilities. This much is pretty straightforward. But the real problem arises where the two differ by a wide margin; and when improvement in one does not get converted into a corresponding improvement in the other. Indeed, in a significant number of cases the observed rank differences between countries are rather large; which, it is asserted, reflect the differences in development strategies and national priorities. Should we then celebrate the cases where HDI is greater than the GNP or the ones when the latter races ahead of the former? Unfortunately, this vital question remains to be answered satisfactorily.

The Human Development Paradigm strongly prefers more of human development, with the same level of economic development, when there is a trade-off between them. Thus, for instance, the most cited 'success' stories in terms of human development have been those of Sri Lanka and Kerala, pre-reform China and Costa Rica as well as those relating to the Transition Economies of Eastern Europe. These 'minority' success stories of human development have been regarded as significant enough to establish the case for an alternative (and more successful) support-led strategy as opposed to the traditional (and presumably less successful) growth-mediated strategy. The support-led strategy, it has been argued, has achieved human development directly by committing large social expenditures. The result has been a miraculous advancement in human development in a very short time. Valuable functioning (reduction in infant mortality rates, substantial increases in life expectancy and literacy) have been achieved, it is argued, much more quickly than if the reliance had been put exclusively or mostly on the rather unreliable trickle down or the spread effects of a fast growth of per capita income. The great economy of the development effort that it supposedly entails makes the support-led strategy more successful than the growth-mediated strategy in achieving the human development targets. Indeed, the Human Development Paradigm has advertised this 'discovery' to be its seminal contribution to development thinking.

14.2. Relationship with the Liberalist Paradigm

This book argues that the paradigmatic claims of the Human Development Paradigm should rest on its unique non-Utilitarian, consequentialist moral philosophy, briefly described in the preceding chapter. It has enabled the Human Development Paradigm, as no competing paradigm has done, to tackle the problems of distributive justice, poverty and human deprivation adequately and with scientific rigor. In this respect its rejection of the Liberalist Paradigm is emphatic and unequivocal. Thus, its quintessentially moralist approach to economic development contrasts sharply with the Liberalist Paradigm's efficiency-only prescriptions. It would deny two fundamental principles of the Liberalist Paradigm—namely, the distribution-wise neutral Pareto-optimality rule as an adequate indicator of human welfare, and the contractarian-liberalist non-consequentialism of Nozick and Hayek that accords absolute priority to the individual's political rights to the exclusion of her/his economic rights. As a logical corollary, the Human Development Paradigm has also come to reject the unfettered market-only prescriptions of the Liberalist Paradigm. By the same token, it has emphasized the role of government in human development (This aspect of the new paradigm is explored in the next chapter). Furthermore, as noted in the preceding chapter, it has highlighted the principle of social responsibility that 'naturally' goes with the exercise of individual freedom. To that end, it has actively advocated a fundamental connection between the poor peoples' and countries' claimable economic rights to a minimum of sustenance and the counterpart obligations of the rich countries and peoples. An important point here is that the rich countries, no less than the poor countries, are required to actively participate in fulfilling these obligations [UNDP (2003b)]. This is perhaps the most forceful refutation of the non-consequentialist individual-moral-rights philosophy that underlies the Liberalist Paradigm—and fundamentally one of the most enduring contributions of the Human Development Paradigm to the global development dialogue.

14.3. The 'New' Strategy of Economic and Human Development

We now come to a more detailed analysis of the positive side of the Human Development Paradigm—of what it includes. As noted in the preceding section, it has questioned the wisdom of growth strategies that aim primarily at maximizing the growth of per capita income as the index of human welfare on the grounds that gains in income do not automatically translate into gains in human functioning and capabilities. Since enhancing the latter is most properly the end of development, a preferable growth strategy would be one, it is argued, which would achieve it directly by focusing on expanding functioning and capabilities.[5] The direct strategy has also been christened as the support-led strategy as opposed to the traditional indirect growth-mediated strategy [Sen (1983); Dreze and Sen (1989); Sen (1999b)].[6] However, one wonders why it should have taken so much wisdom to discover the obvious fact that a direct approach will deliver human development in a much shorter period of time than an indirect approach. The real question to answer is whether human development achievements secured through the direct route are also more durable over the long haul than those achieved through the indirect approach? To be more specific, one must ascertain whether too much human development too early comes at an avoidable cost of economic development. It is to a detailed analysis of this question that we now turn in this and the next chapter.

14.3. (i). The Case for Support-led Growth Strategy

The relative merit of the support-led strategy of economic development seems to be based almost exclusively on cases where achievements in terms of HDI differ significantly from those in terms of GNP. UNDP (2005) cites some striking comparisons with respect to each country's economic development (measured by its GNP level) and human development (measured by its HDI rank *vis-à-vis* others), which make an interesting reading regardless of what they imply for the choice of development strategy. Bolivia has a much lower per capita income than Guatemala but a significantly higher HDI than the latter; Tanzania is among the poorest countries of the world but has an HDI comparable to that of the four-times richer Guinea; Vietnam has the same level of income as Pakistan but a significantly higher HDI (life expectancy in the former is much higher than the latter). Saudi Arabia has four times the income of Thailand but the same HDI ranking; Sri Lanka ranks 96 in 177 countries in terms of HDI though its GDP rank is 112. And there are examples of countries that make progress in terms of GNP but not as much, or not at all, in HDI (Brazil); and of countries that have done distinctly better in terms of HDI but much less satisfactorily in terms of GNP (Sri Lanka and the Indian state of Kerala). There are, however, examples that have recorded improvements in terms of both the HDI and GNP (all the miracle economies and the super-miracle grower, post-reform China) and still others, which have lagged behind both (sub-Saharan Africa and the so-called 'emerging economies'). Does this bewildering medley of cases in which the GNP ranks differ significantly from the HDI ranks justify the human development aficionado's extraordinarily fervid attachment to the new-fangled development strategy? There is no doubt that generalizations about the direct strategy are based on these deviant cases. It would not be unreasonable to assert that whatever one claims about a strategy that achieves one or the other objective, one should prefer the strategy which leads to a better outcome with respect to both. But let us first look at the generalizations made about the superior merits of the direct, or the support-led strategy.

Some Generalizations: (a) the most common generalization that one encounters for the support-led strategy is that since the end of development is to acquire valuable functionings and capabilities (like higher literacy and higher life expectancy), the development policy must directly focus on it. Also, because income and wealth are only the means to achieving them one should adopt HDI rather than the GNP as an indicator of human well-being. (b) Yet another generalization is the following: 'Not only it is the case that economic growth is the means rather than an end, it is also that for achieving some important ends income is not a very efficient means either' [Sen (1983), p. 754].[7] An obvious policy implication of these generalizations is that government policy should henceforth focus on achieving the agreed ends (a higher HDI rank) directly rather than indirectly by accelerating the rate of growth of GNP.[8] This insight is of immense importance because it has directed attention, as nothing else could, on translating economic development success (measured by the growth of per capita income) into human development success (measured by increasing expenditure on education and health). What makes this recommendation especially attractive is that human capabilities can be increased even at low levels of economic development (when the cost of achieving high level of human development is also low). The examples of pre-reform China, Sri Lanka and Kerala have been cited as a convincing demonstration of the proposition that, not waiting for achieving very large increases in GNP, remarkable gains in human development (reducing mortality, especially child mortality, and increasing the quality of life) can be achieved at moderate rates of economic growth by giving priority to the provisioning of basic social services, especially education and health.

The Achievements of the Proposed Strategy: The outcomes of the proposed strategy wherever followed consistently have been too striking to ignore: these countries have been able to achieve higher human development gains than the much richer Brazil, South Africa, Namibia and Gabon, to cite only a few examples. The development experience since 1990 seems to show that increasing the policy focus on human development has been richly rewarded. In the last fifteen years, 2 million less children have died and the chances of children living to achieve age five have increased by 15 per cent.

No less important, 1.2 billion people have gained access to clean water; and world-wide immunization has brought down the death toll, saving lives by an estimated half a million. And, no less impressive, the average literacy rate has increased from 70 to 76 per cent; and compared with 1990, there are 30 million fewer primary school-going children out of school and the average number of years in school has climbed by half a year. Also, the gender gap has declined. It has been pointed out, with a legitimate sense of pride, that the developing countries have steadily converged with the developed countries in terms of their relative HDI ranking, though most of them are far from achieving this objective in terms of GNP [UNDP (2005), p. 1]. These are tremendous achievements, which must be valued regardless of what they do to increasing productivity and growth—indeed, even to suggest otherwise would be a sure sign of a flint-hearted disregard for human suffering. These gains can reasonably be interpreted to show that a support-led strategy works—indeed, the claim is that it works better than a growth-mediated strategy could ever have. No wonder, therefore, that the drift of academic opinion along the rapid stream of accumulating evidence in favour of the new development strategy seems to be unstoppable. The idea that one needs to go beyond GNP gains in order to repair the capability deficits between individuals and nations that stubbornly survive gains in per capita income seems to have struck the right 'chord' in development thinking. Right or not, there is little doubt that this idea has pullulated without much intellectual or policy resistance.

14.4. Does Support-led Strategy Exist Apart from Growth-Mediated Strategy?

But has the strategy struck the right chord? An obvious question seems to be: for instance, should not one prefer a high-growth strategy, such as that the East Asians have pursued consistently, that has also led to miraculous human development achievements in a very short period of time? Why should an income-based strategy be defined as one that leads to a lacklustre human development achievement? These questions will be more fully answered in the next chapter. Here we focus on the support-led strategy and ask: is it legitimate to deduce an alternative strategy from a handful of cases when such claims can be easily refuted by reference to many more striking cases of the miraculous success of the growth-mediated strategy? The logical foundation of such a deduction seems to be rickety at best.[9] The argument in favour of the direct strategy is that it aims at raising human capabilities, which should contribute to achieving high rates of per capita GNP, and then lead to even greater achievements in human development. The paradigm-making examples of the human development, the Indian state of Kerala and Sri Lanka, do not lend support to such an unambiguous deduction. The fact is that the heart-warming achievements of Kerala—life expectancy of 72 years, a fertility rate below the replacement level, a near-universal literacy in the younger age group, relatively low levels of gender inequality, virtual absence of child labour—have been bought at the expense of a significantly weak (or rather weakened) economic growth, and a high level unemployment and morbidity.[10] The case of Sri Lanka is similar: here too high human development has been achieved at the expense of low growth and high unemployment, both of which might have contributed in a significant way to the present civil war conditions there.[11] Indeed, this seems to be the story of all the developing countries that could not achieve high growth rates of per capita income, notwithstanding their impressive gains in human development. Should one then not worry about the adverse consequences of a support-led strategy on growth, just as one does about the adverse consequences of growth strategy that runs up a human-development deficit? An attempt has been made in the next chapter to resolve this issue. But let us look at a related question alluded to above. Can one reasonably think of a virtuous reinforcing circle connecting high growth and high human development?

14.5. Is There a Virtuous Circle: High-Human Development Leading to High Growth and Back?

We now come to a detailed examination of one of the foundational claims of the Human Development Paradigm—namely, that there exists a two-way, mutually reinforcing relationship between economic growth and human development.[12] The line of causation going from growth to human development has is generally taken for granted; but the veracity of the argument in favour of a support-led strategy hinges crucially, if not entirely, on the reverse causation going from human development to growth. More precisely, the hypothesis seems to be that high rate of human development leads to high rate of economic growth and that this feedback is expected to create a virtuous circle in which specific policies can be used to increase the rate of human development, which in turn would accelerate the growth rate of GNP and, thereby, automatically induce further improvements in human development.[13]

14.5. (i). Preliminary Empirical Evidence on Human Development and Economic Growth

It may be interesting to look at the relation between human development and economic growth in Asia and the Pacific Region in order to see the reasonableness of the claim about the existence of a virtuous circle. The choice of the region is most appropriate because it is here that the most heart-warming and mind-boggling episodes of miraculous economic and human development have taken place.

Figure 14.1 does confer a certain degree of plausibility on the human-development hypothesis: namely, high levels of human development have generally been associated with high rates of economic growth. Of the fourteen countries included in the sample here, the relationship seems tight in nine countries. In the top right-hand box, high growth rate of per capita income is associated high level human development (China, Malaysia, Singapore and South Korea). On the other hand, the reciprocal relationship between low human development and low economic growth also holds for India, Pakistan, Nepal, Papua New Guinea, and Bangladesh.

Figure 14.1: Economic Growth and Human Development in Asia and Pacific Region (1965–2000)

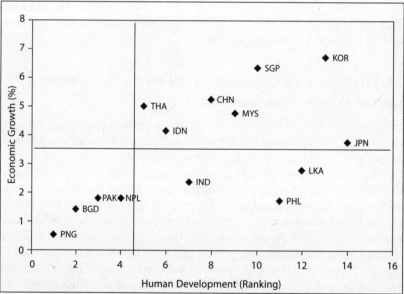

Note: Enrolment rate in secondary schools is used as human development indicator. The countries are ranked on the basis of human development. Average economic growth rate is 3.47 per cent and average enrolment rate is 49 per cent.

◆ Following countries are included in the sample: Bangladesh (BGD), China (CHN), India (IND), Nepal (NPL), Indonesia (IDN), Japan (JPN), Papua New Guinea (PNG), Korea (KOR), Malaysia (MYS), Pakistan (PAK), Philippines (PHL), Sri Lanka (LKA), Singapore (SGP), and Thailand (THA). Due to non-availability of data on enrollment rates, Fiji (FIJ), Hong Kong (HKG), Taiwan (TWN) and Vietnam (VNM) are not included here.

However, as if to muddy the waters for the hypothesis, there are some important countries, like Sri Lanka, the Philippines and Japan, where a very high level of human development has coexisted with a low rate of growth of per capita income; and Thailand and Indonesia, where high growth has been associated with a low level of human development. It follows that no firm generalization is possible with respect to the two-way relationship between growth of per capita income and human development, even though in most cases this association seems to hold. The case of Sri Lanka is most important because its splendid success with human development was the original source of inspiration for the new paradigm. Furthermore, this diagram does not say anything about the chain of causation going from human development to economic growth. This will require some detailed regression analysis, which is presented in Part VI.

14.5. (ii). Human Development Frontier

However, let us pursue the Human Development Paradigm's reasoning for the existence of a virtuous circle a little more closely in terms of the UNDP's concept of the 'human development frontier'.[14] The countries on the human development frontier are seen the most effective 'converters' of economic growth into human development. China, Costa Rica and Sri Lanka are located on the 'human development frontier' [UNDP (1996), p. 67]. But the virtuous circle, which further requires the efficient conversion of human development into economic growth, has not worked in the case of Sri Lanka, Costa Rica and Kerala—the countries whose example suggested the viability of a support-led strategy. It is significant that, of the on-the-frontier countries, the virtuous circle has worked only for China, a miracle-growth country. On the other hand, the virtuous circle has worked in high-growth countries, which are not on the frontier (Malaysia, South Korea, and Singapore). In other words, with the exception of China, the countries with 'strong links' between human development and economic growth have not, as a rule, been located on the human development frontier.[15] These observations again suggest that a support-led strategy does not exist apart from a high growth strategy. Indeed, a more accurate description of the growth and human development linkage would be that a high rate of human development is as likely to ignite a virtuous circle (China) as it is to create a vicious circle that tends to dampen economic development (Sri Lanka, Costa Rica and Kerala) if not supported by a permanent set of policies to increase economic growth and then ploughs it back into human development? In other words, there is no automatic link going from human development to economic growth, or that which travels from high growth to high human development. Direct policies are required to foster strong links between human development and economic development. In other words, a pusillanimous 'trickle down' blights a support-led strategy no less than it does a growth-mediated strategy. There is, however, a more fundamental reason why the way back from human development to economic growth and development is not assured: it is that human capital built by more education and better health is probably a necessary but not a sufficient condition to propel the economy onto a high-growth path.[16] And if it could not do so in the star cases (Kerala and Sri Lanka), it is so much less likely to do so in the less successful cases.[17] Are then the appearances deceptive here as in all cases where correlation is mistaken for causation? That seems to be the case. We must then go beyond appearances. This is done in the next chapter.

14.6. CONCLUDING REMARKS

The analysis presented so far strongly suggests that, on balance, there is a lot more going for the growth-mediated strategy than for the support-led strategy. In fact, the resolution of all the major human development issues is connected directly or indirectly with the growth of per capita income, the importance of which cannot be diminished by scoring philosophical points in the direct-indirect strategy debate. If securing human development is elemental for human happiness, so is growth of per capita income at the highest possible rate. To some, it may be a perfect example of a Hobson's choice; but commonsense suggests that the growth-mediated strategy is definitely a winner if growth rate of per capita income of 6 per cent plus is sustained for decades. This conjecture gets support from two related facts: (a) Cases of self-reinforcing virtuous circle have been observed only in the high-growth economies and most convincingly in the East Asian miracle economies; (b) The growth rate of per capita income has been generally subdued in cases where high rate of human development has been the primary policy objective. Whence it follows that, while high human development goes with high growth, the same is not the case with countries where high human development has been accorded the toriority. The latter event has not happened—and for a solid reason. It would be shown in a subsequent chapter that human development has a significant consumption element in it, which depresses physical investment and growth, even as it reduces poverty. It would, therefore, be more sensible to economize on the research time and money spent on the advertisement of the so-called support-led strategy.

NOTES

1. An example of shooting down Aunt Sally is the following: it has been claimed that Lewis (1955) recognized that the purpose of development was to widen human choices but that he purportedly equated a wider human choice 'merely with greater income' [UNDP (1996), p. 46]. However, as the analysis presented in Part II of the present study shows, this is not what Lewis ever said.

2. Haq (1995), who has been universally credited with the fatherhood of the UNDP's Research Programme, states with his characteristic clarity: 'The defining difference between economic growth and the human development schools has been that the first focuses *exclusively* on the expansion of only one choice—income—while the second embraces enlargement of all human choices—whether economic, social, cultural, or political' (italics added, p. 14).

3. It has been observed that, out of the 173 countries for which comparable data exist there is no difference between the HDI and GNP ranking for four countries, less than a 5-rank difference for 29 countries, more than 20 ranks difference for more than 60 countries, 40-rank difference for 10 countries, and more than 30 ranks difference for 26 countries [Haq (1995), pp. 51–52].

4. The distinction between social achievements and economic development made in the text is due to Dreze and Sen (1995); and Sen (1999b).

5. It may be recalled that Robert McNamara's World Bank in the 1970s had also called for the 'dethronement of the GDP'. However, the anti-GDP rhetoric was used to devise a new direct strategy to fight poverty.

6. At another place, the growth-mediated strategy is referred to as the Blast Strategy (acronym for Blood, Sweat and Tears) and the support-led strategy as the Gala Strategy (acronym for Getting-by-with-Little Assistance) [Sen (1997a)]. The latter strategy is regarded as a more 'friendly' strategy—obviously so, because even a passably rational decision-taker will economize on shedding blood, sweat and tears shedding to achieve stated policy objectives. Sen, however, points out that in fact the strategies lie in between these two extremes and the problem of making a choice between these strategies refers to this mixed-strategy spectrum.

7. The generalizations in the text have been made on the basis of the contrasting performances of Brazil, China, Mexico, South Korea and Sri Lanka with respect to their success in achieving a high level of life expectancy at birth. Later on, Kerala (in India) was added to the list of a handful of countries that achieved exemplary performances in terms of human development indicators, though lagging in terms of growth. However, it appears that Sen's enthusiasm for the direct strategy has subsided with the passage of time.

8. Sen (1983) states: 'If the government of a poor developing country is keen to raise the level of health and the expectation of life, then it would be pretty daft to try to achieve this through raising its income per head, rather than going directly for those very objectives through public policy and social change, as in [pre-reform] China and Sri Lanka' (p. 753).

9. It may be objected that, by the Hume's Law, there are no valid empirical statements on the basis of which general statements can be made. Thus, for instance, no matter how many white swans you observe, it does not entitle you to make the general statement that all swans are white. As Popper (1980) asserts the only valid procedure is, 'to test a hypothesis only after it has been advanced' (p. 30). But we have not pursued this criticism in the text.

10. 'While the social opportunities of living long, healthy, and literate lives have been radically enhanced in an exemplary manner, the opportunities that depend on growth have been more stagnant' [Dreze and Sen (1995), p. 197]. The authors, however, are not so sure about the net outcome of the direct strategy for economic development, taking into account both sides of the 'coin'.

11. The only thing that can still be said about the growth potentialities of the support-led strategy is that, as Dreze and Sen (1995) point out, those who wished to convert their gains in human development into higher income have had to go outside of these countries/ regions. It is not, however, clear whether this is an argument for this strategy or against it. To some extent one may applaud such an eventuality. Out-migrations has helped balance-of-payments problems of these countries/regions by the back flow of worker's remittances. But this is more like an unintended consequence of a high human development and low-income growth strategy. What is clearer is that the gains in skills and human capital have not been ploughed back into greater growth creation.

12. It has been argued that the 'two-way link between human development and economic growth implies a virtuous circle—with good human development promoting economic growth, which, in turn, advances human development' [UNDP (2003b), p. 69].

13. The proposition in the text has been duly illustrated with the help of a schematic representation, entitled: 'From Human Development to Growth—and Back' [UNDP (1996), p. 68; (2003b), p. 70]. It is needless to point out that a visual illustration of a hypothesis does not suffice even as a suggestion about its validity, let alone its proof.

14. The relevant diagram has not been shown in the text.

15. The countries with 'strong links' between human development and economic growth, referred to in the text are: China, Malaysia, Hong Kong, Thailand, Singapore, South Korea, Indonesia, and Japan [UNDP (1996)].

16. The argument in the text is the mirror image of the usual assertion about growth of per capita income: that the latter is a necessary but not a sufficient condition for human development.

17. UNDP (1996) approvingly cites the human-capital models and the endogenous growth theories, which suggest that human capital accumulation is a strong enough force to achieve rates of economic growth by increasing productivity through R&D investment. Indeed, the latter suggest that all that has to be done to achieve high rates of growth (through increasing returns to scale) is for the government to invest in human capital. Yet another important point in this connection is the dubious nature of the proxies used to indicate the human capital: schooling rather than training; schooling rather than enrolment. Furthermore, there seems to be a broad agreement that human capital is not sufficient for sustaining high rates of growth [Temple (1999)].

15

Choice between Support-Led Strategy and Growth-Mediated Strategies

The Human Development Paradigm has from the very beginning displayed a queer mingling of pessimism and optimism. Three strands of thought seem to be clearly discernable. Firstly, its pessimistic predications have rested on a handful of cases where low human development has coexisted with high growth, suggesting that high growth would not always translate into solid human development achievements. Indeed, the growth-human development pessimism was the original inspiration for the support-led strategy. Secondly, it has also asserted that normally human development and economic growth go in the same direction in a mutually reinforcing fashion. True, it has been recognized that some countries have been better than others at converting human development into high growth, and vice versa; and that it is possible for countries to go through 'periods of lopsided human development and lop-sided economic growth'; yet, the normal case has been regarded as the one where human development led to economic growth and back to 'form circles of reinforcing causality' [UNDP (1996), p. 67]. Thirdly, it has persuasively argued that human development expenditures on education and health should be undertaken for their intrinsic worth. What they do to economic growth is an important issue but by no means a decisive one in opting for the support-led strategy.[1] Indeed, if it were decisive then there would be no need for the support-led strategy. A common element of these strands of thought is that trying to achieve solid human development through high income growth is no more than a forlorn hope; but that there exists a direct and a more effective way to translate higher growth into additional increments of human development. Indeed, this seems to be the source of the effervescent optimism it has sought to suffuse throughout the developing world. But, unfortunately, the problem is not that simple. Indeed, a lack of clarity on this issue has been the paradigm's Achilles' heel. The empirical evidence that is usually presented in support of this basic contention is not always conclusive. This book argues that there exists an unavoidable hard-core trade-off between high income growth and high human development achievements. While it is a legitimate concern that human happiness deficits may persist notwithstanding increments in income, there are aspects of human happiness that only the growth of per capita income can provide and which education and health alone cannot adequately take account of [Anand and Sen (2000)]. What the human development literature has not recognized is that a definite opportunity cost is attached to each of these strategies in terms of lost output or human development foregone. Thus, a choice cannot be made for either of these strategies on a priori grounds. The question has to be decided on the basis of empirical evidence. In other words, it is not possible to bypass the quintessential question: How does one choose between the support-led and growth-mediated strategies?

15.1. SUPPORT-LED STRATEGY: THE ACHILLES HEEL OF HUMAN DEVELOPMENT PARADIGM

The fact is that both the pessimistic and optimistic scenarios noted above are problematic. Unfortunately, the evidence against these scenarios seems to be fairly convincing. On the one hand, there have been cases of reversal in human development in the slow-growing economies. Eighteen countries, with a combined population of 460 million (including the countries located in sub-Saharan Africa and the former Soviet Union) suffered negative growth rates (notwithstanding their high rates of human development). They have, of late, suffered from 'unprecedented human developmental reversals' as well; they have scored lower scores in 2003 over what they achieved in 1990 [UNDP (2005), pp. 21–22].[2] On the other hand, there has not been a single case of human development reversal in the high-growth economies. In other words, growth failure leading to a human development failure seems to be more probable than human development failure leading to growth failure. This rather persistent tendency suggests a very important conclusion, which has not been factored in the thinking on human development: if income achievements do not automatically convert into corresponding capabilities without a direct focus on expanding the capabilities, the same is true of capability achievements, i.e. they too do not convert automatically into a higher growth performance without taking direct measures to stimulate growth.

15.2. IS THERE A VIRTUOUS CIRCLE? SOME IMPORTANT REGRESSION RESULTS

We are now in position to test the virtuous circle hypothesis discussed in the preceding chapter.[3] Figure 14.1 failed to establish a presumption about the hypothesis one way or the other. Based on comparable pooled data for eighteen countries of Asia and Pacific region (including East Asia and China), Tables 15.1 and 15.2 seek to verify the Human Development Paradigm's hypothesis about the existence of a virtuous circle between human development and economic growth and the linkage is strong (statistically significant) both ways. In particular, it tests the claim about the strength of the support-led strategy to achieve twin objectives of human development and economic growth. For added clarity, the estimates have also been presented for Asia and Pacific region as a whole, non-East Asian countries and East Asian countries. The non-aggregation of the regression results by regions, perhaps done for the first time in the development literature, should help verify the uniqueness hypothesis, namely, that East Asian miraculous growth experience has been unique to the region so that the development policies used there could not be replicated elsewhere. As pointed out in Parts III and IV many a generalization about the East Asian miracle experience rests on the veracity of such claims. We begin with the analysis of the link going from economic growth to human development.

Table 15.1: Determinants of Human Development in Asia-Pacific Region: From Growth of per capita Income to Human Development (1965–2000)

	All Countries		East Asia		South Asia	
	Coefficients	Elasticity Estimates	Coefficients	Elasticity Estimates	Coefficients	Elasticity Estimates
Constant	-10.875 (1.472)	-	12.921 (1.247)	-	-27.60 (13.265)	-
Growth Rate of GDer capita	0.395 (1.625)	0.032	0.631 (1.615)	0.066	0.206 (0.662)	0.012
Lon (lagged GDer capita)	6.307 (12.226)	0.647*	3.311 (4.872)	0.340*	32.372 (16.926)	3.32*
Population Growth Rate	-5.312 (3.829)	-0.210*	-0.341 (0.16)	-0.012	-2.49 (2.423)	-0.138*
R^2	0.692	-	0.437	-	0.864	-
Number of Observations	307	-	124	-	125	-

Note: t-values are reported in parentheses. Asterisks on the elasticity estimates denote their statistical significance. Except for human development, the data for estimation have been taken, from Penn World Table (PWT)-Version 6.1 (2002). The proxy for human development, literacy rate, is taken from *Human Development Reports*. The data on Vietnam is for 11 years only (since 1989), which partly explains the reduction of the number of observations from the required 630 in this case (18 countries times 35 years).

15.3. The Link Going from Income to Human Development: Asia and Pacific Region

Extensive experimentation with alternative specifications shows that the only meaningful determinants of human development are the two income-related variables (growth rate of per capita income and lagged GDP per capita) and population growth. Table 15.1 shows that the level of lagged GDP per capita exerts the most powerful (and significant) influence on human development with an elasticity of 0.64 that is 1 per cent change in last year's income produces a 0.64 per cent change in human development. Next in importance is population growth, with an elasticity of (-)0.21: that is, human development is negatively related to population growth. The third most important explanatory variable is the growth rate of per capita GDP with an elasticity of 0.03. The corresponding coefficients for all the three variables are highly significant. These findings confirm one of the main contentions of this book namely, that changes in the level and rate of per capita income (along with population growth) make a decisive impact on human development both ways—it pulls up (depresses) human development when income growth is strong (weak).

15.3. (i). The Uniqueness Hypothesis

Table 15.1 offers some interesting insights into the determinants of human development in East Asia and South Asia. It also brings out clearly the inter-regional differences with respect to the relative values of these variables. Two points need to be highlighted here. (a) The information given in the table highlights the importance of sustaining high growth rates of per capita income for long periods in order to achieve successful human development. In particular, it clearly shows that neglecting an active pursuit of high rate of growth of per capita income for securing quick gains in human development would be hazardous, to put it rather mildly. The fact is that it would not be reasonable to expect any significant and lasting improvements in human development if per capita income was also not rising at the same time. True, as the human development literature has pointed out with tiresome repetition, higher income is only a means to an end; but the information in the table says that it is a means without which the end of human development cannot be adequately achieved. (b) There is nothing particularly unique about the East Asian experience with respect to the determinants of human development: with some differences, it is the traditional variables that explain the high growth rates of income in all the developing countries, including East Asia. The level of lagged GDP per capita is a lot more important determinant of human development in South Asia than in East Asia. The relevant elasticity is 3.32 in the former as compared to only 0.34 in East Asia. The level of significance of the corresponding estimated coefficients also reflects the same prediction. The explanation of this large difference might lie in the much smaller pre-existing levels of income and human development achievements in South Asia than in East Asia. The same is the story with respect to population growth. East Asia, more than South Asia, has already achieved miraculous fertility reduction, so that there is not much room for improvement on this count. As expected, the growth of per capita income also has had a somewhat more pronounced impact on human development in East Asia than in South Asia—with an elasticity of 0.066 in the former as compared with 0.012 for the latter. Indeed, the growth of per capita income has exercised only an insignificant effect on human development in South Asia whereas it is significant (though only marginally so) in East Asia. In other words, the growth rate of per capita income seems to be less important than the pre-existing *level* of per capita income in both the regions. But both variables underscore the importance of the income variable, lagged or current, as the primary determinant of human development.

15.4. THE LINK GOING FROM HUMAN DEVELOPMENT TO GROWTH OF PER CAPITA INCOME: ASIA AND PACIFIC REGION

We now turn to testing the strength of the reverse causation—of going uphill from human development to growth of income. The statistical significance of this link is crucial for determining the absolute and relative importance of human development for stimulating the growth of per capita income.[4]

The Human Development Paradigm makes the strong claim (citing the new endogenous growth theory) that human development is one of the most powerful forces propelling growth; and that it has been especially forceful in East Asia, even more powerful than physical capital formation. Table 15.2 tests these claims. It shows that they are simply untenable: human development's contribution to economic growth has been statistically insignificant, though the sign is positive. In other words, human development makes a positive, though only insignificant, contribution to economic growth. Instead, the most potent factors contributing to growth are the traditional one: the investment/GDP ratio, the government expenditure/GDP ratio and openness. Interestingly, reducing inflation rate also contributes positively to economic growth. There is yet another important route through which social expenditure can possibly effect growth of per capita income namely, by stimulating investment. Unfortunately, the information given in Table 19.1 (in Chapter 19) does not support the usual claims that human development helps investment: it shows instead that human development expenditures tend to reduce investment. This suggests that, though greater human development must be made for its own sake (people should be healthy and literate regardless of what it does to growth), it will be unrealistic to expect that it will stimulate investment and growth as well.

15.4. (i). The Uniqueness Hypothesis

It has been claimed that the so-called uniqueness of the East Asian experience lies in the overwhelming contribution of human capital to its miraculous growth. Table 15.2 does not seem to support this claim. It rather shows that the coefficient of human development is statistically insignificant in East Asia as well as non-East Asia. On the other hand, there are big inter-regional differences between the behaviour of the traditional variables (the investment/ GDP ratio and the share of government in total investment). However, it will be wrong to consider them as unique to East Asia. Indeed, the relevant elasticity is higher for South Asia than in East Asia.

Table 15.2: Determinants of Growth of per capita Income in Asia: From Human Development to Growth of per capita Income (1965–2000)

	All Countries		East Asia		South Asia	
	Coefficients	Elasticity Estimates	Coefficients	Elasticity Estimates	Coefficients	Elasticity Estimates
Constant	2.065 (1.666)	-	-0.748 (0.30)	-	-2.212 (1.04)	-
Investment-GDP Ratio	0.176 (3.86)	0.764*	0.22 (2.33)	0.77*	0.361 (3.526)	2.65*
Government Expenditure-GDP Ratio	0.10 (2.806)	0.129*	0.111 (1.94)	0.067	0.044 (2.108)	0.092*
Inflation	0.013 (0.196)	-	0.0095 (1.028)	-	-0.464 (3.799)	-
Inflation-Squared	-0.002 (1.884)	-0.026	-0.003 (2.108)	-0.046*	0.008 (2.383)	-1.261*
Openness	0.036 (3.682)	0.404*	0.067 (2.43)	0.614*	0.066 (2.22)	0.883*
Human Development	0.012 (1.23)	0.149	0.011 (0.533)	0.110	0.014 (0.684)	0.25
R^2	0.36	-	0.375	-	0.494	-
Number of Observations	307	-	124	-	125	-

Note: t-values are reported in parentheses. Asterisks on the elasticity estimates denote their statistical significance. Except for human development, the data for estimation have been taken, from Penn World Table (PWT)-Version 6.1 (2002). The proxy for human development, literacy rate, is taken from *Human Development Reports* [UNDP (various issues)]. The PWT gives data for Vietnam from 1989 only, which partly explains the number of observations below 630 (18 countries times 35 years) Inflation-squared is included as an independent variable to capture non-linearity in growth-inflation relationship.

15.5. IS GROWTH-MEDIATED STRATEGY A WINNER?

We are now in a position to give a fairly definitive judgment regarding the validity and effectiveness of the new-fangled support-led strategy as opposed to the more traditional growth-mediated strategy. Tables 15.1 and 15.2 offer three fundamental lessons for development policy. Firstly, they support the findings that the most enduring human development successes have taken place in countries where the growth of per capita income also increased the fastest namely, the East Asian miracle economies, and of late, the super-miracle Chinese economy. In particular, poverty has fallen most radically in fast-growing countries, and especially in China, both in percentage terms as well as in absolute terms [UNDP (2003b), p. 41]. This much the creators of the Human Development Paradigm have acknowledged. However, this admission has seldom been carried to its logical conclusion.[5] Not sufficient awareness has been shown of the hard fact that additional human development effort would not pay positive dividends, if pushed beyond a certain point; instead, it would submit quickly to the eternal laws of diminishing returns. Table 19.1 (Chapter 19) shows that, helter-skelter human development could negatively affect growth and investment. These results seem to suggest the reason why the countries (Sri Lanka, Eastern Europe) or regions of big countries (Kerala, India), which achieved stellar success in human development, failed to generate solid growth on a lasting basis. Ostensibly, they, thinking that human development will sustain growth as well, did not pay enough attention to the factors that have traditionally contributed to growth everywhere in the world. They forgot that like everything in life, keeping a sense of balance and proportion is the key to achieving maximum economic and human development. The task of development policy is, therefore, to find the 'turning point' through trial and error.

Secondly, it follows from the first point, a support-led strategy, which fails to stimulate growth at the same time, is not likely to be sustained for long periods of time. At best, it is a strategy of converting gains in economic growth into human capabilities. This is a great achievement in itself; and pointing this fact has been marked a big step forward on the road to knowledge about development. It is, however, a grave mistake to make the further claim that this fact also qualifies it as a valid growth strategy. The most that can be claimed for the support-led strategy is that it establishes the pre-conditions to broad-based economic development. But a successful fulfilment of the preconditions of growth is no guarantee that economic growth will actually take place, much less that it will be sustained.

Thirdly, the analysis presented above suggests that long-run growth basically requires a vigorous pursuit of the traditional growth-mediated policies (e.g., increasing the saving and investment rates, investing enough in human capital formation, investing in innovation and research through essentially well-targeted import-substitution policies). Thus, among the determinants of growth, the highest value of elasticity (0.74) attaches to increasing investment rate. Next in importance comes increasing the share of government in total investment expenditure, with an elasticity of 0.129.

15.6. CONCLUDING REMARKS

The analysis presented in this and the previous chapters may appear as too critical of the Human Development Paradigm; but this, in fact, is not the case. Rather, the point is that the Human Development Paradigm's claim to fame lies in showing a rigorous way to tackle the elemental issues of social justice, including poverty reduction. However, its paradigmatic claim would be weak if it were construed as offering an alternative strategy of economic or human development. In particular, there is no valid *prima facie* case for the support-led strategy. Development experience shows that just as economic growth does not promote human development automatically, the same is the case with human development: it too does not convert into economic growth automatically. This is the central point that has often been missed in the human development dialogue.

We must now address the next question: which of these strategies should be chosen if a choice must be made between them? The evidence presented so far supports the superior claims of the growth-mediated policy. The reason is that countries that adopted the traditional development policies (the miracle economies and China) have succeeded in achieving both high economic and human development. On the other hand, the countries that tried to tread the direct road to development (Kerala, Sri Lanka and the former Soviet Union bloc countries) can be cited as examples of lacklustre development. They failed to reach the goal of self-reinforcing process that could convert human development gains into high growth rates and then to high human development and so on.[6] The point is that there is no other road to success that could win for the developing countries the crowning wreath of development success. Judged by the actual outcomes of the development effort under these rival strategies, it can be stated without fear of contradiction that the support-led strategy represents the triumph of pious resolve over what is feasible.

NOTES

1. The UNDP (1996) contains the most extensive exposition of the human development approach on which the later reports have drawn. It states: 'Those who advocate human development—welcome improvements in health or education. But they regard these as valuable in their own right, whether they increase output or not' (p. 54).

2. Truly catastrophic has been reversal in the former Soviet Union: it fell 48 places in its HDI ranking. This is also a country where growth rates have declined disastrously, doing more damage to its economy than it suffered in the Second World War.

3. The regression results presented in Tables 15.1 and 15.2 and the other tables in the subsequent chapters are based on the pooled data drawn from the Penn World Table 6.1, which provides comparable information for 168 countries. (The Penn World Table 6.1 uses purchasing power parity (PPP) adjusted national accounts data, converted to international prices, for 168 countries for the period 1950–2000). For the present study, we have selected eighteen Asia-Pacific countries for which all the relevant data were available (which makes eighteen cross-sections). The time-periods, except for Vietnam, are 1965 to 2000, or thirty-five years. We have used the standard pooled data techniques for estimating the regressions presented in these tables, applying the fixed-effect model, which is equivalent to the Least Squares Dummy Variables approach. We have estimated each equation by incorporating dummy variables to capture structural differences across individual countries and across groups of low, middle and high-income countries. See, Judge, Hill and Griffith (1982) and Asterio (2006) for details of the regression techniques used for analyzing pooled data. As is well known, the pooled data capture the structural changes in the sample countries and enable one to study the dynamic behaviour of the variables included in the estimations, something not achieved by making simple cross-country comparisons based on one or two observation obtained from country surveys. They also provide more efficient and broader sources of variations in the estimates of the parameters by considering much broader sources of variations.

4. It may be noted that the finding: 'the link going from human development to growth is insignificant' is not an argument against increasing social expenditure on education and health, which are intrinsically important.

5. Thus it has been pointed out, though somewhat confusingly, 'economic growth is an important means to human development, and when growth stagnates over a prolonged period, it becomes difficult to sustain progress in human development' [UNDP (2004), p. 128]. Sen (1999b) states the point even more explicitly: 'The support-led strategy is a recipe for rapid achievement of higher quality of life, and this has great policy importance, but there remains an excellent case for moving on from there to broader achievements that include economic growth as well as the raising of the standard features of quality of life' (p. 49). On balance, 'the support-led strategy remains shorter on achievements than growth-mediated success...' [Sen (1999b), p. 49]. It is a short logical step, seldom taken, from these admissions to an acknowledgement of the failure of such a policy for achieving during economic and human development.

6. Indeed, Sen (1983) had also stated: 'Development economics was born at a time when government involvement in deliberately fostering economic growth in general, and industrialization in particular, was very rare, and when the typical rates of capital accumulation were low. The situation has changed in many respects, and while we may deal with different issues, *it does not in any way invalidate the wisdom of the strategies then suggested*' (p. 752; italics added).

16

Human Development Paradigm: The Key Growth-Related Issues

The discussion in the present chapter will show that the Human Development Paradigm's Olympian certitude about the merits of support-led strategy has gradually been replaced by doubts about its efficacy and a greater understanding of the relatively superior merits of the growth-mediated approach to human development. From the original position where no possibility seemed too remote and no goal too distant for the support-led strategy, it seems to have climbed down to a more balanced view of the development process. Partly informed by the light of human reason, but mostly in a bid to find a realistic middle ground between economic development and human development, it has revived some of the traditional themes of economic development namely, import substitution *versus* export expansion; the role of the government in promoting economic and human development and the dynamics of Unequal Exchange. Some of these themes are consistent with its basic logic (the ones that have the effect of enhancing the quality of social justice at the national and global levels); others are not (those policies that in effect emphasize maximizing growth). In the same vein, it now openly acknowledges the shortcomings of the HDI as a reliable indicator of individual well being, especially when inequalities between different countries and between different income groups within the same countries are significant [UNDP (2005)]. Yet the authors of the paradigm seem to be unaware of the logical consequences of these new trends in their thinking. The aim of this chapter is to create such awareness.

16.1. THE TRADE-DEVELOPMENT CONNECTION

The Human Development Paradigm has, of late, strongly revived global interest in the unfair patterns of the international trading system pointing out that the trade-growth linkage has not always worked to the developing countries' advantage.[1] It has also emphasized the need for gradualism in trade liberalization and advocated the imposition of import restrictions with a view to supporting domestic economic activity and helping innovations and technological change, without discriminating against export expansion. It has especially highlighted the need for limited and temporary capital account controls in times of financial crisis such as that ravaged the East Asian 'miracle growers'. And as a logical sequel to these positions it has taken a middle-of-the-road stand on globalization and the WTO-led international trading system, and has highlighted the need for increasing its development content.[2] With a view to achieving these goals, it has explicitly stated, 'It is difficult to find examples of sectors competing successfully in world markets without active state involvement'. Even more significantly, it lays down: 'the aim of industrial policy should be to create conditions under which countries acquire the technological capabilities needed to raise productivity, maximize the advantages of trade and development and dynamic comparative advantage' [UNDP (2005), p. 134]. Even more important is its assertion, 'Trade policy needs to be developed as part of an integrated strategy for poverty reduction and human development. Leaving it to the market is not an adequate approach' (p. 144). The UNDP's powerful advocacy and intellectual support has also successfully revived global interest in those discarded traditional prescriptions and policies whose scientific worth has of late been established. To development connoisseurs, all this would smell like 'old wine in new bottles'; but breaking the spell of a dominant liberalist opinion is a contribution.

16.2. Expanding the Domestic Market through Import Substitution

Continuing down the same evolutionary road, the Human Development Paradigm now seems to endorse the traditional stance on import-substituting industrialization, which aimed primarily at 'creating protected—and so profitable—home markets for domestic entrepreneurs to invest in'. Indeed, 'the data on growth in total factor productivity show that it is wrong to assume that inward orientation produced more dynamic inefficiency than did outward orientation' [UNDP (2003b), p. 37].[3] It also rejects the liberalist argument that import-substituting industrialization fell into disuse through a genuine 'exhaustion' of import-substitution policies; it rather puts the blame where it rightly belongs: on the exogenous shocks which set the development of Latin America, Middle East and sub-Saharan Africa back irrevocably—and on the Liberalist Paradigm's ideological support for *laissez-faire* solutions to development problems. Echoing the Unequal Exchange hypothesis, it blames the WTO for preventing developing countries from an active pursuit of import-substituting industrialization, whereas, the developed countries did the same during their days of under-development. In fact, they are still doing it with respect to their 'sunset industries'. It attributes the early success of

Korea and Taiwan to their policies of 'building up high technological capacity by restricting imports, encouraging reverse engineering of imported technologies and regulating foreign investments'. A study of the more recent examples of fast-growing countries (especially of post-reform China and Vietnam) has led it to accept the traditional wisdom, without saying it explicitly, that *laissez-faire* solution to the development problems leads only to economic stagnation. The only sensible course of action, it now argues, is to combine expansion of the domestic markets with gradual import liberalization. Export fetishism does not figure anywhere among the policies that have historically helped high-growth with equity.

16.3. GLOBALIZATION WITH A PINCH OF SALT

The Human Development Paradigm's new position on globalization also follows from its stance on the trade-growth linkage and its renewed emphasis on expanding domestic markets through import substitution. It recognizes that globalization is a lusty, ineluctable historical process whose march can be stopped only by endangering the prosperity of peoples and nations; and yet it also threatens to jeopardize economic growth and disfigure human development by the quintessential polarity in its unfolding. The Human Development Paradigm has forcefully restated developing countries' fears that globalization seems to be spurring a race to the bottom by grabbing from the poor and giving them to the rich, marginalizing nations already integrated into the world economy, decoupling them from scientific achievements carried out in the developed world and widening the pre-existing disparities in the levels of income and well-being within nations and between nations. These de-equalizing tendencies have reached a point where they have become economically and morally unacceptable—economically, because such tendencies weaken the demand-side forces that have historically stimulated growth; and morally, because within a nation and between nations inequality offends our inborn 'capacity for a sense of justice and a capacity for a conception of the good', as Rawls (1999) would put it.[4] One of the reasons for globalization and human development to diverge is that despite huge strides towards opening up world markets, big swathes of world economy, such as textiles and shipping, still remain only imperfectly accessible to the developing countries. In particular, the large agriculture subsidies that the OECD countries give to their farmers violate the very principles of trade liberalization that the WTO and other international donors keep imposing on the developing countries. More ominously, by wilful applications of the TRIPs Accord, the developed countries have relentlessly deprived the developing countries of their traditional technologies through a 'silent theft' [UNDP (1999)]. Also, insofar as the WTO has prevented the developing countries from copying the technologies of the developed countries, it has closed off the historical route to development for the latecomers since the Industrial Revolution [UNDP (2005)].[5] And, as if to add insult to injury, the developing countries have paid large amounts of royalties (which amount to a hefty $71 billion per annum) to the firms in the developed countries.

To remedy the situation, the Human Development Paradigm has insisted that developing countries combine high growth with integration with the world economy. As examples of an historical trend, it has cited the contrasting examples of two 'successful globalizers', Vietnam and Mexico. Vietnam has liberalized gradually and focused on expanding the domestic market to broaden the export base. The result has been a deeper integration with the world economy, high rates of economic growth, increased equity and lower poverty. On the other hand, Mexico concentrated on fast-track liberalization of its economy. True, it has achieved high rate of exports, but only low rates of growth and high inequity [UNDP (2005), pp. 121–22]. These instances, and many more, illustrate the basic principle that 'integration with the world economy is an outcome, not a pre-requisite of a successful growth strategy' [UNDP (2003a), p. 28].

16.4. A DEVELOPMENT-FRIENDLY WTO

The Human Development Paradigm has increasingly assumed a leadership role in pinpointing the areas where the WTO, which has been responsible for enforcing international trade rules since 1995, needs to be reformed with a view to enhancing its development content. It has powerfully argued that the WTO has intensified, rather than lessened, the dynamics of 'unequal exchange'.[6] Thus, under its not-so-watchful eyes, the classical case of the secular decline in commodity prices has re-emerged with unrelenting ferocity: 'the primary producers [now] are locked in a depression more than that of the 1930s'. The problem has been illustrated by the crisis of the coffee prices, which has caused the income from coffee sales to plummet from $12 billion in 1980 to $5.5 billion in 2003. It has thus 'destroyed the livelihood of twenty million households in which the smallholder production of coffee provides a critical source of income'. In the case of Ethiopia alone, the loss of income to average household has amounted to a $200 per household, in a country where more than one-third of the rural population lives on $1 a day. In Central America the falling coffee prices have caused a loss equal to 1.2 per cent of the GDP; and in Nicaragua the incidence of extreme poverty has risen by 5 per cent among coffee producers, while declining by 16 per cent in the case of non-coffee producers [UNDP (2005), pp. 139–141].

To counteract these baneful tendencies, the Human Development Paradigm has emphasized that international institutions—the WTO in particular—should work for the global good. Its efforts are all the more pertinent because this is not how the present world economic system works. Stripped of the rhetoric of globalization, a commitment to multilateralism and a concern for the developing countries growth and development, the benefits of the world trading system 'are very unevenly shared, while its costs are unevenly distributed' [UN (2000)]. The fact is that the WTO is less sympathetic to the developing countries' interests than its predecessor was (the GATT). As if to show its liberalist leanings, it has increasingly taken 'a one-size fits-all approach—one that invariably reflects the interests of the developed countries' [UNDP (2003b), p. 63]. True, it has some positive aspects, which its supporters have tirelessly advertised. Thus, it has confidently asserted, 'It is clear that, for the first time in history, the world can embrace a rule-based system for economic coexistence, the essential principles of which are generally agreed' [WTO (2004b), p. 5]. Yet appearances are more deceptive here than elsewhere in the liberalist domain. Indeed, in a variety of subtle and not-so-subtle ways it has narrowed significantly the 'development space' for the developing countries. It was for this reason that the Doha Round was demanded. But the recent suspension of the Doha Round negotiations (on 24 July 2006), caused mainly by the developed countries' refusal to budge on agricultural subsidies and their insistence that the developing countries open up their markets for their manufactured goods, is yet again a proof of the deepening dynamics of unequal exchange, with no significant equalizer in sight. To counteract these tendencies, the UNDP has encouraged, and financed, debate and discussion on these issues both at the national and international forums, which have led to a broad consensus that the WTO in its present form does not serve the interests of the developing countries.

16.4. (i). How to Reform the WTO?

The Human Development Paradigm has emphasized that the WTO needs to be reformed in at least four ways. Firstly, it has argued that the TRIPs Accord 'has struck a wrong balance between the interests of the technology holders and the wider public interests'. Indeed, it 'threatens to widen the technology divide between technology-rich and technology-poor countries'; and it has all but foreclosed possibilities of the late-coming developing countries to catch up with the pioneer rich countries [UNDP (2005), pp. 134–35]. Indeed, in this respect, the TRIPs Accord has violated a historical law of economic development namely, the latecomers copying the advanced technology created by the pioneers. Perhaps, the most pernicious effect of the TRIPs Accord has been to raise significantly the prices of the medicines of common use in the developing countries.[7]

Secondly, it has singled out for criticism the Single-Undertaking requirement, whereby, the signatories to the WTO must accept all its provisions as a package deal, on the grounds that it has been more of a hindrance than help for the developing countries. The revised rules for the non-tariff barriers have been extended to all the developing countries, without showing much sensitivity to their development requirements at different stages of economic development. The WTO, it has pointed out, has undermined one of the basic principles of the GATT which was to accord Special and Differential treatment to the developing countries with respect to their receiving unrequited market access to the developed countries markets. In this respect, the WTO has in effect reversed the line of development thinking at the global level since 1955. Reflecting the dominant influence of liberalist ideas, the WTO has encouraged the developing countries to liberalize voluntarily without waiting for a *quid pro quo* from the developed countries.[8] The developing countries have been forced to liberalize trade voluntarily, which has weakened greatly their bargaining position in global trade negotiations. The Human Development Paradigm has persuasively argued, of late, that this unjust clause of the WTO should be moderated in its application, if it cannot be entirely undone [UNDP (2003b)].[9]

Thirdly, the new paradigm has shown that the WTO has greatly limited the possibilities of import-substituting industrialization for the developing countries. True, Article 18-c of the GATT is still available but the WTO does not look favourably at those clauses—in particular, it disfavours Article 18, Part IV and the Enabling Clause—which had enabled the developing countries to enjoy the benefits of unrequited market access to the OECD markets [UNDP (2003b), pp. 55–57].[10] Once again, in order to achieve accelerated economic and human development, these disabilities of the WTO should be removed. In this context, the Human Development Paradigm has commented unfavourably on the TRIPs Accord, which the developing countries had to accept as part of a 'grand bargain' to consummate the Uruguay Round Negotiations. This Accord has practically closed off the industrialization space for the developing countries. It has become very difficult for them to employ the tools that 'successful economies in East Asia and elsewhere once used to maximize the benefits of foreign investment, including the local content requirements, technology transfers, and local employment, and research and development provisions' [UNDP (2005), p. 134]. A highly pernicious result of the application of this rule has been that multi-nationals have all but displaced the domestic firms.[11]

Fourthly, the Human Development Paradigm has highlighted the iniquities of on-going massive agricultural subsidization by the OECD countries. This system has posed a great challenge to the developing countries agricultural development because subsidies enable the developed countries to lower their prices below the cost of production of the developing countries, which puts the latter at a great disadvantage both in their own markets and the international markets. A tacit acceptance of this unjust system has earned for the WTO the unenviable sobriquet of the 'killer of the developing countries' farmers'.[12] Even as the developing countries put pressure on the developed countries, the latter have engaged in a large-scale re-packaging exercise in order to escape the WTO rules. A particularly odious example of the extent to which the developed countries have routinely hit the poor countries and people is the case of US subsidies to their cotton and rice producers. In the case of cotton, these huge subsidies to domestic producers ($4.7 billion in 2005) have tended to lower the international prices of cotton by 9 to 13 per cent and allowed the US producers to dominate world cotton markets and through their price-lowering effects to hurt the developing countries producers very badly. Thus, in Benin alone, the fall in cotton prices in 2001 directly increased the incidence of poverty from 37 to 59 per cent [UNDP (2005), p. 131]. As if to highlight its complicit connivance, the WTO has been a silent observer of these and other undesirable developments that have marred the working of the international trading system.

16.5. Concluding Remarks

The Human Development Paradigm constitutes an important milestone in the historical evolution of knowledge about the complexities of the development process. But the paradigm in its present form is by no means the 'end of history'. Fortunately, no such claims have been made; and it has shown awareness of the shortcomings of its original understanding of the development process: namely, it takes more than making progress in selected human development indicators (education and health) to achieve economic and human development on a lasting basis. An 'unintended consequence' of the Human Development Paradigm's evolution from, as it claims, an essentially 'non-human' approach of the rival paradigms to its own brand of human approach to the development process has been a tacit endorsement of the some of the basic propositions of the Traditional Development Paradigm—though this fact has never been acknowledged. In particular, it has restated its support for such foundational traditional ideas and propositions, as the role of the state in economic development, the inevitability of the import-substitution strategies for economic development, unequal exchange, and the need to go for an exploration of the developing countries dynamic comparative advantage.

All this has refocused the mind on the essential developmental issues and has served to bring development policy back to its original development concerns. But has it? The point made in this book is that its persistent advocacy of the support-led strategy might have diverted attention from the main thrust of development policy. Taking such contradictory postures can only create confusion in policy-making. It is, therefore, essential that the paradigm consciously tries to be of 'one mind' as to the basic elements of development strategy namely, to maximize growth rate of per capita income while paying due attention to social justice and human development considerations. In other words, to make a beneficial impact on development policy it must heal the 'inner split' between its anti-income maximization logic that started it off as a new development paradigm and the income maximization practice (through intensified import substitution, for instance) that it now advocates.

Notes

1. UNDP (2005) forcefully restates its position on the trade liberalization and growth linkage: '...successful trade liberalization and deepening integration are often outcomes of sustained growth with countries lowering tariffs as they grow richer' (p. 119).
2. A detailed restatement of the traditional themes in the human-development context was first set out in UNDP (1999) and UNDP (2003b).
3. UNDP (2003b) also recalls that the most intense practitioners of import-substituting industrialization—India and Pakistan—did quite well in this period partly because they insulated their economies from the de-stabilizing effects of short-term capital movements (they yet had not allowed free mobility of short-term capital). Their example also showed that, 'mechanisms other than import-substitution contributed to the economic collapse' (p. 38).
4. The discussion in the text on the limited reach of globalization draws freely on Naqvi (2004/2006).
5. The misuse of the Intellectual Property Rights Accord has been the most blatant in the case of the pharmaceutical industry. The developed countries multi-nationals have been able to monopolize the industry by including a TRIPs-plus provision in bilateral trade agreements, which strengthen their stranglehold on the pharmaceutical industry. UNDP (2003a) contains a detailed criticism of the TRIPs accord among other aspects of the WTO. See also Naqvi (1996) and (2002).
6. The following is a powerful restatement of the reality of Unequal Exchange that the WTO has carefully hidden behind the façade of its democratic procedures (the one-country-one-vote principle of decision-making). 'Some countries are more able than others to influence the WTO agenda. In the Uruguay Round, developing countries, despite their majority, were unsuccessful in opposing the extension of the WTO rules into areas such as intellectual property rights, investment and services. The agreement on agriculture left most of EU and US farm subsidy programmes intact for the simple reason that it was all essentially a bilateral agreement between the two parties that was forced onto the multilateral rules system. In effect, the world's economic superpowers were able to tailor the rules to their national policies' [UNDP (2005), p. 146].
7. It was to prevent the international pharmaceutical companies from raising the prices of medicine for the developing-country users that their governments adopted the Doha Declaration on Public Health in 2003.
8. The WTO has condescendingly reminded the developing countries, 'that their own trade policy reforms would produce a large share of the benefits to themselves and to other developing countries from global liberalization of trade in agriculture and manufactured

goods. This lesson, that a large part of the economic gains from trade liberalization accrue domestically, should not be overlooked in the context of the reciprocal bargaining for market access' [WTO (2004a), p. 2].

9. The reason for the weakening of the developing country's bargaining position is that GATT/WTO system does not represent the free-trade principle of voluntary unilateral liberalization. Instead, trade liberalization is regarded as a cost rather than a source of gain. Each round of global trade negotiations, therefore, is an occasion for a relentless trading of interests for interests in which each country must be able to 'give' some in order to be able to 'take' some. The Structural Adjustment Programmes by forcing the developing countries to liberalize voluntarily have greatly weakened their capacity to 'take' because they have so much less to 'give' in international bargaining. These matters have been clarified at some length in Naqvi (2002).

10. These issues have been discussed at length in Naqvi (1996).

11. The application of the TRIMs Accord has led to a displacement of the local firms in the automobile components industry in Latin America by the multi-national corporations.

12. The Cancun meeting of the WTO (10 September 2003) was greeted with cries of 'WTO kills the farmers'. As if to prove that it literally kills the farmers, a distinguished and articulate Korean farmer, Lee Kyung Hee, committed suicide publicly in front of the protesters.

17

The Human Development Paradigm: Social Justice, Equity and Poverty Reduction

The preceding chapters strongly suggest that, contrary to popular understanding, the Human Development Paradigm is distinguished not so much by its new-fangled support-led strategy, but by its non-apologetic moral vision. We explain it some detail in this chapter and the next. In this chapter, we discuss it in relation to the broader issues of social change—those relating to the problems of social injustice, poverty and human deprivation—with confidence in its scientific credentials. The next chapter will mostly deal with foundational issues like gender inequity and famines and some other matters. A common element in both the chapters is the recognition that the paradigm offers a message of hope—that these problems can be solved in a reasonably short period of time by a well-focused development policy. What makes it a cut above the rest is its insistence that social justice should be concerned with process of decision-making as well as with the opportunities they offer people to pursue valued outcomes [Sen (1999b)]. As a mark of originality, the Human Development Paradigm does not accept either the Benthamite Utilitarianism, or the distribution-blind Pareto-optimality principle, or the non-consequentialist moral principles, because none of these can handle the problems of social justice adequately.[1] For the same reason it denies that self-interest is the only rational principle of individual or social conduct. Indeed, development policy can be seen as correcting the adverse social consequences of an excessive inebriation with self-interestedness. On the other hand, altruism and an unbending commitment to a cause—even when such motivations do not bring any immediate personal reward—have historically been a potent force for social change, something that is beyond the ken of self-interest maximization.[2] Indeed, without an adequate supply of such hard-core altruism no systemic change could have come about anywhere, at any time in human history.

17.1. REDUCING INEQUALITIES

The nearly universal demand for reducing social and economic inequalities flows naturally, as Rawls (1999) pointed out, from two vital moral powers that men/women possess: 'their capacity for a sense of justice and their capacity for a conception of the good' (p. xii).[3] In a morally oriented social framework that allows all its members the freedom to form, revise and rationally pursue their conception of the good, only the equitable states of the economy will be rationally chosen. To this end, the Human Development Paradigm would focus on promoting a 'well-ordered society'. A distinguishing characteristic of such a society would be that individuals voluntarily work for the betterment of others, especially the least-privileged in the society and that they do not as a rule free ride for their personal gains. The Millennium Declaration (2000) explicitly recognizes it as a 'collective responsibility' of all nations 'to uphold the principles of human dignity, equality and equity at the global level' (p. 1). The UNDP (2005) explicitly states, '[an equitable] distribution [of income and wealth] should be put at the centre of the strategy of human development' (p. 71). The reason for this overarching emphasis on equality is that inasmuch as inequality is bad for poverty alleviation, it is also inimical to growth. It also undermines human development because, with the same HDI (an average indicator of human development), the poor will experience a significantly higher level of human development in a relatively more equal society as opposed to the unlucky ones residing in in-egalitarian countries. Thus, the average HDI rankings, for say, Brazil and Mexico (two very unequal countries) will drop by 52 and 55 places respectively (to 115 and 108), if the average income component of the HDI is adjusted to the average of the poorest 20 per cent of the respective populations (p. 56).[4] This forceful advocacy of equality should have important consequences for development policy in the developing countries. It should also help them to reduce poverty at least by one-half by the year 2015 as part of their global commitment to the implementation of the Millennium Development Goals. An implication of the Human Development Paradigm's moral position is that the quest for equality cannot remain limited to making greater expenditures on health and education. This is because, 'high levels of spending on health have failed to eradicate large disparities in infant death rates based on race, wealth and state of residence' [UNDP (2005), p. 58]. It would also require reforming the basic structure of unequal asset holdings. This is a very important elaboration of the human development concept, which makes it more precise and meaningful.

17.2. Minimizing Poverty and Human Deprivation

Yet another foundational aspect of the Human Development Paradigm is its reasoned focus on the related problems of poverty and human deprivation. The Rawlsian Difference Principle gives the least-privileged of the society most of the social primary goods and resources, and Sen's functioning and capability analysis would discriminate in favour of those in the society (the physically handicapped and those suffering from some debilitating illness) who are less able to convert these resources and primary goods into valuable functionings and capabilities. The Covenant on Economic, Social and Cultural Rights (1976) recognizes 'the right of everyone to an adequate standard of living for himself and his family, including adequate food, clothing and housing and to the continuous improvement of living conditions' (Article 11). One of the central values of The Millennium Declaration (2000)—namely, Solidarity—echoes similar sentiments: 'Global challenges must be managed in a way that distributes the costs and burdens fairly in accordance with the basic principles of equity and social justice. *Those who suffer most or benefit least deserve help from those who benefit most*' (p. 2; italics added). The Millennium Development Goals place human well-being and poverty reduction at the top of global development priorities. However, no less important, indeed revolutionary, is the fundamental shift in global thinking on poverty that the Human Development Paradigm has caused: it is that poverty reduction is not a matter of charity given by the rich to the poor; rather it is a claimable right of the poor.[5] This recognition has created an effective framework of checks and balances within which national governments and the global community could be held accountable for the non-fulfilment of their obligations towards the poor and the needy.

17.2. (i). Poverty as a Capability Deprivation

One of the most important insights the Human Development Paradigm offers is that poverty is not so much a problem of the lowness of income as of the inadequacy of income to achieve the necessary functionings and the capability (or the freedom) to acquire those functioning [Sen (1992)]. This is because the connection between income and capability differs from person to person. Once this point of view is taken, poverty would obviously be seen 'as a serious deprivation of certain basic capabilities' [Sen (1999a), p. 361]. The capability analysis has the merit of explaining adequately, as the income poverty concept cannot, how, in two totally different socio-economic contexts a poor person's relative income deprivation in one place can translate into an absolute capability deprivation at another place. This has implications for some important aspects of poverty. Thus, for instance, African-Americans men living in Harlem, though enjoying income levels much higher than those of poor people in underdeveloped countries have a lesser chance of reaching the age of 40 or more than the Bangladeshi men have. The situation is even worse for African-American women, who have shorter life spans than women in many developing countries in which the income levels are much lower than in the United States [Sen (1999b)]. These observations suggest: (a) poverty is a universal problem and needs attention even in the developed countries; and (b) capability poverty can be much more intense than income poverty depending on the socio-economic location and context of the poor people. The implication for development policy is that poverty must be accepted as a social evil, irrespective of the prevailing inter-country and interpersonal disparities between income and expenditure patterns; and that ameliorative action must go well beyond just raising the income of the target group of poor. Everywhere, it would take transferring more resources to the poor and the physically disabled in order to redress interpersonal capability deficits. Besides being theoretically tighter than alternative formulae, the capability analysis greatly enlarges the information base of the evaluative criteria of human happiness and well-being.

Some Shortcomings of Capability Analysis: While theoretically tight, Sen's principle raises problems of designing and implementing social-welfare programmes on the basis of the capability perspective. Obviously, the capability analysis will be most helpful if the transaction cost for determining inter-personal capability deficits—for instance, giving more to the sick than to the able-bodied person—were typically small or negligible, or if the recipients of the welfare payments could be relied upon to disclose their respective predicaments truthfully. The latter proviso assumes special importance when, because of the disclosure of what Hayek regards as 'private information,' a person might get less than others or nothing at all. The fact is that the cost of collecting information about the incapability's of potential beneficiaries would not typically be negligible, precisely because the potential recipients could be relied upon to give out 'private information' voluntarily. The problem here is the familiar one when information is both imperfect and costly, namely, that moral hazard and assurance problems prevent people from correctly disclosing information about their 'differential and heterogeneous' personal characteristics. Indeed, the possibility of receiving a differential treatment based on physical incapability may lead people to feign it. In extreme cases, the potential recipients of public benefits may self-inflict a physical incapability, as professional beggars do, to enhance their eligibility for additional assistance [Naqvi (2002)]. The policy makers have, therefore, to prepare their incapability reports about the potential recipients based on some costly, time-consuming indirect means of collecting such information rather than doing it by personal interviews of the target group, which too is a time-consuming and costly exercise, apart from being unreliable. Sen (1999a) has himself noted that the 'rough-and-ready' income-poverty analysis may have to be relied upon precisely because 'the choice of the informational base for poverty cannot really be disassociated from pragmatic considerations, particularly, informational availability' (p. 361).[6] However, these observations do not, in any way, detract from the seminal nature of the Human Development Paradigm's contribution to our understanding of one of the most elemental problems that development policy has to face.

17.2. (ii). Poverty and Famine

Yet another fundamental aspect of the Human Development Paradigm is to have shed altogether new light on the nature of hunger and starvation in general and famine in particular. No less important is that it has offered a message of hope—that, notwithstanding the climate of gloomy wretchedness they create, famine and starvation are preventable; and once they come, nevertheless, their duration can be significantly curtailed by timely action. This is an example of making a stitch in time to save literally millions of lives. In this context, an important insight is that hunger and starvation in general, and famines in particular, are symptomatic of an abysmal failure of the economic and political systems of the countries where they occur. The reason is that they have typically been caused less by the inadequate availability of food and more by a lack of accessibility of a large population to food. The Covenant on Economic, Social and Cultural Rights (1976) explicitly recognized this vital point: 'Fundamentally, the root of the problem of hunger and malnutrition is not lack of food but lack of access to available food, *inter alia*, because of poverty, by large segments of the world's population' [Comment No. 12 on Article 11, p. 3]. This is particularly true of the famines. Sen (1981), who has given the most complete and original exposition of the famine problem, has convincingly shown that nearly all the major famines in the twentieth century have occurred amidst plentiful food supplies; and they have been normally caused by a sudden failure of people's 'entitlement failure' below the level where their entitlements set does not include enough food to ensure human survival. It is also a failure of the many ways available in which the society converts (through production, trade and transfers) the endowments of the famine-affected people into food that has usually been the proximate cause of famines (p. 34).[7] Recognizing these facts, the Covenant (Article 11) makes access to food as one of the most basic fundamental rights of all people without which no other right can have much meaning.[8] To this end, it makes it obligatory on all the states 'to ensure for everyone under its jurisdiction access to the minimum essential food which is sufficient, nutritionally safe, to ensure their freedom from hunger' [Comment 12, p. 5]. This reads like a passage from some revolutionary's handbook; and might be one of the reasons perhaps why the Covenant has been observed more in the breach than in the observance.

17.2. (iii). The Nature of Famine

The reasons usually cited in the literature for the occurrence of famines are many, and some of them interrelated. Yet there are some common features about them. Firstly, they come suddenly as a combined result of exogenous shocks that hit only a small section of the population in the same country (not more than 5 per cent on average) and then get magnified. However, the suddenness of the famines is not unrelated to a history of consumption decline of the vulnerable group for decades; nor would it be wise to regard them as 'discrete events'.[9] Secondly, in a typical famine an absolute reduction in the availability of food is only part of the story. What triggers the famine is the precipitate decline in the purchasing power of the famine-afflicted population that deprives it of the means to establish entitlement over the minimum amount of food necessary for human survival. The loss of (exchange) entitlement could come about because the price of food increased sharply enough to cause a sudden collapse in the purchasing power of those poor people who must buy their food in the open market. The calamity might also strike because certain jobs have been eliminated and, in the absence of a social security system, those without jobs simply starve. For all these reasons 'attempts to understand [the famines] in terms of average food availability per head can be hopelessly misleading' [Sen (1999b), p. 168].[10] Thirdly what makes famines scandalous is that their visitation generally escapes media attention and, partly because of that, the rest of the economy carries on its business, as usual. In this sense, famines are also a highly divisive phenomenon. They become even more socially divisive because in such events the inequality of income and wealth increases sharply in the famine-afflicted area. Fourthly, because the famines are avoidable, this very fact makes the job of famine prevention do-able, though by no means easy. This is because terminating a famine then becomes a matter of mobilizing the existing food supplies and of creating temporary job opportunities to restore the purchasing power of the people.

17.3. THE ROLE OF THE STATE

It is obvious that radical institutional changes cannot come about by individual initiative alone. The Human Development Paradigm has, therefore, emphasized state intervention in the quest for social justice and the establishment of a 'well-ordered' society.[11] The focus of intervention would, however, be on reforming the basic social structure of rewards and incentives. Rawls (1999) explicitly states: 'The basic institutions must from the very outset put in the hands of citizens generally, and not of a few, the productive means to be fully cooperating members of the society'. While ruling out a welfare-state solution, he makes clear that such structural changes will come about through the agency of 'liberal socialist regime' [Rawls (1999), p. ix]. In Sen's scheme public policy is aimed at remedying the interpersonal capability deficits—so that those less capable to convert primary social goods or resources into individual happiness receive more than those who are relatively more capable to do so. The important point is that these schemes do not regard an intrusive state as inconsistent with the Human Paradigm's overarching emphasis on individual freedom to choose what is best for her/ him. In this perspective, the focus shifts from the liberalists exclusive emphasis on individual responsibility to a wider effort in which both individual effort and state action shape an essentially egalitarian society. While the state's efforts to rectify the patent imbalances in the structure of property holdings must be seen in the overall perspective of human freedom, it will be misleading to interpret the Human Development Paradigm as one that lays primary responsibility on individual effort and initiative to improve their chances in life.[12] Indeed, the principles noted above hold that it is the primary responsibility of the state (and other non-government institutions) to enable people to lead a life with dignity and equality by enacting institutional reforms that nullify the incentive structure born of hereditary advantages. All this does not minimize the importance of individual initiative and effort to do whatever one can to improve her/his position; but it does reject the liberalist notion that individuals are solely, or even, mostly responsible for their predicament and that their possession of the primary goods or the freedom to choose the best capability set would be strictly proportional to their personal effort to alleviate their suffering. Acknowledging that the sufferings that individuals have to live with and the indignities that they have to submit to are only partly, if at all, due to the lack of their own effort, the state must widen individuals horizons of choice by ensuring that their fundamental economic rights, as defined in the several United Nations documents referred to in this book, are met.

17.3. (i). State Intervention and Famine

As noted above, famine, in effect, signifies a monumental failure of the market mechanism to establish a balance between demand and supply for food in the deprived microcosm because of entitlement failure of a small minority—a balance between the two cannot be restored at a non-negative price [Koopmans (1965)]. The point is that non-market institutions have to play a dominant role in such situations precisely because of the utter failure of the markets for food and other related markets. Indeed, even in normal conditions the food markets are incomplete, so that there is lot of room for making Pareto improvements by government institutions; but in famine conditions these markets simply melt away into economic non-entities.[13] The other reason for government intervention is that one cannot wait for the market to create jobs for the unemployed, and/or to make up for the shortfall in the purchasing power of those affected by the famine. The capacity of the market mechanism to withstand exogenous shocks is greatly reduced in the affected areas as compared with the non-affected areas in the same country, even in the same locality.[14] This asymmetrical adjustment to the shocks, and its slowness, have been among the causes of famine and deaths for some as well as an occasion for making large economic gain for others—the size of this disproportionate incidence of famines on different people in the same locality being determined in large measure by the initial inequalities of income and physical and human assets.[15] However, in this case at least a demonstration that the market fails does not guarantee that the government will succeed. This is because famines also signify a failure of the government to prevent the calamity by establishing safety nets in normal times to help the affected population when famines do arrive, and then its inability to start a series of temporary public-works programmes to provide employment to those afflicted by a sudden and precipitate decline in the purchasing power. A central feature of this multidimensional moral and social failure is that timely action is not taken to prevent such social, economic and moral catastrophes. The markets simply fail to deliver food to those without the necessary purchasing power; and government fails to provide them the jobs and establish the necessary information networks, during and after famines, for fear of an adverse political backlash. The price of the combined failure of the market and the government to solve the problem in time is very high: an 'unusually high mortality risk is associated with a severe threat to the food consumption of at least some people in the area' [Ravallion (1997), p. 1205].[16]

17.3. (ii). Famine as a Challenge to Development Policy

The conjunction of the existence of plenty of food and its failure to reach the worst affected population complicates an apparently simple problem.[17] Complications arise because the visitation of some of worst famines in an environment of food plenty bespeaks a complete breakdown of individual ethics (private hoarders withhold food from the market to make money even as hundreds and thousands die of starvation) as well of the system of governance which fails to move food urgently from areas of food plenty to the famine-afflicted areas. To be effective development policy must, therefore, focus on 'both the elimination of persistent, endemic deprivation and the prevention of sudden, severe destitution' [Sen (1999b), p. 186]. In the long run, a public education programme should make life difficult for the hoarders of food, including heavy punishments for their social crimes. To this end, development policy in fighting famines cannot afford the luxury of taking into account only the broad picture. This is because here a satisfactory situation on the average typically hides extremely unsatisfactory predicament.

Yet another complication for development policy is that it must take into account the essential difference between the problem of poverty reduction and the dynamics of famine. An outstanding, though highly depressing, example of this difference is that a country like China that has achieved remarkable success in reducing inequality, deprivation and poverty, could still experience one of the worst famines of the twentieth century. On the other hand, there are other developing countries (like India and Pakistan) whose record of poverty reduction is anything but stellar and yet these have been spared the odium of famines. It follows that, as noted in the famine literature, the success in poverty reduction is no guarantee against the highly unwelcome visitation of famines, if the government does not take certain rather elementary preventive measures (like the provision of safety nets).[18]

However, it is important that the difference-issue is not over-emphasized. An important point in this context is that the design of an effective anti-famine is not inconsistent with, much less at the expense of, a fruitful anti-poverty policy package. In other words, fighting famine does not necessarily entail any significant opportunity cost in terms of achieving the routine developmental objectives. Indeed, the reverse may turn out to be the case, depending on the type of policy response to a famine situation. For instance, it has been observed that safety nets prevent the productive assets of the famine-hit population from being depleted completely and doing lasting damage to their livelihoods [Osmani (1996)]. In their absence, the famines may exacerbate the inequality of incomes between the famine-hit population and the rest. Furthermore, insofar as inequality lowers the poverty-reducing potential of a given growth rate, safety nets will certainly prevent a bad situation from getting worse. Conversely, the policies that prevent such a scenario raise the long-term growth of the economy and its poverty-reducing potential.[19] Efforts should be made to improve the rural infrastructure, which, among other things, would enhance the speed of response to a famine situation by a greater preparedness to rush food supplies from food surplus areas in the country.

17.4. CONCLUDING REMARKS

This chapter highlights the Human Development Paradigm's seminal approach to the most important human problems that essentially reflect a mingling of economic, social and moral considerations namely, achieving social justice, reducing poverty and alleviating misery and the hopelessness born of utter social and economic deprivation. No less important is the altogether new light it sheds on the tragic phenomena of famines and mass starvation that signify a total failure of the market mechanism. Here we have an ironclad case for urgent state action that focuses on the alleviation of immediate distress through schemes that create employment and strengthen the purchasing power of the people in the affected areas on a priority basis. Yet another contribution of the Human Development Paradigm at a more general level of discourse is to have shown convincingly that many economic issues are best thought of as essentially moral challenges that require a hard-headed economic response. No less important is the fact that it has provided a scientific basis to approach these problems.

NOTES

1. The Pareto-optimality and the non-consequentialist moral principles are not suitable for evaluating the egalitarian credentials of a developing society because they, in one way or another forbid making redistribution of income and wealth on the grounds that it would pave the 'road to serfdom' and/or that it would encourage trampling on people's moral rights and/or because doing so would violate the unanimity principle. The Benthamite principle is also unsuitable for the purpose because it insists on measuring changes in welfare only on the basis of their contribution to total utility. These principles do not consider even a human calamity like a famine that has killed millions as a fit case for public intervention.

2. Adam Smith, the universally accepted *guru* of the self-interest maximization principle (an honour thrust upon him posthumously by his self-interested progeny) has this to say on the place of altruistic behaviour in human conduct: 'How selfish so ever man may be supposed, there are evidently some principles in his nature, which interest him in the fortune of others, and render their happiness necessary to him, though he derives nothing from it, except the pleasure of seeing it' [Smith (1790), p. 191]. This can hardly be read as an ode to the essential selfishness or cupidity of human nature.

3. The demand for social justice and helping the poor also has a deep religious basis. Thus, for instance, Fogel (2000) attributed the Four Ethical Awakenings in the United States to the work of the Gospellers, who believed, 'that the essence of religion became the elimination of poverty and inequality' (p. 121). The point is that a religious commitment to an agreed social objective would strengthen the voluntary human urge to be concerned about others and to actually help those who need it most. For a detailed analysis of Islamic, Christian and Jewish points of view on these issues see, Naqvi (1981); (1994); and (2003); and Wilson (1997).

4. Yet another example of what equalization of income can do to the poor person's chances in life is the following: the income of the poorest 20 per cent in the less egalitarian Guatemala will rise from $550 a year to $1,560 a year if it is set equal to the income of the poorest 20 per cent in the relatively more egalitarian Vietnam [UNDP (2005)].

5. It is interesting to recall that the Human Development Paradigm's position as stated in the text is the exact opposite of the Liberalist Paradigm's: Hayek (1960), representing the latter point of view stated: 'There are good reasons why we should make provisions for the weak or infirm—it is entirely a different matter, however, to suggest that 'those who are poor—are entitled to a share in the wealth [of the rich]...' (p. 101). It may be noted that, as on the question of inequality, the Human Development Paradigm's position gets strong support from strongly held religious beliefs. For instance, Islam clearly states that the poor have a right in the wealth of the rich ('And in whose wealth a due share is included for the needy beggar and those dispossessed' Al-Quran, 70, 24–25). Christian and Jewish traditions have broadly similar positions on this. See Wilson (1997) and Naqvi (2003) on the convergence of the secular and religious philosophies on acknowledging the prior rights of the poor who are deprived to a decent standard of living.

6. Sen (1999a, p. 361) notes that in cases of extreme starvation and when the need for ameliorative action is urgent; the traditional income analysis may have to be preferred to the capability analysis. However, the considerations cited in the text imply that the income poverty may have to be relied upon even in non-extreme cases.

7. Entitlement set is defined as all the commodities bundles that can be procured from all the legal sources at the individual's command [Sen (1981)]. It may be noted that the use of the word entitlement or exchange entitlement is quite different from Nozick's theory of entitlement (1974), which has been discussed at length at different places in the present study.

8. The Covenant emphasized, 'the right to food is indivisibly linked to the inherent dignity of the human person and is indispensable for the fulfilment of other human rights enshrined in the Bill of Human Rights' [Comment 11, p. 2].

9. Thus, the average food consumption of the poor in Bangladesh was on a steady decline for a decade or so prior to 1974–75 famine [Ravallion (1995)].

10. The basic references on famine, in addition to the one cited in the text are: Sen (1981); Dreze and Sen (1989).

11. It is important to note that there are some differences between Rawls and Sen about the scope of state intervention. The former emphasizes that the state confine itself to evolving a system of fair rules within which individuals with different ends can cooperate with mutual advantage; the latter would give a more intrusive role to the state to maximize social good while the individuals exercise their freedom to choose between alternative opportunities [Sugden (1993)].

12. It may be of some interest to note in this context that *World Development Report* (2005) gives a somewhat misleading interpretation of the position that Sen has taken on the state *versus* the individual responsibility issue: '...as in both frameworks [of Sen and Roemer] we acknowledge the central role of individual responsibility and effort in determining outcomes' (p. 79). Roemer's (1996) formula 'equality of resources implies equality of welfare' is not probably concerned with the question of the role of the state, but this is certainly a misinterpretation of Sen's position. He explicitly states: 'the arbitrary narrow view of the individual standing on an imaginary island un-helped and unhindered by others—has to be broadened not merely by acknowledging the role of the state but also by recognizing the function of other institutions and agents' [Sen (1999b), p. 285].

13. An insistence on market solutions in the food markets has historically been one of the factors responsible for letting famines happen and do extensive devastation to human life. The *laissez-faire* policies advocated by Adam Smith, Thomas Malthus, John Stuart Mills not only did not prevent the many famines in British India, but also might have actually been responsible for such tragic situations to degenerate into major human disasters [Ravallion (1997), p. 1206].

14. Basically famines highlight the total inappropriateness of an uncompromising individualistic attitude, which might, in many cases, have obstructed taking effective famine-preventing

measures. Emperor Haile Selassie's dictum that: 'those who don't work starve' meant that there was very little state-arranged relief at the height of the Ethiopian famine of 1973 [Sen (1992), p. 77].

15. Famines in a more fundamental way signify a failure of the neo-classical framework to analyze the famine problem. In fact, competitive equilibrium can peacefully coexist with famines: people can die of hunger in competitive equilibrium for the simple reason that those individuals could not attain a minimum level of consumption necessarily for survival. In other words, famines do not signify a market failure and are not inconsistent with neo-classical Pareto-optimality situation [Coles and Hammond (1995)].

16. The failure to design such preventive policies as the creation of safety nets for the poor allows the famine to take hold, while the failure to come up with suitable remedial policies in time has been responsible for the spread of famine to a larger population.

17. If it is held that total food availability in the country at the time of famine is seldom a proximate cause of famine, as Sen (1981) famously showed, then it may lead to a relaxation, even total neglect, of the national and international efforts to procure sufficient supplies of food available to limit the spread and intensity of famines. Thus, in Ethiopian 1983–85 famine; international aid agencies overestimated the local availability of food (held by private hoarders) that could be mobilized to meet the situation.

18. However, it is important that the distinction between persistent deprivation (an indicator of 'normal' poverty) and sudden destitution (heralding the arrival of a famine) is not overdone. This is because economic policies that lead to perpetuation of poverty also lay the groundwork of the sudden visitation of a famine. Also remedial steps like providing safety nets to the poor on permanent basis would contribute to a resolution, or at least their mitigation, of both the famine-like conditions (in which a substantial part of the population is bypassed by the process of growth) and famines (in which a much smaller population is exposed to extreme deprivation that is also responsible for large number of deaths). Similarly, famines are more likely to occur (indeed, almost always occur) in grossly in-egalitarian countries than in basically egalitarian settings. The political and social atmosphere is one of insensitivity to human distress in the former; while it is one of social awareness in the latter.

19. Compare the statement in the text with the following observation: 'A safety net which can prevent the depletion of productive assets by poor people will entail higher longer term rate of both growth and poverty reduction' [Ravallion (1997), p. 1234].

18

Human Development Paradigm:
Its Moral Motivation

One of the defining characteristics of the Human Development Paradigm is that it does not regard its essentially moral motivation as a source of embarrassment but as an invaluable asset. It helps a deeper understanding of the elemental development issues like unemployment and adds a sense of urgency to their resolution. The key to the success of the paradigm is its non-Utilitarian consequentialist moral philosophy that has sought to replace the self-interest-only doctrine by a wider set of human motivations, (e.g., sympathy, commitment etc.). Rather than trying to reduce human achievements to just one index of welfare (utility, income), it defines human happiness as flowing from a multiplicity of income and non-income factors—such as rights, liberties, and social bases of self-respect, in addition to income and wealth. A striking aspect of the paradigm is the manifest richness of its informational base, the multiplicity of the valuable objectives it explicitly recognizes and the breadth of its evaluative criteria—all of which must be taken into account in any satisfactory evaluation of development success (failure). It also gives special attention to gender inequity, which has for ages inhibited women's steady progress to achieving social, economic and cultural empowerment. Then it highlights the important, but not much noticed issues regarding the relative importance of political and economic rights, the question of fixing the responsibility of the state to offset the socially undesirable consequences of specific economic policies, the relationship between rights and obligations and the nature of social obligations (i.e., their being perfect and imperfect). Above all, it explicitly recognizes that the principles of justice and wisdom must inform progress and reform. All this is a veritable nettle of thorny issues and problems, but a development policy is nothing if it cannot grasp it.

18.1. The Quest for Fairness and Justice

As noted above, one of the basic characteristics of the Human Development Paradigm is its non-Utilitarian consequentialist philosophy. It aims at minimizing social injustice, which is defined as a state, 'when inequalities are not to the benefit of all' [Rawls (1999), pp. 54–56]. The quintessential emphasis on equality follows from the paradigm's moral vision just alluded to: it is that a 'well-ordered society' should not tolerate inequalities with respect to the distribution of income, wealth and social opportunities based on circumstances of one's birth, their inborn talents, or a better physical capacity to enjoy life. It demands that people, as free and equal members of a society, be given equal opportunities to pursue their respective goals and objectives. And to this end, it would reject social systems like hereditary feudalism or ruthless meritocracy that confer initial advantages on privileged individuals based on the circumstances of their birth and early nurture for which they are not 'responsible'. But these initial advantages generally put the recipients on a higher trajectory of lucrative opportunities and social rewards and sow the seeds of social injustice that grow quickly and viciously if not checked in time. A principle of fundamental importance is, therefore, to compensate the losers for all such undeserved inequalities: 'We do not deserve our place in the initial distribution anymore than we deserve our initial starting place in the society' [Rawls (1999), p. 89]. Furthermore, the Human Development Paradigm's reformist agenda aims to keep a balance between different kinds of freedoms, especially between political freedom and economic freedom. This is because 'economic un-freedom in the form of extreme poverty can make a person helpless prey in the violation of other kinds of freedoms' [Sen (1999b), p. 8]. Happily, these basic principles are no longer confined to academic debate only; they form the basic guiding values of the UN, Millennium Declaration (2000) and have been repeatedly mentioned in the global dialogue on economic and human development.

18.2. ELIMINATING GENDER INEQUITY

The Human Development Paradigm has distinguished itself by emphasizing the elimination of gender inequity, ensuring equality between sexes is now regarded as one of the fundamental human rights. It highlights the sordid facts of social life that prevent greater social justice in the aggregate from healing the gender divide, and laments the tendency to side-track a sustained dialogue on this life-and-death issue. Rather than making the policy makers to spring to their feet to take corrective action, the policy response in this respect has generally been moribund and defeatist. Much as we decry this attitudinal defeatism, it must be accepted that the paltry size of the so-called trickle-down effect is most evident in this case. A telling example of such tendencies can be witnessed in East Asian miracle economies, where gender inequities have defied the mighty waves of economic prosperity. The case of China is no less regrettable in this respect. The UNDP (2005) gives prominence to the extant gross gender disparities—especially those in Asia. Thus, in India, the child mortality rate is 50 per cent higher for girls than for boys. The result is that the ratio of females to males is remarkably low (0.93).[1] These girls are among the 100 million 'missing women' in South Asia. Income inequalities and the greater incidence of poverty among women further compound the iniquities of their conditions. In Indonesia, the maternal mortality ratio is four times higher among women in the poorest 20 per cent of the population. It is in recognition of the persistence of gender disparity that Article 3 of the Covenant on Economic, Social and Cultural Rights (1976) made it obligatory on all nations to, 'ensure the equal rights of men and women to the enjoyment of all economic, social and cultural rights set forth in the present Covenant'. The Human Rights Declaration (UNDP, 2000) includes elimination of gender disparity as one of its basic underlying values namely, equality, which explicitly guarantees, 'Equal rights and opportunities of women and men must be ensured' (p. 2).

18.2. (i). The Well-Being and Agency Aspects of Gender Inequity

One of the most important contributions of the Human Development Paradigm to the gender-inequity debate is to have made clear the crucial distinction between the well-being aspect and the agency aspect of gender-based inequities. The two aspects are closely related to each other but are not the same. The well-being aspect focuses on the achievements and opportunities that women have access to; while the agency aspect highlights women's social standing as an effective independent decision taker. 'The well-being aspect is particularly important in assessing issues of distributive justice (including diagnosing economic injustice). The agency aspect [involves] valuing the various things he or she would want to see happen, and the ability to form such objectives and to have them realized' [Sen (1987), p. 59]. The former in a sense denotes the 'deal' a women gets in a society, as a recipient of the benefits or advantages flowing from the implementation of, say, social-welfare programmes; the latter highlights her active role in the making of such decisions and policies. But the worth of the agency aspect is measured mainly by the freedom women enjoy in making decisions regarding such crucial matters as regulating the size of the family. In that respect, the exercise of that freedom is its own reward, in addition to any benefits that may flow from such exercise. It is in this connection that women's freedom to take her own decision to be able to have outside employment is so crucial not only for enhancing her agency but for increasing the overall welfare of the society as well. A large number of cross-country and within-country studies show that women empowerment has had a decisive affect on fertility decline. This is of immense importance to women themselves (they are freed from the burden of frequent pregnancies and the subsequent restrictions on outside the home activities). But it also has wider effects on the rate of social and economic progress. Female literacy, an essential element of woman empowerment, directly contributes to a decline in child mortality, which saves the entire family (especially the mother) from deep emotional stress. Many medical studies show that severe under-nourishment in childhood entails a greater incidence of cardiovascular and other diseases for the grown-ups of both sexes, so that a solution of the problem helps both [Sen (2001)]. It is in recognition of this economy-wide role of women agency and well being that the Covenant on Economic, Social and Cultural Rights (Article 7) stipulates, 'Fair wages and equal remuneration for work of equal value without distinction of any kind, in particular women being guaranteed conditions of work not inferior to those enjoyed by men, with equal pay and equal work'. The UN Millennium Declaration (2000) recognizes 'gender equality and the empowerment of women as effective ways to combat poverty, hunger and disease and to stimulate development that is truly sustainable' (p. 5). It incorporates women rights in several of its Articles—especially, Articles, 3, 6, 7 and 10. The Millennium Development Goals 2 and 3 emphasize gender equality with respect to their access to education and health—which is the well-being aspect—and also their empowerment—which is their agency aspect.

Happily, the progress made on these resolutions and declarations is now regularly monitored. The UNDP's *Human Development Reports* each year record progress with respect to gender inequity—by each country's ranking with respect to the GDI and GEM. Moreover, the *Millennium Declaration Reports* also include extensive coverage of the implementation of the global decisions with regard to ensuring gender equity. But not so happily, the progress made at the national level is at best modest, and in some areas even disappointing. The UN, *Millennium Declaration Report* (2005) states that, notwithstanding the efforts made to repair the gender-deficit since 1990 development policy has a long way to go on this front. Girls still lag behind boys in school enrolment, gender disparities show no signs of declining at higher levels of education, women still have a smaller share of better paying jobs than men, more women than men occupy low-status jobs, and men dominate decision-making at the highest level, and so on (pp. 14–16). Much of this lack of adequate progress can be attributed to the persistence of traditional male-based values, even of male chauvinism. An important step towards reorganizing the existing structure of values is to confront them with facts, and by creating greater awareness of the advantages that accrue to both men and women from the unconstrained (or, at least, relatively less constrained) exercise of the latter's agency [Boserup (1970)]. Yet the repeated reminders of the state of gender inequity such as those cited above would, if continued, help break the ice of age-old bias against women throughout the world.

18.3. POLITICAL AND ECONOMIC RIGHT

The recognition of the economic rights of the individuals in addition to their political rights, as enshrined in the UN's Covenant of Economic and Cultural Rights and Millennium Declaration, has raised some important points both with respect to their separability and enforceability. In particular, the notion of economic rights has long been a topic of debate, mainly because of the difficulty of enforcing them. The reason is that the just demands for fulfilling economic rights are not as clearly definable as political rights because of the complex nature of the domestic and global obligations with regard to the former. Then, protecting each right requires a set of policies that addresses both types separately, but sometimes must do it simultaneously. In particular, economic freedom must be addressed directly and not just indirectly by repairing the political rights. The latter, though a fundamental right, must be supplemented by creating additional opportunities for individuals to make effective use of their freedom to enhance their economic well-being and overall happiness. And to the extent that there are structural constraints on one's capability to convert political rights into economic rights—especially those imposed by the circumstances of one's birth and early nurture—it is the duty of the state to ensure, a la Rawls (1999), that these constraints on personal achievements do not get built into the basic structure of a society. This is a fundamental point because without a restructuring of the system of incentives and rewards based on meritocracy or hereditary privileges, no egalitarian reform, however well intentioned, can command the voluntary support of the people to preserve it. But national governments may not be able to do this fundamental restructuring of the basic institutions all by themselves. Global efforts may be required not only to supplement domestic efforts but also to bring pressures to bear on national governments that are politically too weak to restructure national institutions; or where the basic social institutions do not yet exist to translate individual aspirations into social and political goals. In the present context, an important Millennium goal is to mandate that the, 'responsibility for managing worldwide economic and social development, as well as threats to international peace and security *must be shared among nations of the world and should be exercised multilaterally'* [UN (2000), p. 2. Italics added].[2] The italicized proviso in effect declares that international peace and security are in the nature of global public goods that the market mechanisms cannot optimally provide because the externalities they normally generate cannot be captured by pricing them.

18.4. The Question of Social Responsibility

The quest for social justice raises the problem of fixing the responsibility to achieve it. The nature of the difficulty can be understood better by considering the following real-life problem: who should bear the responsibility to redress social injustice when it arises from the implementation of a set of reformist policies? Thus, for instance, the implementation of the Structural Adjustment Programmes may contribute to increasing the unemployment rate, worsening the distribution of income and wealth, and exacerbating the incidence of poverty. Whose responsibility it is to redress the situation? One would think that the answer will be an unambiguous one: that the state has to take up this responsibility. But believe it or not, answers to this simple question have come bulging with ambiguities: one learns to her/his astonishment that it all depends on the type of moral philosophy one subscribes to. Let us elaborate on the queer chemistry of this enigmatic answer: (a) State inaction would be justified if one is guided by the utilitarian philosophy. This is because if unemployment, skewed distribution of income and wealth and greater poverty do not diminish total utility, then such changes would not matter. (b) Nearer 'home', the same studied insouciance about the adverse social consequences of specific policies will be the right attitude if the state takes non-consequentialism of the Liberalist Paradigm as its moral guide. This is because in the non-consequentialist perspective, the 'badness' of a given situation getting worsened by specific policies is not a matter of policy concern. The focal point of interest would be the 'wrongness' of the situation. Thus, higher unemployment, increased poverty and human deprivation might well be regrettable but they do not trample upon the moral rights of the people. (c) In the Rawlsian perspective if such policies lead to a diminution of the supply of the 'social primary goods', or if they create new inequalities of income and wealth that are not to the benefit of everyone, or if they disturb pre-existing moral and economic equilibrium in a well-ordered society, then some kind of state of action will be called for. (d) State action will be called for with greater intensity if (under pressure from the UNDP) the state weighs its responsibilities for remedial action on Sen's functioning and capabilities scale. The state will then be held responsible for the policies it makes and the specific actions taken to implement those policies; it would then also be logical to demand further that remedial actions be taken once the 'badness' (and not simply its wrongness) of the consequent state of affairs and its extent have been determined. Needless to state the Human Development Paradigm's position on the issue is the relevant one to take. This example should clarify one important contention of this book: it is that without a correct system of moral values it is not possible for development policy to even recognize the urgency of social problems, let alone offer sensible solutions to them (The general principle of responsibility is again discussed in Chapter 22).

18.5. PERFECT AND IMPERFECT OBLIGATIONS[3]

In order to redirect national human and economic development efforts within the overarching framework of the Covenant and the Declaration, and the Goals, the linkage between economic and political rights and the social and personal obligations to fulfil them must be clearly understood. An important problem here is that the nature of the social obligations cannot always be narrowly and perfectly defined (as in the case of legal rights) in the context of economic rights. The reason is that, while the linkage between political human rights and the corresponding obligations can be clearly specified and legislated, the same is not the case with economic fundamental rights. (Bentham called the concept of economic rights as 'non-sense on stilts'). In this well-meaning view, economic rights simply don't exist unless a perfect linkage is established between them and the corresponding individual, social and global obligations. Thus, O'Neil (1996) remarks, 'some advocates of universal economic, social and cultural rights go no further than to emphasize that they can be institutionalized, which is true. But the point of difference is that they *must* be institutionalized: if they are not there is no right' (italics in the original, pp. 131–32). However, Sen (2000) shows at length that there is no warrant whatsoever to jump from a correct demand for making all possible efforts to ensure that these rights are fulfilled to denying them altogether in case they are not perfectly fulfilled. One cannot, therefore, cogently insist on a perfect linkage between economic rights and the corresponding institutional obligations to be able to implement them. 'If the fulfilment of rights is a good thing to happen—the more the better—as it would be in a consequential perspective, the condition of full feasibility couldn't be a condition of coherence.' (p. 498). The problem here is that obligations may be, and are, imperfect or perfect, as Kant (1956) pointed out; and yet this fact does not stand in the way of linking fundamental economic rights to either of them, depending on the nature of the rights in question. In other words, the fact that some economic rights can be fulfilled only imperfectly is not an argument for denying them altogether. A desirable state of affairs would not cease to be so because in practice there will be some shortfalls from attaining it perfectly. One can hardly think of damning ideals simply because they can never be fully realized. A reasonably just society does have its excess baggage of injustices that an imperfect fulfilment of fundamental rights signifies; but that should not prevent a social commitment (in the form of an implicit or explicit contract with the people) to do the best that can be done to fulfil them.

18.6. Concluding Remarks

This chapter has analyzed those aspects of the Human Development Paradigm that differentiate the structure of its values from those held by other paradigms. As pointed out in earlier chapters as well, its contribution in this respect is unrivalled for its originality. It underscores the basic principle of 'shared responsibility', which constitutes one of the 'fundamental values' of the Millennium Declaration and the Millennium Development Goals. The emphasis it places on human responsibility for one's actions, the balancing of rights and responsibilities, the question of perfect and imperfect obligations are all foundational concerns without which a civilized society cannot be run efficiently and equitably—efficiently, because without internalizing the right moral values the cost of policing will be much too high; and equitably, because a just assignment of rights and responsibilities among the people is the essence of social justice. In particular, its enunciation of the fundamental individual economic rights, in addition to political rights, would revolutionize development policy, if and when implemented in the right earnest by national governments and at the global level. An explicit enunciation of the relevant basic moral principles clears the mind of ambiguities about the direction that development policy should take when confronted with situations that normally arise in the implementation of specific policies. The moral of the story related in this chapter, is the following: a society must get its moral philosophy right to avoid the consequences of holding contradictory positions about matters of social concern. If, as the quote from Keynes at the beginning of this book is correct (which the present author regards as the acme of wisdom)—that it is ideas, not vested interests, that matter for good or evil in societies—then it is extremely important to know what kind of ideas define the attitudes of a developing society and what steps it takes to translate these ideas into development policy.

Notes

1. The female-male ratio is generally lower in the developing countries than in the developed countries: as compared with a ratio of 1.05 in North America and Europe. This ratio is 0.96 in North Africa; 0.94 in China, Bangladesh and West Asia; and only 0.91 in Pakistan [Dreze and Sen (1995), p. 141].

2. The other central values underlying the Millennium Declaration are: Freedom, Equality, Solidarity, Tolerance, and Respect for Nature. Freedom demands that, 'men and women have the right to live their lives and raise their children in dignity, freedom from hunger and from the fear of violence, oppression and injustice'; Equality stipulates that, 'no nation and individual can be denied the opportunity to a fair share in the fruits of economic and social progress; Solidarity requires that the costs and burdens of development are shared fairly, and that, 'those who suffer or who benefit least deserve help from those who benefit

most'; Tolerance entails that, 'human beings respect one another, in all their diversity of belief, culture and language'; and Respect for Nature takes showing prudence in the 'management of all living species and natural resources'.

3. This section draws heavily on Sen (2000).

Part VI

Towards a New Development Paradigm

19

The New Development Paradigm I: The Centrality of High and Inclusive Growth

The present chapter attempts to present an outline of a New Development Paradigm and its vision of an effective development policy that excludes from its purview everything that is redundant and nothing that is significant. To be effective it must be fired by messianic impulse and driven by managerial and engineering skills. To this end, it would seek to rekindle the Smithian concern for increasing the wealth of nations and inform it with a determination to improve the quality of distributive justice and reduce the incidence of poverty. It would not seek to achieve one objective at the expense of others; but would pursue these intrinsically worthwhile together as an irreducible set within the framework of a morally acceptable rearrangement of the basic social institutions. Such a comprehensive strategy is also required to meet fully the national obligations under the United Nations Covenant on Economic, Social and Cultural Rights, Universal Declaration of Human Rights and Millennium Development Goals. These global treaties contain within them the most inclusive basis for eliminating poverty and meeting human economic rights within the framework of strongly growing economies in the developing countries. The pursuit of any other legitimate policy objective e.g., macroeconomic stability can best be done within the overarching framework of this globally agreed set of policy objectives. The development experience of more than half a century strongly suggests that it is only when development policy succeeds in this complex manoeuvre that powerful economic forces can spark societal transformations that it is desirable to promote and stand in the door of those which must be resisted. It is argued that this basic understanding of the nature of development policy, its salience and reach, and its evaluative reliability should inform the New Development Paradigm. Its foundations should be raised on the accumulated stock of knowledge about the principal variables that a viable development policy must focus on to achieve the socially agreed ends of development in the shortest possible time. In other words, it must recognize and incorporate the valid core of the preceding paradigms in the making of its vision of social processes. The task ahead is not to start some 'venture into the unknown' from 'square one' but to retread a lot of known territory with a resolute stride, making use of the wealth of available information about the likely consequences of specific development policies. The value judgment here is: throwing out all previous knowledge about the mechanics of development policy and starting anew each time the focus of development policy undergoes a change for whatever reason has been counterproductive before. It will be the more so in the future, if only because the stock of theoretical and empirical knowledge about the development process has grown bigger with the passage of time. Spelling out the dimensions of this challenge and the 'optimal' policy response to it is the task that we set ourselves to achieve in this and the following chapters.

19.1. THE CASE FOR HIGH AND SUSTAINED GROWTH RATE

It was noted above that the Traditional Development Paradigm was in fact committed to Adam Smith's mission to increase the 'wealth of nations' of the developing countries at the fastest feasible rate. To this end, it encouraged the evolution of new growth-oriented institutions that would catalyze rural-based institutions inimical to growth and development. Far-reaching land reforms and industrialization were the main engines of growth and social development. As one would expect, developing countries experienced an unprecedented florescence of economic prosperity, the East Asians the most. But with the intellectual ascension (or rather re-ascension) of Liberalist Paradigm, development policy got imprisoned in the make-believe world of free markets. As any informed observer should have anticipated, the developing countries were consequently pushed off the high-growth path. Then the Human Development Paradigm got development policy to tread the support-led route to human development. Even the global agreement on Millennium Development Goals, which are very strong on attacking poverty and some other highly prized development objectives, do not include a direct mention on such existential development issues as accelerating the growth rate of per capita incomes, the creation of a strong middle class and social justice. The outcome in countries that followed this new-fangled strategy has also been economic stagnation and high unemployment and growing morbidity even as it has achieved remarkable human development success. The hypothesis advanced in this study is that development effort must be refocused on the basics of systemic transformation. It must fertilize its Smithian roots in the knowledge that only those countries that have trained on maximizing the rate of growth of per capita income within the framework of egalitarian institutional change have been crowned with success. The emphasis on social justice has made allies of those whom social injustice had made outsiders in their own environment, and the creation and expansion of an empowered middle class has helped to drive the engine of growth in the direction of production of goods that it needs rather wasting resources on the production of luxuries.[1] Both these elements have, in turn, led to the creation of employment opportunities and a steady human development. Let us then finesse the details of this line of thinking in the light of empirical evidence.

19.1. (i). The Rate of Economic Growth must be High and 'Inclusive'

A solid lesson learned from more than half a century of development history is that the acid test of a successful development policy is whether or not it accelerates the process of 'inclusive' economic growth—as opposed to the 'exclusive' growth associated with rising inequalities of income and wealth— for long periods of time. The emphasis on 'long periods of time' is quintessential because growth spurts lasting for only short periods do not normally produce the desired results. One can debate the many ways in which growth can be made more 'inclusive'; but there should be little confusion about a strictly positive relationship between high growth rates and human happiness if it does become 'inclusive'. It is, for instance, understood that, given a reasonably egalitarian distribution pattern of income and wealth, a sustained annual growth of per capita-income at a rate of at least 3 per cent plus is necessary for reducing poverty significantly. This is also the rate required to achieve conditional convergence with the developed countries.[2] In this context, an important policy objective would be to minimize the time it takes to double per capita income [Naqvi (1992)]. The miracle rate, that East Asia and Botswana achieved, is an annual growth of 6 per cent of per capita income, which doubles it in a period of ten/eleven years. Later on, China has succeeded in performing this feat in five to six years for several decades. The reason for doubling per capita income as soon as feasible is that when this happens the Law of Compound Growth ensures that the time for doubling per capita income gets shorter along the growth path, which thus economizes on the required development effort to achieve target growth in the long run. Yet another fact about achieving and sustaining high rates of economic growth is that developing countries have had a greater chance of making an 'orderly transformation', i.e. attaining a dynamic balance between growth, macroeconomic stability, distributive justice, and poverty reduction only when the economy continues to grow at the 3 per cent plus rate. Contrariwise, the countries growing at a leisurely pace of 1.5 per cent or less (especially countries in the African region) have experienced a disorderly transformation, in which growth, macroeconomic stability and distributive justice and poverty reduction have not followed a predictable course. One of the maxims of a successful development policy is that a high rate of growth is unambiguously superior to a moderate and low rate of growth in terms of its potential to achieve macroeconomic stability, social justice and rapid advances in human development [Naqvi (1995)]. All available evidence points in this direction. During the 1990s, the fastest growing East Asian (at 6.4 per cent) reduced poverty in terms of percentage of people below the poverty line (at $2-a-day) by 14.9 per cent; the South Asian countries growing at a medium high rate (3.3 per cent) also reduced poverty, though at lower rate of 8.4 per cent. However, poverty increased by 0.1 per cent in the slow-growing or stagnating Latin America and the Caribbean (at a rate of 1.6 per cent) and the Middle East and North Africa (at a rate of 1 per cent) [UNDPa (2003), p. 41]. Some interesting regression results are presented in the next chapter on the factors most relevant for poverty reduction in Asia during 1965 to 2000. They show that a 1 per cent growth rate of per capita income reduces poverty by 1.88 per cent. The corresponding elasticity of poverty with respect to the growth of per capita income works out at (-)0.212.

19.2. FACTORS CONTRIBUTING TO 'INCLUSIVE GROWTH': GENERAL DISCUSSION

The analysis presented in this book so far shows that, within an essentially egalitarian framework that favoured land reforms and the rise of a prosperous middle class, the main factors that have contributed to high rates of inclusive growth are: a marked acceleration of the rate of Structural Transformation, a high rate of agricultural productivity, a rapid expansion of the domestic market through import-substituting industrialization, physical and human capital formation and international trade. Structural Transformation tops this short list.

19.2. (ii). Structural Transformation

The foundational nature of the process of Structural Transformation, which no lasting episode of economic or human development could ever bypass, has been highlighted throughout this book and especially in Part II. It is now time to put this concept on a more solid factual and empirical base. Let us review some of the relevant studies, which confirm the fundamental truth of this proposition. Both theoretical and empirical studies have confirmed that Structural Transformation lies at the heart of the development process both in the developing and the developed countries [Dorwick and Gemmel (1991)]. It can, therefore, be rightly regarded as the Fundamental Law of Economic Development. A steady rise in the share of industrial output in total GDP has historically been associated with the rise of per capita income in the developing countries. Thus, in 1950, the median share of manufacturing in developing countries was 10 per cent of total output; by 1980 it had increased to 20–30 per cent of total output in twelve countries in Latin America, Egypt, Sri Lanka, Philippines, Taiwan, South Korea, and China. Somewhat lower in this top league have been Pakistan, India and Thailand [Reynolds (1983)]. Table 2.1 (in Chapter 2) clearly shows this upward trend: it has continued to this day in all the developing countries as they moved up the ladder of economic development, through higher agricultural productivity, a greater diversification of the structure of production and a broadening of the export base—all reinforcing each other. Yet another of its important features is that integration with the world economy promises to be the most lasting and beneficial in those countries where the Structural Transformation has gone the farthest. The New Development Paradigm should continue drawing on this powerhouse of economic development to produce high and sustained growth.[3]

It may be noted that Structural Transformation has historically become self-sustaining by a steady transition to the heavier, higher value-added industries in which the rate of innovation and the knowledge spillover to the rest of the economy are most significant.[4] In this context, it may be noted that there is a robust relationship between equipment investment and growth.[5] The point to grasp here is that the Structural Transformation gradually shifts the locus of activity from low-productivity sectors to high-productivity sectors. It helps all sectors to grow together in a mutually reinforcing fashion through inter-sector input-output linkages. This strategy has been most successful in generating employment, raising the real wage rate, reducing poverty and rectifying imbalances in functional distribution of income.

19.2. (ii). Increasing Agricultural Productivity

It is often forgotten that the rapidity of Structural Transformation has been strongly correlated with a steady increase in agricultural productivity, which helps release more labour for use in industry and other high productivity sectors.[6] Without it, the agricultural real wage would decline, foreclosing the possibilities of a reduction in rural poverty. It is for this reason that land reforms have been regarded as essential for speeding up the process of Structural Transformation. To put this point somewhat differently: a greater speed of Structural Transformation is not inconsistent with a simultaneous increase in agricultural productivity; indeed, the latter has been the necessary condition for the former. Yet another aspect of land reforms has been to help create a strong middle class, which has historically provided strong and continuing demand for industrialization.[7]

19.2. (iii). Priority of Expanding the Domestic Market

It has been recognized that there is no free-trade led option for achieving high rates of economic growth and development. On the other hand, a steady expansion of the domestic market primarily through import-substituting industrialization—and only secondarily by export expansion—has been the historical route for achieving the fastest possible growth.[8] The reason is that an assured domestic market has normally helped exploit strategic complementarities of industrialization, especially the ones needed for greater investment in innovation and technological change [Rodrik (1995)].

19.2. (iv). Physical Capital and Human Capital

There is a broad consensus now that physical capital and human capital formation, a high enough level of saving to finance a large proportion of investment from domestic sources is the prime mobile of economic growth in the developing (as well as developed) countries.[9] The liberalist argument against this growth strategy is that it is not sustainable in the sense that it would inevitably imply a persistently rising capital/output ratio and an ever-rising investment rate, which beyond a point tapers off making the growth rate to falter.[10] But such arguments lack validity because there is no unique pattern of growth. True, the rather moderate growth rate of per capita income was fuelled more by productivity growth than the accumulation of capital in European countries but a rising capital/labour ratio has financed miracle growth rate in Japan, East Asia and China [Nehru and Dhareshwar (1993); Easterly and Fischer (1995)].[11] Two points may be noted here. Firstly, the growth experience of Europe, though an important milestone on the highway to economic progress of nations, is not relevant for the developing countries where the European growth rates of 2 to 3 per cent would normally be counted as rather low, and certainly not enough to achieve the Millennium Development Goals. To put it rather bluntly, the Europeans are not the 'pioneers' of miracle growth. It has rather been pioneered by East Asia and followed the late-comers in the rest of the developing world. Secondly, it is not at all plausible to consider a high rate of capital accumulation for long periods of time without the marginal rate of investment also having been extraordinarily high and without a substantial and rising input of new knowledge into the production process. Where the endogenous theory goes wrong, is to vastly over-rate the importance of human capital in relation to physical capital accumulation (investment and schooling) as primary lever of growth. The reason is that greater expenditure on health and education does not always translate into greater human capital formation. For instance, the pay off for a given human development expenditure would be higher in a more egalitarian country than in a less egalitarian one [UNDP (2005)]. Also, it would translate into high growth only when combined with lot of physical capital formation. Indeed, empirical research does not support the proposition that human capital has been more important than physical capital for sustaining high rates of economic growth. Indeed, the reverse has been the case: in East Asia too, physical capital has been more influential for economic growth than human capital [Bosworth, and Collins (1996)]. The empirical exercise reported in Table 19.1 lends strong support to this point of view. The wisest thing for the New Development Paradigm would, therefore, be to emphasize physical and human capital and do whatever is possible to shore up total productivity growth.

19.2. (v). International Trade and New Ideas

The New Development Paradigm must recognize the importance of new ideas and learning as crucial for sustaining high rates of long-term growth. It has been argued that, mainly because it is a non-rival good and reproducible asset, knowledge is subject to increasing (or non-decreasing) returns to capital.[12] The endogenous growth theory has maintained (perhaps, this is the only valid part of the theory) that new ideas translate into improving the quality of the existing goods and producing new products, which add to growth. The main mechanism through which new products increase long-run growth in developing countries is through international trade (imports). Indeed, this has been cited as one more important reason why restrictions on trade can retard growth. Romer (1994) shows that the welfare costs of restricting the flow of new goods can be substantially higher than is indicated by the static misallocation effects of restricting the flow of a fixed set of goods.

19.2. (iv). 'Pro-poor' Growth

There has been some discussion about changing the sector-pattern of growth in order to make it 'pro-poor'. This, by itself, is a laudable exercise; but, unfortunately, some recent discussions about pro-poor growth seem to suggest that the way to do it is to reverse the process of Structural Transformation—to shift the policy emphasis, at least on the margin, from industrialization to agriculture—on the grounds that the earlier growth pattern of 'forced draft' industrialization was not pro-poor [Lipton and Ravallion (1995), p. 2609]. The liberalist position has been that the distortions between agricultural sector and the industrial sector and the differentials rates of return between the two sectors have been large and persistent. It has, therefore, been argued that the growth rate will be higher and have greater impact on the poor if these distortions are removed by reversing Structural

Transformation.[13] As noted above, such arguments generally ignore the dynamic relationship between industrial expansion and agricultural growth and the fact that the fastest possible rate of industrialization has historically gone hand-in-hand with maximal growth of agriculture.[14]

19.3. FACTORS CONTRIBUTING TO GROWTH AND INVESTMENT IN ASIA AND PACIFIC REGION: AN EMPIRICAL ANALYSIS

Table 19.1 lends broad support to the ideas outlined in the preceding section about the factors responsible for achieving high rates of growth and investment in Asia and the Pacific Region. The table basically highlights the importance of Structural Transformation for development policy, relatively to other variables that have been mentioned in the literature as the basic determinants of growth and investment. The same information has then been disaggregated into East Asia and South Asia. The findings presented in the table throw some new light on some of the old-new propositions about the principal determinants of growth and investment, especially in East Asia as opposed to those in the relatively slower growth of South Asia. It yields the following important findings.

19.3. (i). Contribution of Structural Transformation to Growth and Investment

(1) For Asia as a whole, Structural Transformation has, on average, been highly significant for achieving high rate of investment; but it has been insignificant for growth. The explanation for these results is that industrialization contributes to high rates of economic growth by raising the investment rate. The statistical reason is that investment/GDP ratio variable might have captured at least some of effects of the Structural Transformation on growth. The implied growth elasticity is 0.04. The investment elasticity is 0.54.

(2) Structural Transformation has been one of the most decisive and significant factor in achieving the unprecedented rates of investment in East Asia; and, also the most important factor contributing to growth. The growth elasticity is 1.37 and the investment elasticity is 0.90.

(3) In South Asia, the coefficients and elasticity's for both growth and investment are insignificant. The reason for the differential contribution of Structural Transformation is obvious: Structural Transformation progressed most decisively only in East Asia. Indeed, looking at elasticity, it can safely be inferred that growth and investment rates must have been much higher in East Asia than elsewhere. These results also show that one does not have to go farther than recognizing the elemental importance of Structural

Transformation to find a satisfactory explanation of the growth differential between East Asia and non-East Asia—exactly as the Traditional Development Paradigm had prescribed.

19.3. (ii). Contribution of Openness and Human Development to Growth and Investment

It may be interesting to focus on openness and human development as factors contributing to growth and investment and then compare their significance relative to that of Structural Transformation. The Liberalist Paradigm has highlighted the importance of external trade and the Human Development Paradigm pinpoints human development as the dominant variable explaining the high rates of economic growth especially those in East Asia. Both seem to have erred in downplaying the importance of Structural Transformation.

Openness, Growth and Investment: The estimated coefficients in Table 19.1 show: (1) Openness has been a highly significant contributor to growth. However, contrary to the liberalist contention, it has been an insignificant growth-promoting factor in East Asia but highly significant in South Asia, where the growth elasticity is 2.37. (2) Openness has not had a significant impact on accelerating the investment rate in East Asia but it has been significant in non-East Asia. (3) Openness does not explain miracle investment rates in East Asia; rather it has been associated with the slower investment of South Asia.

Human Development, Growth and Investment: The table brings out two very important points. (1) As noted above, human development contributed significantly to growth in East Asia but not in South Asia. This is broadly in accord with the prediction of the Human Development Paradigm. (2) However, human development has not been a dominant influence on growth of per capita income: the size of elasticity is less than half of that of Structural Transformation. In other words, the latter's contribution completely dominates that of human development. This is not in accord with the Human Development Paradigm's prediction. (3) Contrary to Human Development Paradigm's prediction, social expenditure has not had a positive effect on investment. Indeed, in East Asia, in fact, in Asia as a whole, its contribution to investment has been negative, whereas it has had an insignificant, though positive, effect on investment in South Asia. This may, at first sight, appear to be a surprising, even wrong result, but it is neither. The reason is that in high-growth economies, which have already achieved a high level of human development, additional human development might have substituted for physical investment. In other words, human development seems to include a significant consumption element in it. Now, this is not an argument against pushing for human development, but it does warn against facile thinking, implicit or explicit in the literature, that human development somehow substitutes for physical investment. What the table shows is that physical capital formation, rather than human capital formation, has been the dominant factor in achieving miracle growth in East Asia.

The Dominance of Structural Transformation: Together, these results yield the following generalizations: (1) Structural Transformation has been the dominant mechanism for promoting high rates of economic growth and investment in the miracle growth countries. (2) The expansion of the domestic market, rather than increasing openness, has been by far the most important, and reliable, source of high rates of economic growth and investment. In other words, import substitution has been more important than export expansion as a factor responsible for miracle rates of growth and investment. (3) The slower growth of South Asia has more to do with a lesser degree of expansion of the domestic market through Structural Transformation, and not with any lack of openness. (4) The main difference between the miracle growing East Asia and the slower growing South Asia has been the speed and depth of Structural Transformation; it is neither openness nor human development. (5) Physical capital formation remains the primary engine of growth. The human capital formation seems to have been internalized in these economies in the form of the higher total factor productivity of the miracle growers, but it does not minimize the importance of physical capital formation. (6) Overall, contrary to the general misconception, the East Asian countries seem to have followed the traditional development policy, even more faithfully than the slower-growing non-East Asians. Whether they were conscious of it or not is immaterial in the present context.

19.3. (iii). Other Contributory Factors to Growth and Investment

Table 19.1 highlights two more contributors to growth and investment. (1) The most important factor explaining growth of per capita income in both East Asia and non-East Asia has been an increase in the investment/GDP ratio. It may be noted that the growth elasticity is a little less than 2.5 times higher in South Asia than in East Asia; it is 4.04 in the former and 1.71 in the latter. However, this information has to be interpreted with care.

The much higher elasticity of investment/GDP ratio in non-East Asia than in the East Asia probably reflects the much lower (apparent) efficiency of investment in the former than in the latter.[15] In other words, investment has probably been less efficiently used in South Asia as compared to East Asia, where the investment efficiency has been very high. The fact that government investment/GDP ratio has been a more potent force for growth than Structural Transformation in non-East Asia may be explained as follows. Firstly, to some extent, there must be an overlap here, since industrialization involves more investment. Secondly, investment/GDP ratio includes a wide range of activities including investment in infrastructure and agriculture, both of which are also vital for securing a higher rate of growth. The contribution of the growth of per capita income to investment highlights the obvious point that securing a higher growth of per capita income generates demand for more investment. The other two factors, growth rate of imports and lagged GDP per capita have an obvious interpretation and need not be explained.

19.4. CONVERGENCE AS A POLICY OBJECTIVE

Following the traditional development policy, the New Development Paradigm must accord convergence a central place among the objectives of development policy. As well as achieving success with respect to the wider agenda of human development, the rate of growth of per capita income that developing countries are able to attain, and sustain, with respect to their own potential and relative to the growth rate of the developed countries should be a matter of great importance. Indeed, the two ideas are mutually reinforcing: the steps a country takes to raise its long-term growth rate (especially increasing the saving rate, the physical and human capital formation, lower fertility etc.) determines in a significant way the speed of its (conditional) convergence relative to the growth rates of the advanced countries. The desire to converge with the developed countries reflects non-economic considerations of national pride and self-confidence, but even more importantly, it is also an indicator of development success of a superlative degree. Thus, for instance, the miracle economies of East Asia have narrowed the differential between their GDP relative to that of the United States [World Bank (1993)]. Their irrepressible urge to converge was fuelled by the strong belief that they could attain economic independence only by growing much faster than their erstwhile masters. And there was nothing irrational about it. Baumol (1991) points out that convergence is considered a legitimate policy concern even now among the developed countries 'when their performance threatens to be surpassed by that of other nations' (p. 7). It is even more important for evaluating development success in the developing countries. A higher standing internationally with respect to growth also attracts foreign capital that accelerates the growth rate even further.

19.4. (i). Absolute Convergence versus Conditional Convergence

It may be noted that one of the reasons why convergence as an objective of development policy dropped out of the national development policy has been its alleged non-feasibility. The problem has, however, turned out to be one of definition—whether convergence is defined as absolute or conditional. Taking a sample of 117 countries over a period of 1960 to 1986 to test these competing hypotheses, Pritchett (1995) found no evidence of unconditional convergence. However, it has been shown of late that when the differences between countries with respect to the levels of investment and education are allowed for then conditional convergence turns out to be an empirical reality.[16] Many studies support the general notion of conditional convergence that the neo-classical theory highlighted: for given values of variables like higher initial schooling, life expectancy, lower fertility, etc., long-run growth between countries has been inversely related to their initial level of per capita GDP [Barro (1997)].[17] Thus, convergence is an entirely realistic objective to aim at if it is defined as conditional on the developing countries having strong 'fundamentals' to begin with.[18] These findings explain why the star performer did better than other developing countries in closing the gap between them and the developed countries.[19] However, the fact is that many developing countries besides the star performers have managed to converge with the developed countries. It has been estimated that, during 1960 to 1990, of a sample of sixteen countries, eight improved their position relative to US (Korea, Japan, Thailand, Indonesia, Mexico, Brazil, China and Pakistan, in that order); two held their own (Nigeria and India); and six lost ground (Iran, Argentina, South Africa, Zaire, the Philippines and Bangladesh in that order) [Temple (1999), see, Table 1, p. 115]. The IMF (2000) seems to confirm the conditional convergence hypothesis. Of the ninety-eight countries selected for study during the period of 1970 to 1998, six countries growing at the rate of 3.75 per cent plus achieved 'fast per capita convergence'; and sixteen countries that grew at 2 to 3.75 per cent, managed 'slow per capita convergence' (p. 124). Barro and Lee (1993) estimate that 'convergence occurs at the rate of 3.1 per cent' (p. 276). Incidentally, this is also the rate, which, when sustained over long periods has led to significant poverty reduction. The point is that to make a solid start on the convergent growth trajectory the developing countries need to begin by achieving high rates of investment in physical and human capital, among other measures in the initial period.[20]

19.5. CONCLUDING REMARKS

The present chapter highlights the importance of looking at the central relationship between growth, distributive equity, and poverty reduction as an integrated set of policy objectives that must be achieved *within the overall framework of growth and distribution friendly institutional change.* The italicized phrase underlines the importance of making growth egalitarian and favourable to the poor; for it is only then that we get intimate with the innermost secrets of economic and social progress; and it is only then that cynical bystanders, the common men and women, can be transformed into active agents for societal transformation. With these qualifications in mind, a case has been presented in this chapter to pursue an 'inclusive' high-growth strategy for enhancing economic prosperity and human well being. The point is that, except for a major financial crisis that may call for some limited stabilization, no other consideration should be used as an excuse for slowing down the growth rate of per capita income in the developing countries. The rate of growth must be high enough to achieve convergence with the developed countries. One just has to look at the Chinese rise to a super-power status within a generation and its (legitimate) pride in having greatly narrowed the gap between the size of its economy relative to that of the developed countries—to see what high growth and convergence can do to national self-esteem and to a country's standing in the comity of nations. It is also the country, which has achieved an equally miraculous reduction in poverty both in relative terms as well as absolute terms, highlighting the fundamental negative relationship between high growth and poverty. Vietnam offers yet another example, though less heroic (because poverty remains high there), of the wonders of high and inclusive growth; it has practically erased the bitter memories of decades of war and destruction. India seems to be eyeing the same future as its economy steadies itself on a high growth path. Experience has shown that far better in terms of prosperity and peace it is to make growth rather than war.

Table 19.1: Determinants of Growth and Investment in Asia: 1965–2000 (Focus Structural Transformation)

Dependent Variables	All Countries				East Asian Countries				South Asian Countries			
	Economic Growth		Investment-GDP ratio		Economic Growth		Investment-GDP ratio		Economic Growth		Investment-GDP ratio	
	Coefficients	Elasticity Estimates	Coefficients	Elasticity Estimates	Coefficients	Elasticity Estimates	Coefficients	Elasticity Estimates	Coefficients	Elasticity Estimates	Coefficients	Elasticity Estimates
Constant	-2.17 (1.0)	-	-13.85 (4.6)	-	3.466 (0.5)	-	3.599 (1.3)	-	6.437 (2.0)	-	6.429 (17.)	-
Investment-GDP ratio	0.182 (2.3)	0.7*	-	-	0.151 (3.4)	1.7*	-	-	0.155 (4.2)	4.0*	-	-
Growth rate of GDP per capita	-	-	0.20 (7.6)	0.0*	-	-	0.234 (3.4)	0.0*	-	-	0.210 (3.1)	0.0*
Human Development	0.017 (0.9)	0.21	-0.07 (5.3)	-0.2*	0.06 (1.6)	0.5*	-0.05 (2.4)	-0.1*	0.007 (0.2)	0.15	0.015 (0.9)	0.07
Share of Manufacturing in GDP	0.005 (0.1)	0.04	0.319 (9.5)	0.5*	0.196 (1.6)	1.3*	0.49 (6.7)	0.9*	0.032 (0.4)	0.3	0.005 (0.0)	0.0
Openness	0.034 (2.4)	0.3*	-	-	0.010 (0.4)	0.09	-	-	0.177 (3.9)	2.6*	-	-
Growth Rate of Imports	-	-	0.04 (1.6)	0.0*	-	-	-	-	-	-	-	-
Lon (lagged GDP per capita)	-0.02 (0.0)	-	-	-	-0.460 (1.8)	-	-	-	-1.04 (2.7)	-	-	-
RP2P	0.26	-	0.651	-	0.388	-	0.600	-	0.445	-	0.306	-
Number of Observations	285	-	285	-	112	-	112	-	113	-	114	-

Note: t-values are reported in parentheses. Asterisks on elasticity estimates denote their statistical significance. Except for human development, the data for estimation have been taken from Penn World Table-Version 6.1 (2002). The proxy for human development, literacy rate, is taken from *Human Development Reports* [UNDP (various issues)]. The reduction in the number of observation below the required number (630) has been caused by the non-availability of the comparable data for all the eighteen countries for thirty-five years.

NOTES

1. There may have been some exceptions to the general tendency noted above, but most of these cases are of those countries where the growth rates of per capita income have not exceeded 3 per cent and when their growth rates have not been stable.

2. Barro (1997) has identified the possibility of conditional convergence only, as unconditional convergence does not hold as a historical tendency.

3. The case of sub-Saharan Africa may be seen as an exception to the rule stated in the text: 'it is far more integrated with world economy than many developing countries and Structural Transformation there has gone farther than in the South Asian economies. But integration has not been beneficial to this unfortunate region. However, it may be noted that before the external crisis pulverized it in the 1970s, the higher rate of structural transformation was also associated with higher growth in Africa.'

4. The multi-staged industrialization strategy mentioned in the text is consistent with Chenery, Robinson and Syrquin's (1986) scheme for industrial development.

5. Bradford, De Long and Summers (1991) show that the relationship between equipment investment and economic growth is strong for the developing countries. However, the relationship has been rather weak for the OECD countries. Mahalanobis (1953) had presented these ideas much earlier. They formed the basis of the India's Five-Year Plans.

6. Gollins et al. (2002) estimate that shifting workers from agriculture to non-agriculture in 1960s would have tripled individual agriculture labour's productivity in Malaysia and Korea, and increased it by a factor of nine in Thailand (p. 163).

7. The ideas in the text have been formally presented in Murphy, Shleifer and Vishny (1989b). Earlier, these ideas were strongly presented in Lewis (1955).

8. This is not to minimize the importance of export expansion for stimulating growth, but only to highlight the historical route through which all fast-growing economies have progressed (except for small countries like Singapore and Taiwan). Reynolds (1983) concludes that the manufacturing growth in the post-1950 period was a normal response to the growth of the domestic market and less to (export) promotional efforts: 'Overall, my impression is that the effect of market expansion may have been underestimated in the literature, while that of promotional policies may have been overestimated, especially in view of the fact that these policies had a negative as well as a positive effects (p. 973). This observation also refutes the liberalist contention that East Asian countries developed faster because of export-oriented policies while the rest of the developing countries grew at a slower rate because of their inward-looking policies.

9. Yusuf and Stiglitz (2001) identify the above-noted components of the sources of growth as among the 'settled issues' of economic development.

10. A criticism of the remarkable growth of East Asia is that factor accumulation, rather than productivity growth has fuelled it. The industrialization process has been greatly 'compressed'—trying to achieve in four decades what Europe did in more than a century. The result has been high but inefficient growth [Young (1993); Pack (1988)]. However, as argued in the text, this line of argument is not correct.

11. The productivity estimates use a Cobb-Douglas production function with a unit elasticity of substitution between labour and capital. The most widely used estimate of capital share is 0.4 while that of labour is 0.6. If instead a constant elasticity of substitution (CES) function is used then the unitary elasticity of substitution would not hold and much lower elasticity of substitution may result. In that case the real explanation of declining growth whenever it occurs (e.g., in the Soviet Union) would be a declining marginal product of capital rather than a declining total factor productivity (TPF).

12. The recognition that knowledge is subject to increasing returns is, however, an old idea. Marshall (1890) noted that, although nature is subject to diminishing returns, man is subject to increasing returns—Knowledge is the most powerful engine of production; it

enables us to subdue nature and satisfy our wants'. J.M. Clarke (1923) noted: 'knowledge is the only factor that is not subject to diminishing returns' (p. 120). Lewis (1955) has discussed at length the vital importance of knowledge to growth.

13. The liberalist literature has distinguished between the direct price effects and the indirect effects of overvalued exchange rates on the farm sector; and the direct non-price effects of public sector spending etc on the farm sector. It has been argued that the first type of effects discriminate against agriculture so that the removal of this bias should be growth-promoting and pro-poor [Krueger et al. (1988)]. Whatever may be the validity of such arguments, the fact is that agriculture output has suffered in the wake of the Structural Adjustment Programmes because of the reduction in total public expenditure on agriculture (and industry) [Lipton and Ravallion (1995)].

14. As pointed out in Part II of this book, a fast rate of growth of manufacturing is not profitable unless agriculture is also growing simultaneously—even though the latter's share in the GDP must decline, thanks to the inexorable working of the Engel's Law no matter how fast it grows. Furthermore, agricultural and industrial sectors are linked through the labour markets and the product markets. An increase in the growth rate of industrial sector tends to increase the demand for factors and goods in the agricultural sector and increase the real income of the rural poor, which, in turn, would widen the domestic market for industrial goods. The point in the text is not that the steps taken to increase the incomes of the rural poor must be at the expense of the growth of the manufacturing sector; the argument rather is that the former need not be achieved by reversing the process of Structural Transformation. Indeed, doing so would lower agricultural productivity and the growth rate of per capita income much below the rate required to achieve the desired degree of poverty reduction and attain convergence with the developed countries.

15. Apparent efficiency of investment has been defined as the ratio of growth per capita to investment ratio. See Little, Cooper, Corden, Rajapatirana (1993). It also contains an informative analysis of the country experiences with the efficiency of investment. Thus, Korea scores very high on this scale; but Nigeria is an example where high investment rates contributed only negatively to growth (pp. 353–358).

16. This is referred in the literature as β-convergence—that is, the coefficient of initial level of per capita income must be negative. Another type of convergence is with respect to the cross-country dispersion of per capita income. This is referred to as σ-convergence. See Sala-i-Martin (1996) for a detailed discussion of these concepts and their policy implications.

17. Convergence has to be conditional because as a universal tendency, unconditional convergence cannot be achieved. However, it can be done, if the saving and investment rates and literacy levels are high in the initial period. In that case, a low initial income can provide the necessary stimulus for these countries to grow at a rate faster than that of the richer countries, as predicted by the classical theory. The 'new growth evidence' that seeks to explain the growth experiences of the developed and developing countries since 1960 (with the availability of the Summers-Heston tables that tabulate cross-country evidence on growth) also confirms that the Solow-Swan hypothesis about the diminishing returns to capital is certainly correct; but it does leave out of account several factors that affect growth between countries [Temple (1999)].

18. Many empirical studies have identified the following fundamentals: namely, the ratio of saving and investment to GDP, growth rate of population, the investment in human capital, and the level of the per capita income in the initial period. Thirlwall (1999, pp. 117–122) contains a good summary of the empirical studies on the subject. See also *Economic Journal* (1996).

19. Barro and Sala-i-Martin (1995), on the basis of a cross-country sample of 110 developed and developing countries, it reached a similar conclusion (of conditional convergence) and estimated the speed of convergence to be 2 per cent a year. However, the 2 per cent

convergence rate has been questioned. The estimates range from 0 to 30 per cent. The problem is that the econometric techniques used do not satisfactorily allow for the fixed effects, parameter endogeniety and the adequacy of the unit root tests in short panels [Temple (1999)].

20. The convergence objective can be made less demanding in a technical sense by regarding it as a *catching up* process, i.e. it is that developing countries aim to catch up with the developed countries. Now, for the validity of this objective, one need not bother about whether there are diminishing returns to capital (as the classical or neo-classical theory require).

20

The New Development Paradigm II: Growth, Equality, and Poverty Reduction

As noted in the preceding chapter, the New Development Paradigm must pursue growth, equity and poverty reduction together as an irreducible set of policy objectives. Fortunately, there is now a considerable body of knowledge that supports this prescription. It may be instructive here to recapture the highlights of the recent thinking on this crucial linkage and re-examine some key aspects of it in the light of the development experience of the Asia and Pacific Region.[1] Such a re-examination is needed because, like many other aspects of the debate on development policy, the watershed East Asian experience has changed the course of thinking on this three-way vital linkage as well. There seems to be a consensus now that one of the most striking characteristics of the East Asian growth miracle has been its remarkable success in combining the fastest ever growth of per capita income with an egalitarian distribution of income and wealth, a steep reduction of poverty and convergence with the developed countries [World Bank (1993)]. It has also led to the optimistic view that high rates of economic growth trickle down to the poor when associated with an egalitarian redistribution of wealth (say through land reforms) and a build-up of human capital (through greater spending on education and health).[2] However, there are many aspects of this consensus that warrant a second look. But before we attempt this task, it will be useful to review the relevant literature on the rather complex relationship between growth, inequality and poverty—partly because this literature bestrides the paradigmatic divide, at least, so it appears. It also offers some new insights on this old-new elemental development issue.

20.1. GROWTH AND INEQUALITY

There has been a (minority) view among development economists that growth and inequality could be positively correlated. Kuznets inverted U-hypothesis has often been cited in support of inequality fatalism. But it is argued in this book that Kuznets hypothesis does not necessarily provide blanket support to this view.[3] However, apart from the debate about what Kuznets meant, one can easily cite examples of positive, negative and neutral relationships between growth and inequality. Benabou (1996) finds that there is a negative relationship between inequality and any known measure of distribution. Studies using new sets of data do not seem to support strong and positive relationship between an increase (decrease) in mean income, and increase (decrease) in the income (wealth) inequality.[4] Furthermore, there is much country-specificity in the way that growth affects distribution, which depends on the efficiency with which the adverse effects of growth on equity are mitigated by timely policy intervention. On the other hand, it seems plausible that equity plays a central role in determining the pattern and rate of growth; a regressive distribution of income would depress effective demand and, through the accelerator, adversely affect investment, profits, and growth [Dutta (1985)]. In the same vein, it has been confidently asserted that equalizing income and wealth might as well increase aggregate output in a typical competitive economy, such as would be the case under the efficiency wage hypothesis [Dasgupta and Ray (1987); Dasgupta (1993)]. It has also been shown that 'income inequality is harmful for growth, because it leads to policies that do not protect property rights and does not allow full appropriation of returns from investment' [Persson and Tabellini (1994), p. 617].[5] Three main channels have been identified through which greater inequality harms growth: inequality reduces investment; inequality worsens borrower's incentives; and inequality generates macroeconomic instability [Aghion, Caroli and Garcia-Penalosa (1999)]. These findings will be re-examined towards the end of this chapter.

20.1. (i). Inequality is Hard to Reduce

While it pays handsomely to reduce inequality, actually reducing it through deliberate policy, is more easily said than done. It has been observed that in many countries inequality has been remarkably persistent [Squire (2003)]. Once again, this should not suggest that inequality should be accepted fatalistically as something that will stay with us forever. An important reason for persistent inequality has been the political weakness of the leaders in the developing countries to take decisive steps to implement land reforms or take other meaningful measures to redistribute wealth (through taxation of the rich). As a result, 'it appears that aggregate inequality measured by, say, the Gini index does not typically change dramatically from year-to-year' [Kanbur and Squire (2001)].[6] An extensive study of inequality and growth in forty-nine countries did not yield any systematic relationship between these two variables in 80 per cent of the cases. However, there is the U-relationship (rather than the Kuznets inverted-U relationship) in four cases; and the inverted U-relationship in only five cases [Deininger and Squire (1998), p. 279].[7] A study based on a sample of forty developing countries belonging to Asia, Africa, and Latin America suggests that the inequality (measured by the share of income going to the lowest 20 per cent of the population) and growth relationship would not necessarily follow an inverted U-shaped pattern; the share of the lowest 20 per cent of the population is positively related to the growth of per capita income. It, however, finds that the size of the coefficient is lower for the high-growth countries (those where growth rate exceeds 3 per cent per annum), than for the low-growth (those with a growth rate of less than 1.5 per cent per annum); and that it is the lowest for the medium-growth countries (those where the growth rate lay between 1.5 and 3 per cent per annum) [Naqvi (1995), p. 550]. An interesting aspect of these findings is that they trace a U-like pattern of the relationship between growth and inequality; yet another is that the inequality of income need not worsen initially. 'The current consensus is that several factors influence the effects of growth on inequality: the initial distribution of physical and human assets, preferences, the degree of openness to trade, and the effectiveness of governmental redistributive policies' [Lipton and Ravallion (1995), p. 2606]. Some other studies show that inequality is not systematically related to any particular stage of economic development [Galor and Zeira (1993)]. The general trend of academic opinion seems to have tilted in favour of the view that greater equity helps rather than hinder faster economic growth, but that generally, growth is distribution-neutral [World Bank (2005), p. 86].[8]

20.2. GROWTH AND POVERTY

There seems to be a broad-based agreement about the negative growth-poverty relationship. It has been shown that, given the same level of inequality, growth normally trickles down to reduce poverty. Using a sample of eighty countries over four decades Dollar, Sokolff and Kraay (2002a,b) reach the strong conclusion that a dollar worth of growth leads to a reduction in poverty in equal measure.[9] A similar conclusion is reported in Deininger and Squire (1996): in seventy-seven out of the eighty-eight decade-long episodes of growth, poverty was reduced, given that these episodes were probably distribution-wise neutral. While no influential opinion that questions the necessity of growth for reducing poverty, there are doubts about its sufficiency. The dominant view seems to be that the link between these variables is strong but not automatic; and that it is not safe, at least from the policy point of view, to support the sufficiency thesis, even in the East Asian case. The reason is that there are many more variables explaining growth than those explaining poverty [Barro and Sala-i-Martin (1995); Lin, Justin, Cai and Li (1998)]. A reasonable generalization seems to be that, all else remaining unchanged, 'the growth in the incomes of the poor is similar to the growth of mean income' [World Bank (2005), p. 85]. Once again, these assertions need to be more clearly articulated.

20.3. THE GROWTH-INEQUALITY-POVERTY NEXUS

Rather than viewing the relationship between growth, inequality and poverty in pairs of two, it is probably more meaningful to see it together. Alesina and Rodrik (1994) suggest that growth and distribution tend to reinforce each other. It is now well known that the key factor that makes the difference between the so-called pro-poor growth and that, which is less so, is the behaviour of inequality. An increase in inequality tends to dilute the benefits that accrue to the poor from a given growth rate of per capita mean income. In other words, one cannot predict the extent of poverty reduction just by looking at the growth rate of per capita income alone. What happens to inequality—whether inequality has risen or fallen—must also be factored in to get the final picture [Knowles (2001); World Bank (2005)]. A helpful observation in this context is that there is nothing automatic about growth reducing poverty. It takes deft management of the key variables to make it happen. In particular, to ensure that growth does benefit the poor, development policy must arrange that the rising inequality does not nullify most or all the poverty-reducing impact of growth. The condition for establishing a strong negative relationship between growth and poverty is that the benefits of growth accrue at least as much to the poor as to the non-poor. Preferably, the percentage share of growth going to the poor must rise more than the share of the non-poor with growth in order to maximize the poverty reducing potential of growth. Thus, poverty has reduced by as much as 9.6 per cent per-year when inequality is falling. However, none of this detracts from the centrality of high and sustained growth of per capita income for poverty reduction. Thus, one would be hard put to find a case where a sickly growth rate has been associated with a healthy poverty reduction on a lasting basis. One would equally have to strain credulity to believe that high growth directly increases poverty.

There is fairly reliable statistical evidence to suggest that poverty will be rising, if mean household income is falling, though at widely different rates and depending on whether inequality is rising or falling: poverty will increase by 14.3 per cent per year if inequality is rising as well, but only by 1.7 per cent if inequality is falling [Ravallion (2004)].[10] On the other hand, growth has coexisted with poverty reduction even when inequality has increased [Fields (1989); Squire (1993)], and also, that benefits of growth are felt well below the poverty line [Lipton and Ravallion (1995)]. Indeed, there is fairly strong historical evidence that even small changes in inequality can, for better or for worse, make a very large difference to the size of the impact of growth on poverty [Kanbur and Squire (2001); World Bank (2001)]. Ali and El-Badawi (2002) use a dynamic model to show that the economic growth of the MENA (Middle East and North Africa) region has faltered greatly during the model period of 1975 to 1996, and for most countries of the region growth momentum would not revive without, at the same time, making combined efforts to reduce poverty and inequality. Sirageldin (2000) argues that that poverty could be reduced most successfully if, as part of measures taken to produce higher growth, it focuses on increasing human capital and job creation, which would have the added advantage of improving distributive equity. A plausible explanation for the observed three-way relationship between growth, income distribution and poverty is that 'reductions in the inequality at a given growth rate add a 'redistribution component' to the 'growth component' leading to a faster overall poverty reduction' [World Bank (2005), p. 85]. In addition, the chances of reducing poverty, according to the conventional definition, would be brighter if economic growth is employment generating, associated with high social spending on education and health, and the transfers to the poor are affected through the provisioning of basic social services [Squire (1993)]. These aspects will be examined later in this chapter.[11]

20.4. Growth, Equality and Poverty Reduction as a Package Deal

The really difficult challenge for development policy is to deal with high growth, inequality and poverty reduction synchronously in order to internalize the complementarities and the trade-offs between them. Thus, as argued in Chapter 15, a development policy that seeks to reduce poverty directly, without paying equal or more attention to growth, is most likely to entail a heavy opportunity cost in terms of lost output. Lundberg and Ravallion (1999) focus on the importance of finding a set of policies that take into account both the growth and equality objectives together. They show that land reforms (and financial depth) consistently stimulate growth and also equality, while openness helps growth but harms equality. It is, therefore, important that in order to determine the size of the growth effort required to reduce poverty to a target level (for instance, to achieve the Millennium Development Goal of reducing poverty by half by 2015) one must also have an idea of any increase (decrease) in inequality that such an effort might cause. Aghion, Caroli and Garcia-Penalosa (1999) find that when capital markets are imperfect there is not necessarily a trade-off between equity and efficiency. Recognition of this fact explains 'the negative impact of inequality on growth and the positive effect of redistribution upon growth' (p. 1655). Furthermore, they also argue that in the absence of a virtuous circle of inequality leading to growth which then feeds into greater equality, 'there is considerable scope for permanent redistribution policies in order to control the level of inequality and to foster social mobility and growth' (p. 1657).[12] Bourguignon (2004) finds that the important relationships are not between poverty and growth on the one hand and poverty and inequality on the other; the crucial ones are those that look at reduction of poverty as an outcome of the interactions between distribution and growth.[13] He, therefore, prefers to look at the problem in terms of a 'Poverty-Growth-Inequality Triangle' that treats poverty as a function of distribution and changes in distribution and the growth of mean income (or consumption). An effective development strategy would, therefore, focus on the latter set of variables in order to make a significant impact on poverty. He argues that development strategy impacts on poverty in two steps: the pure growth effect and a pure distribution effect, depending on the initial level of inequality and the level of income.[14]

20.4. (i). The East Asian Experience

The East Asian experience has been cited to support the contention that inequality reduction is best done in the initial period and if successful it puts growth on a more egalitarian growth trajectory [World Bank (1993)].[15] There is evidence about the existence of a 'threshold effect'—that countries with high inequality in the initial period experienced lower growth rates than those with high equality, making due allowance for such factors as initial average income, the inflation rate and the degree of openness [Deininger and Squire (1998); Easterly (2002); Ravallion (2004)]. However, these findings do not offer much insight into the mechanics of inequality reduction once the growth process gets going.

20.5. How to Reduce Poverty? Empirical Evidence from Asia and Pacific Region (1970–2000)[16]

The preceding review of the current literature suggests some important guidelines for the New Development Paradigm about how to go about reducing poverty. However, it needs to be supplemented by some additional important relationships that must be factored in a successful poverty-reduction programme; these are the effects of human development expenditures and inflation on poverty. A regression exercise done for the present study, based on the pooled data for the region, re-examines the entire debate in unusual detail. The focus here is on the Asian experience partly because poverty reduction has been done most successfully in Asia, and also because for quite sometime the region has been a leader in growth-man-ship of the highest quality. Yet another reason is that this exercise would help to decide some important aspects of the differences in the East Asian and South Asian experiences in this regard.

20.5. (i). Poverty Reduction in Asia and Pacific

Table 20.1 brings out a few interesting points about the Asian experience with respect to poverty reduction in Asia as a whole. It also throws some new light on the growth-inequality-poverty debate and highlights the following aspects of the problem. (1) A 1 per cent increase in social expenditure reduces poverty the most: by 0.329 per cent; with an implied elasticity of 0.681. (2) Next in importance as a reducer of poverty has been a reduction in inequality. A 1 per cent reduction in inequality reduces poverty by 0.574 per cent; which implies an elasticity of 0.659. (3) It reaffirms that growth of per capita income makes a decisive contribution to poverty reduction. A 1 per cent increase in growth rate decreases poverty by 1.88 per cent, which gives a growth elasticity of 0.21.[17] (4) Inflation tends to increase poverty. A 1 per cent reduction in inflation reduces poverty by 0.44 per cent. The implied elasticity works out to be 0.153. Thus, in terms of relative effectiveness highest credit for poverty reduction goes to a resolute increase in human development expenditure. It also confirms the recent studies on the negative relationship between inequality and growth. (5) But the most important result that comes out of this exercise is that an anti-poverty policy will be crowned with success once it makes a simultaneous effort to increase human development, reduce inequality, increase per capita income and reduce inflation. The table seems to present a thumbs up report on all the three paradigms on this issue—the Traditional Development Paradigm on the strong relationship between growth and poverty; the Liberalist Paradigm on the need to keep inflation low; and the Human Development on the need to increase human development expenditures. It also supports the current literature's emphasis on reducing inequality to be able to alleviate poverty on a lasting basis.

20.5. (ii). A Comparison of Poverty Reduction in East Asia and South Asia

A breakdown of the regression results by East Asia and South Asia should throw some additional light on the hypotheses about the differential experiences of the East Asia and South Asia regions. (1) A high rate of growth of per capita income has been much more important in reducing poverty in East Asia than in South Asia. The growth elasticity of poverty is 0.463 in the former as compared to 0.118 in the latter. This result highlights the obvious point that poverty reduction has been associated most significantly with a higher growth of per capita income in East Asia than in South Asia. (2) A reduction in inequality and growth rate of per capita income is more important as reducer of poverty in East Asia than South Asia. (3) However, human development has had a more decisive effect on poverty in South Asia than in East Asia. The first and second points show that East Asia has achieved poverty reduction by achieving higher growth of per capita income within an egalitarian social structure, which confirms the widespread consensus on this issue. (3) Reducing inflation has been a more important contributor to poverty reduction in East Asia than in South Asia. This seems to be somewhat strange because the average rate of inflation has been higher in South Asia than in East Asia.

Table 20.1: Determinants of Poverty and Economic Growth in Asia and Pacific Region (1970–2000)

	All Countries		East Asia		South Asia	
	Coefficient Estimates	Elasticity Estimates	Coefficient Estimates	Elasticity Estimates	Coefficient Estimates	Elasticity Estimates
Constant	35.36 (3.843)	-	17.174 (0.470)	-	37.11 (3.563))	-
Growth Rate of GDP per capita	-1.883 (3.362)	-0.212	-1.629 (1.33)	-0.463*	-1.578 (1.92)	-0.118*
Inflation Rate	0.414 (3.914)	0.153	0.523 (3.646)	0.280*	0.173 (2.927)	0.058*
Human Development	-0.329 (4.638)	-0.681	-0.074 (0.201)	-0.286	-0.254 (3.714)	-0.499*
Gini Coefficient	0.574 (2.256)	0.659	0.353 (0.657)	0.594	0.54 (1.782)	0.557*
RP^{2P}	0.688	-	0.72	-	0.53	-
Number of Observations	75	-	21	-	52	-

Note: t-values are reported in parentheses. Asterisks on elasticity estimates denote their statistical significance. Except for human development, the data for estimation have been taken, from Penn World Table (PWT) Version 6.1 (2002). The proxy for human development, literacy rate, is taken from *Human Development Reports* [UNDP (various issues)].

20.5. (iii). Generalizations about the 'Best' Poverty Reduction Strategy

The above-mentioned results should help settle the division of opinion on the elemental growth-inequality-poverty relationship.[18] Firstly, these results question the sufficiency hypothesis—namely, that growth is sufficient to reduce poverty, as for instance Dollar and Kraay (2002) claim. Indeed, it should be easy to understand why the sufficiency hypothesis will not hold. There are many more factors that contribute to poverty reduction other than the growth of per capita income. Thus, a rise in inequity or a serious shortfall in human development or a sharp rise in inflation, none of which is an unlikely occurrence, can nullify the contribution of the growth of per capita income to poverty reduction. Secondly, these results show the positive relationship between distributive equity and poverty reduction that some recent studies reviewed above emphasize; but they also make the additional point that, in relative terms, reducing inequity is much more effective than the growth rate of per capita income in order to achieve success in poverty reduction. The implication is not that one is more important than the other; rather it is that both these objectives of public policy should be aimed at together, in order to achieve success in poverty reduction. Thirdly, these results show that while human development may not be central to achieving faster (especially miracle) growth rates and investment, as Table 15.2 shows, but indubitably is for poverty reduction.[19] This result is in conformity with real-life experiences as well. Thus, Sri Lanka and the Indian State of Kerala have been eminently successful in reducing poverty directly rather than getting the same result as a consequence of higher growth. Once again, the conclusion is not that human development expenditure should be de-emphasized or overemphasized but only that human development should be achieved along with a high rate of growth of per capita income in an essentially egalitarian social set-up—a point that has been established in Chapters 14 and 15. Lastly, a point in favour of the Liberalist Paradigm is that it pays to keep inflation within limits, also because of its poverty-increasing effects. In fact, some country studies show that a given increase in the average inflation rate converts into a higher-than-average inflation rate for the poor. However, these results do not necessarily support liberalist monetary and fiscal radicalism because the poverty-reducing effect of inflation may be more than nullified by its adverse effects on inequity, growth and human development. This is in conformity with the development experience since 1980.

20.6. Concluding Remarks

The present chapter completes the main argument of the preceding chapter that high rate of per capita income, distributive justice and poverty reduction should be pursued together. Add to this the urgency for achieving convergence and you get a fairly complete picture of a fruitful development policy. There are two main reasons for pursuing the proposed integrated approach. Firstly, it internalizes the mutually supportive linkages among the elements of the policy package. For instance, it has been shown that greater equality essentially brings up the income of the poor to the mean income and adds a strong demand side stimulus to growth. Thus, the poor benefit the most when higher average mean income goes with greater equality. In that sense, the distribution of opportunities and growth prospects are determined together; and poverty reduction reinforces growth at the same time as it reduces distributive injustice in the society. Secondly, there may be some substantive trade-offs between the elements of the policy package that must be factored explicitly in order to arrive at an overall picture of economic progress. The important result highlighted in this chapter is that the focus of development policy should be on pursuing poverty reduction as part of a wider effort in which growth of per capita income, greater distributive justice and human development, and a modicum of macroeconomic stability are addressed together.[20] The analysis presented in this chapter strengthens the central point that a successful development policy is one that understood the full complexity and multi-dimensionality of the process of economic and human-development.

NOTES

1. It may be noted that the point of departure of the modern thinking on equity was originally to refute the Traditional Development Paradigm's alleged advocacy of a positive relationship between growth and equity; but it has now come out of that narrow (and wrong) box and has been responsible for (or has at least strengthened) the recent tilt in academic thinking towards egalitarianism.

2. It has been argued that a virtuous circle linking growth, equity and poverty reduction has been at work in the miracle economies: 'High rates of growth provided the resources that could be used to promote equality, just as the high degree of equality helped sustain the high rates of growth' [Stiglitz (1996), p. 169]. For the same reason poverty has been reduced drastically on an enduring basis in East Asia and now in China.

3. As suggested earlier in this book, Kuznets did not suggest that the proposed relationship is something like a law of nature. What he did was to present a historical evolution of economies from the early to the middle to the advanced stages of development. But it is true that there were some development economists who used the classical saving function to suggest that inequality could be good for growth. See Chapters 3 to 6 for appropriate citations.

4. It has been noted that the historical and empirical evidence 'for Kuznets generalization is mixed' [Craft (2001), p. 307].

5. A comparison of the respective experiences of India and Taiwan, both low-inequality countries, experienced very different growth paths during 1960 to 1990. The former did not grow much while the latter virtually exploded with growth. These limited examples would lead one to conclude: there is no evidence of the Kuznets curve in either country; high inequality is not a necessary condition for growth (in Taiwan's case); and low inequality does not necessarily help growth (in India's case). But these limited comparisons are at best suggestive, not conclusive arguments in favour of either of the hypotheses on the inequality-growth relationship. See also, Justin (2000) and Clarke (1993) for a re-examination of the evidence on income distribution and growth.

6. Another study based on a panel data for forty-nine countries shows that thirty-two countries showed no trend, ten showed an increasing trend with respect to inequality and only seven a decreasing trend.

7. In the same vein, Chen and Ravallion (1997) find that inequality was not correlated with increase in mean consumption in forty-three spells (A spell is defined as a period in which at least two observations are available for a country).

8. Part of the problem with the Kuznets hypothesis seems to lie in the underlying assumptions about migration, which permits a variety of generalizations about the growth-inequality relationship. Thus, migration is not assumed to take place only from rural to urban areas but also from the urban to rural areas. Those who go to urban areas for education or to earn extra money might as well return to the rural areas. Furthermore, many others might migrate from the less developed to more developed rural areas, in which case again, inequality would increase but poverty would fall [Stark (1991); Connell (1976)].

9. The main problem with Dollar, Sokoff, and Kraay (2002a,b) is that they rely on cross-country data, which can present only average cross-country experiences. For that reason, they do not capture the individual country experience—something that can be done only for each country's household-level analysis. It has been shown that the results based on household surveys are significantly different from those derived from the cross-country data [Collier and Gunning (1999)].

10. Ravallion emphasizes the importance of reducing inequality in an effective programme of poverty reduction. He shows that with a growth of per capita income of say 2 per cent and a headcount index of 40 per cent a low-inequality country (that with a Gini Coefficient of 0.30) the headcount index will be halved in eleven years; but in a high-inequality country (that with a Gini Coefficient of 0.60) it will take fifty-seven years to achieve the same goal. This, however, seems to be only an illustrative example because a rule of the thumb is that with a per capita income growth of less than 3 per cent poverty does not show any significant decline, if at all.

11. A step further along these lines is the concept of the poverty-equivalent growth rate (PEGR), which is shown to be monotonically related to poverty reduction. In other words, to make sure that growth does benefit the poor, preferably more than the non-poor in all episodes of growth, what needs to be maximized is the PEGR. In other words, 'the PEGR that satisfies the monotonic relation with poverty reduction, therefore, is not only necessary but also sufficient for poverty reduction' [Kakwani and Son (2004), p. 3].

12. The absence of the virtuous circle flows from the fact that a one-time reduction in after-tax inequality might foster investment and growth in the short run; but an upsurge in inequality might be provoked by technological change [Aghion, Caroli and Garcia-Penalosa (1999)].

13. See also Bourguignon, de Melo and Morrison (1991).

14. Pasha and Palanivel (2004) present some interesting evidence on the relationship between growth, inequality and poverty.

15. The pre-East Asia research supporting the hypothesis in the text is reported at length in [Adelman and Morris (1989)].

16. It may be noted the estimation period is shorter (1970 to 2000) here than in the case of other variables included in this study because of the non-availability of data from 1965 to 1970.

17. The finding in the text—that there is a significant negative growth—poverty relationship refutes IFAD's (International Fund for Agricultural Development) 'new development paradigm' which asserts among other things, 'There is no association between the annual rate of growth of GNer capita and changes in either in the share of the lowest 20 per cent or in the percentage of poor people among the rural population' [Jazairy, Alamgir and Pannucio (1991), p. 7].

18. The data for poverty were provided by T. Palanivel of UNDP on the instructions of Dr Hafiz A. Pasha, Assistant Secretary General of the United Nations. The reduction in the number

of observations below 630 (eighteen countries times thirty-five years) to a mere seventy-five is explained by the small number of observations available for poverty (84), literacy (84) and Gini (20). The limited number of observations would cast doubt on the finality of the results reported in the text. But these are the best available pooled data on poverty. One would, therefore, have to produce better data to be able to reject the validity of the reported results.

19. It is interesting that UNDP (2005) stresses the centrality of reducing inequality even to achieve the desired human development goals. It shows that greater human development expenditure is not sufficient for achieving human development goals (p. 58). The argument in the text supports this point of view, but warns against resurrecting the necessity *versus* sufficiency debate in the context of human development.

20. In addition to the regressions reported in the text, an attempt was also made to check on the thesis that structural transformation has increased poverty [Lipton and Ravallion (1995)] and the liberalist contention that openness contributes to poverty reduction. None of these hypotheses could be confirmed. Indeed, inclusion of these variables one-by-one and together spoiled the regressions reported in the table.

21

The New Development Paradigm III: Some Important Issues

In this chapter, we propose to determine New Development Paradigm's position on some of the so-called burning (some burnt-out) issues that have occupied a disproportionate place in the discussions on development policy e.g., the role of the state as opposed to that of the market, the relative merits of import-substitution and export expansion, globalization and economic development, and the contribution of Structural Adjustment Programmes to the economic well-being of the people. For their ideological overtones and absolutism, these coruscating controversies have generated a lot of heat but little light. The point of view taken in this study is that, rather than thinking in absolutist, non-consequentialist terms, it is more realistic to form an opinion on these matters in relative terms—relative to their consequences for human well being and the stage of development reached—based on empirical evidence.

21.1. The Role of the State

It is difficult to avoid for any length of time the ubiquitous debate, sometimes done in an eschatological frame of thought, about the relative merits of the state and markets—the dialogue on development policy being no exception to this general statement.[1] It is, therefore, of some interest to revisit this issue, even at the risk of some repetition. The main question we ask, concerns the validity of the concept of a development state for bringing about a systemic transformation of the developing countries. Table 15.1 (in Chapter 15) clearly shows that government expenditure/GDP ratio has been a significant factor in Asia and Pacific Region during the 1965 to 2000 period—in East Asia as well as South Asia, where the game of economic and human development has been played with religious fervour and, going by the present trends, their future is not going to be any the less translucent. So, then, what useful purpose is served by pillorying the government for performing its appointed role of accelerating the rate of economic and human development? A common element of the usual liberalist answers is that they invariably compare real-life situation with a full-blooded government with a mythical Pareto-optimal situation with no government. These types of comparisons make no sense and have been a waste of time because there has never been a state, nor would there ever be with no government, except theoretically. It is, therefore, more sensible to spend research time and effort on answering the elemental question: what should be the order of priorities of an interventionist government, given that there will continue to be an excess demand for it at all stages of development?

21.1. (i). The Order of Priorities

Firstly, the New Development Paradigm should visualize the state as doing things that it has historically done with remarkable success in the West and the East. Though not rejecting the market institutions as facilitators of mutually beneficial exchange, the development state will need to focus on creating, shaping and guiding the markets, promoting innovations, sparking technological change, and working in various ways for the welfare of the people.

Secondly, no less than in the past, it would have to play a large and decisive role in facilitating the passage of the developing societies to successively higher stages of Structural Transformation—from simple manufacturing to higher value added knowledge-intensive goods, which demand a steady supply of innovation and technological change. In other words, import substitution in the creation and adoption of knowledge must be regarded as a permanent feature of economic and human development. While the markets concentrate on expanding the reach of the established industries and activities, which become privately profitable, the state would have to initiate new lines of activities that carry the economy to an unexplored, higher stage of development.[2]

Thirdly, there is a fair degree of consensus, that it is only by determined state intervention that a society can achieve high and sustained rates of economic growth, distributive justice and speedy poverty reduction together. High rates of inclusive growth typically require achieving higher-than-trend physical and human investments and saving rates, undertaking simultaneous investments in closely linked industries (the Big-Push hypothesis) and taking a series of steps to generate higher-than-normal rates of saving. Greater distributive justice would inescapably entail, as Rawls (1999) insists, transforming the major social institutions that 'distribute fundamental rights and duties and determine the division of advantages from social cooperation' into a 'fraternity' in which 'those better circumstanced are willing to have their advantages only under a scheme in which this works out for the benefit of the less fortunate' (pp. 6 and 90 respectively). And, as Table 20.1 shows, poverty reduction requires human development, reducing inequities, promoting growth, regulating the rate of inflation, among others. Now each of these tasks possesses a large element of externality that precludes entrusting it to the market. Melding these jobs into a consistent policy package is an additional task requiring a lot of information and coordination, which only a socially motivated state can undertake.

Fourthly, a development-oriented state would focus on providing health services to all the people, preventing hunger and famine (and to cut short its duration if they come nevertheless), minimizing human deprivation and alleviating the many iniquities of the human condition, especially those that have historically afflicted women. In this context, special mention needs to be made of the provision of universal basic education, the social benefits of which exceed the private benefits by a large margin because it creates an awareness of the alternative choices that 'rational' individuals must make for enhancing human happiness, which is the very essence of 'development as freedom'.[3] Because universal education is so basic in weaving together the fabric of the society, and so much skill formation and scientific sophistication depend on it, it has historically been provided by the state at an affordable cost.[4] This function of the state is emphasized here because Liberalist Paradigm has strongly recommended that even this activity could best be left to the 'Invisible Hand'.

The exact sequence in which one or other of the above-mentioned heavy duty jobs are undertaken will depend on the stage of economic and human development already reached; but at a minimal level all these jobs will have to be undertaken simultaneously to exploit essential complementary aspects between them in order to minimize the average transaction cost. Thus, for instance, making higher-than-trend social expenditure would benefit from a high rate of economic growth in that the demand for skilled labour will rise at the same time as the supply of it is increasing and so on. However, the point to be noted is that state interventions will be required at all stages of development, though its focus will change.

21.2. IMPORT SUBSTITUTION AND EXPORT EXPANSION

There seems to be an evolving consensus, notwithstanding liberalist nitpicking, that the optimal policy is to keep a delicate balance between import substitution and export expansion activities. Firstly, 'there is strong evidence that simply exporting is not enough to result in or substitute for the creation of strong indigenous learning process' [Bruton (1998), p. 929]. Secondly, the dominant tendency in the developing countries has been to gradually change the composition of domestic demand away from primary production towards manufacturing production. Thus, Chenery, Robinson and

Syrquin (1986) find that the expansion of domestic demand has accounted for 72 to 74 per cent of the increase in domestic industrial output across the developing countries (p. 156). The case of Korea has not been much different. Contrary to what folk wisdom would suggest, the domestic demand expansion from 1955 to 1973 accounted for 53 per cent of growth of industrial output (p. 101). Thirdly, it has been shown that a higher growth rate has been achieved by making greater investment in the R&D sector than by simple export expansion [Grossman and Helpman (1991); Rivera-Batiz and Romer (1991)]. Indeed, not making such expenditures would aggravate rather than lessen the inequities of the international economic system because 'the more asymmetric the trading countries are—in terms of size, extent of a head start, or static comparative advantage—the more likely that growth effects will be asymmetric also. This raises the danger that developing countries may end up with the short end of the stick, as could happen when comparative advantage and/or the market size effects lead to a crowding out of their innovative sectors' [Rodrik (1995), p. 2956]. Fourthly, it is wrong to suggest that there exists off-the-shelf technology that can be readily imported. A substantial domestic investment in technology is required in order to adapt foreign-made technology to local conditions. A full blooming of technology and innovation activities is required before a developing country can become a net exporter of 'new goods' [Hausman and Rodrik (2003)]. The general point is that today's global economy does not single out a single best outcome, arrived at by international competition, in which each country serves the world's best interests by producing just those goods that it can naturally turn out most efficiently' [Gomory and Baumol (2000), p. 5]. A lot of what has been written to prove the superiority of outward orientation to import substitution failed to show 'the mechanism through which exports affect GDP growth' and they also ignored the 'potential determinants of growth' [Edwards (1993), p. 1389]. The fact is that the chain of causation between growth and exports still remains to be finally settled.[5]

Fifthly, even if import-substitution policies did promote some inefficiency, there is no evidence to show that it was large enough to slow down the engine of growth in the developing countries. Finally, it may be noted in this context that there is no presumption that import substitution is inherently more distortion-prone than export expansion, nor is it the case that rent-seeking will be more intense in the former case than in the latter.[6] Indeed, it has been shown that when export subsidies are the dominant form of protection—measured by the DRC's (Domestic Resource Costs) or the EPR's (Effective Protection Rates—they are no less distorted than import restrictions) [Naqvi and Kemal (1991a)].[7]

The empirical evidence presented in Table 19.1 (Chapter 19) shows that import-substituting industrialization has been a significant factor contributing to growth and investment in the Asia and Pacific Region from 1965 to 2000, including East Asia. True, openness has been a significant contributor to economic growth in South Asia—though insignificant in East Asia—but it was much less so than Structural Transformation. In fact, Table 19.1 highlights the dominance of Structural Transformation, not openness, as the key factor in the process of economic development. These tendencies have lasted long enough to continue in the foreseeable future as well. There is, therefore, not much wisdom in continuing the rather pointless debate about the inherent inefficiency of import substitution as opposed to that of export expansion. The fact is that relative emphasis of the one or the other has depended on the stage of development. Lewis's statement (1955) on this issue should have settled this controversy long ago: 'In development programmes all sectors of the economy should grow simultaneously, so as to keep a proper balance between industry and agriculture and between production for the home consumption and production for exports' (p. 283).[8] Table 19.1 also makes clear that there is no warrant whatsoever for the liberalist practice of equating the import-substitution strategy with a slower rate of economic development in non-East Asia as opposed to the alleged export-led nature of the East Asian miracle growers. The fact is that in order for per capita income to grow at the fastest possible rate, both activities have been undertaken with a reasonable degree of balance and coordination among them throughout the developing world, including East Asia. These matters have been discussed at length at different places in the present study; the point to emphasize here is that the export expansion and import substitution controversy should now be finally put aside. The focus of analysis and policy must instead shift to finding the right combination of import-substitution and export-expansion activities, and implementing them at the lowest possible opportunity cost, in different countries at different stages of economic development.

21.2. (i). Shrinking Global Space for Export-led Growth

There is yet another reason why import-substitution activities should not be discriminated against either on grounds of efficiency or growth. It is that export expansion, whatever are its merits, is no longer an open-ended option, if ever it was. Ironically, the developing countries have achieved outward orientation under duress, as part of their obligations under the WTO and the Structural Adjustment Programmes, but they do not now know what to make of their exalted first-best status. The reason is that western protectionism—especially in the form of the indiscriminate and arbitrary application of anti-dumping duties and myriad other import restrictions—remain green as ever. It has been freely used to block the entry of their exports into the OECD markets on one pretext or another. An example of the tenacity of western protectionism is the suspension of all negotiations regarding the Doha Development Round in July 2006 after the failure of six major member countries to make sufficient progress among themselves on the modalities of negotiations on two key areas, agriculture and Non-Agricultural Market Access (NAMA).

That Western protectionism has had adverse consequences for the well-being of the people, especially of the poorest farmers, is no longer in doubt. The evidence is compelling that it has reduced job creation and destroyed existing jobs, lowered the real income of the poor producers in one of the poorest regions of the earth (sub-Saharan Africa), exacerbated inequalities of income and wealth and increased the incidence of poverty. Thus, it has been estimated that, as a net effect of the protectionist measures by the OECD countries, $700 billion worth of extra exports from the developing countries could not materialize. This is equal to four-times the total inflow of foreign direct investment into the developing countries [UNCTAD (1999), p. 143]. The moment of truth seems to have arrived; the developed countries should talk less of free trade; they should rather prove by their action that they really believe in what they have professed, both in the classrooms and across the bargaining table in international negotiations.

21.2. (ii). Adverse Terms of Trade

As a logical consequence of Western protectionism, the Prebisch-Singer scenario seems to have remerged with a vengeance: greater exports buy too little of imports and development. The terms of trade (including the income terms of trade) have moved against the primary and manufactured exports of the non-oil producing developing countries at the rate of about 1.5 per cent per annum since the 1980s. This has cut down their purchasing power to finance the imports required for industrial development. And 'yet the crisis in commodity prices is conspicuously absent from the international trade agenda' [UNDP (2005), p. 139]. There is strong evidence that high growth rates in the developing countries can only be financed by large current account deficits and by large inflows of foreign capital. The former cannot be sustained beyond a certain limit; and the latter has shown more inclination to make arbitrage profits than to serve the interests of the developing countries [UNCTAD (1998)]. The development prospects of the developing countries, therefore, face a double jeopardy; and yet they have little leverage to overcome it.

21.3. Globalization and Development Policy

There is an influential point of view that globalization has been unambiguously good for all countries. Dollar, Sokolff and Kraay (2002a,b) find that propounders of globalization have done significantly better than the ones who are anti-globalization. They claim to show that the former increased their share in world trade in the 1977–97 periods. But even a cursory look at these figures shows that this assertion cannot be true as a refutable proposition. For how would then one explain the predicament of sub-Saharan Africa, whom globalization has trapped in the downward spiral of negative growth and poverty? The region has failed to diversify its exports beyond primary goods and simple manufacturing. It has helplessly witnessed the terms of trade moving inexorably against it and its capacity to import consistently eroded. In general, there seems to be a near-consensus that globalization has contributed to growing inequity between nations and there is a fear that 'international economic integration' might as well sow the seeds of 'domestic and social disintegration' [Rodrik (1997), p. 2].[9] The point is that globalization can never be a source of good so long as it primarily works, as it has so far, in the interest of the developed as opposed to that of the developing countries.

21.3. (i). The WTO and the Global Economic System

Notwithstanding the rhetoric of a democratic and rule-based world trading system, the WTO has not been able to establish its credential as working for a just world economic order. A wiser attitude would be one of scepticism (though not one of hostility) towards the inevitable munificence of the existing world trading system. There is, therefore, need to rewrite 'the rules that govern markets for labour, goods, ideas, capital and the use of resources need to become more equitable' [World Bank (2005), p. 223]. The Doha Development Round recognized the need for doing so; however, the suspension of the negotiations seems to have embroiled the WTO in a major existential crisis. Enough evidence has now become available to question the fairness of the WTO and its utter inability to give birth to a brave and fair new world, as promised.[10] True, the Reciprocity Principle and the Most-Favoured Nations Clause of the GATT, which the WTO has retained, have enormously expanded international trade by matching interests for interests by comparison with a situation if each country could set the terms of international exchange in isolation, without the discipline of the WTO.[11] The limitation of these clauses should, however, be noted. It is that the efficiency of these principles has been constrained by the inherent imbalances of economic and political powers of the trading partners. The fact is that the

Uruguay Round of Trade never intended to make the world trading system more equitable; it was primarily meant to safeguard the interests of the developed countries.[12] It is, therefore, not surprising that, under the not-so-watchful eyes of the WTO, the developing countries have, by-and-large, lost out to the developed countries, and the weaker ones among them have been hurt the most.[13] To move forward the current practice of forcing the developing countries to lower the tariff and non-tariff barriers voluntarily without demanding a *quid pro quo* from the developed countries should be given up. This is because the global trading system is run on the basis of trading of interests against interests. An act of voluntary liberalization in this system would, therefore, be routinely punished, not rewarded because 'unilateral free trade hardly weighs with the people who really matter' [Krugman (1997), p. 113].

21.3. (ii). Capital Market Liberalization and Global Instability

An important negative aspect has been the rather precipitous liberalization of the capital market in the developing countries. There is now a near-consensus that, 'under free capital mobility, no regime of exchange rate will guarantee stable and competitive rates; nor will it combine steady growth with financial stability' [UNCTAD, *TDR* (1999), p. 130].[14] A study of seventy-six currency crises and twenty-six banking crises has found that each time a crisis-ridden country liberalized its capital account and the financial sector without first providing strong regulation and sound banking supervision the outcome has invariably been severe banking and currency crises, even in countries with strong fundamentals [Kaminsky and Rheinhart (1999)].[15] These crises have generally been seriously damaging for the developing countries' growth performance—so much so that now even the IMF routinely advises the developing countries not rush to liberalize their capital markets too soon. It is, therefore, essential to devise some sort of a stabilizing mechanism to shore up the international exchange-rate system. In the absence of effective governance of capital flows and without a global system of exchange rates, the only other feasible option is to resort to temporary controls on short-term capital movements when they threaten the exchange-rate regimes in the developing countries—which, incidentally is an old Keynesian idea.[16]

21.3. (iii). Globalization and Slower Structural Transformation

There is a real danger that a strict application of the WTO rules and procedures will greatly weaken, as it already has, the rate of Structural Transformation as a source of growth in the developing countries. This is because it does not allow infant-industry protection even in case of industries subject to increasing returns to scale and imperfect competition, where the payoff in terms of learning, learning to learn, and knowledge accumulation would be large. But the fact is that industrialization would not be possible without a modicum of protection—especially in case of industries where the steady growth of domestic markets is an important element in their growth. In such cases, 'one cannot use current comparative advantage as the only basis for judgment of how to allocate resources' [Stiglitz (1989b), p. 199]. And yet this is what the WTO does. True, Article 18-c of the GATT is still available but the UR Agreement does not look favourably at those clauses, i.e. Article 18, Part IV and the Enabling Clause—which justify the Special and Differential treatment of the developing countries. It would, therefore, be highly beneficial for the developing countries if the relevant clauses of the WTO were amended suitably to enable them to engage in import substitution, especially in industries that are subject to increasing returns to knowledge.[17] In general, WTO must allow developing countries 'to develop the capacity to enter higher-value added area of world trade' [UNDP (2005), p. 134]. Needless to clarify, these arguments for temporary protection to knowledge-based industries do not constitute an argument for pervasive import licensing and exchange control, like the ones that prevailed in the decades of 1960s and 1970s. Regardless of their merits, these ideas are now part of history and it would be unwise to revive them [Bhagwati (1978); Krueger (1978].

21.3. (iv). Globalization and Inequality

Globalization has displayed an irreducible polarity in its unfolding. While exciting great expectations, it has also turned to dust promises of prosperity for all, spurring rather the race to the bottom. Even as the production-possibility frontier is pushed outwards, causing surges of wealth in advanced countries, the gathering storm of the imbalances of privilege and power, inequality, poverty, and human deprivation threatens the stability, even the viability, of the economies of the developing countries. An essentially inequitable outcome should not come as a surprise because the rules of the game that govern globalization reflect the liberalist world-view of national and global development. Thanks to the in-built inequities of the WTO, globalization has tended to enhance distributive inequities between nations and peoples and erode the poverty-reducing potential of international trade and capital flows.

21.3. (v), Fragmentation of Global Production

Perhaps, one of the most dramatic aspects of globalization has been the 'fragmentation' of the production processes, which, at least theoretically, could enhance the gains from trade of final goods by adding to them those accruing from the trade in intermediate goods as well [Jones (1993)]. However, production fragmentation has not been an unmixed blessing for the developing countries. True, it has increased output; but it has also greatly enhanced the influence of the MNCs to practically dictate the type, quantity, and the location of the goods and services produced by their production networks. This also has had implications for the type of foreign direct investment (FDI) available to the developing countries now. Thus, three-fourths of foreign investment that flowed into the developing countries in the 1990s, when its quintessential beneficence was most emphasized, represented the merger and acquisition activities of the MNCs and added little to the production capacity of the emerging markets that were fortunate enough to receive it. Worse still, arbitrage profit seeking has, by-and-large, been an unstable source of development finance [*TDR* (1999)]. No less reprehensible have been the adverse consequences of the Structural Adjustment Programme on employment and wages, especially of the unskilled workers. The technological change associated with production fragmentation has tended to reduce within-the-industry demand for unskilled workers relative to that for the skilled workers both in the developed and the developing countries. The main reason for this somewhat paradoxical result is that, 'the outsourced activities are unskilled labour-intensive relative to those done in the developed economy, but skilled labour-intensive relative to those done in the less developed economy. Moving these activities from one country to the other raises the average skill-intensity of production in both the locations' [Feenstra (1998), p. 42]. In addition to this bias against unskilled labour is the profound change in the bargaining position of labour relative to that of capital. This might have an impact on the size of wage inequality induced by globalization [Borjas and Ramey (1995)].

21.4. Reforming Structural Adjustment Programmes

The basic principle of reforming the Structural Adjustment Programmes should be the one that Keynes pointed out long ago: the burden of adjustment should primarily be borne by those who can bear it without hurting the development possibilities of the developing countries. To this end, the Structural Adjustment Programmes must, above all, leave enough space for domestic policies to function effectively for achieving maximal (rather than 'sustainable') growth, improving distribution of income and succeeding in poverty reduction. The current practice of imposing on national governments a set of development policies and priorities in the form of notorious terms and conditions, disregarding their own understanding of their economies must be discontinued. True, some important shifts have taken place in the design of the Structural Adjustment Programmes. They now wear a 'human face', in that poverty reduction is mentioned as one of their key objectives and the budgetary targets are set at a more 'realistic' level to allow greater fiscal space for larger development expenditures. Indeed, the emphasis in some countries (mostly in Africa) has shifted from terms and conditions oriented to 'country ownership' and to participatory planning. A conscious effort has been made at the World Bank to hear the 'voices of the poor' of the borrowing nations. Yet, much of these improvements count for little when the needs of the borrowers conflict with those of the richer countries, whose values and priorities have set the form and direction of multilateral lending.[18] As far as the IMF policies are concerned, it is admitted now that they have made the spirit of growth to flee from the developing countries by forcing recessionary policies on them.[19] Thus, notwithstanding some window-dressing, the focus of the Structural Adjustment Programmes remains much the same as before. They are still systematically contract-based—involving high interest rates, too low budgetary targets, higher taxes etc. Their net effect has been to destroy jobs (as happens in fiscal stabilization and privatization episodes) rather than create them, increase distributive inequities and enhance poverty. All this must change.

21.4. (i). Maximal Growth rather than Sustainable Growth

In line with the basic recommendation stated at the beginning of Part VI, the New Development Paradigm should contribute to changing the focus of the Structural Adjustment programmes from sustainable growth (a euphemism for low growth) back to maximal growth. In other words, their primary focus should shift from too much macroeconomic stability to growth, employment creation and poverty. In this context, they need to change their routine insistence on a strict implementation of restrictive monetary and fiscal policies with a view to containing budgetary deficits and lowering the inflation rate to a level where they become inconsistent with maximal growth and employment generation.[20] However, there is merit in keeping inflation rates at a reasonable level within the framework of high and sustained growth.[21] Furthermore, the Structural Adjustment Programmes should not continue with their myopic focus on speedy capital-market liberalization. There is not much substance in the argument that since the capital-scarce developing countries should be the last ones to live with capital-market inefficiency they must be the first ones to liberalize capital markets. Quite the contrary; they must be the last ones to do so as well. Capital-market liberalization has seldom, if ever, promoted growth; they have seldom if ever issued the right signals to guide capital flows into sectors and countries where they make the most contribution to economic growth. In fact, private capital typically flows into privately profitable, rather than into socially profitable activities (into enclave-type activities rather in manufacturing) and into countries that need them least [TDR (1999); Stiglitz (2003)]. The East Asian crisis illustrates very well the adverse consequences of freeing capital markets much too soon. Fortunately, there seems to be a change of heart in this respect; the developing countries are now advised not to rush capital market reforms. It is only that, in most cases, such advice amounts to crying over spilt milk. The developing countries have already opened their economies fully in this respect and it may not be possible for them to do much about them now without inviting adverse reaction from the international financial markets.

21.4. (ii). Focus on Distribution and Poverty Reduction

The New Development Paradigm would seek that Structural Adjustment Programmes pay greater attention to their distributional effects. It is something they have lacked so far. This much has been conceded even by their architects: 'the important issue of the distributional impact of adjustment has received attention in computable general equilibrium models, but it is fair to say that this work has not yet had a wide impact' [Corbo and Fischer (1995), p. 2917].[22] This is unfortunate because promoting an equitable distribution of income and wealth lies at the heart of Structural Adjustment Programmes, if only because a lack of it would imperil domestic political support for them.[23] In fact, these programmes have been extremely unpopular with the people, partly because they have seldom, if ever, reflected their interests.[24] For instance, they have generally forced developing countries to do 'trade liberalization before safety nets were put in place, before there was an adequate regulatory framework, before the countries could withstand the adverse consequences of the sudden changes in market sentiments that are part and parcel of capitalism; forcing policies that led to job destruction before the essentials of job creation were in place; forcing privatization before there were adequate competition and regulatory frameworks' [Stiglitz (2003), p. 73]. The fact is that, for their lack of focus on distributional issues, a faithful implementation of these programmes has invariably led to food riots and protests against increasing the prices of health and education services. In this context, the current policy of withdrawing subsidies on wage goods and increasing the price of food will also have to be revised, if only because it directly increases poverty among the non-producers of food. Also, the IMF's existing hostility to an increase in public expenditure, mostly on ideological grounds, must be given up, if only because lower public development expenditure tend to crowd out private investment expenditure as well, which tends to lower growth and increase poverty.[25]

21.4. (iii). Enhance 'Public Ownership' of Structural Adjustment Programmes

It follows from the above considerations that the New Development Paradigm must emphasize the principle of the public ownership of the Structural Adjustment Programmes. This is what the international donors also assert. But, notwithstanding the rhetoric, the real ownership of the programmes continues to rest with the international donors, who usually safeguard the interests of their corporate paymasters. To make it worse, the current practice is against sharing relevant information about the likely effects of the Structural Adjustment Programmes with the public for fear that this might lead to the derailment of the programmes.[26] This autocratic style of liberalist reforms has everywhere tended 'to undermine representative institutions, to personalize politics, and to generate a climate in which politics becomes reduced to fixes, to a search for redemption. Even if neo-liberal reform packages make good economics, they are likely to generate voodoo politics' [Bresser et al. (1993), pp. 9–10]. All this must change. To this end, the social, economic and political cost and benefits of the programmes must be factored in. Here two things stand out as central to enhancing the chances of their success: (i) the costs and the benefits of the programmes must be shared both by the privileged and underprivileged and; (ii) they must be designed so as to maximize public participation by disseminating the relevant information about them.[27]

21.5. CONTROLLING INFLATION: REGRESSION RESULTS ON ASIA AND PACIFIC REGION (1965–2000)

Controlling inflation has been the focal point of the Structural Adjustment Programmes. To that end, they emphasize reducing the budgetary deficits and keeping the money supply under control. However, both these measures can also have adverse effects on the real variables—especially, the growth rate of per capita income. To evaluate the merits of this aspect of the programmes, an attempt has been made to see the impact of controlling inflation on the growth rate. Table 15.2 (in Chapter 15) sheds some interesting light on the issue. A new variable 'Inflation Square' has been included to account for any possible non-linearity in the inflation-growth relationship. The average figures for all Asia and Pacific region have also been disaggregated to see the differential responses, if any, to changes in the rate of inflation. The following important points emerge from the regression exercise: (a) The effect of inflation on the growth of per capita income has been positive but insignificant. However, it is negatively and significantly related to growth in South Asia. The reason for the latter result is that inflation rate has been substantially higher in South Asia than in East Asia, where the inflation rate has come down as a consequence of high growth; (b) More interestingly, the coefficient of the 'inflation squared' variable has, on average been negative and significant. This means that once inflation crossed a certain threshold level, it has had adverse consequences for growth in both the East Asian and non-East Asian countries. The somewhat obvious result coming out of this exercise is that development policy should find for each country the threshold level of inflation, namely, the level above which inflation tends to hurt growth, but below which it helps it. Obviously, it will be counterproductive to push the inflation rate below the threshold level. This is a rather tedious exercise to undertake on the basis of pooled data for several countries, but should be do-able for individual countries. However, it is clear that these findings do not support the current policy of reducing inflation at whatever cost to output, nor do they encourage laxity about inflation. As always, these results point to a policy of moderation with respect to the maintenance of macroeconomic stability as opposed to a growth-maximization policy.

21.6. CONCLUDING REMARKS

This chapter has delineated with a broad brush the New Development Paradigm's point of view on issues where controversies continue to simmer—namely, the role of the state; the export versus the import substitution issue; globalization and the Structural Adjustment Programmes. The need for gaining clarity has been emphasized because unfortunately the debate about them has been more off balance than enlightened. The main finding of this chapter is that these issues are important but they need not be looked at in a confrontational, either or manner. Instead, the New Development Paradigm must evolve a non-ideological, consequentialist stance that remains focused on the likely repercussions that specific development policies might have on economic growth, social justice and poverty.

On the state versus the market issue, the debate has come full circle: from a moderately intrusive proactive state, to a minimal state, to a 'market-friendly' state, and finally, to a highly intrusive development state. The changes in the academic opinion on what the East Asian miracle really meant has been responsible for these policy reversals in the developing countries. Chastened by the failure of the market-only experiments, the problem is no longer seen as how to minimize the government through whatever means (say through aggressive privatization); it is rather to have an efficient government—

which will surely be non-minimalist—that performs the foundational functions of development because it has access to more (essentially costly) information about the economy than the private sector can be reasonably expected to possess. It is now understood that development states have created new opportunities for the effective working of the market and private initiative, throughout the developing world—indeed, also in the developed world.[28] The New Development Paradigm, recognizing the essential role of the state in economic matters, should, therefore, become of 'one-mind' on this vital issue and steer clear of the essentially wasteful government versus the market debate that the Liberalist Paradigm initiated.[29]

On the import substitution versus the export expansion debate, the East Asian miracle has again set the terms of the development dialogue. The liberalists have regarded, almost without exception, the miracle to have been export-led. This debate has caused an undesirable change in the development strategy that has left in its trail a whole litany of wrong ideas on development. Indeed, it would take a whole project to estimate the damage that the implementation of these false ideas has caused to the economic well-being of people. The proper conclusion for the New Development Paradigm to draw from this sorry episode in the realm of ideas is that such matters had better be decided with reference to their positive contribution to Structural Transformation, which has been shown to be the key factor for quickening the pace of economic development throughout the developing world. From this vantage point, the case for import substitution as an integral part of the development process would becomes stronger still at 'higher' stages of industrial development—namely, when it becomes necessary to move beyond simple manufacturing to heavy industries, where the spillover effect on the rest of the economy is the most pronounced [Bradford, De Long, and Summers (1991)]. This policy shift is required to lay the foundation of durable export expansion in higher value-added products that would at the same time accelerate the growth rate of per capita income, achieve a dynamic balance between different sectors of the economy and strengthen the links between learning and (physical and human) capital accumulation.

On the globalization issue, the basic point is not whether it should be or should not be (it is very much there, like it or not); it is rather that it should be regulated to work for the good of the developing countries where the majority of humankind resides. It should be recognized firmly and honestly that, 'even when not guilty of hypocrisy, the West has driven the globalization agenda, ensuring that it garners a disproportionate share of the benefits, at the expense of the developing world' [Stiglitz (2003), p. 7]. An obvious first step to change the reality would be to link the voluntary liberalization of trade forced on the developing countries as part of the Structural Adjustment Programmes to their negotiating position in the WTO round of negotiations.

In addition to making globalization function efficiently and equitably with respect to the trade in goods, there are far more important issues of the trade in services and knowledge. Steps should also be taken to control, if not eliminate altogether, the flagrant misuse of intellectual property rights by the MNCs, most of which reside in the OECD countries. It is, therefore, an urgent matter that the TRIPs Accord is suitably amended so that it is only the genuine intellectual property rights that get protection under the law. Furthermore, to enhance the equity potential of the WTO, its rules should be modified to permit the adoption of growth-oriented policies.

On the Structural Adjustment Programmes, the moral of the story related above is that the New Development Paradigm should encourage sensitivity to their distributional consequences and their impact on poverty alleviation. But it must remain watchful about the adverse impact of large and growing budgetary and trade deficits and overvalued exchange rates. Furthermore, the policy stance should be to strike a balance between the dictates of controlling the inflation rate and the requirements of high and sustained growth. A wise course of action would be to eschew monetary radicalism and fiscal dilettantism on the one hand and a light-hearted attitude towards macroeconomic stability on the other. To this end, each country must settle on a growth-maximization policy that does not allow the inflation rate to go beyond the 'threshold rate'.

NOTES

1. Thus, for instance, the debate between the neo-Keynesians and the Rational Expectationists revolved around their answer to the following question: can the government help stabilize the economy through active interventionist policies? While the Keynesians advocated interventionist policies because they thought there were deadweight losses or market failures of a macroeconomic nature in the market economy that the government can do something about. The monetarists and the rational expectationists argued the opposite [Tobin in Klamer (1984), p. 10]. There seems to be a close relationship between different phases of the evolution of development policy with those through which mainstream economics has passed. While the Traditional Development Paradigm, and to some extent the Human Development Paradigm, have tended to reflect the Keynesian and the neo-Keynesian positions, the Liberalist Paradigm have sympathized with the Rational Expectationist's and Monetarist's points of view. And, to use a rather helpful Marxian terminology, there is a pressing need in both streams of thought for evolving a synthesis of the thesis and anti-thesis.
2. Indeed, this is how industrialization has progressed. Thus, for instance, the Pakistan Industrial Development Corporation (PIDC), which pioneered industrialization in Pakistan, would open up new lines of activity and sell it to the private sector once it became privately profitable.
3. *Development as Freedom* is the title of Sen's book (1999b).
4. Stiglitz (2003) states the point made in the text forcefully: 'As efficient as the markets may be, they do not ensure that individuals have enough food, clothes to wear, or shelter' (p. 224). See also Stiglitz (2006) for a powerful statement of this point of view.

5. Thus, there is considerable truth in the claim that, 'outward orientation cannot be considered as a universal recommendation for all conditions and for all types of countries' [Singer and Gray (1988), p. 403].

6. Indeed, this was the point of the research about the optimal form of state intervention— namely, that the exchange rate regime should be neutral with respect to the two types of activities [Bhagwati and Ramaswami (1963); Naqvi (1969; 1971)]. However, much of this emphasis on neutrality of the trade regime got lost in the general enthusiasm about the unbounded beneficence of export expansion.

7. In the case of Turkey, rent-seekers had as much incentive under the export-oriented regime to seek export industry status as they had under the tight import restriction regime to obtain import licenses [Onis (1991)]. By the same token, there is also not much force in the liberalist claim that export activities are more efficient and more growth-promoting because the exporters will be engaged in productive profit-seeking due to their greater exposure to external competition; as compared with the wasteful rent-seeking done in the import-substitution activities that cater to a protected market [Krueger (1978)].

8. Later on, he stated the relationship between export expansion and production for the home market in some more detail: 'If the domestic market is too small, it is still possible to support an industrial sector by exporting manufactures and importing food and raw materials. But it is hard to begin industrialization by exporting manufactures. Usually, one begins by selling in a familiar and protected home market, and moves on exporting only after one has learnt how to make one's costs competitive' [Lewis (1978), p. 10].

9. See also Streeten (1998) for an analysis of the de-equalizing effects of globalization.

10. The various issues of the *Trade and Development Report (TDR)* especially those since 1995 bring out the various weaknesses of the post-UR Agreement international trade and payments system.

11. Begwell and Staiger (1999) show that the reciprocity and discrimination principles of the GATT guide governments towards the efficient multilateral trading system by comparison with a situation, 'when governments acting in isolation shift the cost of their intervention onto the trading partner by altering the world prices with their unilateral choices'. Needless to point out, this important property of the GATT principles is conditional on each member regarding it as a means of improving the efficiency of the system. This view, however, ignores the fact that these arrangements have, in practice, been primarily as a means to tilt the system in favour of the stronger partners. The recent breakdown of the Doha Round of negotiations proves, if any proof was necessary, that the developed countries continue to pursue their narrow national interests, in utter disregard of the global interests.

12. The UR-negotiations were not allowed to move forward as long as the developing countries did not give in to the developed countries' demand about safeguarding the so-called intellectual property rights and to open up the former's market to the exports of the latter. In the end, as a reflection of the unequal bargaining power of the developed countries, while an agreement was reached about the free export of financial services and information technology, nothing substantial was agreed to the developing countries' exports of maritime services and construction.

13. A World Bank study concluded: 'Sub-Saharan Africa, the poorest region in the world saw its income decline by 2 per cent as a result of the trade agreement.' [Cited in Stiglitz (2003), p. 61].

14. The 2001 issue of the United Nations Trade and Development Report (*TDR*) puts the problems faced by the developing countries at the doors of the total lack of governance of the international capital flows: 'There is no satisfactory unilateral solution of the exchange rate instability and misalignments in emerging markets, particularly under free capital movement' (p. 67). It, therefore, highlights the urgent need to establish a global system of exchange rates to safeguard the developing countries from the chaotic nature of exchange-

rate regime of the G-3 countries. But, unfortunately, no such scheme for establishing a global architecture for exchange rates is on the cards at present.

15. See Summers (2000) and Demirguc-Kunt and Detragiache (1998) for an analysis of financial liberalization.

16. A related, though distinct, issue concerns the desirability of letting the exchange market find its own level versus the feasibility of exchange-market intervention. (It is a distinct issue because the restrictions on the flow of capital suppress the market forces, whereas, the exchange market intervention works through the market; but it is a related issue because both types of interventions may have the same effect on the foreign exchange market). The consensus in the 1980s was against any intervention in view of the highly integrated nature of the exchange markets all over the world. However, the studies done in the 1990s support the case for market intervention. Sarno and Taylor (2001) conclude: 'Official intervention can be effective, especially if intervention is publicly announced and concerted, and provided that it is consistent with the underlying stance of monetary and fiscal policy' (p. 862).

17. In this context there is need to re-examine Article XVIII and sections A& C of GATT, 1994, and to soften the compensation requirements, which are at present too onerous to take any advantage of these articles. Also, Part IV of GATT together with the 1979 Tokyo Round Enabling Clause can provide a good starting point for a re-evaluation of the UR Agreement [UNCTAD, TDR (1999), p. 132].

18. The rich countries (the shareholders of the Bank) have a strong handle in the form of the replenishment of the triennial IDA to 'foist their values on the Bank's borrowers' [Mallaby (2004), p. 389]. The result is that the so-called fight against poverty has been lost even before it began in the right earnest.

19. And it is accepted now that an expansionary policy was the main force behind the fast recovery of Malaysia, Korea and Thailand from its recession in the late 1990s [Lane, Ghosh, Hamann, Phillips, Scultze-Ghatta and Tsikata (1999)].

20. In a review of the roles of the IMF and the World Bank's activities, Krueger (1998) points out: 'Since balance of payments difficulties are normally symptomatic of unsustainable level of expenditure relative to income, the conditions negotiated in the Fund programme often result in at least a temporary retardation in the rate of growth, if not a recession' (p. 1986). The reality, however, is more unpalatable. The growth rates have been retarded for rather long periods, thereby, increasing unemployment rates and poverty.

21. There is some empirical support for the view that moderate inflation (of say 12–15 per cent) does not hurt growth) and that a policy of pushing inflation rates lower and lower can be positively harmful for long-run growth, employment creation, and poverty reduction [Bruno, Ravallion, Squire and Easterly (1998)].

22. Persson and Tabellini (1994) conclude: 'to date, how income distribution and economic growth are jointly determined in political equilibrium is not very well understood' (p. 613). Rodrik (1996) states: 'Because distributional issues are at the heart of the literature [on policy reforms] discussed here, we need more progress on understanding why institutions for compensating losers from reform are not more common. There are very few papers where the difficulties of compensating the losers are made endogenous to the analytical framework' (p. 39).

23. Rodrik (1996) notes that very few studies in the political economy literature endogenize the difficulties of compensating the losers, and that they seldom discuss 'the institutions for compensating the losers' (p. 39).

24. Instead, in the true spirit of the Liberalist Paradigm, the international donors have insisted that developing countries submit to the pains caused by the Structural Adjustment Programmes in their own interests. Since the common man has generally rebelled against the perverse logic of the IMF—that the more pain the people endure; the better for

them—democratic governance has not been considered suitable for the implementation of these programmes.

25. Joan Robinson (1962) pointed out: 'The argument that public investment, however beneficial, must be less eligible than any private investment, merely because it is public, has no logical basis; it is just a hangover from *laissez-faire* ideology' (p. 126).

26. Thus, for instance, Sachs (1994) counsels: 'If reformers want free prices, they should not stand there and talk about it—they should do it, because everyone will be against free prices until it has been done, until it is an established fact' (pp. 509–10).

27. The case against 'authoritarian conditionality' approach to development is most forcefully stated in [Mallaby (2004)]. Instead, he has argued for a participatory model of development to enhance the voluntary ownership of these models.

28. As has been discussed at length in the preceding chapters, in the overwhelming number of cases the state has intervened on behalf of the private sector, especially where the markets did not exist. For instance, the Pakistan Industrial Development Corporation in Pakistan had it in its charter that it would intervene only where the private investment was shy; and once its investment projects became attractive enough, the same will be sold to the private sector. And this is what actually happened to all the developing economies, including the miracle economies of East Asia. Even in the super-miracle performing China, the state is now fostering the markets though only in phased manner.

29. A recent statement of the liberalist position that it believes in the 'primacy of the markets and the centrality of the institutions', does not correctly capture the sense of the liberalist consensus on development policy [World Bank (2005)]. The fact is that the centrality of institutions has never been the concern of the liberalists. If anything, they have been more concerned with the creation of an institutional framework in which the individual can pursue its own interests as he sees fit.

22

The New Development Paradigm IV: Moral Foundations

This chapter spells out the New Development Paradigm's moral understanding of inclusive growth. This is important 'because people's economic behaviour is influenced by their moral beliefs, and it [is important] to see what impact these beliefs have on economic outcomes' [Hausman and McPherson (1993), p. 679]. Indeed, one can easily recall examples of developing countries, for instance, Singapore, where a conscious effort has been made to reflect moral values (based on Confucian moral principles) in their highly successful development effort. The Human Development Paradigm has pioneered the formal introduction of moral considerations into the economic calculus. However, because of its de-emphasis on income maximization as a desirable end of human (and economic) development, it does not offer a compelling moral case for inclusive growth. Those considerations apply to the New Development Paradigm as well. In this chapter, we supplement that analysis by some aspects of the non-Utilitarian consequentialist philosophy which have generally been left out the standard expositions namely, the Rawlsian conception of a 'well-ordered society' and Sen's principle of 'consequent evaluation' but which have important implications for inclusive growth.

22.1. The Quintessential Morality of Inclusive Growth

To be relevant and effective, development policy must be conducted within the framework of economic principles and ethical norms that strengthen the case for inclusive growth in an integrated and logically consistent framework of analysis. This would mark a definite improvement over the current intellectual fashion to insist on positivism and yet make recommendations that can really be justified on moral grounds. It should be clear to the reader that sticking to positivism, consciously or unconsciously, would not be helpful in addressing adequately some of the most basic development issues e.g., unemployment. Solow (1980) pointed out long ago that without positing some kind of moral considerations it would not be possible to explain why sometimes labour market is not self-clearing. A morally motivated solution would still be socially desirable even if is not optimal (even if labour markets do not clear at the going wage rate).[1] But no less compelling is the moral aspect of the apparently amoral processes through which high rates of per capita income are secured. Making people save and invest at such high rates as have become a routine matter in East Asia and China (investment rates exceeding 35 per cent and saving rates in excess of 40 per cent or so) could not have come about without suffusing a moral commitment among people to work for the good of the society, even though they must suffer a reduction in present consumption for extended periods of time. Similarly, a sense of duty to the society must also be tapped to make them rise in defence of an essentially just system in times of crisis. The recent example of South Korea, for instance, of the common people rising in defence of their systems during the 1996/97 financial crisis is one of the most heart-warming examples of voluntary action spurred by a sense of moral duty to the society. Indeed, one can state it as a general rule that no extraordinary feat of inclusive growth can succeed without filling men/women's hearts with a sense of self-sacrifice for the larger good of the society.

The New Development Paradigm must, therefore, 'settle down' on a helpful normative theory. Fortunately, doing this would not require undertaking a 'venture into the unknown'. The non-Utilitarian consequentialist moral philosophy has brought 'high theory' down from its empyrean heights to help in analyzing real-life development issues scientifically. Indeed, it is no exaggeration to state that without these seminal contributions, it would not have been possible to tackle the problems of distributive justice, gender equity, poverty reduction and human deprivation with full confidence in the scientific credentials of such an exercise. We again cite here Rawls's and Sen's explorations as representative of a large number of similarly motivated contributions.

22.1. (i). The 'Well-Ordered Society'

Chapter 13 gave a fairly complete exposition of the Rawlsian Justice-as-Fairness and the Difference principles, both of which provide a very strong moral case for changing those institutions that are incompatible with the demands of social justice and which fail to accord priority to the needs of the least-privileged in the society. The implementation of these principles requires making a conscious transition from an ill-ordered society to a 'well-ordered society' [Rawls (1999), p. 479]. However, it is important to see that what is 'just' need not be 'good', and that the requirements of each are not the same. An additional requirement is needed for making the two concepts congruent. It is that it is rational and good for each individual to adopt the standpoint of justice. This is because what is 'just' gets invigorated and ennobled by an irrepressible human longing for doing 'good' to others, especially for the least privileged in the society.

The creation of a 'well-ordered society' should, therefore, be the overarching purpose and rationale of a development policy that aims at instituting reforms that are just and good. One of its winning features would be that the 'principles of justice are public' and they 'characterize the commonly recognized moral convictions' held by the members of a society (p. 497). It would, therefore, be perfectly normal for members of a well-ordered society to act with 'deliberative rationality' from the standpoint of justice, above all else. Indeed, in such a society, it would not be rational to act unjustly and selfishly and to be 'a free rider whenever the opportunity arises to further his personal interests' (p. 499). Rather than be apathetic bystanders when the maelstrom of the moment calls for active participation, members of a well-ordered society will feel better off being allies in a common struggle for systemic change. The assumption here is that since the principles of justice and goodness are public and known to every member of the well-ordered society, she/he would normally adhere to what is regarded as normal behaviour rather than incurring the opprobrium of deviating from them. A cumulative effect of combining the principles of justice with the goodness of justice in a well-ordered society would be that in it 'institutions are collectively rational and to everyone's advantage from a suitably general perspective' (p. 497). And its members come to possess (and perhaps be possessed by) a sense of belonging to it, so that it endures over time and is expected to be 'stable' for that reason. One of the basic postulates of such a society is that its members will not be motivated by individual greed. This is because 'we cannot preserve a sense of justice and all that this implies while at the same time holding ourselves ready to act unjustly should doing so promise some personal advantage' [Rawls (1999), p. 498]. All this should help immensely the process of systemic change.

Four important implications of these observations need to be noted. Firstly, it is known that systemic change, which is the essence of successful development, requires making substantial readjustments in the existing *loci* of economic, social and political powers in the society—from the feudal class to the profit-making entrepreneurs and to the middle class. This is a tremendous challenge, which requires making institutional changes that lay the foundations of a society that is both 'good' and 'just'. Secondly, as noted above, sustaining growth at the highest possible rate is inconsistent with large-scale free riding by members of the society. In other words, one cannot lionize self-interest maximization as a way of life and still hope for rapid and well-directed development process. The reason is that making systemic transformation entails commitment to a national cause for extended periods of time. Thirdly, and this is fundamental, one cannot even explain growth and development, let alone social justice and structural change, without explicitly bringing moral motivations into the calculus of development policy. In particular, the dominance of self-interest principle would, in effect, preclude implementation of just development policy. For instance, as noted above, a development policy that aimed at miracle growth and required people making collective sacrifices for the good of the society tomorrow (in the form of achieving large saving and investment rates to finance Structural Transformation) will be impossible to implement without going all the way beyond self-interest maximization behaviour. Fourthly, the market system is inadequately prepared to regulate social life, and that it needs to be supported by some moral code or 'implicit social contract'. More generally, 'ethical behaviour is a socially desirable institution which facilitates the achievement of economic efficiency' [Arrow (1974), p. 354]. Indeed, without it the cost of running a capitalist system will be prohibitively high. On the other hand, moral values like trust, honesty, keeping one's contract, when internalized in a social system, can keep the cost of running a real-life economy much lower. It has been shown that a given output can be secured at significantly lower cost with moral considerations than without them [Reder (1979)].

22.2. Sen's General Principle of Consequential Evaluation

Chapter 13 set out Sen's Functioning-and-Capability analysis, which goes beyond the Rawlsian scheme of social cooperation in that it allows more room for a development-oriented policy. An important aspect of Sen's analysis is that public policy should be geared essentially to repairing the individual's capability deficits with a view to converting primary social goods or resources into personal well-being. Any meaningful egalitarian redistributive scheme must, therefore, give more to those with some physical disability than to able-bodied individuals. These themes find further elaborations in Sen's moral principle of 'Consequentialist Evaluation' (2000).The basic idea here is that, 'one must take responsibility for the consequences of one's actions and choices, and that this responsibility cannot be obliterated by any pointer to a consequence-independent duty or obligation' (p. 482).[2] The principle is quite general in its application—it is relevant for forming a proper evaluative perspective as well as to make informed judgments about specific actions and rules of conduct. An important aspect of the principle should be noted. Within the broader framework of consequentialism, one can legitimately talk of cultural and political rights without having to satisfy the stringent requirement of legal rights. Furthermore, unlike the liberalist disregard of the principle of responsibility, one can require that, 'others pay serious attention to their responsibilities in preventing harm and violation of freedoms and rights' (p. 502). In the present context, the implications of the principle for development policy should also be clear. It is that the government must be concerned with all the consequences of specific government policies for inclusive growth—those on growth, distributive justice and poverty alleviation as an irreducible policy package. The moral principle does not put restrictions on what the government should or should not be doing.

22.3. BEYOND THE SELF-INTEREST PRINCIPLE

The preceding analysis specifically noted the inconsistency of self-interest maximization with inclusive growth. It may be of some interest to elaborate a little on this theme. As noted above, the Human Development Paradigm would explicitly emphasize the essential 'irrationality' of a socio-economic order in which people are guided by self-interest maximization alone. Rawls (1999) sees the problem in the context of his concept of a well-ordered society discussed above: 'if it is a psychological law that individuals pursue only interests in themselves, it is impossible for them to have a sense of justice (as defined by the principle of utility)' (p. 399). The point is that without a sense of justice and the desire to do good to others and the society, no growth-promoting and justice-oriented social change can come about, much less sustained for long periods of time. It is, therefore, essential that, as noted above, the 'background institutions' are restructured to reflect people's desire to act justly. Even though Rawls did not extend his essentially moral ideas to development policy, such an extension is by no means far-fetched. It should be obvious that a broader explanation of human behaviour has the added advantage over a strictly individualistic approach of being able to explain a wider range of human motivation and relate them to the basic national and global developmental problems. Sen (1997b; 1999b) explicitly argues for a plurality of human motivation. For instance, commitment (defined in terms of a person consciously choosing a line of action that may lower her/his personal welfare because helping others is regarded socially as the most respectable thing to do) may well serve as a perfectly rational form of human behaviour—for it is only when 'you give of yourself that your truly give'.[3] Thus, it would be perfectly rational (being an integral part of the maximizing behaviour) to be guided by such considerations as: (a) social commitment and moral imperatives; (b) direct welfare effect (being swayed in ones choice by what others think of him doing a particular act); (c) following the conventional rules.

22.4. GENDER INEQUITY

If one were asked to choose one aspect of our socio-economic life that is regulated predominantly by moral considerations, the unambiguous answer would (or should) be gender equity. It is here that economic forces alone have failed to reduce gender inequities and where there is not much hope to do much, without at the same time, working over time to change the moral and cultural norms of traditionally male-dominated societies in the developing world. While one may debate the desirability of reducing inequality of income and wealth from the point of view of growth, the same is not the case with gender inequity, a reduction in which is most likely to be growth promoting besides making a society worth living. A direct and resolute programme of reducing gender inequality would, therefore, be one of the defining characteristics of the New Development Paradigm. An important consideration in this context is that many central aspects of gender inequity do not get addressed at all if one relies exclusively on improving the general economic conditions of the society. Indeed, there is evidence that steps taken to accelerate general development do not always make a significant impact on increasing female child survival. A more practical way to accomplish this objective is to increase female labour-force participation and literacy rates [Sen (1999b), p. 197]. Similarly, not necessarily related to the growth rate achieved, the fertility rate has declined sharply everywhere as a direct result of the expansion of family planning programmes and a greater involvement of women in economic activities (through granting micro-credit directly to women).[4] Indeed, a virtuous circle can be created if gender inequity is reduced directly; greater participation in economic activities lowers fertility which in turn leads to greater female participation in economic life; and both have an ameliorative effect on growth rates, poverty reduction and social justice. Conversely, a failure to do so can (and does) have the opposite effect of creating a vicious circle in which lower participation rates contribute to high fertility rates, which then compromise a country's growth rate, or at least abbreviates its 'spread effect'. In both cases, it is important to change the existing social institutions, long held ideas, prejudices and traditions that have defied a fair solution of the gender inequity problem.

22.4. (i). The Complexity of Gender Inequity

Having stated the general principles of gender equity, it is important to understand that such recognition is not by itself sufficient to achieve it. The reason is that gender inequity 'is not one homogenous phenomenon, but a collection of disparate and interlinked problems' [Sen (2001)]. An important aspect of this complexity resides in the deeply held social prejudices against women, which are taken to be obvious truths not open to detailed scrutiny. It is, therefore, not surprising that the great exponents of the equality between men and men have been deafeningly silent on the equality between men and women.[5] Indeed, the existence of such prejudices creates a kind of vicious circle that tends to perpetuate the fallen state of women; the existing prejudices against women often condition human thinking, including of women themselves about what they themselves are capable of doing. Their failure to fully participate in the life of the community even when the opportunity to do so presents itself then tends to perpetuate those biases.[6] What this means is that an effective advocacy of this aspect of social development through a reasoned dialogue should be an essential aspect of development policy.

22.4. (ii). The Plurality of Gender Egalitarianism

It is important to see that, as is the case with other important development issues, a pluralistic approach has a better chance of success in reducing gender inequity, if only because no single remedy can address the problem in a satisfactory fashion. To see the difficulties in comprehending the problem and designing public policy to address it, let us consider the following aspects of it. Firstly, the inequities that afflict women are many and varied and each one calls for separate policy action because of its sheer enormity.[7] Each type of inequity needs to be addressed directly and not indirectly by curing some other type of inequity. For instance, achieving success in mortality inequity by minimizing the discrimination against women in the provisioning of better nutrition and ensuring greater access to health facilities would not necessarily repair the damage done to them by natal inequity, which is a new and vicious form of gender bias. Similarly, equality with respect to seeking outside unemployment does not diminish the basic inequity with respect to household work; indeed, it adds to it. The solution to the problem is not just to let more women work outside their home; it also requires assigning to men some of the work that women are supposed to do with a view to equalizing the total burden of work at home and outside the home.

Secondly, family relationship is both cooperative as well as conflicting in all its manifestations. For instance, the fundamental decision of having one or more children, especially if the existing one is a girl-only family, the basic choice about rearing them in a particular way are best made cooperatively by both men and women. The intricacy of these decisions and the environment in which these are undertaken in order to minimize the tensions involved in taking them entails a 'cooperative conflict' situation [Sen (1990)]. As if to add to the complexity of the problem, an equitable distribution of the power to make decisions about the family (e.g., about the family size) between men and women is constrained by the success a society achieves in women empowerment and by the latter's sheer physical strength to carry on the burden of the household and that of outside employment.

Thirdly, there is the cruel problem of the 'missing women' in the sense of being dead because of the gross inequities in the distribution of health and related facilities [Dreze and Sen (1989)].[8] This is a truly tragic phenomenon that is related to the entire attitudinal make-up of the society in which both men and women play their respective parts. Thus, for instance, both contribute, at least so it appears, to perpetuating the prevalence of irrational son preference, and both must bear their share of responsibility.[9] Yet, even this apparently insoluble problem can become tractable if women come to enjoy the necessary freedom to find jobs outside their homes and have more free time at home as well. However, this matter is also not that straightforward because an increase in labour force participation tends to be negatively related to their income: as incomes fall; more women take outside work [Standing (1985)]. In other words, an increase in labour-force, participation rate is not invariably a sign of increasing women prosperity and independence. Related to the gender inequity issue is the phenomenon of the 'feminization of poverty'. This problem also is not easy to resolve because women typically work longer hours to attain the same level of well-being [Lipton and Ravallion (1995)].

22.5. Concluding Remarks

The most important point of this brief chapter is that the New Development Paradigm must be guided by an explicit set of moral principles. Indeed, this should be one of its defining characteristics. We have noted in Part II of this book that, for all its strengths, the Traditional Development Paradigm did not succeed (or more accurately, did not try to undertake the job) in laying out an explicit philosophical framework to support its essentially morally motivated agenda of systemic change. The Liberalist Paradigm ignored the problem mainly because of its inherent positivist orientation. This has perhaps been one of its major failings. The Anti-Liberalist Consensus is, at its best, in the pointing out the weaknesses of the Liberalist Paradigm but its contribution to an understanding of the development process is minimal. The Human Development Paradigm has been the first to spell out a consistent moral theory but it does not possess an adequate development theory. The New Development Paradigm should fill these gaps in our understanding by combining development and moral principles in a logically consistent fashion. It turns out that the principle of commitment to a national cause would add a powerful moral motivation for attaining high growth, poverty reduction and convergence with the developed countries.

NOTES

1. Solow (1980) explains: 'Wouldn't you be surprised if you learned that someone roughly of your status in the profession, but teaching in a less desirable department, had written to your department chairman offering to teach your courses for less money'.

2. More formally, the principle is stated as one of 'situated evaluation', which requires that, 'person making the choice cannot escape the necessity to take note of her own position *vis-à-vis* the actions and their consequences' [Sen (2000), p. 483]. This principle does not make extraneous demands, as the Utilitarianism does, that all consequences other than utility consequences should be ignored.

3. The quote in the text is from Khalil Gibran (1923): 'You give but little when you give of your possessions; It is when you give of yourself that you truly give' (p. 19).

4. One of the most striking cases that illustrate the power of directly involving women in economic activities on lowering the fertility rates is that of Bangladesh, where total fertility declined from 6.1 to only 3.4 in about fifteen years (between 1980 to 1996), as a direct result of the provision of the micro-credit.

5. Thus, Rousseau's famous declaration, 'Man was born free and everywhere he is in chains', obviously applied to men and *not* women. It is one of the ironies of human condition that this great exponent of human liberty, somewhat ungratefully to the woman who educated him, did not think much of equality between sexes. Then an intellectual giant like Nietzsche stated: 'God created woman. And boredom did indeed cease from that moment—but many other things ceased as well. Woman was God's second mistake.' While such views would now be regarded, what Russell characterized, as 'intellectual rubbish'; yet the hold of such openly biased nuggets of folk wisdom on public discussion and debate does not seem to have flagged much with the state of economic development.

6. There are many examples of such attitudes. For example, it is not uncommon that women, who when unmarried are given the best of education by their parents in the hope that it would help them lead an honourable life by taking outside employment, sometimes give in too easily, and sometimes under great pressure from the husband and his family not to take outside employment.

7. Sen (2001) identifies seven types of gender inequity. There is the mortality inequity as the mortality rates are typically higher for women than men in large parts of the developing world. Then there is the natal inequity because of son preference. To make life more difficult for women there are the basic facility inequity, the special opportunity inequity, the professional inequity, the ownership inequity, and, finally, the household inequity.

8. The figure for 'missing women' is arrived at by estimating the differential between the baby girls who are actually born with gender related discriminations, and that could be born without such discriminations. A rough measure of the differential is to take the woman-to-man ratio in sub-Saharan Africa of 1.022 and compare it with the actual ratio in a developing society. Thus, Sen (2001), on the basis of a female-to-male ratio of 0.93, arrives at a figure of 37 million for India and 44 million for China in 1986. For the world as a whole, the figure was then 100 million. Another estimate, by Klasen (1994), is 80 million.

9. Son preference on the ground that sons contribute to family income while daughters don't is irrational because, given equal opportunities, both perform equally well in this and other respects. Its continued existence even in advanced societies (because the son carries family name) is further evidence of its irrationality, in the sense that it is the outcome of long-held traditions rather than of reasoned argument. However, the desire to have a son out of a desire to have both sons and daughters (not all sons or all girls) is not a sign of discrimination against a girl child.

Part VII

A Recapitulation

23

Towards a 'Constructive' Development Policy

This book has traced the evolution of development policy since 1950, when the business of development began in right earnest, down to the present. It has put precise markers to identify the principal inflexion points—the three paradigms, that is—along the evolutionary curve of development policy in the last half a century or so. The general impression that emerges from this elaborate exercise is that the developing world today is better off than it was in the past partly due to the pioneering development efforts made in the first three decades of development and partly because of the human development advancements.[1] But this book also shows at length, that the overall picture could have been prettier still if the incidence of high growth and significant poverty reduction had been greater across countries and across income classes within countries and if the development policy had not undergone sudden change of course in the last quarter of a century or so.[2] In particular, the precipitate shift in the focus of development policy that the Liberalist Paradigm caused has generated an unbroken fog of confusion. It has replaced the great clarity of vision that the Traditional Development Paradigm suffused throughout the developing countries. The Human Development Paradigm has made invaluable contributions to development thinking, in part, by reviving some of the foundational traditional themes and partly by clarifying the moral basis of development policy. But it too has added its own quota of confusion by insisting that human development rather than maximizing the growth rate of per capita income should be the focal variable, strongly implying that the two objectives are either antithetical or that achieving the former objective would, of necessity, lead to a success in the latter. It is, therefore, high time that suitable changes were made in the form and focus of development policy. Part VI gives an outline of the proposed New Development Paradigm, which should make, as the British economist-mathematician Frank Ramsey put it, many things clearer about the development process without claiming to have made anything clear. Whether this effort can be characterized as a *tour de force* is for the readers to decide; but at least some modest success might have been achieved in highlighting, and resolving, the debilitating dilemmas of development policy that have bedevilled policy makers for nearly a quarter of a century. This chapter and the next present a bird's eye view of the major themes analyzed at length in this book.

23.1. Overarching Development Themes

Four overarching themes have dominated the evolution of development policy in the following chronological order: (a) The Traditional Development Paradigm aimed to maximize growth of per capita income associated with an essentially egalitarian systemic change; and it added a sense of infectious urgency so vital for consummating such a momentous enterprise. (b) The Liberalist Paradigm radically shifted the policy focus to 'sustainable' growth of per capita income within the binding constraints of macroeconomic stability and market-friendly reforms. (c) The anti-Liberalist Consensus proved that when markets are incomplete and information is imperfect (which is almost always the case in the real world), unfettered markets produce 'sub-optimal' solutions. It, therefore, rejected the market-only liberalist prescriptions and admitted the socially beneficial role of the state. (d) The Human Development Paradigm, on the understanding that income and wealth are only the means for achieving human happiness, has redirected development policy yet again to maximize human development by expanding social expenditures on education and health. To this end, it proposed a 'support-led', as opposed to the traditional 'growth-mediated', strategy of economic development. In order to break out of the labyrinth of confusing and confused thinking about development, this book has emphasized the need for a New Development Paradigm. It suggests that, as if to trap the light of development, the proposed paradigm should focus on maximizing a morally motivated 'inclusive growth' that pursues growth, equity and poverty reduction simultaneously.

Each of these paradigms is identifiable in terms of one or more of the focal variables, which define pretty precisely its worldview of a successful development policy. We, therefore, describe below the major landmarks in development policy in the last half a century or so from this point of view.

23.1. (i). Growth of per capita Income and Systemic Change

The initiation and maturation of the Traditional Development Paradigm marked the first, and most important milestone in the evolutionary journey of development policy. It correctly understood the key factors that accelerate economic growth, reduce poverty and facilitate the emergence of a strong middle class within the framework of reasonably egalitarian institutions. To this end, it departed from the *laissez-faire* and minimal government model of the colonial times and emphasized government-supported import-substituting industrialization to give priority to expanding the domestic market with a view to broadening the domestic production and export bases. This strategy was designed to achieve the highest feasible rate of growth of per capita income at the same time that it permitted a beneficial integration of the developing countries with the world economy. It aimed to achieve convergence with the developed countries to minimize an unhealthy dependence on foreign sources of supply. The Traditional Development Paradigm also understood the positive linkage between growth, greater equity (including gender equity) and poverty reduction. But, in the absence of an adequate consequentialist non-Utilitarian moral philosophy, its ostensible egalitarianism was not based on an elaborate moral philosophy; nor was it free from ambiguity about the conversion of growth into valuable functioning's and capabilities. However, the rather detailed analysis presented in Part II should have made it clear that, contrary to folk wisdom about the traditional view (which the Liberalist Paradigm has freely advertised); it definitely did not preach or practice bloody-minded 'growth-man-ship'.[3] It rather asserted that growth of per capita income was the fire that raged in the blood of development, and nothing worthwhile could be achieved without it. All empirical evidence suggests that the Traditional Development Paradigm was, by-and-large, successful in attaining high rates of economic growth with greater equity and reduced poverty wherever it was faithfully and imaginatively practiced. The best followers of the traditional policy—especially East Asia and China—have also managed to achieve a significant degree of convergence with the OECD countries.

23.1. (ii). Market Reforms, Macroeconomic Stability and 'Sustainable Growth'

In one of the most dramatic reversals of fortune in the history of ideas, a rather inglorious liberalist-engineered putsch 'dethroned' the Traditional Development Paradigm for its alleged scientific in-exactitude and complete disregard for efficiency considerations.[4] Therefore, the Liberalist Paradigm that ascended the 'throne' decreed that the pursuit of efficiency must take precedence over all other worthwhile objectives of development policies. The rationale for this directive was explained by pointing out that with its inbuilt policy-induced inefficiency, the traditional pattern of growth could not sustain in the long run because it purportedly made exorbitant demands on the developing countries' scarce capital resources. So it was that, inebriated with an idealistic fervour and proselytizing zeal, it sought to create a sort of Tinsel town of free-markets without, or at best minimal, government in which individual freedom to hold onto what he/she acquired or inherited without fear of state intervention reigned supreme. Since then, 'first-best' development policy has been routinely defined as the one that unquestioningly obeys market signals, religiously defends private property (of the rich in effect), punctiliously meets the requirements of strict macroeconomic stability, and dutifully lets the Law of Comparative advantage dictate the pattern of domestic resource allocation. For its romantic attachment to the first-best procedures regardless of their consequences for growth, equity and poverty reduction, the liberalist approach to economics sees reality as it should be (one that conforms to the axiomatically derived rules of utility maximization) [Hahn (1991); Malinvaud (1991)]. It confidently believes in the efficacy of the first-best procedures and probably relies on some kind of a mysterious 'placebo effect' to produce growth in all developing countries regardless of the stage of their development and the state of their institutional preparedness.

The present study argues that the Liberalist Paradigm has probably been right (though only up to a point) in emphasizing the need for guarding against macroeconomic instability, especially when it arises from grossly overvalued exchange rates and uncontrolled budgetary deficits.[5] But it has not been right in substituting 'sustainable' growth for the maximum growth of per capita income and for wilfully slowing down the engine of economic progress. And it has been dead wrong in insisting on the unlimited right to private property in the developing countries, irrespective of the structure of their economies and institutional set-up.[6] Also, its thinking on the vital social issues of distributive justice and poverty reduction has been rather primitive when not downright perverse. It is, therefore, not surprising that the list of its positive achievements is skimpy at best. True, it helped developing countries achieve a semblance of macroeconomic stability e.g., low inflation rates, budgetary and trade deficits and relatively undervalued (though not necessarily 'realistic') exchange rates But this feat has been achieved by killing the goose that laid the golden eggs—one that produced high, even miraculous, inclusive growth. Indeed, in this perspective, high growth is the enemy that must be watched; as soon its onset threatens to upset the apple cart of macroeconomic stability, it is interpreted as a sign that the economy is 'overheating' and must, therefore, be cooled down by restrictive monetary and fiscal policies. Furthermore, it has widened the inequalities of income and wealth within nations and between nations, increased the unemployment rate, and heightened income and non-income poverty. Its utter failure to lift Latin America out of the quagmire of an almost interminable stagnation is a telling proof, if any was needed, of the utter inadequacy of the Liberalist Paradigm to support a genuine development policy. The moral is that a demonstration of the scientific virtuosity of liberalist policies would not be enough to prove their relevance to the problems of development.

Strangely enough, for all its failures and the fact that the academic consensus has moved away from it, the liberalist creed still seems to dominate in the policy-making circles, which have no option but to slavishly accept what the international donors tell them is best for them. One may wonder why people should persist with a set of policies that have failed in practically every crisis-bitten country. Some have blamed it on the unholy alliance of wealthy individuals, corporate interests, and the religious right that has overtaken Western societies since the 1970s [Galbraith (1991)]. On the other hand, the international donors have accused the developing countries for not being steadfast enough in the implementation of painful structural adjustment. The most charitable explanation, which the present study prefers, is that having remained loyal for too long to a set of ideas, the liberalists consider it a perfidy to renounce their faith in its quintessential truth merely because it has led to some unsavoury consequences in the developing countries. Thus, even though ravaged by doubts, they still manage to keep the outward presence of seeming calm.

23.1. (iii). The sub-Optimality of Unfettered Markets

As if to prove the Newton's Third Law of Motion: 'to every Action there is always an opposite and equal Reaction', an anti-Liberalist Consensus was born at about the same time when the Liberalist Paradigm ruled the waves in the developing countries. It restated the classical case against unfettered domestic and global markets with all the theoretical finesse that neo-classical economists (rightly) demand and in a language that neo-classical economists understand. It showed that in all cases when information is imperfect or asymmetric, and markets are incomplete or liable to failure, the free-market solutions would be essentially improvable. What it means is that a well-focused state intervention can nearly always improve the efficiency of (unfettered) market outcomes in the real world. The liberalists make the counter-observation that government failure is always more damaging than market failure. But this is either a vacuous statement or a bad non-sequiter. The reason is that while there is an elaborate theory of market failure there is nothing similar to remedy government failure or one that proves that government failure is always worse than market failure [Stiglitz (1998)]. On the positive side, one of the most interesting aspects of the Anti-Liberalist Paradigm is the demonstration of the essential validity of the Structural Transformation and the Big-Push hypotheses of the Traditional Development Paradigm and their importance for both growth and equity. It makes clear that the failure of the market solutions does not always mean that the state must go out of its way to subvert the markets to achieve economic bliss. The aim should be to achieve a just milieu which judiciously assigns specific functions to each with a view to getting closer to the socially agreed objectives of development policy.

The anti-liberalist theoretical demonstrations have some important implications for development policy. Firstly, it has shown that there is no a priori case for privatization. Indeed, the circumstances when privatization can be so justified are nearly as restrictive as the ones required to prove universal market success. In other words, the efficiency of privatization must be established on empirical grounds, on a case-by-case basis. Available empirical evidence has also failed to establish the beneficence of the privatization worldwide. Instead, it shows that practically in every case, privatization has resulted in job destruction, without doing much to create new jobs. In worst cases, it has ended up in a gross wastage of national wealth in the form of public corruption, asset stripping on a scale before which the much-maligned rent seeking of the public-sector enterprises stands out as the acme of honesty [Stiglitz (2003)]. Secondly, they show that the liberalist case for trade liberalization, especially for capital-market liberalization, cannot be sustained regardless of the conditions prevailing in the developing countries. While the former has led them into a no-win situation *vis-à-vis* the developed countries, the latter has, in most cases, made it impossible for them to work with a sustainable exchange-rate regime. Also, there is not much credible empirical or circumstantial support for the liberalist insistence on export fetishism or for its unmitigated hostility towards import-substitution industrialization.

However, for all its scientific virtuosity, the Anti-Liberalist Consensus has failed to spell out a valid mechanism for growth and development, much less address the quintessential issues of economic growth, distributive justice, poverty reduction and convergence as an irreducible set of policy objectives. The demonstration of the inadequacies of the free-market solutions is not all that there is to guide development policy down the road to systemic change and economic prosperity. Above all, a development policy cannot be cast, as the Anti-Liberalist Consensus does, entirely in an antiseptically positivistic mould. It must rely as much on normative judgments based on socially accepted norms of human conduct as on engineering economic principles. Indeed, it can be stated that, the real task of development policy begins once it frees itself from the will o' the wisp of the market-versus-the government debate.

23.1. (iv). 'Human Development' and 'Support-led Growth'

For the purposes of the present study, the Human Development Paradigm has been defined more broadly than is customary; it includes, besides the UNDP

Research Programme, the entire non-Utilitarian consequentialist moral philosophy and the UN's several treaties and declarations. The purpose of this rather unconventional representation is to bring under one heading several related themes that together better explain the paradigm's basic purpose, salience and reach than what is contained each year in the UNDP's highly influential *Human Development Report*. In this more inclusive mould, the Human Development Paradigm has made an invaluable contribution to development thinking. With a view to putting the people 'at the centre of development', as Streeten (1981) has put it, it has corrected many of the excesses of the Liberalist Paradigm. Less convincingly, it has sought to replace the alleged 'commodity fetishism' of Traditional Development Paradigm with a focus on human development. Furthermore, of late, it has taken a correct, even humane, stand on global issues—in particular, about globalization—that have a direct bearing on the well-being of the developing countries. Of late, it has revived many of the traditional development themes e.g., the critical importance of expanding the domestic market through knowledge-creating import substitution, making use of selective (and temporary) import protection; and of the centrality of the dynamics of unequal exchange, which has made globalization a one-sided game of making the rich richer, and the poor poorer. But it must be stated that this part of its contribution is not strictly consistent with its paradigmatic vision, which is to de-emphasize commodity fetishism. At a methodological level, the Human Development Paradigm's greatest success lies in having developed an essentially pluralistic consequentialist non-Utilitarian moral philosophy, which has saved welfare economics from irrelevance to the welfare of the people. It has also put the immense insights of the normative public-choice theories at the service of development policy. In particular, it has rescued development policy from the deadly nihilism of the Arrowian impossibility theorem and demonstrated the practical 'possibilities' of the rather arcane and esoteric axiomatically derived social-choice procedures, so that one can 'talk about injustice and unfairness without having to face the accusation that such diagnoses must be inescapably arbitrary or intellectually despotic' [Sen (1999a), p. 365].

Regardless of the rather exaggerated nature of some of its claims, the Human Development Paradigm has been immensely successful in convincing policy-makers to greatly enhance social expenditures, i.e. the expenditure on health and education. While it has, mercifully, not cured the world of commodity fetishism, it has rightly argued that the pursuit of human happiness is not always synonymous with material plenitude (even though one wonders who has ever advocated that they are synonymous). It is also perhaps right in emphasizing the need for going beyond crass materialism to find human happiness in ascetic simplicity. Notwithstanding some of their theoretically blemishes, its basic empirically verifiable innovations—the HDI and GDI in particular—have changed development practice permanently, at least so it appears. Even more important than what meets the eye, beneath its apparently cool and calm moral principles, which the Human Development Paradigm displays as its mark of recognition in the realm of ideas, lurks the fierce and passionate longing for social change.

The Human Development Paradigm has advertised support-led strategy as one of its defining, indeed original, contributions to economic knowledge. In fact, it has turned out to be its Achilles heel. There is evidence that by virtue of its central recommendation that human development could be achieved directly not waiting for the forces of growth to gain momentum, it might have weakened them—most pointedly in countries where this recommendation has been implemented faithfully. This book shows at length that, though most valuable is the recognition of the somewhat obvious point that the growth of per capita income is only a means to achieve certain specified ends (many of them being non-monetary in nature); yet it does not render the pursuit of the fastest feasible growth of per capita income and distributive equity any the less urgent because income-related deficiency cannot always be offset by improvements in the literacy and longevity [Anand and Sen (2000)]. The Human Development Paradigm has, in effect argued that, given the knowledge that human happiness can be achieved less painfully, with lesser inputs of material acquisitions and in a shorter time, it is not rational to toil ceaselessly, enduring more pain and suffering than is absolutely necessary. This seems to make sense. On the other hand, one can argue that the proposed strategy aims to leave out the 'heartaches and nightmares' of life and retain only its 'wonderment and joy'. However appealing such an endeavour might be to one's epicurean sensibilities, the fact is that it is not always feasible to do so. It is the quiet urge to surge, rather than the lust for comfort and eternal bliss, that has moved human societies to their destiny. From this point of view, the support-led strategy might be accused of having contravened a 'historical' truth. More recently, Sri Lanka, Eastern European countries and Kerala perhaps tried to re-enact the celestial high drama (of grabbing the apple of their desires much too soon) and were duly penalized by low growth, high unemployment rates, morbidity and all that goes with it. As always, the truth lies between these extremist views. Development inevitably presents a thistle of difficult choices that must be made with full awareness of the painful trade-offs. It is neither wise to race full blast to achieve human development, ignoring the inevitable hardships of economic development, nor it is sensible to condemn oneself to a Sisyphus-like existence of eternal toil, if that can be avoided. The preferred course of action, which this book argues is perhaps the most productive of salutary results, is that one must aim to achieve the highest feasible growth rates and the associated institutional changes that distribute the fruits of economic progress equitably among the people. Achieving that requires making the inevitable sacrifices of present comforts for the sake of higher rate of inclusive growth. At the same time, it should be arranged that a progressively higher proportion of incremental income is made available for social expenditures so to facilitate a steady conversion of higher income into higher capabilities.[7] Fortunately, that seems to be the direction in which the Human Development Paradigm, though not very clear-headedly, has proceeded in practice.

23.1. (v). Maximal (Inclusive) Growth Leading to Systemic Change

One of the most fundamental elements of the proposed New Development Paradigm is an explicit statement of the factors that explain 'inclusive' economic growth; that maximal growth should be achieved within the framework of an egalitarian systemic change and that a generous provision is made for education, health and food security. However, maximal growth of per capita income is the engine that pulls the inclusive growth strategy over high hills and down deep valleys. It has been shown that a developing economy has a greater chance of achieving growth with macroeconomic stability and social justice if its per capita income consistently grows for long enough time at the rate in excess of 3 per cent. In practice, only the countries that could sustain a 4 to 6 per cent growth rate of per capita income for several decades have succeeded in reducing poverty in both absolute and relative terms.[8] To this end, the New Development Paradigm would explicitly recognize that maximizing the rate of Structural Transformation (i.e., increasing the share of industrial output as a percentage of GDP), savings and physical and human capital formation, are the essential building blocks of a durable edifice of widely shared economic progress. No less relevant is its contention that, while the income-creating role of exports is beyond doubt (indeed, this is true by definition); it is the expansion of the domestic market that has led growth in the developing countries.[9] It may be noted in this context that maximal industrial growth is not inconsistent with maximal growth of agriculture.[10]

An important general principle of the inclusive growth strategy is that development policy must be managed in a demonstrably efficient manner. The success of the development effort must be evaluated in terms of its contribution to achieving high rates of economic growth, greater distributive equity and poverty reduction as an irreducible set of policy objectives within the framework of democratic governance that allows individuals the freedom to choose freely the capabilities that one has reason to value from a range of alternatives. When this is done successfully, then, as Rawls (1999) put it, people will have the incentive to support such a system if and when it is threatened by internal dissension or exogenous shocks.[11] To this end, the privileged groups must be called upon to make sacrifices in times of economic difficulty. Such a complex economic manoeuvre implies, at the very least, that inequality of income and wealth is considered as morally wrong unless justified by reference to higher growth that promises to bring good to all.

23.2. CONCLUDING REMARKS

This book has argued that the time has arrived for a New Development Paradigm to change the focus of development policy yet again. It may be appropriate to conclude this chapter by addressing the following question: In what sense is the New Development Paradigm a really new paradigm? This is a fair question to ask because, in the strict sense of the term, it is probably not a paradigm. It does not represent a complete break from the past, nor does it prescribe an altogether new way of doing science. Instead, this book suggests that, in the spirit of making beneficial change in development policy, the new development perspective should essentially be a creative synthesis of the Traditional Development Paradigm and the Human Development Paradigm, adding for good measure, some of the basic, though obvious insights of the Liberalist Paradigm (that the inflation rate and the budgetary and trade deficits should not be allowed to get out of hand). And yet it can confidently claim that like all syntheses, it too would contain more information than its constituent elements possess. Freeing the mind from the influence of 'wrong ideas', it must aim to reclaim the lost path of high growth that did so much good to the developing countries, with the difference that its focus now would explicitly be on an information-rich, and morally motivated 'inclusive' growth, in the sense defined in Part VI. While making paradigmatic claims, the New Development Paradigm does not fail to acknowledge what is right in the preceding paradigms in the belief that there is nothing altogether new under the sun, and that it would be foolhardy to reject all that has been accomplished by the best minds in our profession. This 'generosity' of spirit would save it from wasting time, as the preceding paradigms have done, on differentiating the new from the 'old' ways of thinking and making exaggerated claims for having discovered some altogether new truths not divined before.

NOTES

1. In human development terms, the progress in the last fifty years or so has been unprecedented. 'Indeed, the past generation had yielded more development progress than any since the Industrial Revolution. Since 1960, life expectancy in poor countries had risen from 45 to 64. Since 1970, the illiteracy rate had fallen from 47 to 25 per cent. And since 1980 the number of poor people had fallen by about 200 million that is, at a time when the world population had increased by 1.6 billion' [Mallaby (2004), p. 295]. However, it may be noted that the average picture looks brighter, even in human development terms, only

if China in included, but is dismal if it is excluded. In the rest of the world, if China were excluded from the average picture then, 'the number of people living below the dollar-a-day line actually increased between 1987 and 1998, and not by a small number; 100 million extra people living in abject poverty over this period' (p. 270).

2. In paradigmatic terms it can be stated that the link between observed growth rates and poverty reductions has been weak in countries which observed the rules of the Liberalist Paradigm and the strongest in cases which did not follow the prescriptions of the Liberalist Paradigm. This point has been most convincingly demonstrated in [Stiglitz (2003); (2006)].

3. Gillis, Perkins, Roemer, and Snodgrass (1983) were probably the first ones to have coined the expression 'growth fundamentalism' for the Traditional Development Paradigm. See also King and Levine (1994) for this point of view.

4. Behrman and Srinivasan (1995) somewhat approvingly characterize the change of guards in the realm of development policy as 'dethronement of the dominant paradigm and the elevation, if not enthronement, of openness, competition and the market in development...' (p. 2468).

5. While Liberalist Paradigm's focus on maintaining a regime of macroeconomic stability is legitimate only if it is done within limits, one would be hard put to find any responsible practitioner of the Traditional Development Paradigm who argued otherwise.

6. It has been maintained that the Liberalist Paradigm understood the importance of institutional change [World Bank (2005)]. But this is only partially true because its understanding of institutional change was, and still is, confined to the creation of a legal infrastructure that would adequately safeguard individual amoral rights (in the liberalist sense of the term) to hold on to private property so long as it was acquired through the legally correct procedures of initial acquisition and exchange and if it allowed individuals the freedom to maximize their self-interest. However, this is not the sense in which the Traditional Development Paradigm and the Human Development Paradigm used the term, nor is it the sense in which the New Development Paradigm would use it.

7. Sen (1999b) argues: 'The support-led strategy is a recipe for rapid achievement of higher quality of life, and this has great policy importance, but their remains an excellent case from there to broader achievements that include economic growth as well as the raising of the standard features of quality of life' (p. 49). The argument in the text is to follow the growth-mediated strategy and then spend higher amounts on education and health. Perhaps, in practice these approaches might produce identical results; but that is not so certain.

8. The growth targets mentioned in the text are the observed average growth rates that Asian countries (including East Asia and China) achieved during 1965 to 2000. The 6 per cent growth rate is the miracle growth rate, which doubles per capita income in about eleven years. UNDP (2003a) shows that only the countries that sustained a growth rate of 3 per cent and above (all of which are located in Asia) have succeeded in reducing poverty in both percentage and absolute terms (p. 41).

9. Lewis (1955) set out clearly 'in the later stages of economic growth the dynamic role ceases to be monopolized by foreign trade, and may even pass from it altogether to the home market' (p. 282). Later on empirical studies have confirmed this insight (e.g., Chenery, Robinson and Syrquin (1986)).

10. Lewis (1955) explicitly stated that industrial progress is very much dependent on a fast growth rate of agriculture. However, the requirement that agriculture and industry should grow together does *not* mean that they 'have to grow at the same rate' (p. 278). The point is simple enough but has usually been missed in the usual critiques of the traditional development policy where the differential growth rates of agriculture and industry have been cited as evidence of a bias against agriculture.

11. This is exactly what actually happened when economic development in East Asia was threatened by the financial crisis in 1996–97. In South Korea people came out voluntarily to help the system out of its deepest crisis.

24

The Epilogue

An overarching theme of this book has been to emphasize the urgent need to pull development policy away from the cauldron of pointless controversies, which have by no means enhanced the prestige of the economic profession. Amidst these controversies, logical analysis has been replaced by ideological waffle. As a result, they have not let an informed dialogue on the existential development issues flower. An outstanding example of unhelpful controversies has been the somewhat disconcerting cacophony about what has been universally accepted as the foundational concern of development policy since Adam Smith namely, the maximization of the growth of per capita income in the inclusive sense and the set of policies that make it possible. Development experience should have taught academics and policy makers that there could be no paltering with the spirit of development. A wealth of empirical evidence, some of it cited in this book, has now become available to re-evaluate the development policies pursued so far. It shows rather conclusively that a lot depends on this single achievement: the likelihood of reducing poverty and increasing human development becomes stronger in a regime of high growth than in one marked by low or medium growth. It is a testimony to the economist's febrile mind that the pursuit of high growth has become a hotly contested bone of contention among them. As noted above, in the last quarter of century, development policy has been marked by extraordinary vicissitudes in the realm of thought and policy just because it has not accepted this obvious truth and all it implies (high rates of Structural Transformation, saving and physical and human capital formation etc.).

24.1. Continuity and Change

This book has argued that to have forsaken the high-growth path for whatever reasons has been a monumental mistake. It, therefore, strongly recommends that the interest of developing countries would be best served if development policy in future were spared the pangs of unnecessary paradigmatic change in the structure of development policy, unless the change is warranted by profound changes in the reality. As noted in Parts III to V of this book, two such 'change-of-course' announcements made within the last quarter of a century, have proved to be sand rather than lubricant in the wheels of economic progress. At first the liberal economists and then human development decided to try something altogether different. The Liberalist Paradigm argued that the pursuit of maximal growth could not be fruitful, so that development policy should aim instead to maintain a regime of macroeconomic stability that would, in time, generate 'sustainable' growth through some mysterious mechanism; but the Human Development Paradigm denies the very desirability of the pursuit of maximizing growth in per capita income. Following in the footsteps of Aristotle who exuded wisdom when few did (382–322 BC), it shifted analytical and policy focus to the pursuit of human development on the grounds that maximizing wealth and income itself was not the proper objective of human endeavour.[1] Fortunately, the total failure of the macroeconomic stability-first strategy in Latin America, which once boasted of miracle growth (especially in Brazil), and the economic stagnation in the wake of miraculous human development in Sri Lanka, Kerala and Eastern Europe seem to have blunted the point of either of these reforms.

24.1. (i). Is a New Development Paradigm Warranted?

This book has argued at length that rather than make unnecessary announcements about the advent of a new paradigm, one must aim at changing the surrounding institutions in an egalitarian mould that enhances the connectivity of growth, distributive justice and alleviate poverty. To this end, it must draw upon the existing stock of knowledge of the various facets of the development process and reinterpret it, if necessary, in the light of solid factual and empirical evidence. To illustrate the point, it would have been a grievous mistake if the Traditional Development Paradigm had not supplanted the outmoded patterns of thought and policies of an irrelevant colonial era. However, the same was not the case with the Liberalist Paradigm, which was ideologically inspired, based on perceptions unrelated to the reality in the developing countries. The only remarkable thing about it, however, is that perfectly sane economists have propagated its message with evangelical zeal. Regardless of what its intentions were, the outcome of implementing the Liberalist Paradigm has been to distort development thinking and derail the development process. Fortunately, along its development line, the real world seems to have intruded and it is now not as absolutist in its prognoses and policies as it used to be. Furthermore, the Anti-Liberalist Consensus and the Human Development Paradigm successfully exposed the weaknesses of the Liberalist Paradigm. The former practically destroyed its market-only rhetoric, exposed the weaknesses of the *laissez-faire* ideal and revived interest in some of the forgotten aspects of the Traditional Development; but it did not provide a satisfactory perspective on growth, much less inclusive growth.

The latter clarified the moral basis of economic development and highlighted the need for converting the increments in income and wealth into valuable functioning's and capabilities. However, it too went off the beam when it claimed to have discovered the most direct route to reach human happiness without, at the same time, putting in motion strong mechanisms to achieve the highest possible rate of inclusive growth to facilitate a speedy transformation of the ill-ordered societies into well-ordered societies.

24.1. (ii). Has the Time for a New Development Paradigm Arrived?

The question to be answered is: has the right time for inaugurating a new paradigm arrived? If the analysis of the competing paradigms presented in this book is valid, then the answer is in the affirmative. Firstly, considerable confusion exists regarding the direction of development policy. There are no agreed guidelines, say for achieving the Millennium Development Goals about reducing poverty. One just has to read the annual reports of international organizations like the WTO, the World Bank, the IMF, the UNDP, and UNCTAD to see the wide differences among the opinion makers about how to go about the problem. More often than not they agree only to disagree. The same is true of the wide divergence of opinion about maximizing growth and reducing distributive injustice. We have seen in the preceding chapters that, while their rhetoric is the same, the practical solutions they suggest do not suffice to address these problems in their fullness. Thus, their answers range from a strict compliance with the conditions of the Structural Adjustment Programmes, i.e. the maintenance of strict non-inflationary regimes, a clear definition of property rights, minimum government, and greater openness to greater expenditures on human development. And there are many more solutions that fall in between these polar extremes. We have analyzed at length, both, the irrelevance of some of the questions asked and the inadequacies of the answers given to these questions. A start must be made by cleaning up the Augean Stables in the realm of ideas—a task that this book has undertaken.

Secondly, this dominant opinion still seems to be that of the IMF and the World Bank. Two points may be noted in this connection:

(a) Contrary to the suggestions that, in practice, the Liberalist Paradigm has become irrelevant, the fact is that it is very much alive. For instance, one still encounters the magic-of-the-market argument: 'Once a developing country government establishes the rules of a fair game and ensures their enforcement, it will be advised to stand back and enjoy self-generating growth' [Roll and Talbot (2001)].[2] Nor have things changed at the global level. The rather unedifying debate on the Doha Round of Development has finally revealed the hidden hand of the liberalist forces (the MNCs in particular) working overtime to scupper every deal that might be even passably beneficial to the developing countries. Not only that; while the developed countries have insisted that the developing countries open up their markets to OECD imports, they have failed to give up their scandalously large agricultural subsidies and support to the sun-set industries in which the developing countries have a decided comparative advantage. The Structural Adjustment Programmes, wearing a 'human face', continue to do merrily what they have done in the past—promote sustainable (slower) growth, even if that has meant widening the gulf between the rich and the poor and causing much pain to the common man. It is still insisted with full force that developing countries must themselves carry the cross of their economic misfortunes and that it would not be beneficial to offer their exportable goods any preferential treatment and so on.

(b) There are those who, agreeing that liberalist thinking has not done much good, still propose alternative ways to reduce poverty that are different from it only in form rather than substance. Indeed, they may end up doing more harm than good to development efforts. Thus, for instance, there is a whole research industry working overtime to sell the idea of 'pro-poor growth' to the developing countries. There is nothing wrong with this apparently noble aim (growth should be pro-poor, the more the better); what is wrong is that it seeks to achieve this objective by reversing the direction of Structural Transformation. We have shown in this book that these suggestions are simply wrong-headed and that the proposed change of course of development policy would be counter-productive in the extreme and do a great damage to the developing countries' growth possibilities. There is, therefore, an urgent need to break the spell of liberalist thinking once and for all and offer an integrated vision of economic progress that is jolting as well as polished. The Anti-Liberalist Consensus has done that to the satisfaction of at least some of the neo-classical economists. The Human Development Paradigm has given strong support to some of these ideas. Those insights should help the New Development Paradigm to stake its claim for existence in the context of its programme of inclusive growth.

24.2. WHITHER THE WINDS OF CHANGE?

Before we conclude this chapter and the book, we may fruitfully recall, from Part IV some of the basic principles underlying the New Development Paradigm. It has been shown at length that the new paradigm must internalize the following lessons of successful economic and human development to initiate and sustain high rates of inclusive growth in the future. These matters have been discussed at length at different places in the book; but it may be of interest to recapitulate their highlights in this final chapter.

24.2. (i). The Quintessential Mystery of Development

Development experience testifies to the essentially mysterious nature of the development process, which renders sure-fire formulae based on the certainty of development outcomes useless for implementation. Many a path-breaking development outcome has emanated from areas and activities that could not have been anticipated in advance.[3] On the other hand, fastest growth and development have come about by implementing policies (in particular, the forbidden protectionist policies rather than the first-best market-oriented policies) that are routinely condemned *ex ante* as the surest way to development failure.[4] The liberalist development formulae and beliefs have already done enough damage to the developing countries. Fortunately, their star has expanded and collapsed as the cumulative result of increasingly disgruntled voices of reason. The developing world would, therefore, be better served if these seemingly well-intentioned ideas were quietly consigned to, what Bertrand Russell called, the heap of 'intellectual rubbish'.

24.2. (ii). The Moral Foundations

A successful development policy must achieve clarity with respect to the moral dimension of its basic structure. At the very least, it must not relinquish a basic sense of decency. In this context, New Development Paradigm must, like the Human Development Paradigm, explicitly state its moral stance on the foundational developmental issues. Needless to point out, the moral values it displays publicly would uncompromisingly insist on social justice and equality of opportunity in an essentially non-elitist social milieu. This book, following Sen (1998b), has argued that any analysis of the multi-faceted phenomenon of development would be incomplete without adding to it a non-Utilitarian and consequentialist moral and ethical perspective that saddles individuals with the consequences of the choices they voluntarily make and which is informed by an insatiable curiosity to transform human lives for the better. The aim should be to meet adequately the needs of the least-privileged on a priority basis within a just and fair socio-economic regime, which does not let the circumstances of birth and early nurture to influence an individual's future possibilities of economic and social advancement. In it, individuals would also have the freedom to choose between alternative 'capability sets' to lead a life of reasonable prosperity and happiness of their choice. A generous infusion of these ideas should make development policy intellectually enlightening and morally edifying and enthuse people to defend the system raised on these principles when exogenous shocks or endogenous strains test its viability.

24.2. (iii). Institutional Change

Development experience has brought into the sharp relief the need to 'get the institutions right'.[5] Emphasis on the creation of development-friendly institutions also illustrates the importance of the social and political context in which specific reforms have to be implemented.[6]

24.2. (iv). Focus on Unemployment

A litmus test of successful development policy is its contribution to a significant reduction in the unemployment rate. This is essential for the equity and efficiency of any economic system, the more so of a developing society. A corollary of this obvious observation is that a state of the economy in which high unemployment persists and endured must be rejected, both on moral and economic grounds.[7] It took Keynes to write his epoch-making 1936 book to show that tolerating high unemployment rate on the grounds that it was purely voluntary and that it could be cured by reducing wages was fundamentally an absurd idea. The fact is that it is still an absurd idea: in a world of asymmetric information and incomplete contracts, lowering wages would not cure unemployment even if markets were perfectly competitive, nor would it improve the efficiency of the economy. On the other hand, paying higher (efficiency) wage could add to the economy's productivity. But the moral argument against unemployment is no less potent; it is that the damage done to the withered lives of those thrown out of jobs for securing illusory efficiency gains is likely to be permanent and irreversible (those dying of hunger or committing suicide, a common phenomenon when unemployment is deep enough and lasts long enough, cannot be brought back to life once the economy improves). This is especially the case in developing countries, which do not have an elaborate social security system. The point is that in a well-functioning democratic market framework, a social contract (implicit or explicit) must exist between the government and the public. An integral part of this social contract is that the fruits of economic progress must be fairly shared through the creation of new employment opportunities and/ or by the generous provision of social safety nets; and that when economic progress gets stalled for whatever reasons, then the answer should not be to safeguard the interests of the rich and let the misery of the poor increase through falling wages and rising unemployment.

24.2. (v). Gender Equity

A fruitful development policy must focus on removing gender inequity, if not altogether eliminating it. This point needs emphasis because if there is a case where growth does not 'trickle down' it is with respect to gender equity. Most depressingly, its incidence has not decreased even in cases where stellar growth with distributive equity has been attained. This observation also applies to the goal of poverty reduction on a durable basis, because 'feminization of poverty' is widespread in developing countries, which also exposes female members of the households to extra health risks. Once again, the moral argument against gender inequity should be decisive: a society that tolerates injustices against women and denies them their appointed agency role (as active decision takers in a milieu of social change) no matter on what grounds cannot deem itself civilized.

24.2. (vi). Access to Food

A durable social contract between the state and the people should, among other things, also explicitly recognize the fundamental human right to a minimum of sustenance (especially to food) both at the national and global levels. This recommendation is highlighted here because the UNDP's Research Programme does not include universal access to food as one of basic elements of human development. This omission is all the more surprising because the International Covenant on Economic, Social and Cultural Rights (1976) and the UN's Millennium Declaration (2000) have mandated universal access to food, which, in order of priority comes before all else for upholding human dignity and development.

24.2. (vii). Efficiency and Growth Trade-off

There seems to be a fair degree of consensus that it would not be wise to expect many growth points to flow from the removal of price distortions alone, as some of 'neo-classical development economists' once insisted. Reliable empirical evidence shows that liberalist reforms focusing on this aspect have rarely produced numbers in excess of one-to-two percentage points of the GDP [Srinivasan and Whalley (1986)]. Indeed, there are cases where distortions were reduced and output fell and where output increased notwithstanding the distortions. Latin America and Eastern Europe are instances of the former, and China and East Asia those of the latter. Whence it follows that 'reducing distortions—whether by planning or by eliminating market-induced distortions—is neither necessary nor sufficient conditions for sustained growth' [Hoff and Stiglitz (2001), p. 439]. The point is that tolerating some (static) inefficiency for the sake of higher growth and (dynamic) welfare gains is, as the Traditional Development Paradigm insisted, the only sensible development policy. That is how high economic growth rate has historically been secured in one country after another, including the East

Asian miracle growers; this is how the battle for growth will be won in the rest of the developing countries.

24.2. (viii). Physical and Human Capital

Of direct interest to development policy is the new endogenous growth theory's demonstration of the positive contribution that human capital and knowledge-creation activities—both of which are subject to increasing returns to scale—can make to economic growth.[8] This has been an important contribution, but its basic limitation is that it makes development success turn only, or mostly, on achieving the desired rates of human capital and knowledge formation.[9] This is obviously an incomplete point of view because it ignores the critical importance of high rates of physical capital formation to economic development. Indeed, both human capital and physical capital formation have had a crucial role to play in the development process. Contrary to the popular view, that extra human capital formation made the difference between the growth accomplishments of East Asian miracle growers and the non-East Asian slower growing economies, the fact is that unprecedented physical capital formation played an even more decisive role in the former than in the latter. Extensive regression exercises, some of which have been reproduced in this book, confirm this point of view.

24.2. (ix). Inevitability of Government Intervention

The New Development Paradigm would support balanced and mutually supportive role of the government and the markets, without wasting any more time on the sterile market versus the government debate that has raged since the official launching of the Liberalist Paradigm in the 1980s. The Anti-Liberalist Consensus has made it abundantly clear that the propositions about the un-improvability of the market-only solutions are neither theoretically plausible nor empirically verifiable. At any rate, the market-only remedies have become totally ineffective in a world dominated by multi-nationals, especially by Bechtel, Chevron, Halliburton and Lockheed Martin. The best thing to do now is to recognize the obvious fact that both government and market failures occur routinely in the course of economic development. In each case, there is always room for making Pareto-improvements that would hurt only a small group of (privileged) people while making everyone else better off. True, in cases where this small group of people is influential enough to block the initiation of such Pareto-improvements, government intervention may entail some rent seeking. But that is not an argument for minimizing government or for crowding it out of the development business altogether, if only because significant rent-seeking activity goes on in the private sector as well [Edlin and Stiglitz (1992)]. Thus, one of the jobs of a socially committed and people-friendly state would be (as it has been) to minimize through effective state legislation the incidence of 'fraud' in the private sector that feeds on asymmetric information between different economic agents. The size of the government has to be decided by reference to the magnitude of the development job it must perform for the people, for all the people. It would vary from country-to-country, partly depending on the effectiveness of market institutions. It would, therefore, be more realistic to regard the government 'as an integral element of the economic system, functioning sometimes as a substitute for, and at other times, as a complement to other institutional elements' [Meier (2001), p. 34]. The fact is that the government has played a catalytic role in helping the societal transformation of rural economies into urban industrialized economies by making large investments in the creation of physical and social infrastructure, and in education and research and other public goods and, also, in promoting scientific discoveries, the fruits of which have historically been provided to the society free of charge. This was done in the now developed countries (especially in the United States) and has more recently been done in the fastest growing developing countries. There is no reason why the rest of the developing world should be denied the opportunity to develop with active government support.

24.2. (x). Import Substitution and Export Expansion

For reasons just stated, a fruitful development policy would have little time for the unseemly intellectual mud-slinging that has gone on since 1980 about the relative merits of import substitution versus export expansion policies, for continuing the unending discussions of the rent-seeking characteristic of import substitution regimes, and for giving credence to the overly exaggerated claims about the great advantages of liberalization of trade and capital flows and privatization. A balanced (and maximal) growth of the economy has, historically, required a steady expansion of the domestic market through import-substitution activities while not neglecting to seek out external markets for the higher value added goods that such activities come to produce in time. At any rate, the problem now is not that developing countries should adopt export-orientated policies, because that has, by-and-large, been done—and in many countries, overdone.[10] The problem for them now is: having achieved their first-best status under duress, what should they do with it, given that Western protectionism remains green as ever; and the WTO's rhetoric that it has provided an even playing field for the developed and the developing countries remains just rhetoric. Thus, without prejudice to the on-going export-expansion activities, knowledge-creating import substitution must be accepted as a permanent feature of the development process, with a focus on promoting innovation and technological change and exploring new areas of comparative advantage for the developing countries. That is how human societies, including the Western societies, have progressed in the past; this is how they will grow in economic strength in the future.

24.2. (xi). Inflation, Exchange Rates and Economic Growth

An important element of the proposed development policy should be to maintain a balanced stance on containing inflation in a manner that does not hurt growth and employment creation. The liberalist worry about inflation is not entirely unjustifiable. Development experience in the last forty-five years or so shows that there is not a single case of a developing country in which high growth has been associated with very high rates of inflation on a sustained basis (see Figure 8.1). However, this observation does not necessarily support the liberalist contention that low inflation rates are always, or mostly, associated with high rates of economic growth. Indeed, there have been as many cases of low growth and low inflation (e.g., India, Pakistan, and Kenya) as there have been of low inflation and high growth (e.g., Singapore, and Malaysia). The lesson to be learnt from these real-life experiences is that a low inflation rate is best maintained within the context of a strongly growing economy. Yet another issue, forcefully brought to notice by the Liberalist Paradigm, is that exchange rates should be maintained at a realistic rate, even though it is not always obvious as to where to draw a line under an objectively determined exchange rate.[11] The empirical evidence from Asia during the last forty years or so seems to support the claim that devaluations have had a positive impact on economic growth [Rodrik (1995); Naqvi (2002)]. But it is also common knowledge that the market exchange rates often reflect the effect of speculative factors unrelated to the true opportunity cost of foreign exchange, which mostly remains shrouded in mystery. Indeed, the possibility of devaluation sometimes creates a moral hazard type of phenomenon—it tends to strengthen the speculative forces that lead to devaluation. The destabilizing role of rapid capital-market liberalization on the development effort, which is often imposed as a conditionality of the IMF loans has been noted in this context.

24.2. (xii). Globalization

One of the most important challenges that development policy has faced in modern times is to adopt a winning strategy to deal with the reality of globalization. For a phenomenon as divisive as globalization, it is only wise to fall for a one-sided triumphal picture of the good that globalization has allegedly done, or would do, to the developing countries in particular. The fact is that globalization today is not much different from the *laissez-faire* doctrine that the Keynesian Revolution discredited long ago. What is presented today as an unmitigated good—the liberalist claim that globalization has unquestionably led to high growth and lower poverty worldwide—was correctly seen in the first half of the twentieth century as no more than a projection of the British national interests.[12] In today's world, the situation has grown only worse. Free trade and liberalization are widely regarded today as re-colonization by another name in order to tighten the control on the developing countries' natural resources (especially, oil). Its consequences for the developing countries have been no less disastrous [Juhasz (2006)].[13] Hence, as in the past, it would not be wise to regard globalization as an unmixed blessing for all nations and peoples. Indeed, an unlimited faith in it signifies a kind of intellectual retrogression and a lack of concern for a fair sharing of the gains from international trade and investment. A particularly disturbing downside of globalization has been the marginalization of the unskilled labour in both the developed and developing countries as skill upgrading takes place. Rather than sing paeans of glory of globalization, it must, therefore, be admitted that it has strengthened the dynamics of unequal exchange, widened inequalities of income and wealth between the developed and developing countries, and impaired the latter's capacity to grow to their 'full complements of riches'.[14] Even worse is the case of the impoverishment of sub-Saharan Africa, where the brute struggle for the barest existence has been waged in its meanest form. A corollary of the point just made is that 'the end of *laissez-faire*' should be accepted without any reservations; which also means that it be rejected as a basis for organizing international relations.[15] This recommendation sounds more revolutionary than it in fact is because *laissez-faire* has never been the flagship of world economic system, not even in the nineteenth century that is regarded by some as the Golden Age of *laissez-faire* [Gordon (1971)].

24.3. CONCLUDING REMARKS

It follows from analysis in Part V of this book that the New Development Paradigm would exclude: the Traditional Development Paradigm's lack of clarity about the moral foundations of development policy; the Liberalist Paradigm's unrepentant lionizing of macroeconomic stability in a rather absolutist vein; the Anti-Liberalist Consensus's pedantic claim that development is all about a demonstration of the inevitability of market failure in a wide variety of situations; and the Human Development Paradigm's overarching vision that the Holy Grail of human happiness can be grasped just by making higher social expenditures on education and health, and that doing so will also generate fast enough growth rate required for sustaining the highest achievable rate of human development. But the New Development Paradigm does not reject all that has gone before in order to establish its paradigmatic credential. It would separate the charisma of new ideas of the previous paradigm from the ensuing chaos that their overzealous implementation caused. To this end, it will borrow: from the Traditional Development Paradigm, its basic understanding of the factors that make developing countries move at the fastest possible speed down the road to economic progress with an undivided focus on poverty reduction and a reasonable degree of distributive justice; from the Liberalist Paradigm, its emphasis on fiscal prudence to keep inflation within moderate limits; from the Anti-Liberalist Consensus's pioneering contributions, a clearer understanding of the limits to market success; and from the Human Development Paradigm, the overarching emphasis on human development as a basic development objective in its own right. Having assimilated these desirable aspects of the preceding paradigms, it would then make its own contribution. It would push for inclusive growth as the surest way out of the extant intellectual malaise, both at the theoretical and policy-making levels, and emphasize that human dignity cannot be separated from the quest for material well-being as long as it is morally sound and contributes to enhancing human happiness. Whatever might be the form or shape of economic progress, economic growth must burn brightly and crackle cheerfully like it does in a grate.

To achieve agreed social ends, development theory must reflect an uncanny understanding of reality and of what it takes to change it for the better. This is fundamental because, historically, intellectual advancement and material progress have occurred each time, economic theories displayed a deep understanding of real-life problems. The Keynesian Revolution in the 1930s, which aimed to save capitalism from itself and the establishment of Development Economics in the 1950s in response to meeting the colossal challenges of the post-colonial times are the two outstanding recent examples of the brilliant success of socially oriented research programmes in transforming the lives of the common men and women within a generation as well as making a solid contribution to the endogenous growth of economic science. Unfortunately, since 1980 intellectual fuzziness has beclouded development dialogue. Not only that, the spontaneous, doctrine-less individualism, driven solely by a religious belief in selfishness and greed and an irrational emphasis on possessing rather than giving, has done incalculable harm to the possibilities of human advancement. The slow grind of the vicious circle of poverty has been at work in the developing countries felled by liberalist policies at the domestic and global levels. This dangerous drift into the abyss should be resolutely checked and reversed. We must bring clarity of vision to our development endeavours and go for the 'summits of minds' that the founders of development economics had spanned half a century ago. With wisdom and unremitting sense of destiny and public service, an essentially multi-dimensional development policy, which highlights the togetherness of its various elements, as well as the spaces between them, must tackle the existential problems of economic and human development. To this end, the domestic and world markets must be confined and conditioned to serve the larger good of the developing societies. Efficiency and distributional correctives should be applied in order to ensure that the world socio-economic system does not capsize by the unrelenting fury of untamed markets. And moral correctives are required so that achieving steady increases in economic prosperity does not push the frontiers of demand into a terrain where the rich person's gain is the poor person's loss.

A lot is at stake. This is no time to use misleading idioms like 'collateral damage' to paper over the ugly reality in the developing countries. If there was ever a time to make a fresh start to think logically and practically about the development prospects of the majority of humankind, it is here and now. Economic development is difficult enough even when guided by 'right' policies but with 'wrong' ones success is most unlikely. The New Development Paradigm must, therefore, steer clear of both wild exaggeration and outright self-deception about the precarious nobility of conventional wisdom, which is nothing more than a subterfuge for advancing the interests of the privileged. It must strive instead, for the economic prosperity of the people—of all the people. If that takes turning the existing unjust social institutions upside down, then let the inevitable be done. After all, economic development is a matter of creative destruction, of a fundamental change in the structure of values that sustain human societies and of a revolution in thought and action that renders the most appealing traditional ideas socially unacceptable. Holding a lantern across the divide between unimaginable opulence and abject poverty, it must aim to illumine social consciousness about the many injustices of human condition that have darkened the face of the developing societies.

The great eleventh century poet-philosopher and mathematician, Omar Khayyam, perhaps summarized our present economic and moral predicament, and the way out of it, with his inimitable brevity:

Ah Love. Could you and I with Him Conspire?
To grasp this sorry Scheme of Things entire,
Would not we shatter it to bits, and then
Remould it nearer to the Heart's Desire. (Page 200)[16]

NOTES

1. Aristotle reportedly laid down in his *Nichomachean Ethics*: 'Wealth is not the good we are seeking; for it is merely useful and for the sake of something else' [cited in Sen (1999b)]. Following Sen, practically every UNDP *Human Development Report* has repeated the Aristotelian wisdom. While Aristotle's advice must have made sense in his time when prolonged economic stagnation spanning centuries was common, and the only way to increase wealth was through wars and usurpation of poor people's property, it does not now when earning wealth is not an entirely ignoble occupation. Indeed, it did not make sense even to Adam Smith in 1776. A highly prominent moral philosopher as well, he talked explicitly about increasing the wealth of nations as the primary occupation of economists. All that this somewhat strange practice shows is that economists can be as antediluvian as they please.

2. Williams (2001) makes a similar point. He argues for a minimum government and giving maximum incentive to private initiative to revive growth in the developing countries.

3. This was the basic point of Hirschman's unbalanced growth hypothesis (1958) namely, that new and unexpected opportunities of investment arise as part of the dynamics of development and call for new entrepreneurial initiatives. Much earlier, Schumpeter (1934) had also made a similar point.

4. It has been noted: 'the world's most successful economies during the last four decades prospered doing things that are more commonly associated with failure is something that cannot be easily dismissed' [Hausmann and Rodrik (2003), p. 605)].

5. Stiglitz (2003) gives a graphic description of the havoc that market-friendly policies— stabilization/liberalization/privatization programme—have inflicted upon the transition economies. The social cost of enforcing sure-fire market remedies without creating the supporting institutional infrastructure has been staggering by any reasonable standard of evaluation. The programme to set Russia on the path to economic progress has turned out to be the recipe of its precipitate decline. In particular, 'privatization and the opening of the capital markets led not to wealth creation but to asset stripping' (p. 144).

6. North (1994, 1997) has emphasized the need for 'getting the institutions right', as a precondition for 'right' prices doing their job. It is interesting to recall that, long before North, the Traditional Development Paradigm emphasized the need for creating growth-promoting institutions. Arthur Lewis (1955) devotes a whole chapter to spell out the various types of institutions and institutional constraints that block or facilitate economic growth. He states: 'Institutions promote or restrict according to the opportunities they provide for specialization, and according to the freedom of manoeuvre they permit' (p. 57).

7. It may be noted that, contrary to liberalist thinking, unemployment does not denote an efficient state in the Paretian sense. The reason is that there is room for making Pareto improvements in economies that are characterized by incomplete markets, efficiency wages unemployment (all of which deviate significantly from the textbook competitive model of a market economy). It follows that the existence of unemployment cannot be explained away as being consistent with economic efficiency (i.e., it is efficient for the economy to live with unemployment rather than spend resources on finding jobs for the unemployed) [Greenwald and Stiglitz (1986)].

8. In fact, the Traditional Development Paradigm emphasized the centrality of the human capital formation to economic growth much earlier. The real contribution of the new theory lies elsewhere. It is to have pointed out the mechanisms for 'the diffusion and adoption of new goods and technologies in a developing country' [Bardhan (1995), p. 2992].

9. It is interesting to note that much reinventing of the wheel has taken place here: the authors of the Traditional Development Paradigm had explicitly highlighted the growth-promoting role of knowledge creation. The reader is referred to Chapter 4 of Lewis (1955) for an explicit statement of the role of knowledge creation in the process of growth. Indeed, he

assigns to acquisition of knowledge no less importance than he does to capital accumulation. He however, was careful to recognize both physical and human capital formation as contributors to growth.

10. The overdoing of export orientation in many countries (including East Asia after the 1996/97 crisis) as a source of growth has exposed these countries to exogenous shocks; and in Africa it has had negative effects on its development efforts.

11. An important reason for avoiding overvalued exchange rate is that Dutch Disease prevents the growth of the non-traditional exports. Furthermore, it would not let the process of structural transformation go much beyond the most protected activities. Thus, for instance, overvalued exchange rates would make import of machinery cheaper. Similarly, they would not justify the setting up of such industries domestically. The latter option would not, however, be beneficial to developing countries because these industries generate economies of scale.

12. Robinson (1962) pointed out: 'Free trade doctrine itself, as Marshall shrewdly observed, was really a projection of British national interests' (p. 119); that the Keynesian Revolution broke through the pretended internationalism of the free trade doctrines' (p. 121); and that, 'the variety of problems that face other nations and the abandonment of the pseudo-universalist Free Trade doctrine, is a great advance in enlightenment' (p. 121).

13. Juhasz (2006) shows that free markets and free trade are integral parts of the Pax Americana Project.

14. For a detailed analysis of globalization and its impact on various aspects of economic and human development see [Naqvi (2006/2004)].

15. The *End of Laissez-Faire* is the title of Keynes's book, reproduced in (1971–73). It shows that the nineteenth century doctrine never served the world's interests and that minimum government never formed the basis of political consensus even then.

16. The lines in the text are from *Rubaiyat (Quatrains) of Omar Khayyam* translated by Edward Fitzgerald (1980). Omar Khayyam was born in the latter half of the eleventh century and died in the first quarter of the twelfth century.

Bibliography

Abramovitz, Moses (1952), 'Economic Growth', in a *Survey of Contemporary Economics*, Vol. 2, B.F. Haley (ed.), Homewood, Illinois: Irwin for American Economic Association.

Abramovitz, Moses (1992), 'The Search for the Sources of Growth: Areas of Ignorance, Old and New', *Journal of Economic History*, 53 (2 June), 217-43.

Adelman, Irma (1978), Redistribution before Growth: A Strategy for Developing Countries, Inaugural Lecture for the Cleveringa Chair, Leiden University, The Hague: Martinus Nijhof.

Adelman, Irma (1989), 'Nineteenth-Century Development: Experience and Lessons for Today', *World Development*, 17(9), 1417-32.

Adelman, Irma (1997), 'Editorial: Development History and its Implications for Development Theory', *World Development*, 25(6), 831-840.

Adelman, Irma (2001), 'Fallacies in Development Theory', in G. Meier and J.E. Stiglitz (eds.), *Frontiers of Development Economics*, New York: Oxford University Press.

Adelman, Irma and Cynthia Taft Morris (1973), *Economic Growth and Social Equity in Developing Countries*, Stanford: Stanford University Press.

Adelman, Irma and Sherman Robinson (1989), 'Income Distribution and Development', in Chenery, H. and T.N. Srinivasan, *Handbook of Development Economics*, 2, New York: North Holland.

Aghion, P., E. Caroli, and C. Garcia-Penalose (1999), 'Inequality and Growth Theories', *Journal of Economic Literature*, Dec (37), 1615-60.

Ahmad, Ehtisham and Athar Hussein (1989), 'Social Security in China: A Historical Perspective', The Development Economics Research Program, London School of Economics CP # 4.

Akerlof, George (1970), 'The Market for Lemons', *Quarterly Journal of Economics*, 84(3), 488-500.

Alesina, Alberto and Dani Rodrik (1994), 'Distributive Politics and Economic Growth', *The Quarterly Journal of Economics*, 109(2), 465-90.

Ali A. Ali and Ibrahim A. Elbadawi (2002), 'Poverty in the Arab World: The Role of Inequality and Growth', in Ismail Sirageldin (ed.), *Human Capital: Population Economics in the Middle East*, UK and Cairo: I.B. Tauris and The American University in Cairo Press, 62-95.

Amsden, Alice (1989), *Asia's Next Giant: South Korea and Late Industrialization*, New York: Oxford University Press.

Anand, Sudhir, Amartya Sen and R. Kanbur (1985), 'Poverty under the Kuznets Process', *The Economic Journal (Supplement)*, 95, 42-50.

Anand, Sudhir, Amartya Sen and R. Kanbur (1993), 'The Kuznets Process and the Inequality-Development Relationship', *Journal of Development Economics*, 40, 25-52.

Anand, Sudhir and Amartya Sen (2000), 'The Income Component of the Human Development Index', *Journal of Human Development*, 1(1), 83-106.

Aristotle (1980), *The Nichomachean Ethics* (Translated by D. Ross), Oxford: Oxford University Press.

Arrow, Kenneth (1951), *Social Choice and Individual Values*, New York: John Wiley and Sons (2nd edition in 1963).

Arrow, Kenneth (1972), 'Gifts and Exchanges', *Philosophy and Public Affairs*, 1(4), 343-63.

Arrow, Kenneth (1973), Some Ordinalist Notes on Rawls Theory of Justice, *Journal of Philosophy*, May, 70, 245-63.

Arrow, Kenneth (1974), 'Limited Knowledge and Economic Analysis', *The American Economic Review*, 61(1), 343-63.

Arrow, Kenneth (1979), 'The Property Rights Doctrine and Demand Revelation under Incomplete Information', in Michael J. Boskin (ed.), *Economics and Human Welfare: Essays in Honor of Tibor Scitovsky*, New York: Academic Press Inc, 23-39.

Asian Development Bank (2003), *Key Economic Indicators of Developing Asian & Pacific Countries*, ADB: Manila.

Asterio, Dimitrios (2006), *Applied Econometrics: A Modern Approach Using Microfit and E-views*, London: Palgrave, Macmillan.

Aw, B.Y. and G. Batra (1994), 'Productivity and the Export Market: A Firm-level Analysis', The University of Pennsylvania (Memo).

Balassa, Bela and Associates (1971), *The Structure of Protection in Developing Countries*, Baltimore: John Hopkins Press.

Balassa, B. (1978), 'Exports and Economic Growth: Further Evidence', *Journal of Development Economics*, 5, 181-190.

Balassa, B. (1981), 'Adjustment to External Shocks in the Developing Countries', World Bank Staff Papers, No. 472.

Balassa, B. (1988), 'Interest of the Developing Countries in the Uruguay Round', *The World Economy*, 11, 39-54.

Baldwin, Robert E. (1956), 'Patterns of Development in Newly Settled Regions', *The Manchester School*, XXIV, 161-79.

Baran, Paul (1957), *The Political Economy of Growth*, New York: *Monthly Review Press*.

Bardhan, Pranab (1988), 'Alternative Approaches to Development Economics,' in Hollis B. Chenery and T.N. Srinivasan, *Handbook of Development Economics: I*, Oxford: North Holland, 39-71.

Bardhan, Pranab (1993), 'Economics of Development and the Development of Economics', *Journal of Economic Perspectives*, 7(2), 129-42.

Bardhan, Pranab (1995), 'Contributions of Endogenous Growth Theory to the Analysis of Development Problems: An Assessment,' in Behrman and Srinivasan, *Handbook of Development Economics*, III b, Amsterdam: Elsevier Science B.V.

Bardhan, Pranab (1996), 'Efficiency, Equity and Poverty Alleviation: Policy Issues in Less Developed Countries', *Economic Journal*, 106(438), 1344-56.

Barro, Robert J. (1993), 'Losers and Winners in Economic Growth', *World Bank's Annual Conference on Development Economics*, Washington: D.C.: World Bank.

Barro, Robert J. (1997), *Determinants of Economic Growth: A Cross-country Empirical Study*, NBER Working Paper No. 5698, Cambridge, Mass: National Bureau of Economic Research.

Barro, Robert J. and Xavier Sala-i-Martin (1995), *Economic Growth*, New York: McGraw-Hill.

Bauer, P. and B.S. Yamey (1957), *The Economics of the Underdeveloped Countries*, Chicago: University of Chicago Press.

Bauer, P. and B.S. Yamey (1984), 'Remembrance of Studies Past: Retracing First Steps', in Meier, G.M. and Dudley Seers, *Pioneers in Development*, New York: Oxford University Press (for the World Bank), 27-43.

Baumol, William (1986), 'Productivity Growth, Convergence and Welfare: What the Long-run Data Show', *American Economic Review*, 76(5), 1072-85.

Baumol, William (1991), 'Towards a Newer Economics: The Future Lies Ahead', *The Economic Journal*, 101:104, 1-8.

Baumol, William (2002), *The Free Market Innovation Machine*, Princeton N.J.: Princeton University Press.

Bebchuck, Lucian, Jesse Fried and David Walker (2002), 'Managerial Power and Rent Extraction in the Design of Executive Compensation', *University of Chicago Law Review*, (cited in *The Economist*, 13-19 July 2002, p. 64).

Begwell, Kyle and Robert W. Staiger (1999), 'An Economic Theory of GATT', *American Economic Review*, 89(1), 214-248.

Behrman, J. and T.N. Srinivasan (1995), *Handbook of Development Economics*, Vol. III-b, New York: Elsevier Science B.V.

Bell, Clive (1990), 'Development Economics', in John Eatwell, Murray Milgate and Peter Newman (ed.), *Economic Development (The New Palgrave)*, London: Macmillan Press Ltd, 1-20.

Benabou, Roland (1996), 'Inequality and Growth', *NBER Macroeconomic Annual*, II, 11-74.

Bergson, Abram (1938), 'A Reformulation of Certain Aspects of Welfare Economics', *The Quarterly Journal of Economics*, 52(Feb), 314-44.

Bhagwati, Jagdish (1965), 'The Pure Theory of International Trade', *Surveys of Economic Theory (Growth and Development)*, New York: St Martin's Press, 156-239.

Bhagwati, Jagdish (1978), *Anatomy and Consequences of Exchange Control Regimes*, Cambridge MA: Ballinger.

Bhagwati, Jagdish (1982), 'Directly Unproductive Profit-Seeking (DUP) Activities', *The Journal of Political Economy*, 90(5), 988-1002.

Bhagwati, Jagdish (1988), *Protectionism, Cambridge, Mass: The MIT Press*.

Bhagwati, Jagdish and V.K. Ramaswami (1963), 'Domestic Distortions, Tariffs and Optimum Subsidy', *Journal of Political Economy*, 71(Feb) 44-45.

Bhagwati, Jagdish and T.N. Srinivasan (1979), 'Trade Policy and Development', in R. Dornbush and J.A. Frankel, *International Economic Policy*, MD: Johns Hopkins University Press.

Bhagwati, Jagdish and T.N. Srinivasan (1980), 'Revenue-Seeking: A Generalization of the Theory of the Theory of Tariffs', *Journal of Political Economy*, 88, 1069-1087.

Bhagwati, Jagdish and T.N. Srinivasan (2002), 'Trade and Poverty in the Poor Countries, *The American Economic Review (Papers and Proceedings)*, 92(2), 10-185.

Binmore, K. (1987; 1988), 'Modeling Rational Players, I and II', *Economics and Philosophy*, 3 and 4, 179-214, 9-55.

Binswanger, H. and Rosenzweig M. (1986), 'Behavioral and Material Determinants of Production in Agriculture', *Journal of Development Studies*, 22(3), 503-539.

Binswanger, H. Deininger, K. and Feder, G. (1995), 'Power, Distortions, Revolt and Reform in Agricultural Land Reforms', in Behrman, J. and Srinivasan, T.N., *Handbook of Development Economics*, New York: Elsevier Science B.V.

Birdsall, Nancy and Miguel Szekely (2003), 'Bootstraps and not Band-Aids: Poverty, Equity, and Social Policy', in John Williamson and P.B. Kuczynski, *After the Washington Consensus*, Washington, D.C.: Institute of International Economics; 49-73.

Blanchard, Olivier (1997), *The Economics of Post-War Communist Transition*, Oxford: Clarendon Press.

Blaug, Mark (1983), *The Methodology of Economics, or How Economists Explain*, Cambridge: Cambridge University Press.

Borjas, George and Valerie Ramey (1995), 'Foreign Competition, Market Power, and Wage Inequality', *Quarterly Journal of Economics*, 90(4), 1075-1110.

Boserup, Easter (1970), *Women's Role in Economic Development,* London: Allen and Unwin.

Bosworth, Barry and Susan M. Collins (1996), 'Economic Growth in East Asia: Accumulation versus Assimilation', *Brookings Papers in Economic Activity*, No. 2, 135-203.

Balassa, B. and Associates (1982), *Development Strategies in Semi-Industrialized Economies,* Baltimore: MD: Johns Hopkins Press.

Bourguignon, Francois (2004), 'The Poverty-Growth-Inequality Triangle,' a paper presented at the Development Dinner Organized by the World Bank Islamabad Office, Pakistan (16th June).

Bourguignon, Francois Jaime de Melo and Christian Morrison (1991), 'Poverty and Income Distribution during Adjustment: Issues and Evidence from the OECD Project', *World Development*, 19(11), 1485-1508.

Bradford, Colin, and Branson, W.H. (1987), *Trade and Structural Change in Pacific Asia*, Chicago: University of Chicago Press for NBER.

Bradford, J., De Long and L.H. Summers (1991), 'Equipment, Investment, and Economic Growth', *The Quarterly Journal of Economics*, 106(2), 445-502.

Brandt, Willy (1980), *North-South: A Program for Survival*, London: Pan Book.

Bresser Pereira, Luiz Carlos; Maravall, Jose Maria and Adam Przeworksi (1993), *Economic Reforms in New Democracies: A Social-Democratic Approach*, Cambridge: Cambridge University Press.

Bruno, Michael (1996), 'Inflation, Growth and Monetary Control: Non-linear Lessons from Crisis and Recovery', Paolo Baffi Lecture (Rome: Bank of Italy).

Bruno, Michael Martin Ravallion and Lyn Squire (1996), 'Equity and Growth in Developing Countries: Old and New Perspectives on the Policy Issues', Policy Research Paper # 1563, Washington, D.C.: World Bank.

Bruno, Michael Martin Ravallion and Lyn Squire and W. Easterly (1998), 'Inflation Crises and Long-run Growth', *Journal of Monetary Economics*, 41(Feb.), 3-26.

Bruton, Henry (1998), 'A Reconsideration of Import Substitution', *Journal of Economic Literature*, 36:2, 903-36.

Buchanan, Allen (1985), *Ethics, Efficiency, and the Market*, Littlefield, USA: Rowman and Allenheld.

Buchanan, James (1985), *Liberty, Market, and the State: Political Economy in the 1980s*, Sussex: Wheatsheaf Books Ltd.

Buchanan, James and W.C. Stubblebine (1962), 'Externality, '*Econometrica*, 29, 371-84.

Buchanan, James and Gordon Tullock (1962), *The Calculus of Consent*, Ann Arbor: The University of Michigan Press.

Calabresi, Guido (1968), 'Transaction Costs, Resource Allocation, and Liability Rules', *Journal of Law and Economics*, April, 67-74.

Calvo, G. (1989), 'The Incredible Reforms', in G. Calvo (eds.), *Debt, Stabilization and Development, Essays in Honor of Carlos-Diaz-Alejandro*, New York: Basil Blackwell.

Campos, Nauro, F. and Falrizio Coricelli (2002), 'Growth in Transition: What We Know, What We Don't, and What We Should', *Journal of Economic Literature* 30(3), 793-836.

Cardoso, Eliana and Albert Fishlow (1992), 'Latin American Development: 1950-1980', *Journal of Latin American Studies*, 24, 197-217.

Caves, R.E. (1965), 'Vent for Surplus Models of Trade and Growth', in R.E. Baldwin et al. (eds.), *Trade, Growth and the Balance of Payments*, Chicago: Rand McNally.

Chakravarty, Sukhamoy (1969), *Capital and Development Planning*, Cambridge: MIT Press.

Chen, Shaohua, and Martin Ravallion (1997), 'What Can New Survey Data Tell Us About Recent Changes in Distribution and Poverty', *World Bank Economic Review*, 40: 357-376.

Chenery Hollis, B. (1955), 'The Role of Industrialization in the Development Programs', *American Economic Review (Papers and Proceedings)*, 45(May), 40-57.

Chenery Hollis, B. (1965), 'Comparative Advantage and Development Policy', in American Economic Association and the Royal Economic Society, *Surveys of Economic Theory: Growth and Development*, II, New York: St. Martin's Press and London: Macmillan.

Chenery Hollis, B. (1980), 'Trade Shares and Economic Growth', *American Economic Review (Papers and Proceedings)*, 70(2), 281-287.

Chenery Hollis, B. and Michael Bruno (1962), 'Development Alternatives in an Open Economy', *Economic Journal*, 72, 79-103.

Chenery Hollis, B., Michael Bruno, and M. Syrquin (1975), *Patterns of Development, 1950-1970*, London: Oxford University Press.

Chenery Hollis, S. Robinson, and S. Syrquin (1986), *Industrialization and Growth: A Comparative Study*, Washington D.C.: The World Bank.

Chenery Hollis and T.N. Srinivasan (1988), *Handbook of Development Economics*, New York: Elsevier Science Publishers.

Chhibber, A. (1989), 'The Aggregate Supply Response: A Survey', in I. Commander (ed.), *Structural Adjustment in Agriculture: Theory and Practice*, London: Overseas Development Institute.

Clark, Colin (1984), 'Development Economics: the Early Years', in Gerald M. Meirs and Dudley Seers, *Pioneers in Development*, New York: Oxford University Press (for the World Bank).

Clarke, G.R.G. (1993), 'More Evidence on Income Distribution and Growth', mimeo, Department of Economics, University of Rochester.

Clarke, J.M. (1923), *Studies in the Economics of Overhead Costs*, Chicago, Ill: University of Chicago Press.

Coase, A.W. (1960), 'The Problem of Social Cost', *Journal of Law and Economics*, 3, 1-44.

Coats, A.W. (1971), *The Classical Economists and Economic Policy*, London: Methuen.

Coles, Jeffery L. and Hammond, Peter J. (1995), 'Walrasian Equilibrium Without Survival: Existence, Efficiency and Remedial Policy', in Basu, Kaushik, Prasantha Pattnaik and K. Suzumura, *Choice, Welfare and Development*, Oxford: Oxford University Press.

Collier, Paul and William Gunning (1999), 'Explaining African Economic Performance', *Journal of Economic Literature*, 37(1), 64-111.

Connell, J., Dasgupta, B. Laishley, R. and Lipton, M. (1976), *Migration from Rural Areas: The Evidence from Village Studies*, Delhi: Oxford University Press.

Cooper, Richard N. (1987), 'Industrial Policy and Trade Distortion', in Dominic Salvatore (ed.) *The New Protectionist Threat to World Welfare*, Amsterdam: North Holland.

Cooter, D. (1990), 'The Coase Theorem', in Eatwell, Milgate and Newman, *Allocation, Information, and Markets (The New Palgrave)*, London: Macmillan Press LTD.

Corbo, V. and Rojas, P. (1992), 'World Bank-Supported Adjustment Programs: Country Performance and Effectiveness', in Corbo, V. and S. Fischer, S.B. Webb, *Adjustment Lending Revisited: Policies to Restore Growth*, Washington: D.C.: World Bank.

Corbo, Vittorio and Stanley Fischer (1995), 'Structural Adjustment, Stabilization and Policy Reform: Domestic and International Finance' In J. Behrman, and T.N. Srinivasan (eds.), *Handbook of Development Economics IIIb*, New York: Elsevier Science B.V.

Craft, Nicholas (2001), 'Historical Perspectives on Development', in G.M. Meier and Joseph E. Stiglitz (eds.), *Frontiers of Development Economics*, New York: Oxford University Press.

D'Souza, Juliet, Robert Nash and William Megginson (2000), 'Determinants of Performance Improvement in Newly Privatized Firms: Does Restructuring and Corporate Governance Matter?' Working Paper, U. Oklahoma.

Darby, M.R. and E. Karni (1973), 'Free Competition and the Optimal Amount of Fraud', *Journal of Law and Economics*, 16(1), 67-88.

Dasgupta, P. (1993), *An Enquiry into Well-being and Destitution*, Oxford: Oxford University Press.

Dasgupta, P. and Ray, Debraj (1987), 'Inequality as a Determinant of Malnutrition and Unemployment', *The Economic Journal*, 96, 1011-1034.

Davidson, David (1986), 'Judging Interpersonal Interests', in Jon Elster and Aanund Hylland (eds.), *Foundations of Social Choice Theory*, Cambridge: Cambridge University Press.

De Long, B. (2003), 'India Since Independence: An Analytic Growth Narrative', in Rodrik, Dani (ed.), *In Search of Prosperity: Analytic Narratives on Economic Growth*, Princeton University Press, Princeton, New Jersey.

Deininger K. and Squire L. (1996), 'A New Data Set Measuring Income Inequality', *World Bank Economic Review*, 10(3), 565-591.

Deininger K. and Squire L. (1998), 'New Ways of Looking at Old Issues: Inequality and Growth', *Journal of Development Economics*, 57:259-287.

Demirguc-Kunt, A., and Detragiache, E. (1998), 'Financial Liberalization and Financial Fragility', paper presented at the Annual World Bank Conference on Development Economics, Washington, D.C.: World Bank.

Diakosavvas, S. and Scandizzo, P.L. (1991), 'Trends in Terms of Trade of Primary Commodities, 1990-1982: The Controversy and its Origins', *Economic Development and Cultural Change*, 39, 231-264.

Diamond, P. and James A. Mirrlees (1971), 'Optimal Taxation and Public Production I: Production Efficiency; and II: Tax Rules'. *American Economic Review*, 61, Jan and June 8-27 and 261-8.

Diaz-Alejandro and F. Carlos (1975), 'Trade Policies and Economic Development', in Peter Kenen (ed.), *International Trade and Finance*, New York: Cambridge University Press, 93-150.

Dollar, David and Sokolff, K. (1990), 'Pattern of Productivity Growth in South Korean Manufacturing Industries, 1963-1979', *Journal of Development Economics*, 33, 309-327.

Dollar, David, K. Sokolff and Art Kraay (2002a), 'Spreading the Wealth', *Foreign Affairs*, Jan/Feb, 81(1), 1-13.

Dollar, David and Lant Pritchett (1998), *Assessing Aid: What Works and What Does Not and Why*, Washington, D.C.: World Bank and Oxford University Press.

Dollar, David, K. Sokolff, and Art Kraay (2002b), 'Growth *is* Good for the Poor', *Journal of Economic Growth*, 7(3), 195-225.

Domar, Evsey D. (1946), 'Capital Expansion, Rate of Growth and Employment', *Econometrica*, 14, 137-47.

Dorwick, Steve and Norman Gemmel (1991), 'Industrialization, Catching up and Economic Growth: A Comparative Study across the World's Capitalist Economies', *The Economic Journal*, 101:405, 263-75.

Dreze, Jean and Amartya Sen (1989), *Hunger and Public Action*, Oxford: Clarendon Press.

Dreze, Jean and Amartya Sen (1995), *Economic Development and Social Opportunity*, London: Oxford University Press.

Durant, Will (1961), *The Story of Philosophy*, New York: Simon and Schuster.

Dutta, A. (1985), 'Stagnation, Income Distribution and Monopoly Power', *Cambridge Journal of Economics*.

Dworkin, R. (1981a), 'What is Equality? Part I: Equality of Welfare', *Philosophy and Public Affairs*, 10(3), 185-246.

Dworkin, R. (1981b), 'What is Equality? Part II: Equality of Resources', *Philosophy and Public Affairs*, 10(3), 283-345.

Easterly, William (1992), 'Endogenous Growth in Developing Countries with Government-induced Distortions', in V. Corbo, S. Fischer and S. Webb (eds.), *Adjustment Lending Revisited, Policies to Restore Growth*, Washington D.C.: World Bank.

Easterly, William (2002), 'Inequality Does Cause Underdevelopment: New Evidence', Working Paper 1, Centre for Global Development, Washington D.C.

Easterly, William, Carlos Alfredo, and Klauss Schimdt-Hebbel (1994), *Public Sector Deficits and Macroeconomic Performance*, New York: Oxford University Press.

Easterly, William and Stanley Fischer (1995), 'The Soviet Economic Decline', *The World Bank Economic Review*, 9(3), 341-371.

Easterly, William and Ross Levine (1997), 'Africa's Growth Strategy: Policies and Ethnic Division', *The Quarterly Journal of Economics*, 112(4), 1203-50.

Easterly, William (2001), *The Elusive Search for Growth: Economist's Adventures and Misadventures in the Tropics*, Cambridge, M.A.: MIT Press.

Economic Journal (1996), 'Controversy on Convergence and Divergence of Growth Rates', *Economic Journal*, 106(437), 1016-1069.

Economist (1991), 'The Poor Man's Plague', September 21, p. 21.

Economist (2002), 'Coming Home to Roost', *The Economist*, 29 June-5 July, 69-71.

Economist (2002), 'Convergence, Period', *The Economist*, 20-26 July, 68.

Eckstein, Otto (1957), 'Investment Criteria for Economic Development and the Theory of Inter-temporal Welfare Economics', *Quarterly Journal of Economics*, 71, 56-85.

Edlin, Aaron and J.E. Stiglitz (1992), 'Discouraging Rivals: Managerial Rent-seeking and Economic Inefficiencies', Stanford University, California: Department of Economics.

Edwards, Sebastian (1989), 'The International Monetary Fund and the Developing Countries: A Critical Evaluation', *Carnegie-Rochester Conference Series on Public Policy*, vol. 31, Autumn, 7-68.

Edwards, Sebastian (1993), 'Openness, Trade Liberalization, and Growth in Developing Countries', *Journal of Economic Literature*, 31(September), 1358-1393.

Emmanuel, Aghiri (1972), *Unequal Exchange: A Study of the Imperialism of Trade*, New York: Monthly Review Press.

Esfahani, Hadi S. (1991), 'Exports, Imports, and Economic Growth in Semi-industrialized Countries', *Journal of Development Economics*, 35(1), 31-57.

Evenson, R.E. and L.E. Westphal (1995), 'Technological Change and Technology Strategy', in J. Behrman and T.N. Srinivasan, *Handbook of Development Economics*, Amsterdam: Elsevier Science B.V.

Farrell, Joseph (1987), 'Information and Coase Theorem', *Journal of Economic Perspectives*, 1(2), 113-119.

Feder, D. (1983), 'On Exports and Economic Growth', *Journal of Development Economics*, 12, 59-74.

Feenstra, R.C. (1990), 'Trade and Uneven Growth', NBER Working Paper, 3276.

Feenstra, R.C. (1998), 'Integration of Trade and Disintegration of Production', *Journal of Economic Perspectives*, 12(4), 31-50.

Fehr, Ernst and Urs Fishbacher (2003), 'The Nature of Human Altruism', *Nature*, 425 (October), 785-791.

Fei, John C.H. and Gustav Ranis (1963), 'Innovation, Capital Innovation, and Economic Development', *The American Economic Review*, 53(3), 282-313.

Fei, John C.H. and Gustav Ranis (1964), *Development of the Labor-surplus Economy: Theory and Policy*, Homewood, IL: Richard D. Irwin.

Fei, John C.H. and Gustav Ranis and S.W.Y. Kuo (1980), *Growth with Equity: Taiwan's Case*, New York: Oxford University Press.

Feldman, Allan M. (1991), 'Welfare Economics', in John Eatwell, Murray Milgate, and Peter Newman, *The World of Economics (The New Palgrave)*, London: Macmillan.

Fields, G. (1980), *Poverty, Inequality and Development*, New York: Cambridge University Press.

Fields, G. (1989), 'Changes in Poverty and Equality in Developing Countries', *World Bank Research Observer*, 4, 167-186.

Findlay, Ronald (1979), 'Trade, Development and the State', in Gustav Ranis and Paul T. Shultz (eds.), *The State of Development Economics*, New York: Basil Blackwell, 78-95.

Fitzgerald, Edward (1980), *Rubaiyat of Omar Khayyam*, Glasgow and London: Collins (Khorasan Edition).

.Fleming, J. Marcus (1955), 'External Economies and the Doctrine of Balanced Growth', *Economic Journal*, 65(June), 241-56.

Fogel, R.W. (2000), *The Fourth Great Awakening and the Future of Egalitarianism*, Chicago: the Chicago University Press.

Forbes, Justin (2000), 'A Reassessment of Relationship between Inequality and Growth', *American Economic Review*, 90(4), 869-887.

Frankel, J., and D. Romer (1999), 'Does Trade Cause Growth?', *The American Economic Review*, 89(3), 379-399.

Friedman, Milton (1962), *Capitalism and Freedom*, Chicago: University of Chicago Press.

Friedman, Milton (1968), 'The Role of Monetary Policy', *American Economic Review*, 58(1), 1-17.

Frost, Robert (1965), *The Road Not Taken*, USA and Canada: Holt, Rinehart and Winston.

Fudenberg, D. and E. Masken (1990), 'Evolution and Cooperation in Noisy Repeated Games', *The American Economic Review, Papers and Proceedings*, 80(2), 274-9.

Furubotn, Eirik G. and Svetozar Pejovich (1972), 'Property Rights and Economic Theory: A Survey of Current Literature', *Journal of Economic Literature*, 10(4), 1137-62.

Galbraith, John Kenneth (1991), 'Economics in the Century Ahead', *The Economic Journal*, 101:404, 41-46.

Galenson, Walter and Harvey Leibenstein (1955), 'Investment Criteria, Productivity, and Economic Development', *Quarterly Journal of Economics*, 69(3), 343-70.

Galor, O. and J.Zeira (1993), 'Income Distribution and Macroeconomics', *Review of Economic Studies*, 60, 35-52.

Gerschenkron, A. (1952), 'Economic Backwardness in Historical Perspective', in B. Hoselitz (ed.), *The Progress of Underdeveloped Countries*, Chicago: The University of Chicago Press.

Gibbon, Henry (2000), 'Editor's Letter', *Privatization Yearbook*, London: Thomson Financial, 1.

Gibran, Khalil (2004), *The Prophet*, New York: Alfred Knopf (originally published in 1923).

Gillis, M., D. Perkins, M. Roemer and D. Snodgrass (1983), *Economics of Development:* New York: Norton.

Gollins, Douglas, Stephan Parente, and Richard Rogerson (2002), 'The Role of Agriculture in Development', *The American Economic Review, Papers and Proceedings*, 92(2), 159-165.

Gomory and Baumol (2000), *Global Trade and Conflicting National Interests*, The MIT Press: Cambridge, MA.

Gordon, Scott (1971), 'The Ideology of Laissez-Faire', in A.W. Coats (ed.), *The Classical Economists and Economic Policy*, London: Methuen.

Graff, J. De V. (1990), 'Social Cost', in John Eatwell, Murray Milgate, Peter Newman, *The New Palgrave: The World of Economics*, U.K.: Macmillan Press Limited.

Greenhalgh, S. (1985), Sexual Stratification: the Other Side of Growth with Equity in East Asia', *Population and Development Review*, 11(2), 265-314.

Greenwald, Bruce and J.E. Stiglitz (1986), 'Externalities in Economies with Imperfect Information and Incomplete Markets', *The Quarterly Journal of Economics*, 101:2, 229-64.

Greenwald, Bruce and J.E. Stiglitz (1988), 'Pareto Inefficiency of Market Economies: Search and Efficiency Wage Models', *American Economic Review*, 78(2), 351-355.

Grilli, E. and M.C. Yang (1988), 'Primary Commodity Prices, Manufacturing Goods Prices, and the Terms of Trade of Developing Countries: What the Long Run Shows', *The World Bank Economic Review*, 2, 1-47.

Grossman, Gene and Elhanan Helpman (1991), *Innovation and Growth in a Global Economy*, Cambridge: MIT Press.

Grossman, Gene and Elhanan Helpman (1994), 'Endogenous Innovation in the Theory of Growth', *Journal of Economic Perspectives*, 8:1, 23-44.

Haberler, Gottfried (1950), 'Some Problems in the Theory of International Trade', *Economic Journal*, 72(June), 223-40.

Haberler, Gottfried (1959), *International Trade and Economic Development*, Cairo: National Bank of Egypt.

Hahn, Frank (1991), 'The Next Hundred Years', *Economic Journal*, 101: 104, 47-50.

Hahn, Frank and Martin Hollis and R.C.O. Mathews (1965), 'The Theory of Economic Growth', *In Surveys of Economic Theory*, Vol. 2, London: St. Martin Press.

Hahn, Frank and Martin Hollis (1979), *Philosophy and Economic Theory*, Oxford: Oxford University Press.

Haq, Mahbubul (1995), *Reflections on Human Development*, New York: Oxford University Press.

Harberger, Arnold (1993), 'Secrets of Success: A Handful of Heroes,' *American Economic Review*, 83(2), 343-50.

Harris, John R. and Michael P. Todaro (1970), 'Migration, Unemployment, and Development: A Two-Sector Analysis', *The American Economic Review*, 60(1), 125-42.

Harrod, Roy (1939), 'An Essay in Dynamic Theory', *Economic Journal*, 49(139), 14-33.

Harsanyi, John, C. (1977), 'Morality and the Theory of Rational Behavior', *Social Research*, 44 (4), 623-56.

Harsanyi, John, C. (1982), 'Morality and the Theory of Rational Behavior', in Sen and Williams (eds.), *Utilitarianism and Beyond*, Cambridge: Cambridge University Press.

Hausman, Daniel and Michael S. MacPherson (1993), 'Taking Ethics Seriously: Economics and Contemporary Moral attitude', *Journal of Economic Literature*, 37(2), 671-731.

Hausmann, Ricardo and Dani Rodrik (2003), 'Economic Development as Self-discovery', *Journal of Development Economics*, 72, 603-633.

Hayek, F.A. (1944/1994), *The Road to Serfdom*, Chicago: Chicago University Press.

Hayek, F.A. (1945), 'The Use of Knowledge in Society, '*American Economic Review*, Sept (35), 519-530.

Hayek, F.A. (1960), *The Constitution of Liberty*, London: Routledge and Kegan Paul.

Heckscher, Eli, F. (1933), 'The Effects of Foreign Trade on the Distribution of Income', in Ellis, H.S. and L.A. Metzler, *Readings in the Theory of International Trade*, Philadelphia: Blackiston.

Helleiner, G.K. (1986), 'Outward Orientation, Import Instability and African Economic Growth: An Empirical Investigation', in S. Lall and Frances Stewart (eds.), *Theory and Reality in Development: Essays in Honor of Paul Streeten*, London: Macmillan.

Heilbroner, Robert L. (1990), 'Analysis and Vision in the History of Modern Economic Thought', *Journal of Economic Literature*, 28:3, 1097-114.

Heston, A., Robert Summers and Betina Aten (2002), *Penn World Tables Version 6.1*, Center for International Comparisons at the University of Pennsylvania (CICUP).

Hirsch, Fred (1977), *Social Limits to Growth*, London: Routledge and Kegan Paul (Reprinted with a Foreword by Tibor Scitovsky, 1995).

Hirschman, Albert (1958), *The Strategy of Economic Development*, New Haven, CT: Yale University Press.

Hirschman, Albert (1958), 'Investment Criteria and Capital Intensity Once Again', *Quarterly Journal of Economics*, 72, 469-71.

Hirschman, Albert (1981), 'The Rise and Decline of Development Economics', in A.O. Hirschman (eds.), *Essays in Trespassing: Economics to Politics and Beyond*, Cambridge: Cambridge University Press.

Hirschman, Albert (1984), 'A Dissenter's Confession: The Strategy of Economic Development Revisited', in D. Seers and G.M. Meier (eds.), *Pioneers in Development*, New York: Oxford University Press, 87-114.

Hirschman, Albert (1985), Against Parsimony: Three Easy Ways of Complicating Some Categories of Economic Discourse', *Economic Philosophy*, 1(1), 7-12.

Hirschman, Albert (1988), 'Two Hundred Years of Reactionary Rhetoric: The Case of the Perverse Effect', in Grethe B. Peterson (ed.), *The Tanner Lecture on Human Values*, X, Salt Lake City; University of Utah Press.

Hobday, Michael (1995), *Innovation in East Asia*, Aldershot: Edward Elgar.

Hoff, Karla and Joseph Stiglitz (2001), Modern Economic Theory and Economic Development', in G.E. Meier and Joseph Stiglitz (eds.), *Frontiers of Development Economics*, New York: Oxford University Press, 389-459.

International Monetary Fund (1999), *World Economic Outlook*, Washington D.C.: IMF.

International Monetary Fund (2000), *World Economic Outlook*, Washington: D.C.: IMF.

Islam, Nurul (1967), 'Comparative Costs, Factor Proportions and Industrial Efficiency in Pakistan', *The Pakistan Development Review*, 7(2), 213-246.

Islam, Nurul (1970), *Studies on Commercial Policy and Economic Growth*, Karachi: Pakistan Institute of Development Economics.

Jazairy, I.M., M. Alagir, and T. Panucio (1991), *The State of World Rural Poverty*, New York: New York University Press (for International Fund for Agricultural Development (IFAD)).

Johnston, Bruce and John Mellor (1961), 'The Role of Agriculture in Economic Development,' *The American Economic Review*, 51(4), 566-93.

Jones, Leroy and IL Sakong (1980), *Government, Business, and Entrepreneurship in Economic Development: The Korean Case*, Cambridge, MA: Harvard University Press.

Jones, Ronald (1993), 'The New Protectionism and the Nature of World Trade', *The Pakistan Development Review*, 32(4), 398-408.

Judge, G.G., R.C. Hill, W.E. Griffiths, H.L. Ltkepohl and T.C. Lee (1982), *Introduction to the Theory and Practice of Econometrics*, New York: John Wiley.

Juhasz, Antonia (2006), *The Bush Agenda*, New York: Reagan Books.

Jung, Woo and Peyton Marshall (1985), 'Exports, Growth, and Causality in Developing Countries', *Journal of Development Economics*, 18(2), 1-12.

Kakwani, Nanak and Hyun H. Son (2004), 'Pro-poor Growth: Concepts and Measurement', Paper Presented at the Nineteenth Annual General Meeting & Conference, PSDE (January 13-15), Islamabad: Pakistan.

Kaldor, Nicholas (1955), 'Alternative Theories of Distribution,' *Review of Economic Studies*, 23.

Kaldor, Nicholas (1967), *Strategic Factors of Economic Development*, Ithaca: New York: Cornell University Press.

Kaminsky, Graceila and Carmen M. Rheinhart (1999), 'The Twin Crises: The Causes of Banking and Balance of Payments Problem', *American Economic Review*, 89(3), 473- 500.

Kanbur, Ravi and K. McIntosh (1990), 'Dual Economies', in Eatwell, Milgate and Newman, *Economic Development (The New Palgrave)*, London: Macmillan, 117-19.

Kanbur, Ravi, K. McIntosh and Lyn Squire (2001), 'The Evolution of Thinking about Poverty: Exploring the Interactions', in G.M. Meier and Joseph E. Stiglitz (eds.), *Frontiers of Development Economics*, New York: Oxford University Press.

Kant, Immanuel (1948), *Groundwork of the Metaphysics of Morals*, translated in 1948 by H. Patton, New York: Harper and Row.

Kant, Immanuel (1956), *Critique of Practical Reason*, (tr. L.W. Beck), New York: Bobbs-Merrill.

Kemp, Murray C. and M. Ohyama (1978), 'On the Sharing of Trade Gains by Resource-poor and Resource-rich Countries', *Journal of International Economics*, 8(1), 93-115.

Keynes, John Maynard (1932), *Essays in Persuasion*, New York: Harcourt Brace.

Keynes, John Maynard (1936), *The General Theory of Employment, Interest and Money*, New York: Harcourt Brace.

Khan, Ali (1980), 'The Harris-Todaro Hypothesis and the Hecksher-Ohlin-Samuelson Trade Model', *Journal of International Economics*, 10(4), 527-48.

Khan, Ali (2003), 'Composite Photography and Statistical Prejudice: Leavy-Peart and Marshall on the Theorist and the Theorized', Department of Economics, the Johns Hopkins University.

Khan, Ali and Syed Nawab Haider Naqvi (1983), 'Capital Markets and Urban Unemployment', *Journal of International Economics*, 15, 367-385.

Khan, Mohsin (1990), 'The Macroeconomic Effects of Fund-supported Programs', *IMF Staff Papers*, 37(2), Washington: DC.

King, Robert and Ross Levine (1994), 'Capital Fundamentalism, Economic Development, and Economic Growth', *Carnegie-Rochester Series on Public Policy*, 40(June), 259-92.

Klamer, Arjo (1984), *Neo-Classical Macroeconomics: Conversations with the Neo-Classical Economists and their Opponents*, Sussex: Wheatsheaf Books Ltd.

Klasen, Stephan (1994), 'Missing Women Reconsidered', *World Development*, 22.

Klein, Lawrence R. (1978), 'The Supply Side', *The American Economic Review*, 68:1, 1-17.

Klein, Lawrence R. (1985), *The Economics of Supply and Demand*, Oxford: Basil Blackwell.

Knowles, S. (2001), 'Inequality and Economic Growth: the Empirical Relationship Reconsidered in the Light of Comparable Data', Paper Presented at the Wider Conference on 'Growth and Poverty', Wider: Helsinki.

Komiya, R. (1959), 'A Note on Professor Mahalanobis' Model of the Indian Economic Planning,' *Review of Economic Studies*, 41(Feb), 29-35.

Koopmans, Tjalling (1965), *On the Concept of Optimal Growth, in the Econometric Approach to Development Planning*, Amsterdam: North Holland.

Kornai, Janos (2000), 'Ten years after the Road to Free Economy, The Author-Self-evaluation' (mimeo), Harvard University.

Krueger, Anne O (1974), 'The Political Economy of the Rent-seeking Society', *The American Economic Review*, 64:3, 291-303.

Krueger, Anne O (1978), *Liberalization Attempts and Consequences*, Cambridge, MA: Ballinger.

Krueger, Anne O (1981), 'Aid in the Development Process', *World Bank Research Observer* (Jan).

Krueger, Anne O (1983), *Trade and Employment in Developing Countries, Vol. 3: Synthesis and Conclusion*, Chicago: University of Chicago Press (for National Bureau of Economic Research).

Krueger, Anne O (1990), 'Asian Trade and Growth Lessons', *American Economic Review*, Papers and Proceedings, May, 108-112.

Krueger, Anne O (1990), *Government Failures in Development*, NBER Working Paper No. 3340, April.

Krueger, Anne O (1993), *Political Economy of Policy Reform in Developing Countries*, Cambridge, MA and London: The MIT Press.

Krueger, Anne O (1995a), 'Policy Lessons from Development Experience Since the Second World War', in Behrman, J. and T.N. Srinivasan (eds.), *Handbook of Development Economics*, Elsevier Science BV. 2497-2552.

Krueger, Anne O (1995b), *Trade Policies and Developing Nations*, Washington D.C.: Brookings Institution.

Krueger, Anne O (1997), 'Trade Policy and Economic Development: How We Learn?' *The American Economic Review*, 87(1), 1-22.

Krueger, Anne O (1998), 'Whither the World Bank and the IMF?' *Journal of Economic Literature*, 36(4), 1983-2020.

Krueger, Anne O and Tuncer, B. (1982), 'Growth of Factor Productivity in the Turkish Manufacturing Industries', *Journal of Development Economics*, 11, 307-326.

Krueger, Anne O, Schiff, M. and Valdes, A. (1988), Agricultural Incentives in Developing Countries: Measuring the Effect of Country wide and Economy-wide Policies', *World Bank Economic Review*, 2; 255-271.

Krueger, Anne O Schiff, M. and Valdes, A. (1991), *The Political Economy of Agricultural Pricing* (Vols. a, b and c), Baltimore and London: Johns Hopkins Press.

Krugman, Paul (1992), 'Towards a Counter-Revolution in Development Theory', Washington: World Bank Conference on Development Economics.

Krugman, Paul (1997), 'What Should the Negotiators Negotiate About?' *Journal of Economic Literature*, 35(1), 113-120.

Krugman, Paul (1999),'Towards a Counter-Counterrevolution in Development Theory', Annual World Bank Conference in Development Economics.

Kuczynski, Pedro-Pablo and John Williamson (2003), *After the Washington Consensus*, Washington, D. C.: Institute of International Economics.

Kuhn, Thomas (1962), *The Structure of Scientific Revolutions*, Chicago: University of Chicago Press.

Kuznets, Simon (1955), 'Economic Growth and Income Inequality', *The American Economic Review*, 45:1, 1-28.

Kuznets, Simon (1956), 'Quantitative Aspects of the Growth of Nations: 1. Levels and Variability of Growth Rates', *Economic Development and Cultural Change*, 5, 5-94.

Kuznets, Simon (1957), 'Quantitative Aspects of the Growth of Nations: 2. Industrial Distribution of National Product and Labor Force', *Economic Development and Cultural Change*, 5(supplement): 3-111.

Kyle, Bagwell and Robert Staiger (1999), 'An Economic Theory of GATT', *The American Economic Review*, 89(4), 215-248.

Kyle, Bagwell and Robert Staiger (1961), 'Economic Growth and the Contribution of Agriculture: Notes on Measurements', *International Journal of Agrarian Affairs* (April).

Laffont, Jean-Jacques (1989), 'Externalities,' in J. Eatwell, M. Milgate and P. Newman (eds.), *Allocation, Information and Markets, the New Palgrave*, London: Macmillan.

Laffont, Jean-Jacques and Eric Maskin (1982), 'The Theory of Incentives: An Overview', in Hildebrand, Werner (eds.) *Advances in Economic Theory*, Cambridge: Cambridge University Press.

Lakatos, Imre (1970), 'Falsification and Methodology of Scientific Research', in Imre Lakatos and A. Musgrave (eds.), *Criticism and Growth of Knowledge*, Cambridge: Cambridge University Press.

La Porta, Rafael and Florenico Lopez-de Silanes (1999), 'Benefits of Privatization—Evidence from Mexico', *Quarterly Journal of Economics*, 114(4), 1193-1242.

Lal, Deepak (1983), *The Poverty of Development Economics*, London: Institute of Economic Affairs, Hobart Paperback.

Lane, T., A. Ghosh, J. Hammann, S. Phillips, M. Schulze-Ghatta, and T. Tsikata (1999), 'IMF-Supported Programs in Indonesia, Korea, and Thailand,' Occasional Paper 178, International Monetary Fund.

Lange, Oscar (1936-37), 'On the Economic Theory of Socialism' *Review of Economic Studies*.

Leibenstein, Harvey (1957), *Economic Backwardness and Economic Growth*, New York: John Wiley.

Leontief, Wassily (1983), 'Technological Advance, Economic Growth, and the Distribution of Income', *Population and Development Review*, 9(3), 403-410.

Lee, J.H. (1992), 'Government Interventions and Productivity Growth in the Korean Manufacturing Industries', Paper Presented at NBER Conference on Economic Growth, Cambridge, MA.

Lewin, Shira (1996), 'Economics and Psychology: Lessons for Own Day from the Early Twentieth Century,' *Journal of Economic Literature*, 34: 1293-1322.

Lewis, Arthur (1954), 'Economic Development with Unlimited Supplies of Labour,' *Manchester School*, 22,139-91.

Lewis, Arthur (1955), *The Theory of Economic Growth*, London: Unwin University Press.

Lewis, Arthur (1966), *Development Planning*, London: George Allen and Unwin Ltd.

Lewis, Arthur (1972), 'Reflections on Unlimited Labor', in L.E. Marco (ed.), *International Economics and Economic Development*, New York: Academic.

Lewis, Arthur (1978), *The Evolution of the International Economic Order*, Princeton, NJ: Princeton University Press.

Lewis, Arthur (1984a), 'The State of Development Theory', *American Economic Review*, 74:1, 1-10.

Lewis, Arthur (1984b), 'Development Economics in the 1950s', in G.M. Meiers and D. Seers (eds.), *Pioneers in Development*, New York: Oxford University Press, 121-137.

Linder, Staffan B. (1961), *An Essay on Trade and Transformation*, New York: John Wiley.

Lin, Justin, Fang Cai and Zhou Li (1998), 'Competition, Policy Burdens, and State-Owned Enterprise Reform', *The American Economic Review*, 88, 422-27.

Lipsey, R.G. and Lancaster (1956), 'The General Theory of Second Best', *Review of Economic Studies*, 26, 11-32.

Lipton, M. and M. Ravallion (1983), 'Labor and Poverty', World Bank Staff Working Paper#616, Washington, D.C.: The World Bank.

Lipton, M. and M. Ravallion (1995), 'Poverty and Policy', in Behrman, J. and T.N. Srinivasan (eds.), *Handbook of Development Economics IIIb*, Elsevier Science B.V.

Little, I.M.D. (1982), *Economic Development: Theory, Policy and International Relations*, New York: Basic Books.

Little, I.M.D., Tand James A. Mirrlees (1969), *Manual of Industrial Project Analysis in Developing Countries*, London: Oxford University Press.

Little, I.M.D., Tibor Scitovsky and Michael Scott (1970), *Industry and Trade Regimes in some Developing Countries*, London & New York: Oxford University Press.

Little, I.M.D., R. Cooper, Max Corden and S. Rajapatirana (1993), *Boom, Crisis and Adjustment*, Oxford: Oxford University Press.

Locke, J. (1952), *Second Treatise on Civil Government*, Edited by P. Laslettz (2nd, Rev. Edition), Indianapolis: Bobbs-Merrill.

Lora, E. (2001), *Structural Adjustment Reforms in Latin America: What has been Achieved and How to Measure it*, Research Department Working Paper 446. Washington, D.C.: Inter-American Development Bank (December).

Lucas, Robert E., Jr. (1972), 'Expectations and the Neutrality of Money', *Journal of Economic Theory*, 4, 103-24.

Lucas, Robert E., Jr. (1988), 'On the Mechanics of Economic Development', *Journal of Monetary Economics*, 22:1, 3-42.

Lucas, Robert E., Jr. (1990), 'Why does Capital not Flow from the Rich to Poor Countries', *American Economic Review*, 80, 92-96.

Lucas, Robert E., Jr. and Thomas Sargent (1978), 'After Keynesian Macroeconomics', in *After the Phillip's Curve: Persistence of a High Inflation and High Unemployment*, Boston: Federal Reserve Bank of Boston, 47-72.

Lundberg, Mattias and Martin Ravallion (1999), 'Growth and Inequality: Extracting Lessons for Policy-makers', Policy Research Department, World Bank, Washington, D.C.

Maddison, Angus (1970), *Economic Progress and Policy in Developing Countries*, London: George Allen and Unwin.

Maddison, Angus (1991), *Dynamic Forces in Capitalist Development*, Oxford, UK: Oxford University Press.

Maddison, Angus (2001), *The World Economy: A Millennial Perspective*, Paris: Organization For Economic Development and Cooperation.

Mahalanobis, P.C. (1953), 'Some Observations on the Process of Growth of National Income', *Sankhya*, 12:4, 307-12.

Malinvaud, Edmond (1984), *Mass Unemployment*, New York: Basil Blackwell.

Malinvaud, Edmond (1991), 'The Next Fifty Years', *The Economic Journal*, 101: 404, 64-68.

Mallaby, Sebastian (2004), *The World's Banker*, A Council of Foreign Relations Book, New York: The Penguin Press.

Malthus, Thomas, R. (1798), *An Essay on the Principle of Population*, London: W. Pickering(1986).

Mansfield, Jane (1990), *Beyond Self-Interest*, Chicago: Chicago University Press.

Marshall, Alfred, (1890/1969[1920]), *Principles of Economics* (8th Edition), London: Macmillan.

Meier, Gerald M. (2001), 'The Old Generation of Development Economists and the New', in G.M. Meier, and Joseph E. Stiglitz (eds.), *Frontiers of Development Economics*, New York: Oxford University Press, 13-50.

Megginson, William L. and Jeffry M. Netter (2001), 'From State to Market: A Survey of Empirical Literature', *Journal of Economic Literature*, 39(2), 321-389.

Mellor, John W., and Bruce F. Johnston (1984), 'The World Food Equation,' *Journal of Economic Literature*, 22(2), 531-74.

Mellor, John W. (1986), 'Agriculture on the Road to Industrialization', in John P. Lewis and V. Kallab (eds.), *Development Strategies Reconsidered*, USA: Transaction Books (for Overseas Development Council).

Metzler, Lloyd (1949), 'Tariffs, Terms of Trade, and the Distribution of National Income', *Journal of Political Economy*, 47(1), 1-29.

Michaely, Michael (1977), 'Exports and Growth: An Empirical Investigation', *Journal of Development Economics*, 4(1), 49-53.

Michaely, Michael, Papageoriou, D., and Choski, A., (1989), 'The Design of Trade Liberalization', *Finance Development*, 26(1), 2-5.

Milanovic, Branko (2002), 'True World Income Distribution, 1988 and 1993: First Calculations Based on Household Surveys Alone', *Economic Journal*, 112 (476), 51-92.

Mosley, P. Harrigan, J. and Toye, J. (1991), *Aid and Power: The World Bank and Policy-Based Lending*, London and New York: Routledge.

Mueller, Dennis C. (1989), *Public Choice*, Cambridge: Cambridge University Press (First Edition, published in 1979.

Murphy, Kevin, Andrei Shleifer, and Robert W. Vishny (1989a), 'Income Distribution, Market Size, and Industrialization', *Quarterly Journal of Economics*, August, 537-64.

Murphy, Kevin, Andrei Shleifer, and Robert W. Vishny (1989b), 'Industrialization and the Big Push', *Journal of Political Economy*, 97(5), 1003-26.

Myerson, Roger, and Mark Satterthwaite (1983), 'Efficient Mechanisms for Bilateral Trading', *Journal of Economic Theory*, 29: 265-285.

Myerson, Roger (1990), 'Mechanism Design', in Eatwell, Milgate and Newman (eds.), *Allocation, Information and Markets*, London: Macmillan Press Limited.

Myrdal, G. (1956), *An International Economy: Problems and Perspectives*, Westport CT: Greenwood Press.

Myrdal, G., (1957), *Economic Theory and Underdeveloped Regions*, London: G. Duckworth.

Myrdal, G. (1968), *The Asian Drama*, Hammondsworth, UK: Penguin Books.

Myrdal, G. (1984), 'International Equality and Foreign Aid in Retrospect', in Gerald Meier, Dudley Seers (eds.), *Pioneers in Development*, New York: Oxford University Press, 151-165.

Naqvi, Syed Nawab Haider (1963), 'The Balance of Payments Problem and Resource Allocation in Pakistan—A Linear Programming Approach', *Pakistan Development Review*, 3(3), 349-370.

Naqvi, Syed Nawab Haider (1964), 'Import Licensing in Pakistan', *Pakistan Development Review*, 4:1, 51-68.

Naqvi, Syed Nawab Haider (1966), 'The Allocative Biases of Pakistan's Commercial Policy', *Pakistan Development Review*, 4:4, 465 - 89.

Naqvi, Syed Nawab Haider (1969), 'Protection and Economic Development', *Kyklos*, 22(1), 124-54.

Naqvi, Syed Nawab Haider (1970), 'Foreign Capital Requirements and External Indebtedness of a Developing Country', in E.A.G. Robinson and Michael Kidron, *Economic Development in South Asia(1970)*, International Economic Association Conference, held at Kandy, Ceylon (now Sri Lanka), 504-524.

Naqvi, Syed Nawab Haider (1971), 'On Optimizing 'Gains' from Pakistan's Export Bonus Scheme,' *Journal of Political Economy*, 79(1), 114-27.

Naqvi, Syed Nawab Haider (1981), *Ethics and Economics: An Islamic Synthesis*, Leicester: The Islamic Foundation.

Naqvi, Syed Nawab Haider (1992), *On Raising the Level of Economic and Social Well Being of the People*, Islamabad: Pakistan Institute of Development Economics.

Naqvi, Syed Nawab Haider (1993), *Development Economics: A New Paradigm*, New Delhi, Newbury Park, London: Sage Publications.

Naqvi, Syed Nawab Haider (1994), *Islam, Economics and Society*, London: Kegan Paul.

Naqvi, Syed Nawab Haider (1995), 'The Nature of Economic Development', *World Development*, 23:4, 543-56.

Naqvi, Syed Nawab Haider (1996), 'The Significance of Development Economics', *World Development*, 24:6, 975-987.

Naqvi, Syed Nawab Haider (2002), *Development Economics—Nature and Significance*, New Delhi, Newbury Park, London: Sage Publications.

Naqvi, Syed Nawab Haider (2003), *Perspectives on Morality and Human Well being*, Leicester: The Islamic Foundation.

Naqvi, Syed Nawab Haider (2004), 'International Trade and Economic Governance in Asia', Background Paper, New Delhi: UNDP Asia and Pacific Regional HDR Initiative.

Naqvi, Syed Nawab Haider (2006/2004), 'Globalization and Human Development: An Overview', in Ismail Sirageldin (ed.), *Sustainable Human Development, In Encyclopedia of Life Support Systems (EOLSS)*, Developed Under the auspices of the UNESCO; UK: EOLSS Publishers, Oxford.

Naqvi, Syed Nawab Haider (2006), 'A Perspective on Development Policy', *IASSI Quarterly*, Vol. 24; 3 and 4 (forthcoming).

Naqvi, Syed Nawab Haider and A.R. Kemal (1991a), *Protection and Efficiency in Manufacturing: A Case Study of Pakistan*, San Francisco: ICS Press.

Naqvi, Syed Nawab Haider and A.R. Kemal (1991b), 'The Privatization of Public Sector Enterprises', *Pakistan Development Review*, 30(2), 105-144.

Naqvi, Syed Nawab Haider and A.R. Kemal (1999), 'Privatization, Efficiency, and Employment in Pakistan', in Anthony Bennett (ed.), *How Does Privatization Work*, London: Routledge, 228-49.

Nehru, J. (1941), *Toward Freedom. The Autobiography of Jawaharlal Nehru*, Boston: Beacon Press.

Nehru, J. (1946), *The Discovery of India*, New York: The John Day Company.

Nehru, Vikram and Ashok Dhareshwar (1993), 'A New Data Base on Physical Capital Stock: Sources, Methodology, and Results', *Revista de Analisi Economico*, 8(1), 37-59.

Newbery, David and Michael G.Pollitt (1997), 'The Restructuring and Privatization of Britain's CEGB—Was it Worth It?', *Journal of Industrial Economics*, 45, 269-303.

Noll, Roger (2000), 'Telecommunication Reform in Developing Countries', in A. Krueger (ed.), *Economic Policy Reform: The Second Stage*, Chicago: The University of Chicago Press.

North, Douglass, C. (1990), *Institutions, Institutional Change, and Economic Performance*, Cambridge, UK: Cambridge University Press.

North, Douglass, C. (1994), 'Economic Performance through Time', *American Economic Review*, 84(3), 359-68.

Nozick, Robert (1974), *Anarchy, State and Utopia*, Oxford: Basil Blackwell.

Nurkse, Ragnar (1953), *Problems of Capital Formation in Underdeveloped Countries*, New York: Oxford University Press.

Nurkse, Ragnar (1958), 'Comment on Viner's Stability and Progress: the Poorer Countries' Problems', in D. Hague (ed.), *Stability and Progress in the World Economy*, London.

O'Neil, Onora (1996), *Justice and Virtue*, New York: Cambridge.

Odagiri, H. and Goto, A. (1993), 'The Japanese System of Innovation: Past, Present and Future', in R.R. Nelson (ed.), *National Innovational Systems: A Comparative Analysis*, New York: Oxford University Press.

Ofer, Gur (1987), 'Soviet Economic Growth: 1928-85', *Journal of Economic Literature*, 25(4), 1767-1833.

Ohlin, Bertil (1933), *Inter-regional and International Trade*, Cambridge, MA: Harvard University Press.

Olson, Mancur (1971), *The Logic of Collective Action*, Cambridge, Mass: Harvard University Press.

Onis, Z. (1991), 'Organization of Export-oriented Industrialization: the Turkish Foreign Companies in Comparative Perspective', in T. Nas and M. Odekon (eds.), *Politics and Economics of Turkish Liberalization*. London: Associated Press.

Osmani, S.R. (1996), 'Famine, Demography and Endemic Poverty', *Journal of International Development*, 8(5), 597-623.

Pack, Howard (1988), 'Industrialization and Trade', in Hollis Chenery and T.N. Srinivasan, Handbook of Development Economics, Vol. 1, New York: North Holland, 334-380.

Pack, Howard (1994), 'Endogenous Growth Theory: Intellectual Appeal and Empirical Shortcomings', *Journal of Economic Perspectives*, Vol. 8, No. 1, 55-72.

Pack, Howard and Larry Westphal (1986), 'Industrial Strategy and Technological Change: Theory versus Reality', *Journal of Development Economics*, 22: 87-128.

Papanek, Gustav and Oldrich Kyn (1986), 'The Effects of Income Distribution of Development, Economic Growth, and Economic Strategy', *Journal of Development Economics*, 23(1), 55-66.

Pasha, Hafiz A. and T. Palanivel (2004), 'Pro-Poor Growth: The Asian Experience', Paper Presented at the Annual General Conference and Meeting of the Pakistan Society of Development Economists, Islamabad, Pakistan.

Pearson, R. (1987), Transfer of Technology and Domestic Innovation in the Cement Industry, in J.M. Katz (ed.), *Technology Generation in Latin American Manufacturing Industries*, London: Macmillan.

Perkins, Dwight (1988), 'Reforming China's Economic System', *Journal of Economic Literature*, 26(2), 601-45.

Perkins, Dwight (1994), 'Completing China's Move to the Market', *Journal of Economic Perspectives*, 8, 23-24.

Persson, T. and G. Tabellini (1994), 'Is Inequality Harmful for Growth', *American Economic Review*, 84, 600-621.

Popper, Karl R (1980), *The Logic of Scientific Enquiry* (tenth, revised edition), London: Hutchinson.

Prebisch, Raul (1950), *The Economic Development of Latin America and its Principal Problems*, New York: Department of Economic Affairs, The United Nations.

Prebisch, Raul (1984), 'Five Stages in My Thinking on Development', in D. Seers and G.M. Meier (eds.), *Pioneers in Development*, New York: Oxford University Press, 175-191.

Price Waterhouse (1989), *Privatization: The Facts*, London: Price Waterhouse.

Pritchett, L. (1991),'Measuring Outward Orientation in Developing Countries: Can It Be Done?' World Bank, Mimeo.

Pritchett, L. 1995), 'Divergence: Big Time,' *World Bank Policy Research Working Paper* No. 1522, Washington, D.C.: World Bank.

Przeworksi Adam (1991), *Democracy and the Market: Political and Economic Reforms in Eastern Europe and Latin America*, Cambridge: Cambridge University Press.

Ranis, Gustav (1988), 'Analytics of Development: Dualism', in Hollis Chenery and T.N. Srinivasan, *Handbook on Development Economics*, 1, Amesterdem: North Holland, 74-91.

Ranis, Gustav (1989), 'Labor Surplus Economies', in John Eatwell, Murray Milgate and Peter Newman (eds.), *Economic Development, The New Palgrave*, London: Macmillan.

Ranis, Gustav and J.C. Fei (1961), 'A Theory of Economic Development', *American Economic Review*, LI, 533-65.

Ranis, Gustav and Syed Akhtar Mahmood (1992), *The Political Economy of Development Policy Change*, Cambridge, MA and Oxford: Basil Blackwell.

Ravallion, Martin (1995), 'Household Vulnerability to Aggregative Shocks: Differing Fortunes of the Poor in Bangladesh and Indonesia', in Basu, K., Pattnaik, P., Suzumura, K. (eds.), *Choice, Welfare and Development*, Oxford: Oxford University Press.

Ravallion, Martin (1997), 'Famines and Economics', *Journal of Economic Literature*, 35(September), 1205-1242.

Ravallion, Martin (2004), 'Pro-Poor Growth: A Primer', World Bank Policy Research Paper, 3242.

Rawls, John (1985), 'Justice as Fairness: Political Not Metaphysical', *Philosophy and Public Affairs*, 14-3,223-251.

Rawls, John (1993), *Political Liberalism*, New York: Columbia University Press.

Rawls, John (1999), *A Theory of Justice*, (Revised Edition), First Published in 1971, Oxford: Oxford University Press.

Ray, Debraj (1998), *Development Economics*, Princeton, NJ: Princeton University Press.

Reder, Melvin (1979), 'The Place of Ethics in the Theory of Production', in Michael Boskin (ed.), *Economics and Human Welfare: Essays in Honor of Tibor Scitovsky*, New York: Academic Press, 133-146.

Reynolds, Lloyd (1977), *Image and Reality in Economic Development*, New Haven: Yale University Press.

Reynolds, Lloyd (1983), 'The Spread of Economic Growth to the Third World: 1850-1980', *Journal of Economic Literature*, 21 (September), 941-980.

Ricardo, David (1817), *On the Principles of Political Economy and Taxation*, P. Sraffa (ed., 1951), Cambridge: Cambridge University Press.

Rivera-Batiz, L.A. and Romer, P.M. (1991), 'Economic Integration and Economic Growth', *Quarterly Journal of Economics*, 106: 531-555.

Robertson, Dennis (1940), *Essays in Monetary Economics*, London: Palgrave.

Robinson, Joan (1956), *The Accumulation of Capital*, London: Macmillan.

Robinson, Joan (1962), *Economic Philosophy*, England: Penguin Books.

Robinson, Joan (1979), *Aspects of Development and Underdevelopment*, Cambridge: Cambridge University Press.

Robinson, Sherman (1976), 'A Note on the Hypothesis Relating Income Inequality and Economic Development', *American Economic Review*, 66, 436-440.

Robbins, Lionel (1935), *An Essay on the Nature and Significance of Economic Science* (2nd Edition), London: Macmillan.

Rodan, Rosenstein (1943), 'Problems of Industrialization of Eastern and South-eastern Europe', *The Economic Journal*, 53:2, 202-11.

Rodan, Rosenstein (1957), *The Objectives of U.S. Economic Assistance Programs*, Washington, D.C.

Rodan, Rosenstein (1984), 'Natura Facit Saltum: Analysis of the Disequilibrium Growth Process', in G.M. Meir and Dudley Seers (eds.), *Pioneers in Development*, New York: Oxford University Press, 207-221.

Rodrik, Dani (1995), 'Trade and Industrial Policy Reforms', in J. Behrman and T.N. Srinivasan (eds.), *Handbook of Development Economics*, Amsterdam: Elsevier Science BV.

Rodrik, Dani (1996), 'Understanding Economic Policy Reforms', *Journal of Economic Literature*, 34(1), 9-41.

Rodrik, Dani (1997), *Has Globalization Gone Too Far?* Washington DC: Institute of International Economics.

Rodrik, Dani and Arvin Subramanian (2004), 'From 'Hindu Growth' to Productivity Surge: The Mystery of the Indian Growth Transition', National Bureau of Economic Research, (Working Paper 10376), Cambridge, MA 02138.

Roemer, John E. (1996), *Egalitarian Perspectives*, Cambridge: Cambridge University Press.

Roll, R., and Talbott, J. (2001), 'Why Many Developing Countries are Just Aren't'? Unpublished Paper, November 13.

Romer, P.M. (1986), 'Increasing Returns and Long-run Growth', *Journal of Political Economy*, 94:5, 1002-37.

Romer, P.M. (1990), 'Endogenous Technological Change', *Journal of Political Economy*, 98(5), S71-102.

Romer, P.M. (1994), 'New Goods. Old Theory, and the Welfare Costs of Trade Restrictions', *Journal of Development Economics*, 43(1), 5-38.

Rondinelli, Denis and Max Iacono (1996), *Policies and Institutions for Managing Privatization*, International Training Center, ILO, Turin, Italy.

Rosen, Sherwin (2002), 'Markets and Diversity', *American Economic Review*, 92(1), 1-15.

Rosenthal, Elisabeth (2003), 'Bias for Boys Leads to Sale of Babies in China', *New York Times* (Sunday, 20 July).

Rousseau, J.J. (1964), *A Discourse On The Origin of Equality, in the First and Second Discourses*, R.D. Masters (ed.), New York: St. Martin's Press.

Rostow, W.W. (1953), *The Process of Economic Growth*, Oxford: Clarendon Press.

Rostow, W.W. (1956), The Take-off into Self-sustaining Growth', *Economic Journal*, 66(261), 25-48.

Rostow, W.W. (1984), 'Development: Political Economy of the Marshallian Long Period', in Meier, G.M. and Dudley Seers, *Pioneers in Development*, Oxford University Press, 229-261.

Roth, Alvin and J. Murnighan (1982), 'The Role of Information in Bargaining: An Experimental Study', *Econometrica*, 50, 1123-42.

Rothschild, Michael and Joseph Stiglitz (1976), 'Equilibrium in Competitive Insurance Markets: An Essay on the Economics of Imperfect Information', *Quarterly Journal of Economics*, 90, 629-50.

Russell, Bertrand (1973), *Roads to Freedom*, London: Unwin Books (First Edition, 1918).

Sachs, Jeffrey D. (1987), 'Trade and Exchange Rate Policies in Growth Oriented Adjustment Programs' in V. Corbo, Morris Goldstein, and Mohsin Khan, *Growth-oriented Programs*, Washington: D.C.

Sachs, Jeffrey D. (1994), 'The Political Challenge of European Transition: The Case of Poland', Unpublished Paper.

Sachs, Jeffrey D. (1999), 'Helping the World's Poorest', *The Economist*, 14 to 20 August, 17-20.

Sachs, Jeffrey D. and Andrew M. Warner (1997), 'Sources of Slow Growth in African Economies', *Journal of African Economics*, 6,335-76.

Sala-i-Martin, X.X. (1996), 'The Classical Approach to Convergence Analysis', *Economic Journal*, 106(437), 1019-1036.

Samuelson, Paul A. (1939), 'The Gains from International Trade', *The Canadian Journal of Economics and Political Science*, 5, 195-205.

Samuelson, Paul A. (1947), *Foundations of Economic Analysis*, Cambridge, MA: Harvard University Press.

Samuelson, William (1985), 'Comments on Coase Theorem', in Roth, Alvin, *Game Theoretic Models of Bargaining*, New York: Cambridge University Press.

Sappington, David and Joseph Stiglitz (1987), 'Privatization, Information and Incentives', *Journal of Policy Analysis and Management*, 6:4, 567-92.

Sarno, Lucio and Mark P. Taylor (2001), 'Official Intervention in the Foreign Exchange Market: Is it Effective and If So, How Does it Work?' *Journal of Economic Literature*, 39(3), 839-868.

Schmalensee, Richard, (1991), 'Continuity and Change in Economics Industry', *Economic Journal*, 101(404), 115-21.

Schumpeter, Joseph, A. (1934), *The Theory of Economic Development*, Cambridge, Mass, Harvard University Press.

Shleifer, Andrie and Robert Vishny (1989), 'Management Retrenchment: The Case for Manager-specific Investment', *Journal of Financial Economics*, 25, 123-29.

Schultz, Theodore W. (1956), 'The Role of Government in Promoting Economic Growth', in Leonard D. White(ed.), *The State of Social Sciences,* Chicago: Chicago University Press.

Schultz, Theodore W. (1964), *Transforming Traditional Agriculture*, Chicago: The University of Chicago Press.

Schultz, Theodore W. (1981), 'The Economics of Being Poor', in Theodore W. Schultz (ed.), *Investing in the People: The Economics of Population Quality*, Berkeley and Los Angeles: University of California Press.

Scitovsky, Tibor (1954), 'Two Concepts of External Economies', *Journal of Political Economy*, 62(April), 143-51.

Scitovsky, Tibor (1990), 'Balanced Growth', in John Eatwell, Murry Milgate and Peter Newman (eds.), *The New Palgrave: A Dictionary of Economics*, 1(A-D), London: Macmillan, 10-26.

Shleifer, A. and R. Vishny (1999), *The Grabbing Hand: Government Pathologies and their Cures*, Boston: Harvard University Press.

Sen, A.K. (1976-77), 'Rational Fools: A Critique of the Behavioral Foundations of Economic Theory', *Philosophy and Public Affairs*, 6, 317-44.

Sen, A.K. (1981), *Poverty and Famine: An Essay in Starvation and Deprivation*, Oxford: Clarendon Press.

Sen, A.K. (1983), 'Development: Which Way Now', *Economic Journal*, 93(Dec), 745-762.

Sen, A.K. (1987), *On Ethics and Economics*, Oxford: Basil Blackwell.

Sen, A.K. (1990), 'Women and Cooperative Conflict', in Irene Tinker, *Persistent Inequalities*, New York: Oxford University Press.

Sen, A.K. (1992), *Inequality Re-examined*, New York: Clarendon Press.

Sen, A.K. (1993), 'Markets and Freedoms', *Oxford Economic Papers*, 45.

Sen, A.K. (1997a), *Development Thinking at the Beginning of the 21st Century*, London: The Economic & Social Research Council (The Development Economics Research Program).

Sen, A.K. (1997b), 'Maximization and the Act of Social Choice', *Econometrica*, 65, 745-779. Reprinted as Chapter 4 in Amartya Sen, *Rationality and Freedom*, New Delhi: Oxford University Press.

Sen, A.K. (1999a) 'The Possibility of Social Choice', *American Economic Review*, 89:3, 349-78. Reprinted in Amartya Sen (2002c), *Rationality and Freedom*, New Delhi: Oxford University Press.

Sen, A.K. (1999b), *Development as Freedom*, Oxford: Oxford University Press.

Sen, A.K. (2000), 'Consequential Evaluation and Practical Reason', *The Journal of Philosophy*, xcvii (9), 477-502.

Sen, A.K. (2001), 'Many Faces of Gender Inequality', *Frontline*, 18(22), 4-14.

Sen, A.K. (2002a), 'Open and Closed Impartiality', *The Journal of Philosophy*, 9909(2), 445-69.

Sen, A.K. (2002b),'How To Judge Globalization', *The American Perspectives,* Winter, A2-A6.

Sen, A.K. (2002c), *Rationality and Freedom*, New Delhi: Oxford University Press.

Singer, Hans W. (1950), 'The Distribution of Gains between Investing and Borrowing Countries', *American Economic Review (Papers and Proceedings)*, 40:2, 473-85.

Singer, Hans W. (1984), The Terms of Trade Controversy and the Evolution of Soft-financing: Early Years in the UN, in G.M. Meier and Dudely Seers (eds.), *Pioneers in Development*, New York: Oxford University Press, 275-303.

Singer, Hans W. and Patricia Gray (1988), 'Trade Policy and Growth of Developing Countries: Some New Data', *World Development*, 16(3), 395-403.

Sirageldin Ismail (2000), Elimination of Poverty: Challenges and Islamic Strategies, Keynote Address, *Islamic Economic Studies*, Vol. 8, No. 1 (October 2000), 1-18.

Sirageldin, Ismail (2000), 'Elimination of Poverty: Challenges and Islamic Strategies', Evolutionary Perspective,' in M.K. Tolba (ed.), *Our Fragile World*. London and Paris: EOLSS Publishing Co. Ltd.

Sirageldin, Ismail (2007), *Human Prospects in the Twenty-First Century: Freedom or Serfdom*. (Forthcoming) London, UK: I.B. Tauris. [Processed: Isirag@aol.com]

Smith, Adam (1976[1776]), *An Enquiry into the Nature and the Causes of the Wealth of Nations*, reprinted by R.N. Campbell and A.S. Skinner, Vol. 1, Book 11, Oxford: Clarendon Press.

Smith, Adam (1790), *The Theory of Moral Sentiments*, republished and edited by D.D. Raphael and A.L. Macfie, Oxford: Clarendon Press.

Solow, Robert M. (1957), Technical Change and the Aggregate Production Function, *Review of Economics and Statistics*, 39(3), 312-332.

Solow, Robert M. (1980), 'On Theories of Unemployment', *The American Economic Review*, 70(1), 1-11.

Solow, Robert M. (1994), 'Perspectives on Growth Theory', *Journal of Economic Perspectives*, 8(1), 45-54.

Souza, D' Juliet and William Megginson (2000), 'Sources of Performance Improvement in Privatized Firms: A Clinical Study of the Global Telecommunication Industry', Working Paper Univ. of Oklahoma.

Squire, Lyn (1993), 'Fighting Poverty', *American Economic Review*, 83(2), 377-82.

Squire, Lyn (2003), 'Equity, Growth, and Human Development', *Online Encyclopedia of Life Support Systems*, EOLSS-UNESCO.

Srinivasan, T.N. (1993), 'Long-run Growth Theories and Empirics: Anything New?' in T. Ito and A. Krueger (eds.), *Lessons from the East Asian Experience*, Chicago: Chicago University Press.

Srinivasan, T.N. and Whalley, J. (eds.) (1986), *General Equilibrium Trade Policy Modeling*, Cambridge, MA: MIT Press.

Srinivasan, T.N. and Jagdish N. Bhagwati (2001), 'Outward Orientation and Development: Are Revisionists Right?' in Deepak Lal and Richard Shape, *Trade, Development, and Political Economy: Essays in Honor of Anne Krueger*, London: Palgrave.

Standing, Guy (1985), *Labor Force Participation and Development*, Geneva: ILO.

Stark, O. (1991), *The Migration of Labor*, Oxford: Basil Blackwell.

Stern, E. (1991), 'Evolution and Lessons of Adjustment Lending', in V. Thomas et al. (eds.), *Restructuring Economic Distress: Policy Reforms and the World Bank*, Oxford: Oxford University Press.

Stern, Nicholas (1989), 'The Economics of Development: A Survey', *The Economic Journal*, 99(September), 597-685.

Stern, Nicholas (1991), 'The Determinants of Growth', *The Economic Journal*, 101:104, 122-133.

Stern, Nicholas and Francois Ferreira (1993), *The World Bank as 'Intellectual Actor'*, The Development Economics Research Program series, London: London School of Economics.

Stigler, George J. (1981), 'Economics or Ethics' in Sterling McMurrin (ed.), *Tanner Lectures in Human Values*, II, Cambridge: Cambridge University Press.

Stiglitz, Joseph (1986), 'The New Development Economics', *World Development*, 14(2), 257-265.

Stiglitz, Joseph (1987), 'Learning to Learn, Localized Learning and Technological Progress', in P. Dasgupta and Stoneman (eds.), *Economic Policy and Technological Performance*, Centre for Economic Policy Research, Cambridge University Press.

Stiglitz, Joseph (1988), 'Economic Organization, Information, and Development', in Hollis Chenery and T.N. Srinivasan (eds.), *Handbook of Development Economics I*, New York: North Holland.

Stiglitz, Joseph (1989a), 'On the Role of the State', in A. Heertje, *The Economic Role of the State*, Amsterdam: Bank Insinger de Beaufort, NY.

Stiglitz, Joseph (1989b), 'Markets, Market Failures and Development', *American Economic Review, Papers and Proceedings*, 79(2), 197-203.

Stiglitz, Joseph (1991), 'Another Century of Economic Science', *Economic Journal*, 101(Jan), 134-141.

Stiglitz, Joseph (1996), 'Some Lessons from the East Asian Miracle', *Research Observer*, 11(2), 151-177.

Stiglitz, Joseph (1998), 'The Private Uses of Public Interests: Incentives and Institutions', *Journal of Economic Perspectives*, 12(2), 3-22.

Stiglitz, Joseph (2003), *Globalization and Its Discontents*, New York and London: W.W. Norton.

Stiglitz, Joseph (2006), *Making Globalization Work*, England: Allen Lane.

Stiglitz, Joseph and A. Weiss (1981), 'Credit Markets in Markets with Imperfect Information', *American Economic Review*, 71(June), 393-74.

Stiglitz, Joseph and Marilou Uy (1996), 'Financial Markets, Public Policy, and the East Asian Miracle', *Research Observer*, 11(2), 249-276.

Strachey, Lytton (1984), *Eminent Victorians*, England: Penguin Books.

Streeten, Paul (1959), 'Unbalanced Growth', *Oxford Economic Papers* (New Series), 11(2), 167-190.

Streeten, Paul (1981), *Development Perspectives*, London: Macmillan.

Streeten, Paul (1989), 'International Cooperation', in Hollis Chenery and T.N. Srinivasan, *Handbook of Development Economics*, 2, New York: North-Holland, 1153-1186.

Streeten, Paul (1993), 'Markets and State: Against Minimalism', *World Development*, 21(8), 1281-1298.

Streeten, Paul (1998), 'Globalization: Threat or Opportunity', *Pakistan Development Review*, 37:4, 51-85.

Sugden, Robert (1993), 'Welfare, Resources and Capabilities: A Review of Inequality Re-examined by Amartya Sen', *Journal of Economic Literature*, 31(Dec), 1947-62.

Summers, Lawrence H. (2000), 'International Financial Crises: Causes, Prevention, and Cures', *American Economic Review, Papers and Proceedings*, 90(2), 1-16.

Summers, R. and Heston, A. (1988), 'The Penn World Tables (Mark 5): An Extended Set of International Comparisons, 1950-1988', *Quarterly Journal of Economics*, 106, 327-368.

Heston, A., Summers. R. and Aten B. (2002), *Penn World Table Version 6.1*, Center for International Comparisons at the University of Pennsylvania (CICUP).

Sutton, J. (1986), 'Non-cooperative Bargaining Theory', *Review of Economic Studies*, 53, 709-724.

Syrquin, Moshe (1988), 'Patterns of Structural Change', in Hollis B. Chenery and T.N. Srinivasan (eds.), *Handbook of Development Economics*, I. New York: Elsevier Science Publishers, 203-273.

Temple, Jonathan (1999), 'The New Growth Evidence', *Journal of Economic Literature*, 37(1), 112-156.

Thomas, V. et al. (1991), *Restructuring Economies in Distress: Policy Reform and the World Bank*, Oxford and New York: Oxford University Press.

Thirlwall, A.P. (1999), *Growth and Development* (6th Edition), London: Macmillan Press.

Timmer, Peter (1973), 'Choice of Techniques in the Rice Milling in Java', *Bulletin of Indonesian Economic Studies*, 9(2), 57-76.

Timmer, Peter (1988), 'The Agrarian Transformation', in Chenery, H. and T.N. Srinivasan, *Handbook of Development Economics I*, New York: North Holland.

Tinbergen, Jan (1956), *Economic Policy: Principles and Design*, Amsterdam: North-Holland.

Tinbergen, Jan (1958), *The Design of Development*, Baltimore: Johns Hopkins University Press.

Tinbergen, Jan (1985), *Production, Income and Welfare*, UK: Wheatsheaf Books.

Tullock, Gordon (1986), *The Economics of Wealth and Poverty*, Brighton, Sussex: Wheatsheaf Books.

UN (1966), *Covenant on Economic, Social, and Cultural Rights*, General Assembly Resolution, 2200A (XXI) 16 December, New York.

UN (2000), *United Nations Millennium Declaration*, A/RES/55/2, 18 September. Adopted by the General Assembly, New York: United Nations, [http://www.un.org/millennium/declaration/ares 55e.pdf].

UN (2005), *The Millennium Declaration Goals Report*, New York: United Nations.

UNDP (1996), *Human Development Report*, New York: Oxford University Press.

UNDP (1999), *Human Development Report*, New York: Oxford University Press.

UNDP (2000), *Human Development Report, 2000*, New York: Oxford University Press.

UNDP (2003a), *Human Development Report, 2003*, New York: Oxford University Press.

UNDP (2003b), *Making Global Trade Work for the People*, London and Sterling, Virginia: Earthscan Publications Ltd for the UNDP.

UNDP (2004), *Human Development Report, 2004*, New York: UNDP.

UNDP (2005), *Human Development Report (2005): International Cooperation at the Crossroads*, New York: United Nations Development Program.

UNCTAD (1998), *Trade and Development Report*, New York: United Nations.

UNCTAD (1999), *Trade and Development Report, 1999*, New York: United Nations.

UNCTAD (2001), *Trade and Development Report, 2001*, New York: United Nations.

UNCTAD (2002), *The Least Developed Countries Report: Escaping the Poverty Trap*, Geneva.

UNIDO (1996), *Industrial Development Global Report (1996)*, Vienna: Oxford University Press.

Uzawa, H. (1961), 'On a Two-sector Model of Growth, Part 1', *Review of Economic Studies*, 30, 105-18.

Varian, Hal (1974), 'Equity, Envy, and Efficiency', *Journal of Economic Theory*, 9(1), 63-91.

Vickers, J. and G. Yarrow (1988), *Privatization: An Economic Analysis*, Cambridge, M.A.: MIT Press.

Vickers, J. and G. Yarrow (1991), 'Economic Perspectives on Privatization', *Journal of Economic Perspectives*, 5(2), 111-132.

Viner, Jacob (1958), 'Stability and Progress: The Poorer Countries' Problems', in D. Hague (ed.), *Stability and Progress in the World Economy*, London.

Visaria, P. (1980), 'Poverty and living Standards in Asia: An Overview of the Main Results and Lessons of Selected Household Surveys', Working Paper #2, Living Standards Measurements Study, Washington, D.C.: The World Bank.

Wade, R. (1990), *Governing the Market: Theory and the Role of the Government in East Asian Industrialization*, Princeton, N.J.: Princeton University Press.

Wade, R. (2006), 'Question of Fairness', *Foreign Affairs*, September/October (a review of Ethan Kapestein's book, *Economic Justice in an Unfair World, Princeton University Press.)*

Waverman, L., and Murphy, S. (1992), 'Total Factor Productivity in Automobile Production in Argentina, Mexico, Korea, and Canada: The Impacts of Protection', in G.K. Helleiner (ed.), *Trade Policy, Industrialization and Development*, Oxford: Oxford University Press.

Waverman, L., and Murphy, S. (2001), 'Winners and Losers', *The Economist*, 28 April-24 May, London, 73-75.

Waterston, Albert (1965), *Development Planning*, Baltimore: Johns Hopkins Press.

Watkins, M.H. (1963), 'A Staple Theory of Economic Growth', *Canadian Journal of Economics and Political Science*, 29, 141-158. 1978.

Westphal, Larry E. (1978), 'The Republic of Korea's Experience with Export-led Industrial Development', *World Development*, 6(3), 347-82.

Westphal, Larry E. (1990), 'Industrial Policy in an Export-Propelled Economy: Lessons from South Korean Experience', *Journal of Economic Perspectives*, 4: 41-59.

Whitehead, Alfred N. (1972), *Symbolism: Its Meaning and Effect*, New York: Capricorn Books.

Williamson, John (1990), *Latin American Adjustment: How Much Has Happened*, Washington, D.C.: Institute of International Economics.

Williamson, John (2003), 'Overview: An Agenda for Restarting Growth and Reform', in Kuczynski and Williamson (eds.), *After the Washington Consensus*, Washington, D.C.: Institute of International Economics, 1-19.

Wilson, Rodney (1997), *Economics, Ethics and Religion: Jewish, Christian and Muslim Thought*, New York: New York University Press.

World Bank (1978), *World Development Report, 1978*, New York: Oxford University Press.

World Bank (1982), *World Development Report, 1982*, New York: Oxford University Press.

World Bank (1987), *World Development Report, 1987*, New York: Oxford University Press.

World Bank (1990), *World Development Report, 1990*, New York: Oxford University Press.

World Bank (1990), *Adjustment Lending Policies for Sustainable Growth*, Policy and Research Series Papers, 14.

World Bank (2003), *World Development Indicators*, Washington: D.C.

World Bank (1991), *World Development Report (The Challenge of Development)*, New York: Oxford University Press.

World Bank (1993), *The East Asian Miracle*, London: Oxford University Press.

World Bank (1999), *World Development Report (1998/99): Knowledge for Development*, New York: Oxford University Press.

World Bank (2001), *World Development Report: Attacking Poverty*, New York: Oxford University Press.

World Bank (2005), *Equity and Development (World Development Report, 2006)*, New York: Oxford University Press.

WTO (2004a), *Coherence in Global Economic Policy-making and Cooperation between the WTO, the IMF and the World Bank*, Geneva: WTO.

WTO (2004b), *Future of the WTO*, Geneva: WTO.

Yaqub-Khan, Sahabzada (2006), *Strategy, Diplomacy and Humanity* (compiled and edited by Anwar Adil): Inter-cultural Forum, Takshila Research University, San Diego, United States and Islamabad, Pakistan.

Yergin, Daniel and Joseph Stanislaw (1998), *The Commanding Heights: the Battle between Government and the Marketplace That is Remaking the Modern World*, New York: Simon and Schuster.

Young, Alwyn (1993), *The Lessons From the East Asian NIC's: A Contractarian View*, NBER, Working Paper No. 4482.

Yusuf, Shahid and Joseph E. Stiglitz (2001), 'Development Issues: Settled and Open', in Gerald G. Meier and Joseph E. Stiglitz (eds.), *Frontiers of Development Economics*, Washington: World Bank.

Index